Syria After the Uprisings

Syria After the Uprisings
The Political Economy of State Resilience

Joseph Daher

Haymarket Books
Chicago, Illinois

First published in 2019 by Pluto Press in London.

This edition published by
Haymarket Books
P.O. Box 180165
Chicago, IL 60618
773-583-7884
www.haymarketbooks.org
info@haymarketbooks.org

ISBN: 978-1-60846-924-6

Distributed to the trade in the US through Consortium Book Sales and
Distribution (www.cbsd.com) and internationally through Ingram Publisher
Services International (www.ingramcontent.com).

This book was published with the generous support of Lannan Foundation
and Wallace Action Fund.

Special discounts are available for bulk purchases by organizations and
institutions. Please call 773-583-7884 or email info@haymarketbooks.org
for more information.

Cover design by Melanie Patrick.

Library of Congress Cataloging-in-Publication data is available.

10 9 8 7 6 5 4 3 2 1

Contents

Acknowledgements

I am very much indebted in the writing of this thesis to my family (my parents, my brother and my wife) for their support and love through these past years. I would like to thank especially my mother Juliet and my wife Paola, who supported and encouraged me constantly in my work. I would also like to mention and thank my daughters Yara and Tamara who without knowing it calmed me down in times of stress by their presence and lovely smiles.

I finally would like to dedicate this book to my father Nicolas, who passed away in September 2014, with all my love and gratitude. He always has been a true inspiration for me and continues to be in my daily life. His great humanism, large heart, generosity, courage, honesty, humour, knowledge, etc ... have very much influenced me in my various activities and works.

By dedicating this book to him, I cannot but also dedicate this book to the people of Syria, from where our family originally comes. They have suffered enormously since the beginning of the revolutionary process in March 2011, from massive destruction and displacements and grave human rights violations. My deep thoughts are with them and also with all those activists that have struggled for a democratic, social and inclusive Syria.

Introduction

Syria has been at the center of world news since March 2011, following the beginning of a popular uprising in the country and its violent repression. The Syrian civil war evolved increasingly over the years into a war involving multiple local, regional, and international actors. The majority of observers and scholars have analyzed the Syrian conflagration through a geopolitical lens or in sectarian terms, equating religious communities with political positions and in both viewpoints ignoring the political and socioeconomic dynamics at the root of the conflict.

This book views the origins and developments of the Syrian uprising that began in March 2011 as a part of wider popular uprisings in the Middle East and North Africa (MENA). These events and processes are the result of the confluence and mutual reinforcement of various sites of dissatisfaction, struggle, and popular mobilization. These battles are intertwined and have enabled different sectors of these societies to join forces in rebelling against authoritarian and corrupt regimes, which are deemed responsible for the continual deepening of the social crisis.

Although the war is not finished and some territories were still outside the domination of the regime at the beginning of 2019, the regime's survival and maintenance was nearly achieved, despite being significantly weakened and having important internal contradictions. This book aims to look at the reasons and roots of the resilience of the Bashar al-Assad regime.

What is the nature of the regime built by the Assad family? Who were the actors involved in the uprising, and how did they organize themselves? How did the regime react to repress the protest movement? Was the opposition able to present a credible alternative to the regime? What was the role of Islamic fundamentalist and jihadist movements? How did regional and international interventions influence the uprising in Syria? What were the reasons behind the development of a peaceful uprising into an armed civil war with regional and international components? We start this analysis from the internal dynamics specific to Syria and put them into a comprehensive framework, which includes regional trends and international issues. These questions are intrinsically linked.

Activists from Syria have also asked themselves these questions. In a 2015 study led by the nongovernmental organization (NGO) Dawlaty that included 139 nonviolent activists, one of the "several factors that led to the creation of gaps within the non-violent movement, which opened the door for militarization and increased suspicion of the movement by some parts of Syrian society" was notably the fact that

> activists suffered from the impression that the Syrian regime would fall quickly, just like Mubarak's in Egypt and Bin Ali's in Tunisia ... When the regime showed that it was not going anywhere anytime soon, the problem of flight, withdrawal, and resorting to militarization emerged. The Libyan revolution, with its international intervention, became an attractive model for some ... (Dawlaty 2015: 18)

We will see that the challenges faced by the initial large and inclusive protest movement in Syria had the capacity from the outset to provide an alternative to the Assad regime. We will also analyze the reactions and adaptations of the Syrian regime in order to repress the popular movement.

To analyze the resilience of the regime, I will address first the nature of the uprising in depth, taking into account its main economic, social, and political characteristics in a local and international arena and on a *longue durée* perspective. We examine the origins and key developments of these events by attempting to reconstruct the stages of their development. This will be done in connection with an analysis of societal changes that influenced Syria's core classes, ethnic and religious minorities, and various groups with diverse interests, without neglecting the regional and international political arena. This study is inspired by a historical, materialist approach that begins by studying Syrian society and its transformations in order to analyze and explain events. In doing so, it will also consider external factors that favored the outbreak of protests, such as the overthrow of Tunisian and Egyptian dictators. This approach will take into consideration the impact of various economic policies—which have been implemented over decades, particularly since the 1960s—on economic and social spheres, as well as their impact on the Syrian class structure, as well as on the country's multisectarian and multiethnic mosaic.

It is impossible to understand the Syrian uprising or the regime's reaction without a historical perspective and approach dating back to the seizure of power by Hafez al-Assad in 1970. We will analyze the regime established under Hafez al-Assad and its evolutions under his son Bashar al-Assad, who succeeded him in 2000.

Three key theoretical arguments are advanced in the following discussion. The first concerns the shifting terrain of class and state formation in Syria since the rise to power of Hafez al-Assad—the beginning of the era of economic opening—and its relationship to the political practice of the state. While neoliberal policies led to an impoverishment of significant parts of Syrian society, they have also helped enrich a layer of the country's business community from various religious sects, from or closely connected to the ruling elite. The political practice of the state became increasingly responsive to the concerns of this layer, to which it holds close social, political, and financial ties. This was reflected by its economic policies, as well as its repressive behavior and attitude toward opposition members and sections of the bourgeoisie not linked to the state.

The second theoretical argument concerns the ways in which Syria evolved in a particular regional context, which had consequences on the uprising. I draw upon materialist analyses of imperialism to show how the intervention of foreign actors influenced the nature of the uprising and dynamics regarding the Syrian state.

Finally, we tackle the issue of sectarianism and its dynamics in order to explain its role in the uprising. Various local and regional actors involved in the uprising have used sectarian policies to mobilize popular constituencies and as a tool to reach their objectives.

Structure of the book

This work is organized into seven chapters. Chapter 1 tackles the roots of the authoritarian and patrimonial[1] state established with Hafez al-Assad's seizure of power in 1970. Next, the transition period following the death of

---

[1] Elements of understanding can be found in the patrimonial nature of the regime's apparatus in Syria according to Gilbert Achcar (2013), in which the centers of power (politics, the military, and the economy) within the regime were concentrated in one family and its clique (namely, the Assads), similar to Libya or the Gulf monarchies. Thus, the regime was pushed to use all the violence at its disposition to protect its rule. He described the patrimonial state in the traditional Weberian definition as an absolute autocratic and hereditary power, which can function through a collegial environment (i.e., parents and friends) and that owns the state: its armed force, dominated by a praetorian guard (a force whose allegiance goes to the rulers, not to the state), economic means, and administration. In this type of regime, it is a type of crony capitalism that develops, dominated by a state bourgeoisie. In other words, the members and people close to the ruling families often exploit their dominant position guaranteed by the political power to amass considerable fortunes.

In addition to the patrimonial nature of the state, and reinforcing this pattern, was the rentier characteristic of many of the states of the region, including Syria. *Rent* is defined as a regular revenue that is not generated by the work carried out or commissioned by the beneficiary. Therefore, most of the patrimonial states in the MENA region are generally characterized by a deeply corrupt, trilateral "power elite," as explained by Achcar (2016: 7) as follows:

> [A] triangle of power constituted by the interlocking pinnacles of the military apparatus the political institutions and politically determined capitalist class (a state bourgeoisie), all three bent on fiercely defending their access to state power, the main source of their privileges and profits.

Hafez al-Assad and the arrival to power of Bashar al-Assad is analyzed. During Bashar's era, Syria experienced the reinforcement of the patrimonial nature of the state in the hands of the Assad family, through its neoliberal policies, and the replacement of sections of the old guard by relatives or close individuals of the new ruler. The socioeconomic consequences of neoliberal policies are also observed throughout the reigns of the two dictators.

In Chapter 2, the nature and dynamics of the actors in the protest movement during the first years of the uprising, and then in the subsequent militarization, are analyzed. The situation of near-dual power, or at least a potential alternative to the regime created by the deepening of the revolutionary process and the establishment and expansion of local councils managing affairs locally, is studied. The inclusive message and behavior of the majority of local opposition organizations and committees were the most feared threat by the regime, which characterized the protest movement as a foreign conspiracy led by "extremist terrorists" and "armed gangs." The gradual escalation of violence and repression by the regime's forces led to the defections of increasing numbers of soldiers and officers, as well as civilians taking up arms. This resulted in the establishment of the Free Syrian Army (FSA). The FSA was first characterized by its plurality among its numerous groups, which expanded throughout 2011 and 2012. The dynamics of the FSA's networks evolved as a result of the regime's harsh repression and the networks' division, as well as the latter's lack of organized support. Finally, the gradual process of marginalization of FSA networks is examined, occurring notably because of their increasing dependence on foreign governments, absence of any form of centralization to coordinate more effectively, and competent and rooted political leadership that can unite the various armed components of the opposition around a specific political program.

Chapter 3 addresses the mobilization of the regime's popular base to support repression, especially the roles of crony capitalists and security services. Damascus officials used sectarian, tribal, and clientelist connections to quell the protests. Various strategies of repression and violence are analyzed. Through providing state services and employment, the regime also produced a form of dependence on the part of large sections of the population, particularly against the background of the deepening war and acute socioeconomic crisis. At the same time, Damascus showed flexibility toward some regions that were generally more supportive of the regime by providing them with more autonomy, or at least more political space to their local populations.

Chapter 4 looks at the failure of the opposition in exile to constitute a credible, democratic, and inclusive alternative that could express the demands of the protest movement. Divisions fomented by a number of foreign actors progressively marginalized the various bodies of the opposition in exile. The subsequent rise of Islamic fundamentalist and jihadist movements was linked to the weakening and division of FSA networks and those of civilian and democratic groups and activists, and the inclusive message of the uprising lost its appeal among some sections of the Syrian population. The role of first the regime, and then of foreign actors, in the expansion of Islamic fundamentalist and jihadist movements is explored in detail, along with the role played by some FSA networks' corrupt behavior and the failure of the various states claiming to support the uprising to assist it financially, militarily, and politically. The intervention of regional states claiming to support the uprising only deepened the divisions within the political and armed opposition groups.

In Chapter 5, the involvement of the Kurdish population and Kurdish political groups in the uprising is examined. Large swaths of Kurdish youth fought alongside other sectors of the Syrian people against the regime in the uprising through the establishment of local coordination committees, while Kurdish political parties, with few exceptions, were initially unready to engage with the protest movement. Throughout the uprising, the cooperation between the Arab and Kurdish coordination committees and youth either ceased or was very much diminished. The reasons for this were principally rooted in the actions of the main representatives of Syrian Arab opposition in exile, rejecting the national demands of Kurdish political parties. Furthermore, the increasing influence of the Democratic Union Party (known by its acronym PYD, because in Kurdish, its name is *Partiya Yekîtiya Demokrat*), with the blessing of the Assad regime, on the Kurdish political scene in Syria increasingly marginalized the links with other sections of the opposition and the wider uprising. The rest of the chapter concentrates on the rise of the PYD, its clashes with various armed opposition forces, and finally the establishment of the Rojava (which means "the West" in Kurdish) self-administered region under its authority.

In Chapter 6, the internationalization of the Syrian uprising and the interventions, direct or indirect, of various international and regional actors are examined. The massive involvement of Damascus's allies Russia, Iran, and Hezbollah, as well as its political consequences, will be described in detail. The Syrian regime's increasing dependence on Russia and Iran made it more inclined to accept their political, economic, and cultural influence. On the other hand, the policies of the so-called friends of Syria (the Gulf Monarchies, Turkey, and Western states) will be analyzed. The question of the willingness of the United States and other Western countries to intervene in Syria to overthrow the regime is explored, while the Gulf Monarchies' and Turkey's political projects are characterized by competition and lack of unity. The establishment of a so-called caliphate by the Islamic State (IS) had consequences on the priorities of Western countries toward Syria, which increasingly concentrated on the war on terror in Syria, rather than support for the opposition. Meanwhile, the establishment and expansion in Kurdish-inhabited regions of the PYD also progressively changed the Turkish government's orientation in the conflict. The Gulf Monarchies were increasingly challenged by other factors, such as Saudi Arabia's military intervention in Yemen since spring 2015 and tensions that exist between Qatar and Saudi Arabia due to their divergent policies during the uprisings.

In Chapter 7, we first focus on the human and socioeconomic consequences of the war. The expansion of the war economy permitted the rise of new economic actors linked to the regime. Finally, we look at reconstruction as a major project embarked upon by the regime and crony capitalists in order to consolidate their political and economic power, as they reward foreign allies for their assistance with a share of the market. Reconstruction, however, faced several internal and external challenges for the future.

Geography and demography of Syria

Syria had a population of around 24 million people prior to the uprising in the beginning of 2011. About 56 percent of the population was urban by 2010, with an annual growth rate of nearly 2.5 to 3 percent in the years prior to the uprising (Nasser and Zaki Mehchy 2012: 3; World Bank Group 2017: 21). In 2011, 58 percent of the population in Syria was constituted of people below the age of 24 years (IFAD 2011).

Arab Sunni Muslims comprised between 65 and 70 percent of the total population, while the remainder was split among various Islamic minorities, including Alawites (10–12 percent), Druze (1–3 percent), Shias (0.5 percent), and Ismailis (1–2 percent); various Christian denominations (between 5 and 10 percent); and ethnic minorities, including Kurds (between 8 and 15 percent), Armenians (0.5 percent), Assyrians (between 1 and 3 percent), Turkmens (between 1 and 4 percent), and other groups.

Important foreign populations also exist, especially Iraqis and Palestinians prior to the uprising. Around 500,000 Palestinian refugees were registered in Syria in 2011, and between 1.2 and 1.5 million Iraqi refugees from the U.S.-led invasion of Iraq in 2003 resided in Syria (UNRWA 2011; World Bank 2017: 13).

1. The Construction of a Patrimonial Regime

Introduction

Traditional large landowners and merchants dominated Syria until the 1960s. Following independence in 1946, nationalist and leftist forces were growing and increasingly challenging the ruling classes of the country. The rise of Arab nationalism, including the Ba'th Party, led to the unity of Syria and Egypt between 1958 and 1961 with the creation of the United Arab Republic (UAR). The coup of 1961, resulting in the end of the UAR, was only a short setback before the domination of the political and economic elite of Syria was completely undermined. The Arab nationalist military coup d'état in 1963, dominated by Ba'thist elements, and successive policies until 1970 achieved significant populist socioeconomic gains. The rise to power of the Ba'th Party following the 1963 coup marked the end of the political dominance of the urban bourgeoisie, drawn predominantly from the Arab and Sunni Muslim populations of the country, and inaugurated a new era in which the new regime was dominated by social forces from the rural and peripheral areas and by religious minorities, notably the Alawis, Druze, and Isma'ilis (Haddad 2012a: XIV).

The arrival to power of Hafez al-Assad in 1970 marked the beginning of the building of a patrimonial state and of violent waves of repression against all forms of dissent within the Syrian political scene, from Islamic movements to nationalist, leftist, and liberal organizations. When Hafez al-Assad passed away in June 2000, his son Bashar succeeded him. A few hours after the announcement of the elder Assad's death, the Syrian parliament reduced the minimum age for the presidency from 40 to 34, thereby permitting Bashar to occupy this position "legally." Within a month and a half, a referendum had been organized, and he was elected with an official 97.3 percent of the vote (Perthes 2004: 7). Sa'ad Eddin Ibrahim's reference to Syria as *Jumlukiya*, which combined the Arabic words for "republic" (*jumhuriya*) and "monarchy" (*malikiya*), described this process very well (as cited in Stacher 2011: 198).

Hafez al-Assad (1970–2000): The roots of the patrimonial regime

Hafez al-Assad became president in a referendum in 1971, and from that point, he built a political system around himself in which powers were concentrated in his hands. The sphere of control of the state and its hold over society developed considerably; new institutions were established and existing ones transformed so as to conform to the emerging hierarchical and despotic structure.

Al-Assad built a strong regime through a neopatrimonial strategy that concentrated power in a presidential monarchy bolstered by his bloc of Alawi military men, in which we can find many of his family members commanding the top of the army and security forces. This patrimonial core was connected to society through bureaucratic and party populist corporatist institutions that went past sectarian and urban/rural divisions, integrating a constituency that cut through the middle class and the peasantry and represented the interests of a sizable regime coalition (Hinnebusch 2012: 97).

From the 1970s, Assad built a close network of associates to consolidate his regime. Members of Assad's own family and clan, and from the Alawi sect, had a comparative advantage in this respect. Out of 31 officers appointed by Hafez al-Assad to lead the Syrian armed forces between 1970 and 1997, no fewer than 19 (61.3 percent) were Alawi, of which eight were from his own tribe and four others from his wife's tribe (Batatu 1981: 331). All military units, as well as most security services, were under the command of Alawi loyalists from the president's own tribal and regional background (Perthes 1995: 181). Many Alawis from the *dakhel* ("hinterland"; i.e., the Homs-Hama region), considered then, and still did on the eve of the uprising in 2011, that the security services were managed and dominated by coastal Alawis and that urbanized Dakhel Alawi lacked the political connections of the coastal ones. Similar complaints could be heard in the army. To reach a high rank and influential position, one needed to be from a particular clan (Khaddour 2013a: 12; Goldsmith 2015a: 151–153). The differences between these two groups diminished with the development of the armed conflict in the country after 2011, with the strengthening of a sense of shared group affiliation and restored social cohesion across the Alawi population as a whole (Khaddour 2013a: 12), although without eliminating the socioeconomic disparities and diversity within it.

Palestinian researcher Hanna Batatu (1998: 215–226) argued that the increasing sectarian tensions in Syria in the 1970s, against the backdrop of the rising conflict between Islamic fundamentalist movements and the Assad regime and Syria's intervention in Lebanon, increased Assad's dependency on his kinsmen for political survival and thus strengthened the Alawi identity of the regime. The "Alawitization" of the officer corps was particularly reinforced after the 1979 attack on Alawi cadets in Aleppo's school of artillery by Islamic militants, and even more so, following the Hama massacre in 1982, as discussed later in this chapter (Seale 1988: 329; Van Dam 2011: 98–102). Since the early 1980s, Alawis dominated command positions in the armed forces. Sectarian representation was especially ascendant in the Republican Guard, the fourth Armored Division, the Air Force Intelligence, and the Military Security, all of which were critical for regime survival (Bou Nassif 2015: 7–9). Recruitment for employment in the state sector was another instrument by which the regime linked itself to the Alawi population, massively targeting Alawi from rural areas who were the principal beneficiaries of public sector expansion.

Dissident voices within the Alawi population were eliminated. Assad targeted possible Alawi military challengers to his rule, as well as those who had relations with the Sunni Damascene bourgeoisie, including General Muhammad Omran, assassinated in Lebanon in 1971. Salah Jadid, who had ruled Syria from 1966 to 1970, was also imprisoned from 1970 until his death in 1993.

The Alawi population did not benefit disproportionately from economic policies favoring them against other populations, according to Alasdayr Drysdale's analysis (1981: 109). The Ba'thist regime's commitment to reducing regional and urban inequalities improved life in the countryside through comprehensive land reform, extensive irrigation and land reclamation projects, and the establishment of cooperatives and new factories. Alawi who lived in the highlands complained that the bulk of peasants in their areas were destitute and still depended on erratic weather conditions for tillage (Batatu 1998: 341).

More generally, the Assad regime tried to minimize all visible signs of Alawi religiosity and promoted assimilation into the Sunni mainstream. Bashar and Hafez al-Assad both performed public prayers in Sunni mosques, while Sunni mosques were built throughout Alawi majority–populated areas. They promoted a policy of "Islamizing" the Alawis (Hinnebush 1996: 211). The regime prohibited any form of civil representation to establish a Higher Alawi Supreme Council and did not refer publicly to the Alawi religion. For example, the Alawis follow the same religious laws as the Sunni community regarding the law of personal status (marriage, divorce, inheritance, etc....) and receive a Sunni religious education in schools, media, and public institutions, just as other Islamic minorities do, except the Druze community (Syria Exposed 2005; Said, 2012; Wimmen 2017: 73).

Sunni high leaders also held important posts in the elder Assad's regime, including Chief of Staff Hikmat al-Shihabi, Minister of Defense Mustafa

Tlass, Vice President Abd Halim Khaddam, and all the prime ministers during his rule. These and other Sunni members of the president's inner circle had not secured their positions as representatives of the Sunni majority, but rather because they were longtime loyal followers of Assad (Perthes 1995: 182). Sunnis were present at all levels of state institutions. Significant numbers of urban Sunnis, mainly from Damascus, were coopted into the top ranks of the party, and many nonparty technocrats were incorporated into the government (Hinnebush 2001: 83). That said, all these personalities, except Rif'at al-Assad (the brother of Hafez) until his exile, drew their authority and strength from Hafez al-Assad and had no or very little power base of their own. The center of decision-making remained ultimately with the president (Batatu 1981: 332).

Ba'th and corporatist organizations

According to Syria's 1973 constitution, the Ba'th was the leading party in the Syrian state and society. However, it lost all of its ideological credentials with the arrival to power of Hafez al-Assad, who transformed it into an instrument of social control and of mobilization for the president (Perthes 1995: 154). The party saw the end of internal elections and their replacement by a top-down system, while elements opposing the regime policies were repressed (Seurat 2012: 59).

The post-1970s period was characterized by mass enrollment in the party with the objective to broaden the popular base, even admitting former Muslim Brotherhood (MB) members and rural notables (Perthes 1995: 155), and the use of the party as the main instrument for extending the regime's control over society. From a total party membership of 65,398 in 1971, it rose to 1,008,243 by June 1992 (Batatu 1998: 174). The party was transformed into a framework for clientelism; ideology was substituted for patronage as the dominant cement of the regime, and the party was a major front of it (Hinnebush 1990: 166). This transformation can be extended to other state institutions too:

> Assad is an organization man, mistrustful of the masses and of revolutionary adventures. He relies on the large power structure of the country: the armed forces, the bureaucracy, the Ba'th party, and the public sector—perhaps in that order. These instruments are used to control, preempt, and police, not to mobilize. (Richards and Waterbury 1990: 201)

The party, however, maintained an enduring purpose in connecting the regime and its constituency. First, it still performed individual interest articulation, negotiating with the bureaucracy to rectify constituent complaints, to place clients in jobs, and usually to smooth the decrepit functioning of the bureaucratic state. Second, the party sustained its policies of recruiting popular elements into the elite (Hinnebush 2001: 82–83).

The use of popular corporatist organizations also increased considerably. Following the 1970 coup, the trade unions were progressively denatured in order to assist the regime rather than defending working class interests. The 1972 conference of the General Federation of Trade Unions (GFTU) characterized the role of the unions in the Ba'thist state as "political" (Perthes 1995: 174); in other words, it abdicated any independent and autonomous political role for the unions and subordinated any material demand to a higher imperative: to increase production (Longuenesse 1980). The major political role of the GFTU evolved toward mobilizing their membership for constant productive efforts and to build support for regime policies among the working class. GFTU, however, continued to play a notable social role for the benefit of its membership and other segments of the population by providing some services, usually free or comparatively cheaper than other institutions, especially in the field of public health (Perthes 1995: 174–176).

The number of members in peasants' unions increased considerably. In 1972, their numbers reached 213,000, or 40 percent of the rural workforce. After 1973 and near the end of the agricultural reform program, the energy of the peasants was now channeled toward production rather than their own economic and political interests (Metral 1980). The Peasant Union and cooperatives increasingly served the interests of their wealthier members (represented by peasants with medium-sized holdings), whereas rural, landless peasants and small landholders were left without any organizations defending their interests. Thanks to their position in the cooperatives, the Peasant Union and the party, middle class peasants became the leading class in the countryside politically, without entering its wealthiest stratum (Perthes 1995: 87).

Selective and progressive liberalization

Under the new regime, good relations with conservative Arab and Western states were encouraged, while the private sector was pushed to play a larger role in the economy and foreign capital was invited as investments in the country. The regime started a process of winning the favor and support of the private sector by implementing various economic liberalization measures directly after the coup. The private-sector contribution to gross domestic product (GDP) growth rose from 30 percent in the 1960s to 37 percent in 1980 (Seifan 2013: 4), while throughout the 1970s, private investments grew faster than those of the public sector (Perthes 1995: 51). However, this controlled economic *infitah* did not challenge the predominant role of the state and public sector as the main pillars of the economy (Matar 2015: 19).

The early 1980s marked the beginning of the fiscal crisis that erupted in 1986. Real gross national product (GNP) had diminished by about 20 percent by the end of the decade (Perthes 1992b: 210). As the regime fell short of revenue, it responded through austerity measures and progressive, although limited, privatization and liberalization.

The regime's strategy regarding economic liberalization was to expand and shift its patronage networks progressively to the private sector, while controlling access to resources and the market to restrict and limit privatization to selected members and organizations. Thanks to this close intertwining of public with private interests, the state became a machine for the accumulation of considerable resources, enriching the close circles of Assad, his family, and his most faithful lieutenants in particular. The informal networks and nepotism, which bound the various sectors of the state to the business community, multiplied, giving birth to a new class of bourgeois rentiers. This "new class" was connected to all sorts of business with the state. In wealth and influence, they soon surpassed the country's mainly petit bourgeois trade sector and remnant of the old pre-Ba'th, commercial bourgeoisie (Perthes 1992b: 214).

A new push for liberalization of the economy was made in 1991, developed under a process of reforms called *al-ta'addudiyya al-iqtisadiyya* ("economic pluralism"), which officially acknowledged the role of the private sector alongside the public sector. The symbol of the new liberalization process was Decree No. 10, 1991 (Haddad 2012a: 7). This investment law decree was intended to promote and encourage national and foreign private investment in sectors of activity that previously had been under the monopoly of the public sector (Perthes 1995: 58; Marzouq 2013: 39). The private sector, which represented about 35 percent of gross fixed capital formation between 1970 and 1985, increased to 66 percent in 1994 (Hinnebush 1997: 261).

The distribution of investment projects by economic sector licensed under Law No. 10 during 1991–2005 did not serve its initial purpose to boost productive sectors of the economy: 60 percent in transport projects, 37 percent in industrial projects, and 3 percent in agricultural projects (Matar 2015: 123). This law served the interests of the new class, organically linked to the state, which needed to invest its wealth in the various sectors of the economy. Decree No. 10 thus constituted the springboard by means of which the various networks of businessmen in the country were able to launder its accrued income (Haddad 2012a: XIV). The share of salaries and wages in the GDP diminished considerably, reaching 40 percent in 2004, while rents and profits represented approximately 60 percent (Khaddam 2013: 77).

The transition from a command economy to crony capitalism was thus accelerated during the 1980s with the gradual abandonment of a centrally directed economy. The new liberalization policies were coupled with new austerity measures in the 1990s. Government spending as a portion of GDP dropped dramatically, from 48 percent in 1980 to 25 percent in 1997 (Goulden 2011: 192). The end of the 1990s witnessed growing socioeconomic problems, with poverty reaching 14.3 percent in 1996–97 (Matar 2015: 109). Inequality was also increasing in Syrian society. By the end of the 1990s and the beginning of 2000, the upper 5 percent of the country was estimated to control about 50 percent of the national income (Perthes 2004: 10).

There was also a gendered consequence to these policies. The total number of women in the workforce had expanded in the 1980s and beyond, focused particularly on the state-controlled, public economic sector. The percentage of women employed in industry in the public and private sectors increased from 13.4 percent in 1971 to 23 percent in 1981, but then decreased dramatically during the 1980s and 1990s, reaching a level of 9.8 percent in 1995. The same evolution occurred in the service sector, in which the percentage of women workers increased from 18.7 percent in 1970 to 47.2 percent by 1981, and then it decreased to 30.2 percent in 1995 (Perthes 2004: 10). In the public sector, the percentage of women always had been higher than in the private sector, but the latter's size and contribution in the 2000s was much higher than the public sector (the ratio was 70:30).

No opposition allowed

Through these three decades in power, Syrian society came increasingly under the control of the regime in all its various components. The Ba'th Party was the only political organization, which had the right to organize events, lectures, and public demonstrations and to distribute a newspaper on the campus of a university or military barracks. Even the political parties allied to the regime in the National Progressive Front (NPF) did not have the right to organize, make propaganda, or have even a small official presence in these institutions (Seurat 2012: 138).

Politically, the Islamic fundamentalist forces led by the MB represented the most significant menace to the regime from 1976 until the Hama massacre in 1982. Hafez al-Assad first tried to coopt some sectors of the MB throughout the 1970s and sought some form of understanding with the movement, although these efforts were combined with periods of violent repression (Seale 1988: 188; Pierret 2011: 245; Lefèvre 2013: 87).

Alongside the repression endured by their members, the hostility of the MB was deepened through the years by the growing domination of Alawi personalities of key regime institutions, especially in the army and security services. This was reflected in the increasing concentration of MB attacks on the Alawi identity of the regime, rather than (as in the 1960s) on its more "atheist" features. In 1979–80, the MB called for an armed revolt to overthrow the regime and establish an Islamic State (Porat 2010; Seurat 2012:145). The MB presented themselves as the natural spokesmen of the country's Sunni population and characterized their fight with Syria's rulers as a struggle between Sunni and Alawi (Batatu 1982: 13). They sought to generate a form of Sunni solidarity that cut across class and regional divisions. The leadership of the party attempted most particularly to win the support of the upper land-owning class, which had suffered significantly from the Ba'thist policies of the 1960s. The networks connecting the MB and the rich landowners, which had been established in the 1950s, were revived. Rich nobles began supplying significant funding to the MB and engaged with them in plans to overthrow the regime. They were also supported politically, and even financially, by four countries with different political considerations, but all sharing hostility to the Assad regime: Iraq, Egypt, Jordan, and Saudi Arabia (Lefèvre 2013: 50, 129).

By the end of the 1970s and the beginning of the 1980s, increasing military confrontation occurred between the jihadist group Fighting Vanguard and the regime's forces, taking an intense sectarian and violent turn. The Fighting Vanguard was a faction officially separate from the MB, although the boundaries were not clear between the two entities, and leaders and members of both organizations shared deep relations during that period (Pargeter 2010: 82; Lefèvre 2013: 120).

The first targets of the regime following Hafez al-Assad's rise to power, however, were the nonviolent, democratic, leftist, and secular opposition. These groups posed a significant threat to the regime throughout the 1970s and 1980s, as they had large support particularly among trade unions, professional associations, and the middle class. These movements and organizations were composed of members reflecting the diversity of the Syrian society, including important minority elements. Following the military intervention by the Syrian regime in Lebanon in 1976 against the Palestinian resistance and the Lebanese National Movement (LNM), which they condemned in strong terms, these movements and organizations stepped up their opposition to the regime (Middle East Watch 1991: 9). At the same time, crackdowns intensified against trade unionists affiliated or identified with these opposition parties (Middle East Watch 1991: 14). In 1980, all professional associations were dissolved by decree (Seurat 2012: 100). The regime then established new professional associations and appointed new leaders who mainly acted as corporatist arms of the state and the ruling party (Middle East Watch 1991: 19).

The 1980s also were characterized by intermittent conflicts and repression against Palestine Liberation Organization (PLO) members and Palestinians more generally. The regime's jails held approximately 2,500 Palestinian political prisoners in the summer of 1990 (Middle East Watch 106–108). The leftist opposition and critics within the Ba'th Party were also the target of security forces.

The turning point, however, was in February 1982 with the Hama uprising, followed by massive and bloody repression. A general insurrection was called from the minarets of the city, following an ambush by fighters in the Fighting Vanguard and the MB against regime security forces in the old city. Guns and ammunition were captured from police stations and approximately 100 government and party representatives were assassinated (Lawson 1982). Weapons were distributed en masse, and an Islamic tribunal was established (Seurat 2012: 113). Regime forces crushed the armed rebellion and imposed a violent, collective punishment on the city. Estimates of the number killed varied from 5,000 to 10,000, and many thousands more were injured. More than a third of the city was destroyed, leaving between 60,000 and 70,000 people homeless (Middle East Watch 1991: 20; Lefèvre 2013: 120).

Following the Hama massacre, all organized Syrian opposition was almost completely crushed. Arrests of political activists and human rights defenders continued, particularly targeting left-wing and democratic groups throughout the 1990s.

Integration of the bourgeoisie and conservative layers of society

The repression of popular organization and opposition political parties went hand in hand with the increased connection and collaboration among sectors of the predominantly Sunni urban business community through policies of economic rapprochement and controlled liberalization (Perthes 1992b: 225). Private-sector representative institutions such as the Chamber of Commerce and Industry were reinvigorated in the mid- and late-1980s, just when economic networks started to solidify (Haddad 2013: 84).

This was increasingly translated into the institutions of the state. In parliamentary elections organized in May 1990, two members of the Damascus Chamber of Commerce and one of the Aleppo Chamber of Commerce were elected, with one of the new deputies clearly characterizing himself as a representative of businesses (Perthes 1992a: 15–18). In the People's Assembly, a greater voice and space were given to businessmen, religious sheikhs, and some traditional tribal leaders among the nonparty and independent elements. They occupied 33.2 percent of the seats in Parliament in 1994 (Batatu 1998: 277).

The regime also developed a religiously conservative discourse, in contradiction to the secular image that it claimed to represent. Assad multiplied the number of allegiances to Islam (Seurat 2012: 88), and during a speech to Syrian Ulama, he affirmed that the Corrective Movement, political reforms initiated following his coup d'état in 1970, was necessary to preserve the Islamic identity of the country against the Marxist drifts of his predecessors (Pierret 2011: 244). In 1973, he ordered a new printing of the Koran with his picture on the cover (Talhamy 2009: 566). The regime built 8,000 new mosques throughout the 1970s, 1980s, and 1990s, established around two dozen institutes of Islamic higher education, and developed some 600 quasi-official religious institutions in all Syrian governorates and cities to replace those that had been used by the MB for recruitment (Khatib L. 2011: 90). The regime was trying to encourage a conservative Islamic establishment to channel Islamic currents and legitimize itself (Hinnebush 2001: 83).

They also started to sponsor and institutionalize alternative Islamic groups that were willing to cooperate. The Naqshbandi Kuftariya Sufi order under Sheikh Ahmad Kuftaro's and Sheikh Sa'id al-Buti's groups became the two most prominent Islamic factions and expanded considerably in the 1970s (Khatib L. 2011: 90). At the same time, during the 1970s, the Qubaysiyyat female Islamic movement, established by al-Sheikha Munira al-Qubaysi as an autonomous female branch of the Naqshbandi order, was granted its first permission to establish an elementary school/preschool in Damascus (Imady 2016: 73). Syrian authorities also encouraged the activities of Sheikh Saleh Farfour and its al-Fatih Islamic Institute.

The rise of the Islamic charitable sector reflected a period of détente between the Ba'th regime and the Islamic trend, which started in the mid-1990s in the hope of strengthening the regime's legitimacy by ameliorating relations with domestic and regional Islamic forces. In 1994, for example, leaders of Jama'at Zayd, an Islamic organization, came back from their exile in Saudi Arabia and became leading players in private welfare, attracting significant popularity among the Damascene middle class and higher strata, which provided the group with an important capacity to attract funds from the private sector (Pierret and Kjetil 2009: 596).

Prisoners associated with the MB and the Islamic movement's opposition were liberated by the regime, and some were even coopted by Damascus as independents in Parliament, such as when Ghassan Abazad, an Ikhwan leader from Dar'a who brokered the return of MB members exiled in Jordan, won a seat in Parliament in the beginning of the 1990s (Hinnebush 1996:

211). This was happening in the background of new, secret negotiations between the regime and the MB following the election of Ali Sadreddine al-Bayanouni as chair of the MB in Syria in 1996 (Lefèvre 2013: 175).

This rapprochement with religious conservative layers of society was accompanied by censorship and attacks on literature criticizing religion, while self-declared atheist writers were asked to respect the sensibilities of Muslim believers (Khatib L. 2011: 89).

There was also a rapprochement between Alawi and Shi'a doctrines following Assad's arrival to power. Historically, this began in the 1930s, but it increased considerably with the consolidation of the relationship with the Islamic Republic of Iran (IRI) after 1979. Hundreds of Hawzaz and Husseiniya were constructed, financed, and supervised by Iran, and thousands of Iranian clerics were allowed into Syria to act as teachers and guides to the Alawi population (Khatib L. 2011: 94). Iranian missionaries in Syria were able to convert a few thousand people in the country, notably in some of the villages in the northeastern area of the Jazirah, close to the Shi'a religious sites Uwais al-Qarni mosque and Ammar ibn Yasir shrine, where the missionaries had established a base. Bashar al-Assad ultimately put an end to this Shi'a proselytism in 2008, following criticisms of Sunni religious authorities and clerics (Balanche 2018: 14).

The regime similarly encouraged a policy of rapprochement with tribal[1] sheikhs, whose powers had been weakened by previous Ba'th policies of land redistribution. Some Bedouin tribes were also called upon by the regime to play a role in the repression of the military insurrection of the MB between 1979 and 1982. Hafez al-Assad formed alliances with several common tribes (or Shawi)[2] that inhabited the rural areas of the country, particularly Deir ez-Zor, where the Ougeidat tribe joined the army and intelligence services in large numbers (Wilcox 2017). In the city of Aleppo, it was the Berri tribal family that took care of the repression against the MB, and it was greatly rewarded by the regime with control over border traffic of all kinds (Donati 2009: 299). Since the 1980s, the position of Minister of Agriculture have been generally granted to a Bedouin, as are senior appointments to the Ministry of Interior and the Ba'th Regional Command, while some Bedouin tribal leaders also become deputies in Parliament (Chatty 2010: 46). The Syrian regime allows the leaders of tribes a greater

---

[1] According to Khedder Khaddour (2017c), "A tribe, in the Syrian context, is a sociopolitical unit based upon extended families living in a defined territory, usually entire towns and city neighborhoods."

[2] According to Dr. Haian Dukhan (cited in Mateo and Wilcox 2017), "the word Shawi comes from the fact that these tribes raised sheep and goats whereas the noble tribes raised camels. The noble tribes, of course, despised the common tribes."

degree of influence over local communities of tribal background and provides them with certain privileges.

Bashar al-Assad's era until 2011

Following the death of his older son, Bassel, in a car crash in 1994, Hafez al-Assad began the process of preparing the succession to his other son, Bashar. Hafez al-Assad died in June 2000. In the decade prior to the 2011 uprising, the patrimonial nature of the state in the hands of the Assad family and relatives (including extended family) was strengthened greatly through a process of accelerated implementation of neoliberal policies and the replacement of sections of the old guard by relatives or individuals close to Bashar al-Assad.

There was, however, a wind of hope among sectors of the country with the rise to power of Bashar al-Assad. The notorious political prison of Mezzeh in Damascus, a symbol of the brutal political repression of the regime, was closed in September 2000, while around six hundred political prisoners were released in November 2001 (Ghadbian 2015: 93). Human rights organizations and forums for debate also multiplied at the beginning of this new reign. The political parties of the NPF were authorized to publish their own weekly newspapers, in addition to opening provincial offices (Perthes 2004: 20).

In early 2001, the first privately owned newspaper, *al-Dommari*, owned by caricaturist Ali Ferzat, was authorized to resume publication by the regime after nearly 40 years. The pan-Arabist newspapers *al-Hayat* and *al-Sharq al-Awsat*, as well as Lebanese, Jordanian, and Gulf Arab titles and a small number of private magazines, were progressively made available (Ghadbian 2015: 93). However, the country was still far from having any pluralistic and free press. In September 2001, the Syrian regime adopted a new Press Law (Decree No. 50/2001), which provided the government with sweeping controls over virtually everything printed in Syria (Human Rights Watch 2010). The authorities did not hesitate to censor content that it considered unacceptable (George 2003: 133).

The phenomenon of discussion forums, which was the most salient feature of the opportunity taken by activists and opposition members to express themselves, rapidly increased, and by 2001, there were more than 170 across the country that engaged large numbers of participants (Abbas 2013: 18).

Some youth movements, gathering university students from middle class and popular backgrounds, also came out of these forums, such as the movement of activists against globalization in Syria (known as *ATTAC Syria*) and the gathering of young Democrats called *Shams* (Hamsho 2016). At the same time, clandestine student organizations emerged in Aleppo and Damascus, where they were the best organized. They denounced the corruption of university professors by launching boycott campaigns against them or gathering signatures, while demanding more autonomy and democracy within student associations and unions. Student movements also mobilized on some social issues; for example, in February 2004, around 500 students demonstrated against a decree abolishing the obligation of the state to employ engineers and architects after they graduated. In response to this protest, 64 students were expelled from Aleppo University because of their political activities, while a campaign of repression followed against the hidden student committees of Aleppo and Damascus and a number of clandestine associations (Gauthier 2005: 103; Emancipations 2015).

These student committees also supported the Palestinian Intifada, including protests, between 2000 and 2003. The regime saw with some concern the organization of actions in solidarity with the Intifada and in some cases launched a campaign of intimidation (and even arrests) against students who organized and took part in the various demonstrations and sit-ins, forcing them to put an eventual end to their activities. The authorities were scared that if these demonstrations continued, the protests might extend their concerns to a domestic agenda (Abdulhamid 2005: 36; Emancipations 2015).

Syrian civil society and political organizations were thus mobilized from the mid-2000s, calling for reforms and a democratization of the state. This was the meaning of the Declaration of 99 or the Committee to Revive Civil Society (announced by a press release under the name of the Declaration of 1,000), which comprised intellectuals, artists, writers, researchers, and even representatives of some political parties. The Declaration of 99, published in the Lebanese press in September 2000, called on the authorities to put an end to martial law, liberate political prisoners, and provide political freedoms. Some signatories were even allowed to publish articles in local state-controlled press, particularly al-Thawra, that were critical of the regime (Abbas 2013: 18; Perthes 2004: 13).

During the same period, some 20 deputies established an "independent Parliamentary Bloc," while 70 lawyers published a statement demanding an end to the state of emergency in place since 1963, the independence of the judiciary, and the legalization of political parties (Perthes 2004: 16). Regular protests in front of tribunals in Damascus and Aleppo were held during this period, while Kurdish political organizations multiplied their actions against the regime's policies and denounced the continuous political, economic, and cultural discrimination against the Kurds in Syria (Gauthier 2005: 102–103; Tejel 2009 112–114).

The regime's officials progressively launched a brutal counterattack at the rhetorical level through the press, accusing opposition members of being backed by foreign countries and being antinationalist. Some of their aggression was even physical, such as the arrests or assaults of activists (George 2003: 48). By the end of summer 2001, ten of the most prominent leaders of civil society were imprisoned, and all the forums for debates except for one were closed (Landis and Pace 2009: 121). The state's media increasingly avoided using slogans such as "*al-islah wa-l-tajdid*" ("reform and renewal"), which had been used to characterize the new era, and instead switched to "*al-tatwir wa-l-tahdith*" ("development and modernization") (Perthes 2004: 18–19).

In 2005, more than 250 major opposition figures and political parties signed the "Damascus Declaration," a manifesto that called for "a democratic and radical change" in Syria based on dialogue, the end of the state emergency, and the release of political prisoners. The signatories to the declaration included the National Democratic Alliance (a nationalist and left-liberal-wing alliance of five parties), the committees for the revival of civil society, the Democratic Kurdish Coalition, the Kurdish Democratic Front, and a number of independent personalities such as former MP Riyad Seif. The MB supported the Damascus Declaration, but in 2006, they joined forces with 15 other opposition groups, along with Abdul Halim Khaddam, the former vice president of Syria who had just defected from the regime (as discussed later in this chapter), in the establishment of the National Salvation Front (NSF). The "Damascus Declaration" did not join this new coalition, which was roundly criticized by several of its prominent signatories (Porat 2010: 4).

In December 2007, the National Council of the Damascus Declaration was established in Syria, with the participation of 163 members. A few days after, the regime launched a campaign of arrest against the Declaration's members and twelve members of its leadership were prosecuted and sentenced in 2008 to prison terms ranging from three to six years (Perrin 2008; Kawakibi and Sawah 2013: 13; Sawah 2012: 10). Arrests of political activists continued until the end of the 2000s. The Damascus declaration and its leadership were increasingly poisoned by divisions (Carnegie 2012c).

In April 2009, the leader of the Syrian MB, Ali Sadr al-Din al-Bayanuni, announced an end to their participation in the NSF. The Syrian Ikhwan were seeking a form of understanding and reconciliation with the regime. This process started a few months earlier, with al-Bayanuni's announcement during the January 2009 Israel-Gaza war of a "suspension of resistance activities in the struggle against the Syrian regime," following a meeting held at this same time between Bashar al-Assad and Sunni religious leaders, including Sheik Yusuf al-Qardawi, an influential personality affiliated with the MB (Porat 2010: 1–4). The beginning of the uprising in Syria in March 2011 would end this process with the MB calling in April to support the protest movement.

More generally in the years preceding the start of the uprising, a new generation of young activists was rising in Syria, but often they were not involved in traditional political parties. These activists carried out a series of community activities around social and economic issues. Between 2004 and 2006, a wave of sit-ins developed at the initiative of these young political activists and civil society organizations, dealing with various issues relating to democratic and social rights. They also launched various civil campaigns, including a campaign to oppose so-called honor crimes or to confer to women the right to pass their citizenship to their children. In these campaigns, the civil rights activists used new media (blogs, emails, and text messages) and social networking sites such as Facebook and Twitter, which were forbidden in Syria (Sawah 2012: 14). These campaigns were an opportunity for young people to come into direct contact with the street and opened new channels for dialogue with the public on various issues (al-Aous 2013: 25).

Activists were also involved in social assistance to the victims of the drought that hit eastern Syria. Hundreds of thousands of people left their home towns and villages and came to the Damascus countryside. Civil society activists started to organize the provision of food, shelter, and toys and education for the children of the displaced population, risking their own safety by doing so as the regime opposed any social solidarity outside its umbrella. Young men and women challenged the regime's restrictions to provide assistance and drew a development plan to help them return to their schools and homes (Sawah 2012: 2).

Women's rights organizations were similarly developing their activities, particularly in the campaigns mentioned here. The al-Thara Group was the first one to engage in women's and children's rights. Its website was very prominent, attracting great interest from civil activists (al-Aous 2013; Kawakibi and Sawah 2013). Large sections of this new generation of activists would play an important role in the beginning of the uprising in 2011.

Bashar's conquest of the old guard

Following Bashar al-Assad's arrival to power in 2000, a collective leadership with the old guard remaining from his father's era was established. Bashar's first years were concentrated on consolidating his power against the clientelist networks of the old guard. He introduced his loyalists into the army and security forces and incorporated reforming technocrats into government in a tug of war with the rest of the Ba'th Party leadership over appointments. In less than two years, approximately three-quarters of the 60 top political, administrative, and military officeholders were ousted. All editors-in-chief of the state-run media were replaced. A few months later, nearly all provincial governors and provincial heads of the Ba'th were removed.

In 2002, elections for lower-level party leaderships generated an important turnover among functionaries. That same year, the government enacted a decision to retire all civil servants over the age of 60. This decree, which included 80,000 employees, permitted younger cadres to be upgraded and provided new opportunities for new entrants. Some exemptions to forced retirement were necessary, especially in the foreign ministry, where diplomats with accumulated experience were insufficient, and in the security apparatus. This reorganization provided the means for the new leadership around Assad to achieve rapid domination over the public sector. In the new Parliament of 2003, although the general political coloring was not modified because the majority share of the Ba'th Party in the chamber was already fixed, 178 out of 250 deputies were newcomers (Perthes 2004: 8).

This turn was also reflected in the increasing undermining of Ba'thists in official positions, while the nomination of liberal technocrats increased. Ghassan al-Rifai, a World Bank economist with a PhD from the University of Sussex, became Minister of Economy and Foreign Trade; Muhammad al-Atrash, who held a doctorate in economics from the University of London and served in the past as an adviser of the World Bank, became Minister of Finance; Isam al-Zaim, who has been a researcher at the National Council for Scientific Research in Paris, became Minister of Industry. Later, Abdallah Dardari, holding a master's degree from the University of Southern California and former assistant resident representative for the United Nations Development Programme (UNDP) in Syria, became Minister of Planning. Later, he was promoted to Deputy Prime Minister for Economic Affairs (Hinnebush 2015: 29; Zisser 2007: 67).

Within the Ba'th Party, a massive turnover in leadership and cadres reached its summit at the tenth Ba'th Party Congress in 2005, when the old guard, led by Abdel Halim Khaddam, was cleared from power. The resignation of the first vice president, Khaddam, the second-most-important figure in Syria and one of the closest allies of Hafez al-Assad, was the most significant change. Bashar al-Assad had marginalized him politically since the beginning of the 2000s. In the same year, Ghazi Kana'an, an associate of Khaddam and former interior minister following the Syrian army's withdrawal of Lebanon in 2005, was found dead in his home, allegedly after committing suicide. Other figures of the old guard were also replaced (Hinnebush 2015: 37), mostly by technocrats without any base of support.

In removing these elements, Assad considerably curtailed the difficulties for his new reforms, but that also undermined influential and powerful interests with clientelist networks that included key sections of society in the regime. The army and security forces were not spared by these turnovers, as they were key institutions to secure Bashar's power. Hostile figures of the old guard had been dismissed by his father before his death, so Bashar was able to designate their successors. Old-guard military barons and intelligence bosses, including Alawi generals Ali Aslan and Adnan Badr Hasan, Shafiq al-Fayyad, and Ibrahim al-Safi, were ousted from the Central Committee, while Maher al-Assad, brother of Bashar, and Manaf Tlass, a close friend and associate of Bashar and son of former defense minister Mustafa Tlass, saw their membership renewed (Hinnebush 2015: 29, 38).

Bashar al-Assad also appointed family members in senior positions in the army, such as his brother Maher, the de facto commander of the fourth Armored Division; his cousin, Zou al-Himma Shalish, in charge of units responsible for the security of Bashar and his family; another cousin, Hafez Makhlouf, who headed the internal branch of the General Security Directorate 's Damascus branch; yet another cousin, Hilal al-Assad, was commander of the Military Police in the fourth Armored Division; and Assad's brother-in-law, Asef Shawkat, the strongman in the intelligence apparatus until his death in 2012 (Bou Nassif 2015: 17).

Although some old-generation figures from the era of Hafez al-Assad still played a role in Bashar's regime, this was the most important change in the membership of the political elite for 30 years, across almost all spheres of state power. According to researcher Volker Perthes (2004: 9), this turnover was necessary because

> [f]rom the president's perspective, such a thorough renewal and rejuvenation of the political and administrative elite was necessary not only to gather support for his ideas about reform, but also to increase, albeit gradually, the number and weight of people within the institutions of power who owed their position, and thus their loyalty, to him not to his father or to the old regime...

Weakening state institutions and corporatist organizations

New members with antagonistic aspirations entered the Ba'th Party, while its decline as a channel for recruitment to top offices and reduced numbers of cadres resulted in a diminishing role of the party in Syrian society. The party's policymaking was monopolized by small circles of leaders linked to the regime, with no possibility to challenge it from below (Wael Sawah, cited in al-Om 2018: 161). The weakening of the Ba'th was witnessed at all levels. Political mobilizations were no longer the prerogatives of the Ba'th but were privatized. For example, in 2007 during the referendum to confirm the presidency of Bashar al-Assad, it was mostly the networks of Rami Makhlouf and of other rich tycoons close to the regime that mobilized regime supporters (Donati 2013: 47–48). In 2010, Assad, in a new move to consolidate his power, disbanded the second-rank branch and subbranch leaderships, further undermining the apparatus on the eve of the uprising against the regime (Hinnebush 2012: 100).

In addition to the Ba'th Party apparatus, Assad weakened workers and peasant unions, viewed as obstacles to neoliberal economic reform. The regime increasingly starved the various populist corporatist organizations of funds and attacked their powers of patronage, but with dire consequences. As explained by Raymond Hinnebush (2012: 98–99):

> [T]his debilitated the regime's organized connection to its constituency and its penetration of neighborhoods and villages. The gap was partly filled by the security services, which however were underpaid, corrupt and lax, moreover, Assad curbing of their ability to dispense patronage and legal exemptions, such as tolerance of smuggling, reduced their ability to coopt societal notables such as tribal elders, symptomatic of this was the mid-decade outbreak of several localized sectarian/tribal conflicts (between Bedouin and Druze in Suwayda, and between Alawis and Isma'ilis in Masyaf), which manifested an erosion of the regime. Where citizens would once have gone to local party or union officials for redress or access, increasingly they approached tribal, sectarian and religious notables.

As argued by Ammar Abdulhamid (2005: 37), regarding the 2005 clashes between Alawi and Isma'ili populations in the town of Masyaf:

> [D]espite the fact that at the heart of all these issues lie some well documented socioeconomic grievances, the fact that the rioting took place along sectarian and ethnic fault lines is pretty telling.

Previously, sectarian tensions existed in some mixed regions as a result of the regime policies and repression of the late 1970s and 1980s. In the coastal areas, the neoliberal policies after 2000 exacerbated the competition among popular classes over dwindling public resources and increased social inequality. This competition took on sectarian colors on some occasions. Individuals from the Alawi popular classes occupied strong positions in the security sector and in the army, which helped them access professional and material advantages, particularly in the public sector, and they benefited from systemic corruption in the public sector as a result of regime patronage policies. The Alawi population was overrepresented in the state apparatus. A study from 2004 showed that 80 percent of employed Alawis worked in the military, state-led industry, or the public sector.

In the governorates of Lattakia and Tartus, the proportions of the working population employed in the civilian public sector (54.6 percent and 39.5 percent, respectively) were higher than the national average (26.9 percent). In comparison to other religious sects, the Alawi were far more represented in this sector. In Lattakia, of the male workforce, 81 percent of Alawi was employed in the public sector, compared to 57 percent of Christians and 44 percent of Sunnis (Balanche 2015: 91–92). During the first phase of the uprising in 2011, protesters in mixed Sunni-Alawi cities, such as Baniyas, Lattakia, and Tartus, raised this issue, demanding the rectification of alleged pro-Alawi sectarian biases in employment in state industries and public administrations.

Youssef Abdo (2018), a former employee at the Afforestation Development Office project in the governorate of Tartus, stated in an interview:

Among around 60 employees in the Afforestation Development Office project affiliated with the Tartus governorate in the village of Derdara, the quasi-totality were Alawi, except me |Sunni| and one Christian. A similar sectarian disproportion was present in the offices of the Directorate of Agriculture in Tartus. Although these areas were in far majority inhabited by Alawi population and could explain a majority of Alawi employees, there was however a recruitment system of "wasta" linked to familial and tribal connections favoring Alawis in the office. This system of recruitment based on wasta favorising Alawi was less extreme in the mixed areas of Tartus and Lattakia's governorates, although the number of Alawi employees were generally more important...

This situation led some sections of the population to perceive the Alawi population as a whole as inextricably connected to experiences of unfair privilege, and quite often to abusive practices as well, such as protection rackets or the extortion of bribes for access to public services.

This overrepresentation in the public sector, however, did not reflect a special socioeconomic position in society; a growing number of Alawis were left outside the circle of communal privilege. The Alawi popular classes suffered just like others during the liberalization of the economy, the end of subventions, and high inflation. The Alawi Mountains was one of the most impoverished regions, after the North-Eastern regions, which were populated mainly by Kurdish people. A report of the International Crisis Group (ICG) in 2011 stated that

> the Alawi countryside remains strikingly underdeveloped; many join the army for lack of an alternative; members of the security services typically are overworked and underpaid. Young members of the community for the most part joined the security apparatus solely because the regime offered them no other prospects. Ordinary Alawi rarely benefited, from high-level corruption, least of all under Bashar.

The increased patrimonial nature of the state and the weakening of the Ba'th Party apparatus and corporatist organizations rendered cliental, tribal, and sectarian connections all the more important. This trend manifested itself throughout the country, and not only on the coast. In the city of Aleppo, the regime continued to sustain its connections to two tribal leaders, in addition to other networks, to exercise its control and domination. The Berri tribal family, whose collaboration with the regime went back to the 1980s, managed the security apparatus of the city and also benefited from border traffic, while the Shahada played a more political role and held a seat in Parliament. In Raqqa, tribal families allied with the Assad regime benefited from the privatization of state farms in the Jazirah in the 2000s (Donati 2009: 299). The number of tribal clashes, however, increased during Bashar al-Assad's rule as a result of neoliberal policies that impoverished even more rural areas, and also because the patronage systems that developed between Hafez al-Assad and the rural communities were weakened (Wilcox 2017).

In the case of Suwayda, mainly inhabited by the Druze population, the regime managed the region by compromises with local notables. The governor and the heads of the army and security services were from other Syrian provinces in order to avoid collusion with the local population, but the key positions in the governorate administration, directions of state bodies, and the party cell in Suwayda were vested to members of large Druze families. For example, after a period of deprivation in the 1970s and 1980s in terms of public investments from the state, a member of the Atrash family was appointed in the 1990s to head the powerful Ministry of Local Administration and Environment, resulting in a boom of public investment in the Suwayda region, including improved services and the creation of thousands of administrative jobs. The state also relied on the religious elites, especially the three "al-Aql" sheikhs who are the highest religious representatives of the Druze community. These civil and religious elites provided the interface between the regime and the Druze population (Roussel 2006: 148; Balanche 2018: 15).

Similarly, the efficiency of the Syrian Arab Army (SAA) was weakened considerably in the years following Bashar's arrival to power. Its funding fell considerably, its lucrative activities in Lebanon ended after its withdrawal in 2005, and its arms and equipment fell far behind those of Israel (in terms of technology and capacity to go to war). The combat-preparedness of the SAA steadily deteriorated throughout the 1990s and fell to a dramatic low on the eve of the 2011 uprisings. The neglect of the armed forces was even more striking considering the preferential treatment and status extended to the units controlled by Assad's kin and composed nearly entirely of Alawis, especially the Republican Guards, fourth Division, and eleventh Division, which enjoyed generous funding, special training, advanced weaponry, privileged status, and access to top leadership (Abbas 2011; Bou Nassif 2015: 13–14; Kattan 2016).

According to Hicham Bou Nassif (2015: 11), "Sunni officers suffered from more discrimination in the military under Bashar al-Assad than under his father." The Sunni officers interviewed by Bou Nassif explained that Hafez al-Assad's control over his generals was stronger than his son's. The regime became more decentralized under Bashar, with several powerful military barons maneuvering for power and battling to position their Alawi followers throughout the various sectors of the armed forces. Consequently, the Sunnis' number of prominent appointments in the military decreased even more in the decade prior to the uprising (Bou Nassif 2015: 11).

The implementation of neoliberal policies also negatively affected the living conditions of many military personnel, pushing many officers from the lower ranks to seek additional jobs in the private sector due to high inflation and depreciation of real wages, while influential, high-ranking officers benefited from contracts with private interests as the market opened up, accumulating substantial amounts of wealth. Disparity within the army increased significantly, affecting its cohesion. The weight of military economic institutions also weakened with the liberalization of the economy. The Military Housing Institution (MHI) was one of the largest economic establishments in the country, employing 100,000 and 50,000 temporary workers in the 1980s and monopolizing more than 85 percent of the domestic market in construction contracts. It saw an important decline in the 2000s. In 2011, it employed 25,000 workers and lost more than 35 percent of its market share. The MHI and the second military construction enterprise (MATA), which also played a significant role in construction projects, remained the most important in the construction sector and maintained its monopoly in some segments of the economy (Said S. 2018: 62–66).

In short, seeking to strengthen and consolidate its power within the regime that he inherited, Assad continuously weakened the regime and the state's institutional capacities to preserve its connections and power over society.

The acceleration of neoliberal policies

Unlike his father, Bashar allowed the World Bank and the International Monetary Fund (IMF) to intervene in the process of economic liberalization (Matar 2015: 111). The Ba'th Party, at its tenth regional conference in 2005, adopted the social market economy as a new economic strategy. In other words, the private sector would become a partner and leader in the process of economic development and in providing employment instead of the state (Abboud 2015: 55). The aim was to encourage private accumulation principally through the marketization of the economy while the state withdrew in key areas of social welfare provision. Doing this aggravated already-existing socioeconomic problems.

The attraction of foreign investment and the return of Syrian funds held outside the country by nationals and expatriates, especially in the service sectors, were fundamental to this new economic strategy. Legislative Decree (LD) No. 8 was ratified in 2007 to promote more investment in the country, and it became the main legal framework behind private investment, supplanting the old Investment Law No. 10, passed in 1991 (Matar 2015: 112–113). In addition, the Syrian Investment Agency (SIA), a new investment authority, was established, which took the place of the investment bureau that had been functioning since the beginning of the 1990s. Foreign direct investment climbed from $120 million in 2002 to $3.5 billion in 2010. Investment inflows drove a boom in trade, housing, banking, construction, and tourism (Hinnebush 2012: 100). Only 13 percent of all foreign and domestic investments throughout the 2000s were in manufacturing areas (Abboud 2015: 55). Industry and mining accounted to 25 percent of the GDP, but manufacturing production contributed to only 4.4 percent of the GDP in 2011, already suffering from the beginning of the uprising as its contribution to the GDP diminished from 6.9 percent in 2009, while the average size of manufacturing establishments in 2006 was around 4.8 workers per establishment in Syria. The manufacturing sector was constituted by 99 percent of Small and Medium Enterprises (Matar 2015: 12).

The financial sector developed similarly, with the establishment of private banks, insurance firms, the Damascus stock exchange, and money exchange bureaus throughout the 2000s. The first measure to liberalize the banking sector was taken in 2001, granting the right for the establishment of private banks for the first time after 40 years of a state-controlled banking system. The ruling elites and the commercial bourgeoisie, such as Rami Makhlouf, Nader Qalai, Issam Anbouba, and Samir Hassan, were the major shareholders of many private banks, rather than comparable market competitors. The rebirth and development of private banking were essential for the state bourgeoisie. It allowed them to operate their bank accounts and conveniently transfer their deposits outside the country. Previously, they had to smuggle or convert their wealth into dollars and store it in private Lebanese banks (Matar 2015: 117).

The opening of private banks also increased the regime's access to growing pools of investment capital in the Gulf Monarchies (Donati 2013:38). By the end of 2011, more than twenty private banks existed parallel to the specialized public banks,[3] and they accounted for 27 percent of total banking assets worth $40 billion (Butter 2015: 7).

The Syrian regime progressively eliminated trade barriers with the implementation of the Greater Arab Free Trade Area (GAFTA), signed in 2005, along with bilateral agreements with its neighbors Turkey and Iran. Trade liberalization witnessed a more significant increase in the importation of foreign products, rather than the export of Syrian products. Exports grew by 34 percent between 2005 and 2010, while imports saw a surge of 62 percent during the same period (Seifan 2013: 116). Trade liberalization (especially the treaty with Turkey and the export of massive Turkish products) did play a negative role in the dislocation of productive resources and in the termination of many local manufacturing plants, particularly those situated in the suburbs of the major cities where many protests in 2011 initially began (Matar 2015: 115).

The share of the private economy continued to rise, contributing to up to 65 percent of GDP (and more than 70 percent, according to other estimates) in 2010. More than 70 percent of the labor force in Syria worked in the private sector (Achcar 2013: 24). The public sector remained the largest single employer in Syria, accounting for around 28.5 percent of the workforce in 2008 (World Bank 2011:46).

Neoliberal policies satisfied the upper class in Syria and foreign investors, especially from the Gulf Monarchies and Turkey, at the expense of the vast majority of Syrians who were hit by inflation and the rising cost of living. During this period, the regime also significantly reduced taxes on the profits of the private sector, both groups and individuals, from 63 percent in 2003 to 35 percent in 2004, and then for a second time in 2005 so that it now ranges between 15 and 27 percent. These measures were implemented despite the fact that tax evasion was already very prevalent, reaching 100 billion Syrian pounds (SYP) in 2009, according to some estimates (Seifan 2013: 109). Small- and medium-sized enterprises, which made up more than

---

[3] These are the Real Estate Bank, the Agricultural Cooperative Bank, and the Industrial Bank.

99 percent of all businesses in Syria, were also mostly negatively affected by marketization and the liberalization of the economy (Abboud 2017).

Economic growth was chiefly rent-based, dependent on oil export revenues, geopolitical rents, and capital inflows, including remittances. The share of productive sectors diminished from 48.1 percent of GDP in 1992 to 40.6 percent in 2010 (Marzouq 2013: 40), while the share of wages from the national income was less than 33 percent in 2008–09 compared to nearly 40.5 percent in 2004, meaning that profits and rents commanded more than 67 percent of GDP (Marzouq 2011).

In the decade following Bashar's rise to power, the significance of the service sector role increased, while that of agriculture diminished considerably (as discussed later). The service sector's share in value added increased from 41.9 percent in 2000 to 55.5 percent in 2008. During the 2000s, the share of tertiary employment rose from 42.8 percent to 52.8 percent. This sector represented 84 percent of the growth registered during this period. In 2008, over half of Syrian workers were employed in the tertiary sector, while 30 percent worked in the industrial sector, which included the construction industry to up to around 15 percent (World Bank 2011: 46).

These liberalization measures were accompanied by the diminution of subsidies, the halting of public-sector employment expansion, and the reduction of its role in internal investment. Social security spending in the 2000s was reduced considerably by the cutbacks to the pension system. Spending on healthcare and education had not risen in accordance with population growth. The shares of the education and healthcare sectors, expressed as a percentage of GDP expenses, were approximately 4 percent and 0.4 percent, respectively, before 2010. The regime had embarked on the gradual privatization of schools (particularly universities and colleges) and of the health system (Marzouq 2013: 49–50). This process was accompanied by the reduction of the quality and quantity of public health services, which forced the people to turn to the private sector to access basic services. Subsidies were also removed on key food items, as well as on gas and other energy sources. Price liberalization meant that products essential to everyday life were increasingly unaffordable for most low-income families (Abboud 2015: 55).

Land: "Feudalism returns"

Meanwhile, the ownership of land was increasingly concentrated in a small number of hands. A Syrian satirical newspaper put it well in 2006: "[A]fter 43 years of socialism, feudalism returns" (cited in Goulden 2011: 192). In agriculture, the privatization of land took place at the expense of several hundreds of thousands of peasants from the northeast, particularly following the drought of 2007–09, in which 1 million peasants received international aid and food supplies, while 300,000 persons were driven to Damascus, Aleppo, and other cities. However, this social catastrophe should not be perceived as simply the consequence of a natural disaster. Even before the drought, Syria had lost 40 percent of its agricultural workforce between 2002 and 2008, dropping from 1.4 million to 800,000 workers (Ababsa 2015: 200). The sector's share of employment in the country fell from 32.9/30 percent in 2000 to just 14/13.2 percent by 2011 (Nasser and Zaki Mehchy 2012: 3; World Bank Group 2017: 9).

The liberalization measures regarding agriculture under Bashar al-Assad took place starting at the end of 2000, with the privatizing of state farms in the north after more than four decades of collective ownership. The real beneficiaries of these privatization processes, nevertheless, were investors and entrepreneurs that became able to unlawfully rent these former areas of the state, according to researcher Myriam Ababsa (2006: 224).[4] Former owners were able to recover a portion of their properties, but above all, a class of entrepreneurs and investors close to the regime built massive fortunes, benefiting from state-subsidized irrigation on fertile land and leading to the creation of large latifundia estates (Ababsa 2006: 229). At the same time, the growth and intensification of land exploitation by big agribusiness companies facilitated the corruption of local administration, which accompanied the agricultural crisis.

Other laws benefiting landowners at the expense of peasants also reduced the agricultural workforce. An agrarian relation law was passed in 2004 (Law 56) that allowed landowners to terminate all tenancy contracts after three years, permitting them to expel peasants from the land that they had been working on for two generations in exchange for meager indemnities (which often went unpaid) and replace them with temporary workers. Implemented in 2007, this law resulted in the expulsion of hundreds of tenants and workers, especially on the coast in Tartus and Lattakia (Ababsa 2015: 200). Peasants and farmers also suffered from the reduction or elimination of subsidies on fuel and basic food needs (ICG 2011: 23).

In 2008, 28 percent of farmers were exploiting 75 percent of the irrigated land, while 49 percent of them had only 10 percent—evidence of the inequalities within this sector (FIDA 2009: 2). Small farmers with land on

---

[4] Decision No. 83 of December 16, 2000, provides for the division of state farms into 30 irrigated donums (3 ha) and 80 nonirrigated donums (8 ha), to be distributed first to former owners and beneficiaries of the agrarian reform, and then to the workers of the farms and to the holders of exploitation contracts (*muchakrin*). It should be noted that this was not a transfer of ownership, but rather the granting of ten years' use of the land, under which the beneficiary acquires full ownership. Therefore, it was forbidden to sell or rent these lands in the meantime (Ababsa 2006: 218).

the outskirts of cities were selling their smallholdings for increasingly large amounts, as funds from abroad (particularly the Gulf monarchies) poured into the country. Law No. 15 of 2008 facilitated the foreign ownership of land. Between 2004 and 2006, property prices in Syria as a whole increased by some 300 percent (Goulden 2011: 192).

Neoliberal policies and despotic upgrading

The neoliberal policies and deepened processes of privatization created new monopolies held by relatives and associates of Bashar al-Assad and the regime. Rami Makhlouf, the cousin of Bashar and the richest man in Syria, represented the mafia-style process of regime-led privatization. His economic empire was vast, including telecommunications, oil and gas, as well as construction, banks, airlines, and retail (Seifan 2013: 113). Makhlouf was also the main shareholder of the Cham Holding Company, while holding more than 300 licenses as an agent for big international companies (Sottimano 2016). According to various sources, he controlled (whether directly or indirectly) nearly 60 percent of the Syrian economy, thanks to a complex network of holdings (Leverrier 2011).

The Assad-Makhlouf alliance could include external actors into their *asabiyya*[5] (group solidarity or social bond), such as Muhammad Saber Hamsho, who is still a significant Syrian businessman in the country. A few years prior to the uprising in 2011, he became a powerful political and economic figure as a result of his association with Maher al-Assad, the brother of Bashar, following his marriage to the sister of Maher's wife. He was "elected" as a deputy in Parliament in 2003 and 2007, while the Hamsho Group participated in wide areas of the economy, from information technology (IT) equipment to tourist infrastructure (Donati 2013: 40). Before the uprising in 2011, many other examples of members of the ancient state bourgeoisie transforming into private bourgeoisie existed, such as Mustafa Tlass and sons, the sons of Abdel Halim Khaddam, and the sons of General Bahjat Sulayman (Matar 2015: 110). The role of the new businessmen issued from the state bourgeoisie and the high officials became prominent in the economic life of Syria, increasingly taking positions previously occupied by the traditional bourgeoisie.

According to the economist Samir Seifan, based on a list of the 100 most important businessmen in Syria published by the economic magazine

---

[5] This notion originates in the work of the 14th-century scholar from North Africa, Ibn Khaldoun, and implies a particular social bond that connects tribal and familial groups across a region. Khaldoun's concept was later developed by Middle East scholars to encompass group solidarity based on social networks constructed through family and personal relationships (Roy 1996: 6).

al-*Îqtisâd wa al-naql*, 23 percent were children of high officials, or they were their partners or acted as their "facades" or "interfaces"; 48 percent were new businessmen, the majority of which had close and corrupt relationships with the security services; 22 percent were from the traditional bourgeoisie from before the nationalization policies of the 1960s, which for some also had corrupt relationships and partnerships with the leaders of the state; and 7 percent had their main business activities outside Syria. In terms of religion, 69 percent were Sunni, 16 percent Alawi, 14 percent were Christians, and 1 percent were Shi'a, while there were no Druze, Isma'ili, or Kurds on the list. It is important to note that of the ten wealthiest businessmen in Syria, the majority were Alawis, and most were closely linked to the Assad family, such as Rami Makhlouf. In terms of regional distribution, the wealthiest businessmen were most frequently from Damascus, followed by Aleppo, Lattakia, and finally the cities of Homs and Hama, while there was not a single businessman from the regions of Raqqa, Deir ez-Zor, and Hasakah on the list (Seifan 2013: 112–113).

The regime thus expanded its predatory activities from having control over "rents derived from the state" to a position that permitted it to dominate "private rents" without any transparency. These new incomes also enabled ruling elites to establish a network of associates, whose loyalty they bought with market shares and protection (Donati 2013: 39–40).

From 2005, the number of business associations increased, mostly in the form of joint ventures between local businesspeople and foreign countries, and were generally controlled by businessmen with close links to the regime (Haddad 2013: 84). The entrepreneur Imad Greiwati, who emerged during Bashar al-Assad's era, led the Federation of Chamber of Industry, which was established in 2006 (Donati 2013: 41). The elections to the Chambers of Commerce in 2009 also reflected the increasing influence of businessmen with close links to the regime. This was embodied by the appointment by presidential decree of the Damascene entrepreneur Bassam Ghrawi, who was close to Bashar al-Assad as secretary-general of the Damascus Chamber of Commerce. He also occupied the position of secretary-general of the Federation of Syrian Chambers of Commerce (Donati 2013: 41). Kamil Ismail al-Assad, a relative of Bashar, was president of the Lattakia Chamber of Commerce and Industry, and Tarif Akhras, a relative of Asma al-Assad and among the largest exporters in Syria, was president of the Homs Chamber of Commerce and Industry (Valter 2018: 52; *International Business Publication* 2010: 192).

The creation of holding companies (al-Cham, controlled by Rami Makhlouf, Muhammad Sharabati, and *al-Sourya;* and later the Syria Qatari Holding Company, founded in 2008 and based in Damascus, which was equally owned by the regimes of Syria and Qatar) constituted another step in the renewal of the regime's networks in the business world. Holding companies were the instruments for the state bourgeoisie to conduct private business with the new commercial bourgeoisie. Al-Cham had 70 members, including mostly entrepreneurs close to the regime and families of the Syrian business bourgeoisie, and capital of USD 350 million. *Al-Sourya* had a capital of USD 80 million and involved 25 young entrepreneurs, including the sons of former regime and Ba'thist officials, gathered around Haytham Joud, the nephew of a prosperous Sunni entrepreneur from the city of Lattakia who was connected with the regime during the Hafez era (*The Syria Report* 2016k). *Al-Sourya* also established the Syrian Business Council, which consisted of a network of 280 businessmen who took advantage of their privileged positions to consolidate and expand connections with the Syrian diaspora and Arab business communities. The involvement and participation in the Syrian economy of these foreign actors (especially from the Gulf monarchies) reinforced the regime's position, while the line between public and private players was blurred by the regime's manipulation.

The previous agreement between the regime and business community deepened as the members of these two holdings secured capital, networks, and political support for the regime. In return, they enjoyed economic benefits from the market expansion, took the most profitable projects, and benefited from the regime's political protection. Outside this entrepreneur network linked to the regime, other businessmen who were not close to or connected with the regime also sought to benefit from the expansion of the market and neoliberal policies. They were tolerated, so long as they did not challenge the regime politically, because of the investments that they carried out in the less lucrative sectors, and also because they brought in foreign partners whose capital was sought after by the regime (Donati 2013: 42).

For example, the Sanqar family, despite its wealth and links to regime power [Omar Sanqar was close to Hafez al-Assad and an independent member of Parliament (MP) between 1990 and 1998 (Wieland 2012: 170)], lost to Rami Makhlouf its lucrative license to import luxury cars. In another case, Ghassan Abboud, a wealthy businessman who established a satellite channel called Orient TV in 2008, had to close the Damascus office in 2010 when he refused to hand over the majority of shares to Rami Makhlouf, and the security forces raided the office. The first opposition-held conference after the beginning of the uprising in July 2011 was organized by Ammar al-Qurabi's National Organization for Human Rights in Syria and funded by Abboud, as well as Ali and Wassim Sanqar (Marchand 2011). Such maneuverings by the crony capitalists against the assets and contracts of other sections of the bourgeoisie were common, illustrating the precarious and dependent status of this elite segment vis-à-vis the regime (Abboud 2013: 2).

Economic liberalization did not lead to the strengthening of an independent middle class of capitalists that would challenge dictatorship and lead to democracy, as promoted by a strand of academic literature in the 1990s. Neither did the new civil society, made up of associations and so-called NGOs constituting a new elite linked to business networks close to the regime, encourage democratization. Syria Trust for Development, an umbrella association set up with the sponsorship of Asma al-Assad in 2007, symbolized this process (Kawakibi 2013: 172), blocking the emergence of an autonomous and democratic civil society. The rapid growth in the number of development government-organized NGOs (GONGOs) went hand in hand with the repression of activists (Donati 2013: 44).

The researcher Salam Kawakibi (2013: 173–176) explained that these GONGOs had three main purposes. The first was to replace the state as the provider of social services in the framework of increasing neoliberal policies. The second was to establish new corporatist structures to satisfy emerging social groups and to tie them to the regime by providing them with both material (employment) and moral (doing good) benefits and creating their own network of clientele to broaden the popular support for the regime, directing it toward a more liberal one. Finally, they attracted important sources of foreign funding.

Similarly, new private media was far from creating a space for open and democratic debate. Syria's most influential media tycoons were a collection of wealthy businessmen with close connections to the regime's political, military, and business establishment. Rami Makhlouf established the *al-Watan* newspaper. Majd Bahjat Sulayman, owner of Syria's largest media empire, was the executive director of Alwaseet Group and chairman of the United Group for Publishing, Advertising, and Marketing (UG). Ayman Jaber and Muhammad Saber Hamsho, along with a number of other Syrian businessmen, established Dunia TV, later renamed the Sama satellite channel (Iqtissad 2015b).

In this way, the regime constituencies shifted toward the higher liberal classes. This form of crony or mafia capitalism, in which economic opportunities depended on loyalty to the regime, alienated and marginalized some elements of the bourgeoisie that lacked those connections and therefore did not constitute a strong element of regime support. No large business venture was possible without the participation of crony capitalists linked to the regime.

Role of the private sector and religious charities

The responsibility of social services to ease rising inequalities was given increasingly to private charities, and therefore bourgeois and religious conservative layers of Syrian society, especially religious associations. In 2004, of 584 charitable organizations, 290 were registered Islamic organizations, most of which were active in Damascus and its suburbs. Of the more than 100 charitable organizations in the capital, approximately 80 percent were Sunni Muslim before the uprising in 2011 (Pierret and Selvik 2009: 601). These groups served about 73,000 families, with a budget of approximately USD 18 million (Khatib 2011: 119).

Neoliberal policies strengthened religious associations in Syria, both Islamic and Christian, as well as their networks of diffusion, increasing their role in society at the expense of the state. In 2009, out of 1,485 associations, 60 percent were charities, the vast majority of which were religious (Ruiz de Elivra 2013: 30). Bashar continued a strategy of fostering Islamic conservative sectors, just as his father did. The Islamic orders of the Kuftariyya and the Qubaysiyyat, as previously mentioned, largely maintained their activities in the same way. On the eve of the uprising, the Qubaysiyat owned around 200 schools. The support for the Qubaysiyyat reached a peak when one of their members was appointed as an official religious adviser of the minister of *Awqaf* (the minister in charge of religious endowments), in early 2008, when "an Office of Women's Religious Instruction" was established (cited in Kannout 2016: 28).

One of the most successful and notorious Islamic associations was the Jama'at Zayd, which, as discussed previously, had deep-rooted ties to the Damascus Sunni bourgeoisie, conducted by the Rifa'i brothers, Ussama and Sariya (Pierret and Selvik 2009: 603). The association also collaborated occasionally with the authorities before 2011. The Zayd movement was allowed by the Ministry of *Awqaf* to raise funds for its charitable project at the exit of Friday Prayer (Pierret and Selvik 2009: 608) and obtained control over new mosques at the expense of others. Also, some of their members attained important positions in official religious institutions (Pierret 2011: 115).

Bashar's new regime boosted during this period its use of Islamic symbolism and vocabulary in an attempt to build up its legitimacy and popularity among pious Sunni Muslims. This was used to mobilize the support of large sectors of Syrian society against a hostile international political scene and threats against Damascus after the U.S.- and UK-led military invasion of Iraq in 2003 and the isolation Syria faced following the assassination of former Lebanese prime minister Rafic Hariri (Pinto 2015: 158–159). As explained by researcher Lina Khatib (2012: 33), Bashar promoted the idea of *takrees al-akhlak wa nashr thaqafat al-tasamuh, wa isal al risala al-haqiqiya lil-islam* (which means "diffusing morality, spreading the culture of tolerance, and communicating the true message of Islam" in Arabic) in many of his addresses, interviews, and conference presentations. He increasingly presented himself and the Syrian regime as patrons of moderate Islam against

"Islamic extremism." He projected the image of a leader faithful to Islam and a guardian of the Islamic religion in Syria. The state-controlled media commonly reported Bashar's participation in holiday prayers in mosques across the country, while images portraying him as a pious Muslim proliferated throughout the country (Pinto 2015: 158).

This was accompanied by a continued policy of détente, started by Hafez al-Assad at the beginning of the 1990s, toward opposition Islamic fundamentalist groups through the release of political prisoners, and the tolerance of Islamic publications and movements so long as they refrained from political involvement. In 2001, for example, Sheikh Abu al-Fath al-Bayanuni, the brother of the former head of the MB, was authorized to come back after 30 years in exile, and his son, a rich businessman, participated in the establishment of a mall (Pierret 2011: 115). In 2003, Assad lifted a long-standing ban on religious practice in the military barracks (Khatib 2011: 116). In 2006, the military academy welcomed religious authorities to lecture cadets for the first time since the Ba'th Party's accession to power in 1963 (Khatib 2012: 34). Bashar also offered Islamic groups and pro-regime clerics an unprecedented level of access to the state-run broadcast media (Moubayed 2006).

In 2006, the state issued a decree increasing the number of official Islamic institutions in Syria—which numbered in the thousands—by endorsing the establishment of a Sharia faculty at the University of Aleppo, in addition to the existing one at the University of Damascus (Khatib 2011: 117).

Prior to the onset of the uprising, the country disposed of around 976 Islamic schools and institutes and over 9,000 active mosques, of which some 7,000 were said to be uncontrolled by the Ministry of *Awqaf* (Khatib 2011: 162). Since the middle of the 1990s, Islamic groups had been able to ally themselves with Syria's influential and affluent business class, though they also did so with religious Syrians who became wealthy through their time working in the Gulf states. As a result, the groups were more able to provide services in both well-off and less-affluent districts. Regarding education, almost 200 of the country's 400-odd private educational institutions were said to be influenced by Islamic groups. In Damascus, as many as 25 percent of school students were taught by teachers with an overtly religious agenda, and moreover had to take extracurricular classes—outside the control of the state—about Islam (Khatib 2011: 137–139).

These policies coincided with the censorship of literary and artistic works, the promotion of a religious literature that filled the shelves of libraries, and Islamization of the field of higher education (Pierret 2011: 115). Feminist activists and groups were publicly accused by religious conservative movements close to the regime of heresy, of seeking to destroy society's morality, and of propagating Western values, the notion of civil marriage, the rights of homosexuals and lesbians, and total sexual freedom (al-Aous 2013: 25). For example, on April 11, 2005, the pro-regime Sheikh al-Buti waged a virulent attack on women's rights and feminist activists, describing them as "dirty agents," "traitors," "dwarfs," and "slaves whose masters seek to eradicate the Islamic civilization from its roots" (cited in al-Hallaq 2013b).

This Islamic revival helped Islamic groups to recruit new members, especially among the youth. Their message was the only one besides that of the regime that was allowed in the public sphere, and they benefited at the same time from funds arriving from the Gulf region, the welfare associations, the provision of social services, and volontariat work. The regime's strategy of encouraging quietist (or unchallenging) Islamic conservative sectors in society led to an expansion of Islamic schools and charities, conservative clothing, and mosque attendance. Further, Islamic intellectuals and businessmen were incorporated into Parliament, among them influential personalities such as Sheikh Muhammad Habbash, while official acknowledgment was provided to the Qubaysi movement that preached Islam among upper class Damascene women (Hinnebush 2012: 105).

In the April 2007 legislative elections, all the main lists of independent candidates in Damascus contained a majority of businessmen, each accompanied by a religious figure (Pierret and Selvik 2009: 601). The regime also engaged in a coordinated effort to build alliances with the intertwined business and religious elite of formerly oppositionist Aleppo: It nominated the Aleppo mufti Ahmad Badr al-Din Hassun as the new Grand Mufti of Syria, and Aleppo benefited from his alliance with and economic opening to Turkey, which brought in new investments (Hinnebush 2012: 105). Sheikh Ahmad Badr al-Din Hassun came from a well-known family of Aleppo sheikhs and had many followers in the Sunni bourgeoisie of the city (Pinto 2015: 162). The researcher Raphael Lefèvre (2013: 156), describing this rapprochement with Islamic conservative sectors of the society, wrote that "in the first ten years of Bashar al-Assad's rule, the regime did more to accommodate conservative Syrian Muslims that at any point before."

This policy of accommodation to the Islamic conservative sectors of society did not mean that all were politically incorporated into the regime. The regime sought to control these movements by repressing some and favoring others. Some sought accommodation with the regime by establishing links with the security services or the Ministry of *Awqaf,* and they were allowed to spread their networks, at the risk of losing credibility among the public. At the same time, prominent figures within the Islamic movement, such as sheikhs Salah Kuftaro and Sariya al-Rifa'I (as well as some of the latter's followers), became more critical of some of the features of the state, especially following Bashar's arrival to power. Their attacks concentrated particularly on the secular aspects of the regime and secular groups and personalities (Khatib 2012: 45; Moubayed 2006).

The regime also facilitated the presence of jihadist movements in Syria, whose influence increased in the country after the American- and British-led war on Iraq in 2003. Islamic fundamentalists and jihadist groups started advertising and recruiting in the country's urban centers, looking for men to fight for the resistance against the American and British intervention in Iraq (Lister 2015: 34). It was estimated in 2008 that Syrian nationals represented the third-largest contingent of foreign jihadist fighters and the highest number of jihadist prisoners at the Camp Bucca jail in Iraq. The country also served as the entry point for 90 percent of all foreign insurgents traveling to Iraq as of December 2008 (Lefèvre 2013: 148). A rapid and vast foreign-fighter recruitment and facilitation network in Syria was established for the express objective of supplying the jihadist insurgency in Iraq. At this time, Syria's Grand Mufti, Sheikh Ahmad Kaftaru, issued a fatwa making it *fardh ayn* (religiously obligatory) for all Muslims, both male and female, to resist the occupying forces using any possible means, including suicide bombings (Lister 2015: 39).

The Syrian regime's collaboration with jihadists served a particular geopolitical purpose, including as a tool to push the United States to collaborate and normalize its relations with Damascus, as well as diverting jihadists into a war against foreign occupiers in Iraq. Due to the progressive halt in the collaborations and/or complicity with jihadists to help them travel to Iraq from 2008, Syria became the target of jihadist attacks. This also led to a revolt of Islamic fundamentalist members in July 2008 in the Sednayya prison, close to Damascus, and for the first time in several years, Syrian security services started a campaign of repression and arrest of members of jihadist networks within the country (Lister 2015: 44–45). The danger of jihadist networks was real. More than 8,000 jihadists traveled through Syria to Iraq from 2003 to 2011 (Khatib 2011: 189). These networks and experiences from Iraq would feed the development of jihadist networks following the beginning of the 2011 uprising in Syria.

This provoked repressive measures by the regime aimed at other sections of the Islamic sector. In 2006, the director of Damascus *Waqf*, Muhammad Khaled al-Mu'tem, issued a decree that banned religious lessons from Syria's mosques, with Koranic lessons reduced to once or twice rather than being given on a daily basis (Khatib 2012: 48). In August 2008, the minister of *Awqaf*, Muhammad Abd al-Sattar, enacted three important decisions regarding the charitable activities in Syria. First, the regime forbade charities and mosques to hold the *mawa'id al-rahme* (charity tables) during Ramadan. The objective was to prevent merchants, rich businessmen, and religious men who funded these events from using these public celebrations for their own benefit, as well as putting an end to collective mass gatherings. Second, at the end of 2008, anyone working in a clerical role, such as imams or prayer leaders at mosques and teachers at religious institutions, was compelled to step down from any official post he might hold in a charitable institution. This decision was made to prevent any religious Sunni figure from holding too much political capital (Ruiz de Elivra 2012: 23–24). Finally, the regime did not hesitate, as a measure of coercion, to dissolve a charity's board of directors.

The regime continued to try to limit the autonomy and influence of some Islamic groups that had attained increasing importance in the previous years. In June 2009, Salah Kaftaru was imprisoned on charges of embezzlement, and only two months earlier, his brother, Mahmud, had been arrested and imprisoned for 13 days (Imady 2016: 79–80). In 2010, a verbal decree was enforced banning around 1,000 *munaqabat* (women with a full-face veil, or niqab) from teaching. A few days later, *munaqabat* were also forbidden from registering as students at the university level (Khatib 2012: 30). The culmination of these measures was to come with Decree No. 48, enacted on April 4, 2011, which proclaimed the creation of al-Sham Higher Institute for Religious Sciences, while effectively nationalizing three religious colleges, once funded and administrated by associations presided over by religious scholars (Imady 2016: 79–80). In 2011, the Ulama of Damascus were at their lowest point organizationally and lacked a large popular base, leaving them unable to play a crucial role in the growing protest movement.

Socioeconomic consequences of neoliberal policies

Bashar's policies led to an expansion of poverty and wealth inequality. The GDP increased at an average of 4.3 percent per year from 2000 to 2010 in real terms—in other words, doubling from USD 28.8 billion in 2005 to around USD 60 billion in 2010 (World Bank Group 2017; Statista 2018). However, only a very small stratum of the society benefited from this growth. In 2007, the percentage of Syrians living below the poverty line was 33 percent, which represented approximately 7 million people, while another 30 percent were just above this level (Abdel-Gadir, Abu-Ismail, and El-Laithy 2011: 2–3). Even the regime-controlled Syrian General Federation of Trade Unions in 2009 deplored the fact that

> the rich have become richer and the poor poorer ... low income earners who make up 80 percent of the Syrian population are looking for additional work to support themselves ... (cited in Hinnebush and Zinti 2015: 293)

The labor force participation rate for people aged 15 years and older declined from 52.3 percent in 2001 to between 39 and 43 percent in 2010. This was a direct result of the failure of the neoliberal policies of the regime, which was unable to absorb potential entrants to the labor market, especially young graduates. The diminution in the labor force participation rate took place in both rural and urban areas but was sharper in rural areas. Women suffered massively, with a labor force participation rate of women aged 15 and older decreasing from between 21 and 20.4 to 13.2/12.7 percent between 2001 and 2010—one of the lowest rates in the world. The male participation rate also diminished from 81 to 72.2 percent during the same period (Nasser and Zaki Mehchy 2012: 3; SCPR 2016b: 35; World Bank Group 2017: 9).

The general unemployment rate was estimated by 2010 at around 25 percent, rather than the official 8.6 percent announced by the state (Nasser and Zaki Mehchy 2012: 3–10; World Bank Group 2017: 9–10). The youth unemployment rate was 48 percent in 2011 (IFAD 2011).

Economic liberalization also affected the labor market. Prior to the uprising, the informal sector was a significant contributor to the Syrian economy. It was estimated to account for about 30 percent of employment (1.5 million individuals) and about 30–40 percent of GDP, according to estimates in the tenth five-year plan. It was noteworthy that more than 50 percent of informal-sector workers were between the ages of 15 and 29, revealing the decreasing opportunities available for Syrian youth during the liberalization periods (ILO 2010: 3). The informal sector was concentrated in internal trade, restaurants, hotels, construction, real estate, agriculture, and manufacturing, while the formal labor was mostly based in the service and industrial sectors and, to a lesser degree, in storage and telecommunications. The majority of the formal labor was in the public sector.

Poor suburban neighborhoods expanded considerably, while urban real estate speculation unleashed by the influx of Gulf capital, together with an end to rent controls, drove the cost of housing beyond the means of large sectors of the middle class (Hinnebush 2012: 102). This pushed many Syrians into marginal areas of cities, where they were often forced to live in informal housing. This situation led to a housing crisis, a shortfall of around 1.5 million formal homes according to the Syrian Economic Center in 2007 (cited in Goulden 2011: 188–190), with sections of the population becoming homeless or living in informal areas (Hinnebush 2012: 102).

The regime's solution to the crisis was to outsource the problem to the private sector, as it did increasingly with the economy as a whole. But the private sector invested in luxury housing targeting rich Syrians (within the country and the diaspora), foreigners, and tourists. Investments in luxury tourist and residential developments attracted around USD 20 billion in investments from the beginning of the 2000s to mid-2007, while it was estimated that USD 24 billion would have been the cost of upgrading all the country's informal housing to a decent level (Goulden 2011: 192). The failure of this solution pushed the regime to engage in a process (Law No. 33, passed in 2008) of granting property rights to informal residents in exchange for a fee to local authorities, which was largely unsuccessful.

An estimated 30 to 50 percent of the population lived in informal housing (Goulden 2011: 188). In Aleppo, 29 informal settlements (out of a total of 114 neighborhoods registered by the municipality) occupied about 45 percent of the city's inhabited area and were home to an estimated total population of 2.5 million (Ahmad 2012: 8). These neighborhoods, in addition to often being poorly constructed (and therefore dangerous to live in), lacked medical services, with few public health facilities (Goulden 2011: 201).

The proportion of poor was higher in rural areas (62 percent) than in urban areas (38 percent) (FIDA 2009: 4), while just over half (54.2 percent) of all unemployment was found in rural areas (IFAD 2011: 1). The most impoverished areas of the country were those populated mostly by Kurds, such as in the Jazirah, despite producing two-thirds of the country's grain (70 percent wheat) and three-quarters of its hydrocarbons (Ababsa 2015: 201). The Jazirah was the region with the highest level of poverty, hosting 58 percent of the country's poor before the 2004 drought. By 2010, the impact of four consecutive droughts since 2006 had been dramatic for both small-scale farmers and herders. In the affected regions of the Jazirah, the income of these groups dropped by as much as 90 percent (United Nations 2011: 5).

Conclusion

The establishment of the modern patrimonial state occurred under the leadership of Hafez al-Assad, through various means such as sectarianism, regionalism, tribalism, and clientelism, which were managed via informal networks of power and patronage. This came with harsh repression against any form of dissent. These tools allowed the regime to integrate, bolster, or undermine groups belonging to different ethnicities and religious sects. At the local level, this meant the collaboration of various actors with the regime, including state or Ba'th officials, intelligence officers, and prominent members of local society (clerics, tribal members, businessmen, etc.). As argued by academic Heiko Wimmen (2017: 70):

> These officials would provide their loyalty and material proceeds to the leadership in return for franchises of authoritarian power. Thus the main currency in this system of dispersed rule, and the key to

accessing privilege and resources, was not so much sectarian affiliation but rather loyalty to the regime and usefulness for its maintenance
of power...

The rise to power of Hafez also opened the door to economic liberalization, in opposition to the radical policies of the 1960s.

Bashar al-Assad's arrival to power in 2000 considerably strengthened
the patrimonial nature of the state with the increasing weight of crony capitalists. The accelerated neoliberal policies of the regime led to a further
shift in the social base of the regime, constituted originally by peasants,
government employees, and some sections of the bourgeoisie, to a regime
coalition with crony capitalists at its heart—the rent-seeking alliance of
political brokers (led by Assad's mother's family) and the regime supporting
the bourgeoisie and higher middle classes. This shift was paralleled by the
disempowerment of the traditional corporatist organizations of workers and
peasants, as well as the cooptation in their place of business groups and
higher middle classes.

The absence of democracy and the growing impoverishment of large parts
of Syrian society, in a climate of corruption and increasing social inequalities, prepared the ground for the popular insurrection, which thus needed
no more than a spark. Full of confidence, Bashar al-Assad declared in an
interview with the *Wall Street Journal* (2011) following the overthrow of
President Ben Ali in Tunisia:

> Despite more difficult circumstances than in most Arab countries,
> Syria is stable. Why? Because you must be very closely linked to the
> beliefs of the people.

The Syrian leader was very wrong to believe that his regime would not
be affected by these waves of protest.

2. Popular Uprising and Militarization

Introduction

In this chapter, we analyze the protest movement in Syria, characterized in the beginning by its inclusive and democratic message and considerations, as well as the way in which it progressively managed large swathes of territory as the regime withdrew or was expelled from them. The political movements and practices of the coordination committees, youth networks, and groups within the protest movement were the biggest challenge and threat to the regime, which deemed all opposition activists and demonstrators as Salafist armed groups in an attempt to discredit the movement and pacify the population. The beginning of the uprising witnessed the birth of many youth and civilian organizations, composed of diverse ethnic and sectarian groups, while acts of civilian resistance multiplied.

The uprisings brought together different groups in society. On the one hand were the popular classes, who wished to change their material conditions and bring about more democracy. On the other were some limited parts of the bourgeoisie and higher middle classes, who saw their interest in the promotion of a more liberal state, free of the reigning families who held political power and the growing economic benefits arising from it. As put by Hinnebush (2012: 106), "the social base of the uprising was those excluded from or only precariously incorporated into the regimes' new coalition."

Damascus from the beginning chose harsh repression of the protest movement, which led to a rising number of defections among conscript soldiers and officers who refused to shoot peaceful protesters. Increasingly, civilians also took up arms. At the end of summer 2011, the FSA was established, as well as a myriad of other brigades. Armed resistance against the regime was nearly generalized by the end of 2011, creating new dynamics in the uprising.

The militarization was largely driven by the violent repression of the regime; sections of the opposition resorted to armed self-defense. The first constituted armed opposition groups often had a purely local dynamic and served to defend their hometowns and areas from aggression by the armed security services. Armed opposition groups increased rapidly and fell under the FSA network, which never acted as a single, unified institution and was characterized by its pluralism in the first years of the uprising. This dynamic changed progressively with the establishment of larger groups, foreign interventions, and the growing influence of Islamic fundamentalist armed groups.

Syria was nevertheless witnessing a revolutionary situation, with attempts by various opposition groups to challenge the sovereignty of the regime.

The internal dynamics of the uprising, first sparks...

At the national level, starting in January 2011, a few events such as the painting of graffiti, small demonstrations, and other actions of dissent against the regime occurred before the beginning of the first massive demonstrations, encouraged greatly by the uprisings in Tunisia and Egypt and the subsequent overthrow of those countries' dictators. During this same period, many human rights advocates and activists had to face a series of tactics of intimidation and the close monitoring of their emails, blogs, and telephone conversations. Some of them were warned not to leave the country (Williams 2011).

While campaigns of intimidation, arrests, and repressions by security forces against activists and demonstrations were underway, official newspapers in Syria (*al-Thawra*, *Tishrin*, and *al-Ba'th*) were celebrating the regional uprisings. Official media especially praised the overthrow of Hosni Mubarak in Egypt, stressing that his departure greatly troubled Israel, with which Egypt signed a peace treaty in 1979 (*Orient le Jour* 2011a). The regime was attempting to divert popular attention with the spectacle of foreign political events and promote its own narrative while excluding other television networks, such as al-Jazeera, from the media space.

In addition to repression, the regime implemented some social measures in response to the protests. Ministers were told to listen to citizen complaints, and local officials displayed uncharacteristic interest in popular needs (ICG 2011: 5). The regime announced in mid-February the creation of a National Welfare Fund of USD 250 million. Long awaited, the fund was intended to help some 420,000 families, while increasing by 72 percent the heating allowances for public servants and pensioners (about 2 million people). In the beginning of March, the Syrian regime also took a series of measures to bring down the prices of basic foodstuffs (*Orient le Jour* 2011b).

On March 8, Bashar al-Assad rushed to the province of Hasakah to announce the launch of the Tigris River diversion project to develop the northeastern region of Syria affected by the droughts of the last few years, after more than three decades of delays. The project cost USD 3 billion and was expected to irrigate large tracts of land, develop agricultural production, and create jobs for thousands of people (Yazigi 2016b: 2).

These measures, however, would not be enough. The country was facing a structural economic crisis, not a temporary one.

On March 15, more than 100 protesters demonstrated in the *suq al-Hammidiiya* and Hariqa in the heart of the capital, chanting slogans calling for freedom and an end to the emergency laws. The demonstration was dispersed by security forces, and six protesters were arrested (BBC News 2011b). It was the first time that the slogan "Allah, Syria, and Freedom" was chanted, as a response to the slogan of the supporters of Bashar al-Assad, "Allah, Syria, and Bashar." On the day after, March 16, relatives of a number of political prisoners organized a rally in front of the Ministry of the Interior, gathering approximately 150 people. A total of 34 people were arrested (BBC News 2011a).

In the same week, the true spark of the uprising was lit in the southern city of Dar'a, which quickly became a symbol of the popular resistance. On the night of February 22, 2011, a few students scribbled slogans on the school wall in Hay al-Arbeen District, inspired by the revolutions in Tunisia and Egypt: "No teaching, No School, Till the end of Bashar's rule," "Leave, Bashar," "Your turn is coming, Doctor," and the famous "The people want the fall of the regime." The children were spotted by security forces and were arrested with other young students (Evans and al-Khalidi 2013). On March 18, the boys' families and several hundred local citizens demonstrated throughout the city, demanding the liberation of the children, a crackdown on corruption, and the implementation of real democratic reforms in the country (Daraafree Syria 2011; SyriaFreePress 2011). On the same day, protests in different areas of Syria were witnessed, such as in the small town of Baniyas, located on the coast near Tartus, with protesters notably chanting, "Sunni, Alawi, we all want freedom" (Shaam Network S.N.N. 2011a; Darwish 2016d; Abdo 2016). Similar demonstrations erupted in Damascus, Aleppo, Homs, Lattakia, Raqqa, Qamishli, and Hama.

Demonstrations in some localities also raised other specific demands, although always under a general umbrella of reforms and freedom. Residents of Baniyas, for example, requested the cancellation of regime measures that discriminated against female employees of the education ministry wearing a niqab. In Dar'a, resentment concentrated on a number of officials who were seen as particularly incompetent, brutal, or corrupt, and the 2008 decree that subjected land sales in cities close to border areas to the approval of security officials, who ran a large-scale extortion scheme (ICG 2011: 5). Demands of protesters in mixed Sunni-Alawi cities, such as Baniyas, Lattakia, and Tartus, were also directed at the alleged pro-Alawi sectarian biases in employment in state industries and public administrations (Balanche 2011; Abdo 2018). In Homs, the first demonstration at the

Khaled Ibn al-Walid Mosque, which drew around 2,000 protesters, was initially to condemn the local governor. He had been the target of increasing criticisms in the past years, notably because of his corruption, arbitrary land expropriations, suspicious real estate contracts, and especially his urban project "Homs Dream" (*The New York Times* 2011; *Orient le Jour* 2011c; Wimmen 2017: 78–79), which would have forcefully displaced populations, mostly popular classes, from some areas of the city's center to make way for expensive commercial malls and buildings for higher strata of the society.

March 18, 2011, was the first day of the Syrian uprising, called the "Friday of dignity," in tandem with the Friday of the same name in Yemen. The events in Dar'a marked a turning point, like the "Friday of Rage" on January 28 in Egypt.

Popular protests expanded in the next days to other cities of Syria. In the following weeks, several Ba'th Party offices in various cities were torched by protesters, while portraits of Bashar al-Assad—and his father, Hafez— were torn apart (42maher 2011a). On Friday, March 25, slogans to overthrow the regime were chanted for the first time (Tansîqîyya madîna Nawa 2011; 42maher 2011b). A few days earlier, the local mobile telephone agency belonging to Bashar's cousin, billionaire Rami Makhlouf, was burned down. This attack was a clear symbol of the corruption and the nepotism of the regime, while protesters chanted, "We'll say it clearly, Rami Makhlouf is robbing us" (Shadid 2011). On March 27, in a rare act of defiance in the People's Chamber, which is usually constituted by loyalists of Bashar, Dar'a MP Youssef Abou Roumiye accused the security forces of opening fire without mercy, and criticized the president for not coming to the region to apologize (Abazeed 2011).

Protests continued to grow, and the first general strike since the beginning of the uprising occurred in the city of Dar'a on April 5, protesting the continuation of the repression (*Orient le Jour* 2011c). Massive demonstrations occurred in various cities in the following months, such as Hama in June. Meanwhile, attempts to transform the center square of Homs into an Egyptian Tahrir Square, as between 10,000 and 20,000 demonstrators gathered for several hours, were repressed violently by the regime's security services; numerous protesters were murdered during their expulsion from the square (*The Guardian* 2011; Silent whisper2009 2011). Similarly, efforts to reach the city center in Damascus were repressed by the regime's security forces. The uprising would then extend gradually in the following months to all regions of the country—despite (or perhaps because) of the tactics deployed by the regime. Indeed, this violent and growing repression by the security services would progressively radicalize the protest movement, which moved from demanding reforms to demanding the fall of the regime.

The outbreak of the uprising in the city of Dar'a was symbolic because it was known as a bastion of the Ba'th. A number of senior dignitaries of the party originated from there, including Vice President Faruk al-Shareh; tribal leader Mahmoud Zoubi, who served as prime minister from 1987 to 2000; and Sulayman al-Qaddah, head of the party between 1985 and 2005 (Lister 2015: 15). These men embodied the bankruptcy of the state and its elites, who had for years abandoned to their own fate the rural classes and the out-lying cities they themselves came from, to the benefit of policies promoting the bourgeois classes and higher social strata of Damascus and Aleppo.

Social classes in the uprising

The most important components of the uprising were economically mar-ginalized Sunni rural workers, urban employees, and self-employed workers, who bore the brunt of neoliberal policies, especially since 2000. Idlib, Dar'a and other mid-sized towns, as well as other rural areas where the revolts broke out, are all historical strongholds of the Ba'th Party, and benefited from the policies of agricultural reforms in the 1960s (Seifan 2013: 123). There was a continuous impoverishment of rural areas since the 1980s and the droughts from 2006 accelerated rural exodus, as we have seen. This situation was exacerbated by an annual population growth rate of around 2.5 percent that affected particularly small- to mid-sized towns in rural areas, in which population often multiplied by five to ten times since the 1980s. Public services provided by the state in these towns did not increase—on the contrary, they often even diminished with the neoliberal policies, leading to a deterioration of living conditions (Baczko, Dorronsoro, and Quesnay 2016: 46–47). As Suzanne Saleeby (2012) argued, the initial protests were based largely on the perceived erosion of the Ba'th-peasant social contract. In the main towns of Damascus and Aleppo, the geog-raphy of the revolts was mapped closely to their socioeconomic divisions.

The Damascus suburbs and towns surrounding the capital, where pro-tests were prevalent since the beginning of the uprising, were known as the *poverty belt*, while the map of opposition-held neighborhoods in Aleppo from summer 2012 was nearly exactly that of the impoverished working-class Sunni neighborhoods: densely packed, poorly planned, and featuring relatively recent urban growth (Stack and Zoepf: 2011; Kilcullen and Rosenblatt 2012). Western Aleppo, on the other hand, with its better ser-vice provisions, was composed mostly of middle-class public employees, some sections of the bourgeoisie, and some minorities.

Except the Kurdish and Assyrian areas (see Chapter 5), the minority towns and rural inhabited areas did not witness similar mass mobilizations as these abovementioned areas, although forms of dissent and protests did occur, for example, in Salamiyah (Darwish 2016b), populated mostly by Isma'ilis, and Suwayda, populated mostly by Druze (Ezzi 2013). Many activists of Christian background were also engaged in antiregime activities in the country. In the Christian neighborhoods of Damascus, they were more cautious. They generally worked in partnership with like-minded activists from across the city, and their activity was not restricted to any specific area (Sabbagh 2013: 80).

Another important segment of the uprising consisted of the university students, young graduates, and sectors of the lower and middle classes in major cities such as Damascus, Aleppo, Homs, Lattakia, Deir ez-Zor, Suwayda, Hasakah, and Raqqa[1]. The number of students in higher education increased massively since the 1970s, enrollment figures for Syrian tertiary education grew from around 7 percent in 1970 to 26 percent in 2010 (World Bank 2018). Students, therefore, represented a significant and distinct social force. They would be a particular important section of the protest movement at the beginning of the uprising. The Union of Free Syrian Students (UFSS) was established on September 29, 2011, in opposition to the regime and for a civil and pluralistic democracy. They grew rapidly in numbers, and many Syrian universities established a branch (LCC 2011a; Syria Untold 2013a; Hassaf 2018). They faced repression by the official pro-regime student union members and the security services. By July 2012, a quarter of all the individuals killed in the protest movement were university students, according to the UFSS (2012).

Finally, large sections of the bourgeoisie, without strong connections to the regime, initially adopted a more passive, wait-and-see attitude, especially in Damascus and Aleppo. Most were reluctant to take part in the movement except through ambivalent means that did not put them in the spotlight (Abbas 2011), although some did participate directly. In the summer of 2011, in the city of Deir ez-Zor, a strike was launched by traders in support of the uprising. It led to violent repression by the security services. The crackdown resulted in protests by the Chamber of Commerce and Industry of the city, which issued a statement denouncing the repression and concluding with: "Long live Syria free! Glory to the martyrs!" According to Jihad Yazigi (2013), the fact that these positions were taken in secondary cities of the country was not surprising, given the relative decline of these urban centers, as well as the physical and political distance of their elites from Damascus and Aleppo who had largely benefited from the economic liberalization of the previous decades. Some sections of the

---

[1] Syria had five government universities in 2011: Damascus, Homs, Aleppo, Lattakia, and Deir ez-Zor, with regional branches in Dar'a, Suwayda, Idlib, Tartus, Hama, Hasakah, and Raqqa.

Syrian bourgeoisie and wealthy elites in exile established the Syrian Business Forum, which openly aligned with the opposition. They supported efforts for relief and humanitarian aid, while playing a political role within larger opposition politics. In Damascus and Aleppo, the vast majority of the bourgeoisie was more inclined toward the Assad regime (Abboud 2017).

The passive support of some sections of the bourgeoisie toward the uprising soon was replaced by a desire to return to stability under the rule of the regime, following events notably including the looting of Aleppo's industrial zones. This followed the conquest of eastern parts of the city by various opposition armed groups in the summer of 2012. The Damascus bourgeoisie feared that a similar fate would befall their institutions and properties if opposition armed forces took over large areas of the capital.

The rise of the IS and jihadist fundamentalist movements from 2013 also pushed most sections of the traditional bourgeoisie and the higher middle-class strata of Damascus and Aleppo into supporting the regime, or at least to remain neutral, despite its crimes and unpopularity. In 2015, the fall of the city of Idlib to various opposition armed groups led by the Jaysh al-Fateh coalition, dominated by Jabhat al-Nusra and Ahrar al-Sham, led to the systematic looting of public and private properties (Saråj al-Dîn, Mû`min 2015; *The Syria Report* 2015d). This widespread looting demonstrated for many the inability of the opposition to administer regions outside the regime's domination.

With the deepening of the war, many business elites decided to leave Syria and transfer large portions of their capital outside the country. According to Samer Abboud, total withdrawals from Syrian banks amounted to around USD 10 billion by the end of 2012, the majority of which was reinvested in neighboring countries. Some transferred their activities to Turkey, Jordan, Egypt, and the UAE. Thus, major industrial facilities, or parts of them (such as those held by Nestlé, which had sustained a fire; the Bel Group, a French cheese producer; and Elsewedy Cables Syria), were relocated (al-Mahmoud 2015). Syria's neighbors benefited from the considerable cash injections flowing from the establishment of new companies and production plants by Syrian businessmen, as well as joint ventures with local partners. The majority of those business elites who left the country were not connected to the new networks and opportunities provided by the war economy, while the networks that had previously ensured access to power were now challenged or disappearing (Abboud 2013: 6).

Political tendencies at the beginning of the uprising

Some activists taking part in the uprising had been involved in the various struggles against the regime before 2011. A great majority of them were

secular democrats from all communities, including ethnic and religious minorities. Some of them played an important role in the grassroots
committees and in the development of peaceful actions against the regime,
and they were mostly young individuals from lower- and middle-class layers,
often graduates and users of social media. The grassroots civilian opposition was indeed the primary engine of the popular uprising. They sustained
it for numerous years by organizing and documenting protests and acts of
civil disobedience, and by motivating people to join the protests. The earliest manifestations of the coordinating committees were neighborhood
gatherings in locations throughout Syria. Committees would typically begin
with about 15 to 20 people and then often expand to include hundreds (Abi
Najm 2011; Khoury 2013: 3).

These committees slowly developed internal structures, and several of
them played a particularly important role on a national level, especially the
Syrian Revolution Coordinators Union (SRCU), UFSS, and the Local
Coordination Committees (LCCs). The cadres of these committees were
generally highly educated and globalized male and female youth, including
some human rights activists and lawyers. Some coordination committees
were not affiliated with any higher coalition, which did not prevent them
from collaborating with other coordination committees in neighboring areas.

The coordination committees organized the popular resistance, including
protests, campaigns of civil disobedience, and strikes, while increasingly
playing a humanitarian role and providing services after the militarization
of the uprising. In 2011 and 2012, an upsurge of civilian activities was witnessed in neighborhoods, villages, and cities liberated from the regime
forces, and demonstrations were attended by large numbers of participants.
Protesters and activists would describe the activities alongside protests as
"carnivals of the revolution." The relative absence of regime forces allowed
civilian activities to spread (including discussions, debates, seminars, and
meetings), and connect with their counterparts in various Syrian cities
(Darwish 2016b). Examples of self-organization in areas freed from the
regime's security forces, even on a temporary basis, also started to appear.

Between mid-December and December 30, 2011, general strikes and
civil disobedience paralyzed large parts of the country (LCC 2011b, 2011c).
The campaign was called "The Strike of Dignity" and involved numerous
actors, such as LCCs and other organizations (Syria Untold 2013c). Regime
security forces responded violently against attempts of shopkeepers to participate in the strikes (al-Jazeera 2011).

These organizations also provided humanitarian assistance for those suffering from the increasing destruction caused by the repression and
fighting, especially in providing relief to internally displaced persons (IDPs).
They also documented human rights violations in the country committed

by the regime's forces and all armed groups. They issued numerous political statements in the first years of the uprising, and in the case of the LCCs, also published a newspaper called *Freedom! Here We Come (Tli'na A'l Horriyeh)* (Abi Najm 2011; Carnegie 2012c). Other coordination committees and youth groups also formed at the beginning of the uprising, gathering together numerous youth activist networks that increasingly collaborated through coalitions in various campaigns and civil actions.

The regime targeted these networks of activists. Large numbers were imprisoned, killed, or forced into exile. They nevertheless played an important role in the ongoing revolutionary process by trying to articulate between the various forms of popular resistance to the regime. By early 2012, there were approximately 400 *tansiqiyyat* (coordinating committees), despite intensive campaigns of repression by the security forces (Khoury 2013: 3).

There were other groups who opposed the regime, in which religious clerics played a significant role in certain neighborhoods and areas. Political views varied considerably among the sheikhs who had joined the uprising, from Salafist to more liberal trends (Hossino 2013).

Finally, elements of the more traditional opposition were also involved in the protest movement, among them some Kurdish political parties, left-wing groups, nationalists, liberals, and Islamic networks. Many former activists or political opposition members acted in an independent manner in various LCCs and new structures established within the uprising, rather than through political organizations.

An inclusive platform

In the first years of the uprising, many emphasized inclusiveness and challenged sectarianism, shouting slogans such as "The Syrians are one." At the same time, since the beginning of the uprising, some small sectarian groups existed and developed alongside the increasingly bloody repression of the regime while promoting a sectarian political platform. Some demonstrators in Dar'a and Lattakia, and later in Hama as well, at the start of the uprising chanted, for example, "No to Iran, No to Hezbollah, We want a Muslim who is afraid of God" (Shaam Network S.N.N. 2011b; Tansîqîyya al-Lâziqîyya 2011; No Iran 2011). Despite debates over its meaning,[2] this

---

[2] The academic Joshua Landis explained that the slogan "We want a Muslim who is afraid of God" was used by the MB in the 1970s and 1980s to discredit the Syrian regime, as well as by Saddam Hussein against Iraqi Shi'as. In reaction to his explanation, one Internet user answered, "Someone who is said to be 'afraid of God' in the wider context of Syrian society means someone who is virtuous and morally righteous, not necessarily religious. This phrase is quite often used in marriage context, i.e., 'I would like to find my daughter a young man who is afraid of God.' The

chant was seen by many (especially but not exclusively Shi'as and Alawis) as a sectarian, anti-Shi'a slogan that implied that Assad, as an Alawi, was not a true Muslim. A few months later, in October 2011, in a neighborhood of Homs, the slogan "No to Iran and no to Hezbollah" was accompanied by "We want King Abdallah" of Saudi Arabia (Sadam al-Majid 2011).

In June 2011, in the town of Halfaya, in Hama's countryside, protesters waved Turkish flags and chanted, "Our constitution is the Koran, end Hezbollah and Iran ... our leader is Adnan." This referred to the Salafist Adnan Arour, who was based in Saudi Arabia after he fled Syria following the Hama Massacre in 1982, and had an important audience among some sections of the opposition (Shaam Network S.N.N. 2011c). He became famous at the beginning of the uprising for his numerous appearances on two Saudi-owned Salafist satellite channels, which devoted most of their airtime attacking Shi'a Islam and were widely viewed in Syria. He opposed the regime, but he did so by promoting a sectarian campaign against Alawis. The slogan raised by the protesters of Halfaya was a Sunni sectarian position that lacked appeal for the majority of the Syrian population.

These examples, however, were the exception in Syria during this period, while the dominant argument was for the unity and freedom of the Syrian people and against sectarianism.

Religious spaces, symbols, and vocabulary also played a role in sections of the protest movement. In the protests and demonstrations, political slogans demanding freedom, justice, and the end of the Assad regime were associated with the chanting of *Allahu akbar* (God is great) and *La ilah illa Allah* (There is no god but God). The demonstrations started in mosques because these were the only spaces where protesters could gather and organize out of sight of the security forces (Pinto 2017: 125). This did not prevent local grassroots organizations from being particularly attentive to the issue of sectarianism and communicating an inclusive message to all Syrians. Faced with attempts by the regime to divide the protest movement along sectarian and ethnic divisions, activists on the ground reacted by displaying slogans and chants promoting the unity of the Syrian people and organizing campaigns from this perspective.

Slogans such as "We are all Syrians, we stand united" were repeated constantly in the demonstrations and on social networks such as Facebook or Twitter. At the beginning of the uprising, a placard at the entry of the mosque in Dar'a read, "No to Sectarianism, we are all Syrians." In

---

underlying logic behind this meaning stems from the belief that anyone who fears God will not be able to commit the sins that evoke his wrath, hence will always be morally righteous." The Internet user might be quite right about the meaning of *Afraid of God* on its own, but it becomes or is understood as sectarian when combined with *Iran*, *Hezbollah*, and *Muslim* in the same sentence.

demonstrations on Friday, April 8, in the northeastern city of Qamishli, Kurdish youths chanted: "No Kurd, no Arab, and Syrian people are one. We salute the martyrs of Dar'a." And the most prominent chant raised in the Rifa'i Mosque in Damascus on April 1 and in the demonstration in Damascus University was "One, one, one, the Syrian people are one!" This would become one of the most popular slogans of the uprising. Most protests emphasized the unity of Syria and its diversity with chants such as "Not Sunni nor Alawi, we want freedom" (Wieland 2015: 231) or "No to sectarianism, yes to national unity" (Kalo 2014). In opposition to accusations by the regime of Sunni sectarianism and of being all Salafists, the protesters rejected them and stressed the involvement and participation of religious and ethnic minorities. For example, a banner in a demonstration in Zabadani in April 2011 said, "Neither Salafi, nor Muslim Brotherhood … My sect is freedom." They often used irony, such as one placard in Baniyas in April 2011 that read, "Was the martyr Hatem Hanna a Salafi Christian?" in reference to a Christian protester killed by the security forces (Pinto 2017: 128).

Solidarity among different religious sects and towns existed from the beginning of the uprising. The city of Salamiyah, the majority of which is inhabited by the Isma'ili population, welcomed around 20,000 displaced individuals from Hama during the summer of 2011. These were mostly Sunni, fleeing the repression of the regime against the city. The settling of the displaced Hamwis in Salamiyah was itself a form of political struggle: the fact that the Hamwis, nearly all coming from a Sunni background, found refuge in Salamiyah, full of religious minorities, and the fact that it was the activists of Salamiyah who broke the siege on Hama, demonstrated a solidarity built from below (Darwish 2016b; Anonymous C 2017).

Palestinians from Yarmouk Camp joined at the beginning of the protests "demonstrations and rallies in several neighborhoods of Damascus such as Midan, Hajar al-Asswad, al-Qadam [neighborhoods near the Yarmouk camp], or a bit further in Douma and Harasta," according to camp activists Tareq Ibrahim (2013) and Abu Zeed (2014). They added that before the camp became the target of regime forces, the neighborhood welcomed "displaced civilians from nearby targeted areas" and humanitarian assistance was organized for them by the camp's youth.

Feminist activist Razan Ghazzawi (2018) explained that Damascus and its province witnessed a high level of participation in 2012 of women from religious minority backgrounds and, to a lesser extent, nonveiled Sunni women, as they were considered less suspect by the regime's authorities than conservative veiled Sunni women, and therefore not searched at military checkpoints. These women took advantage of this situation to smuggle into different areas suffering from the regime's sieges and repression medication, food, and other necessary items, as well as smuggling out activists:

> At the end of 2012, regime started to notice that women from minority backgrounds and nonveiled Sunni were playing an important role in support of activists and opposition-held areas and started to impose more security restrictions and control much more systematically at checkpoints everyone.

Other initiatives of various groups and youth organizations throughout the country made a special point to reject sectarianism and support the revolution. One activist stated that in this period, the nonviolent movement

> made each one of us (protesters) feel that she became Syrian again. We felt at home in each city where we held demonstrations ... Our loyalties were unified and we all belonged to one family: the Syrian Revolution. (Dawlaty 2015: 19)

Women's participation, challenging patriarchy

The first two years saw important participation from women in demonstrations and other opposition activities. Women were instrumental to the civil disobedience movement from its earliest stages (Syria Untold 2014c; Anonymous A 2014).

The activities of women and women's groups were wide and diverse. Some organizations and committees coordinated women-only demonstrations almost daily and organized themselves in grassroots cells to deliver assistance and relief to the families of detainees, those killed, or FSA soldiers. Some groups, such as Syrian Women for the Syrian Intifada (SANAD) supported grassroots activists who were fired because of their political stance or were forced to remain in hiding upon learning that they were wanted by the regime. They raised funds and supported activists in their work in aid, media, or securing medicine (Ghazzawi 2014; Ghazzawi, Afra, and Ramadan 2015: 11; Anonymous A 2014; Anonymous B 2014). They also engaged in work promoting coexistence and rejecting sectarianism. They participated in several grassroots initiatives, from emergency and humanitarian assistance to the publication of local newspapers such as *Enab Baladi* in Douma and Daraya (Syria Untold 2013e, 2013f).

Women also began to organize their own groups within the opposition bodies in which they were marginalized. A study of women's peace activism by the Badael foundation noticed a significant rise in the number of women's groups in 2012, with the establishment of eleven in just one year. Initially, these groups focused on various forms of emergency aid, but gradually became more specific to women's rights, including programs empowering women on the economic and educational levels, documenting human rights violations, especially those involving women, and raising awareness of gender-based violence (Ghazzawi, Afra, and Ramadan 2015: 11). Significant groups of women activists played an important role in their localities and regions, such as Women's Coordination Committee of Salamiyah (Tansîqîyya Salamîyya 2011; Syria Untold 2014f; Darwish 2016b), the movement of the Daraya Free Women's initiative (Abd al-Hak 2011; Syria Untold 2013f), Syrian Women for the Syrian Intifada–SANAD (Ghazzawi 2014), and women's organizations in Douma (Ghazzawi, Afra, and Ramadan 2015) and Qamishli (Darwish 2016a).

Another important element in the involvement and participation of women in the uprising was the issue of breaking social codes and over-coming traditional barriers.[3] Female activists often agreed that the beginning of the revolution opened the door for women to challenge restrictive social conventions, whether those conventions were legal, familial, religious, or social (Dawlaty 2015: 39; Anonymous A 2014).

In some areas, however, this was made more difficult for security reasons, but also because of conservative religious trends. Women revolutionaries, for example, were given mandatory male protection, while some demonstrations were segregated from men or women were simply prohibited from participating (Kannout 2016: 37). Women in the uprising also encountered other difficulties. Razan Zaytouneh, the prominent revolutionary and human rights activist and one of the founders of the LCC, explained that an LCC activist told her that the coordination committee had a bad reputation in his town because people said it was led by women, which undermined the position of its activists. She argued that "women's roles were distinguished, but only one Committee is led by a woman, which is natural since it is Daraya's Women Assembly" (cited in Kannout 2016: 42). The lack of women in the local LCCs was exemplified in a survey distributed to the LCC units throughout the country regarding the numbers of female members among their activists. Razan Zaytouneh explained the results of the survey:

---

[3] The women of Zabadani explain in a video, for example, that their demonstrations were not only against the political regime, but also against the traditions and costumes of a conservative society that the revolution helped them overcome. These women were able to break social norms and overcome traditional barriers in order to be a vital part of the Syrian uprising (Kayani WebTV 2012).

Only 16 Committees responded, and the result speaks for itself [...] all the rest of the Committees have no female members at all. The ones that had more than 4 members were those of Shahba, Jdeidat Artouz, Hanano, Misyaf, Hasakah, and Inkhel! LCCs with 2–4 female activists were those of Ariha, Atareb, and al-Sanamayn, while those with 1–2 female activists were Kafrouma and Zabadani. The rest: zero women. (cited in Kannout 2016: 42)

Women were excluded from decision-making positions such as representation in local LCCs, despite the fact that four out of eight members of the LCC's Executive Bureau were women.

There was also a gendering of roles assigned to women in the activities within the protest movement, despite their deep involvement in the uprising in various fields. The feminist activist Kannout (2016: 43) explained that this was

justified by comments of the sort of women's inclinations are different than men's, so they better do what men leave behind or what requires a "feminine touch." ... such as banner preparation, medical relief, distribution of food baskets, and cooking for the rebels.

Women's associations also raised the issue of representation of women in local councils within the country and other activism.

The participation of women in the protest movement diminished throughout the years with the violent repression of the regime, increasing militarization of the uprising, and rise of Islamic fundamentalist and jihadist forces.

Organization of the protest movement

By the end of 2011 and the beginning of 2012, regime forces started to withdraw or were expelled by opposition armed groups from an increasing number of regions. In the void left behind, the grassroots organizations began to evolve into ad hoc structures of local government, in which on many occasions LCC activists were the main nuclei of the local councils. In some regions that were liberated from the regime's armed forces, civil administrations were also set up to compensate for the absence of the state and take charge of its duties in various fields, like schools, hospitals, roads, water systems, electricity, and communications (Khalaf, Ramadan, and Stolleis 2014: 9). Omar Aziz (2011), a 63-year-old anarchist activist who was arrested in October 2012 and died under torture in a regime jail in February 2013, was the first to call for the establishment of local councils in October 2011. In Damascus and its surroundings, his ideas and calls for self-governing councils likely inspired their establishment, but the reality on the ground and the need for activists and local populations to organize society politically and cooperate with armed opposition groups greatly contributed as well.

According to researcher Rana Khalaf, the first Local Council was established in the city of Zabadani in the end of 2011, with the main objective of coordinating among civilians and armed opposition groups. This then developed into a prototype of local governance emulated throughout the opposition-controlled areas of the country (Khalaf 2015: 46). Local councils developed rapidly as well in the countryside of Damascus in the beginning and middle of 2012, such as in Douma (Local Council of Douma 2016; Khaddour 2015a: 10), which was inhabited by more than half a million persons originally, although the numbers diminished through the years.

Similar examples of effective local councils also existed in the north of the country, such as Manbij, in the northeast of Aleppo Governorate (Munif 2017; Zaman al-Wasl 2013a; Khoury 2013: 5) and Raqqa (Arhim 2013; Syria Untold 2013d, 2013g), until both cities fell under occupation by the Islamic State and the Levant (ISIL) in 2014. The province of Aleppo and the city, where the armed insurgency found itself with several million individuals under its control following the regime's forced expulsion from these areas between mid-2012 and early 2013, also witnessed the expansion of local councils and self-governance (Baczko Dorronsoro and Quesnay 2013; Zaman al-Wasl 2013a; Chouikrat 2016).

This did not mean that there were no shortcomings of the local councils, such as the lack of representation of women or of religious minorities in general. In a study on civil activism in Syria in 2014, female participation was attested to be weak. Four Local Councils reported female representation of up to 17 percent. They were located across the Hama, Raqqa, and Aleppo areas (Khalaf, Ramadan, and Stolleis 2014: 20). The lack of women's participation continued in most of the Local Councils throughout the uprising. According to a study conducted by Omran for Strategic Studies (2016: 16) between January and May 2016 on 105 local councils (out of 427 throughout Syria), only 2 percent of members were female.

Other problems existed as well. Huda Yahya (2017), an activist from Idlib countryside, although describing local councils as mini-governments replacing the state's institutions and concerned with the provision of public services to the civilian population, argued that

> these councils have shown some forms of disorganization, undemocratic practices, representation of families, and underrepresentation of women. They have also failed to win the trust of the citizenry...

Furthermore, councils were far from well established everywhere in opposition-held areas and were at different stages of development depending on their security situation, access routes to border areas, amount of time since their establishment, and existence of other competing structures or spoilers (Khalaf 2015: 46). Civil councils were also not always completely autonomous from military groups, often relying on them for resources (Darwish 2016c: 2), or because the council members were largely selected according to the influence of local military groups (Baczko, Dorronsoro, and Quesnay 2016: 158).

Council members were also often chosen rather than elected, based on the influence of local military leaders, clan and family structures, and elders. According to researcher Agnes Favier (2016: 11),

> the majority of local councils (over 55 percent) did not emerge through elections but were established by "elite self-selection" mechanisms (i.e., a group of leaders including rebel fighters, notables, tribes, families, and revolutionary activists agree to share the local council seats among themselves by consensus without elections).

Another problem that was encountered was the need for particular professional and technical skills. For example, in the government of Idlib Province, one of the conditions to be elected was to be a university graduate. This allowed higher classes to monopolize the representation of these councils (Baczko, Dorronsoro, and Quesnay 2016: 282).

Despite these limitations, local councils were able to restore a minimal level of social services in their regions and enjoy some level of legitimacy. The role of local councils continued throughout the years, despite the multiple threats and deepening of the war, in various opposition-controlled territories. The numbers of Local Councils, however, diminished continuously throughout the years because of the military advances of pro-regime forces capturing opposition-held territories and the attacks of Islamic fundamentalist and jihadists armed groups against civilian councils, replacing them with their own.

Organization of the political opposition

The establishment and formation of political opposition alliances in Syria very much followed the inheritance of previous schisms. After the beginning of the uprising in the country, figures such as Burhan Ghalioun, Michel Kilo, Hussein al-Awdat, Aref Dalila, Habib Issa, Abdul-Aziz al-Khair, and Hazem Nahar called on all opposition parties to unite, despite their political and personal differences, to develop a common vision. The National

Coordination Body for Democratic Change (NCBDC) was established in Damascus in June 2011, bringing together fifteen political parties and several independent figures.[4] Members of the NCBDC were committed to three principles: "no" to foreign military intervention, "no" to religious and sectarian instigation, and "no" to violence and the militarization of the revolution (Amir and Fakhr ed Din 2012; Carnegie 2012d).

A few months later, the Syrian National Council (SNC), which was called the "National Salvation Council" in its first meeting in mid-July 2011, was established in Istanbul on October 2, 2011. The SNC was formed by a coalition of groups and individuals, including signatories of the Damascus Declaration (2005), the Syrian MB, various Kurdish factions, and representatives of the LCC. The LCC's leadership, however, had an ambiguous attitude toward the SNC, according to a former founding member of the LCC, Ciwan Youssef. The decision by the leadership to join the SNC followed pressing demands from Burhan Ghalioun, the first president of the SNC, and of the People's Party (a former Communist Party Political Bureau led by Ryad al-Turk), a founding member of the SNC, to boost the legitimacy of the opposition coalition within the country. At the same time, the LCC did not want to get too involved politically within the new opposition body regarding its decisions and policies. However, this situation would not last.

The coalition was initially supported massively by Qatar and Turkey, which respectively funded and hosted the SNC on its territory. The new coalition was also welcomed by Western powers and Gulf monarchies. It became the main point of reference for countries backing the opposition, while some businessmen opposed to the Assad regime, supported it financially from the beginning. On April 1, 2012, over 100 countries in the so-called Friends of Syria group recognized it as "the umbrella organization under which Syrian opposition groups are gathering" (Carnegie 2013a). The SNC very early on adopted a critical stance toward some internal opposition groups such as the NCBDC because they advocated for negotiation and dialogue with the regime and refused external intervention.

The SNC has been criticized since its establishment for being dominated by a large Islamic component, including the Syrian MB and a second Islamic bloc consisting of the "Group of 74," mostly former MB members (including many businessmen). With nearly one-quarter of the council's 310 seats, the MB was indeed the largest and most coherent faction within the SNC

---

[4] At its inception, the NCBDC encompassed opposition figures and parties from leftists and Arab nationalist backgrounds, in addition to the Syriac Union Party and two Kurdish leftist movement, including the Democratic Union Party (known as the PYD) (Carnegie 2012d).

(Carnegie 2013a) and was supported by Qatar and Turkey. Doha facilitated the access of MB members to its channel, al-Jazeera. The MB also controlled two of the SNC's central offices in charge of military affairs and humanitarian assistance, which provided them with millions of dollars of donations to constitute and/or strengthen their own support networks in Syria (O'Bagy 2012a: 16; Phillips 2016: 110; Youssef 2018). Faruk Tayfur, a leader of the Syrian MB, was the president of the Syrian Association for Humanitarian Aid and Development, founded in Istanbul in 2012 and the only one recognized by the SNC at this period (Diaz 2018: 214). Building on exile structures, the Islamic fundamentalist movement was rapidly able to play a central role in the SNC (Becker 2013: 2). The SNC was divided from within between competing interests and policies, which were strengthened by the foreign actors' intervention in the council, while it lacked any legitimacy on the ground.

The relations between the LCC and the SNC, which initially supported the opposition body and the nomination of Burhan Ghalioun as president (Youssef 2018), gradually deteriorated. On May 17, 2012, the LCC issued a statement accusing the SNC of betraying "the spirit and demands of the Syrian Revolution" and marginalizing its representatives. The LCC announced its formal withdrawal from the SNC on November 9, accusing the council of being under MB control and of failing to reform into a truly representative structure (Carnegie 2012c), although the head and two members of their bloc in the SNC opposed the decision (Carnegie 2013b).

A few months earlier, in February 2012, 14 leftist and democratic organizations and political forces, with a mix of veteran opposition activists and youth, established a coalition called *al-Watan*.[5] The coalition was created with the objective of participating in the revolution and reinforcing it to overthrow the regime and build a civil and democratic state (Abi Najm 2011). The organizations belonging to this coalition were targets of the regime's repression early on. The coalition disappeared progressively because of the severe repression of the majority of its members and its impossibility to organize, although some member organizations were still operating in some regions throughout the uprising.

---

[5] These organizations were (1) Harakat Ma'an for a Free and Democratic Syria; (2) the National Gathering; (3) the National Bloc in Syria; (4) the Citizenship Movement; (5) the Coalition of Syrian Left; (6) the National Committee Democratic Action in Jaramana; (7) Vision for Change; (8) the Revolutionary Left in Syria; (9) the Support Committee of the Syrian Revolution; (10) Helem (Dream); (11) the Gathering "al-Tarîq"; (12) the National Initiative in the Jabal al-Arab; (13) Cadres of the Communists in the Jabal al-Arab; and (14) the Civil Enlightenment Movement.

On November 11, 2012, the SNC joined the new, broader opposition coalition of the National Coalition of Syrian Revolutionary and Opposition Forces (known as the Coalition for short), and was awarded 22 seats out of 63 in the coalition's governing political council. About a half-dozen other SNC members were also given seats, considered as independent national figures or representatives of minorities. The coalition was established at the Doha meeting as a response to increasing pressure from the United States and other Western states for the formation of a Syrian opposition coalition that was more diverse and inclusive than the SNC. The main goal was to create a coalition that would be able to win more widespread international recognition and, along with recognition, increased financial and material support. This new coalition included representatives from the LCCs and initially had the support of large sections of the FSA (Carnegie 2013b).

This would not last very long. In the spring and summer of 2013, criticisms were growing from within the protest movement against the Coalition. The Revolutionary Movement in Syria, a coalition of various local committees within Syria, representing the Syrian Revolution General Commission, the LCCs in Syria, the Syrian Revolution Coordinators' Union, and the Supreme Council for the Leadership of the Syrian Revolution issued a statement in May 2013:

> The revolutionary forces that have signed this statement will no longer bestow legitimacy upon any political body that subverts the revolution or fails to take into account the sacrifices of the Syrian people or adequately represent them. We consider this statement to be a final warning to the Coalition, for the Syrian people have spoken ... (LCC 2013a)

The Coalition repeated the same mistakes as the SNC, failing to win internal support within Syria, whether from civilian activists or opposition armed groups.

At the same time, soon after its foundation, the Coalition established many structures in Turkey with the purpose of assisting local councils: the Assistance Coordinating Unit (ACU), whose objective was to provide humanitarian aid inside Syria (December 2012); the Local Administration Council Unit (LACU), which aimed to help standardize the local councils under a unified framework (March 2013); and, with the formation of the Syrian Interim Government (November 2013), its Ministry of Local Administration, Refugees, and Humanitarian Relief created the General Directorate for Local Councils (March 2014). All these units, however, were politicized and polarized according to personal interests and partisan agendas and were backed by rival regional sponsors, particularly the Saudi kingdom and Qatar. Therefore, at the height of regional rivalries in 2013 and 2014, these structures mostly operated in competition with each other, seeking to secure their presence and impose their influence on local councils inside Syria through financial support (Favier 2016: 11).

There were still many criticisms of the dominating role of the MB. For example, Mustafa Sabbagh, a former SNC member who was elected as the Coalition's secretary-general, had deep ties to the MB, although he was listed as an independent member of the SNC. Sabbagh was part of the SNC's military bureau and reportedly one of its most important distributors of MB funding to the Syrian opposition during the early stages of the uprising (O'Bagy 2013: 25). The nomination of Ghassan Hitto, a personality chosen by Qatar and close to the MB, as the prime minister of the Coalition confirmed this trend (Karouny 2013) and led several figures to suspend their membership in the Coalition.

From May 2013, however, Qatar's domination over the Syrian Coalition was progressively eclipsed by that of Saudi Arabia. This was the result of several factors, notably the resignation after five months of the Coalition's president, Ahmed Khatib, because of his complaints that external interventions were preventing him from working effectively and the increasing frustration by Western powers of the new opposition body's incapacity to create links within Syria (Phillips 2016: 122). The final straw in galvanizing the Western powers behind the move to rein in Qatar by promoting Saudi leadership was the appointment in mid-March of Hitto (Karouny 2013; Lefèvre 2017: 75). In early May, a twelve-member delegation from the Syrian coalition visited Saudi Arabia for an unprecedented official meeting that lasted two days. Prior to this meeting, Saudi authorities had consistently declined to meet the opposition, despite repeated requests. In the meeting, Riyadh called on the Coalition's delegation to expand its membership significantly (Hassan 2013a). At the end of May, after a week of tense discussions, the Syrian Coalition announced the inclusion of 54 new members, nearly entirely backed by Riyadh (Phillips 2016: 122), including independents such as Ahmed al-Jarba, a tribal leader and future president of the Syrian Coalition, new representatives of the revolutionary movement, largely from the Islamic spectrum, 15 members from the FSA, and a liberal bloc led by opposition figure Michel Kilo (Becker 2013: 2).

Even the MB, perhaps sensing the changing winds, sought good relations with Riyadh. Syrian Brotherhood deputy leader Mahmoud Farouq Tayfour traveled to the Saudi kingdom to meet with the Saudi foreign minister, Saud al-Faysal, in one-to-one talks. According to sources close to the opposition, Tayfour gave assurance to the Saudi minister that "Syria's

Brotherhood will definitely not be like Egypt's Brotherhood" (cited in Hassan 2013a).

These changes were also the result of regional developments to the detriment of Qatar. Sheikh Hamad bin Khalifa al-Thani gave up his post as emir of Qatar to his son in late June 2013, and more than a week after, on July 3, the Egyptian defense minister and head of the Supreme Council of the Armed Forces, Abdel-Fattah al-Sisi, announced the removal in a military coup of MB and Qatari ally President Muhammad Morsi, following mass protests against Brotherhood rule that demanded his resignation. Saudi Arabia, the UAE, and Kuwait rushed to congratulate the Egyptian military and pledge USD 12 billion to Egypt in the wake of Morsi's ouster in 2013 (Khan and Lebaron 2015).

On July 6, the Syrian Coalition with its new members elected as its head a new pro-Saudi executive, Ahmad Jarba,[6] a tribal leader from the Shammar clan of the northeastern Syrian province of Hasakah, known for its close links with the Saudi kingdom. Jarba defeated businessman Mustafa Sabbagh, a point man for Qatar. The previous pragmatic decisions of the Syrian MBs favoring the Saudi kingdom allowed the election of Tayfour as one of the vice presidents of the Coalition (Reuters 2013). On July 8, Ghassan Hitto resigned as prime minister of the Coalition, to be replaced in September by the pro-Saudi Ahmed Tu'mah (Phillips 2016: 123).

In January 2014, most of the Brotherhood's members of the Coalition voted for Saudi candidate Ahmed al-Jarba when he ran for a second term as president. The pragmatism of the Syrian Ikhwan movement even permitted the party to escape the consequences of a Saudi decision to designate the MB as a terrorist organization. Thousands of Syrian members of the Brotherhood continued to live in Syria, while Saudi authorities did not oppose the election of Muhammad Walid, a Syrian surgeon practicing in Jeddah before he moved to Istanbul following his nomination, as the new leader of the Syrian MB. After his election, he thanked Saudi Arabia for "protecting" the Syrian Brotherhood in their exile and for "supporting" the Syrian revolution. He also equated the kingdom to a "strategic powerhouse for all Muslims in the world" and supported its policies against Iran and its military intervention in Yemen (Lefèvre 2017: 75–76).

Ahmed Jarba's term expired in July 2014, and he was succeeded by his confidant, Hadi al-Bahra. Bahra's nomination was apparently the result of a power-sharing agreement that left the Coalition's presidency under Saudi

---

[6] Al-Jarba was one of the original members of the Damascus Declaration and was imprisoned at least twice by the Syrian regime for his political activities.

control but gave the Qatari faction the position of secretary-general and one of the three vice presidencies (Oweis 2014: 2).

In an attempt to unite various sections of the opposition for future negotiations with Assad's regime, Saudi Arabia organized a conference in Riyadh in December 2015, which gathered civilian and armed opposition groups and individuals to establish a joint document and select a team to negotiate with the Assad regime about a political transition. The High Negotiations Committee (HNC) was established in this conference, composed of 34 members. The Coalition had nine representatives, another five were drawn from the NCBDC, and nine others were listed as independents. Ultimately, eleven members were selected from the armed opposition groups, the FSA's networks, and Islamic fundamentalist groups, such as Muhammad Alloush of the Jaysh al-Islam (Lund 2015e).

The HNC attended and participated in the various peace talks held in Geneva from 2016, but they were unsuccessful, notably because of the regime's intransigent refusal of any transition in which Bashar al-Assad would not be included, as well as their own political limitations. The military victories of the regime since 2016 weakened the HNC even more, while fortifying the will of the regime. The HNC was not even invited to the peace talks in Astana, Khazakstan, in 2016 and afterward, sponsored by Russia, Iran, and Turkey. Only some armed opposition groups, led by Muhammad Alloush, were represented.

In the autumn of 2017, HNC, under Saudi Arabia's increasing pressure, included the "Moscow" and "Cairo" platforms[7] to unite the opposition even more widely in negotiation talks with Assad's regime.

The divisions within the opposition continued and were even exacerbated by foreign powers throughout the years, especially the Qatari-Saudi rivalry. Regional actors prioritized their own interests rather than devoting their efforts to rendering the opposition more effective. The rapprochement of Arab states and some Gulf monarchies, especially UAE, with the Syrian regime by the middle to the end of 2018 (see Chapter 6) only further weakened the opposition in exile.

Militarization and the establishment of FSA networks

From the first days of the uprising, the regime dealt with the demonstrations with extreme violence. The reaction to the earliest protests was very

---

[7] The Moscow and Cairo platforms each comprise a handful of activists and are named after the cities where they first convened. They do not control territory on the ground or have strong links with armed groups engaged in the war.

harsh, with around 100 people killed in the week after the first demonstration in Dar'a (*Orient le Jour* 2011d). Security services continued on this path and gradually escalated their repression during the ensuing months, while arresting political opponents. In the beginning, the regime tried to coopt some sections of the opposition, or at least calm them, through various symbolic measures and openings. But these attempts did not change the strategic decision by Damascus to continue its harsh repression.

This led to a rising number of defections among conscript soldiers and officers who refused to shoot at peaceful protesters, while at the same time, initial unorganized and occasionally armed resistance against the security services was starting to emerge toward the end of May and beginning of June 2011 in some localities. In the following months, the FSA was established, as well as a myriad of other brigades. Armed resistance against the regime was nearly generalized at the end of 2011, creating new dynamics within the uprising. The first constituted armed opposition groups often had a purely local dynamic and served to defend their hometowns and areas from aggression by the armed security services.

The first instance of significant armed rebellion came in June, when local militiamen, probably in coordination with Syrian army defectors, killed a large number of regime security forces in Jisr al-Shughour, a northern town at the foothills of the mountainous Turkish border (Halliday 2012a: 11). On June 9, 2011, as regime security forces closed in on the rebellious town, Lieutenant Colonel Hussein Harmoush announced that he and his companions, around 150 soldiers, were defecting from the army to "protect the unarmed protesters who demand freedom and democracy," adding, "peace, peace, no divisions, one, one, one, the Syrian people are all one" (Freedom for Syria-Antakya 2011). They also proclaimed the creation of the Free Officers Movement.

In July 2011, the defecting Air Force colonel Ryad al-As'ad announced—from a refugee camp in Antakya Province in Turkey—the establishment of the FSA, explaining its mission as protecting the revolution and the Syrian people in all its components and religious sects (Ugarit NEWS Channel 2011). There was an increasing number of desertions from the army, in particular of ranking soldiers refusing to fire on peaceful demonstrators. In late September 2011, As'ad announced the unification of the Free Officers Movement and the FSA, following reports of Harmoush's kidnapping by regime security services somewhere near his sanctuary in southern Turkey.[8]

---

[8] Syrian state media aired an interview in mid-September in which Harmoush recanted his previous statements, saying that the opposition was indeed "armed gangs" murdering people. He went on to say that the first people to contact him after his defection were the MB and exiled former Syrian vice president Abdul Halim Khaddam. Both statements bolstered the regime's

In the autumn of 2011, more and more activists started to embrace and support the nascent FSA and the need for help from foreign actors. On September 9, 2011, protests were held in the name of "international protection"; on October 28, under the slogan "Establish a no-fly zone," similar to the one imposed in Libya; and on December 2, "Buffer zone is our demand" (ICG 2012b: 2; Phillips 2016: 84). Later in December 2011, the FSA established official relations with the exiled political opposition, the SNC, formalizing its status as Syria's main armed opposition (Lister 2016b: 6).

The members of FSA units generally originated from the majority component of the uprising: marginalized (informal and formal) workers of the cities and countryside (Darwish 2016b, 2016e), members of the popular classes who had suffered from the acceleration of neoliberal economic policies and the repression of the regime. The armed opposition was made up partly of defected soldiers from the Syrian army, but the vast majority were civilians who had decided to take up arms (Halliday 2012a: 13; Solomon 2012a). Some brigades were loosely gathered under a common umbrella, such as the FSA, but most were locally organized and only active in their hometowns. Lacking unity and centralization, they coordinated on specific battlefields, but rarely on political and strategic decisions. They generally gathered together along village or extended family lines, with little ideological cohesion.

Fighters tended to be conservative and practicing Sunni Muslims from popular neighborhoods in rural and urban areas, but they were not motivated by a particular religious fundamentalist ideology linked to al-Qa'ida or other Islamic fundamentalist movements, as claimed by regime propaganda (Jaulmes 2012; al-Jazeera English 2012; Legrand 2016: 1). Names adopted by some armed groups in the summer and autumn 2011 with a religious Sunni connotation, such as Khalid Ibn al-Walid, who was the Muslim Arab conqueror of Syria in the seventh century, or Umar Ibn al-Khattab battalion in Deir ez-Zor, reflected the social milieu of their members, who were usually rural, socially marginalized, and commonly practiced their religion.

With this said, the FSA was initially characterized by the variety of its members' political views, and to some extent its ethnic and sectarian compositions. The Kurdish Salah al-Din Brigade fighting in Aleppo and northern Syria initially defended a democratic program for all Syrians without discrimination (Hossino 2013). The National Unity Brigades

---

argument that a foreign conspiracy was responsible for unrest in Syria. The consensus among political and armed opposition members was that Harmoush was responding to threats or torture, and he was revered as a hero despite this damaging interview. Harmoush was executed in January 2012 (Halliday 2012a: 15).

(Kata'ib al-Wahda al-Wataniyya) were established in the countryside of Damascus in 2012 and had democratic and inclusive aspirations. The spokesman of this group declared in the first line of a statement, "Religion is for God, and the homeland is for all," while adding, "the National Unity Brigades operate for the sake of a civil, democratic state for all ethnicities and social identities" (Darth Nader 2012). Two battalions, Oussoud al-Ghouta and Oussoud Allah, were linked to Arab nationalist and socialist political parties in Douma, where they had a historical presence in competition with Islamic fundamentalist movements (al-Dik 2016: 190–191). Among religious minorities, involvement in the armed opposition was present but very limited, and most often on an individual basis.

In a survey of the opposition carried out by the International Republican Institute and Pechter Polls of Princeton, New Jersey, in June 2012, most of the armed opposition fighters favored a democratic system or process. The survey reported that 40 percent preferred a transitional government in Damascus, leading to elections, while 36 percent declared that they wanted a constitutional assembly, as in postrevolutionary Tunisia, leading to elections (cited in Hassan and Weiss 2015: 181).

By early 2012, the armed groups of the FSA were demonstrating increasing effectiveness and were able to remain in control of key regions near Damascus and central Homs. The FSA achieved these victories by forcing the regime to fight in many locations at once, stretching the security forces thin and increasingly pushing the regime to prioritize some areas. Successes of FSA brigades resulted in its steady growth, pushing the Assad regime to increase its use of violence considerably by using its artillery in 2012 (Halliday 2012a: 11). By March 2012, around 60,000 Syrian soldiers had defected (Lister 2016b: 5).

Civilian and armed protest movement, collaboration, and problems

The violent repression by the regime against peaceful demonstrators and the leaders of the protest movement (who were killed, arrested, or forced into exile) provoked a general radicalization of the uprising and helped to empower activists who were more inclined to armed resistance. More and more groups of citizens took up arms to defend their demonstrations and homes against the *Shabihas*,[9] the security services, and the army. Some

---

[9] Initially, the term *Shabiha* was used in the 1980s in the home village of the Assad family, Qardaha, where individuals belonging to the extended Assad family and their entourage were known to act extrajudicially, operating large-scale smuggling operations and using tactics of intimidation against the inhabitants of the coastal region. However, since March 2011, the word

military brigades were established with previously civilian activists (Darth Nader 2012; Darwish 2015: 68–69; Darwish 2016e).

Similarly, among the various coordination committees, which were previously determined to continue their peaceful struggle, many shifted their position in light of the increasing militarization of the uprising and the violent repression of the regime. In mid-2012, the SRGC called for foreign military intervention and now actively supported military groups inside Syria, such as the various FSA groups, with logistics, funds, and intelligence on the ground (Carnegie 2012e). The LCC increasingly provided logistical and technological support to FSA groups, as well as intelligence regarding regime activities and the Syrian army's movements and whereabouts, while continuing to focus on using peaceful resistance to topple the regime (LCC 2012a).

In August 2012, the LCC launched a new campaign called "A Revolution of Dignity and Morals," focusing on the principles and goals of the Syrian revolution that all individuals opposed to the Assad regime would commit to, including civilians and opposition armed groups. A code of good conduct was created at the initiative of the LCC for the FSA battalions, which notably included an article demanding respect for international law and opposition to sectarianism. This statement of good conduct was signed by a large number of armed opposition groups (LCC 2012b) but would progressively fade away with the continuation of the war throughout the years.

In a similar attempt, Farzand Omar, a cardiologist and human rights activist from Aleppo, launched the National Coalition to Protect the Civil Peace in late 2012 to unite secular civil society groups and aid organizations with secular-minded armed opposition brigades. He brought together FSA democratic forces such as the Salah al-Din Brigade, the National Unity Brigades that operated during this period in parts of Idlib and Hama, and small Christian brigades that existed near the city of Qamishli with their counterparts in aid organizations, schools, and grassroots movements (Hossino 2013). The initial relation between the grassroots activists and the armed opposition depended generally on the dynamics between FSA units and local councils.

Several reasons existed for the tense relationship between activists and FSA battalions in some areas. First was the FSA fighters' lack of roots with the local population when originating from other regions. This was quite clear in the case of Aleppo Province, where there was a flagrant difference

---

Shabiha has been used by both the media and the opposition to designate any armed paramilitary group or militia with links to the army, the secret service, or the Ba'th Party. Shabihas are generally individuals (civilians) who are de facto neighborhood or village strongmen with connections to influential individuals inside the regime (Khaddour 2013a: 8–9).

in the way that the revolution progressed in Aleppo city and the country-side. In the countryside, there was greater support for the uprising since the beginning, and LCCs were established very rapidly to organize revolutionary activities. As soldiers defected from the army, LCCs from their hometowns provided them with safety (Khoury 2013: 6–7). In contrast, in Aleppo city, support for the uprising was more hesitant and conflicted, partly because the regime retained solid control of security over the city until mid-2012, and partly because large segments of Aleppo citizens were unwilling to oppose the regime openly. The exception was a large section of Aleppo university students who had been protesting against the regime since the earliest days.

About 80 percent of the armed opposition groups that captured eastern Aleppo were fighters coming from the Syrian countryside (Solomon 2012c). The rural and urban divide in Aleppo was very deeply rooted in historical factors. Many bourgeois and middle-class Aleppo urbanites characterized the protesters in the first demonstrations at the university and rural Aleppo as *Abu Shehata*, a derogatory term literally meaning "Men wearing slippers," referring to the (lower) social class of the protesters, or as not originally from the city, but rather from rural backgrounds and other parts of Syria. At the same time, sections of the rural armed population saw the city as wealthy and elitist. One opposition fighter declared that "in Aleppo they only think about trade, about money" (Solomon 2012a). Both Damascus (although more diverse) and Aleppo's poorer neighborhoods shared similar characteristics, in that they were relatively religiously conservative, with a predominantly Sunni Muslim working-class population with transplanted villagers long ignored by the regime and deprived of services and economic opportunities (Stack and Zoepf 2011; Kilcullen and Rosenblatt 2012).

In some cases, the areas controlled by FSA battalions were characterized by lawlessness, with some groups involved in theft and robbery. In 2012, in the demonstrations held by LCCs and other civilian activists, a growing number of placards criticizing the FSA could be seen, with messages such as "The gun that has no culture kills and does not liberate," "The FSA, correct your path," and "Our mistakes are more dangerous to our revolution that the bullets of the regime." Moreover, activists and LCCs focused on various demands, including unification of the FSA, calls against sectarianism, and calls to preserve the objectives of the revolution (LCC 2012c). In some cases, activists complained of the sectarian attitudes of some individual fighters. In Aleppo, activists from the Alawi sect working with the Kurdish-Arab Fraternity Coordination Committee were subjected to sectarian harassment carried out by armed opposition factions linked to the FSA (Syria Untold 2014b).

The increasing militarization weakened the protest movement considerably. However, there were some cases of more or less successful cooperation between the civilian and armed opposition, especially when the armed opposition submitted to the control of the local councils. In the town of Daraya, the FSA factions were under the direct authority of the Local Council, and any military operation had to be coordinated with it. The city also disposed of only one financial treasury, which managed the donations and financial assistance given to the city. The Local Council was in charge of distributing the funds, which were allocated to various services such as the support of the FSA factions, relief and humanitarian operations, and the distribution of daily aid to the besieged population in the city. The Local Council also ordered the militias to avoid any kind of human rights violations and any extremist sectarian statements or behavior (Dawlaty 2015: 33). Daraya was often mentioned as an example of collaboration between the Local Council and armed opposition groups.

Attempts to unify the FSA

In late 2011 and early 2012, provincial military councils connecting local groups to the national FSA leadership started to emerge, representing a new level of operational coordination within Syria's armed opposition movement. The military councils in Homs, Hama, Idlib, Dar'a, and Damascus experienced mixed success: They were not able to win the support of every major armed opposition group operating in the country, but at the same time they did command a critical mass of the opposition battalions operating under the umbrella of the FSA. In some cases, the development of military councils took place in concert with the growth of civilian councils, which coordinated the activities of local activists organizing protests throughout Syria. They were able at some points to coordinate political and military components of the uprising inside the country (Halliday 2012b: 10–17). Throughout the uprising, however, the various FSA units were never able to unite formally and act as a single organization, despite various attempts from local and foreign initiatives.

One element preventing unity and centralization was the lack of organized support and funding. For example, in the case of Deir ez-Zor, it was reported that

the first operations of the FSA were funded through social networks, relying heavily on donations, for example, or the use of savings. Many weapons and ammunition were taken from Assad's army … (Darwish 2016b)

The Syrian armed opposition was neither well armed nor well funded. Fighters bought weapons on the black market from arms dealers and smugglers from Iraq, Lebanon, and Turkey. They also seized weapons from security forces in attacks on regime arms depots. Sometimes they even purchased them from corrupt officers within the security apparatus. Otherwise, most of the fighters armed and funded themselves as individuals or small groups (al-Jazeera 2012).

The lack of willingness of Western states to support the FSA armed groups still very much existed in the beginning of 2012. In a late February 2012 interview with CNN, General Martin Dempsey, U.S. chairman of the Joint Chiefs of Staff, declared that it was "premature to take a decision to arm the opposition movement in Syria, because I would challenge anyone to clearly identify for me the opposition movement in Syria at this point" (Halliday 2012a: 9).

In the first Friends of Syria meeting in Tunis in February 2012, the Saudi foreign minister, Prince Saud al-Faisal, described the arming of the FSA as an "excellent idea," while Qatar's foreign minister, Sheikh Hamad bin Jassim al-Thani, called for the creation of an Arab force to "open humanitarian corridors to provide security to the Syrian people." At the same time, the SNC increasingly dropped its initial objection to arm FSA units, and in March 2012, it announced the establishment of a military body to oversee and organize armed opposition groups within the country under a unified leadership (Reuters Staff 2012). The bureau never became functional, however, and was the first of a series of failed ephemeral joint commands that tried to establish a center of organization and funding for the armed opposition groups.

This position worsened the situation of FSA groups on the ground, which were obliged to seek support and funding elsewhere, especially from the Gulf monarchies. This would have significant consequences in furthering a process of Islamization of the uprising and of the armed opposition groups. As described by Steven Heydemann (2013a: 5):

> In the case of the US and Europe, the political risks thought to accompany direct engagement with the armed opposition or participation in any form of military action, including the creation of safe zones, has led Western governments to cede leadership and influence to Saudi Arabia, Qatar, and Turkey in providing financial, political, and military support for the opposition—even though they have done so in ways that directly undermine Western interests in preventing sectarian radicalization and political fragmentation on the ground.

The preference of religiously conservative Gulf funders was also reflected in the attitudes adopted by the armed opposition brigades. In June 2012, a small group of militants took the name of Sheikh Hajaj al-Ajami, a Kuwaiti Salafist who had provided them with significant funds. This situation not only generally strengthened Salafist factions, but it pushed other armed opposition groups and fighters to join these religious fundamentalist brigades in order to be provided with essential weapons and ammunitions. Some FSA groups increasingly started to adopt symbols, rhetoric, and facial hair affiliated with Salafism to receive funding (ICG 2012b: 10). Following the summer of 2011, symbols traditionally associated with Islamic militancy had come to the fore.

An emblematic example of this process was the case of the FSA-aligned Faruq Brigades, which began in Homs as a movement of army defectors phrasing their propaganda in a nonreligious military and nationalist vocabulary. The group then switched to a black logotype over crossed swords, and several unit leaders grew Salafi-style chin beards (Lund 2012: 11). In another case, one opposition fighter from the town of Qusayr in Homs Province explained that his group was given money on the condition that they all "grew beards," in keeping with the Islamic religion (Sherlock 2012a).

Many opposition members denounced the role played by Islamic groups, from hardline Salafists to the exiled MB, in bankrolling many battalions that shared their religious outlook (Solomon 2012c). Mulham al-Drobi, a member of the Brotherhood's executive committee, said in May 2012 that the Syrian MB opened its own supply channel to the armed groups, using resources from wealthy private individuals and money from Arab Gulf monarchies, including Saudi Arabia and Qatar (DeYoung and Sly 2012). The Revolutionary Shields Commission represented at one point in 2012 one of the prominent factions supported by the Syrian Ikhwan, while other groups throughout the country were established by the MB (Sherlock 2012a; Abu Rumman 2013: 25). Voices criticizing the behavior of the MB among FSA groups increased at this period.

In April 2013, the joint command of FSA issued a statement denouncing the attempts by the MB to monopolize and hijack the revolution (Syria Direct 2013). This created a situation in which competition increased among FSA units as they fought for resources. A fighter described these circumstances as follows: "When it comes to getting weapons, every group knows they are on their own … It's a fight for resources" (Solomon 2012c). Organizational cohesion suffered increasingly because of this competition and the variety of financiers with different agendas. Infighting between Syrian armed opposition groups surfaced more consistently by April 2012 (Halliday 2012b: 28). By acting independently, and often through multiple independent channels relying on personal contacts, regional states (i.e., Turkey, Qatar, and Saudi Arabia) contributed to the decline of the FSA, according to analyst Charles Lister (2016a: 8). He added that there was never a centralized policy put into place to avoid the chaotic situation that followed, when Qatar, Turkey, and Saudi Arabia each threw in money and weapons in the hope of backing the best proxies. (cited in Young 2017)

Failed attempts to centralize and unify opposition armed groups

After numerous failed attempts at unification, including the February 2012 higher Revolutionary Council and the September 2012 Joint Command, armed opposition commanders from the FSA established a new centralized leadership body called the Supreme Joint Military Command Council, or the Supreme Military Command (SMC), on December 7, 2012, bowing to intense pressure from Qatar and Saudi Arabia (Macfarquhar and Saad 2012). The foreign backers expressed three main goals behind the creation of the SMC: to unite forces in the country to prevent anarchy; to sideline external elements and limit their influence over the fate of the Syrian people; and to prevent extremist elements from taking over centers of power in the country. The SMC represented the convergence of international interests, and especially an agreement between Qatar and Saudi Arabia, as the armed opposition groups' most important backers, to channel their support through one organization (O'Bagy 2013: 16–18).

The SMC was officially operating on behalf of the Syrian Coalition. The Coalition and the SMC cosigned a document stating that the organizations' mutual goal was the overthrow of the regime in Damascus and the dismantling of the security apparatuses. The SMC maintained close relations with the Coalition in the hope of receiving better support and resources by cultivating its relationship with it, as it was recognized internationally. A few months after the establishment of the SMC, at the end of February 2013, U.S. president Barack Obama's administration officially announced that it would provide food and medicine, with U.S. advisers supervising the distribution to Syrian opposition fighters with the SMC via the Coalition. The Central Intelligence Agency (CIA) used SMC-linked channels to begin ferrying in small-scale lethal supplies, with a variety of Croatian-made weapons (purchased by Saudi Arabia) first appearing in the country in January 2013. This assistance, however, fell short of the arms capability requested (DeYoung and Gearan 2013; Lister 2016b: 8). In addition, Qatar and Saudi Arabia continued to bypass the SMC and directly fund groups on the ground for their own political interests. Their competition and rivalries, therefore, continued to increase divisions among the armed opposition groups.

The SMC failed to establish itself as an effective force and progressively fell apart as a result of internal disputes between and within the General Staff and the SMC. In June 2015, the Syrian Coalition's president, Khalid Khoja, ordered the SMC to be dissolved (Lund 2015c).

Even before the dissolution of the SMC, since 2013, Western and regional states supportive of the opposition had been establishing military operation commands in Jordan and Turkey to coordinate the provision of finance, weapons, logistical supplies, and intelligence to vetted FSA groups. Each was composed of military officials from more than a dozen countries. While the command center in Jordan, known as a Military Operations Center (MOC), had operated independent of the SMC, the facility in Turkey [the Müşterek Operasyon Merkezi (MOM)] had worked primarily through General Salim Idriss. From October 2013, regional states, led by Saudi Arabia first and then Qatar and Turkey, supporting Syrian opposition armed groups collaborated with the United States (specifically, the CIA) to facilitate a series of mergers of smaller factions into larger ones. These larger factions would be capable of operating on a provincial or cross-provincial level.

This merging process between FSA-affiliated groups was supported by the United States, but this did not materialize into any dramatic larger provision of arms and weaponry, although these groups had relations with Washington. Instead, as explained by Lister (2016a: 14):

[T]hese relations had largely been sustained by noticeable levels of external support from Turkey and Gulf States, at times overseen or permitted by the U.S. It was thus regional states that filled the vacuum left by a lack of determined American effort...

The marginalization and fragmentation of FSA networks, submitted to various local and foreign influences, did not prevent throughout the following years new initiatives to try to form a so-called national army by uniting various opposition armed forces, from FSA units to Islamic fundamentalist movements such as Ahrar al-Sham and Jaysh al-islam, but excluding jihadists (Jabhat al-Nusra and IS) and People's Defense Corps (YPG) Kurdish forces. FSA organizational unity remained even more difficult as regional states, especially Qatar, Saudi Arabia, and Turkey, maintained their continuous competition, with the aim of gaining influence over the various armed groups.

The weakening of FSA forces continued, therefore, and they increasingly became proxies for foreign states, fell under the domination of Islamic and jihadist fundamentalist forces, or both.

Marginalization of FSA networks

From the middle of 2015, most nonjihadist and non-Salafist armed opposition groups had been marginalized in the military struggle against the regime, first by repression by Assad's forces and foreign allies, Russia, and Iran, and second as a result of pressure from their regional backers to deescalate the fight against Assad to concentrate on other enemies instead. Finally, the domination on the military field and attacks of jihadist and Salafist armed groups contributed to the general weakening of autonomous FSA forces.

The main foreign backers of the armed rebellion established, as mentioned earlier, the Jordan-based MOC and the Turkey-based MOM to support a selection of FSA factions. Their assistance had been limited, irregular, and with strings attached. Each state created and developed its own channels to support armed factions individually outside these operation centers, without coordinating with other countries. Throughout the uprising, foreign backers increasingly pressured local FSA groups to target other secondary armed groups in peripheral military confrontations to serve their own interests rather than focusing on the regime. This damaged the local legitimacy of the FSA groups, to the benefit of the regime as well as Salafist and jihadist forces (Legrand 2016: 1–2).

Jordan and Turkey increasingly used local FSA and other armed opposition factions, composed of thousands of fighters, to guard their borders. This situation facilitated significant gains by regime forces in some regions and provided an opportunity for jihadist factions to present themselves as the only ones still fighting on the battlefield. The MOC suspended payment of salaries on several occasions to Southern Front rebels to pressure them to fight various jihadist forces. Meanwhile, Turkish troops, alongside armed opposition forces ranging from FSA units to Islamic fundamentalist forces, launched a military campaign within Syrian borders in late summer 2016 to prevent the sister organization of the Kurdistan Workers' Party (PKK) in Syria, the Democratic Union Party (PYD) (see Chapters 5 and 6), from extending its control along Turkey's borders. Turkish military intervention showed the changing priorities of Ankara regarding Syria, from regime change to a counterterrorist strategy against PYD and IS, directing its Syrian armed proxies in service of an agenda unrelated to opposing the regime. Ankara even asked some armed opposition forces to withdraw from eastern Aleppo, under siege by pro-regime forces at this period, to join its military campaign.

Meanwhile, Washington facilitated the supply and assistance of weapons to some FSA factions if they concentrated on fighting IS, such as the Southern Front in the region of Dar'a and various FSA factions in the Tanf area, a Syrian border-crossing with Iraq that is close to the Jordanian border (Oweis 2016: 6; al-Khalidi 2017a). At the same time, in mid-February 2017, the domination of Salafist and jihadist forces and the marginalization of FSA forces in northwestern Syria led the CIA-coordinated military aid for FSA-vetted armed opposition forces in these areas to be frozen (al-Khalidi, Perry, and Walcott 2017). In September 2017, after regime troops, backed by Iranian militias and heavy Russian air cover, regained a string of border posts with Jordan that it had abandoned in the early years of the conflict, two FSA groups, Usoud al-Sharqiya and Martyr Ahmad Abdo, were ordered to stop fighting the Syrian army and Iranian-backed militias in southeastern Syria by their backers from the CIA and neighboring states that supported them, which included Jordan and Saudi Arabia. They were asked to pull out of the area and retreat into Jordan (al-Khalidi 2017b).

Israel also supplied some small, local, armed opposition factions, such as the Knights of the Golan, near its border with cash, food, fuel, and medical supplies since 2013, in order to create a zone free of IS and to prevent pro-Iranian and Hezbollah forces from entering areas that could be used to transport weapons to military bases in southern Lebanon and the Syrian side of the Golan. In total, there were roughly 800 opposition fighters in more than a dozen villages in the Syrian-occupied side of the Golan Heights (Jones 2017).

The marginalization, fragmentation, and infighting between FSA networks and opposition armed groups more generally, while subject to different local and foreign influences, also made it less and less popular in many areas (Enab Baladi 2018a). In areas outside the control of the regime and the IS, particularly in Idlib, Damascus countryside, and Aleppo Province, local councils and activists launched campaigns between 2015 and 2017 to stop internal infighting, to attempt to put an end to the authoritarian practices of armed opposition groups against civilians, and to prevent these forces from meddling in civilian affairs. They often demanded that armed opposition groups evacuate their military headquarters and transfer ammunition depots far from civilian communities for the protection of the people and their property, in order to try to avoid turning the city into a battlefield (SMART News Agency 2017).

Another phenomenon through the years that weakened the FSA networks was FSA leaders and fighters switching sides to fight for the regime. Their reasons included opportunism, material ambitions, and the prospect of financial gain. Many had accumulated significant fortunes from the war economy and entered into obscure partnerships with regime officers. Other opposition leaders chose to enter reconciliation agreements with the regime that gave their fighters immunity and protected populated civilian areas from more destruction and aerial bombardment. The abandonment of international allies or protection also pushed some FSA units to seek an understanding with regime officials (Zainedine 2018). However, reconciliation deals did not prevent the regime's forces from subsequently arresting or killing former FSA members (see Chapter 3).

Conclusion

Protesters were inspired by the uprisings in Tunisia and Egypt and saw an opportunity to launch a similar revolt in Syria following the events in Dar'a. There was less fear among large sectors of the society, especially for the youth, who had not lived through the repression of the 1980s. The repressive measures of the regime against the protest movement and the lack of political progress, in terms of human rights and reforms with real changes on the ground from Bashar al-Assad, opened the door for a radicalization of the protesters' demands, evolving from reforms to the fall of the regime. In the first two years of the revolution, coordination committees succeeded in organizing national campaigns through their networks of activists in villages, neighborhoods, towns, and cities. Although each region remained isolated from each other to a certain extent, messages of solidarity were exchanged between them.

Different forms of resistance had different social, economic, and political roots. In Aleppo, rural and urban was clearly the main dividing line during the uprising. The protest movement was perceived, at least by some sections of the middle and business classes of the city, as being led by rural and religiously conservative people challenging their wealth and lifestyle. The shelling by armed opposition forces of West Aleppo, targeting civilians and nonmilitary infrastructure, only further alienated those sections of the population, although eastern regions of Aleppo suffered far more violence at the hands of the regime and Russian air forces. Similar dynamics played out to some extent in Damascus.

Second, significant sectors of religious minorities, particularly Alawis and to a lesser degree Christians, also remained passive due to fears of Salafism and jihadism or of a political vacuum in which they would be vulnerable, such as in Iraq post-2003. This is not to say that no members of religious minorities participated in the uprising, but rather that they represented only a small section of their community.

The protest movement suffered from some limitations. No united leadership represented it, and instead coordination committees and youth organization were set up, which was "the biggest mistake," as the former option would have "prevented the movement from fracturing," according to a study of more than 100 nonviolent activists (Dawlaty 2015: 25). The political opposition formed in exile was unable to play this role for various reasons (see Chapter 4), ranging from internal division, growing corruption, and interventions of foreign states (Saudi Arabia, Qatar, and Turkey). The high level of repression against activists and members of coordination committees, especially killings and forced disappearances, considerably weakened the human resources of the uprising and isolated many activists who survived in their villages, neighborhoods, and regions. Some of these activists got involved in the emerging local councils, which played an important role in managing their areas during the Syrian uprising.

Some have criticized the militarization of the uprising for leading to dependence on foreign support, increased Islamization, and subsequent disaster, while others argue that only armed resistance was capable of toppling the regime. Veteran opposition activist Rateb Sh'abo (2016), although critical of the militarization, stated the dilemma as follows:

> It is clear that the "decision" to militarize the Syrian Revolution has resulted in an everlasting disaster ... Having said that, it is equally obvious that maintaining a peaceful revolution against a regime obsessed with its own survival, which viewed the battle against political change as an existential one, is practically impossible. This is to say that the fierce debate and the war of certainties that persisted around the revolution between the defenders of militarization on the one hand, and those weeping over peacefulness on the other, had little meaning.

In conclusion, the failure to constitute an independent and organized social and political force with some forms of centralization created a vacuum in which other internal and external actors were able to intervene and instrumentalize the opposition, armed and civilian, to the detriment of the protest movement. Despite these limitations, a revolutionary process was opened in Syria, as witnessed by the intrusion of large popular masses on the political scene, challenging radically the rule and structures of the regime.

3. The Regime's Repression

Introduction

The regime responded to the revolutionary situation by portraying it as the work of a foreign conspiracy seeking to nurture a sectarian civil war. In a speech in January 2012, Bashar al-Assad identified the demonstrators with the al-Qa'ida terrorists of 9/11 (cited in Pinto 2017: 127). At the same time, since the first days of the uprising, the regime violently repressed the protest movement and especially targeted the peaceful, nonsectarian, and democratic activists. Many of them were arrested and tortured to death in prison; others had to flee the country. As a result of this violence, the protest movement moved progressively toward more radical positions by calling for the overthrow of the political system.

As in the 1970s and 1980s, the domination by the security services of the Syrian political system still very much existed. Prior to the beginning of the uprising in March, news was leaked that Bashar al-Assad had formed a Special Committee to study the possibility of protests spreading to Syria and how to thwart them. The committee concluded that the reason for the overthrow of the Tunisian and Egyptian heads of state was the failure to crush the protests at the moment of their outset. Thus, the security option had been the preferred response even before the mass protests started, according to researcher Hassan Abbas (2011).

The lessons from Egypt and Tunisia learned by Damascus were an example of what Heydemann and Leenders (2011) call "authoritarian learning," in which an authoritarian regime adopts ideas, practices, frames, or policies from other countries. The regime's actions were also rooted in its structure and previous experiences.

The changes within the structure of the Assad regime, especially following Bashar's ascension to power, forced it to rely on a limited social base, much smaller than in the 1970s, with no nationally popular organizations to assist it in its repression; therefore, it was more reliant on sectarian, tribal, and clientelist links for the mobilization of its popular base through various informal and patronage networks. Crony capitalists affiliated with the regime first mobilized people to demonstrate in support of the government, and moreover played an important role in the development and funding of pro-regime militias. But the security services played the most important role in establishing and expanding such militias. Finally, the role of the state's continued provision of services is important in this context. Throughout the war, the state remained the largest employer and provider of services in Syria.

Mobilization of popular base

a) Crony capitalists and businessmen
There were no mass defections by crony capitalists and businessmen close to the regime; throughout the conflict, they played an increasingly political role. They first funded the regime's orchestrated mass rallies and public relations campaigns (Haddad 2012b), while private media organizations owned by some of them defamed the protest movement and promoted state propaganda (Abbas 2011; Iqtissad 2015a). Later, they were increasingly involved in the funding of pro-regime militias (as discussed later in this chapter) and in the funding of various services, including medical treatment or weddings, for militiamen, soldiers of the SAA, and members of the security services (Eqtisad 2017). Rami Makhlouf, through his company Syriatel, was especially involved in these kinds of services. By mid-2018, he also established the Nour Microfinance Foundation, whose mission included the provision of financial services to low-income individuals who lack collateral for bank loans (Kharon Brief 2018).

Early sanctions by various international and regional states did not encourage Syria's integrated elite to abandon the regime, with the exception of a few individuals such as Manaf Tlass. No individual under sanctions allied himself with or otherwise joined the opposition. The sanctions incentivized some businesspeople to become more integrated with the regime as economic opportunities arose during the conflict. The integrated elite, from all sects, remained firmly entrenched in Syria (Abboud 2013: 3; Younes 2016).

The Assad regime punished businessmen who openly supported the uprising by confiscating their property or bringing spurious legal charges in newly established so-called counterterrorism courts (Kattan 2014). Firas Tlass, who fled the country after voicing his support for the opposition, saw his assets seized (*The Syria Report* 2014a). In August 2014, Tlass's company MAS was formally transferred to state ownership (al-Iqtisadi 2014b). The regime also seized the assets of those who had a direct relationship with Bashar al-Assad but did not demonstrate their support as expected. Imad Ghreiwati, one of Syria's most influential business personalities, saw his assets and those of his family seized by the state. He has resided in Dubai since his resignation in 2012 from his position as the head of the

Syrian Federation of Chambers of Industry (Baladi News 2017). Similarly, the assets of Mouaffaq al-Gaddah,[1] one of the biggest Syrian investors in the UAE, and who was previously provided with government land in Damascus for free, were seized in 2014 under the accusation of "funding terrorist organizations" and "participating in bringing weapons into Dar'a" (*The Syrian Observer* 2013; al-Iqtisadi 2014a). His name was withdrawn from the terrorist list in May 2018, perhaps demonstrating his reconciliation with the regime. Most of these people, however, have never made any official statements opposing the regime or in support of the uprising.

These measures served to discipline the Syrian business community, especially within the country, but outside it as well. In a meeting in July 2018, as the regime regained much territory, Jamil Hassan, head of the Air Force Intelligence administration, declared that more than 150,000 security files of wealthy people and Syrian businessmen who "aided the terrorists" had been compiled, and that these people would be dealt with through harassment and pressure, pending the full withdrawal of their funds, which will be used to "rebuild what they destroyed" (*The Syrian Reporter* 2018). Whether or not these actual numbers were true, it is certain that pressure on business to serve regime interests will remain.

b) Weakening of the army

In March 2011, the SAA was at a low level of combat and operational professionalism as a result of decades of corruption. It was weakened considerably during the uprising, with various estimates that its numbers fell from between 220,000 and 300,000 to as few as 80,000 or 100,000. By the beginning of 2018, more than 119,000 pro-regime forces died in military confrontations, including 62,000 members of the SAA (Balanche 2016; Davison 2016; Zaman al-Wasl 2018b).

Security forces identified potential defectors. Commanders suspected of being a risk, even those who held significant positions, were suspended at the first sign of trouble. Manaf Tlass, for example, was discharged from command of his Republican Guard brigade and even put under house arrest before he defected. No major military units defected with their leaders. The security apparatus also enforced compliance with orders by killing or imprisoning and torturing soldiers who failed to follow orders to shoot at demonstrators (Halliday 2013: 13). This explained partially why most of the defections occurred on an individual basis or in small groups. Thousands

---

[1] Al-Gaddah is a businessman who built his wealth in the UAE and returned to Syria in the mid-2000s as the economy opened up. He invested, in particular, in several real estate projects in the upscale Yaafour District outside Damascus.

of soldiers and officers were detained on suspicion of harboring sympathy for the revolution (Bassiki and Haj Hamdo 2016).

Bashar acknowledged in July 2015 that the army had a shortage of personnel and had to abandon some areas in order to better defend what he called "the important regions of Syria that the armed forces hold onto so it doesn't allow the collapse of the rest of the areas" (cited in Bassam, al-Khalidi, and Perry 2015). By "the important regions of Syria," he was referring to Damascus, Homs, Hama, and the coastal area around Lattakia.

Desertions and lack of will to serve from Syrian youth explained the difficulty in recruiting new soldiers. Many left for Europe or other countries after receiving call-up papers or orders to report for reserve duty. From March 2012, local media outlets reported that the regime was banning all Syrian males aged 18 to 42 (and sometimes up to 50) from traveling abroad without the permission of the military recruitment department (*The Syria Report* 2012; We Are All Syria 2017). Thousands of men hid out of fear of forceful conscription.

Throughout the years, propaganda for the army in state media, recruiting posters all over Damascus, and various amnesties for deserters and draft dodgers did not change any of this. The regime continued to suffer from a lack of personnel, and this situation was increasingly problematic, especially following the recapture of new areas in 2016 by pro-regime forces and regime allies.

The regime announced in November 2016 the establishment of its first official volunteer-based military force, the Fifth Assault Corps, aimed at "fighting terrorism," and which would be deployed alongside other army units and foreign allied forces. Russia was the main driving force in the creation of this unit by managing and funding it. Targeted initially for recruitment were civilians who were not already drafted for military service, army deserters, and government workers. The Fifth Corps provided recruits with a monthly salary and case settlement for those who had previously deserted their military posts. Volunteers with government jobs were offered yearlong contracts and continued to receive their government salaries and benefits in addition to their Fifth Corps pay. These conditions were particularly enticing for large segments of Syrian youth who were facing high unemployment and rising inflation. At the same time, the regime employed massive propaganda to promote the Fifth Corps, such as leaflets in regime-produced bread bags, advertisements on state television and in newspapers, and religious calls to foster recruitment. The Ministry of *Awqaf* ordered the head imams of mosques in regime-held areas to mobilize youth to join (al-Masry 2017). The Fifth Corps also increasingly integrated into its ranks fighters involved in pro-regime militias, such as the National Defence Forces (NDF), and former opposition armed groups that had reached an agreement with the regime. In mid-2018, this unit consisted of tens of thousands of troops, including pro-regime conscripts, members of volunteer militias created by the regime, and Russians, together with members of former opposition armed factions that signed agreements with Russia (Semenov 2017; Oudat 2018).

Syrian militias, Lebanese Hezbollah units, Iranian and Iraqi volunteers, and private military companies, rather than the SAA, undertook actions against opposition armed groups; only a fraction of SAA forces (between 20,000 and 40,000 soldiers) could reliably be deployed in offensive operations. These units consisted largely of elite forces, such as the Republican Guard, Special Forces, and Fourth Armored Division, that recruited heavily among Syrian Alawis (Kozak 2017). On this issue of repressing the protest movement and insurgency, Bashar relied, as his father did, on a limited number of military units, mostly composed of Alawis and often led by individuals with family or tribal connections to the ruling family.

According to a Russian military expert, Syria's General Staff had no coherent short-term or midterm strategic plans. Assad's generals did not believe that their troops could bring the country to order without military assistance from foreign states. They did not have any projects to large-scale operations, given the ostensibly high combat capabilities of the illegally armed groups, lack of ammunition and modern equipment, and a fear of heavy losses and a negative outcome from the fighting. He added that the majority of SAA units were positioned at about 2,000 fortified checkpoints throughout Syria in 2016 (Khodarenok 2016). Thus, over half of the army operated with no connection to their units. Sitting inside these checkpoints, the regulars were mostly undertaking defensive duties and extorting money from the locals. The only exception to this situation was the Syrian Arab Air Force, which conducted a significant number of sorties daily (reaching 100 some days in 2015), over 85 percent of which were bombing runs. The Air Force's contribution to the overall fire damage was about 70 percent. The air strikes were conducted by several dozen fighter/bomber jets and around forty army aviation helicopters (Khodarenok 2016).

At the same time, army recruits selected for officer training increasingly took on a deepened sectarian and localized identity: They were exclusively Alawi and largely came from the coastal regions of Lattakia and Tartus, while Alawi from Homs chose to join the NDF instead of the army. Since 2011, 10,000 new students enlisted in Syria's military education program, which was reduced from three to two years. While the officer corps had long facilitated the enrollment of Alawis, it was by no means a purely Alawi institution. Before the 2011 uprising, for instance, the Military Academy in Aleppo and the Military College in Homs welcomed several hundred applicants per year from various backgrounds, although an entry quota system for the Military College favored recruits from Alawi-populated provinces (Hama, Homs, Lattakia, and Tartus). The army's transformation to security-vetted Alawi aspirants was not openly recognized but became the army's de facto recruitment policy (Khaddour 2016a).

This did not prevent the regime from efforts to recruit young Sunni men applying in regime-held areas to fight in the SAA (Alous 2015). Furthermore, in some cases, reconciliation agreements absorbed former armed opposition groups, in their quasi-totality composed of Sunni fighters, into the regime's local militias—mainly the NDF or the SAA (Ezzi 2017)—although far from systematically (as discussed later in this chapter).

Similarly, the SAA, Syrian security forces, and militias still included influential Sunni figures in regime and affiliated institutions. In the SAA and security forces, we found:

- Ali Mamlouk, the head of national security, supervising all other security agencies
- General Fahd Jassem al-Friej, the former Minister of Defence and Deputy Commander-in-Chief of the Army and the Armed Forces (July 2012–January 2018) (Karouny 2012)
- Major General Mahmoud Ramadan, commander of the Thirty-Fifth Special Forces Regiment, assigned to the protection of Western Damascus
- Brigadier General Jihad Muhammad Sultan, the commander of the Sixty-Fifth Brigade that guarded Lattakia
- Colonel Khalid Muhammad, a Sunni from Dar'a, in charge of securing Damascus for Department 40 of Internal Security
- Muhammad Deeb Zeitun, the head of state security
- Muhammad Rahmun, the head of political security
- Mahmoud al-Khattib, the head of the investigative branch of the political directorate
- General Ali Diab, the head of the military security branch in Hasakah
- General Hayez al-Moussa, installed in the autumn of 2016 as governor of Hasakah

Among militias, the commander of the NDF in Dar'a was a Sunni man of Palestinian origin, and the commanders of the NDF in Qunaytra, Raqqa, and Aleppo were likewise Sunnis. One of the regime's leading anti-IS fighters who received support from regime security branches was Muhana al-Fayad. He led the large Busaraya tribe between the Deir ez-Zor and Hasakah areas and was also an MP (Alam 2016; Malik 2016; Zaman al-Wasl 2018a).

These senior Sunni officers were hired, promoted, and maintained as individuals. Sunnis in state institutions could also be found as the head of foreign intelligence, the minister of defense, senior officers in air force intelligence, the minister of interior, the head of the ruling Ba'th Party, the majority of Ba'th Party leaders, and the president of the Parliament. (at least until 2017 when Hamoudeh Sabbagh, a Chrsitian, was elected). In addition, the posts of vice president and foreign minister have been occupied by Sunni personalities since the 1980s.

Their success nonetheless had little to no impact on their broader communities, as shown by Emile Hokayem (2016), but were totally based on the sectarian, tribal, and clientelist politics of the regime. In some cases, subordinates could challenge their authorities in the security services, empowered by their strong links and connections with the Assad family (Belahdj 2013: 20).

The army remained intact, despite these problems. The defections within the army at the beginning of the uprising did not affect its organization. Aside from occasional cases of high-ranking defectors who were already outside the trusted security circles, the majority of defections were noncommissioned officers or conscripts. They mainly joined the FSA or fled the country with their families (Kattan 2016). There were defections in the infantry, but no major fighting unit broke away en masse. The core of the officer corps remained on the side of the regime, or at least did not defect. This was the case across sectarian lines.

There were a variety of reasons for this, including reliance on some limited brigades, mostly composed of Alawis, to combat the insurgency and therefore not directly involving Sunni officers, as well as socioeconomic advantages. Army officers had access to a benefits system that linked nearly every aspect of their professional and personal lives to the regime, placing them in an antagonistic relationship with the rest of society. In the neighborhood of Dahiet al-Assad, or "the suburb of Assad," northeast of Damascus and the site of the country's largest military housing complex, officers were given the opportunity of owning property in Damascus. As many army officers, both Sunni and Alawi, hailed from impoverished rural backgrounds, home ownership in the capital would have been beyond their financial reach (Khaddour 2015b).

The army remained central to the regime's survival due to its investment in various functions other than direct military combat. Throughout the war, it was the central platform for coordinating and providing logistical support to the various pro-regime militia forces deployed around the country, notably by sourcing and distributing weapons to paramilitary groups. The army was also the second-largest landowner in the country after the Ministry of Local Administration; it ran the military construction company, the largest construction company in Syria, and the military housing establishment, which was the largest developer and permitted the army to continue providing officers with housing, allowances and other benefits. Finally, the army continued to play a major role in symbolically legitimizing the regime's leadership of the country (Khaddour 2017a).

c) Security services and establishment of militias
The military weakness of the SAA led to the creation of militias throughout the country, mainly at the initiative of the security services and crony capitalists. These militias replaced those of the Ba'th Party and other popular corporatist organizations, which assisted the army and secret service to repress the MB insurgency in the early 1980s (Khaddour 2013a: 20). Popular corporatist organizations of the regime, used in the 1980s to oppose the protests and demonstrations, were no longer relevant in terms of numbers or significance to the regime of Bashar al-Assad. On the contrary, it had implemented policies to weaken them considerably. The Ba'th Party had become too bureaucratic and inert to be used for this purpose, and many defected from the party at the beginning of the uprising. Politically, the role and influence of security services steadily increased throughout the uprising.

The role of Air Force Intelligence claimed center stage in 2011. Air Force Intelligence immediately assembled pro-Assad militias and launched a hunt for dissidents. The influence of Jamal Hassan, head of the Air Force Intelligence, grew in parallel with the regime's dependence on his organization, which gradually moved to a more conventional battlefield role (Lund 2016c). He even dared to criticize Bashar al-Assad for having shown too much restraint in the beginning of the uprising, unlike his father, Hafez, who he argued had acted "wisely" in Hama in 1982 by eliminating the opposition completely (Sputnik News Araby 2016).

The militiafication of the conflict started with the establishment of the Popular Committees. Some of these groups spawned spontaneously, but they were usually recruited by intelligence services and pro-Assad businessmen to break up demonstrations alongside the security forces. The security branches in various regions began organizing them and providing them with arms, cars, and security cards. The National Security Bureau, headed by Major General Ali Mamlouk, oversaw the Popular Committees nationally. It divided the regions into sectors under the responsibility of the branches of the security services in Damascus and its surrounding countryside. Each branch of the security service assumed direct supervision and distribution of weapons to groups of young men to establish armed groups in charge of representing the authorities and respect for the law in the regime-controlled areas (al-Sheikh 2013).

The Popular Committees assisted the security branches and SAA in raids and operations to find and repress wanted men, while providing security at regime facilities and managing checkpoints. They received both cash and weapons from the regime's security services (Halliday 2013: 18). Its members earned monthly salaries ranging between SYP 20,000 and SYP 25,000, and they also gained privileges such as access to gas, other fuel, and bread (al-Sheikh 2013). These groups often had a bad reputation, and many complaints were directed against them because of their thuggish behavior and abuse (Mashi 2012).

The regime also encouraged the establishment of vigilante groups in neighborhoods. The security services gathered young men from the neighborhoods and organized them to control the area, while also providing information about what was happening around them in order to identify activists. They were generally given a licensed gun and a security pass. Checkpoints and neighborhood vigilante groups multiplied rapidly throughout 2011 (Sabbagh 2013: 83). In mid-2012, the regime started to systematically arm more such groups in Damascus, while some of its members received training lasting one to three months in military camps in Iran and Lebanon (Reuters 2012c).

To a lesser extent, the Ba'th Battalions, recruiting with no ideological basis, were created by former Aleppo Ba'th Party chief Hilal Hilal when he was coorganizing the defense of the city in the summer and autumn of 2012. The Ba'th Battalions were also used by security services to control neighborhoods and quell protests. The group remained strongest in Aleppo, but branches were established in various areas of the country, including Damascus, Lattakia, Tartus, and Hasakah (Lund 2015b). In 2017, a number of al-Ba'th Brigades, especially in Homs and Hamas, were created by university students loyal to the regime and acted under the leadership of the Fifth Corps in the SAA. The students in these battalions had 18-month contracts, which would exempt them from mandatory military service. Members also received a salary of USD 200, or more based on their qualifications (Zaman al-Wasl 2017c).

In 2013, the regime with the significant political, economic, and military assistance of Iran established the *Quwat al-Difaa al-Watani* or NDF, numbering between 100,000 and 150,000 fighters in the following years (Kozak 2017; Lund 2015b). This force appeared as an umbrella organization and reshaped all Shabiha units and popular committees. The contractual arrangement on which it was based stated that the regime would provide financial compensation for volunteer members, and that these would officially retain their civilian status. The NDF was also set up because many young men throughout Syria were evading military service for the army. Some found the conditions of the new paramilitary forces attractive and joined the NDF instead of the army because they could remain within the borders of their home province and were required to work only limited and

THE REGIME'S REPRESSION / 83

regular hours. Only a few NDF units were deployed in areas far outside their places of origin. Recruitment to the NDF sometimes also was on the basis of a deeply divisive and sectarian strategy in some regions. The new paramilitary force ultimately became strong, managing many checkpoints and conducting regular security patrols (Ezzi 2013: 64; Massouh 2013: 95–96).

Alongside the establishment of the NDF, other militias existed, such as the Local Defense Force (LDF), created first in Aleppo in around 2013–14. The LDF units were restricted to fighting in their areas of origin. The LDF units were set up with the assistance of Tehran, and sometimes Hezbollah, which played a part in training and advising them. LDF members were considered to be part of the official Syrian armed forces (al-Tamimi 2017a).

The creation of these militias created a particular dynamic in the coastal areas inhabited by Alawis, as Alawis provided the main personnel for both the army and the militias. The regime established militia recruitment centers in villages on the coast under the patronage of four main militias: the NDF, Suqur al-Sahara, al-Ba'th Brigades, and al-Bustan. These were chiefly headed by former and current Alawi army officers and particularly recruited among Alawi populations. The Shi'a Lebanese movement Hezbollah mobilized and recruited Alawis as well, although for purely military objectives and not to build any political base (Khaddour 2016b: 13–14).

Other members of religious minorities, particularly Christians and Druzes, also joined NDF units. Sunnis were recruited in some areas according to previous clientelist and tribal connections consolidated by the regime in the previous decades. In the city of Aleppo, recruits to the NDF led by former businessman and landholder Samy Aubrey were from the city's own youth, from loyalist villages as well as local clans and tribes such as the Berri, whose leader Zeno was executed as armed opposition forces first stormed Aleppo in the summer of 2012 (Schneider 2017). Aubrey used the NDF and other militias for personal reasons as well, including for protecting and expanding his own business interests. Members of Aubrey's extended family, such as the local construction magnate Muhammed Jammoul, have also been accused of abuses in Aleppo (Zambelis 2017).

Pro-regime Palestinian-based militias were also established, such as the Palestinian Liberation Army, the Galilee Forces, and al-Quds Brigades in Aleppo. The latter was probably the most important of these. It was established under the supervision of the engineer Muhammad al-Sa'id, with members originating from the Nayrab refugee camp, which had suffered sieges by opposition forces in 2012 and 2013, and Handarat refugee camp in Aleppo. They openly operated as an auxiliary to pro-regime forces since 2013 and were constituted of several hundred soldiers (al-Tamimi 2015b). They played an important role in fighting alongside regime and foreign Shi'a militia forces in the fall of 2016 to conquer the opposition-held areas of East Aleppo, which was finally recaptured in December 2016, in the campaign to recapture Deir ez-Zor in the end of 2017, and in other military campaigns. In October 2018, the militia was even recruiting in eastern Ghouta a few months after the region fell to the regime by offering people high salaries and exemption from serving in the army (Syria Call 2018).

Another decisive element that facilitated the recruitment of Sunni fighters to regime forces in Aleppo was the unprecedented early 2013 decree allowing conscripts from Aleppo to serve their mandatory military service inside the city itself, and optionally with a loyalist militia of their choice. In the past, the regime always had mandated that conscripts serve in regiments well away from their hometowns, with no exceptions, but that changed after the uprising began. Many, therefore, took the opportunity to join up, as they could go back home every day, instead of deserting. This considerably expanded the ranks of loyalist militias such as the Ba'th Brigades, which was almost entirely Sunni and in 2013 became the second-most-powerful regime unit in Aleppo, after the elite Republican Guard (Dark 2014a).

Similarly, in the region of Idlib, long-standing regime allies led the small pro-Assad militia networks that emerged from 2012 onward, and all of them were local Sunni from Idlib. Three central figures, all Sunnis, played an important role in their establishment. First, Khalid Ghazzal, who was a Ba'thist businessman with long-standing ties to the Syrian intelligence services and who worked with the regime to identify and liquidate MB sympathizers during the 1979–82 insurgency. He raised money to pay Popular Committees consisting of his relatives, Ba'thists, and other residents of Idlib. Second, Jamal Harmoush,[2] who established Popular Committee factions which were then turned into the NDF. Finally, Jamal Suleiman managed a vigilante group given Popular Committee status by the security agencies in 2011. As the conflict deepened, this growing force was provided with heavier weapons and increasingly took on a more conventional military role in policing the city and its outskirts. With the conquest of the city by Jaysh al-Fateh in March 2015, many of the city's Popular Committee chiefs fled along with their paymasters, and these forces crumbled (Lund 2016b).

In the region of Hasakah, the regime also established pro-regime militias relying on their links with local Arab tribal families, such as al-Maghawir militia (or the Commandos), in which the regular SAA was also deeply involved. The central personality in the al-Maghawir militia was Muhammad

---

[2] Harmoush was a distant relative of Lieutenant Colonel Hussein Harmoush, one of the first officers to defect from the SAA.

al-Fares, a sheikh of the Tai tribe and former member of the Syrian parliament, whose clansmen in the Qamishli area long operated as a regime proxy (Lund 2015a). The Islamic Revolutionary Guard Corps (IRGC)–Quds Force and Hezbollah trainers were reportedly working to build the capacity of these loyalist militias (Jamestown Foundation 2015).

With the increasing military advantages of pro-regime forces on the battlefield at the end of 2016, some tribal leaders who had joined the opposition now were turning their back on them and rejoining the regime, and in some cases establishing militias to fight opposition armed forces. Sheikh Nawaf al-Bashir, leader of the Baggara tribe in Syria's eastern Deir ez-Zor Governorate and a former member of the Syrian parliament, who in 2012 defected from the regime, came back to Damascus in January 2017 and pledged loyalty to Assad. He then opened recruitment offices in Aleppo and Homs to recruit Arabs for a pro-regime militia backed by Iran and headed by Muhammed al-Baqir to play a future role in Deir ez-Zor, Bashir's hometown (Van Wilgenburg 2017a). More generally, the fears of many local Arab tribes in the Jazirah areas under the PYD's control, combined in some instances with fears of a Shammar resurgence (see Chapter 5), drove support for the Assad regime. Many founded militias that were closely allied with the SAA (Khaddour 2017b).

Pro-regime businessmen also established militias. Although initially a charitable foundation, the al-Bustan association controlled by Rami Makhlouf developed a security branch from the beginning of the uprising, recruiting mostly Alawis from the coastal areas in Lattakia and Tartus. Makhlouf also armed some sections of the Syrian Social Nationalist Party under the leadership of Issam Mahayri (Massouh 2013: 93), as well as the Tiger Forces militia from 2013 under the leadership of General Suheil al-Hassan, an Alawi intelligence officer and celebrity among regime supporters. The Tiger Forces were an elite unit, better equipped than the regular army, composed of several thousand men,[3] mostly Alawi officers from the Fourth and Eleventh Divisions, but also some Sunni groups and subgroups[4]. The regime's Air Force Intelligence Directorate also recruited and trained

---

[3] The Tiger Forces' offensive units were estimated at roughly 4,000 infantry, while there were an unknown number of artillery and armor crewmen. The total number of affiliated individuals was likely much higher than 4,000 (Waters 2018: 1).

[4] There were two groups and a number of subgroups that consisted of Sunni individuals: the small Abu Arab Groups from Harasta, Damascus; the Bani 'Az tribe-based Mubarak Groups from Abu Dali, Idlib; the Sahabat Regiment, which partially recruited from Kawkab, Hama; the Ali Taha Regiment's Maskana Group from the mixed Sunni-Christian neighborhood in Homs; and the Khattab, Ma'ardes, and Taybat al-Iman subgroups of the Tarmeh Regiment, each from their respective towns in north Hama (Waters 2018: 4).

civilians (mostly Alawis) to join this special force (Khaddour 2016a; Schneider 2016; Waters 2018). Makhlouf was also suspected of funding other militias, such as Dar'a Qalamoun, Kataib al-Jabalawi, Leopards of Homs, and Dir' al-Watan (Hayek and Roche 2016).

Muhammad and Ayman Jaber funded the Desert Hawks Brigade (*Liwa Suqur al-Sahara*) and the Sea Commandos (*Mughaweer al-Bahr*), originally established in early 2013. With the hundreds of millions of dollars that they secured through lucrative business deals with the regime, they recruited former soldiers from the SAA's Special Forces and offered them generous wages. They purchased most of the equipment for their mercenaries from Western arms dealers. The Sea Commandos provided thousands of fighters to assist Assad's army in the battle to recapture Palmyra from IS in 2016. They also participated in regime offensives in other regions, including the Raqqa and Homs countrysides. Their militias received training from Russian and Iranian armed forces in Syria (Ahmed 2016; Khaddour 2016a; Enab Baladi 2017a). George Haswani, a native of Yabrud near Damascus who was involved in buying oil from IS-controlled fields, leading to his blacklisting, was another businessman close to the regime funding the Qalamoun Shields, which included between 2,000 and 4,000 militants fighting close to the Lebanese border (Ahmed 2016; Fadel 2016; Khaddour 2016a).

The Military Service Law, the legal framework officially governing the army, made the use of paramilitary groups possible because it allowed "auxiliary forces" and "other forces that are necessitated by circumstances" to fight alongside the army. Militias were included in the latter category because they were characterized as autonomous armed groups operating in the military's framework (Khaddour 2016a).

Private militias also appeared when the regime relinquished its role in protecting commercial facilities and convoys, leaving investors to establish their own security companies to protect their businesses. In August 2013, a legislative decree legalized private security companies for protection and guarding services under the supervision of the Ministry of Interior (Zaman al-Wasl 2013b; al-Mahmoud 2015). Many of the private security companies were owned by businessmen close to Assad's inner circle, according to journalist Nour Samaha (2016). In August 2016, the Syrian regime approved the establishment of a private tourism security company that would "offer services to protect tourist groups and those who wish to take advance of its service," including Syrians returning from abroad, businessmen, and journalists. Their tasks could also include protecting properties, including hotels operated by Syria's Tourism Ministry (Now 2016). In the beginning of 2019, 78 licensed private security companies were operating in Syria (Khatib 2019).

The importance of the militias increased throughout the war. By 2015, their numbers reached between 125,000 and 150,000 members (Barnard,

Saad, and Schmitt 2015; Balanche 2016). There were several intertwined reasons for this situation. The first was the weakness and deterioration of the SAA, as we have seen. The second was the degradation of the fiscal position of the regime, which was lacking funds to fight the war. Finally, the worsening economic situation in the country pushed the majority of Syrians into poverty. Fighting with one of the militias was often the best-paying job available to men, while it also offered the possibility for fighters to remain in their region and offered amnesty to draft dodgers (Hayek and Roche 2016). In addition, and unlike soldiers in the army, they were often allowed and even encouraged to loot houses when attacking opposition-held areas (Reuters Staff 2013).

Large differences existed between the numerous pro-regime militias. Some of them had almost every major weapon system in the army's prewar arsenal, along with many weapons delivered by Iran and Russia (Hayek and Roche 2016), while others were poorly disciplined semicriminal or sectarian gangs in civilian attire (Lund 2015b). There were attempts by the regime, following Russian pressure, to try to integrate some of these militias, such as the NDF, into the army, notably by the establishment of the Fourth and Fifth Corps (al-Masry 2017).

From the beginning of 2018, some militias were disbanded, mostly because their financial patrons stopped funding them, as the regime increased the pressure to stop the activities of their militias and some militiamen joined the army (Zaman al-Wasl 2018b). Throughout that year, other pro-regime militias saw their contracts ended as the regime retook control of large areas of the country (Enab Baladi 2018p). However, the majority of pro-regime militias, especially the most significant, would not be easily dismantled in a postconflict phase because they have become an integral part of the regime's power structure and increasingly would operate under the umbrella of the army's regular forces (Khaddour 2018).

d) Religious establishments

A few weeks after the beginning of the uprising, in April 2011, the regime sought to reach the religiously conservative sectors of the society by closing the country's only casino and scrapping a ruling that banned teachers from wearing the niqab. Sheikh al-Buti had spoken out on both issues before the uprising. Ironically, regime supporters had initially used the demands of some protesters for the reinstatement of banned teachers wearing the niqab as a proof of their religious extremism (Wimmen 2017: 72). The regime also promised the establishment of a national institute for Arabic and Islamic studies with campuses throughout the country, as well as the creation of an Islamic satellite channel based in Syria that teaches "true Islam," in the words of pro-regime Sheikh al-Buti (Qureshi 2012: 76). The regime also met with a number of religious dignitaries from different towns to try to appease the protest movement.

The majority of the Sunni high religious establishment stood by the authorities, particularly long-standing allies of the regime such as the Ministry of Religious Endowments (*Awqaf*), led by Abdul Sattar Sayyed, Grand Mufti Ahmad Hassun, and Sheikh al-Buti. They had much to lose from Assad's possible downfall, as they were deeply linked to the regime. Al-Buti immediately condemned the protests as a foreign conspiracy and praised the army at a time when it was already responsible for the deaths of thousands of civilians. He died in a bomb attack while giving a mosque lesson in March 2013. Few scholars were as vocal as al-Buti in their support for the regime, but many warned against discord or took refuge in silence (Pierret 2014: 5).

Throughout the uprising, the influence and organizational activity of the Kaftariyya and the Qubaysiyyat, the two Sunni religious movements closest to the regime, were reduced to Damascus. Most of the schools that were built by their members outside Damascus were either closed down or destroyed. In Damascus, the complex of Abu al-Nur became home to a branch of the al-Sham Higher Institute, which was managed and supervised by the Ministry of *Awqaf*. The Sufi-order component of the Kaftariyya headed by Rajab Deeb remained silent on his position toward the uprising, as did many of the elder disciples of Kaftaru who remained alive. Al-Qubaysi, the head of the Qubaysiyyat, opted for a similar silent position, which all the members of her inner circle adopted as well (Imady 2016: 81–82).

The regime also used Sunni religious clerics in the so-called reconciliation agreement with opposition groups. A combination of coercion and enticement was used to replace opposition administrative bodies with local authorities loyal to the regime. The agreement was implemented in several areas, and many members of the reconciliation delegation were sheikhs and imams of mosques, the large majority of whom were appointed by the government's Ministry of *Awqaf* during the period leading up to the uprising in 2011 and afterward were involved in the opposition, most often in Islamic movements. The regime rehabilitated these imams through their control over the restoration of services to opposition areas, reproducing official pro-regime religious establishments as they existed before the war. Merchants and traditional dignitaries were also often included in the reconciliation delegation (Ezzi 2017; Lund 2018a). The regime expanded as well local religious networks sympathetic to it in areas it had reconquered to consolidate its hold over religious institutions.

In September 2018, Decree No. 16 was signed by Bashar al-Assad and was widely perceived as strengthening the role of the Ministry of Religious Endowment by revising and expanding its responsibilities and its internal structure as a way to compensate it and religious groups linked to it for standing by the regime's side during the uprising. It extended the powers of the ministry at different levels. It was also a tool to try to prevent uncontrolled religious mobilization. First, the decree permitted the ministry to establish its own commercial establishments, whose revenue would go directly to its treasury without passing through the Central Bank or the Ministry of Finance, giving it complete financial independence. It could now outsource its property, set up tourism projects (like restaurants, hotels, and cafés), and rent its land to investors. Decree No. 16 provided also for full tax exemptions for the workers in the religious field of the Ministry and *waqf* properties. The Ministry of *Awqaf* was already the richest institution in Syria due to a constant flow of charity funds and its large tracts of property that had been registered as religious endowments since the Ottoman Empire.

The decree also allowed the ministry to govern financial and educational institutions, in addition to governing artistic and cultural production and authorizing a group called The Religious Youth Group to train and supervise preachers, monitor public vice, and make *zakat* an obligatory tax for Sunni Muslims.[5] It established preuniversity Sharia schools and religious councils in mosques, independent of the Ministries of Education and Higher Education. It also led to the strengthening of the ministry's role, at the expense of the Grand Mufti, in a power struggle of influence and material benefits (notably over control of financial donations to religious charitable institutions) between the two Sunni religious institutions. The decree authorized the minister of *Awqaf* to appoint the Grand Mufti of the republic, a right previously vested in the presidency, and limits his tenure to three years, renewable only through the minister's approval, while stripping the mufti of the right to chair the Higher Awqaf Council, which every mufti has enjoyed since 1961, giving the job to the minister instead. The decree provoked significant opposition and criticism, from both loyalist and opposition circles, denouncing a deepening of the process of Islamization of Syrian society[6] (al-Akhbar 2018; Rose 2018; Zurayk 2018). The decree was submitted to numerous amendments by MPs that limited some of the ministry's powers (notably the tax exemption for workers in the religious affairs and the freedom from influence of other ministries) but confirmed the expansion of the ministry's reach in society.

The leadership of the various Christian churches was also considered to have strong links to the regime, particularly those living in Damascus and

---

[5] This article was also seen as a clientelistic move. The minister's son benefited from the decree as his youth movement, created a few months ago, was mentioned, thus giving it official recognition. According to the new amendments, the name of this group was changed to Young Imams.

[6] Despite its call to "fight Wahhabi and Muslim Brotherhood thought" and appeals for religious "moderation," the decree was viewed as extending the role of the ministry in all affairs of the society.

Aleppo (Wieland 2012: 90). In the first statement on March 29, 2011, of the Council of Bishops in Damascus regarding the situation in Syria, it described the situation in the country as "a foreign conspiracy with domestic hands, agitated by biased media," while adding, "We congratulate our great people on the reforms started by President Dr. Bashar al Assad, our homeland protector, and hope that such reforms will be continued" (cited in Sabbagh 2013: 78). On June 16, 2011, the Council of Bishops in Damascus published another statement stressing that it did not want to see Syria turn into a second Iraq (Sabbagh 2013: 78–79; Wieland 2012: 90).

In the first year of the uprising, church leaders continued to issue pro-regime statements, while also appearing on official television channels and writing articles for pro-regime newspapers. Some clergymen also supported the formation of vigilante groups encouraged by security services in Christian neighborhoods. For example, the Reverend Gabriel Daoud was famous for being the link between the Christian militias in both Homs and Qamishli and General Ali Mamlouk, head of the National Security office, and carried out a number of visits to Syrian regime officials to establish Christian paramilitary groups. In October 2016, Mor Ignatius Aphrem II, patriarch of the Syriac Orthodox Church, issued an official decision to stop Daoud from practicing his work in the Syriac church because of his military activities (All4Syria 2016). The increased militarization of the uprising led to diminishing appearances and statements in favor of the regime (Sabbagh 2013: 81), as Christian dignitaries did not want to see retaliation against Christian populations. This tendency would again change throughout the years as the regime consolidated its power.

The regime had also developed cooperative relations with the three Sheikhs al-Aql, who were the most important religious personalities in the Druze community. At the beginning of the uprising, this triumvirate consisted of Hussein Jarbua, Hammud al-Hinnawi, and Ahmad al-Hajari, with Jarbua regarded as *primus inter pares* (Gambill 2013). Two had died by 2014 and were replaced by younger relatives, with only Hammud al-Hinnawi remaining from the older generation (Lang 2014). Sheikh al-Hinnawi and Sheikh Hussein Jarbou were broadly supportive of the regime and denounced the protest movement as "a foreign plot" (Choufi 2012); however, they refused early on to denounce Druze army defectors as demanded by the regime.

Sheikh Ahmad al-Hajari was more nuanced in his positions and even expressed his dissatisfaction with the regime's repression of protesters, although without calling to join the protest movement. He also refused to issue a statement in support of Bashar al-Assad. Sheikh Ahmad al-Hajari passed away in strange circumstances in the aftermath of a car crash in March 2012. Some say that the regime ordered his assassination

(Metransparent.net 2012; Aboultaif 2015; Gambill 2013). His successor, Sheikh Hekmat al-Hajari, was a staunch supporter of the regime and had close relations to the security services. Following the death of Hussein Jarbua, Sheikh-aql Yusuf Jarbua replaced him. He also backed the regime, although he issued a fatwa condemning all civilians who fought with regime forces outside Suwayda (Ezzi 2015).

The general tendency among the three sheikhs since then was continuing to support the regime. They issued a statement setting red lines and banning any statement against "the homeland and the leader of the homeland, its institutions, and the Syrian Arab Army" (Ezzi 2015). They also excommunicated Sheikh al-Bal'ous, who headed the movement of Rijal al-Karama (Men of Dignity) (discussed later in this chapter) and adopted an independent path from both the regime and the opposition and at one point had a very important influence in the Suwayda region (Ezzi 2015). Sheikh Jarbua and Sheikh Hanawi were also involved in the pro-Assad Dir' al-Watan faction that was competing for influence with the Sheikh al-Bal'ous movements of Rijal al-Karama (al-Tamimi 2015a).

Strategies of repression: sectarianism and violence

The spread of sectarianism was a key part of undermining the inclusive message of the uprising. Massacres were committed by pro-regime militias and/or Shabihas, mostly with Alawi backgrounds in some specific areas, targeting poor Sunni villages and popular neighborhoods in mixed regions, particularly Homs and Hama provinces and the coast, where Alawi and Sunni populations lived side by side (Darwish 2016d; Satik 2013: 398).

According to Paulo Gabriel Hilu Pinto, the dynamics of repression and the regime's strategic use of violence were central to the sectarianazation process:

> The regime also used a selective distribution of violence in order to deepen sectarian fault lines among the protesters, dividing and isolating them. Whenever the protests occurred in mixed Sunni/Alawi or Sunni/Alawi/Christian cities, such as Lattakia and Baniyas, even when members from all communities took part in the protests, military and paramilitary violence was directed mainly to Sunni neighborhoods. (Pinto 2017: 135)

The objective was increasing fear and sectarianism between local communities and on a larger scale. This was particularly clear in Homs and in some cities of the coastal region, such as Baniyas. One of the first appearances of the Shabiha was in Homs. The security forces worked to mobilize

Alawis, particularly the young and unemployed, to prevent any opposition in their areas, and moreover sent them to Sunni areas of Homs to lead demonstrations in support of the Assad regime (Khaddour 2013a: 13).

The position of large sections of the Alawi population in Homs to stand in favor of the regime or not join the opposition was reinforced following several incidents in the city early in the uprising that targeted Alawi individuals and sometimes their families (Satik 2013: 400). Killings were highly publicized, and footage of mutilated bodies and funerals was given extensive television coverage (Khaddour 2013a: 15). The regime's propaganda accused armed Salafist groups of committing these crimes, while at the same time having a hidden hand in provoking sectarian tensions in the city (Satik 2013: 400). Regime officials also spread rumors among Alawis and Sunnis living close by, particularly in Homs, about future attacks on each other's neighborhoods (Dibo 2014).

The development of the Shabiha phenomenon in Homs can be attributed more to the Alawi community's militarization than to any planned strategy to defeat the uprising, at least initially (Khaddour 2013a: 13). Alawis constituted a quasi-majority of these Shabiha militias in Homs, Lattakia, Baniyas, and Jableh (Satiq 2013: 398), but Shabiha could include all sects and ethnicities.

The Shabihas played a major role in the regime's strategy to further sectarianize the country and transform the popular uprising into a sectarian war. They were often embedded with the SAA troops in offensives against villages and neighborhoods. For example, in May 2012, Shabihas accompanying the army went house to house in the town of Taldou, in the Houla region of Homs, after it suffered bombardment, slitting the throats of more than 100 people, including women and children (Hassan and Weiss 2015: 137).

The Syrian Network for Human Rights (SNHR 2015: 8) noted that regime forces and its allies committed 49 sectarian massacres that resulted in the killing of 3,074 persons between March 2011 and June 2015. Attacks on Sunni mosques, which were the often-public sanctuaries for protesters, were perceived as proof of the regime's sectarian bias rather than attempts to extinguish centers of dissent (Wimmen 2016).

In minority-inhabited regions, the regime first sought to recruit and mobilize Shabihas of the same community (often unemployed young men with criminal backgrounds) to take care of the repression against protesters. Security services would not directly intervene, and thus the demonstrations were portrayed as local conflicts. This was the case in Suwayda in majority Druze and Christian areas, such as Bab Touma in Damascus (Ezzi 2013: 46). In Jaramana neighborhood in Damascus, Druze and Christian communities also formed militias that manned checkpoints at entrances to the neighborhood by fall 2012 (Reuters 2012c).

The establishment of Popular Committees also expanded to regions that had been largely untouched by protests, such as in the Wadi Nassara.[7] They were initially faced with significant opposition because most people thought their presence was getting them involved in unnecessary problems (Massouh 2013: 94). This situation, however, changed progressively after opposition armed groups in mid-2012 took over al-Hosn, al-Zara, and Krak des Chevaliers, which are close to the villages of Wadi Nassara. Out of fear, and after several incidents that increased tensions in the area, local youth started to join the SAA and pro-regime militias, including the NDF or the armed branch of the Syrian Social Nationalist Party, which had a large following in this region (al-Monitor 2014a). The fears of the local community only increased when the area was taken over by the Jihadist organization Jund al-Sham, which killed tens of Syrian Christians in August 2013 (Mashi 2013a).[8]

Other events also reinforced the fear of local communities, such as the departure of many Christians from Homs, and to a lesser extent Qusayr (see Chapter 4), and their arrival in Wadi Nassara following the deepening of the war in these two cities and interventions of armed opposition groups (al-Monitor 2014a). Marmarita, the largest Christian town in Wadi Nassara, swelled, for example, from a population of 7,000 to 30,000 in 2014 (Choufi 2014).

Similarly, in Jaramana, in the Damascus suburbs, popular committees initially were criticized by many locals for acting as a criminal gang by forcing people to pay protection money, harassing displaced persons, and committing crimes (Sinjab 2012). Criticisms were toned down after Jaramana, and to a lesser extent Bab Touma, became the targets of several car bombings and shelling by armed forces (Sherlock 2012b; The Guardian 2013). Human Rights Watch (2015) collected information on 17 car bombings and other improvised explosive device (IED) attacks between January 2012 and April 2014 in Jaramana.

Groups allied with the regime were also mobilized to control populations from various backgrounds. In the Yarmuk camp in Damascus, it was the Popular Front for the Liberation of Palestine–General Command (PFLP-GC), headed by Ahmed Jibril, a longtime ally of the Assad regime, that in the beginning was in charge of controlling the camp and crushing any sign of dissent (Satik 2013: 398; Ibrahim 2013; Abu Zeed 2014; Salameh

---

[7] The Wadi Nassara (meaning "the Valley of the Christians" in Arabic) region is in the countryside of western Homs. Most inhabitants are Christians, and its largest village is Marmarita.

[8] Similarly, large numbers of Sunni Arab residents of al-Hussein village at the foot of the Crac des Chevaliers were not able to return after the regime's forces recaptured the castle in spring 2014 (Balanche 2018: 26).

2014). In the Christian neighborhood of Aziziya, in Aleppo, the Armenian party Tashnag, which held demonstrations in favor of the regime, organized its own militia early in the uprising to control the area and retaliate from incursions of FSA and other opposition armed groups that had captured large areas of neighboring Jdayde (Balanche 2015: 40).

The regime also used the strategy of fear among some religious minorities to mobilize local civilians to pursue repressive actions and campaigns. A young Christian man of Bab Touma recalled, for example:

> When saboteurs wanted to start a demonstration from the Umayyad Mosque, the security service called some young men, including me, and told us that the Muslim Brotherhood would demonstrate there and then move towards Bab Touma and Bab Sharqi to enter Christian quarters. We had to surround the mosque and help security forces prevent them. On that day, we brought some knives; they were the only arms we were allowed to hold. We cordoned off the mosque waiting for them to come out, but those who came out looked like regular worshippers. They seemed afraid. I did not see any one try or intend to break through. I was surprised at their fear. When I looked around, I realized that we along with the security men were the source of their fear. (Sabbagh 2013: 82)

He explained why he and his friends were chosen: "[W]e were local young men who got involved in every dispute. The security service knew us and knew about our strength and enthusiasm to step in" (Sabbagh 2013: 82). According to testimonies gathered by researcher Randa Sabbagh (2013: 87), most newly armed people had previously been jobless and had a criminal record. In a similar fashion, journalist Lina Sinjab (2012) interviewed a journalist from Jaramana, who declared that in her locality:

> The security people recruited all the convicted criminals in prison, released them under an amnesty and armed them under the pretext of protecting the area from armed Salafist gangs.

Raed Abu Zeed (2014), a Palestinian activist in the Yarmouk camp in Damascus, explained as well that a few months after the beginning of the uprising in his neighborhood:

> The Syrian security services and allied Palestinian faction PFLP-GC started arming some local militias composed of criminals who had been released from prison recently in a presidential amnesty, and they were receiving attractive salaries to repress protests and target activists…

Activists in regions inhabited by minorities suffered repression, but generally experienced far from the worst of the regime's gunfire and killing sprees. Mazen Ezzi (2013: 49) saw this behavior as a result of the regime's strategy of not antagonizing religious minorities. The heaviest fire, ranging from sniper attacks to barrel bombs, was reserved for Sunni-majority cities and areas where demonstrations were massive (al-Hallaq 2013a: 105), while Sunni-populated areas with no protests were not generally targeted by the regime's repression.

Sunni-inhabited areas that witnessed massive protests were also on some occasions completely destroyed by the regime. Entire neighborhoods were wiped out, using explosives and bulldozers, in 2012 and 2013 (e.g., in Damascus and Hama, two of Syria's largest cities). Regime officials and pro-regime media outlets claimed that the demolitions were part of urban planning efforts or removal of illegally constructed buildings. But as described by a report of Human Rights Watch (2014a):

The demolitions were supervised by military forces and often followed fighting in the areas between government and opposition forces. These circumstances, as well as witness statements and more candid statements by government officials reported in the media indicate that the demolitions were related to the armed conflict and in violation of international humanitarian law, or the laws of war.

The report added that these demolitions "served no necessary military purpose and appeared intended to punish the civilian population." The governor of the Damascus countryside, Hussein Makhlouf, explicitly stated in an October 2012 interview that the demolitions were essential to drive out opposition fighters in his governorate. Thousands of families lost their homes (Human Rights Watch 2014a).

The regime had a clear interest in portraying the uprising as sectarian and led by religious extremists. It scared religious minorities to make them side with the regime, and some sections of the Sunni population, especially more liberal segments.

Sectarian demographic change?

Some opposition sources accused the regime of seeking a demographic change in Syria by removing Sunni Muslims from sensitive areas (McDowall 2016). According to this argument, the regime was trying to diminish the percentage of Arab Sunnis who may have posed a threat to its rule, and repopulate majority-Arab Sunni territories with other religious communities, especially foreign and native Shi'a. As we have seen, the dynamics of repression and the regime's strategic use of violence were central to the sectarianization process, fostered by sieges and forced displacement. By the end of 2015, more than 80 percent of Syrians who had left the country were Sunni Arabs, which is unsurprising because of the community's majority status and the fact that most fighting occurred in the Sunni Arab-dominated areas where the uprising erupted (Balanche 2018: 21).

The case of Homs is an example of forced displacement of populations by the regime's forces and the conflict leading to a significant demographic change. Before the uprising, Homs was the third-largest city in Syria, with an estimated population of between 800,000 and 1.3 million people. The population was decimated by the conflict, with only around 400,000 remaining. Much of the city's built environment was damaged or destroyed: As of 2014, 50 percent of Homs's neighborhoods had been heavily damaged, and 22 percent had been partially damaged (Azzouz and Katz, 2018).

In January 2018, Homs governor Talal Barazi told the Associated Press that 21,000 families had come back to the city (cited in Hayden 2018). The residents who have returned had to use in their great majority their own money or assistance from the United Nations to fix their homes just enough to be livable. However, many former inhabitants were denied permission to return to their homes, with officials citing lack of proof that they had indeed lived there, which was as a result of the torching of the Land Registry office in Homs (Chulov 2017). Although a small number of formal residents came back, many displaced persons complained that the government made returning harder by demanding returnees to appear on state television—considered as a form of public humiliation—or by stipulating that they bring their army-age sons (Solomon 2017).

Alongside this situation, the Iranian regime was accused of actively participating in a demographic change scheme in some areas, while denunciations have been raised at the wave of purchases made by Iranian traders of a large amount of Syrian real estate in a number of cities (al-Souria Net 2016e) (see Chapter 7). These elements, regardless of their scale or their degree of realism according to area, increased sectarian tensions significantly.

There have been sectarian massacres and forced displacement by regime forces and their allies against impoverished Sunni populations in various areas who were involved in the uprising, or at least suspected of sympathies toward it. Similarly, indigenous and/or foreign sectarian Shi'a militias (and sometimes their families) have been located in areas considered sensitive for security and political reasons, such as in Qusayr and some areas of rural Damascus (Iqtissad 2016; Zaman al-Wasl 2017e). The city council of Qusayr announced in October 2018 a reconstruction plan for the city, and property owners had one month to submit objections. However, large numbers of its inhabitants had found refuge outside the country, and very few would be able to claim any rights or object within a month, leading in practice that many faced expropriation (see Chapter 7) (*The Syria Report* 2018d).

This policy, however, was not a strategic and systematic policy on a national scale. The regime's strategic objective through its repression measures was not demographic change per se, but to quell the protests and end all forms of dissent.

The regime took multiple approaches to recapturing and administering opposition-controlled areas, which varied according to circumstances. From late 2016 and early 2017, as the regime was increasing its control on newly conquered territories, it sought to recruit locals to establish new pro-regime militias in these areas. For example, in Barzeh, a Damascus suburb, young residents joined the new Qalamoun Shield force, supported by Syria's military intelligence, to fight IS in July 2017 (Zaman al-Wasl 2017f), while pursuing the policy of reconciliation agreements in opposition-held areas. There were also cases of former FSA fighters joining pro-regime militias such as the NDF-linked Golan Regiment established in 2014 (Samaha 2017b). This process continued throughout 2017 and 2018 as the regime increased its control over former opposition-held areas.

At the same time, these agreements did not prevent regime security forces from subsequently arresting former FSA members or civilians who had accepted the reconciliation, on the pretext that they carried out crimes. Some disappeared or were killed in "unknown circumstances." Between July and November 2018, for example, pro-regime forces detained at least 23 former opposition commanders and opposition figures across Dar'a province after retaking control of the area (a-Noufal and Clark 2018).

But the demographic narrative downplays the support of sections of Arab Sunni populations for the regime, especially in Damascus and Aleppo, and the Arab Sunnis within the regime's institutions. Pro-regime Sunni militias existed since the beginning of the uprising, and new ones were being established in 2017 and 2018 to fight alongside the regime's forces and its allies.

Around a million people from Aleppo and Idlib, the vast majority being Arab Sunnis from various socioeconomic backgrounds, have settled during the war in the provinces of Tartus and Lattakia (Sada al-Sham 2017), challenging the notion of a possible Alawistan for Alawis to withdraw to. More generally, some 80 percent of IDPs resided in regime-controlled areas (Balanche 2018: 20). In several former opposition areas retaken by regime forces, such as Zabadani and al-Moadmiyeh, inhabitants were generally allowed to return, according to Human Rights Watch (2018b).

Probably more than other religious and ethnic communities in the country, Syrian Arab Sunnis did not have a single political position but were formed through various elements (class, gender, regional origin, religious or not, etc…) and were politically diverse. The regime was not opposed to Sunni populations or a particular Sunni identity per se, but to hostile constituencies, which have been primarily from Sunni popular backgrounds in impoverished rural areas and midsized towns, in addition to the suburbs of Damascus and Aleppo.

Islamic fundamentalist and jihadist movements (such as the IS, Jabhat al-Nusra, Ahrar al-Sham, and Jaysh al-Islam) have also engaged in sectarian massacres and demographic changes in some regions (see Chapter 4), although not to a similar level.

Women also targeted by the repression

Security apparatus and Shabihas also targeted women, whether or not they were participating in the uprising, living in areas considered as supporting the revolution. They have used rape as a powerful weapon of repression and terror. Since the spring of 2011, women have been assaulted and/or raped by militiamen at checkpoints. Worse, campaigns of rape by pro-regime militias were enacted inside houses while the families were present. In addition, women imprisoned in the regime's prisons have been subjected to inhuman and degrading sexual abuse.

Various human rights organizations reported more than tens of thousands of rape cases in the regime's prisons (Tahrir Institute for Middle East Policy 2017). These findings suggest an organized crime of great magnitude. The systematic, planned, and large-scale nature of these assaults made these rapes crimes against humanity. The reported statistics were considered conservative because in many cases, survivors do not wish to expose themselves to the stigma and taboos surrounding rape and sexual violence. Violence and torture suffered by women in prison, therefore, were very difficult to document.

Imprisoned women were doubly victimized and isolated: by the regime, but also by their own families and society that rejected them, and in some cases went even further by killing them. The patriarchal structures of society come to reinforce the torture organized by the Assad regime, which itself played on these structures: rape was knowingly used to "dishonor" the whole family, and even the clan or the neighborhood (Cojean 2014; Loizeau 2017). A woman activist from Daraya reflected on this situation:

> While they [the local population] considered the detention of men a Medal of Honor, they believed that the detention of women is a sign of disgrace and dishonor, due to the likability of rape that might encumber families and break their backs … (cited in Kannout 2016: 38)

Crushing democratic alternatives

The regime acted to prevent the cross-sectarian unity of the Syrian people by violently repressing demonstrations, such as during the Homs sit-in that could have transformed into a Tahrir Square. The objective of the security services in some cities, such as Homs and Lattakia, was first to maintain the protests only in Sunni majority–inhabited areas and not to allow its development in other areas, and then to crush them altogether (Satik 2013: 403).

The regime specifically targeted opposition urban centers and highly populated neighborhoods, especially those held by non-IS forces, in order to force its residents to leave for regions under the regime's control and where it had the most support. According to Khaddour (2016b: 6),

the outcome of these internal migration flows directly played in the regime's favor: it depopulated rebel-held areas, increased the number of Syrians living under the regime, upheld regime propaganda over the increasing popular support for Assad, and justified its indiscriminate bombings in opposition areas.

The objective was also to destroy burgeoning attempts by the democratic sectors of the protest movement to create and organize its own viable alternative to the regime's provision of essential state functions, including via sieges[9] and bombings of opposition-held areas (Berti 2016).

Along with these destructive military means, the regime centralized many of its administrative functions, distributing critical services from the capital cities of Syria's governorates, where its affiliated forces were deployed, rather than from outposts in the countryside as it had done prior to March 2011. State institutions were relatively well protected by regime security forces and affiliated militias. By doing this, the regime encouraged masses of displaced civilians to travel to regime-controlled areas to benefit from particular public services, in addition to looking for security as opposition-held areas were being bombed (Khaddour 2015a: 6–7).

Later in the uprising, the Assad regime increasingly promoted the strategy of forging local agreements with cities and/or districts that had been besieged and continuously bombed to displace forcefully the local population, or at least large numbers of them, opposed to the regime. They did this to

---

[9] Regime sieges prevented goods from entering the areas, and civilians were forbidden from leaving through the use of military checkpoints or antipersonnel landmines. Besieged Syrians starved to death in some cases.

pressure individuals to leave their homes to go to regions under the regime's control rather than other areas held by the opposition. In practice, this meant targeting opposition-held areas to destroy their infrastructure and cut opposition supply lines, as well as deliberately attacking civilians and targeting hospitals, schools, or markets. One example of this was the campaign against medical personnel and facilities. There have been 382 attacks on medical facilities in Syria between March 2011 and June 2016, according to data collected by Physicians for Human Rights. Of those strikes, at least 344—or 90 percent—were conducted by the Syrian regime or Russian forces. These forces also killed more than 700 medical personnel in Syria (Williams 2016). Preventing civilian access to basic goods and services, including humanitarian aid, was another widely employed tactic to guarantee either that civilians were forcibly displaced or that the opposition eventually was forced to surrender both territory and population (Berti 2016).

The regime also used the reconciliation deals to destroy opposition institutions by forcibly dismantling their political and service bodies in the newly submitted areas. Most of the individuals who were forcefully displaced in Idlib in these reconciliation agreements were active in creating civil service bodies, local opposition councils, and civil society organizations. The regime previously considered the local civilian opposition councils and popular organizations as being among the greatest threats to its return to opposition-held territories. This was because these institutions had enabled the opposition and local communities to self-organize, providing the population with an alternative to state institutions when it came to the provision of key services (Ezzi 2017).

The role of public employees

Military and economic assistance from Iran and Russia was the crucial element that sustained the regime's survival (see Chapter 6). But the ability of the Syrian state to remain the provider of essential public services, even in the many areas that were outside the regime's control, was nevertheless also a key factor in its resilience. The pro-regime newspaper *Sahibat al-Jalala*[10] estimated in September 2016 that the number of civil servants and other beneficiaries of government salaries or pensions living in opposition and other areas outside regime control was around 300,000, out of a total 2

[10] The editor-in-chief was Abdul Fattah al-Awad, who held several government positions, including the editor-in-chief of *al-Thawra* newspaper, and he often wrote for *al-Watan* newspaper, controlled by Rami Makhlouf (al-Akhbar 2016).

million to 2.5 million in the country (or 12–15 percent) (*The Syria Report* 2016i).

Despite the loss of territory, the regime made it a priority to maintain the functioning of state-owned agencies, therefore keeping large sections of the Syrian population reliant on its authority. Due to the conflict and its destruction, Syrians who were already heavily dependent on the state before the uprising became even more so. The state was by far the country's largest employer during the war (Khaddour 2015a: 3). Salaries for civil servants and public-sector employees declined in real terms since 2011 but remained important in nominal terms, representing 25 percent of the 2016 budget (*The Syria Report* 2016b). Salaries of state and military employees and pensioners were increased on several occasions, although not enough to compensate for rising inflation, since the beginning of the war in 2011 (Enab Baladi 2018g).

While subsidies were declining for most products and services, state-owned public agencies remained the primary providers of essentials like bread, subsidized fuel, healthcare, and education (Khaddour 2015a: 3). The provision of state services, in contrast to the perceived chaos in some areas controlled by the opposition, was among the most powerful sources of regime legitimacy (Yazigi 2016c: 3–4).

The regime also implemented new laws during the war to try to win the loyalty—or at least the neutrality—of the civil service and the army, the two key institutions of the regime. In November 2015, a new law regulating rents banned eviction for civil servants and soldiers and their families (*The Syria Report* 2015f). In mid-January 2017, a presidential decree confirmed thousands of employees working under temporary contracts as civil servants (up to 40,000, according to the Ministry of Social Affairs). The decree stipulated that children of "martyrs" (in other words, fighters who died while fighting for regime forces under temporary annual contracts), as well as employees under "youth contracts" would be confirmed as full civil servants starting February 1, 2017. By becoming civil servants, they would receive bonuses, health insurance, pensions, and other benefits (*The Syria Report* 2017b). In September 2018, a decree exempted martyrs and injured people from up to SYP 1 million of debt for low-income loans in public banks (Sabbagh 2018). In the end of December 2018, the state issued a new decree, after the one released in June of the same year, that once again raised the salaries of military personnel and the pensions of retired military personnel in general by 8 percent of their monthly salaries (SANA 2018i).

At the same time, state employment was also used as an instrument to build and buy allegiances, and the share of public-sector jobs going to Alawis—already disproportionately large relative to their share of the population before 2011—increased. In December 2014, the government announced that 50 percent of new jobs in the public sector would go to families of the so-called martyrs, who were predominantly Alawi (Yazigi 2016c: 4). This led to some conflict between the families of those killed because of discrimination in favor of those who died in the security forces over those in the army or militias (al-Souria Net 2016d). In October 2018, the Council of Ministers excluded all those who failed to perform military and the reserve service from applying for public employment recruitment process, despite a presidential amnesty a few weeks earlier that had pardoned them if they settled their status with the authorities (Damas Post 2018d). In February 2019, several measures for wounded and demobilised members of the military and the security services had been adopted, while a month letter a new decree was issued that doubled the compensations paid to parents of deceased members of the security services aligning them with those of the military. Members of the security services and of the army who were killed after March 15, 2011 receive every month now to 100 percent of their children's salary from 50 percent previously.

Rising tensions and discontent in regime-held areas

The growing sectarian tensions between Sunni and Alawis did not mean that no tensions existed between the Alawi population and the Assad regime. The rising death toll in the army included many Alawis; insecurity and growing economic hardships created tensions and fueled animosities among Alawi populations. In October 2014, Prime Minister Wael Halqi inaugurated several upscale retail and tourism projects in the coastal city of Tartus, worth a combined USD 100 million, including a 30,000-square-meter commercial mall costing around SYP 10 billion (USD 52 million) owned by businessman Ali Youssef Nada. These inaugurations angered partisans of Bashar, who considered the construction of these projects to be indecent while the country was devastated by war. These criticisms were expressed with an increasingly palpable bitterness even in the pro-regime media, particularly after considerable losses among the soldiers and the death of about 50 children in attacks on Homs. The promotion of other tourist projects added to it. Loyal supporters accused the regime of abandoning them "while approximately 60 percent of the population of Tartus cannot afford to shop [in the new mall]," said one indignant message on a pro-regime Facebook page (AFP and *Orient le Jour* 2014c; *The Syria Report* 2014b).

In August 2015, more than 1,000 people carried out a sit-in at the roundabout of al-Ziraa in Lattakia to protest the murder of Colonel Hassan al-Sheikh in front of his children by Sulayman al-Assad, the son of Bashar al-Assad's cousin, because the colonel's car had passed his car on the road. The protesters raised photos of the colonel and demanded the trial of

Sulayman (SOHR 2015a). On October 2 of the same year, an important demonstration in pro-regime districts in the city of Homs took place against officials, notably the governor of the province,[11] Talal Barazi, a businessman who had been appointed in July 2013 and a known regime supporter, following an explosion that killed dozens of children (*The Syria Report* 2013b). This protest occurred one month after the arrest of pro-regime activists at the origin of a protest campaign called "Where are they?" against the abandonment by the regime of a military base in the north of Raqqa Province and the massacre of hundreds of SAA soldiers by the IS (Dark 2014b). In January 2016, the head of the Homs security council, Louay Mouala, was finally removed following the protesters' demands and demonstrations criticizing city authorities for not guaranteeing security, but the civilian governor, Talal Barazi, remained in place (Khaddour 2017c). One month later, however, protestors in Zahra neighborhood in Homs demanded the overthrow of the governor following a terrorist attack that killed dozens of people and injured hundreds (Homs 2016).

In July 2016, authorities refused to allow a sit-in by regime supporters in the coastal regions to protest the government's decision to increase fuel prices by about 40 percent, fearing that demonstrations would spread across pro-Assad areas after a number of loyalists organized a protest the month before in Damascus (al-Souria Net 2016b). In late September 2016, the destruction of dozens of small cafés and shops in Jableh generated discontent in this coastal city, which was traditionally supportive of the regime. The shop owners went on to burn tires as some skirmishes took place with the security services that had come to destroy the shops. The decision to demolish the stalls was officially made on the basis that they were established illegally, although the shops had been operating for years and paying rents to the city council. On social media, pro-regime supporters converged on one explanation—that the shops were destroyed to make way for a large real estate development, likely a resort (*The Syria Report* 2016h).

The opposition website Zaman al-Wasl (2017d) described 2016 as the hardest year for coastal cities since the beginning of the uprising. Problems ranged from a lack of security and the spread of lawless Shabiha groups, as well as a lack of public services and rising consumer prices. Armed individuals and gangs committed killings, abductions, and looting, as well as bullying and humiliating residents, even those loyal to the regime. The state of corruption in Lattakia's justice system became widespread, including bribery and unfair verdicts. Rotten and expired food also spread widely in the coastal areas, particularly in Lattakia, but the locals had no other

[11] Governors are the formal representatives of the Syrian president across the country's provinces.

option than to eat this produce because of its low price. Unregulated and expired drugs proliferated throughout the pharmacies, most of it smuggled by Shabiha and members of different regime forces. On January 15, 2017, dozens demonstrated in front of the Electricity Directorate in Lattakia to protest electricity cuts of up to 23 hours a day (Hourani 2017). Finally, the weakness and corruption of the state security forces facilitated terrorist bombings in various cities and towns in the coastal area.

In May 2017, a call by the regime for the recruitment of new army reservists from Tartus sparked a new wave of anger among locals in the coastal city. The governorate of Tartus was already suffering from a shortage of youths and men under the age of 50 as a result of their joining pro-regime forces, emigrating, or dying on the battlefield. A Facebook user wrote in a post addressed to the regime:

> Why people should fight with you? For a grain of potatoes and a loaf of bread? If someone dies for you, you give him a clock as compensation that only costs 100 Syrian pounds ... We are not slaves to the rulers and those hungry for power ... (Zaman al-Wasl 2017g)

In the coastal region, wounded and disabled former regime fighters also voiced their discontent with the regime, which had neglected them, offering them no support or jobs to help regain their independence. The families of fighters were generally poor and often dependent on female relatives to support the household financially (Zaman al-Wasl 2017h).

In January 2019, as a reflection of the continuous discontent and frustration among the regime's popular base on the coast because of the worsening of the socioeconomic situation and lack of basic services, a video of a former fighter in the Assad regime's security forces residing in the city of Tartus appeared, saying "Long live Syria, and down with Assad" (al-Souria Net 2019).

There were growing frustrations among the Alawi population toward the regime, most of whom were not linked to Assad family members or their Alawi cronies. Corruption and repression continued, and many who had stood by the regime began to reconsider their staunch support of it—at the same time, however, they were not indicating that they were thinking of joining the ranks of the opposition.

Adaptation of regime policies

Faced with the growing frustrations of the coastal Alawi population and the effects of the war on them, the regime adopted new forms of governance in these regions to secure continuing support. The regime allowed the establishment of local charity organizations, which multiplied rapidly, with the objective of supporting the communities that suffered heavy losses and continuing to privatize social services. The new charities started to appear from 2011 and were mostly initiatives of individuals linked to the state bureaucracy and the regime through employment, familial, and other networks. These addressed the immediate needs that would have been met by the state before the uprising (Khaddour 2016b: 11–12).

These new organizations assumed an intermediary role through which the regime could link with the coast, including sects other than the Alawis. They contributed to the expansion of the regime's networks of organization and domination over the local population in a changing context of war. The charities allowed the regime to meet needs at the local level and contain resentments over the high toll of losses on the battlefield. This made, according to Khedder Khaddour (2016a: 11–12), "coastal Alawis and the regime mutually dependent on one another for survival," while adding,

> through the charities, the regime has not only been able to redeploy a human network, but also to perpetuate its political culture in and domination over coastal Alawi communities...

Indeed, Alawis on the coast remain entrenched in the regime system as the emerging forms of local governance, such as the charities, were set up through and operated with the active collaboration of regime networks.

At the same time, the investments of the state in these regions increased. Many of these projects were launched and even completed months or years earlier, and their announcement served to ease rising frustrations toward the regime. The combined value of projects announced in 2015 reached nearly SYP 30 billion (nearly USD 70 million) for the Tartus and Lattakia provinces, while the city of Aleppo was assigned SYP 500 million (around USD 1,16 million), despite the latter being much more affected by the war and in greater need of support (*The Syria Report* 2015g). At the beginning of 2015, the University of Tartus was established, becoming the seventh state-run university in the country. The University of Hama, the only other university to be established after the beginning of the uprising, was created in 2014 in response to an inflow of displaced persons from other parts of the country (*The Syria Report* 2015j).

In April 2016, the government announced a new series of investments in Tartus and Lattakia totaling around SYP 37 billion (around USD 86 million), respectively receiving SYP 17 billion and SYP 20 billion (*The Syria Report* 2016d). The Syrian government also increased by up to 260 percent the price at which it bought tobacco from its farmers, most of whom were based in the coastal area and mountains, where this product represented a significant share of economic activity (*The Syria Report* 2017d).

This policy continued in 2017. In mid-April, a delegation including twelve ministers and led by Prime Minister Imad Khamis spent five days in the province of Tartus to inaugurate several large development projects. Because many projects announced in previous years failed to materialize, the prime minister established a follow-up committee with the responsibility of providing a bimonthly report on the implementation of the various projects announced during the visit. The delegation also met with local councils of the governorate and with business leaders, and honored the families of 80 martyrs from the SAA (Syria Report 2017g).

Prime Minister Khamis made another visit in October to the coastal areas, once more promising new investment projects in the region (*The Syria Report* 2017o). In 2017, SYP 5.2 billion were spent in the coastal area, out of a total of SYP 11 billion allocated to the reparation of roads and construction of new ones across the country (*The Syria Report* 2018a).

Despite these investments, many projects announced by the government in the months and years before had not yet materialized. In October 2017, the private newspaper *al-Watan*, owned by Rami Makhlouf, published an article severely criticizing the performance of the government following Khamis's visit to the coastal areas. The paper denounced the fact that in most sites he visited, little or no progress had been achieved yet, especially in Tartus. The article claimed that no answers were provided to many demands from families of martyrs, and criticized the limited number of appointments to government jobs of those disabled in the war—both sensitive issues for the regime (*The Syria Report* 2017o). Far from an independent source, *al-Watan*'s article reflected a popular mood among regime loyalists.

The announcement of new projects in Tartus and Lattakia continued in 2018 with great fanfare. In October, Khamis inaugurated new projects worth up to SYP 27 billion, according to SANA (2018f, 2018g).

The regime was adapting its policies toward the coastal regions' population to win their support (or at least neutrality). The level of discontent remained high, though, due to the continuing rising death toll and harsh socioeconomic conditions.

Tolerance of criticism from independent pro-regime media

The uprising saw an upsurge of independent media run by opposition activists. Pro-regime media outlets and Facebook pages also multiplied significantly, further affecting the media landscape. The new outlets were mainly Internet-based, and social media sites such as Facebook were used to produce content without acquiring an operating license. The pro-regime Facebook pages, often based on a network of people from a particular village, neighborhood, or city and operating autonomously, generally reinforced the regime's narrative, becoming key sources of information on military movements and local incidents often not covered in state media.

Researcher Antun Issa (2016: 18) explained:

> They represent the "mood" of the communities that support the government, and thus can be viewed as a barometer of support for the regime...

This was also the case when these sites raised criticisms against aspects of the regime, such as its official media, or condemned some of its actions, including looting by its soldiers (Hayek and Roche 2016; Issa 2016: 19).

In February 2017, new criticisms were raised against the government following a countrywide fuel crisis, especially in Lattakia Province, where most gas stations closed. Many minibus drivers announced an open strike in the city. Most of the civilian population was denied fuel because militia, security, and army personnel monopolized the limited fuel available. The loyalist social media pages blasted the Khamis government and the oil ministry for their repeated hollow promises to secure fuel for citizens (Zaman al-Wasl 2017b).

In the beginning of 2019, pro-regime pages on social media were inflamed with posts and messages featuring strong criticisms and insults of members of the Assad government. Indeed, even Assad did not escape blame (al-Souria Net 2019).

The regime did not engage in any form of repression against these media outlets, despite their occasional criticism. The fact that such criticisms were allowed to occur revealed a media environment that had become more representative and reflective of the community's views, rather than simply a propaganda machine dominated by the regime and associated elites. Media freedom in regime-held regions remained more restricted than in the opposition-controlled areas, at least before the rise of the IS and other jihadist groups. The new media were laying the foundation for a shift in Syria's media culture in a postwar context. While opposition media have been and will continue to be repressed, it is difficult to envisage the regime targeting its own online supporters, who have been instrumental in promoting its narrative. Even within the regime's sphere of control, a more open media culture could survive, and some form of tolerance of criticisms against the regime may continue (Issa 2016: 19).

The case of Suwayda: between control and autonomy

The weakening of the regime increased local autonomy in Suwayda, which still depended on the regime in terms of food, fuel, and services, all of which came to the governorate via the Damascus Suwayda road. Since the beginning of 2013, the main concern for the majority of the Druze population in Suwayda was to stop the mandatory military service of Druze youth outside the governorate. By the advent of 2015, more than 1,500 Druze in the SAA had died. In the first half of 2015, there were many recorded cases of locals in Suwayda Province attacking military police stations and conscription centers, attempting to release their sons who had been arrested at checkpoints to conscript them into the army (Ezzi 2015). The regime withdrew the military intelligence chief of Suwayda after protests led by Druze religious sheikhs in April 2014 (Lang 2014). In August 2016, a number of Suwayda residents tried to storm the governorate building to protest the murder of a resident by NDF fighters. A sit-in was organized outside the building, demanding that the killers be executed and the security situation reassessed (Orient News 2016).

It was in this atmosphere that Sheikh Wahid Bal'ous became a very popular figure among the local Druze population. He was leading a group called Rijal al-Karama (Men of Dignity), which was committed to protecting the Druze in the province, while opposing both the regime's security institutions in Suwayda and reactionary Islamic groups. Sheikh Wahid Bal'ous led campaigns to oppose the recruitment by the SAA of men originating from Suwayda, to prevent them being sent to fight outside the province, and to impede the regime from withdrawing heavy weapons from the governorate and leaving it defenseless. The Rijal al-Karama grew into a significant group with a military force, including 27,000 who refused to serve in the SAA (Ezzi 2015).

Bal'ous also launched campaigns against corruption. He advocated a "third-way" line that called for reform within the existing regime system in Suwayda Province rather than revolution (al-Tamimi 2015a, 2015c). Even following Bal'ous's assassination in the summer of 2015 (with some pointing to the killing as the work of regime loyalists), Rijal al-Karama continued to expand and became the key military actor in the Suwayda Province. The movement maintained a position of neutrality and acted to prevent the entry of any armed opposition group from outside the province, while prohibiting forced conscription in the province (al-Tamimi 2017b).

Druze pro-regime militias still existed in the region, however, such as Humat ad-Diyar, which was led by the son of a former sheikh who received support and funding from the regime and from Druze groups in Lebanon, the NDF, or Dir al-Jabal, a 1,000-strong militia whose members carried military identification cards and permission to carry arms issued by the Syrian Ministry of Defense (Ezzi 2015). In addition, thousands of Druze served in the regime's army (Gambill 2013).

Demonstrations and protests increased considerably in the province after the assassination of Bal'ous (Rollins 2016). Occasional protests continued in Suwayda throughout the years against the regime, its policies, corruption, and lack of services (I'lâm al-sûwaydâ` 2016; Noufal and Wilcox 2016a; Szakola 2016).

The regime responded in various ways. It increased its investments in the region. In 2014, more than SYP 6 billion (USD 25 million) were spent on the water, health, and electricity sectors in the governorate, though in reality, most of the funds came as subsidies for the electricity sector rather than investment in new projects. Other announcements included compensation of SYP 20 million (around USD 85,000) to be provided to about 1,430 farmers who had suffered from the cold wave in the winter of 2014–15, or SYP 70 million in 2014 for microenterprises (*The Syria Report* 2015a). In 2015, Suwayda hosted 17 investment projects by the SIA, the highest for all of Syria that year. The regime also had to deal with an attitude that increasingly affirmed the Druze identity of the region, including checkpoints with Druze flags and insignia (Ezzi 2015).

However, tensions remained between the local population and the regime. Anger was at its highest in the summer of 2018, after IS killed at least 250 civilians in an attack in which local Druze fighters, mostly from the Rijal al-Karama militia, eventually drove back IS militants after hours of fighting, although not before the jihadists captured more than two dozen local women and children and withdrew into the desert. Regime forces intervened only after 36 hours of fighting. The outrage of the local population deepened because the IS attack occurred just after a Russian delegation visited the province, requesting that 50,000 local men turn themselves over for military service. There were accusations by some local activists that the Syrian government withdrew large numbers of their forces from the province—paving the way for the IS attack. In some cases, locals expelled Syrian government officials from funeral ceremonies for those killed in the attack (Clark and Hamou 2018; Suwayda 24 2018).

Because the region did not join the opposition, however, the regime was prepared to make some concessions by granting more autonomy to some local forces and tolerating some level of dissent. But this situation probably will not last, especially as the regime has been consolidating its power throughout the country. At the beginning of 2019, there were increasing reports of military and political reinforcements by the regime's troops and security services in Suwayda. There was a "tacit approval" by the heads of the Druze religious community, Sheikhs Akl, of the growing presence of the regime's forces, provided that they did not prosecute the estimated

40,000 individuals from the province who were refusing to join the SAA (Halabi 2019).

Conclusion

The regime's strategy of repression and survival largely drew on its main base of support: crony capitalists, security services, and high religious institutions linked to the state. At the same time, it used its patronage networks through sectarian, clientelist, and tribal links to mobilize support on a popular level. Through the war, the deepening Alawi sectarian and clientelist aspects of the regime prevented major desertions, while patronage bound the interests of disparate social groups to the state.

The regime's popular base demonstrated the nature of the state and the way that the power elite related to the rest of society, or more precisely in this case its popular base, through a mix of modern and archaic forms of social relations, not through civil society. The regime relied mostly, but not solely, on coercive powers. It also counted on the passivity of large numbers of urban government employees and more generally members of the middle-class strata in the two main cities of Damascus and Aleppo, although their suburbs were often hotbeds of revolt. This was part of the passive hegemony imposed by the regime.

Moreover, this situation demonstrated that the regime's popular base was not limited to sectors and groups issued from the Alawi and/or religious minority populations, although these were important. Rather, it included those from various sects and ethnicities who pledged their support to the regime. More generally, large sections of the regime's popular base were increasingly acting as agents of regime repression. As argued by Steven Heydemann (2013b: 71), "regime-society relations [were] defined to a disturbing degree by shared participation in repression."

This resilience came at a cost, however, in addition to the regime's increasing dependence on foreign states and actors. The regime's existing characteristics and tendencies were amplified. Crony capitalists considerably increased their power as large fractions of the Syrian bourgeoisie left the country, massively withdrawing its political and financial support to the regime. This situation compelled the regime to adopt more and more predatory behavior in its extraction of increasingly needed revenue. At the same time, the clientelist, sectarian, and tribal features of the regime were reinforced. The regime's Alawi identity was strengthened, especially in key institutions such as the army and to a lesser extent in state administrations.

The authority of the state was also weakened, as were its institutions, allowing more space for militias. At the same time, in the case of Suwayda Governorate, the province was able to gain more autonomy as Damascus sought to calm tensions. Assad's regime did not see Suwayda as challenging or threatening its rule in any long-term or radical way, as the great majority of the region's local population was unlikely to join the opposition. This relative autonomy was more and more challenged, however, as the regime strengthened its power in the country and conquered new territories.

In other words, the end of the war and the defeat of armed opposition would not ensure the end of the regime's problems or challenges to reach a form of stability, which could only be authoritarian.

4. The Failure of the Opposition: The Challenges of Fundamentalism and Sectarianism

Introduction

This chapter first addresses the limitations and subsequent failure of the opposition in exile to constitute a credible, democratic, and inclusive alternative and to echo the initial popular and egalitarian aspirations of the protest movement. The establishment of a large and disparate coalition of opposition forces did not change this situation. The various bodies of the opposition in exile, SNC and the Syrian Coalition, also experienced divisions under the interventions of foreign actors and progressive submission to their interests. This situation allowed the increasing development and expansion of the Islamic fundamentalist movements, at the expense of the armed opposition forces linked to the FSA's local networks and civilian and democratic groups and activists.

The repression by regime forces against the democratic sections of the protest movement, both in its civilian and armed components, was the main reason for its weakening. The protest movement and its civilian institutions, along with the appeal of its democratic and inclusive alternative, however, were also undermined by the rise of Islamic fundamentalist and jihadist movements. These repelled not only many religious and ethnic minorities, but also sectors of the Arab Sunni populations. Large sections of the Sunni middle class and the bourgeoisie in Damascus and Aleppo were not appealed to by these movements, but not only as the regions in rural areas and midsized towns controlled by these groups witnessed numerous protests and dissent against their authoritarian practices.

These reactionary Islamic movements also attacked the democratic activists and imposed their authority on institutions developed by locals in areas liberated from the regime. In general, the influence of these extremist forces became stronger in many areas, limiting the activities of other activists. From the end of 2013, popular organizations' activities and presence progressively diminished through the years as a result of this situation in areas beyond the realm of the regime (Khalaf, Ramadan, and Stolleis 2014: 16).

The regime initially encouraged and favored the rise of Islamic fundamentalist and jihadist movements in order to sectarianize the uprising and
transform its propaganda into a reality, characterizing the protesters as
sectarian and religious extremists. At the same time, the Arab Gulf monarchies and Turkey also assisted these groups for their own political
reasons. Their expansion was equally the result of the divisions, problems,
and weaknesses of the FSA networks, as seen in chapter 2.

The opposition in exile and the failure to present an inclusive alternative

The obstacles facing the uprising were mounting through the years, and
the overthrow of the regime became increasingly unlikely. The SNC
and then the Coalition, however, were also unsuccessful in uniting the
various opposition groups and representing a political alternative that
could match the aspirations of the protest movements on the ground,
despite their recognition on the international scene. Similarly, they were
unable to appeal to many within the country or to Syrian refugees. This
was due to a lack of a political strategy to win popular support, as well as its
dependence on foreign powers and its early attempts to encourage foreign
intervention in Syria initially to impose a no-fly zone, or perhaps a buffer
along Syria's border with Turkey (Peterson 2011). The SNC, and representatives of the MB in particular, discussed with the Turkish authorities in
November 2011 the possibility of a no-fly zone imposed by their air force
(AFP 2011). From February 2012, the SNC officially retreated from its
initial refusal to external military intervention in Syria and the arming of
the opposition armed groups. These became central demands of the coalition toward Western and allied regional powers. Meanwhile, it was
unable to provide strategic political leadership, empower local civil administration, assert credible authority over armed opposition groups,
deliver humanitarian relief, or devise a political strategy to split the regime
(Sayigh 2013).

The unwillingness of foreign powers to intervene directly in Syria to
topple the regime pushed progressively the SNC and then the Coalition to
legitimize the various Islamic fundamentalist forces as their influence was
growing within the country. The former president of the Syrian Coalition,
Moaz al-Khatib, justified in March 2013 the influx of foreign jihadists into
Syria as a counterweight to the presence of Russian and Iranian military
experts and Hezbollah fighters, and considered them brothers and honored
guests (al-î`tilâf al-watanî li-qûwa al-thawra wa al-mu'ârada al-sûrîya
2013). Jabhat al-Nusra was characterized as part of the revolutionary movement by SNC president George Sabra, a member of the liberal People's

Party (the former Communist Party–Political Bureau led by Ryad al-Turk), in a statement in response to the United States listing the jihadist group as a terrorist organization (Ali 2015). Michel Kilo refuted initially all accusations against Jabhat al-Nusra that described it as a fundamentalist organization (Syrian4all 2013). He also rejected any comparison between IS and Jabhat al-Nusra, arguing that the latter was a movement for "an Islamic electoral system" and wanted to reach an Islamic state by national consensus, while the former wanted to achieve this goal through despotism (Radio Rozana 2014).

Jaysh al-Islam, a Salafist organization, was integrated into some of the exiled opposition's official bodies, while Ahrar al-Sham participated in some meetings and discussions but did not join them. These two organizations were guilty of numerous human rights violations, including attacks on activists and authoritarian rule in the areas they controlled. The Coalition did not condemn these practices or mobilize to demand the release of kidnapped activists (as discussed later in this chapter). In July 2013, Zahran Alloush, the military commander of the Islamic Front (IF) and leader of Jaysh al-Islam, declared:

> The mujahidin of al-Sham will wash the filth of the rafidha[1] and the rafidha from al-Sham, they will wash it forever, if God wills it, until they cleanse Bilad al-Sham from the filth of the majus who have fought the religion of God. So go oh mujahidin to support your brethren, go to support your brethren, we, in Liwa al-Islam [former name of Jaysh al-Islam], welcome the mujahidin from all over the world to be an aid and support for us, to fight in our ranks, the rank of sunna (traditions of Muhammad) the sunna of the messenger of God, which raise the banner of tawhid [pure monotheism] high, until the humiliation and destruction is upon the majus, the enemies of Allah. (cited in Smyth and Zeilin 2014)

Hassan Aboud, leader of Ahrar al-Sham, explained in an interview:

> What is happening in Syria is that the country has been ruled by a Nusayri idea, a Shi'a group that came to power and started discriminating against the Sunni people. They prevented them from practicing their religion and painted a picture of Islam that is far from what

---

[1] This term is in reference to Twelver Shi'a, *Rafidha* means rejectionist and refers to the Shi'a because, according to those who use the term, they do not recognize Abu Bakr and his successors as legitimate rulers after the death of Islam's Prophet Muhammad. In the Syrian context, *rafidha* has been used to denote Iran also (Zelin and Smyth 2014).

Islam is, with traditions and practices that are not Islamic at all. It wanted to wipe true Islam from the country ... (Abu Arab 2013)

Despite their authoritarian and sectarian practices, Muhammad Alloush, who served as the political leader of Jaysh al-Islam from January 2016 to May 2016 following the death of his cousin Zahran Alloush, was the chief negotiator for the Saudi-based HNC in peace talks with the Assad regime in Geneva. Alloush resigned on May 30, 2016, claiming that the talks were a "waste of time" because the regime was not willing to pursue "serious negotiations" (Stanford University 2016). He remained a member of the HNC itself, however, and was a key actor in other peace negotiations sponsored by Russia, Turkey, and Iran in late 2016 and 2017.

Ahrar Sham was also initially included in the HNC list, and its delegate, Labib Nahhas, attended the signing ceremony in Riyadh. The leadership of the Salafist group, however, issued a public statement directly after the closing ceremony saying that they were withdrawing from the conference. Ahrar Sham had already criticized the inclusion of some groups such as NCBDC, viewed as too close to Russia, while they considered the final statement as too secular-leaning and opposed the inclusion of actors perceived as hostile to Islamic forces (Lund 2015e). Ahrar Sham, however, participated in the Turkish-led military offensive against Afrin in January 2018, with the support of the Syrian Coalition (see Chapter 6).

The SNC and the Coalition also failed to provide any socioeconomic alternative in the interests of the popular classes, instead promoting neoliberal policies and a "balanced free-market economy" (Syrian National Council 2011), not dissimilar from those of the regime. In 2013, a group of leading Syrian experts affiliated with the opposition published a policy document called the Syria Transition Roadmap, in which it called for the privatization of Syria's publicly owned companies; price liberalization; lifting subsidies; downsizing of the public sector; the return to their rightful owners of all assets (land, corporations, factories, houses, and buildings) nationalized by the Ba'th Party; and Syria's entry into multilateral institutions such as the World Trade Organization (WTO) (Syrian Center for Political and Strategic Studies and Syrian Expert House 2013: 202–215). Their conclusion was as follows:

thus, Syria needs to gradually abandon its state-led, dirigiste economic model in favor of a market-based one ... The key objective here is to enhance the Syrian economy's productivity and competitiveness, and thus to put it on a path toward where growth and employment generation are led by the private sector. (Syrian Center for Political and Strategic Studies and Syrian Expert House 2013: 203)

These recommendations emphasized the influence of the former bourgeoisie and landowning families among the leadership of the political opposition.

Critics also complained of the lack of female representation in opposition institutions. Women were often limited to symbolic representation (Syria Untold 2014e), with no real responsibilities in the SNC, the Coalition, and then the HNC. The SNC counted just 24 women out of 444 members, and the Coalition only three women (Hossino and Kanbar 2013).

Activist Khawla Dunia declared in March 2014 that the situation of Syrian women was in a constant state of degradation,

> not only in terms of rights, which is the case for both sexes, but, more importantly, in terms of the lack of balance between the sacrifices and the achievements. (cited in Syria Untold 2014d)

Female participation in the HNC at its 2015 establishment was limited to two representatives of the 33 members. Female activists often characterized opposition groups as "unreliable," "discriminative," and "elitist" when it came to women's rights, similar to the Assad regime, and only having female representatives holding "decorative positions" with no effective role in the decision-making process (Ghazzawi, Afra, and Ramadan 2015: 19).

The domination of the Muslim Brotherhood and other conservative forces was also reflected in the opposition's approach to women's rights issues. For example, in the July 2012 opposition conference held in Cairo under the sponsorship of the Arab League, the National Covenant document on women's rights stated the following:

> The Constitution guarantees the elimination of all forms of discrimination against women, and seeks to create the required legislative and legal environment that enables their political, economic, and social empowerment, in accordance with all relevant international conventions, as well as in harmony with the culture of the society. (al-Awsat Asharq 2012)

That last phrase, "in harmony with the culture of society," was added in response to the demand of conservative Islamist groups and individuals. The phrase was widely denounced by feminists as being a justification for curtailing their rights. More generally, many feminist activists have criticized the fact that individuals in the SNC, and subsequently in the coalition and the HNC, inevitably yielded to Islamic fundamentalist pressures, sacrificing women's rights in the process (Abdeh 2018; al-Hallaq 2018).

Feminist activist Lama Kannout (2016: 59) explained that from the beginning of the uprising, "seculars would inevitably yield to Islamists, sacrificing women's rights in the process."

Some of the members of the Coalition or opposition members adopted sectarian positions. Opposition member and former MP Mahmoun Homsi declared at the beginning of the uprising, "You despicable Alawis, either you renounce al-Assad, or else Syria will become your graveyard," adding, "Down with the despicable political Shi'a'. From this day on, you will see what we Sunnis are made of" (MEMRI 2011). The SNC did not condemn this language.

On July 1, 2013, Anas Ayrout, a Salafist sheikh, member of the Coalition, and leader of the Syrian Islamic Liberation Front, called on fighters to target Alawi villages in coastal areas. He declared that they "must concentrate on their villages, their homes, their strongholds. We must strike at their infrastructure, and prevent them from living a normal and peaceful life … We have to drive them out of their homes like they drove us out. They have to feel the pain that we feel…" (cited in Oweis 2013a). A member of the SNC, Saleh al-Mubarak, supported the attack on Lattakia's countryside, affirming that "the battle may be moved to the ruling family's heartland, and the Alawis be given notice that they cannot be safe if the rest of the people are unsafe" (cited in Mouzahem 2013).

Some pro-uprising media were also guilty of sectarian messaging. Orient TV, owned by Syrian businessman-in-exile Ghassan Abboud, known for his sectarian diatribes,[2] presented the massacre in May 2015 of more than 40 civilians, including children, by IS fighters in the mixed town of Mabujah in Hama province, composed of Sunni, Isma'ili, and Alawi, as members of the regime's forces. The presentation of the events provoked a major controversy, as it was used to justify a later sectarian crime (Arif 2015).

The Coalition also refused to recognize Kurdish national rights and expressed chauvinist attitudes toward Kurds. Coalition members also supported Ankara's hostility and military aggression against the PYD/PKK, characterizing the Kurdish Party as a terrorist group (see Chapters 5 and 6).

The lack of inclusiveness of the Coalition and exiled opposition was seen once more in the General Principle of the transition plan submitted by the opposition's HNC in September 2016, in which it exclusively named Arab Islamic culture as the source "for intellectual production and social relations

---

[2] One of his Facebook posts, for example, attacked Alawi and other religious minorities (see Abboud 2015).

amongst all Syrians" (High Negotiation Commission: 2016: 9). Some groups affiliated with the HNC, notably Kurdish and Assyrian ones, denounced this as not reflecting the diversity of the Syrian population.

The Coalition was further afflicted by internal rivalries and dissensions, and defections increased throughout the years. In December 2016, Samira Masalmeh, the deputy president of the Coalition, declared that she was unaware of the methods by which the political body received money and requested that an inquiry be made on its spending. In addition, she stated that her work concentrated on fighting "extremist ideas" within the group, but that she had been stopped from speaking by some "extremist groups" present as a bloc within the Coalition (Enab Baladi 2016c). Following these statements, Masalmeh was turned over to the body's legal committee for internal investigation (Zaman al-Wasl 2017a). She resigned shortly afterward.

In his own resignation from the Coalition in January 2017, veteran opposition activist Fayez Sara enumerated several problems, including its inability to enact reforms in the bloc's political institutions as some blocs and individuals imposed their control over the temporary government. He criticized the unwillingness of the Coalition to take any position on the "Islamic" forces—from IS to Jund al-Aqsa and Nusra—which played an "evil" role in implementing the Assad regime's policies. He added that the Coalition had been established with the same problems as the SNC, including regional and international interventions that shaped it according to their agendas and involved figures and groups among them (Madar al-Youm 2017).

The increasing focus of the major international and regional state actors on the "war on terror" and consensus around Bashar al-Assad remaining in power also diminished the significance of the Coalition and even pushed some of its members to make peace with the regime. Bassam al-Malak, a Damascus trader and former member of the Damascus Chamber of Commerce prior to the uprising in 2011, announced his withdrawal from the Coalition in August 2017 and his return to Syria (cited in Syria News 2017).

Similarly, the Coalition's growing dependence on foreign actors increasingly caused problems as the interests of these states diverged. In November 2017, the head of the Syrian opposition's HNC, Riyad Hijab, the chief negotiator, Muhammad Sabra, and eight other members announced their resignation from the committee ahead of the Riyadh Conference to unite the opposition due to international pressure to accept that Bashar al-Assad will remain in power, according to Suheir al-Atassi, one of the members who resigned (*Middle East Monitor* 2017b).

Gulf monarchies fostering a sectarian framework

Gulf support for the SNC and the Coalition was paired with a sectarian orientation. The monarchies and their media promoted a sectarian narrative of the uprising and worked to transform it into a sectarian conflict between Shi'a and Sunni, while hosting many Salafist sheikhs who would use Gulf channels to promote their divisive speeches. As soon as March 25, 2011, the influential MB-linked Qatar-based Egyptian Salafist Sheikh Yusuf al-Qardawi, host of a weekly program on al-Jazeera television, declared:

> The President Assad treats the people as if he is Sunni, and he is educated and young and he might be able to do a lot, but his problem is that he is prisoner of his entourage and religious sect ... (Satik 2013: 396)

In August 2012, the Bahraini MP Abd al-Halim Murad declared that it was possible to achieve victory against the slaughter of the "rancorous" Safawis, a reference to the Safavid dynasty that ruled Iran from 1501 to 1736 and Shiitized Iran (Smyth and Zeilin 2014).

In May 2013, Sheikh Yusuf al-Qardawi declared a jihad on the Syrian regime at a rally in Qatar, calling for Sunni Muslims to join the fight against Assad and his Shi'a base, and called Alawis "more infidel than Christians and Jews" (Pizzi and Shabaan: 2013). Qardawi added "How could 100 million Shi'a [worldwide] defeat 1.7 billion [Sunnis]?" (Pizzi and Shabaan: 2013). This statement was later praised by Saudi Arabia's Grand Mufti Abdul Aziz al-Sheikh (al-Arabiya 2013). Similarly, the *Râbitat al'âlam al-îslâmi* (Muslim World League), an association of Islamic clerics established in 1962 and serving as a political instrument of Saudi Arabia in foreign policy, repeatedly characterized the Syrian regime as a "rogue Nusayri regime" and "stressing the obligation of supporting the Muslims of Syria and saving them from the sectarian conspiracy," in other words from the Shi'a (Muslim World League 2013).

Gulf television also fueled sectarian tensions. Faisal al-Qassim, a presenter on al-Jazeera, hosted a segment discussing whether Syria's Alawi population should be subjected to genocide, while al-Arabiya welcomed Syrian Salafist cleric Adnan al-Arour, who once promised to "chop [Alawis] up and feed [them] to the dogs" (cited in Carlstrom 2017).

Private donations from the Gulf supported Islamic fundamentalist armed movements. The Popular Commission to Support the Syrian People, associated with the wealthy Ajami family in Kuwait, funneled millions of dollars in funds and humanitarian aid to Salafist movement like Ahrar al-Sham. Ahrar publicly thanked the commission for sending USD 400,000 (McCants 2013). The Salafi cleric, Dr. Shafi al-Ajmi, was among the most vitriolic purveyors of sectarianism in Kuwait, calling for the torture of Syrian soldiers and demonizing the Shi'a (Wehrey 2013: 3). In Saudi Arabia, sheikhs of the Saudi Islamic fundamentalist movements Sahwa[3] became significant funders of the Syrian armed opposition, mostly Islamic groups. In May 2012, Saudi officials prohibited several Sahwa prominent sheikhs from collecting money for Syria outside official channels. Private donations, however, continued to be transferred to Syria through Sahwa networks, while fundraisers adopted a lower profile. Salafist armed groups were the main beneficiaries, especially the Syrian Islamic Liberation Front, supported politically by the Saudis and the Sahwa. Some sheikhs close to the Sahwa, such as Muhammad al-'Arifi and Abdallah al-Ghunayman, also argued in favor of Saudis going to fight in Syria. Members of the Sahwa networks portrayed the Syrian uprising from its outset in sectarian terms: a religious war between Sunnis and 'a Nusayri regime whose strongest allies are Shi'a and Jews (Lacroix 2014b: 4–5).

With the militarization of the uprising, foreign influence increased. Armed factions brandishing an Islamic identity were favored by Islamic donors, such as states and individuals from the Gulf, while the battalions of the FSA were increasingly weakened. In these conditions, more and more fighters joined Islamic groups, and these gained ground over the years, while the democratic and secular voices were marginalized.

A similar trend was occurring, to a lesser degree, among civilian activists. Activists in Salamiyah claimed that one well-known Arabic-language broadcasting organization refused to broadcast video footage of one of the revolutionary campaigns in the city because it included no images of flags bearing the Shahada (the testimony to Islam symbol). They also argued that some channels, mainly in the Gulf, would screen footage of revolutionary activities in Syria only if it contained Islamic speeches and slogans

---

[3] The Saudi Islamic fundamentalist movement, known as the Sahwa, was influenced by the MB and its ideological views, while maintaining a close, nonconflictual relationship with the Saudi kingdom for a few decades. At the beginning of the 1990s, they demanded the opening of the political system, criticized the call made by King Fahd for infidels to assist the kingdom during the liberation of Kuwait from the Iraqi occupation, and advocated for the Islamization of state policies in the economic, social, political, media, and military spheres. The Sahwa was reintegrated to the Saudi religious and social spheres after a period of repression, in exchange for which Sahwa leaders avoided all criticism of the government. The MENA uprisings that began in 2011 challenged that accommodation, as the Sahwa was tempted to seize the opportunity and make a renewed political stand (al-Rasheed 2010: 185; Lacroix 2014a).

(al-Hallaq 2013a: 109). More generally, criticisms were raised that Islamic actors were interviewed much more often than secular opposition figures or intellectuals. In Dar'a at the beginning of the uprising, for example, activists complained "that satellite networks were marginalizing prominent leftists" (cited in Nir Rosen 2012).

Establishment of Islamic fundamentalist groups

The release of significant groups of jihadists and Islamic fundamentalists by the Assad regime started as early as the end of March 2011, with the liberation of 260 prisoners from Sednayya Prison—a great majority of whom were known Islamic fundamentalists and jihadists (Lister 2015: 53). On May 31, Assad announced an amnesty to free Syria's political prisoners. In reality, his amnesty was selective, keeping the vast majority of protestors and activists in prison, while a great number of Salafist jihadists were released.

Three of these men would become founders of the most important Islamic fundamentalist brigades:

- Zahran Alloush, son of a famous Syrian Sheikh based in Saudi Arabia, established Liwa al-Islam in Damascus suburbs in Douma in March 2012. Liwa al-Islam's first base of recruitment was a prewar network of Salafi activists, ex-prisoners, and friends and students of his father at the Tawhid Mosque in Douma. The group also benefited from the financial support of Gulf-based Salafi preachers like Adnan al-Arour, in exile in Saudi Arabia and an old acquaintance of the Alloush family. Al-Arour praised Zahran Alloush in several appearances on Saudi TV channels (Fî sabîl âllah 2015). Liwa al-Islam had a Salafi orientation and called for an Islamic state. The group presented itself as an independent jihadi militant group, although collaborating with FSA groups (Lund 2017a). In September 2013, following the merger under the leadership of Liwa-al-Islam of at least 50 groups operating mainly around Damascus, the movement changed its name to Jaysh al-Islam (Hassan 2013c). This merger was engineered by Saudi intelligence to build a force that could act as a counterweight to Jabhat al-Nusra and ISIS (Oweis 2013b).
- Hassan Aboud participated in the establishment of Kataib Ahrar al-Sham, officially founded in late 2011 in the region of Idlib and Hama, although some secret cells had reportedly been active in the region soon after the beginning of the uprisings (Abou Zeid 2012). The organization was originally composed of former prisoners, including Iraq war veterans from the Sednayya Prison. Funding was quickly secured from foreign sympathizers such as Hajaj al-Ajami and other Gulf clerics, many

of whom were linked to the Salafi Umma Party in Kuwait (Lund 2014c), and from private sources in Kuwait, Qatar, and Saudi Arabia (Lister 2015: 56–58; Solomon 2012b). The principal objective of the movement was to wage jihad against Iranian-led efforts to project Shi'a power across the Levant and to replace the Assad regime with an Islamic state, according to its founding statement (ICG 2012b: 15). Ahrar al-Sham always made clear that it was a separate entity from the FSA. Despite some connections to the al-Qa'ida movement—some of its leaders had worked with Osama bin Laden in Afghanistan—Ahrar al-Sham was not a transnational jihadi group. It consistently declared that its struggle was limited to Syria and sought to ally itself pragmatically with all groups fighting the regime, from Jabhat al-Nusra to the FSA (Abu Arab 2013; Lund 2014d). Ahrar al-Sham repeatedly referred to the Taliban as an example of a successful Islamic project and issued on August 1, 2015, a statement mourning the death of Taliban founding leader Mullah Muhammad Omar (Lister 2016a: 28).

- Ahmad Issa al-Sheikh established the Liwa Suqur al-Sham in November 2011 as an FSA brigade, but it rapidly adopted a Salafist orientation. He called for the establishment of an Islamic state, while the group's media promoted a message rejecting any national and pan-Arab identity, as national unity between Sunnis, Alawis and Christians were forbidden under Islamic law (ICG 2012b: 17–18).

A famous picture showed these three figures standing in a row, all smiles, not long after being freed by Assad's amnesty in spring 2011.

Future ISIL members were also released at this time, including Awwad al-Makhlaf who was at one point a local emir in Raqqa, and Abu al-Ahir al-Absi, who was jailed in Sednayya Prison in 2007 for membership in al-Qa'ida. In mid-July 2014, al-Absi became IS's provincial leader for Homs (Hassan and Weis 2015: 145). In early February 2012, the Syrian regime released Abu Musab al-Suri, an important jihadist ideologue and a top al-Qa'ida operative with significant experience fighting the Assad regime in the late 1970s and early 1980s (O'Bagy 2012b: 15). These were just a few examples of a larger phenomenon.

Establishment of Jabhat al-Nusra

By August 2011, several Islamic fundamentalist armed groups had formed in Damascus and northern Syria. The Islamic State in Iraq (ISI) had sent a senior commander, Abu Muhammad Jolani, a Syrian from Damascus, along with six other ISI commanders who were a mixture of Syrians, Iraqis, and Jordanians, to set up a Syria-based wing. In the weeks following Jolani's arrival in Syria, he initiated contact with several small ISI-connected cells. The ISI devoted about 50 percent of its budget to its new Syrian front, while additional support was transferred from preexisting al-Qa'ida private networks in the Gulf (Lister 2015: 56–68).

The ISI branch carried out its first operation, a double suicide bombing, outside Syrian military intelligence facilities in southwest Damascus in the neighborhood of Kfar Souseh on December 23, 2011, killing at least 40 people (Casey-Baker and Kutsch 2011). A second attack was carried out on January 6, 2012, when a suicide bomber detonated explosives near several buses transporting riot police in the al-Midan District of Damascus, killing 26 (Shadid 2012). The ISI claimed credit for the first attack at the announcement of the official establishment of its branch in January 23, 2012, under the name Jabhat al-Nusra li-Ahl al-Sham min Mujahidin al-Sham fi Sahat al-Jihad (The Support Front to the People of the Levant by the Mujahideen of the Levant on the Fields of Jihad), through its media wing, al-Manara al-Bayda. The second attacks were not claimed until February 26. The organization's third attack occurred in Aleppo on February 10, when two Syrian fighters detonated their explosive-laden vehicles outside security buildings in the al-Arkoub and New Aleppo neighborhoods of Aleppo, murdering 28 people and injuring over 200 others. This operation and the one on January 6 were carried out to "avenge the people of Homs," who were under siege by the regime (Lister 2015: 64).

In the video announcing the formation of Jabhat al-Nusra, Jolani declared war on the Assad regime. He added that this was only half of the struggle, with the other being the establishment of Islamic law across the *Bilad al-Sham*.[4] He also said that Jabhat al-Nusra was an organization composed of mujahidin from various fronts, indicating international and likely Iraqi operational influences. The organization's vocabulary pointed to a common phraseology with al-Qa'ida, while the *Shumukh al-Islam* online forum, also used by al-Qa'ida and ISI, became the main distributor of its media. At the same time, Jolani was careful to hide his organizational links with the al-Qa'ida branch in Iraq (Lister 2015: 51, 59, 64; Hassan and Weiss 2015: 149–150).

Jolani also denounced Western states and their assistance to sectors of the Syrian opposition, warning the opposition to refuse any such offers from abroad. He attacked the Arab League and Turkey for being too close and submissive to the orders of the United States, and he said that the

---

[4] *Bilad al-Sham* refers to Greater Syria and generally includes Syria, Lebanon, Palestine, and western Iraq.

establishments of the state of Israel in 1948 and the IRI in 1979 were part of an ongoing struggle against Sunni Islam.

Jabhat al-Nusra portrayed itself as the Sunni community's aggressive defender against the "Alawi enemy" and its "Shi'a agents." From the beginning, it had used a sectarian rhetoric, employing derogatory terms such as *rawafidh* (the plural of *rafidhi*, literally meaning "rejectionists") in reference to the Shi'a, a practice commonly used among Iraqi Salafi jihadi insurgents, and the word *Nusayri*[5] instead of *Alawis* (ICG 2012b: 11).

Following its establishment in January 2012, Jabhat al-Nusra received statements of support from famous jihadi ideologues (Lister 2015: 59–60; O'Bagy 2012b: 31). Beginning in 2012, the al-Qa'ida leader Ayman al-Zawahiri called on Muslims in Iraq, Jordan, Lebanon, and Turkey to join the uprising against Assad's "pernicious, cancerous regime," and warned Syrian opposition fighters not to rely on the West for help (*The Guardian* 2012). Jabhat al-Nusra stepped up its operations throughout the country in March 2012, participating in small-scale battlefield operations by fledging insurgent organizations, joining guerrilla-style ambushes and conducting assassinations, and planting IEDs in suburban Damascus and in rural areas of Idlib, Hama, and Homs (Lister 2015: 71).

Al-Nusra presented itself as a local Syrian jihadist organization struggling against the Assad regime, trying to forge alliances with other military forces with similar objectives, avoiding enemies, and abstaining, at least in the beginning, from an extreme implementation of a very conservative understanding of Sharia and targeting of religious minorities. This was the line followed by the al-Qa'ida leadership between 2011 and 2013 in various countries (Lister 2015: 67). This strategy was the result of the failures of al-Qa'ida in the past to win great popularity in Iraq because of its violence or applying an extreme form of Sharia too rapidly (Hassan and Weiss 2015: 150; Lister 2015: 56–58).

The efforts to present Jabhat al-Nusra as Syrian and more or less moderate, in comparison to the previous practices of al-Qa'ida in Iraq, did not prevent its unpopularity at the beginning of the uprising. The general atmosphere within the nascent protest movement was at odds with al-Qa'ida's politics. In early 2012, al-Nusra had difficulty finding allies on the field. They were even accused by some of being a creation of the regime. Protesters in the streets rejected the use of suicide bombings against state buildings.

---

[5] *Nusayri* refers to the founder of the Alawi religion, Abu Shuayb Muhammad Ibn Nusayr. It is used to characterize the Alawi religion as following a man and not God, and therefore not divinely inspired.

The suicide-bombing tactics targeting city squares and locations with significant civilian populations were adopted less and less frequently, and a shift toward other forms of military operations was increasingly practiced by al-Nursa throughout 2012. The jihadist movement tried to reduce its civilian casualties and to limit operations strictly to military targets. Unlike al-Qa'ida in Iraq, Jabhat al-Nusra demonstrated in the first two years of the uprising a keen sensitivity to public perception. Zawahiri's advice and the lessons from the Iraq war were being taken into account. Jabhat al-Nusra made efforts to avoid alienating the larger population and garner popular support (O'Bagy 2012b: 36–37; Lund 2012: 29). The fact that the group was primarily composed of Syrians also influenced the behavior of its members who were attentive to the discontent of local populations.

In April and May 2012, Al-Nusra was included for the first time in a major offensive by FSA forces against Damascus. Damascus's northern suburbs increasingly became a base for Nusra recruitment. The organization multiplied operations against the regime in this area, while also claiming activities in Hama, Idlib, Dar'a, and Deir ez-Zor (Lister 2015: 73). By June, it had attained a rate of 60 attacks per month, up from only seven in March (ICG 2012a: 11).

By mid-2012, a number of foreign jihadist organizations issued a call to support the Syrian uprising and encouraged jihadists to join the fight (O'Bagy 2012b: 30–31; Lister 2015: 73). Jabhat al-Nusra was endorsed by several internationally or locally prominent jihadi thinkers and was seen by most of the global salafi-jihadi community as "their" group in Syria (Lund 2012: 25).

In mid-2012, foreign fighters were arriving in Syria in a more organized way. Most of the newly rising jihadist groups, composed mostly of foreigners, stood apart from the FSA, adopting an aggressive sectarian perspective and refusing the nationalist orientation of most of the FSA brigades as well as the Syrian revolutionary flag, insisting instead on the black jihadi flag (Macfarquhar and Saad 2012). The isolation or relative weakness of jihadists in Syria until mid-2012 was reflected in an interview with Omar al-Chichani, head of the military organization of the IS, published in the first edition of the movement's newspaper, *Sana al-Cham*. He explained that he arrived in March 2012 and was surprised to see

people smoking, shaving their beards instead of letting it grow. They listened to songs. And flags of the revolution did not contain the formula of the oneness of God, la ilaha illa Allah. I wondered where I fell! All of these have seemed to me discouraging … (Sana al-Sham, cited in Syria Freedom Forever 2013c)

At that point, on-the-ground media coverage in English, French, Arabic, German, and other languages reported between 800 and 2,000 foreigners in Syria, representing less than 10 percent of opposition fighters. The majority had come at the beginning of 2012 from neighboring countries such as Lebanon, Iraq, and Jordan. A smaller North African contingent hailed from Libya, Tunisia, and Algeria. The presence of Westerners during that period was minimal. Foreign fighters were mainly joining jihadi organizations such as Jabhat al-Nusra (Zelin 2012). Those who had fought in Iraq and Afghanistan brought military skills to the insurgency, such as in the construction of roadside IEDs and vehicular-borne IEDs. These tactics were introduced by Jabhat al-Nusra and Kataib Ahrar al-Sham (ICG 2012b: 19).

Establishment of ISIL in Syria

On April 9, 2013, a voice message from the ISI leader Abu Bakr al-Baghdadi publicly announced that Jabhat al-Nusra was only a cover for and extension of the ISI (Hassan and Weiss 2015: 184). In his message, Baghdadi declared that the two jihadist organizations would now work under a single name: ISIL. Two days later, the leader of Jabhat al-Nusra, Abu Muhammad Jolani, admitted that he had fought in Iraq under Baghdadi's command and that Jabhat al-Nusra had benefited from funds, weapons, and fighters sent by the ISI. Jolani thanked the ISI but rejected Baghdadi's call for unification, seeking to guarantee the jihadi identity of Jabhat al-Nusra by ending his statement with a renewal of allegiance to al-Qa'ida's leader Ayman al-Zawahiri, a potential arbiter who he knew would be favorable to him (Caillet 2013).

Increasing defections, infighting, and a breakdown in operations began to occur as members became more and more divided over who commanded the battlefield. Two months after Baghdadi's declaration, Al-Zawahiri's ruling came in the form of a letter in which he wrote that Baghdadi was wrong to declare the merger without consulting or even alerting al-Qa'ida's leadership. At the same time, he argued that Jolani also committed a mistake to announce his rejection of ISIL and his links to al-Qa'ida without the organization's permission. Al-Zawahiri dissolved ISIL and declared that Syria would hold institutional space for Jabhat al-Nusra, headed by Jolani, while Baghdadi's jurisdiction would be limited to Iraq. He appointed Abu Khaled al-Suri, a former member of al-Qa'ida and at the time a member of Ahrar al-Sham, as an al-Qa'ida delegate to act as an arbiter between the two entities (Atassi 2013; Hassan and Weiss 2015: 184–185).

Al-Baghdadi disapproved of al-Zawahiri's letter and refused to submit to his orders, insisting that the border between Syria and Iraq was an artificial and illegitimate boundary imposed by Western imperial powers at the end of World War I (Hassan and Weiss 2015: 185–186).

Most of Jabhat al-Nusra's fighters joined ISIL, especially the non-Syrian volunteers. It was estimated that 80 percent of *muhajirin* (foreign fighters) in Syria joined the ranks of ISIL (Ghaith 2013). In early May 2013, the majority of the Muhajirin wa-Ansar Army, a group largely composed of fighters from the Caucasus and Central Asia, also merged with ISIL. Its emir, Omar al-Shishani, swore allegiance to Baghdadi and was appointed *wali* (governor) of the Aleppo, Idlib, and Latakia regions. ISIL was also bolstered by Syrian tribes pledging allegiance to Baghdadi, especially in the northern Aleppo and Raqqa regions. In Deir ez-Zor, Jabhat al-Nusra was able to win the support of tribes because many of the group's commanders were themselves from the region. Many tribal leaders also sought to protect their control over oil wells, the profits of which had greatly enriched both the tribes and al-Nusra (Caillet 2013).

In the initial period before summer 2013, however, the relationship between the two actors varied widely by region, with some areas seeing protracted opposition between the two groups and others seeing frequent collaboration.

Islamic fundamentalist and jihadist forces increasingly dominating the military scene

The first six months of 2012 witnessed the emergence and expansion of Islamic fundamentalist and jihadist forces among the armed opposition in Syria. These forces were able to thrive in a political scene in which opposition groups lacked financial and institutional support, whether from Western states or from the leadership of FSA. While Western states offered moral support to opposition groups, they failed to provide FSA forces with the weapons necessary to mount a serious offense against regime forces. Groups unrelated to the FSA were able to expand under these conditions, securing their own funding largely via private networks from Gulf monarchies. During this period, members of a leading Homs activist group explained in a report of the International Crisis Group (ICG) that "donations from Syrian expatriates and other Arabs in Gulf countries helped fuel a growing Islamist trend among militants as of early 2012," while most of the funding received by armed groups in Homs was sent from Islamic fundamentalist movements to other Islamic groups (ICG 2012b: 9–10). By July 2012, local FSA leaders were complaining that their own leadership in Turkey was not able to provide similar support and funding (ICG 2012a: 10).

Other elements favored a climate in which Islamic fundamentalist and jihadist movements were able to develop. Some FSA fighters became disillusioned with the disorganization of the groups under its wing and their inability to strike at the regime, while Salafist (Jaysh al-Islam and Ahrar Sham) and/or jihadist organizations such as Jabhat al-Nusra had greater military experience, higher salaries, and stronger organizational cohesion (Ghaith Abdul-Ahad 2012). The corruption within segments of the opposition, notably the SNC and the Coalition, and of some armed opposition groups' commanders, also led fighters to join jihadist groups perceived as less corrupt and suffering less from internal divisions (Lund 2012: 20). In addition, the multitude of independent groups claiming to be FSA or FSA-affiliated was problematic. There were around 1,200 opposition armed factions at the beginning of 2013 in Syria, according to David Shedd, No. 2 in the U.S. Defense Intelligence Agency (Atlas 2013). The factionalism, profit-making, and incompetence of the FSA groups started to alienate people at the end of 2012 (Hassan and Weiss 2015: 225), and Islamic fundamentalist and jihadist forces increasingly gained a foothold as they proved to be a more effective opposition, both in terms of governance and fighting, than the various FSA battalions.

This situation increasingly pushed armed FSA groups to collaborate with Islamic fundamentalist forces against Assad's forces, though not without difficulties and even occasional clashes. As a consequence of these developments, many FSA groups began to Islamicize their political rhetoric, and new military coalitions emerged that were dominated by Islamic rhetoric both on and off the battlefield (Lister 2015: 71–72; Rafizadeh 2014: 319). The chemical attacks on the Damascus suburbs constituted a turning point in this regard.

Ghouta chemical attacks—a turning point...

On August 21, 2013, the regime used chemical weapons to attack opposition-controlled areas of the Damascus suburbs of Eastern and Western Ghouta, killing more than 1,000 civilians. Following this chemical attack, U.S. president Barack Obama declared that before launching a widely anticipated military strike against regime forces, he would first solicit congressional authorization for use of force (The White House 2013). This decision was understood by many to imply that any U.S. military action would be contingent on a majority vote in a chronically divided U.S. Congress. This resulted in a sharp decline in morale among Washington's allies in the Syrian opposition, who had hoped for the implementation of the president's "red line"[6] on the use of chemical weapons. Had the United States intervened,

[6] The attack occurred one year and one day after U.S. president Barack Obama's "red line" remarks on August 20, 2012, in which he warned: "We have been very clear to the Assad regime,

the relevance of FSA forces and the Coalition would likely have improved, undermining the regime's military capacity.

Within weeks, the situation changed dramatically, as Washington reached an agreement with Moscow to get rid of and destroy the regime's chemical weapons by the end of June 2014. This agreement contributed to making U.S. threats of military intervention appear even less credible, while Bashar al-Assad was made a partner in an internationally monitored disarmament process. The hopes of the Syrian Coalition, which had been riding on the arrival of U.S. military support to transform the situation on the battlefield to their advantage, were dashed. These developments dealt a serious blow to the Syrian Coalition, as its presumed ability to attract a Western military intervention had earned it some significant support among armed opposition forces, including Islamic fundamentalist forces such as Jaysh al-Islam and Suqur al-Sham that had collaborated previously with the SMC and other FSA groups.

Washington's decision not to intervene and instead to make an agreement with Moscow had significant consequences within the armed opposition as a whole. FSA battalions saw even less incentive to distance themselves from jihadist groups such as Jabhat al-Nusra which, despite its ideological differences, had proven itself very effective in battle against the regime forces. Second, the central role of Western powers in any potential international political settlement increased suspicions and fears of an agreement that would benefit opposition exiles at the expense of armed opposition groups actively fighting within Syria (ICG 2014c: 2–3). Islamic fundamentalist and jihadist movements were thereby strengthened with an increasingly discredited FSA, and exiled opposition was seen as out of touch or linked to Western countries.

In September 2013, 11 groups signed a statement calling for the opposition to Assad to be reorganized under an Islamic framework based on Sharia law and to be run only by groups fighting inside Syria. Signatories ranged from various movements, including Jabhat al-Nusra, Ahrar al-Sham, Liwa al-Tawhid, and Jaysh al-Islam. These signatories rejected the authority of the SNC and the exiled administration of Ahmad Tumeh (Solomon 2013).

In mid-November 2013, the Islamic Front (IF) was established by some of the most significant Islamic fundamentalist organizations: the Suqur al-Sham Brigade, the Army of Islam, the Ahrar al-Sham Islamic Movement, the Liwa al-Tawhid, Liwa al-Haq, the Kataib Ansar al-Sham,

---

but also to other players on the ground, that a red line for us is we start seeing a whole bunch of chemical weapons moving around or being utilized. That would change my calculus. That would change my equation" (CNN 2012).

and the Kurdish Islamic Front. This new Islamic coalition was formed following a process that had started in September of the same year, when several of these movements mutually distanced themselves from the Coalition, its exile government, and the SMC (Lund 2013a). The IF charter won the support and approval of multiple significant Salafist ideologues, including the Jordan-based Iyad al-Qunaybi (a consistent Jabhat al-Nusra advocate) and London-based Abu Basir al-Tartusi (Lister 2015: 106).

Some of these groups within the IF did not hesitate to attack democratic groups and activists and sections of the FSA as well. In addition, the IF sought a coalition with the rising ISIL to attack Kurdish civilians and the YPG (Lund 2014a). Groups within the IF were backed by various regional powers. Both al-Tawhid and Ahrar al-Sham enjoyed friendly relations with Qatar and Turkey, while Jaysh al-Islam was supported by Saudi Arabia. The alliance remained an umbrella organization rather than a full union, with each organization maintaining its own separate structure (ICG 2014c: 18–19; Lund 2014b).

Qatar, Turkey, and Saudi Arabia, all of whom felt betrayed by the U.S. policy reversal following the chemical attack against Syrian civilians in Ghouta during the summer of 2013, were pivotally significant in encouraging the IF's establishment as a clear protestation against what Western policy had allowed to take place in Syria (Lister 2016b: 12).

On December 9, 2013, elements of the IF took control of the SMC's storage facilities close to the Bab al-Hawa crossing on the Turkish border, which were full of weaponry provided by Saudi Arabia and Qatar, as well as vehicles, body armor, and medical supplies from the United States, the United Kingdom, France, and other countries. This large border crossing between Turkey and Syria's Idlib Province had long been a major entry point for supplies to opposition armed groups. As a result, the United States and United Kingdom suspended support to the SMC (Lund 2013b; ICG 2014c: 4). This episode represented the beginning of the end of the SMC and pushed toward a further decentralization of the FSA and its leadership, despite failed attempts for new forms of centralized unity in the following years.

Each military victory for the regime and its allies strengthened the Salafist and jihadist movements within the armed opposition. A few years later, the fall of Eastern Aleppo in December 2016 at the regime's hands reinforced the jihadist and Islamic fundamentalist presence in the northwest region of the country, as divisions and clashes among armed opposition forces continued to multiply. Meanwhile, local populations in opposition-held areas were increasingly angered by the division and infighting between the various armed opposition groups, calling for unity among them in the wake of the defeat in Eastern Aleppo in December 2016, as well in the following years.

Rising competition from Islamic and jihadist fundamentalist forces

The repression of the regime was the most decisive factor in preventing a democratic alternative to develop in Syria, while the internal division among FSA groups and inaction of Western powers undermined the secular opposition to the benefit of Islamic fundamentalist and jihadist forces. At the same time, the rise of these forces on the military scene was accompanied by their increasing significance in areas controlled by opposition groups. This growing influence was secured through the establishment of their own institutions, such as Sharia council or committees, that oversaw the management of resources and government facilities (Hassan and Weiss 2015: 225). Sharia councils began to emerge in areas liberated from regime forces, challenging the previous local councils. While initially able to restore stability and security in some areas liberated from the regime (Sly 2013), Sharia councils were reported to have been the scene of unfair, unlawful, and retributional trials (Hanna 2016). These Sharia councils had the role of implementing the authority of Islamic fundamentalist and jihadist and Islamizing laws and the local population, while "legitimizing" the repression of rival forces and activists (Pierret 2013).

In various towns and neighborhoods, local councils also suffered the interventions of armed opposition factions, especially Islamic fundamentalist forces throughout opposition-held areas. The judiciary, which fell within the framework of the tasks that these local councils were trying to achieve, were subjected to many transformations. Most of the judicial institutions that began as independent civil "tribunals" were turned into "Sharia Committees or Councils" under pressure from military opposition factions. A great number of armed opposition factions established such councils, which did not recognize any other authority except their own. This contributed to the decline of the local councils, their influence limited to civilians while they had no authority over the fighters of the armed opposition. Repression against FSA leaders and civil society activists also increased under the Sharia councils, with many imprisoned under charges of espionage and apostasy (al-Haqq 2016). The councils also expelled religious clerics from the areas that they dominated who did not share their ideas, replacing them with clerics who subscribed to their own brand of jihadist and Salafist teachings (Darwish 2015: 65–69).

Salafist and Jihadist organizations also created their own religious police. In Idlib, the Jabhat al-Nusra led Hay'at Tahrir al-Sham (HTS) first created a Hisbah agency (religious police) and then a Committee for the Promotion of Virtue and Prevention of Vice, which imposed a number of restrictions on clothing, barbershops, smoking, listening to music, and mixing at parties.

The committee's actions also included the monitoring of behavior inside hospitals, health centers, and schools through daily patrols. At the hospitals, this included surveillance of medical staff to ensure that they complied with Sharia-friendly clothing, with violators of the committee's rules being sanctioned (Souriatna 2018). In June 2017, HTS also established the Sawa'id al-Khair, or "Goodwill Corps," affiliated with the religious morality police to enforce its laws on the streets and to monitor people (Arfeh 2018). Similarly, Jaysh al-Islam created the Promotion of Virtue and the Prevention of Vices institution, a form of religious police, in Eastern Ghouta. For roughly USD 200 a month, informants were required to report violations ranging from publicly opposing Jaysh al-Islam and cursing to committing "blasphemy" and the wearing of "indecent clothing" by women (Zaza 2017). This had a significant impact on the spread of anarchy and chaos, with various competing opposition armed groups trying to impose their own authoritarian orders on each other's zones of influence, according to Sabr Darwish (2016e: 3).

Similarly, there was competition regarding the control and the provision of resources in different opposition areas. In some areas that they controlled, members of the Nusra jihadist groups often seized supplies intended to be distributed among the local councils, leaving them without enough goods to provide for their own neighborhoods (Arfeh 2016). Jaysh al-Islam also took increasing authority over food supplies through its control of tunnels (as discussed later in this chapter), while also monopolizing employment in Douma in the following years. The group established an employment center where applicants were matched with available jobs, almost all of which it controlled. Jaysh's approval was required even for private initiatives, such as the opening of shops, charities, and pharmacies (Zaza 2017).

Both militarily and politically, access to these resources proved vital. The control of border crossings with Turkey, for example, became a priority for some armed opposition groups to accumulate capital. The Northern Storm Brigade, affiliated with the FSA, used its seizure of the Bab al-Salama crossing with Turkey in 2012 to control key supply and distribution routes for armed opposition groups in what became a profitable side business to its smuggling and kidnapping activities. This crossing was by far the most important on the Syrian-Turkish border, as it was the passing point for most trade and humanitarian assistance into Syria. After rising tensions with other battalions over Bab-al-Salama, the group was finally forced to negotiate an agreement with the Liwa al-Tawhid to share control over the border (and presumably its profits), while diminishing the taxes and expenses imposed on objects and people traveling through the crossing (Abboud 2016; Baczko, Dorronsoro, and Quesnay 2016: 140). Ahrar al-Sham eventually became the sole controller of the Bab al-Hawa crossing, and from 2015 to

2016 was earning between USD 3.6 and USD 4.8 million a month (Tokmajyan 2016: 3). The border crossings were often among the main reasons behind military infighting between various armed opposition groups, notably the conflicts between HTS and Ahrar al-Sham in July 2017 and onward.

Similarly, the oil economy also became a site of confrontation and struggle among opposition groups. Between 2012 and 2013, a new oil economy emerged in eastern and northern Syria. Tribes and clans in Deir ez-Zor and southern Hasakah took over the wellhead operations of dozens of fields. Most of these were in the former operating areas of Shell (al-Furat) and Total (Jafra). The new operators negotiated agreements with the dominant military groups in the region over the sale of crude oil to traders, who then transported the oil to trading and refining hubs close to the Turkish border, at Manbij, Ras al-Ayn (Serekaniye), and Tal Abbyad. Opposition armed groups and their local warlords established clusters of basic refineries in these regions, placing orders with Turkish steel fabrication plants for the pipes, cylinders, and tanks required (Butter 2015: 7).

Various groups benefited financially from the exploitation of these oil fields. Initially, the oil economy in the Jazirah came under the domination of Jabhat al-Nusra and Ahrar al-Sham, under the patronage of the Sharia courts that these movements established in the main towns. ISIL began to penetrate the oil business in early-to-mid-2013, at the same time as it drove out its rivals from the city of Raqqa (Butter 2015: 18). By the end of 2014, the oil and gas fields were divided among the Syrian regime, PYD Kurdish forces, and IS. IS controlled the majority of oilfields, as well as several gas fields in the country in 2015, which they progressively lost through the years as a result of the military advances of pro-regime forces, but above all of the Syrian Democratic Forces (SDF) led by the Kurdish YPG armed forces (see chapter 5), with U.S. assistance. By the end of 2018, the SDF-controlled area contained 90 percent of Syria's oil and gas reserves, including the Conoco natural gas facility, which had the largest capacity of any gas field in Syria before the conflict, and the Al Omar oil field, Syria's largest and most lucrative (Kabalan 2018; Osseiran 2018).

Some armed opposing factions also profiteered from the sieges, not hesitating to seize the best and most crucial supplies for battalion members as popular organizations and local councils struggled to meet civilians' basic needs. For example, some opposition armed groups in the besieged region of Eastern Ghouta dug tunnels to the Barzeh and Qaboun neighborhoods and engaged in profitable trafficking of different goods. Jaysh al-Islam and its surrogate businessmen gained near-monopolistic control over food imports throughout the period when they were dominating these areas, especially after 2016. Traders were allowed to bring nonfood items like cigarettes into Eastern Ghouta and sell them privately at a higher profit (Lund 2016d). The control of the tunnels resulted in conflict among different armed opposition groups. Ghouta was the scene of many street protests in which civilians accused various armed opposition groups of profiteering and seizing food and other products for themselves instead of overcoming intergroup divisions and uniting to fight the regime (Lund 2017c).

Internal conflicts and growing rivalries between various forces also increased progressively from mid-2015 onward, especially in northern areas controlled by Jaysh al-Fateh's coalition and in the suburbs of Damascus. Infighting in Idlib Province and the suburbs of Damascus among armed opposition forces spurred repeated protests by locals. Demonstrators called for armed factions to put forth a united front against regime forces, while simultaneously rejecting the authoritarian rule of armed opposition groups in their regions.

The fall of Eastern Ghouta in March 2018 was also the result of continual rivalries and infighting among different groups controlling these areas, especially between Faylaq al-Rahman and Jaysh al-Islam. Even as regime forces launched their offensive in these areas, the infighting continued, with both Jaysh al-Islam and Faylaq al-Rahman accusing each other of betraying Eastern Ghouta (Lund 2018a).

Internal infighting among armed opposition groups also erupted repeatedly in the northwest of the country.[7] From the middle to the end of 2018, tensions and infighting in these areas largely centered around two main opposition armed blocs, with the jihadist coalition of HTS (led by former al-Qa'ida group Jabhat al-Nusra) on one side, and a loosely affiliated coalition of Turkish-backed opposition armed factions (dominated by Salafist groups such as Jaysh al-Islam and Ahrar al-Sham alongside other Islamic and former FSA groups) under the umbrella of the National Liberation Front (NLF) on the other. By the end of 2018, HTS wielded authority over roughly 60 percent of Idlib Province. New clashes occurred between these two groups in the beginning of January 2019. HTS extended its control over new areas by capturing nearly a dozen towns and villages from rival Syrian opposition factions (Clark and Hourani 2019). HTS's military conquests led to the collapse of NLF factions Harakat Nour a-Din al-Zinki in Western Aleppo and Ahrar al-Sham in northern Hama Province's Sahel al-Ghab region. At the same time, the Syrian Salvation Government, the HTS-affiliated governance body, extended its authority over the areas captured by assuming administrative, civil, and judicial duties (Abdulssattar Ibrahim, Hamou, and al-Maleh 2018).

---

[7] The northwest can be subdivided into three areas: al-Bab, Afrin, and Idlib.

Growing opposition among activists

From 2013, opposition grew against these Sharia councils, who were controlled for the most part by Islamic fundamentalist and jihadist movements from alternative local councils and democratic youth organizations. The various coordination committees and other democratic organizations increasingly condemned the exactions and human rights violations of these groups. On July 28, 2013, the LCC (2013c) wrote a statement to the effect that "the tyranny is one, whether in the name of religion or of secularism," rejecting the authoritarianism of both the Islamic fundamentalist groups and the regime. On August 2, 2013, the LCC addressed a new message to these groups, saying:

> in a unified message from the revolution to the entire world, we are confirming that the kidnapping of activists and essential actors of the revolution, unless they serve tyranny, hinder the freedom and the dignity of the revolution … (cited in LCC 2013d)

Protests to denounce the authoritarian and repressive policies of Islamic fundamentalists and jihadist groups multiplied throughout the areas liberated from the regime's authority. In September 2013, for example, a statement signed by eleven civilian groups[8] representing the protest movement in Damascus's countryside, rallied strongly around Razan Zaytouneh, who

> was threatened and harassed by members of armed factions in eastern Ghouta of Damascus Province, for no other reason than being an independent and unveiled woman who is among the grassroots leadership cadres of our revolution … (Syria Non-Violence Movement 2013)

In addition, the statement said that

> on September 9, 2013, fighters reportedly members of the Liwa al-Islam Brigade shot live fire in front of the door of Zaytouneh's home.

---

[8] These were Revolution Coordination and Liaison Office of Eastern Ghouta; Eastern Ghouta United Relief Office, Middle Sector; United Syrian Services Office in the Eastern Ghouta; Local Council for the Revolution in the City of Kafr Batna; Local Council for the Revolution in the City of Saqaba; Local Council for the Revolution in the City of Ayn Terma; Local Council for the Revolution in the City of Harasta; Local Council for the Revolution in the City of Hazzah; Local Council for the Revolution in the City of Douma; Local Council for the Revolution in the City of Hamouriya; and Local Council for the Revolution in the City of Irbeen.

Three days later, members of armed Jihadist factions began a public smear campaign against Zaytouneh, slandering and libeling her by accusing her of being an agent of the Syrian regime, in a manner to incite potential violence against her ... (Syria Non-Violence Movement 2013)

In mid-October, a new clash erupted between local councils and organizations with the leader of Jaysh al-Islam, Zahran Alloush. A "Statement of the Civilian Movement in Syria Regarding the Remarks of Mr. Zahran Alloush, Commander of the Army of Islam" was published, in which these groups stated their rejection

of any attempt by any party to impose authoritarianism upon decision-making and upon the work of citizens. We also reject any attempt to make compliance with any institution not elected by the people, no matter how powerful or wealthy the institution, a benchmark for the public good or a gauge of patriotism or an indicator of the ability to perform civic duty today ... (cited in Syria Freedom Forever 2013b)

This statement was issued after Zahran Alloush pronounced that the establishment of the expanded Douma Civilian Council was divisive because it ought to have taken the Consultative Council that is associated with him as its sole reference point.

In December 2013, important figures of the protest movement and of the democratic aspirations of the uprising, Razan Zaytouneh, Wael Hammdeh, Samira Khalil, and Nazem Hammadi, were kidnapped from their workplace, the Center for Documentation of Violations in Douma, by armed, masked men. Jaysh al-Islam was widely believed to have been behind their kidnapping and subsequent assassination (Mroue 2018b).

Opponents of Jaysh al-Islam were increasingly repressed, with many who were openly critical of the organization's activities imprisoned. By 2014, reports started to trickle out from the Repentance Prison in Douma, a secret jail where opponents of the Jaysh al-Islam were tortured and killed on the orders of the group's religious tribunals (Lund 2017a). In Eastern Ghouta, women activists started to organize the Mother's Movement, in which they demonstrated on numerous occasions for the release of their children who were imprisoned by Jaysh al-Islam (Ghazzawi; Muhammad, and Ramadan 2015: 27). Until the regime's total reconquest of Damascus of Eastern Ghouta in April 2018, Jaysh al-Islam's authorities continued to target various civil society organizations and close their offices, suppressing or altogether ending their activities. In August 2017, for example, *Rising for Freedom* magazine was outlawed in Douma, and two of its journalists were imprisoned by a court controlled by Jaysh al-Islam over an article published earlier in the year.

Numerous other cases of activists being arrested, repressed, and kidnapped by Islamic fundamentalist forces have been documented. Moreover, throughout 2013, the authoritarian behavior of IS members came under increasing opposition by local populations, especially in Raqqa (Syria Untold 2013b). After the departure of Jabhat al-Nusra and the consolidation of the IS presence in Raqqa in the summer of 2013, an intimidation campaign was launched by the jihadist organization against local activists and journalists in the city, forcing many of them to flee for fear of detention, torture, and assassination (Syria Untold 2014a). Firas Hajj Saleh and Father Paolo Dall'Oglio were among the activists kidnapped by the jihadist group. Rami Jarrah, the codirector of the media organization Activists News Association (ANA), declared that at this point, there were almost no more media activists left in Raqqa and that "across the whole of the north there have been around 60 documented media activist abductions by IS, with the crackdown worsening in the last two months" (Beals 2013).

In 2014, the consolidation of ISIL in the eastern part of Syria eliminated nearly all forms of peaceful activism within its jurisdiction.

Women's participation threatened

Similarly, the participation of women in the uprising also suffered. The role of women decreased significantly over time, becoming mostly reduced to humanitarian aid and relief (Dawlaty 2015: 39). Activist Yara Nassir explained in early 2014 that Syrian women "continue to be hammered by the regime's oppression on the one hand, and by new impositions on the other," while adding that

> the situation is dramatic, as women continue to suffer in areas under regime control, while in many liberated areas they are pushed out of public spaces and decision-making processes. Women continue to look for a civil space where they can freely develop and express themselves. The fact that the revolution did not incorporate women's rights at its core is part of the problem. Gender equality was not at the center of the movement for change. (Syria Untold 2014c)

In the words of activist Razzan Ghazzawi, "while male activists were able to enter liberated or disputed areas, women face all kind of restrictions," and she added that women had to "take extra precautions and security measures to protect themselves from all kinds of dangers." Ghazzawi denounced this situation and male activists' failure to challenge and condemn "these obstacles that are being put in the face of their, supposedly, partners in the revolution" (Syria Untold 2014c).

These kinds of behaviors were expanding in the opposition-held territories, especially with the rising influence of Islamic fundamentalist and jihadist forces. In Eastern Ghouta, for example, women activists explained that the situation changed negatively when Jaysh al-Islam took power, preventing their organizing activities from taking place and imposing restrictive social codes. In the first years of the revolution, female activists were respected and enjoyed a relatively high level of communication and access to negotiations with some armed opposition factions, particularly local FSA groups, which sometimes even helped to implement and facilitate female activists' projects (Ghazzawi, Mohammad, and Ramadan 2015: 20).

However, even among FSA forces, some limitations were put in place. For example, civil activist Mahwash Sheiki (2017) recounted that

[o]ne of my veiled friends who was excited about the revolution told me that once, after enduring extenuating circumstances, she managed to visit Daraya to deliver aid. At the time, neither Daesh nor the Nusra Front controlled the area. It was the Free Syrian Army, which we had hedged our bets on, who stopped and arrested her for traveling without a *mahram* (a non-marriageable male kin).

More generally, the spread of extremist forces led to the increasing exclusion of women from public life and constraints on their rights to work and seek education, as well as their freedom of mobility (Kannout 2016: 56). Journalist Zaina Erhaim (2014) also wrote about her experiences in the areas controlled by opposition armed groups, mostly Islamic fundamentalist groups. In her account, she chronicled the restrictions imposed on the women's movement, including being forced to wear the niqab and be accompanied by a man while passing through checkpoints. Similarly, Ghazzawi (2018) stated that in Idlib Province,

I was prevented from doing my work [humanitarian work for the benefit of displaced persons, teaching children of refugees, and other activities] on some occasions and even threatened by Islamic fundamentalist and jihadist groups because I was not veiled.

In Idlib's region, Jabhat al-Nusra tried to limit women's role in society, enforced gender separation in the workplace, and targeted women's economic empowerment groups, as in the case of the center of Mazaya (Syria Untold 2015; Enab Baladi 2016a). Jabhat al-Nusra also attempted to prevent women from Idlib Province from attending college in Aleppo, while their members stood outside schools distributing long black hijabs for female students to wear (Ghazzawi 2018). At the end of December 2015 in Idlib Province, the courthouse of al-Fateh Preaching and Awqaf, which was one of the institutions of Jaysh al-Fateh, issued a statement calling on women to comply with religiously "legitimate" dress (i.e., long black hijabs) in the streets and public markets (Kannout 2016: 57).

Similarly authoritarian and reactionary measures were put in place after the establishment of Free Idlib University by Jaysh al-Fateh. In November 2015, the university imposed gender segregation policies, with female students being barred from studying subjects such as civil and mechanical engineering, and even from entering the medical institute in an emergency. On the other hand, only female students could be admitted to the midwifery institute. The university's administration imposed "Sharia clothing" on women at Free Idlib University in January 2016, threatening to "prevent those who do not wear Islamic dress from entering the university and doing exams." Female students who did not adhere to the Islamic dress code set forth by the *Rijal al-Hisbah* (the so-called religious police) were publicly reprimanded and banned from attending class. Female lecturers were also targeted by the Islamic authorities (Damascus Bureau 2016).

Coordination committees and other women's organizations tried to remain visible as advocates for women's causes and as participants in the broader uprising, but their role continued to be undermined. One famous women's organization in this field was Women Now for Development (2012), directed by the feminist activist Samar Yazbeck. Its objectives were to enable Syrian women to become active members of society, both economically and socially, and to become key partners in the political decision-making process at the local and international levels (Syria Untold 2016c).

Sectarianism, Islamic fundamentalism, and minorities

Among Syria's religious minority communities, a sense of fear of and uncertainty about any kind of political change was present from the uprising's very beginnings. While the reasons may have varied somewhat within each sect, as well as across class and gender, the general sense of unease and worry about the uprising was markedly present in these communities. Large sectors of Alawis working in public administrations, the army, and security services were scared to lose their jobs in the case of regime change, or to become the target of revenge given their close affiliations with the Assad regime or even simply because of their sect. Other sects, such as Christians, Druze, and Shi'a, also feared the fall of the regime and a form of chaos prevailing in the country that could make them easy targets of opposition groups.

For instance, many in the Christian community had in mind the case of Iraq, in which Iraqi Christians became the target of Islamic fundamentalist and jihadist forces. More than half of the Christian population in Iraq left the country following the U.S.- and British-led invasion in 2003, and their numbers were still diminishing (Ufheil-Somers 2013). Among Christians, this fear and uncertainty most often translated into a form of passivity and neutrality toward the protest movement.

The military's repression of popular demonstrations, heightened sectarian tensions, and the sharp rise in sectarian killings and abductions increased this fear and had dramatic consequences on the relations among religious sects. In the province of Homs, sectarian violence expanded rapidly from the summer of 2011, with revenge killings and attacks between Alawi and Sunni populations becoming more common. Consequences were dramatic with regard to relations between the two communities. Before the uprising of March 2011, the neighborhoods of Homs used to be segregated by religious sect, whether Sunni, Alawi, Christian, or Shi'a, but the general atmosphere of the city was pluralistic and peaceful. It was possible to encounter minority-owned businesses, such as Sunni-owned shops in Alawi neighborhoods. The population in some of the newer areas built in the mid-1990s was mixed (Khaddour 2013a: 11). This pluralism became increasingly contentious when, a few months following the beginning of the uprising, groups of *Shabiha* from outlying villages started taking over the houses and businesses of Sunnis in areas witnessing protests. Most of these Sunni families were forcibly evicted and expelled from the neighborhoods. The Shabiha looted and sold their belongings in what became known locally as the "Sunni market" (Khaddour 2013a: 18).

Religious tensions were growing and open hostility could be heard among some protesters. Author Johnathan Little documented several instances of hostility against the Alawis among protesters in Homs and al-Qusayr in 2012, and even cited individuals who were part of the FSA, claiming their admiration for Osama bin Laden or the Jordanian jihadist Abu Musab al-Zarqawi, because the latter "came to Iraq to confront Iran and the Shi'as" (cited in Littell 2015: 48). The word *Nusayri*, a pejorative term for the Alawi sect previously used by these groups, became increasingly common among fighters of the Syrian opposition (Zelin and Smyth 2014). There were also cases of FSA units arresting people at FSA-held checkpoints on the basis of their religious sect, as minorities—especially Alawis—were considered at the time to be de facto affiliated to the regime (Anonymous C 2017).

Some Alawi and minority activists increasingly voiced their fear and experiences with hatred, discrimination, and violence against minorities in regions controlled by Islamic fundamentalist groups. This runs in contrast to the beginning of the uprising, when protesters warmly welcomed minorities (Wieland 2015: 242). While not reaching similar levels of violence in Homs, cases of abductions and kidnappings increased in the beginning of the uprising in various regions and between local communities such as in Suwayda, a majority-Druze city, and Dar'a, a majority-Sunni city, and between Christians and Muslims in Qusayr in Homs Province (Satik 2013: 407).

In the city of Qusayr,[9] the increasing presence of foreign jihadi fighters in the first half of 2012, alongside the rise in kidnappings and abductions of Christians, rendered the presence of the community more and more difficult. In mid-June, St. Elias Church was turned into the headquarters of an Islamic fundamentalist group (Ashkar 2013), while in the summer of 2012, following the complete conquest of the city by armed opposition forces, the local preacher-turned-brigade leader, Abdel Salam Harba, called through the mosques of the city on the Christians to leave under the pretext of supporting Bashar al-Assad and because they refused to carry weapons to fight the regime (Putz 2012; Wood 2013). The local FSA in Qusyar expressed their shock at the news and rejected the ultimatum, saying that it was not responsible and did not share Harba's sentiments in any way (cited in Ashkar 2013). Harba threatened Christians again in a mosque sermon on October 12, 2012, saying that "there is nothing left for them in Qusayr ... there is no return for them to Qusayr," and that "Qusayr Christians are traitors."

Most of the Christians left Qusayr in the summer of 2012 following the ultimatum, with few remaining in the town until December 2012 (Ashkar 2013). Christians started to come back to the area only after the SAA and Hezbollah regained control of al-Qusayr in June 2013, despite the wide-scale destruction of the city. A minority of the local Sunni population, who were mostly not involved with the opposition, also returned (Mashi 2013b), while the majority still have not returned to date.

From mid-to-late 2013, researchers Baczko Dorronsoro and Quesnay (2016: 324–325) described a situation with mounting sectarianism in some opposition-held areas, particularly ones with growing Islamic fundamentalist and jihadist influence. Minorities became regular targets of looting and attacks because they were suspected or accused of collaborating with the regime. These actions led large numbers of religious minorities to join regime-controlled areas. Even minority activists who had been opposed to the regime from the beginning of the uprising were not welcome in certain areas or even were threatened by some groups. This does not mean that the majority of the local population in opposition-held areas shared these

[9] Qusayr was a town of 30,000–40,000, located a few miles from the Lebanese border. It was once around three-quarters Sunni Muslim and one-quarter Christian.

feelings. Quite the contrary, in fact—it was the influence and control of Islamic fundamentalist and jihadist forces, along with some factions from the FSA, that created such an unwelcoming situation for minorities. Growing sectarian sentiments negatively affected the uprising (Khoury 2013: 7).

Sectarian attacks and military campaigns increased against religious minorities as 2013 progressed and during the following years as well, with suicide bombings targeting Christian and Alawi neighborhoods of Damascus more often (Lister 2015: 153), or the numerous attacks and kidnappings of Assyrian populations in the Jazirah by the IS. This included the IS offensive that drove 3,000 Assyrians from their villages and kidnapping hundreds more in February 2015 (Isaac 2015).

Another example of sectarian attack was in the summer of 2013, when a coalition of armed opposition groups led by Ahrar al-Sham, ISIL, Jabhat al-Nusra, Jaysh al-Muhajireen wal-Ansar, and Suqur al-Izz launched a large-scale offensive in the countryside of Lattakia Province. They occupied more than ten Alawi villages for several days in August, during which they committed numerous massacres. Human Rights Watch collected the names of 190 civilians who were killed by these opposition forces in their offensive on the villages, including 57 women, 14 elderly men, and at least 18 children (Human Rights Watch 2013).

Similar attacks occurred during the next few years. In May 2016, multiple coordinated explosions rocked two highly secure cities on Syria's coast, Jableh and Tartus, killing more than 120 people and injuring scores of others in grisly suicide bombings that targeted civilians at bus stations and a hospital. After the bombings, and as an act of what they called "retaliation," a group of young men, mostly affiliated with NDF's militias, set fire to a displaced persons' camp south of Tartus, the al-Karnak camp, which contained about 400 Sunni families who had fled to the area (Noufal and Wilcox 2016b).

A Human Rights Watch report (HRW 2015) documented indiscriminate attacks with car bombs, mortars, and unguided rockets by armed opposition groups between January 2012 and April 2014 in the following areas: in central Damascus and Sayyida Zeinab and Jaramana in Damascus Countryside Governorate, in the neighborhoods of al-Zahra, Akrama, al-Nazha, and Bab Sba` in the city of Homs, and in the village of Thabtieh, near Homs.[10] The areas, which Human Rights Watch found to be the most prone to attacks from opposition forces, are populated predominantly by religious minorities, including Shi'a, Alawi, Druze, and Christians, and

---

[10] These neighborhoods were selected by Human Rights Watch because they were among those most prone to attack by opposition groups and because of their ability to visit them.

were in close proximity to neighborhoods under opposition control. Exceptions were Bab Sba`, a predominantly Sunni neighborhood with some Christian residents, and central Damascus, a mixed neighborhood of various faiths. The report concluded that

> Human Rights Watch found that in the areas we could visit, neighborhoods under government control inhabited predominately by religious minorities were subject to more indiscriminate attacks by opposition groups than areas that were largely majority Sunni. Public statements by opposition armed groups provided strong evidence that these groups considered the religious minorities to be backing the Syrian government or that the attacks were in retaliation for government attacks on Sunni civilians elsewhere in the country. (HRW 2015)

This demonstrated the increasing sectarian practices among the Syrian opposition armed forces.

The prevalence of sectarian rhetoric and ideology could be seen in the domination of Islamic fundamentalist and jihadist forces on the battlefield. Following the chemical weapons attacks in Ghouta, Jolani issued a statement on August 25, 2013, in which he announced that Jabhat al-Nusra would execute retaliatory attacks against regime and pro-regime regions under the Islamic concept of *qisas*. The action was deemed "Operation Volcano of Revenge," meaning equal retaliation, or "an eye for an eye." One Alawi village would be attacked for every chemical-loaded rocket fired into East Ghouta, Jolani declared (Lister 2015: 164). The seizure of the city of Ma'lula was presented by Jabhat al-Nusra's official account as part of the "Eye-for-an-Eye" revenge campaign. One of Nusra's photos for the attack on Ma'lula was published on Facebook with a verse from the Qur'an stating: "Allah give us patience and victory over the infidels." In November 2015, two days after attacks from regime planes killed at least 40 people in a market in the town of Douma in the suburbs of Damascus, Jaysh al-Islam caged Alawi army officers and their families in cells and displayed them in the streets. This was supposedly done to shield the area from further bombardment (Mackey and Samaan 2015).

In August 2016, armed opposition groups in Aleppo named their attempt at breaking the siege of the city after Ibrahim Youssef. A member of the militant jihadist force Fighting Vanguard, which opposed the regime in the 1970s and 1980s, Youssef headed the group that seized the Aleppo Artillery School in June 1979, separating the Alawi and Sunni cadets before executing up to 83 of the Alawis (Lefèvre 2016). During the military offensive in Aleppo, a spokesman for the Jabhat al-Fateh al-Sham-led forces declared that they would do the same to Alawis. None of the participant groups, which ranged from FSA battalions to jihadists, objected to the name choice, demonstrating the Islamization of the armed opposition forces (Hassan 2016). A few weeks later, militant factions in the Hama countryside dubbed their military offensive on regime-held positions the "Invasion of the Martyr Marwan Hadid." Hadid was the Fighting Vanguard's charismatic founder and first leader, who often referred in a derogatory way to Alawis as "Nusayri dogs" and called for the establishment of an Islamic state in Syria (Lefèvre 2016).

The rising influence of Islamic fundamentalist and jihadist forces pushed minorities, among others, to leave cities in advance for fear of violence or retaliation. The conquest of the city of Idlib in March 2015 by the armed opposition led by Jabhat al-Nusra and Ahrar al-Sham saw the departure of nearly all of Idlib's Christian population, who fled the city shortly before its capture. Of those who remained, many had their homes looted and/or were killed by Jabhat al-Nusra. Father Ibrahim Farah and a young pharmacist were kidnapped. The remaining families in Idlib were used as media pawns, including a woman who appeared in an official video from the group praising the insurgents' treatment of Christians in Idlib. Of those still in the city, the families decided to flee stealthily, coordinating with some Muslims in the city to escape to the province of Hama (Slaytin 2015).

A large number of civil servants and others not directly tied to the regime fled as well. The reasons were multiple: they preferred Assad to Jaysh al-Fateh or simply to escape the fighting and, later, aerial bombardment by the Syrian Arab Air Force (Lund 2016b). The Red Crescent in Idlib buried about 300 bodies in a mass grave on April 9, which also contained bodies of individuals deemed as thugs and killed by Jabhat al-Nusra's militants (Slaytin 2015). At the end of 2018, the ruling authorities of the Salafist jihadist coalition HTS in Idlib confiscated properties belonging to displaced Christian families in the territories under its control.

From the perspective of large segments of Syria's minority communities, as well as some segments of its Sunni population, the rise of these forces and their progressive domination of the opposition military scene rendered the initial objectives of the uprising for democracy, equality and social justice as no longer existent. The growth of the IS, Jabhat al-Nusra, and others benefited the regime politically by undermining other opposition groups, while reinforcing the idea that only the regime could rescue the country from a frightening, extremist alternative. The rise of Islamic fundamentalist groups raised fears among large sectors of the population, not only religious minorities, while pushing even more Alawis into the regime's hands as they became the targets of increasingly frequent suicide bombings with a suspected or explicit sectarian motive.

Similarly, some opposition figures, especially among Alawis, started to retreat from their previous position, such as Nabil Suleiman, who distanced himself from the revolution. Fateh Jamous, the longtime leader of the Party of Communist Action who had been imprisoned between 1982 and 2000 and again between 2003 and 2006, declared during the vote for the new constitution in May 2012 that the opposition's objective should not be to seek to overthrow the regime, but rather to pave the way for a peaceful transition. He rejected the Coalition and acted as secretary-general of the Peaceful Change Path Party, within the so-called official opposition which the regime publicly accepted (Wieland 2015: 235).

Conclusion

The opposition groups in exile, the SNC and the Coalition, were unable to constitute a credible alternative or act as a representative of the initial objectives of the protest movement and its diversity. They also failed to provide a political strategy and leadership to unite the opposition and lead efforts to overthrow the regime. The successive failures of these groups further contributed to Islamic fundamentalist and jihadist groups' domination of the military scene in Syria.

The growth of these forces reduced the protest movement's capacity to communicate an inclusive and democratic message to large segments of the Syrian population, especially among people who were not involved directly in the protest movement but who sympathized with the initial goals of the uprising. These groups also targeted activists involved in the uprising and attacked the democratic components of the protest movement to impose their own objectives and authority, which were opposed to the uprising's initial objectives of democracy and equality.

There was a clear strategy by the regime to favor the creation of Islamic fundamentalist and Salafists jihadist organizations. Their existence would help to discredit the uprising, while repressing democratic components of the protest movement and of FSA forces. The regime was able to take advantage of the fear that these groups generated among large segments of the population who were scared of these kinds of forces. The Syrian regime opted for the strategy of allowing the development of these organizations, including IS, in order to present the only alternative to the regime as an Islamic fundamentalist state. Its propaganda had suggested this ultimatum since the beginning of the uprising, with the goal of increasing divisions within the opposition. Between April 2013 and summer 2014, the Syrian air force largely abstained from bombing discernible IS buildings and installations in the city of Raqqa. In a study conducted by the Carter Center, it was established that prior to IS military advances throughout Syria and Iraq in July and August 2014, the Syrian regime had

> largely abstained from engaging (IS) unless directly threatened ... Prior to this (IS) offensive, the Syrian government had directed over 90 percent of all air raids against oppositions positions ... (cited in Hassan and Weiss (2015: 198)

IS was not the prime concern of the Syrian regime, Syrian foreign minister Walid al-Muallem reportedly admitted, stating that opposition armed groups—who were also fighting the jihadist groups—posed a greater threat to Damascus's rule (The New Arab 2016b).

Each defeat of the democratic sectors of the protest movement, both civilian and armed, strengthened and benefited the Islamic fundamentalist and jihadist forces on the ground throughout the years, which progressively dominated the military scene. The growth of these forces provoked various internal conflicts between different members of the armed opposition, including between Islamic forces.

The various Islamic fundamentalist and jihadist movements defended an Islamic state despite their differences on how to reach this objective. This was, of course, an exclusionary project and was not appealing to various groups within Syrian society (i.e., religious minorities, women, or those who had a different understanding of Islam).

Similar to the Syrian MB in the 1980s, they probably had been successful in widening the gap between the regime and large sections of the population, but they were unable to decisively destabilize the regime. Their sectarian propaganda and open endorsement of violence against minorities had scared away segments of the population who did not identify or agree with this ideology. Furthermore, instead of dividing the Alawi population, and thus weakening their foothold in the army and security services, their anti-Alawi rhetoric and sectarian violence scared the vast majority of Alawis into rallying behind Assad (Batatu 1982).

In this context, democratic activists were not only threatened by regime forces, but by other factions within the opposition, especially Islamic fundamentalist and jihadi groups who rejected the initial democratic aspirations of the uprising. These forces were particularly effective in establishing civil structures as a counterbalance to local councils and coordination committees, repressing any dissent from them to consolidate their own ideology and goals.

The dual opposition faced by the democratic protest movement was symbolized in the summer of 2013 with the arrest of Maisa and Samar Saleh by the Assad regime and IS, respectively. On April 23, the Syrian activist

Maisa Saleh was arrested by regime forces in the Saruja market, in the heart of Damascus. She was known for her active participation in peaceful protests and civil disobedience initiatives. On August 8, her sister, Samar, was detained in the area of Tahuna, Aleppo, for demanding a civil state and equality for all citizens by IS (Syria Untold 2013d). Similarly, there were numerous cases of activists during the uprising who were jailed first by the regime, and later by Islamic fundamentalist forces.

As this history shows, the original protest movement and its democratic objectives were challenged from multiple sides, not only by the regime, although the latter remained the most dangerous actor in the country.

5. The Kurdish Question in Syria

Introduction

The first Syrian Kurdish parties were established in the 1950s. They emerged from an atmosphere of increasingly aggressive and chauvinistic Arab nationalism and growing frustration with Kurdish members of the Syrian Communist Party, whom many saw as being uninterested in or even actively opposing Kurdish national rights (Tejel 2009: 48). The vast majority of these new Kurdish movements adopted socialist ideologies, although the tribal elite remained well represented among their leadership. The notable exceptions to this dynamic, as previously noted, were the Kurdistan Workers' Party (known by its acronym as PKK)[1] and subsequently the Democratic Union Party (PYD), which from the beginning sought to represent the Kurdish popular classes and considered the tribal elite as collaborators in the colonization of Kurdistan (Van Bruinessen 2016: 7). To a lesser extent, the Yekiti Party was also able to have a large following in the 1990s and 2000s before it suffered from internal divisions.[2]

This chapter chronicles the participation of the Kurds and Kurdish political forces in the Syrian uprising. Kurdish protesters initially organized in a similar fashion than in other areas through the establishment of LCCs. However, the collaboration between the Arab and Kurdish coordination committees and youth dwindled over time and eventually ceased because of division and disagreement with Syrian Arab opposition groups, as well as rising Arab and Kurdish ethnic tension more generally.

Over time, the PYD, with the benevolent attitude of the Assad regime, gained increased control over the Kurdish political scene in Syria. PYD was able to take advantage of the divisions among the various international actors intervening in Syria, notably in receiving the assistance of the United States (and to a lesser extent Russia) to advance its own political interests.

---

[1] The PKK was formed in the late 1970s in Turkey, and its ideology was originally a fusion of Marxism, Third Worldism, and Kurdish nationalism, but the group's ideology evolved beyond that, reflecting the influence of American social theorist Murray Bookchin, a thinker advocating "libertarian municipalism."

[2] The Yekiti Party was created in 1992 following the unification of several Kurdish groups from leftist and nationalist origins. Students, intellectuals, and liberal professionals dominated their ranks, although members of all strata could be found (Tejel 2009: 112).

However, this support from foreign actors waned over time, or at least seemed less guaranteed. The PYD-led autonomy over Kurdish regions became a frequent point of contention among numerous regional and local actors.

The Kurdish question in Syria was an important element in understanding the development of the Syrian uprising and the increased divisions among opposition groups over time.

Kurdish issue before 2011: repression and forms of cooptation

In the 1950s and 1960s, Kurds in Syria were the primary scapegoats of rising Arab nationalism in Syria, including during the UAR[3] and afterward with the Ba'thist rule from 1963. They were often portrayed as hired agents working at the service of powerful foreign enemies, especially U.S. and Zionist imperialism (Tejel 2009: 41).

They suffered discriminatory and repressive policies. For example, the first measures of the "Arab Belt" plan started in 1962, which consisted of a *cordon sanitaire* (a type of guarded area) between Syrians and neighboring Kurds around the northern and northeastern rim of the Jazirah, along the borders with Turkey and Iraq. An "exceptional census" of the Jazirah population in 1962 resulted in around 120,000 Kurds being denied nationality and declared foreigners, leaving them, and subsequently their children, denied of basic civil rights and condemned to poverty and discrimination (Seurat 2012: 181).[4]

The Assad regime continued its discriminatory policies toward the Kurds and maintained an institutionalized racist system against Kurdish populations in Syria. Between 1972 and 1977, a policy of colonization was implemented in predominantly Kurdish regions of Syria as part of the Arab Belt plan. Around 25,000 "Arab" peasants, whose lands were flooded by the construction of the Tabqa Dam, were sent to the High Jazirah, where the Syrian regime established "modern villages" adjacent to Kurdish villages (Seurat 2012: 183).

---

[3] The UAR authorities launched a harsh campaign of repression against the main Kurdish party of that period, the Kurdistan Democratic Party of Syria (KDPS), in August 1960. More than 5,000 individuals were arrested and tortured, while about 20 of its leaders were imprisoned and charged with separatism (118; Allsopp 2015: 21; Tejel 2009: 49). Some of the leaders of the movement traveled to Iraqi Kurdistan to seek refuge (Allsopp 2015: 77).

[4] Between 120,000 and 150,000 Kurds are classified as noncitizen foreigners (*ajanib*) on their identity cards and cannot vote, own property, or obtain government jobs (but are not, however, exempt from obligatory military service); and as the so-called *maktumin* (unregistered), who cannot even receive treatment in state hospitals or obtain marriage certificates. The *maktumin* are not officially acknowledged at all and have no identity cards.

Meanwhile, the regime developed a policy to coopt certain segments of Kurdish society—especially with mounting opposition in the country at the end of the 1970s and the beginning of the 1980s, as mentioned in Chapter 1—and to serve foreign policy objectives. Some Kurdish elites participated in the regime's system, such as Kurdish leaders from the religious brotherhoods like Muhammad Sa'id Ramadan al-Buti and official sheikhs such as Ahmad Kuftaro, mufti of the republic between 1964 and 2004 (Pinto 2010: 265). Several Kurds held positions of local authority, while others reached high-ranking ones, such as Prime Minister Mahmud Ayyubi (1972–76), or Hikmat Shikaki, chief of military intelligence (1970–74) and chief of staff (1974–98). However, this was on the condition that they not demonstrate any particular Kurdish ethnic consciousness in their rhetoric or political strategy. Some Kurds were also absorbed at the end of the 1970s and into the 1980s into elite divisions of the army or linked to specific military groups serving the regime. Another form of cooptation was the complicity of local security services with certain families of active Kurdish smugglers in the Jazirah on the Syria–Turkey and Syria–Iraq frontiers (Tejel 2009: 66–67).

This policy of cooptation included some Kurdish political parties as well. The Assad regime established a sort of alliance with the PKK, and the Kurdish PKK leader Abdullah Öcalan became an official guest of the regime at the beginning of the 1980s as Syrian and Turkish tensions flared up. The PKK was authorized to recruit members and fighters, reaching between 5,000 and 10,000 persons in the 1990s (Bozarslan 2009: 68; Allsopp 2015: 40) and launching military operations from Syria against the Turkish army. PKK had offices in Damascus and several northern cities (McDowall 1998: 65). PKK militants took de facto control over small portions of Syrian territory, particularly in Afrin (Tejel 2009: 78). Other Kurdish political parties also collaborated with the Syrian regime. Among these were the Patriotic Union of Kurdistan (PUK),[5] led by Jalal Talabani, who had been in Syria since 1972; and later in 1979, the Kurdish Democratic Party (KDP),[6] affiliated with the Kurdish leader Masoud Barzani (Tejel 2009: 72–78).

The condition sine qua non of support from the Syrian regime was the abstention of the Kurdish movements of Iraq and Turkey from any attempt at mobilizing Syrian Kurds against Assad. Damascus was able to instrumentalize these Kurdish groups by using them as a foreign policy tool to

---

[5] The PUK was originally a leftist Iraqi-Kurdish political party that splintered from the KDP in the mid-1970s.

[6] The KDP is the oldest Kurdish political party in Iraqi Kurdistan. It was founded in 1946 in the Kurdish region of Iran where the Iraqi Kurds, led by Mustafa Barzani, were taking refuge (The Kurdish Project 2017).

achieve some regional ambitions and, at the national level, by diverting the Kurdish issue away from Syria and toward Iraq and Turkey.

Relations between the Kurdish political parties and the Syrian regime increasingly worsened through the late 1990s and into the early 2000s. An improvement in Turkish–Syrian relations prompted Syrian security forces to launch several waves of repression against the remaining PKK elements in Syria (ICG 2013: 12). Following the exile of Öcalan in 1998 and imprisonment of many PKK members, the party's activists tried to establish new parties, with the double objective of evading state repression and providing social support for its thousands of members and sympathizers. The PYD was created in 2003 as a successor to the PKK in Syria (Tejel 2009: 79), part of the party's regional strategy to establish local branches in neighboring countries. Relations were similarly weakening with KDP and PUK from 2000 as Damascus was trying to normalize relations with Baghdad, which meant an end to its interference in Iraqi Kurdish affairs (ICG 2011: 21).

In 2004, the Kurdish uprising began in the town of Qamishli and spread through the predominantly Kurdish-inhabited regions of the country— Jazirah, Afrin, but also in Aleppo and Damascus, where demonstrations were severely repressed by the security forces. The regime appealed for the collaboration of some Arab tribes of the northeast that had historical ties to the regime. Around 2,000 protesters were arrested and 36 killed, while others were forced to leave the country (Lowe 2006: 5). The Kurdish *Intifada*, as well as developments in Iraqi Kurdistan that saw increased autonomy and the raising of Kurdish flags and symbols, boosted Syrian Kurdish people's morale and confidence in mobilizing for their rights and strengthened the nationalist consciousness of the youth and their will for change.

The Kurdish Youth Movement in Syria (known by its Kurdish acronym, TCK, which stands for "*Tevgera Ciwanên Kurd*") was clandestinely established in March 2005, the year after the repression of the Kurdish uprising, and became the largest of the political youth groups after 2004. It would go on to be one of the key actors in the 2011 protests in Kurdish-majority areas (Schmidinger 2018: 76).

Kurds continued to assert themselves by organizing events celebrating their ethnic identity and protesting against anti-Kurdish policies of the regime. Kurdish students of various political groups were also very active throughout the years on university campuses, particularly in Damascus and Aleppo.

The beginning of the Syrian uprising—March 2011

Protests in predominantly Kurdish areas started as early as late March 2011, such as in Amuda and Qamishli, where demonstrators called for freedom and brotherhood between Arabs and Kurds and solidarity with Dar'a (Kurd Watch 2012a; Aziz Abd El-Krim 2016; Darwish 2016a; Hassaf 2018). Demonstrations spread rapidly to other Kurdish-inhabited cities.

The protest movement in these areas emerged around preexisting youth groups such as the TCK or newly established LCCs, who saw themselves as part of the national protest movement against the regime. Throughout the year 2011, as explained by a Syrian Kurdish activist, Alan Hassaf (2018),

> The Kurdish coordination committees coordinated and cooperated with their counterparts in other Syrian cities across the different networks available.

Continuous protests occurred during the following month, although the regime sought to win the backing (or at least the non-opposition) of Kurdish political parties through various other means. In early March 2011, for example, the Ministry of Social Affairs decided to normalize the status of Kurds in all employment matters, while also revoking Decree No. 49, which had impeded the transfer of lands in border regions affecting Kurdish populations (Kurd Watch 2013b: 4). On March 20, the regime acknowledged and celebrated the Kurdish New Year, which was broadcast on state television and extensively covered by the national news agency (ICG 2011: 22). In the years that followed, Nowruz would be celebrated with much publicity by the regime (Sabbagh 2016b). However, the Kurdish Coordination committees canceled Nowruz festivities in March 2012 and transformed them into protests calling for the overthrow of the regime (Abdallah, al-Abd Hayy, and Khoury 2012).

Bashar al-Assad issued a decree in April 2011 following meetings with Kurdish representatives in which Syrian nationality was granted to persons registered as foreigners (*ajanib*—while unregistered Kurds, or *maktumin*, were excluded from this provision) in the governorate of Hasakah, while 48 prisoners, mainly Kurds, were also released.[7] Despite these decisions, several hundred people peacefully marched in various cities such as

---

[7] The ability to assess the implications of the 2011 decree is hampered by the fact that the country has entered a violent conflict, compelling large segments of the population to leave the country. Meanwhile, there were complications to the application of this decree. In addition, one of the main criticisms of Decree No. 49 was that, not being retroactive, it offered no compensation for the stripping of ownership or land rights as a consequence of the loss of nationality in 1962 (Al-Barazi 2013: 24). Although tens of thousands of Kurds were able to obtain Syrian citizenship after the decree passed, there were 19,000 of them who remained deprived of citizenship, while another 46,000 were unregistered in 2018 according to the NGO Syrian for Truth and Justice (Sheikho 2018).

Qamishli, Amuda, and Hasakah, chanting, "We do not want only nationality, but also freedom" (*Orient le Jour* 2011e).

From the summer of 2011, the demonstrators frequently raised the Kurdish flag alongside the Syrian one. In October, massive demonstrations occurred in the city of Qamishli following the assassination of the prominent Syrian Kurdish political activist Mishal Tammo. He was a member of the Kurdish Future movement and had recently been released after spending more than two years in a regime jail, having also served as a member of the executive committee of the newly formed SNC. Upon news of his death, thousands of protesters took to the streets to express their anger and chanted to topple the regime (Nono Ali 2011).

Mass demonstrations continued in Qamishli, and they reached their peak in mid-2012, after which they decreased considerably due to the militarization of the uprising and the PYD's progressive domination of larger swathes of the city (Darwish 2016a).

The collaboration between Arab and Kurdish youth groups and LCCs continued until approximately March 2012. After this period, Kurdish activists started using their own slogans that made reference to Kurdish-specific issues and that had not been previously accepted as general slogans. However, the use of some religious slogans by various Arab groups also became a point of contention (Kurd Watch 2013b: 4; Hassaf 2018).

A number of Kurdish activists and committees initially welcomed the establishment of the FSA. However, they grew increasingly at odds with it following the foreign aid and sponsorship that some FSA groups received from foreign powers, Turkey in particular, and their increasingly religious extremist practices and hostile attitudes toward Kurdish political demands and symbols (Youssef S. 2016; Abd el-Krim 2016; Hassaf 2018). Similarly, there were complaints that many Arab activists had either tacitly supported or engaged in anti-Kurdish rhetoric since the beginning of the uprising. Kurdish activists were accused of being separatist and wanting Kurdish independence. If Kurdish activists ever voiced criticism over some of the opposition's practices or mentioned Kurdish national rights, they were often blamed for betraying the Syrian revolution. As one Kurdish activist from Aleppo put it, seeing Arab revolutionaries treat them like the regime pushed them increasingly toward the PYD (Lundi Matin 2018).

Kurdish Youth committees nevertheless were still able to organize effective demonstrations and protest actions against the Syrian regime and diffuse Arab–Kurdish tensions in many areas during the first years of the uprising (Tansîqîya al-tâkhî al-kûrdîya 2011; All4Syria 2013). At the same time, the influence of the majority of Kurdish youth committees progressively declined on the ground and throughout the uprising.

Kurdish protesters were not limited to so-called corporatist demands, such as the bestowing of Syrian nationality onto Kurds lacking any citizenship; rather, they were part of a much larger protest movement throughout the country. This point was argued by a number of Syrian Kurdish activists who saw this movement as their own, one in which they saw themselves as full and active participants in building a new Syria for all (Youssef S. 2014; Abd El-Krim 2016; Hassaf 2018). This did not mean that traditional Kurdish national demands were sidelined by the youth and protesters, but rather were integrated into their larger vision and struggle against the Assad regime.

Despite their activism in the uprising, the Kurdish LCCs faced skepticism and opposition from traditional Kurdish political parties, almost all of whom were unwilling to participate or play a leading role in antiregime protests (ICG 2013: 9). Only the Kurdish Future Movement in Syria, led by Mishal Tammo, and the Yekiti Party publicly supported the uprising from the beginning. Many youth members of the party were among the organizers of the protests in Kurdish-inhabited regions (Kurd Watch 2013b: 4; Othman 2016). The Kurdish Political Congress,[8] founded in 2009, grew in number with the onset of the uprising in spring 2011. In late April, it established the National Movement of Kurdish Political Parties with the inclusion of three new parties, including the PYD. By May 2011, the National Movement of Kurdish Political Parties announced its platform, which included an end to one-party rule in Syria, equality for all citizens, and a secular state (Kajjo and Sinclair 2011).

A new conference was organized in October 2011 gathering together the majority of Kurdish political parties, independents, Kurdish youth organizations, Kurdish women's organizations, human rights activists, and professionals with the objective of uniting the Kurdish opposition in Syria (Allsopp 2015: 201). This led to the establishment of the Kurdish National Congress (KNC), which followed the creation of the SNC. The KNC was formed in Erbil, Iraq, under the sponsorship of Massoud Barzani, the president of the Kurdistan Regional Government (KRG) of Iraq (Carnegie 2012b) and an important ally of Turkey at the time. Barzani had large influence among several Syrian Kurdish opposition groups. The stated mission of the KNC was to find a "democratic solution to the Kurdish issue

---

[8] Ten Kurdish political parties established in 2009 what became known as the Kurdish Political Congress: the Syrian Democratic Kurdish Party; the Kurdish Left Party, the KDP in Syria; the Kurdish Democratic Front; the Kurdish Democratic National Party in Syria; the Kurdish Democratic Equality Party in Syria; the Kurdish Coordination Committee; the Kurdish Yekiti Party in Syria; the Azadi Kurdish Party in Syria; and the Kurdish Future Movement (Hossino and Tanir 2012).

while emphasizing that it was part of the revolution" (Hossino and Tanir 2012: 3).

Problems still existed within the KNC, particularly given how independent activists and youth organizations had relatively little power compared to political parties. In the initial executive committee, 45 people were elected, including 20 party representatives and six representatives of Kurdish youth organizations. The executive committee was then expanded to 47 to integrate the new political parties, which entered the council, in January 2012.[9] Some Kurdish youth groups also became absorbed into existing political parties, losing their independence and often diminishing their participation in activism, while other youth movements that remained independents were increasingly marginalized within the KNC by the dominant parties (Allsopp 2015: 203–204). Other organizations and parties remained only symbolically affiliated with the KNC, while others left it or ceased to cooperate with it (Halhalli 2018: 40; Hassaf 2018).

Two parties attending the founding conference opted not to join the KNC: the Kurdish Future Movement and the PYD. The Future Movement cited four points of objection to the KNC: the failure of the KNC to commit to the overthrow of the regime; the failure to adopt stronger support for the youth; demands for the Kurds that should remain unhindered from external influence or interests; and the argument that independent activists should have stronger representation in the council (Allsopp 2015: 204). The PYD attended the founding conference of the KNC after its inception in October before deciding to boycott the group and join the NCBDC (Hossino and Tanir 2012). The PYD was very suspicious of Turkey's role and influence in the establishment of the SNC, but of the KNC as well, as its sponsor was Barzani, who was a close ally of Ankara. Turkish military and Barzani's peshmergas (fighters) had both targeted PKK positions in Iraq at different times.

In December 2011, the PYD established the People's Council of Western Kurdistan (PCWK) as an alternative to the KNC that it refused to join. The PCWK was described by the organization as an elected local assembly designed to establish civil institutions and provide various social services to the population it served (ICG 2013: 13). The conference statement supported the popular uprising in Syria and elsewhere in the region, "aimed at establishing a pluralistic democracy" (PCWK 2011). The five organizations within the PCWK [the Rojava Movement for a Democratic Society (TEV-DEM), the Western Kurdistan Democratic Society Movement, the Yekitiya Star women's organization, the Union of Families of Martyrs, the Education

---

[9] The Kurdistan Union Party in Syria, the KDP in Syria, and the Kurdistan Democratic Concord Party joined the KNC in early 2012.

and Language Institution, and the Revolutionary Youth Movement of Western Kurdistan] were all connected to the PYD. The PCWK was in reality an umbrella organization for PYD-affiliated groups and movements (Allsopp 2015: 205).

PCWK activities had the objective of mobilizing support for the PYD in regions witnessing a vacuum of authority by establishing civil institutions such as the People's Local Committees, which were in charge of specific activities in Kurdish-populated areas under its control, as well as security institutions, including the People's Protection Committees and the YPG (ICG 2013: 14).

A contract of civil peace was signed between the PYD and the KNC in January 2012 to prevent new clashes, but it was nevertheless not implemented, and many examples of violent attacks and repression by PYD supporters occurred against other Kurdish activists (Hossino and Tanir 2012; Human Rights Watch 2014; Abdelkrim 2014; Othman 2016; Youssef S. 2016; Hassaf 2018; Kurd Watch 2018). Kurdish youth movements and independents started to oppose PYD domination and control over Kurdish-inhabited areas (ICG 2013: 10; Allsopp 2015: 210), while clashes between PYD and KNC supporters multiplied.

The demonstration of Amuda became a notorious case of the harsh repression of protesters by YPG forces. On June 17, 2013, Asayish forces in Amuda arrested three activists. To protest these incarcerations, Kurdish opposition groups and supporters staged a protest by establishing a tent in the town's main square, which developed into a hunger strike (Syria Freedom Forever 2013a). On June 27, 2013, YPG forces shot into a crowd of protestors in Amuda, killing three men (Zakwan Hadid 2013). PYD security forces killed two more men that night in unclear circumstances, and a third the next day. On the night of June 27, YPG forces also detained around 50 members or supporters of the Yekiti Party in Amuda, and beat them at a YPG military base (Human Rights Watch 2014: 4). Following these incidents, the LCC (2013b) published a statement "Regarding the Acts of Violence Against the Kurdish Syrian Civilians," in which it condemned such practices.

Demonstrations in the Kurdish-inhabited regions were increasingly divided according to each party or alliance; in Qamishli, Amuda and Hasakah, for example, as many as three to five separate protests were organized every Friday (IRIN 2012; Allsopp 2015: 211; Schmidinger 2018: 90).

The PKK remained fiercely critical of Barzani's party, the KDP, and affiliated groups, for the feudalism and corruption with which they were associated. The KDP, for its part, blamed the PKK and its sister organization, PYD, for their violent politics and unwillingness to collaborate with others except as the leading partner (Van Bruinessen 2016: 11). At the same time, the PYD maintained a hostile position toward the SNC, which it viewed as a puppet of Turkish foreign policy, branding the Kurdish groups and figures that joined it as "collaborators." PYD leaders argued that the SNC had not sufficiently answered the Sunni-Alawi question in post-Assad Syria, and the Kurdish issue and their objective was to facilitate the intervention of foreign powers in Syria, particularly Turkey (see Chapter 6), and establish a moderate Islamic regime, which would oppress Kurds (Hossino and Tanir 2012).

Regime attempts to coopt the PYD and control Kurdish regions

Soon after the beginning of the uprising in 2011, the PYD leadership was able to return to Syria, despite the party being forbidden in the country. Saleh Muslim, the leader of the PYD at that period, came back to Syria, to the city of Qamishli, in April 2011. He had taken refuge in a PKK camp in Iraq in 2010 after his and his wife's imprisonment in Syria (Carnegie 2011).[10]

With the return of PYD's leadership to Syria, the organization started to pursue political and paramilitary activities to mobilize support among Syrian Kurds. In this framework, the PKK transferred between 500 and 1,000 armed fighters to create the PYD's military wing, the YPG (ICG 2013: 2), which functioned as an army. In October 2011, the regime freed several Kurdish political prisoners, and soon after, Damascus allowed the PYD to open six Kurdish "language schools" in northern Syria, which the group used primarily for political work. In March 2012, the PKK was able to transfer between 1,500 and 2,000 of its members to Syria from the Qandil enclave, while Turkey was taking a hostile position toward the Assad regime in mid-end 2011 (Cagaptay 2012; IRIN 2012). Assad's regime allowed PYD to develop and extend its influence to pressure Turkey. Militarily, the PKK's Qandil leadership exerted authority over the YPG throughout the uprising, whose leadership was dominated by Syrian and foreign (i.e., Kurdish fighters from other nationalities) PKK fighters trained at that base (ICG 2014a: 5; Grojean 2017: 125).

The Syrian regime had partially withdrawn its forces from some Kurdish majority-inhabited areas by July 2011, or at least was not obstructing any

[10] His leadership was reconfirmed at the extraordinary fifth Congress of the PYD, held on June 16, 2012, at which the party's Central Committee was expanded and dual leadership was introduced to increase and promote the representation of women in the party. Asiyah Abdullah was elected cochair of the party (Carnegie 2012a). At the seventh Congress of the PYD in September 2017, held in the town of Rmeilan in Syria's northeast, a new leadership was elected. Shahoz Hasan and Aysha Hisso replaced Saleh Muslim and Asya Abdullah as the new PYD cochairs (Arafat 2017b). However, Saleh Muslim remained a key and influential figure in the party.

activities in these regions. The PYD and Kurdish forces that would join the future KNC competed to represent Kurdish interests in Syria. The ability of the PYD to organize freely in Syria raised suspicions that the party had settled an agreement with the regime that permitted it to reestablish a presence and operate openly in Syria. In return, the PYD would cooperate with security forces to crush antiregime protests in Kurdish-majority areas and marginalize other Kurdish political parties to win a hegemony over the Syrian Kurdish political scene. PYD was very eager to fill the power vacuum left by the regime (IRIN 2012; ICG 2013: 2; Grojean 2017: 123).

Similarly, during this period the PYD increasingly resorted to social media to project its antiregime credentials and support for the uprising, especially from early 2012 onward (IRIN 2012; ICG 2013: 14). During this period, tensions between the regime and the PYD became more noticeable in some areas, with a gunfight breaking out in Kobani between PYD and regime supporters, as well as members of the Air Force Intelligence Service. In addition, a military court in Aleppo sentenced four PYD supporters to a 15-year prison sentence for membership in the organization. Further, before the vote on the constitutional referendum by the Assad regime on February 26, 2012, the PYD urged a boycott of the polls, claiming that the new constitution did not offer anything to the Kurds (Hossino and Tanir 2012).

Rather than being just an Assad proxy, the PYD was playing a mutually beneficial role for itself and the Assad regime. It sought to take advantage of the lack of security and to expand the land it controlled to try to achieve its political objectives and enforce some form of Kurdish autonomy in Kurdish-majority regions. On the other end of the spectrum, the regime was able to concentrate its military forces on other regions witnessing protests and armed resistance, while PYD was generally hostile to the various opposition armed groups, preventing them from entering their areas. The presence of PYD along the northern frontier of the country also deprived some Syrian opposition forces of their bases and supply lines in Turkey. As previously mentioned, PYD's expanding influence was also a tool for Damascus to use to pressure Turkey, whose hostility to the regime and intervention on behalf of Syrian opposition forces were both rising.

Refusal of any self-determination for the Kurds

The historical quandaries surrounding the Kurdish question reappeared with the popular uprising.[11] The Syrian Arab opposition rejected the demands

---

[11] Although the Declaration of Damascus in 2005 explicitly recognized the Kurdish issue, the four Kurdish parties that were signatories were still not satisfied by the way the far majority of

of the Kurdish opposition, both from the KNC and the PYD. In mid-July 2011, Kurdish representatives at the Istanbul gathering walked out in protest after the refusal of their request to change the name of the country from the Syrian Arab Republic to the Republic of Syria (Kajjo and Sinclair 2011).

Relations between the SNC and the KNC were difficult from the beginning. The SNC's first chairman, Burhan Ghalioun, refused the KNC's main demand for federalism in a post-Assad Syria, calling it a "delusion." Ghalioun also infuriated Syrian Kurds by comparing them to the "immigrants in France" in November 2011, implying their exteriority to Syria (Abdallah, Abd Hayy (al-) and Khoury 2012). In response to the continuous refusal of Kurdish demands within the opposition, on March 30, 2012, Kurdish protesters named the Friday demonstrations the "Friday of Kurdish Rights" (Allsopp 2015: 206).

Tension between the KNC and the SNC increased considerably following the SNC's publication of its "National Charter: The Kurdish Issue in Syria" in April 2012. The document eliminated language recognizing a Kurdish nation within Syria that had been included in the draft's final statement of the Friends of Syria meeting in Tunisia. This resulted in the withdrawal of the KNC from unity talks with the SNC, after which they accused Turkey of excessively influencing the SNC's policy (Carnegie 2012b). Within Syria, in response to the SNC denial of Kurdish national rights, youth groups and parties held banners reading, "Here is Kurdistan" on April 20, while two weeks before, April 6 demonstrations were designated as the "Friday of putting Kurdish Rights above any council" (Allsopp 2015: 206).

The Syrian Arab opposition dealt a new blow to the KNC by refusing its demands to include a reference to the "Kurdish people in Syria" in its Cairo meeting in July 2012 (Sary 2015: 9). The KNC then joined the Syrian Coalition on August 27, 2013, hoping for improvements but failing to see any concrete changes. The SNC and the Coalition continued to act negatively toward Kurdish parties and interests. The KNC was included in the HNC (KNC 2016a) following the Riyadh Opposition Conference in December 2015. This did not prevent their continued denial of Kurdish rights and of chauvinist comments from members of the Syrian Arab opposition of the Coalition. For example, on March 29, 2016, the chairman of the opposition's delegation of the HNC in Geneva, former general As'ad al-Zo'abi, said on Radio Orient television that

---

the Syrian political parties and human rights associations limited the Kurdish question to the single issue of the census in 1962 and the Kurds deprived of their citizenships. The majority was not ready to recognize the Kurds as a separate nation, nor was it willing to listen to demands for federalism and decentralization (Tejel 2009: 127).

The Kurds made up 1 percent of the population and they only wanted to get their papers during the era of President Hafez al-Assad to prove they are "human beings" ... (Smart News Agency 2016)

In response to these comments, considered racist by many Kurds, demonstrations were organized in various Kurdish-majority cities in protest (SMART News Agency 2016).

At the same time, the SNC and the Coalition continued to adopt a harsh attitude against the PYD, considered by many as an enemy of the revolution. George Sabra, president of SNC at the time, declared in January 2016 that PYD was not part of the opposition and was very close to the regime politically, in addition to being part of PKK, which was classified as a terrorist organization. The statement thereby endorsed the official position of Turkey toward the group (al-Jazeera English 2016).

In the autumn of 2016, the great majority of the Syrian Kurdish political movements, including both the PYD and KNC, were angered by the transition plan proposed by the opposition's HNC in September 2016. The KNC (2016b) stated clearly that

this document is not part of a solution, but rather a danger to a democratic, pluralistic, and unified Syria guaranteeing cultural, social, and political rights to all its ethnic, religious, and linguistic groups.

They added,

Whoever reads the document notes immediately that point 1 of the "General Principles" exclusively lists the Arab culture and Islam as sources for intellectual production and social relations. This definition clearly excluded other cultures—be they ethnic, linguistic, or religious—and sets the majority culture as the leading one. As Syrian Kurds we feel repulsed by this narrow perception of the Syrian people. The similarities between this definition and the chauvinist policies under the Assad regime are undeniable.

A new confrontation took place in March 2017 during a further round of peace negotiations in Geneva, when representatives of the NCBDC and HNC refused to transfer a document written by the KNC to the UN special envoy, Staffan de Mistura. This document confirmed Kurdish representation in the negotiation process and demanded an inclusion of the Kurdish question and the interests of other segments of Syria's population into the agenda of negotiations. In reaction, they suspended their participation in the negotiations and with the HNC's meetings (KNC 2017).

The NCBDC has not been very different than the SNC and the Coalition on the Kurdish question. Their original position envisaged a "democratic solution to the Kurdish issue within the unity of Syria's land that does not contradict that Syria is part and parcel of the Arab world." In February 2012, the Kurdish parties belonging to the NCBDC (with the exception of the PYD) withdrew and decided to join the KNC. The NCBDC modified its position slightly in April of the same year, endorsing the implementation of "decentralized principles" in a future Syria, but with no change from Kurdish parties to reenter the fold (Carnegie 2012b). They, however, maintained their opposition to a federal system in Syria.

The FSA had no official position, but most of its leadership was hostile to Kurdish national rights and demands. Colonel Riad al-As'ad, an FSA leader, declared that the group would not permit any territory to be separated from Syria and that "we will never leave Qamishli ... We will not accept one meter of Syrian soil seceding and will go to war" (cited in *Dunya Times* 2012).

The beginning of PYD self-administration

In June 2012, Barzani mediated a power-sharing agreement between the two leading Kurdish groups, KNC and PCWK. Known as the Erbil Declaration, it stated that they would rule Syria's Kurdish regions together during the transition and created the Supreme Kurdish Committee in the pursuit of this objective (Kurd Watch 2012b). The Erbil Declaration remained a dead letter, though, as the position of the PYD in Syria was strengthened and reinforced its unwillingness to share power with other Kurdish political forces.

On July 19, 2012, 17 months after the beginning of the uprising, the regime's forces withdrew from nine Kurdish-dominated towns and handed over control to the PYD. PYD members claimed that the regime's representative left after being given an ultimatum to leave or else be attacked by the party in the following 24 hours, while the SNC and some Kurdish rivals accused the PYD of making a deal with the regime (ICG 2013: 14; Ayboga, Flach, and Knapp 2016: 56–57).

The withdrawal of Assad's regime forces was most probably the result of a tacit agreement with the PYD, which was allowed to come back and organize a few months after the start of the revolt. The regime needed all its armed forces to repress the demonstrations elsewhere in the country and did not want to open a new military front, though it maintained a small presence in some cities, such as Qamishli and Hasakah. This also was part of the regime's strategy to divide the uprising along ethnic and sectarian lines, as the PYD initially adopted a neutral position toward large segments of the opposition forces and was less eager to collaborate with popular organizations and activists in Arab-inhabited areas, while trying to dominate and control the Kurdish population in Syria.

The PYD took over the regime's municipal buildings in at least five of its strongholds—Kobani, Amuda, al-Malikiyah (meaning "Derek" in Kurdish), Afrin, and Jinderes—replacing Syrian flags with its own. The PYD's control of these territories, so close to the Turkish border, alarmed the Turkish government. The Turkish prime minister at the time, Recep Tayyip Erdogan, warned against any plans for an autonomous Kurdish region in Syria before the visit of PYD leader Salih Muslim to Ankara for discussions in July 2013 (Naharnet 2013). Despite the assurances given by the PYD leader to the Turkish administration that his group's call for a local administration in Syria's Kurdish regions would not mean a division of Syria (Khoshnawi 2013), relations worsened between both parties very rapidly, strengthened as well by the end of the peace process in Turkey between the PKK and Turkish government.

PYD's total control over the Kurdish-majority regions led the organization to refuse the power-sharing proposition of the Erbil declaration submitted by Barzani. Instead, they proposed to establish a temporary independent council to manage West Kurdistan (northeastern Syria) until the end of the war in Syria to meet the needs of the local population, improve the economy, and deal with attacks of the Assad regime, Islamic forces, and the Turkish army. The PYD refused peshmerga fighters—affiliated with Barzani's KDP—entry into the country if they were not under its own leadership with the YPG. The KNC disagreed with these conditions and reiterated the importance of cooperation and understanding with the revolutionary forces and national opposition in Syria (IRIN 2012; ICG 2014a: 2–3).

The increasing political and military hegemony of the PYD and the inability of the KNC to project influence inside Syria further weakened the organization and deepened internal divisions. Some parties within the KNC saw cooperation with the PYD as the unique way to maintain a power base in Syria and to defend itself against opposition, Islamic, and jihadist forces attacking Kurdish-populated regions. The launch of the campaign "Western Kurdistan for Its Children" by the PYD in the summer of 2012 against the attacks by opposition armed groups and Islamic fundamentalist and jihadist groups against the cities mostly inhabited by Kurds also diminished criticisms of the party and temporarily united Syrian Kurds across the political spectrum (ICG 2014a: 3). The Syrian Kurdish activist Shiyar Youssef (2016) explained:

Even those most critical of the PYD started to see it as the "lesser of two evils" following the attacks of FSA, Islamist, and jihadist forces against Kurdish-populated areas. I know many Kurdish activists in Qamishli, Amuda, and other areas who, before these developments, used to organize demonstrations and write against the PYD, but have now suddenly started volunteering in the ranks of the YPG to fight against the Islamists because if they won, they would impose their rule and their values that are alien to the local population...

Similar arguments were put forward by other activists (Abd El-Krim 2016; Hassaf 2018), leading to a strengthening of PYD's claim to being the sole viable protector of Syria's Kurds against outside threats. This sentiment among large sections of Kurds in Syria only increased throughout the uprising.

The relations between the KNC and PYD continued to deteriorate, as no space on the political scene was provided for the KNC and its various factions. The border between Syria's and Iraq's Kurdish area, controlled by the patron of the KNC, Barzani, became an arena for this intra-Kurdish competition. Fearing that the PYD would increase its influence and role by taking control of aid distribution, the KRG in Iraq would close crossings periodically on its side of the border, preventing the entry of supplies. As a result, living conditions deteriorated rapidly in Syria's Kurdish areas.

By mid-2013, populations were suffering from significant shortages of electricity, water, food, and gas, leading to a stream of departures for Iraqi Kurdistan. Moreover, during the same period, several Kurdish-inhabited areas in northeastern Syria were suffering attacks by Islamic fundamentalists and jihadist groups. On August 15, the KDP opened the border, but only to close it again three days later. In this period, between 40,000 and 70,000 Kurds fled to Iraqi Kurdistan. The number of refugees in Iraqi Kurdistan reached nearly 200,000 by early August 2013. Relations worsened further, as the KDP forbade PYD members from entering Erbil Governorate and repressed some of its members; in response, the PYD prevented pro-Barzani leaders from crossing into Syria and repressed its supporters (IRIN 2013; Eakin 2013; ICG 2014a: 10–11).

The PYD and the Assad regime

As the PYD expanded its control in Kurdish-populated areas, regime forces maintained a presence in the largest enclaves nominally under the party's control, most notably Qamishli and Hasakah. State services remained Damascus's responsibility, for example, as the regime continued to pay salaries to state employees and manage administrative offices, giving them an important edge (ICG 2014a: 9). The Qamishli airport, which became the country's second-largest airport (only behind Damascus) in 2016, remained under the control of the SAA (*The Syria Report* 2016f). The YPG was accused of coordinating with the regime on some occasions, or at least timing some attacks to distract the opposition and force them to fight on multiple fronts (Haid 2017a).

On various occasions, Saleh Muslim denied any alliance with Damascus and affirmed that since September 2011, the PYD had called for the fall of the regime and all of its related symbols (Kurd Watch 2013a). At the same time, PYD officials recognized that they had made a tactical decision in not confronting regime forces, yet they refuted accusations of collusion, describing themselves as a "third current" between an "oppressive regime and hardline rebel militants" (ICG 2014a: 7). Their position must also be contextualized within the framework of a hostile Syrian Arab political opposition in exile, represented first by the SNC and then by the Coalition, and of large sectors of armed opposition groups in northern Syria. These actors were allied with Turkey and were considered a staunch enemy by the PYD/PKK, and they largely refused to consider Kurdish national demands in Syria.

At the same time, TEV-DEM—dominated by the PYD—kept discreet lines open with regime officials in Damascus and focused their efforts on combating IS and establishing a form of localized government (Sary 2015: 4). In Damascus, regime officials repeatedly refused any form of Kurdish autonomy in Syria.

As argued by a report of the ICG (2014a: 7–8):

> There is little doubt that the PYD is engaging the regime in a conciliatory rather than confrontational manner and has pursued a modus vivendi that serves both, at least for the short term. Its initially rapid advance was dependent on Damascus's June 2012 withdrawal from Kurdish areas; this was mutually beneficial, regime forces to concentrate elsewhere in the north, while the PYD denied Kurdish areas to the armed opposition.

Relations between the Assad regime and PYD continued to be nonconfrontational for years, although localized armed clashes continued to erupt on occasion, especially in the city of Qamishli, where the regime retained a presence. In December 2015, after the YPG-led Syrian Democratic Forces (SDF) (discussed further later in this chapter) signed a truce with the opposition operation room of Fatah Halab, SDF and regime troops clashed, and Sheikh Maqsood became the target of regime airpower. In mid-to-late August 2016, two Syrian SU-24 attack planes targeted Kurdish forces in the city of Hasakah. A U.S.-led coalition scrambled its own jets in the area to protect American advisers who were working with Kurdish forces and to intercept Syrian jets, but the regime planes had left by the time they arrived. Pentagon spokesman Captain Jeff Davis said that "this was done as a measure to protect coalition forces" (The New Arab 2016a). This allowed the YPG forces to take near-complete control of Hasakah after a cease-fire, ending a week of fighting with regime forces and consolidating the Kurds' grip on Syria's northeast (Perry and Said 2016).

Despite the weakening of its influence following the armed confrontations, the Syrian regime sent Ministers of Health Nizar Yazigi and of Local Administration and Environment Hussein Makhlouf to Hasakah as a means of reaffirming its bid for influence in the northeastern province, where they visited various officials (al-Sultan 2016; The Syria Report 2016d). These tensions between the regime and the PYD could also be observed in the struggle over languages taught in Syrian educational institutions in the northeast. The PYD wanted to impose Kurdish teachings in state schools, while the regime threatened to freeze the salaries of teachers that taught any curriculum other than the official one. In cases where the Kurdish Party imposed its own curriculum, the regime did end up forcing some schools to close (Jamal, Nelson, and Yosfi 2015; The Syria Report 2016i).

In mid-October 2016, the regime appointed a new governor for the province of Hasakah, Jayed Sawada al-Hammoud al-Moussa, a former military and security official known for his brutality against civilians.[12] His military record sent a clear message to the PYD that the regime was escalating its efforts (SANA 2016b; Zaman al-Wasl 2016c). The incoming governor cut all financial support to the National Hospital of Hasakah, the largest in the region, after the refusal of Kurdish police forces and other partisan security forces to leave the building by the start of 2017. The National Hospital of Hasakah operated at less than 15 percent capacity compared to its level of activity just a few months before, and entire departments closed their doors. The unprecedented rollback in services affected the more than 1 million residents of Hasakah city, particularly those who were unable to afford medical care at one of the provincial capital's five private hospitals (Abdulssattar Ibrahim, Nassar, and Schuster 2017).

Meanwhile, during the same period in March 2017, the Syrian regime and supporters of the ruling Ba'th Party formed a new paramilitary group, recruiting from local tribesmen and government employees in northern Hasakah Province to gather a force of around 3,000 fighters. The creation of the group built on heightened resentment toward the PYD administration

---

[12] He participated in the repression of civilians, particularly in the Qalamoun Mountains along the Damascus-Homs Highway, where troops under his command reportedly committed several massacres against civilians, in particular in the town of Dumeir (Zaman al-Wasl 2016c).

(Zaman al-Wasl 2017d). Other pro-regime militias with similar designs and intentions were also established in this region.

In mid-June 2017, new clashes occurred between regime forces and the SDF, as both were capturing IS-held territories and getting dangerously close to each other territorially. U.S. warplanes also shot down an SAA jet during this period in the southern Raqqa countryside because it dropped bombs near SDF positions (Al-Khalidi and Spetalnick 2017).

One month later, in mid-September, the Russian air force targeted SDF positions, causing injuries on the eastern side of the Euphrates River in Syria, near Deir ez-Zor (Van Wilgenburg 2017b). During the same period, high regime official Bouthaina Shaaban declared the Syrian government's readiness to fight the SDF:

> Whether it's the Syrian Democratic Forces, or Daesh (Islamic State), or any illegitimate foreign force in the country … we will fight and work against them so our land is freed completely from any aggressor … I'm not saying this will happen tomorrow … but this is the strategic intent … (Dadouch and Perry 2017)

SDF forces suffered a new attack carried out by the Russian and regime forces against their positions in Deir ez-Zor Province on September 25 (SDF General Command 2017).

In the midst of worsening military and political tensions between Damascus and its allies on one side and the PYD on the other side, Syrian foreign minister Walid Moallem affirmed at the end of September that the Syrian government was open to negotiations with Kurds over their demand for autonomy within Syria's borders. This declaration was merely rhetorical, as it did not provide any clearly defined sense of autonomy as used by officials in Damascus and rather sought a form of understanding with the PYD. The Syrian foreign minister released this statement on the same day of the Kurdish independence referendum in Iraq, which the Syrian regime rejected on the basis of its support for Iraqi unity (Reuters 2017d; Tejel, cited in Souleiman 2017).

In mid-December 2017, Bashar al-Assad characterized the SDF as "traitors," and an "illegitimate foreign force" supported by the United States that must be expelled from Syria. He made similar statements throughout 2018, to which the SDF General Command responded, stating that his dictatorship is "the definition of treason" and the people were rebelling against his "authoritarian oppressive security regime" (Rudaw 2017b). The regime also repeatedly declared that Raqqa, under SDF control after IS expulsion, was still an occupied city, and it promised to restore the authority of the state throughout the country (SANA 2017f).

Despite occasional clashes between 2012 and 2016, both actors maintained a pragmatic nonaggression pact and tactically collaborated on some occasions where there was strategic overlap (geography, particular periods, etc....). Deep strategic disagreements nevertheless existed and would reappear from 2017 onward as IS forces in these areas were progressively eliminated and the regime regained numerous territories throughout the country. In addition, Damascus refused to concede regions rich in natural resources, especially agricultural and energy resources.

The PYD, the opposition, FSA, and Islamic fundamentalist forces

Large segments of the Syrian Arab opposition, in addition to considering the seizure of Kurdish-inhabited areas in July 2012 as, in effect, a gift from Damascus, accused the PYD of acting in dishonest ways by breaking ceasefires, in some cases allegedly at the regime's behest (ICG 2014a: 8). Anti-PYD sentiment among the Syrian Arab opposition increased over time and certainly contributed to violence that ultimately positioned Kurds against the Arab opposition from mid-2012 onward. These clashes were fueled by mistrust, competition for scarce resources (land along the Turkish border, oil and gas in Hasakah), and the growing influence and presence of jihadi groups fighting alongside FSA units.

This also led to the expulsion of the PYD-linked FSA, *Jabhat al-Âkrad* (Kurdish front), from several FSA–Jabhat al-Nusra mixed areas in the summer of 2013. YPG forces and Kurdish civilians suffered serious abuses at the hands of groups such as IS and Jabhat al-Nusra (Human Rights Watch 2014: 15–16). For more than a year, Jabhat al-Nusra, Islamic fundamentalist groups, and FSA-affiliated groups imposed a blockade on isolated Kurdish enclaves in Afrin and Kobani, to pressure the YPG fighters to give up their territory (Van Wilgenburg 2014a). This situation prompted a number of Kurds in Syria to join the YPG. Kurds from Turkey also came to the YPG's assistance by crossing the border into Syria through Qamishli (Itani and Stein 2016: 7).

Clashes between FSA groups and the PYD declined significantly in late 2013; a truce reached in Afrin encouraged mainstream armed opposition groups west of Aleppo city to concentrate their fight against the regime there (ICG 2014a: 8). In March 2014, a new situation emerged, and a rapprochement occurred between the FSA and PYD. They found a common enemy in IS in the countryside of Aleppo. This was a reversal of the situation of summer 2013. PYD leader Salih Muslim was now accusing the regime of supporting jihadist attacks against the Kurds (Van Wilgenburg 2014b). Jabhat al-Akrad again cooperated with the FSA against the IS, carrying out operations in Tal Abbyad, Jarablus, and Aleppo (Van Wilgenburg 2014a).

In September, the threat of a continued IS advance west and north from its stronghold towns of al-Bab, Manbij, and Jarablus encouraged the establishment of an alliance between the YPG, six FSA battalions, and Liwa al-Tawhid (Lister 2015: 285). The siege of the Kurdish-majority city of Kobani provoked the forced displacement of about 200,000 people in the surrounding villages before reaching Kobani. The city was defended by the YPG, as well as at least three battalions of Arab fighters, including the revolutionary battalion of Raqqa, the battalion of "the northern Sun," and the battalion of Jarablus. On October 4, the FSA sent additional fighters to defend Kobani. In a statement on October 19, 2014, the YPG acknowledged their participation in resisting the siege of Kobani by IS:

> The resistance shown by us, the Kurdish People's Protection Units (YPG), and the factions of the Free Syrian Army (FSA) is a guarantee for defeating IS's terrorism in the region. Counterterrorism and building a free and democratic Syria was the basis of the agreement we signed with factions of the FSA. As we can see, the success of the revolution is subject to the development of this relationship between all factions and the forces of good in this country ... We also confirm that there is coordination between us and the important factions of the FSA in the northern countryside of Aleppo, Afrin, Kobani, and Jazirah. Currently, there are factions and several battalions of the FSA fighting on our side against the ISIL terrorists. (General Command of the YPG 2014)

The battle for Kobani exacerbated tensions with the Turkish government, as Ankara prevented people from crossing into Syria to fight with the YPG, although they eventually did allow peshmerga forces from Kurdistan Iraq to do so (Itani and Stein 2016: 7).

Despite other infrequent collaborations, such as in the Operation Room of Fateh Halab and YPG in the northern Aleppo countryside in December 2015 (SOHR 2015b; Enab Baladi 2015), relations deteriorated once again between the various Syrian Arab armed opposition forces and the YPG. The YPG's jurisdiction continued to expand in northern Syria as it increasingly clashed with FSA units and Islamic and Salafist jihadi groups. Additional PKK members, including non-Syrians, descended from the mountains of Qandil to join the struggle. At the same time, for Kurds looking for means to defend their communities, cooperation with the YPG was often the only option. Indeed, as battles expanded with Salafi and jihadist armed groups, the YPG's role as a unique viable protector of Syria's

Kurds was further strengthened (ICG 2014a: 5–7). The YPG expanded its control over Kurdish-populated areas along the border with Turkey and throughout much of Hasakah Province in the northeast.

Several factors increased the hostilities between the YPG and the PYD. There was the PYD's support for Russian military intervention in September 2015 on the side of the Assad regime, as well as the military assistance provided by Russian airplanes to the YPG against Arab armed opposition groups in February 2016 in Afrin's region to seize a number of opposition-held areas and Arab-majority towns in northern Aleppo, including Tal Rifaat. Finally, the collaboration of the YPG with regime forces to impose the siege of Eastern Aleppo city on July 28, 2016, increased the hostilities between both groups. Throughout 2016, opposition forces and YPG forces in Aleppo clashed on a number of occasions, while Sheikh Maqsud was under siege for several months by the opposition armed forces in Aleppo (Shocked 2016).

By the end of November and the beginning of December 2016, during the pro-regime force's offensive on Eastern Aleppo and its eventual capture, YPG forces, which officially characterized these clashes as "fighting between Syrian regime forces and Turkey-backed SNC" (ANHA Hawar News Agency 2016), participated in the battle by taking control of some neighborhoods and handing them over to the regime. In exchange, the YPG was allowed to retain control of Sheikh Maqsud and Ashrafia, which are predominantly Kurdish (Orton 2016; SOHR 2016). However, this would not last, as the regime's forces encircled the neighborhoods. By December 2017, the Syrian flag was raised in these neighborhoods and YPG was forced to accept the partial return of regime forces. In late February 2018, YPG forces completely withdrew from the city of Aleppo to participate in the defense of Afrin (as discussed later in this chapter) (Schmidinger 2018: 258).

Some of the armed opposition (both FSA units and Islamic fundamentalist forces) participated in the offensive against Afrin in January 2018 (see Chapter 7). Under the command of Ankara, they justified their involvement, saying that the Kurds were in fact regime allies and that it was important to keep Syria united against separatist groups such as the PKK/PYD (Rudaw 2018c). Videos of Syrian fighters emerged during this period showing racist and hate-filled rhetoric against the Kurds, as well as slogans in favor of Saddam Hussein and Erdogan (Facebook 2018a, 2018b).

Civilian residences and shops in Afrin were looted and the statue of Kawa, a symbolic figure in the New Year's celebration of Nowruz, was torn down. The mutilated corpses of Kurdish YPG soldiers and civilians were displayed on social media. At the end of 2018, it was estimated that around 151,000 people had been uprooted from their homes in the Afrin region because of the Turkish "Olive Branch" military operation in January 2018 and the subsequent occupation. The majority were displaced to the Tal Refaat, Nubul, Zahra, and Fafin areas of Aleppo governorate (UNHCR 2018). YPG forces decided to withdraw from the city of Afrin in mid-March 2018 to permit civilians to leave the city, while announcing the beginning of their armed resistance all across the province of Afrin (Schmidinger 2018: 260).

Tensions only heightened over time between PYD and the various opposition armed groups, leading to more frequent clashes, as well as deepening ethnic divisions between Arabs and Kurds. The situation further deteriorated in December 2018, when armed opposition groups signaled their readiness to participate in a Turkish-led operation against the regions east of the Euphrates River in Syria controlled by the PYD after Ankara warned Kurdish forces of retaliation (Dadouch 2018). The Syrian coalition also supported this offensive, despite the opposition of the Kurdish members and groups within its governing body.

Rojava self-government

By November 2013, the PYD assumed de facto governing authority, managing a transitional administration in what it—and the Kurds more generally—at the time called *Rojava* (western Kurdistan). Rojava included three noncontiguous enclaves: Afrin, Kobani, and Cezire (Jazirah region in Hasakah Province). The joint-interim administration was composed of local and legislative assemblies and governments, as well as a general assembly including Kurdish, Arab, Syriac, and Assyrian representatives from all three cantons. The stated goal was an autonomous administration within a federated Syria (ICG 2014a: 15). At the end of September 2017, at the seventh Congress of the PYD, participants confirmed federalism as the most appropriate solution for the region (Arafat 2017b).

The implementation of the Rojava project was characterized as a form of "democratic autonomy" or "self-administration," whose military and police forces would guarantee security, manage tribunals and prisons, and provide humanitarian assistance. The PYD advocated self-governance at the local level, unified more by a common vision of societal reform than by the rule of a centralized government (ICG 2014a: 2, 12).

However, despite the public emphasis on pluralism, PYD also dominated politically local institutions. As described by the ICG (2014a: 13):

> Members and leaders of the people's councils, theoretically responsible for local governance and including representatives of all Kurdish political parties as well as non-Kurdish populations in mixed areas,

are appointed by the PYD. Likewise, the movement maintains overall decision-making authority, consigning the councils other than for distribution of gas and humanitarian aid to a largely symbolic role...

The commune's institution was also one of the key elements in the new Rojava system to enforce the rule of PYD-linked organizations. Organizations and NGOs outside PYD's framework had to go through the commune system (or other Rojava institutions) to be allowed to operate in these regions (al-Darwish D. 2016: 18).

The PYD implemented similar policies in the expansion and institutionalization of its military forces. Recruitment campaigns were opened to individuals of various backgrounds, while ensuring that they remained under the PYD's command. The YPG opened military academies that provided recruits with three months of training, both tactical and ideological. The YPG also tried to integrate non-Kurds (e.g., Arabs, Syriacs, and Assyrians) within its ranks and under its leadership. It eventually agreed to incorporate non-Kurdish fighters into Rojava's security system as independent brigades capable of maintaining and directing their own leadership while acting under YPG command (ICG 2014a: 14).

Rojava's administrations also established People's Tribunals, which lacked trained prosecutors and judges, as almost no Kurds had been accepted into these professions in the Syrian Ba'th system. The tribunals were established in conjunction with a police force, the Asayish, that worked to implement law and order (Human Rights Watch 2014: 14). The tribunals, consisting of PYD-appointed personnel, administered justice across Rojava under a hybrid penal code. Both tribunals and police forces were heavily criticized by rival Kurdish factions, activists, and human rights organizations for their numerous violations of human rights (ICG 2014a: 14).

In March 2014, the Social Contract of Rojava was published and intended to act as a provisional constitutional charter for the region. The Social Contract charter devoted Articles 8 to 53 to basic principles of rights, representation, and personal freedoms matching the provisions of the Universal Declaration of Human Rights. In addition, the PYD promoted a progressive standard for gender equality in its governance structures, with gender parity in all administrations and the establishment of a ministry for "Women's Liberation"—a standard that has been largely adhered to, including within the military (Sary 2015: 11–12; Perry 2016). Article 28 stated clearly that "women have the right to organize and to remove all kinds of discrimination based on sex" (cited in Sheikho 2017).

The charter emphasized the cultural and ethnic equality of the various populations in Rojava. It also pointed out that decentralization was a response to the multitude of religious, ethnic, and regional conflicts in Syria, as well as to the dictatorship, while emphasizing the full integrity of Syrian territory within a federal system (Sary 2015: 11–12; Perry 2016). The diversity of the population living in PYD-controlled areas demonstrated this inclusiveness. This did not prevent tensions between PYD administrations and other communities, including Arab Sunni populations (as discussed later in this chapter). Christian representatives and churches also protested several decisions by the PYD administrations on various occasions when they felt that their interests were being endangered.

In September 2015, 16 Armenian, Assyrian, and Christian organizations published a statement opposing the bill of the Legislative Council of the Jazirah region, an institution established by the PYD to legislate in one of the three districts under its control. These organizations confiscated the property of residents who left the region officially to "protect" these assets from seizure by third parties and to use them to the benefit of the community. Within a few weeks, the PYD was forced to backtrack, and assets owned by Christians were handed over to various churches (Ulloa 2017; Yazigi 2017: 10). In the same statement, the organizations also argued "any interference into the church's private schools in Jazirah province is unacceptable" (cited in Ulloa 2017: 10). In August 2018, the authorities of the self-administration announced a decision to shut down more than a dozen private schools managed by the Assyrian church and other Christian denominations across Syria's northeast that had yet to adopt the Kurdish-led authority's newly established curriculum. The decision was finally canceled following significant opposition and demonstrations (Edwards and Hamou 2018).

Intimidation and violence against Christian and Assyrian opposition personalities similarly occurred at the hands of YPG forces, including the assassination of David Jendo, an Assyrian leader in the Khabour region in April 2015 (Ulloa 2017: 11). However, these figures were targeted because of their political opinions, not their ethnic or sectarian origins.

YPG forces had been accused on several occasions of discriminatory and repressive policies against Arab populations in some villages in northeast Syria, a point that YPG refuted by claiming that some residents had links with IS (Nassar and Wilcox 2016). Military offensives led by YPG forces on several occasions resulted in the forced displacement of populations. For example, the capture of the city of Tal Rifaat from Arab opposition groups by SDF forces, with the help of Russian air power in February 2016, led to the displacement of the local Arab population (around 30,000 persons), who fled to the Turkish border (al-Homsi 2017). However, a UN Independent International Commission of Inquiry on Syria in March 2017 found no evidence to substantiate accusations by some Syrian Arab opposition actors and AK Parti (AKP) members in Turkey that YPG or SDF forces systematically sought to change the demographic composition of territories under their control (Rudaw 2017a).

The PYD's effectiveness in the provision of social services was also a critical factor in building local legitimacy. The PYD local administrations, called the Democratic Autonomous Administration (DAA), were able to provide services including fuel, education, jobs, electricity, water, sanitation, customs, healthcare, education, and security. The DAA was quite successful in meeting local needs and making up for shortages in key items like gas cylinders and food that were unavailable in the market. In providing these goods, PYD was able to create a dependency upon the local population and strengthen its position among the population within their jurisdiction (Khalaf 2016: 17–20).

New institutions were also created to license business investments, schools, and media outlets. The PYD also established new educational structures, like that of the Mesopotamian Social Sciences Academy. The region's first university was established in October 2015 in the Afrin District, with 180 students (Yazigi 2016c: 5; Khalaf 2016: 17). In the summer of 2016, the University of Rojava in Qamishli was inaugurated. Classes were to be taught in Arabic, Kurdish, and English and include a faculty of medicine, a college of education and science, and a college of engineering (Abdulhalim, Mohammed, and Van Wilgenburg 2016). In the schooling system, an entirely Kurdish school curriculum for the first three years of schooling was introduced in September 2015 in Qamishli and extended progressively to other areas, while the old Ba'thist curriculum had been replaced. The overwhelming majority of the schools in Syria's northeastern Hasakah Governorate were controlled by the PYD-led administration. The exceptions were a handful of schools inside regime-held areas and a number of private Christian schools in Hasakah and Qamishli (Shiwesh 2016). According to journalist Mahir Yilmazkaya (2016), who sympathized with the PYD, the Kurdish Language Institution went from one teacher and twelve students in 2012 to 1,700 teachers and 20,000 students in 200 schools in May 2016.

The DAA's administration also promoted women's rights and participation at all levels—an accomplishment even its critics acknowledged, albeit with contradictions. Civil activist Mahwash Sheiki (2017) from Qamishli, one of the founders of the women's association Komela Şawîşka, acknowledged that improvements had been made in the area of women's rights, despite characterizing the PYD as a "totalitarian ideological party that doesn't accept others with different ideologies":

In theory and according to the laws and general principles issued by the DAA, the accomplishments are great. As women civil activists, perhaps we used to call for these rights without having much hope of seeing them recognized ... what the DAA has approved matches laws passed in First World countries relating to women's rights...

Yet the most important principle the DAA has stuck to was the principle of equal participation in all institutions. This has been followed to the letter, as it is also part and parcel of the structure of the PYD...

The PYD has been able to [mobilize] and include marginalized groups in the area, including women as they were thrust into the military and political life. This change was not natural but forced, and it was not accompanied by the development of women as independent entities with their own needs, rights or obligations. Also, the change did not come about due to a change in the socioeconomic system. In fact, it was the result of a top-down party decision to bring women in large numbers into the fold of the ideology. This has been greatly successful...

In this perspective, she went on explaining that women's rights and participation in Rojava was unique and distinct from other regions across Syria, whether under the regime or the "liberated" areas controlled by opposition forces. With regard to laws tied to women's rights and empowering women militarily and politically, she argued that "this doesn't mean women are fully empowered because empowerment to people and individuals also means economic and social empowerment as well as spreading democracy" (Sheiki 2017).

This testimony could be extended to other areas of the PYD's interventions in the three cantons of Rojava. These interventions were characterized by dynamics from above rather than radical change and participation from below, although there was not always complete separation between the two. As argued by activist Shiyar Youssef (2016) regarding the PYD's rule over these areas:

On one hand, it seems that the experience has begun to achieve commendable gains, such as secular management of the state apparatus, ensuring greater rights for women and the participation of minorities in administration, a greater participation and more agency for the local population in the management of their affairs, especially with the absence of a strong, established state. And we should remember here that the PYD is learning from a rich experience of self-governance that their comrades in Turkish Kurdistan have been living through. On the other hand, however, the experiment may well end with the strengthening of the PYD's dominance and the increase of oppression in the name of protecting these gains, along with their gradual squandering in return for narrow political interests. This is a real and possible danger.

Thomas Schmindiger (2018: 135), specialist on the Kurdish issue and author of the book *Rojava: Revolution, War, and the Future of Syria's Kurds*, similarly stated that his field research led to this intermediate situation, in which "the headquarters of the PKK in Qandil has the final say in decisive questions," while adding that "the council system does play an important role in the small daily administrative decisions and the supply of population."

However, some actors did not recognize PYD's administrative bodies or viewed them with suspicion. A majority of KNC parties condemned these institutions as PYD-dominated, comprised of an assortment of Kurdish, Arab, Syriac, and Assyrian personalities who had little to lose from engaging in the project (ICG 2014a: 15).

These new institutions lacked legitimacy in the eyes of significant segments of Syrian Arabs living within their jurisdiction. For instance, Sheikh Humaydi Daham al-Hadi al-Jarba, the head of the Arab tribe al-Shammar, was nominated as co-governor of Jazirah Canton in Rojava in 2014. His son became the commander of the al-Sanadid forces, one of the main Arab militias fighting alongside YPG forces. The al-Sanadid forces were previously known as Jaysh al-Karama and were accused of expelling and arresting people for supporting the revolution (Orient News 2015). As early as 2013, Daham al-Hadi al-Jarba had made an alliance with the YPG to keep the opposition and jihadi-Salafist organizations out of the Shammar areas on the Iraq-Syria border (Orton 2017). The al-Shammar tribe of Humaydi Daham al-Hadi al-Jarba in the Hasakah Province maintained good relations with the Kurdish population in the Jazirah, as it was one of the few tribes that refused to participate in the repression alongside the regime's security forces during the Kurdish uprising in March 2004. Daham also had good relations with the Kurdish leader Masoud Barzani before his nomination as president of the Iraqi Kurdistan region in 2005 (Van Wilgenburg 2014c). He resided in Erbil from 2003 and returned to Syria in 2009 (Orton 2017). His collaboration with the PYD allowed him to maintain control over oil resources following the withdrawal of the regime's forces and local security agencies (Khaddour 2017b).

However, Daham al-Hadi al-Jarba's role was largely symbolic, meant to showcase the inclusion of different ethnicities. Real power remained in the hands of the PYD. Even Ciwan Ibrahim, the general head of the Kurdish security police in northern Syria, argued that only a few Arabs support this tribe (al-Shammar) (cited in Van Wilgenburg 2014c).[13] Politically, they had little if any common ground, as demonstrated by the response of Hadiya Yousef, copresident of Jazirah Canton, regarding the political views of Daham al-Hadi al-Jarba. "Hadi is certainly not a feminist ... but he supports us" (cited in Enzinna 2015). In a question regarding his collaboration with Yusuf, Daham al-Hadi al-Jarba answered, "I didn't ask to share power with a woman ... They [the PYD] made me do it" (cited in Enzinna 2015).

Similarly, following the conquest by SDF of Manbij in August 2016 and Raqqa in October 2017, both cities occupied by IS, the PYD-appointed new local councils, which represented the ethnic and religious diversities of the city, had a gender quota (Ayboga 2017), in which some of the tribal dignitaries of the city were represented. The Raqqa civil council was led by a dual leadership: Leila Mustafa, a Kurdish woman from the border town of Tal Abbyad, and her male Arab counterpart Mahmoud al-Borsan, a former member of the Syrian parliament and leader of the influential Walda tribe in Raqqa (al-Hayat 2017; Lund 2017e). They delegated 20 of the seats in the council to representatives of local Arab tribes as well (al-Maleh and Nassar 2018). In Manbij, the main Arab representative on the council was Faruq al-Mashi, Muhammad al-Mashi's cousin, an MP in the Syrian parliament. The al-Mashi family, who collaborated with PYD prior to the SDF's recapture of Manbij and returned to the area after they took control, were accused of having violently attacked demonstrators at the beginning of the uprising in 2011 in their role as Shabiha in the city (Khalaf 2016: 20). For his part, Faruq al-Mashi denied in an interview any support for the regime, declaring:

> ...together with my tribe positioned myself against the regime, but rejected armed aggression. But many were in favour of them and the Arabs were of divided opinions. Hardly anyone was on the side of the regime ... (cited in Ayboga 2017)

However, in both cases, PYD was the dominant actor. Symbolic of the situation, huge portraits of PKK founder Abdullah Öcalan were displayed in Raqqa's central square, Naeem. Meanwhile, SDF commanders dedicated the victory to Öcalan and the Women's Coalition (Reuters 2017f), following

---

[13] The Shammar is nowadays a relatively small tribe in Syria (its main branches are in Iraq and the Arabian Peninsula), but it has historically been prestigious and powerful, and before the establishment of the modern Syrian state, it exerted effective control over the northeast of what today is Syria (Khaddour 2017b).

the conquest of the city in mid- to late October 2017 and the expulsion of IS by SDF forces supported by U.S. air strikes.[14]

Under this arrangement, the prominence of tribal leaders in the Rojava institutions was generally preserved rather than challenged. Researcher Khedder Khaddour (2017c) explained that the YPG:

> relied on local tribal networks to manage the populations under their control, but leaders of tribal communities frequently have used these armed groups to pursue their own material interests and position themselves advantageously with respect to other tribal actors ... the efforts of the PYD to deal separately with each Arab tribe—and the similarity of this strategy to that adopted by the Islamic State—reflect a legacy of Syrian state policies that aimed to create divisions between the tribes and even among their members. It displays a concern for the threat, however remote, that a unified Arab tribal population might pose to outside actors.

As argued by researcher Haian Dukhan (cited in al-Maleh and Nassar 2018), "allegiance of the tribes to different parties historically has been determined by pragmatist patronage relations—access to land on which livestock can graze, representation in local governance institutions, as well as employment opportunities." The SDF has indeed not been the only actor trying to mobilize Raqqa's tribes according to their own interests.

However, despite the nomination of Daham as cogovernor of Jazirah Canton and other tribal leaders in civil councils, many heads of local Arabs tribes remained fearful of the designs of the PYD and were drawn to Operation Euphrates Shield, a Turkish military initiative coordinated between FSA and Islamic groups to prevent SDF and Kurdish forces from expanding west of the Euphrates River or remaining close to the regime. It was also not uncommon throughout the uprising to see tribal leaders change their loyalties and pledge allegiance according to the shifting balance of power and current dominating actors. SDF has faced dissent on various occasions from local tribes in regions under its authority (al-Maleh and Nassar 2018).

In addition, scholar Kheder Khaddour explained that the PYD had faced difficulties in coopting educated urban elites who operated in autonomy

---

[14] However, the cost in terms of human lives and infrastructures was terrible. Overall, at least 1,800 civilians were killed in the fighting, while more than 80 percent of the city was uninhabitable or completely destroyed (Oakford 2017). Around 312,000 people had fled Raqqa Province as a whole as a result of the military offensive (Lund 2017e).

from the original tribes to which they belonged, even in cities like Qamishli that had been under its control since the summer of 2012 (Lund 2017e).

At the same time, the decentralized decision-making process promoted by the Rojava administration was far from a resounding success, as Asayish and other security forces generally bypassed other organizational structures, citing security reasons. This led to delays in project implementation and negatively affected economic growth (Sary 2016: 14). The revenues of the PYD-administered areas depended mostly on oil and gas production to cover their expenses. According to a report issued by Jihad Yazigi (2015), oil revenues were reaching USD 10 million per month. The other sources of income were the provision of services (i.e., from its water and electricity operations and food and other products sold). The DAA also increased taxes from sources such as construction permits, land, business revenue, cars, agricultural income, border trade, and even passage of people to and from Rojava. Furthermore, the DAA continued to receive financial support from diaspora networks and support groups (Khalaf 2016: 18).

However, in 2016, the PYD local administration still lacked control over large sectors of the economy that were once heavily managed by the Syrian regime. The provision of wheat remained closely monitored by the administration, but merchants and importers, as well as those benefiting from the war economy and monopoly of goods, became the decisive power in the market (Sary 2016: 13). The PYD self-administrative regions, despite calling for social justice and establishment of agricultural cooperatives, did not witness any significant change. Private property was officially enshrined in the charter, a provision that safeguarded the privileges of landowners while encouraging them to invest in agricultural projects sponsored by the Rojava authorities (Glioti 2016). There was also an integration of some of the old elites and businessmen in new institutions established by the PYD, including Akram Kamal Hasu, one of the wealthiest entrepreneurs in these regions who went on to become the prime minister of the canton of Jazirah as an independent (Schmindiger 2018: 129).

Announcement of the federal system

On March 17, 2016, the Federal Democratic System of Rojava, in areas of northern Syria controlled by the PYD, was officially established following a meeting of more than 150 representatives of Kurdish, Arab, and Assyrian parties in the city of Rmeilan in northeastern Syria. Participants voted in favor of the union of three cantons (Afrin, Kobani, and Jazira). During the Rmeilan meeting, a constituent assembly of 31 members was elected, with two copresidents: Hadiya Yousef, a Kurd who was jailed for two years prior

THE KURDISH QUESTION IN SYRIA / 179

to the uprising, and Mansour Salloum, a Syrian Arab (Said 2016; Kurdish Question 2016).

The Assad regime and the Coalition both stated their opposition to this announcement, while Washington (despite its support for the PYD), Turkey, and the Arab League declared that they would not recognize this newly declared federal entity (Said R. 2016; Sly 2016). A total of 69 armed opposition groups, including Jaysh al-Islam and various FSA forces, also signed a statement opposing the Kurdish federalist project (DW 2016). The majority of the Syrian Arab forces opposed to the Assad regime saw federalism as a step toward separatism and division (al-Souria Net 2016a; Syria Freedom Forever 2016).

In reaction to this announcement, opposition member Michel Kilo declared that Syrians will not allow the establishment of an entity similar to Israel on Syrian soil and that there is no Kurdish land in Syria, only Kurdish citizens (ADN Kronos International 2016). Kilo's statement was reminiscent of the discourse of the 1960s, which compared Kurds to Israel, as mentioned previously in this chapter.

Although a federal system in Syria remained a demand of the majority of Kurdish parties in the country, the KNC opposed this position, arguing that such a system had to be established following discussions with and explanations for the actors behind the Syrian Arab opposition. Similarly, many Kurdish activists criticized the process, describing it as a decision primarily taken by the PYD, with no democratic character or consultation taken with other Kurdish parties and activists (Youssef 2016).

Even Riza Altun, considered the PKK's foreign minister, was critical:

We [the PKK] also criticized them for announcing it prior to the completion of a proper groundwork for its announcement, which gave the impression that it was being imposed as a fait accompli, and that is harmful. The plan should have been explained prior to the announcement being made. We prefer the use of North Syria Federation and call for the removal of Rojava from the name because Rojava denotes a federation of Kurdish identity. North Syria is home to all of its constituents, and the freedom of Kurds there is contingent upon the degree of liberty enjoyed by other inhabitants of the region ... (cited in Noureddine 2016)

In December 2016, the federal system switched its name to the Democratic Federal System of Northern Syria. The removal of the word *Rojava* sparked a wave of anger among various Kurdish groups within the country and in the diaspora.

In July 2017, the PYD-led self-administrative unit announced the organization of elections in the three federally administrative provinces (al-Jazirah,[15] al-Furat,[16] and Afrin)[17] divided into three rounds (Arafat 2017a). The first round of voting was held on September 22, for the leaders of all local communes (around 3,700). The second round, in December, was for representatives to the town, city, and regional councils. The third and final round was to be held in January 2018, but it was postponed and still has not occurred.

On December 5, 2017, the High Electoral Commission of the self-administrative units announced during a press conference in Amuda that turnout for the second phase of local council elections had reached 69 percent. The elections included 21 parties that represented Kurds, Arabs, Christians, and Assyrians from Rojava, with more than 12,000 candidates. The Democratic Nation Solidarity List, which was led by the ruling PYD and accompanied by its allies, won large majorities of seats—more than 4,600 out of 5,600—in all three regions that went to the polls in December. The Kurdish National Alliance in Syria (Hevbendi), which included the Yekiti and former members of the KNC, participated in the elections and won 152 seats. A third list, the Syrian National Alliance List, had eight seats and won a number of formal independent seats as well (Drwish 2017b; Schmidinger 2018: 133).

However, some criticism was raised by Kurdish opposition parties about the lack of free participation in the process. The KNC announced that it was boycotting the elections, describing them as illegitimate. Some Arab opposition members linked to the opposition in exile also boycotted the process. Another problem occurred with the population called al-Ghamar Arabs (meaning "The Arabs of the floods" in Arabic), who were relocated from Raqqa Province to Hasakah Province in advance of the creation of the Euphrates Dam in the 1970s and were barred from the third round of voting. Fouzah Youssef, copresident of the Democratic Federation of northern Syria's Executive Committee, characterized the arrival of the al-Ghamar Arabs to Hasakah Province in the 1970s as "a racist and unfair policy against the Kurds" (cited in Abdulssatar Ibrahim and Schuster 2017).

[15] Jazirah included Hasakah and Qamishli cantons. Hasakah Canton comprises the towns of Hasakah, Darbasiya, Serekaniye (Ras al-Ayn), Tel Tamir, Shadi, Arisha, and Hula. Qamishli Canton comprises the towns of Qamishli, Derik, Amuda, Tirbesiye, Tel Hamis, and Tel Barak.
[16] Al-Furat included Kobani Canton and its towns (Kobani and Sirrin), and Tal Abbyad Canton and its towns (Ain Issa and Suluk).
[17] Afrin includes Afrin Canton and its towns (Afrin, Jandairis, and Raqqa), and Sheba Canton and its towns (Tal Rifaat, Ehraz, Fafeyn, and Kafr Naya).

To consolidate its power, the PYD did not hesitate to practice repressive campaigns and measures against outspoken or oppositional individuals and political parties within its own areas, while YPG forces targeted some independent local media, such as Radio Arta on at least two occasions (2014 and 2016) (Human Rights Watch 2014: 1–2). The KNC's president, Ibrahim Berro, was arrested in August 2016 at an Asayish checkpoint in Qamishli and exiled to Iraqi Kurdistan the day after (Sary 2016: 13). In fact, there have been occasional protests against the PYD and their practices in Rojava.

Furthermore, since October 2014, mandatory conscription was decreed for citizens between 18 and 30 years old to enlist in the Defence Service and join the YPG for six months in areas under its control. The KNC rejected the conscription law and promoted a voluntary appeal instead, arguing that a draft would lead to a mass youth migration out of Kurdistan (Yekiti Media 2014), while a number of Syriac Christian, Arab, and Kurdish political parties, as well as civil society and human rights organizations, also opposed this law. This decision had caused the departure of sectors of youth from all communities to escape imprisonment for refusal to serve (Syria Direct 2014; Ahmad and Edelman 2017). Similarly, in some Arab-majority territories under Kurdish control, mandatory conscription was often refused, especially as infighting between PYD and FSA forces increased. In November 2017, for example, residents and activists in the city of Manbij in Aleppo's eastern countryside organized a strike in protest of a new forced conscription issued by the SDF's legislative council. The SDF issued a statement the day after the strike, on November 6, suspending the decision to impose compulsory conscription on the inhabitants of Manbij and called instead on the residents to voluntarily join "the self-defense army" (Osman 2017).

Some autonomous actors in the Kurdish political and social scene from the PYD were still trying to make their voices heard. An independent media scene was trying to develop in PYD-controlled areas, despite facing tough competition from better-resourced and more numerous party-affiliated media outlets (such as Ronahi TV, Orkes FM, and Hawar News Agency) (Issa 2016: 13).

As we have seen, the DAA was led more by a dynamic from above and controlled by the PYD in an authoritarian way. The many portraits of the Kurdish PKK leader Abdullah Öcalan that covered the walls of PYD government offices were a testament to this reality. However, other significant changes were taking place, particularly regarding the rise of women's participation in society, as well as the codification of secular laws and greater inclusion of religious and ethnic minorities. The authorities and services provided by the PYD also benefited from having significant support and sympathy among wide sectors of the local population.

The PYD and international arena: from collaboration to threats

The PYD's lack of international legitimacy—a by-product of its association with the PKK, characterized as a terrorist organization by the United States and most European states—has always been its Achilles' heel since the beginning of the uprising, preventing its participation in the Geneva conferences. Moreover, the KNC's participation in the Coalition and opposition bodies isolated the PYD and challenged its overall aspirations (ICG 2014a: 21–22).

In mid-2015, things started to change, and closer relations and collaborations, although limited mostly to the military field, began to appear with some international actors. In the framework of its broader strategy of "IS first" and the complete failure to assist FSA forces in combating IS, Washington, on the initiative of the Pentagon, increasingly supported the PYD and the YPG-led coalition known as the SDF, established in October 2015 officially as a response to fight the "terrorism represented by the IS, its sister [organizations], and the criminal Ba'th regime" according to its statement (Jaysh al-Thûwar 2015). This new group was dominated by YPG, while other groups [i.e., Syriac and FSA groups like the army of revolutionaries Jaysh al-Thûwar (Mustapha 2015)] within it played an auxiliary role. The SDF was in fact established to provide a legal and political cover for American military support for the PKK-affiliated group PYD in Syria (Lund 2015d). The SDF became Pentagon's premier partner force against the IS in Syria from this point onward.

At the same time, the domination of YPG Kurdish commanders on the rest of the armed units at some occasions in the following years did pose significant issues, notably with SDF Arab units feeling marginalized in the decision-making process, a dynamic that led to the eventual resignation of some of these personalities and units. For example, in June 2018, it clashed with formerly allied Arab rebel faction Liwa Thuwwar a-Raqqa, resulting in the arrest of some 200 fighters from the faction (al-Maleh and Nassar 2018).

In December 2015, the Syrian Democratic Council (SDC) was formed as the political branch of the SDF. The new coalition, also led by the PYD, was copresided by Riad Darar, an Arab political opponent of the Assad regime,[18] and Ilham Ahmed, a member of TEV-DEM. The SDC was

[18] He was a political activist from 2000 onward, working with civil society groups. He was imprisoned by Assad's regime for five years (2005–10) for his political views and accused of supporting the Kurdish cause. He was a founding member of the NCCDC, from which he later resigned in August 2014 (Drwish 2017a).

mainly comprised of Arab, Kurdish, and Assyrian political forces, along with others from the Kurdish-inhabited region in northern Syria. The SDC supported a federal, democratic, and secular state, but it remained relatively weak politically (Drwish 2017a).

Despite the military support provided by Russia and the United States since mid-2015, the PYD was submitted to increasing pressure. Moscow expressed the necessity for YPG Kurdish forces to collaborate directly and in a more systematic way with regime forces against IS (Rudaw 2015). In August 2016, the Turkish army intervened directly in Syria in coalition with Syrian armed opposition forces acting as proxies for Ankara, in a military campaign called Operation Euphrates Shield, with the support of various international actors, including the United States and Russia (see Chapters 4 and 6). Deputy Prime Minister Nurettin Canikli even acknowledged in the beginning of December 2016 that Turkey "would not have moved so comfortably" without the rapprochement with Russia, which effectively controlled parts of northern Syrian airspace (Osborn and Tattersall 2016).

Similarly, interactions between U.S. officials and YPG commanders remained largely informal and limited to the fight against IS. The United States maintained the PKK on its terrorist list throughout these years and voiced strong support for Turkey's fight against the Kurdish group. They also avoided providing economic support to YPG-PYD-controlled areas, which would further upset Turkey (ICG 2017: 14). On several occasions, Washington even pledged to take back weapons supplied to YPG after the defeat of IS, but failed to take any measures toward this end (Reuters 2017c). As expressed by PKK leader Riza Altun in 2016, regarding the U.S. behavior toward the Kurdish issue in Syria, "the US' role is double-edged depending on its interests, and the relationship with Washington is therefore tactical in nature" (cited in Noureddine 2016).

PYD faced contradictory interests from Russia and the United States. Both actors supported the armed branch of the party, YPG, as a proxy force to achieve their respective political interests (Barrington and Said 2016). At the same time, neither power was prepared to jeopardize its relationship with Turkey. The rapprochement at the end of 2016 among Iran, Turkey, and Russia threatened its interests even more. Russia was unable or unwilling to override a Turkish veto of PYD participation in January 2017 peace talks in Kazakhstan (Stewart 2017).

Russia was trying to regulate relations between the PYD's forces and the Assad regime in 2016 and 2017 (Yalla Souriya 2016; Haid 2017a). Russian military officials hosted a meeting at the end of 2016 in their air base at Hmeimim with various representatives of the Kurdish movements, including both the Tev-DEM and the KNC, to mediate future relations between themselves and the Assad regime. The regime's authorities submitted a list of conditions that would regulate relations between Damascus and the Kurdish enclave, which the regime refused to recognize. Notably, the regime extended its support for the Kurds in the country on the condition that they abandon their demand for a federal system and hoist the Syrian flag on all government buildings and offices (Rudaw 2016). These demands, perhaps unsurprisingly, remained unheeded. The Turkish military offensive, assisted by Syrian armed opposition forces and the support of the Syrian Coalition (2018) on Afrin in January 2018, demonstrated the growing threats on the territories ruled by the PYD and on Kurdish populations more broadly.

The intervention occurred with the relative acquiescence and passivity of the main powers involved in Syria. Moscow, which controlled large parts of Syrian airspace, gave Turkey the green light for the invasion and withdrew its armed forces[19] from the areas targeted by Turkish forces in the cities of Nubl and Zahra, both of which were under regime control. Russian officials had demanded that the YPG hand over Afrin to the Syrian regime to stop the Turkish attacks on the region (Asharq al-Awsat 2018; Shekhani 2018). Damascus and the PYD did reach an agreement in mid-February that would allow regime-aligned militia forces to enter the city, but the Kurdish group refused to cede total control of Afrin to the regime or to hand over heavy weaponry. The deal only signified that pro-regime militias would join YPG fighters in manning their checkpoints. This was not satisfactory to Moscow or Ankara. Russia also saw the operation as a way to deepen the wedge and contradictions between Ankara and Washington in light of the latter's support for the YPG. For its part, the United States remained rather passive, stating that it understood the security concerns of Ankara that gave advance warning of their operation (Gall, Landler, and Schmitt 2018; Rudaw 2018a).

The YPG condemned Russia and Turkey directly for the occupation and blamed the international community for its silence on the dire situation facing the city. They also promised that "the resistance in Afrin will continue until every inch of Afrin is liberated, and the people of Afrin will return" (cited in ANF News 2018). Erdogan, for his part, reiterated that Turkish forces would press their offensive against Kurdish YPG fighters along the length of Turkey's border with Syria, and if necessary, into northern Iraq (Caliskan and Toksabay 2018).

---

[19] In September 2017, Russia had deployed military forces to operate as a military police to prevent new clashes and possible conflicts between the Syrian opposition armed units, backed by Turkey, and the Turkish army on one side, and on the other side the SDF. Therefore, they were sent to enforce a new buffer zone in the Tal Rifaat area (Iddon 2017).

Following the conquest of Afrin, the two main Syrian Kurdish political actors, PYD and KNC, boycotted the Sochi conference in Russia, called the Syrian National Dialogue Congress, to advance peace negotiations in Syria held at the end of January 2018. The Sochi meeting was rendered meaningless after Russia failed to oppose Turkey's military offensive in Afrin, and indeed collaborated with Ankara. The KNC decided not to participate after Moscow refused to accept its demand of including the Kurdish cause in Syria as one of the key agendas of the congress, and furthermore after Moscow's cooperation with the Turkish offensive against Afrin (Rudaw 2018b).

In June 2018, Washington and Ankara agreed on a plan for the withdrawal of YPG Kurdish fighters from the northern Syrian city of Manbij, to be replaced by American and Turkish troops. Turkish and U.S. forces have been conducting joint patrols near Manbij from November 2018. PYD officials were increasingly critical of Washington because of this agreement and the U.S. acceptance of the Turkish occupation of Afrin. In addition, U.S. president Donald Trump has announced on different occasions his willingness to withdraw U.S. forces from Syria once IS was defeated, though without setting a specific date and often providing confusing or contradictory messages on the issue (see Chapter 6) (Abdulssattar Ibrahim and al-Maleh 2018). This worried PYD leadership, who were concerned about the social and political future of territories under its control.

Faced with regional and international pressures on the one hand and by the regime's increasing willingness to reconquer all of Syria on the other, PYD officials increasingly sought a form of reconciliation with Damascus to maintain its institutions and preserve its organizational structure within the country. As argued for example by Aldar Khalil, cochair of the TevDEM, linked to the PYD, "Conditions have changed. It's time to find a solution with Damascus." Having seen the situation change in favor of the regime, some PYD officials had already declared their readiness to dialogue with the regime by the end of 2017 (Zaman 2017). At the same time, at different occasions in 2018, Damascus allowed the PYD to organize demonstrations relating to the party and showing solidarity with Öcalan in areas controlled by the regime, such as in the Kurdish neighborhoods of Sheikh Maqsoud in Aleppo (November) and Zor Afar in Damascus (January) (Enab Baladi 2018q).

In this context, alongside increasing pressure from abroad, especially Turkey, the SDC publicly acknowledged for the first time that it had entered into talks with the Syrian regime for a road map leading to a democratic and decentralized Syria. However, as SDF officials themselves recognized, major challenges stand in the way of future talks—notably the continuous absence of recognition of Kurdish rights and a federal political system

(Abdulssattar Ibrahim and al-Maleh 2018). At this time, despite continuing talks, regime officials did not accept any of the conditions of the PYD, while states' officials and medias continued to attack the Kurdish Party. In January 2019, the PYD was seeking Russian mediation for talks with Damascus following Trump's announcement of the U.S. coalition's pullout of Syria in order to prevent any invasion of Turkish forces against the regions they controlled (see Chapter 6). Russia had declared on numerous occasions that the Syrian regime must take control of the country's northern provinces, notably to regain control of Syria's oil reserves.

Conclusion

The eruption of the popular uprising in Syria allowed the emergence of the Kurdish national question in ways unseen previously in the history of the country. Kurdish independent youth groups and networks initially played an important role in the protest movement, but they were weakened considerably over the years.

The PYD took the uprising as an opportunity to become the dominant Kurdish political actor in Syria. PYD-governed areas were hailed for their inclusion and participation of women in all sectors of society, including the military struggle, the secularization of laws and institutions, and to some extent, the integration and participation of various ethnic and religious minorities. However, the authoritarian practices of PYD forces against rival Kurdish political actors and activists from other communities were criticized.

The increasing insularity of the Kurdish popular movement within the protest movement was the result of two elements. First, the PYD pursued a policy of strengthening its political influence through its own armed forces to control Kurdish-majority areas and enforce a form of Kurdish autonomy that would link the Rojava cantons geographically. This was done by maintaining a nonconfrontational attitude toward the regime, which was busy fighting on other fronts. The regime saw the expanding influence of the PYD as a tool to pressure Turkey.

The other element explaining the increasing isolation of the Kurdish issue from the uprising was the belligerent political positions of the Syrian Arab opposition in exile, represented first by the SNC and then by the Coalition, dominated in both cases by the MB and forces allied or sympathetic to Turkey's AKP government. Within the country, the great majority of Arab armed opposition groups were against the political demands of the Kurdish people in Syria and their political representative. They also supported military offensives from Turkey and/or opposition armed groups against YPG and targeting Kurdish civilians. This was accompanied by

Arab chauvinistic statements against the Kurds. More broadly, the SNC and the Coalition failed to propose an inclusive program that could appeal to the Kurds, resulting in deepening ethnic tensions between Arabs and Kurds. This situation increasingly pushed young Kurds in the arms of the PYD, seen as the sole defender of the Kurdish population in Syria.

From the middle of 2016, the Rojava cantons were more and more under the threat of political changes on the international and regional scene. The successive victories of pro-regime forces from 2016 in the northern regions also complicated the situation for PYD, while threats mounted against it. In December 2018, for example, YPG forces announced their withdrawal from Manbij and allowed Syrian regime forces to assert control over the areas of the city formerly controlled by Kurdish forces (YPG 2018) after Turkish threats to launch an offensive against PYD-controlled areas east of the Euphrates River. This followed Trump's initial announcement to withdraw 2,000 U.S. troops from Syria, although without providing any timeline and subsequently modifying his plans (see Chapter 6). The SAA did not enter the city, but it was present in its outskirts, while the city was still controlled by U.S.- and SDF-allied forces. The Russian military police also began patrolling around the city. At the same time, as the regime was consolidating its power in the country and threats were mounting against the PYD-controlled regions, some former partners of SDF were increasingly seeking a form of reconciliation with Damascus. In February 2019, Sheikh Hamidi Daham al-Hadi Jarba, cogovernor of Jazirah Canton, traveled from Qamishli Airport to the Russian Hmeimim military base in Latakia Province to reconcile with the Assad regime and negotiate the integration of its militia with the SAA (Jesr Press 2019).

Just as the rise of the uprising in Syria had pushed the regime to seek occasional and temporal agreements with the PYD, this threat was increasingly disappearing as its position strengthened and it recovered new territories with the assistance of its allies. The regime, therefore, could once more turn its forces against Kurdish inhabited regions or increasingly undermine its autonomy, especially with international actors, Russia and the United States, progressively abandoning the Kurdish group as their objectives differed from the latter after periods of collaborations.

As we have seen, the destiny of the Kurdish people in Syria was inextricably linked to the causes and conditions of the Syrian uprising. Therefore, their future was in danger and facing multiple threats, similar to the rest of the protest movement.

6. Syria, International Relations, and Interventions

Introduction

The internationalization of the Syrian uprising occurred quite rapidly, with the direct involvement of international and regional actors early on. Prior to 2011, Syria was in a process of rapprochement with Western countries after a period of isolation on the international political scene. In 2008, this situation changed with the election of French president Nicolas Sarkozy, who broke with his predecessor, Jacques Chirac, and the U.S. policy of isolating Damascus. By 2009, Syria had successfully positioned itself between two networks: It simultaneously maintained close relationships with Iran and Russia, its two closest allies, while reviving a period of détente with Western states such as France and the United States. In February 2010, the Obama administration nominated Robert Ford as Syrian ambassador to the United States, a post that had been vacant for five years.

This position between Damascus's allies and Western states, or at least Assad's attempts to reach it, was challenged very rapidly with the eruption of the uprising in Syria and the development of protests throughout the country. Damascus became increasingly dependent on Russia's and Iran's assistance, which grew significantly in the country. On the other hand, lack of unity and a coherent political project by the so-called friends of the Syrian People[1] nurtured divisions within the opposition, while their objectives evolved increasingly throughout the uprising.

The main dynamics of international imperialist and regional interventions were initially motivated by geopolitical considerations rather than economic objectives. Syria was at the center of many geopolitical games in the region, and its overthrow could change the balance of forces in significant ways. Assad's regime benefited from these divisions on the international scene and the assistance given by his allies to remain in power. It was undoubtedly the most important aspect of the resilience of the regime.

The regional political environment in the Middle East witnessed major changes on the eve of the uprisings, particularly with the failures of U.S.-led

---

[1] This was the name that these countries gave to the conferences in support of the exiled opposition SNC and then the Syrian Coalition.

military invasion in Iraq in 2003 and the willingness of the Obama administration to partially withdraw from the region to concentrate on the challenge represented by China. This situation allowed other international and regional actors to play an increasingly significant role in the MENA region.

Assad seeking allies and opposing international sanctions

The international sanctions imposed on Syria by Western powers, Turkey, and the Gulf monarchies, as well as the deepening of the war over time, forced the regime to seek quick and comprehensive assistance from its allies on the regional and international scene. Throughout the war, Syrian officials attempted to increase relations and meetings with investors and officials from states characterized as friendly, especially the BRICS[2] countries, which stood by the regime on the international stage. Russia was certainly the most significant ally of Syria among the BRICS countries, but China's relationship with Syria during the uprising proved important as well.

Prior to the uprising, China was ranked as Syria's third-largest importer in 2010, delivering notably USD 300 million in arms from 2007 to 2010 (Human Rights Watch 2012). From 2011 on, Beijing repeatedly referred to its policies of mutual nonintervention, respect for sovereignty, and nonaggression in its decision to side with the Assad regime during the uprising. Chinese officials stood with Russia diplomatically, vetoing six out of seven resolutions submitted to the UN Security Council (UNSC) to condemn the Syrian regime for using force against their civilians between March 2011 and April 2017 (Hindy 2017). However, China played only a small role in international attempts to end the war, including through the UNSC and the International Syria Support Group, despite having appointed a special envoy to the crisis in March 2016. Similarly, in terms of material support for Damascus, China sold only 500 antitank missiles to Damascus in 2014 (Hindy 2017). At the same time, Beijing became increasingly worried that Uighurs[3] would end up fighting for jihadist groups in Syria and Iraq (Blanchard 2016).

By 2017, China had become Syria's biggest trading partner. Chinese companies provided various equipment and raw materials to Syria, especially Syrian industrialists, because of the European sanctions imposed on

---

[2] The BRICS countries are Brazil, Russia, India, South Africa and China.
[3] Uighurs are a mostly Muslim people who speak a Turkish dialect and hail from China's far-western region of Xinjiang. The Uighur population suffers massive repression by the Chinese state; according to some reports, 1 million Uighurs were held in what resembled a "massive internment camp" in August 2018 (Nebehay 2018).

Syria (Euro News 2017). In the autumn of 2018, after the Damascus International Fair, the Ministry of Public Works also signed contracts with Chinese companies to buy a total of 94 heavy machines, mainly dedicated to the construction sector, for a value of SYP 7 billion, equivalent to around USD 15.3 million (*The Syria Report* 2018s). Several Memorandums of Understanding were also signed between China and Syria, in which Beijing notably provided humanitarian and technical assistance to Damascus worth more than USD 70 million, including the delivery of hundreds of electric generators (*The Syria Report* 2018v). In addition, the China National Petroleum Corporation held major stakes in the Syrian Petroleum Company and al-Furat Petroleum, the two largest Syrian oil firms (Hemenway 2018).

Taking China's participation into account, the regime was above all dependent on its close allies Russia, Iran, and Hezbollah. This dependency would grow at all levels throughout the uprising.

Russia

Russia was an old ally of the Syrian regime, and Moscow's commitment to Damascus and Assad himself has been very clear since the beginning of the uprising in March 2011. Russia has repeatedly vetoed and blocked attempts within the UNSC to impose sanctions and other punitive measures on the Assad regime. Moscow considered the possible overthrow of the Syrian regime a major threat to its own regional interests, viewing such an outcome as weakening its influence in the region and bolstering the U.S. position and that of its allies, while expanding the influence of Islamic fundamentalist movements, which the Russian government observed as a potential challenge to its position not only in the greater Middle East, but also in the Caucas and Central Asia (Heydemann 2013a: 4–5). This did not prevent Russia's Federal Security Service from facilitating the safe passage of Islamic fundamentalist networks from the North Caucasus to Syria, presumably as a way to expel them from their own regions. The number of terrorist attacks in the North Caucasus was in fact reduced between 2014 and 2015, from 525 to an estimated 260. Russian special services, however, were worried about returning jihadists (cited in Valenta and Valenta 2016).

The Western military intervention and overthrow of Libyan dictator Mu'ammar Qaddafi also contributed to Russia's position of refusing any UN resolution that would authorize intervention against the Assad regime. Russian officials considered that they had been deliberately misled in the case of Libya, where Washington persuaded Moscow not to veto a UNSC resolution against Qaddafi. U.S. secretary of state Hillary Clinton had described the operation as a humanitarian mission to prevent the slaughter of Libyan civilians by the regime's forces. But as North American Treaty Organization (NATO) forces increased and expanded their air-bombing campaign, it became clear that the international intervention was mainly focused on getting rid of Qaddafi's regime (Valenta and Valenta 2016). Russia's defense sales company, Rosoboronexport, lost at least USD 4 billion worth of contracts, and the energy company Gazprom was deprived of several billion dollars more in exploration and extraction deals signed with Qaddafi's regime before his 2011 overthrow (Blas and Champion 2016). Moreover, Russia lost a political ally with the overthrow of Qaddafi, who had maintained relatively good political relations with Moscow.

The Assad regime has long been an avid consumer of Russian weaponry. According to the Stockholm International Peace Research Institute, Russia represented 78 percent of Syria's weapons purchases between 2007 and 2012, while from 2007 to 2010, Russian arms sales to Syria reached the total sum of USD 4.7 billion—more than twice the figure for the previous four years. In addition to these sales, Russian companies had USD 20 billion worth of investments in Syria on the eve of the uprising (Borshchevskaya 2013), particularly in the energy sector (Syria Report 2017h). In 2004, Moscow also agreed to write off USD 9.8 billion in Syrian debt to the former Soviet Union (Rainey 2015), out of the estimated USD 13.5 billion owed by Syria, and postponed the payment of the remaining USD 3.61 billion.

The Russian naval center in the city of Tartus was also an important asset for the country's geopolitical interests, as it was the only military base outside the former Soviet Union with direct access to the Mediterranean Sea. This naval center boosted Russia's operational capacity in the region. Following Bashar al-Assad's visit to Moscow in 2005 and the growing relationship between the two countries, renewed Russian-Syrian military cooperation took place, including renovating the port of Tartus to accommodate larger ships, a process that began in 2008 and was completed in 2012. According to navy experts (*Global Security* 2016), the facility was being renovated to serve as a foothold for a permanent Russian naval presence in the Mediterranean Sea. This aligned with Russian president Vladimir Putin's vision for his third term, in which he made the expansion of Russian sea power a pillar of his campaign (Borshchevskaya 2013).

Even prior to the uprising, the importance of the Tartus naval base was on the rise in Syria. The Russian military expanded its small naval facility there to be able to handle bigger warships and transport vessels amid a general buildup of Russian forces. In mid-2015, 1,700 Russian military specialists were deployed, a dramatic increase in personnel at a facility that until 2012 was staffed by a handful of military personnel and civilian contractors (Bodner 2015). The military expansion in Syria was part of a bigger Russian expansion that included establishing military bases in several other countries (al-Saadi 2015b).

The Russian state continued to ship substantial volumes of small arms, ammunition, spare parts, and refurbished material to pro-regime forces (Heydemann 2013a: 4). In January 2014, it stepped up its supplies of military gear to the Syrian regime, including armored vehicles, drones, and guided bombs (Saul 2014). Russian military personnel also trained some soldiers and advised officers in the SAA (Kureev 2016), while developing relations with pro-regime militias, including the Palestinian Quds Brigade in Aleppo (Toumaj 2016) and the Jaber brothers' militias (Hayek and Roche 2016). In August 2015, new Russian military equipment arrived in Syria, while Moscow was simultaneously enhancing its intelligence-sharing program with the Syrian regime. In the same month, a deal was signed between Moscow and Damascus that allowed Russia to establish its Hmeimim Air Base to launch operations (Stratfor 2015). This agreement between Moscow and Damascus, which either party could terminate with a year's notice, also gave great autonomy to Russian military forces in Syria by allowing its military personnel and shipments to pass in and out of Syria at will and not be subject to controls by Syrian authorities, while Syrians could not enter Russian bases without Russia's permission. Finally, Russia disclaimed any responsibility for damage caused by its activities inside Syria (Birnbaum 2016).

Following this deal, another level of Russia's military involvement was reached on September 30, 2015, when Russian jets conducted their first raids in Syria. The military operation was aimed at recapturing territories lost by the Assad regime to various opposition forces (Bassam 2015). The Russian state justified its direct massive military intervention in Syria by couching it within the framework of a war on terrorism, particularly against IS, and to protect the Syrian state. However, the main motivation was to support the crumbling Assad regime politically and militarily and crush all forms of opposition to it. This was witnessed in the rather low proportion of Russian air strikes in Syria that targeted IS. In the first quarter of 2016, 26 percent of Russian air strikes in Syria targeted IS (AFP 2016a). That dipped to 22 percent in the second quarter and 17 percent in the third quarter. As argued by Alex Kokcharov, principal Russia analyst at the Information Handling Services Markit company,

> Russia's priority is to provide military support to the Assad government and, most likely, transform the Syrian civil war from a multi-party conflict into a binary one between the Syrian government and jihadist groups like the IS ... (AFP 2016a)

Moscow built up substantial ground forces in various locations in Syria, with estimates of at least several thousand troops in 2016, including several private military companies (including E.N.O.T. Corp, Wagner, and Morgan Security Group PMC) that also took part in the fighting (Hayek and Roche 2016; Spencer 2016) and Russian military police, along with modern weaponry and infrastructure (*Moscow Times* 2016). While Russia deployed the S-300 air defense missile system to ensure the safety of its naval base in Tartus, Russian navy ships off the Mediterranean coast in the autumn of 2016 deployed S-400 air defense missiles and the short-range Pantsir system. Moscow also sent three missile ships to reinforce its naval forces off the coast of Syria (The New Arab 2016c). In January 2017, Russia and Syria signed agreements to prolong Moscow's control of the strategic Tartus port. The 49-year deal allowed Russia to dredge the Mediterranean port, install floating berths, and carry out repair work. The deal could be extended for another 25-year period automatically if neither side objected (DW 2017). In April 2019, Russian officials declared the renting of the Tartous port would also include the expansion and modernization of its supply of facilities for the Russian's fleet.

By late 2016 to early 2017, Russian military police were deployed in Syria to train their colleagues to carry out joint patrols, including in "de-escalation zones"[4] (AFP 2017) and areas that witnessed the so-called reconciliation agreements between the regime and armed opposition forces. President Putin personally honored members of private military companies, despite the fact that such firms were illegal in Russia. However, at the end of December 2016, he signed a legal amendment regarding Law No. 53 that permitted the deployment of Russian mercenaries around the world and allowed the subcontracting of private military firms by the Russian military (Dobbert and Neumann 2017; Mardasov 2018).

Russia also used military intervention in Syria as "a way to showcase its weaponry for export sales," according to Omar Lamrani (cited in Brown 2017), an analyst with Stratfor, especially its SU-34 fighter jet and cruise missiles. Vladimir Shamanov, a former Russian commander and current MP, mentioned in February 2018 during a parliamentary session that more than 200 new weapons developed by Moscow scientists had been tested in Syria (The New Arab 2018b).

In August 2018, a total of 63,012 Russian military personnel "received combat experience" in Syria, including 25,738 ranking officers and 434 generals, as well as 4,349 artillery and rocket specialists, according to Moscow (AFP 2018).

---

[4] Agreements signed by Russia, Turkey, and Iran calling for an end to hostilities between armed opposition and pro-regime forces in four regions.

Russia's economic role in Syria also increased markedly after 2015. New trade and market opportunities for Russian investors opened up during this time, most notably in the sale of cereals and wheat. The Russian company Adyg Yurak, based in the province of Adygea, became a key actor in Russian–Syrian economic relations and established privileged relationships with numerous regime figures, including the rising businessman Samer Foz, the owner of Aman Group (see Chapter 7) (*The Syria Report* 2017j). In September 2018, Syrian state entities also signed contracts worth USD 19.7 million to buy heavy machinery from Russia that would be used by the construction industry in Syria (*The Syria Report* 2018q).

Moscow's goal was to capitalize on Syria's oil and gas reserves and other industries, which attracted the interest of Russian companies. In December 2016, the Russian company Europolis, owned by a businessman close to Vladimir Putin, signed a deal with the regime stipulating that the Europolis would receive a quarter of all oil and gas reserves from Syrian territory recaptured by the regime. In exchange, Russia would provide mercenaries that would contribute to the fight to evict IS from these areas (*The Syria Report* 2017k).

In June 2017, Damascus awarded the Russian company Stroytransgaz[5] a contract to extract 2.2 million tons of phosphate per year from its mines in central Syria for a period of 50 years. Stroytransgaz, among the most active Russian companies in Syria prior to the uprising, received 70 percent of the revenues, while the government received only 30 percent (*The Syria Report* 2017i). Total exports of phosphate before the war in 2010 were estimated at more than USD 200 million. From 2009 to 2011, Syria supplied almost a fifth of imports of phosphate from the European Union (EU), but those sales collapsed during the war. By the beginning of 2018, as the regime was continuously consolidating its power, some EU countries were once again starting to purchase phosphate from Syria, though still far below prewar levels. Greek imports increased from December 2017 to April 2018, from 5,000 to 16,900 tons, at an estimated value of nearly 900,000 euros (Marks 2018).

Stroytransgaz won several other contracts for infrastructure projects that year, including two gas-processing plants.[6] In June 2018, it took over development and management of the General Fertilizers Company (GFC), one

---

[5] The company was owned by Gennady Timchenko. Stroytransgaz and Timchenko were both placed on the U.S. sanctions list in 2014 after the invasion of Crimea by Russia.
[6] The mine had total estimated reserves of some 1.8 billion tons, but the deal covered a specific block that had reserves of 105 million tons. The Syrian party to the agreement was the General Establishment of Geology and Mineral Resources, which was the parent entity of the General Company for Phosphate and Mines (GECOPHAM), the state company directly involved in phosphate extraction (*The Syria Report* 2018k).

of Syria's large fertilizer complexes near Homs. The agreement involved the investment of USD 200 million of Stroytransgaz to rehabilitate and upgrade the three plants run by GFC that produce urea, triple super phosphate, and ammonium nitrate. Eventually, the production would increase and the fertilizers would be sold in the local and export markets. In exchange, Stroytransgaz would take control of the management of the company and collect 65 percent of its profits for a period of at least 25 years, extendable to 40. The remaining 35 percent would go to the government (Kayali 2018; *The Syria Report* 2018n). In January 2019, the Homs Governorate Council announced the reopening of the phosphate fertilizer plant, after years of suspension, with a daily production capacity of 400 tons of phosphate fertilizer (Enab Baladi 2019a).

Damascus and Moscow have signed a series of agreements covering various sectors in the past few years; however, outside the energy and mining sectors, few have materialized. Russian officials repeatedly told their Syrian counterparts that they would need to secure funding for any development project, while private investors demonstrated little interest in investing in Syria outside the above mentioned sectors.

The Assad regime's dependency on Russia increased considerably throughout the war, while closely coordinating military and diplomatic moves with Moscow. This has not prevented a few small disagreements or incidents between the two actors. Damascus, for example, has on several occasions undermined Moscow's efforts to form a national unity government in Syria by indicating their unwillingness to engage with any opposition groups and figures—even those who called for dialogue with the regime and maintained close connections with Russia (al-Saadi 2015b). Similarly, Russia was more inclined to promote a national cease-fire in the country and an international political settlement to the conflict, while the Assad regime disagreed. Damascus preferred local cease-fires to a national one, wishing to achieve each one on its own terms in conquered or contested areas, while simultaneously exploiting the resulting calm to deploy forces toward escalation efforts elsewhere (Bonsey 2017). Assad's ability to obstruct these initiatives demonstrated his ability to mantain some degree of limited autonomy from Russian influence.

The military intervention in Syria helped Russia become the decisive foreign actor in the country and the postconflict settlement, while demonstrating Russia's new military and political capabilities on the international scene. More generally, it pushed the frontier of geopolitical rivalry and competition between Moscow and the West (or NATO) away from the Russian border, while making clear that any action on the behalf of the United States or NATO needed to take Russian interests into account to achieve a viable solution.

Iran

The Iranian regime had increased considerably its standing and influence in the region, primarily through the IRGC, in the decade prior to the Syrian uprising. The failure of U.S. and British intervention in 2003 and their subsequent occupation of Iraq permitted Tehran, and Shi'a Islamic Fundamentalist movements in particular, to gain major influence in the country, especially increasing their domination over various state institutions and expanding religious and militia networks in the country. Iran also augmented its influence through the growing popularity of Hezbollah in Lebanon, particularly after its self-declared victory following Israel's war against Lebanon in 2006. It also strengthened relations with other political parties in the region, including in Yemen and the Palestinian Occupied Territories.

Iran's expanding influence in the region has been led in particular by the IRGC, which constitutes a military–political force, and to some extent a state within a state in Iran. It controls a major sector of the national economy and embodies the armed expression of Iranian expansionism that has manifested itself through intervention in Iraq, Syria, and Lebanon (Houcarde 2008; Achcar 2018).

Iran has been a key ally of the Assad regime and Bashar al-Assad, warning against the overthrow of the regime and saying that Assad's fate was a red line. Damascus has been essential in providing and resupplying Hezbollah, Iran's proxy in Lebanon, which plays an important role in achieving territorial security vis-à-vis Israel and the United States. The Assad regime protected these supply routes, and officials in Tehran were unlikely to entertain the possibility that any non-Assad Syrian entity would do the same (Lister and McCants 2014). Tehran also saw a real danger in losing one of its key regional allies if the Syrian uprising succeeded. Not only would this spell defeat for a close friend of Iran, it would greatly benefit their regional rivals, especially the Gulf monarchies (Aboudi 2013).

On the ground, the security and intelligence services of the IRI had been advising and assisting the Syrian regime since the beginning of the uprising. Tehran provided essential military supplies to Assad and helped established pro-regime militias on a national level. Iran's head of IRGC, Qasem Suleimani, played a direct role in the creation of the NDF's networks, one of the earliest examples of Tehran taking the lead at a local level to back Assad regime forces (Hayek and Roche 2016).

From mid-2012 to mid-2013, Iran also helped the Assad regime establish and form numerous local and regional militias, including the Damascus-based factions within the Liwa Abu Fadl al-Abbas (LAFA) network, whose commanders were Iraqi Shi'a living in Syria who had settled in the country starting in the early 1980s when fleeing Saddam Hussein's regime (Hage Ali 2017). The various militias of the LAFA network increasingly recruited foreign fighters, particularly Iraqi Shi'a, but also Pakistanis and Afghanis (10,000–20,000 Afghan Shi'a) sent and organized by the IRI (Spencer 2016; Majidyar 2017a). The LAFA factions fought throughout Syria against armed opposition fighters alongside other pro-regime militias (Hayek and Roche 2016).

The initial IRGC contingent in Syria of 1,000–1,500 grew to approximately 3,000 in the autumn of 2015, parallel to the beginning of Russia's direct military intervention and air-bombing campaign in the country. The Iranian regime once again increased deployments to Syria over the course of 2016 to participate in the operation to encircle and recapture the neighborhoods of Eastern Aleppo (Bucala 2017: 4). Iranian officials also decided to allow Russian troops to use the Shahid Nojeh Air Base in Hamedan to bomb targets in Syria, which was an unprecedented move by the IRI and a further testament that securing the upper hand in Syria was crucial to Tehran's regional foreign policy (Geranmayeh and Liik 2016: 4). Iran has also increasingly built up its infrastructures in Syria, establishing three main bases that oversaw operations in large parts of Syria—one near Aleppo in the north and two south of the capital, Damascus—as well as seven smaller tactical bases near active front lines, where Iran and its proxies had a presence (Barnard, Hubbard, and Kershner 2018).

The Iranian intervention in Syria also has been very expensive for the country's economy, with costs ranging from at least USD 16 billion to USD 48 billion in military and economic aid since 2012 (Farhang, cited in Daragahi 2018; Hatahet 2019: 3). In comparison, the cost of the Russian involvement was estimated at USD 2.4 million to USD 4 million a day according to IHS Jane's Information Group, a renowned intelligence provider for the defense industry and governments, which amounted to USD 2.5 billion to USD 4.5 billion since September 2015 (Hatahet 2019: 3). Notably, the IRI provided four important loans to the Assad regime between 2013 and 2017:

- The first loan, which amounted to USD 1 billion, came in January 2013 after regime revenues had already plunged to 50 percent of their prewar levels. The Assad regime dedicated this first loan to pay for imported food commodities and to prop up the Syrian regime's official foreign reserves. The agreement was signed between the Commercial Bank of Syria and Bank Saderat, Iran's export finance bank. Both institutions are state-owned and under U.S. sanctions.
- A second, more robust loan of USD 3.6 billion occurred in August 2013. This money was earmarked primarily for the purchase of crude oil and derivatives, after the Syrian regime lost almost all of the oil fields in the

east of the country. According to the International Energy Agency, Syria imported an average of 30,000 barrels of crude oil per day from Iran in 2013.

- In June 2015, the IRI approved a new credit line of USD 1 billion to the Syrian regime, which was used to help finance imports and offset the sharp drop in the value of the SYP.
- In January 2017, the IRI granted a new credit line of USD 1 billion to the regime. The new loan went to pay for Syria's imports. Half would be allocated to oil supplies, while the other half would be allocated to agricultural and industrial inputs, all of which had to be procured from Iran or through Iranian companies (al-Saadi 2015a; *The Syria Report* 2015e; *The Syria Report* 2017e).

These agreements strengthened the economic and investment ties between the two regimes, which were relatively weak and mostly unimplemented until the outbreak of protests in 2011. Trade between the two countries grew from approximately USD 300 million in 2010 to USD 1 billion in 2014 (al-Saadi 2015a). According to the Ministry of Economy, Iran was Syria's main supplier in 2014, representing some 34 percent of the country's total imports, while it accounted for less than 2 percent in 2010 (*The Syria Report* 2015e). Iranian exports surged again following the two Iranian credit lines granted to Damascus in 2013 and 2015. In some sectors, such as electricity equipment and machinery, Syria became heavily dependent on Iran (*The Syria Report* 2015e).

In June 2018, adviser of the Iranian foreign minister Hussein Sheikh al-Islam declared that more than 50 percent of Iranian companies won bids for hydroelectric power in Syria (Enab Baladi 2018h). However, Iranian private companies showed little interest in investing in the Syrian market, as only one Iranian limited liability company (LLC) and representative office in the Syrian capital opened between 2011 and 2015 (*The Syria Report* 2015e).

In April 2016, the preferential trade agreement between the two countries finally came into force, with customs duties applied on all goods traded between the two countries reduced to 4 percent. Tehran was clearly favored as Iranian exports were 20 times larger than Syrian exports in 2016 (*The Syria Report* 2016h). Syria's reliance on Iranian funds allowed Tehran to secure an agreement in 2011 to create a pipeline that would transport Iranian gas through Iraq and Syria, destined for Europe (al-Saadi 2015a), while providing it with new economic opportunities.

In mid-January 2017, five main economic agreements were reached between Damascus and Tehran, while a sixth was expected to be finalized in relation to the possible transfer of the management of one of Syria's ports to an Iranian company. All the agreements involved the transfer of significant Syrian resources and assets to Iran without clear compensation. One of the five agreements pertained to the transfer to Iran, on a long-term lease basis, of the al-Sharqiyeh phosphate mines located near Palmyra. The other three agreements involved the transfer of Syrian lands on a lease basis to Iranian companies.[7] Finally, an agreement led to the award of a mobile phone license to the Mobile Telecommunication Company of Iran (MTCI), which was also known under its brand name Hamrahe Aval.[8] MTCI is a subsidiary of the Telecommunication Company of Iran (TCI), which has a monopoly over Iran's landline network, and was privatized in 2009. The company is owned and operated by a consortium of companies, including Mobin Trust Consortium and Toseye Eatemad Mobin, both affiliated with the IRGC (Hamidi 2017; *The Syria Report* 2017c; Francis and Sharafedin 2017). However, in September 2017, during the Damascus International Trade Fair, the Syrian minister of telecommunications Ali al-Zafir raised doubts about this contract, arguing that his government was discussing "with several countries that are friendly with Syria, including with Iran, the prospects of investing in a third mobile phone operator" (cited in *The Syria Report* 2017m). Resistance to MTCI's possible license came from two main elements: competitors such as Syriatel, controlled by Rami Makhlouf, who was unwilling to see more competition in his sector; and from the security services, which were rather uneasy and worried about the prospect of the Iranian military gaining access to the country's telecommunications network (Yazigi 2019: 22).

These agreements demonstrated the increasing influence of Iran in the Syrian economy and evolution in relation to the two actors in favor of Tehran, but also in terms of security with the control of a telecommunications network by a company affiliated with the IRGC. It is interesting to note that in 2010, Damascus began a process of awarding a third license as part of a drive to attract global companies and expand the size of the Syrian market. Six companies presented bids—France Telecom, Turkcell, Etisalat, Qatar's QTEL, Saudi Telecom, and Iran's Toseye Eatemad Mobin. The government shortlisted five of these, excluding the Iranian company. In early 2011, several bidders withdrew, citing dissatisfaction with the terms of the contract, before the beginning of the uprising eventually led the government to scrap the deal altogether (*The Syria Report* 2016m).

---

[7] Some 5,000 hectares would be used for the development of agricultural crops, another 1,000 hectares for cow breeding, and 5,000 hectares for oil storage tanks and reservoirs—but the location of these lands were not specified (*The Syria Report* 2017d; Francis and Sharafedin 2017).
[8] In Persian, *Hamrahe Aval* means "The First Companion," a reference to Ali bin Abi Taleb, a companion of the Prophet Muhammad and the first imam in Shi'a Islam.

Other economic agreements continued to be concluded throughout the years. In May 2018, for example, the General Federation for Syrian Farmers concluded a contract with the Iran Tractor Manufacturing Company to purchase 3,000 agricultural tractors with 47-horsepower (HP) and 75-HP engines (*The Syria Report* 2018l).[9] Tehran also participated in various reconstruction projects throughout the country (see Chapter 7).

In February 2018, Major General Yahya Rahim Safavi, Supreme Leader Ayatollah Ali Khameini's top military adviser, declared that Iran would recover the costs of its investments in the Syria war by exploiting the country's natural resources, highlighting Tehran's economic interests for the spoils of war in Syria (The New Arab 2018a).

However, Iranian officials and media raised some criticisms in early 2018 at the lack of implementation of economic agreements concluded in previous years, notably some of the agreements mentioned previously. By June 2018, some evolutions occurred as Iran was granted the right to develop its phosphate reserve by the adoption in the Syrian parliament of a text ratifying "the agreement signed between the Syrian and Iranian governments pertaining to the development of the phosphate mines located near Palmyra" (cited in *The Syria Report* 2018m).

One week later, during a visit to Tehran by the Syrian minister of economy and foreign trade, Muhammad Samer al-Khalil told the Iranian minister of economic affairs and finance, Masoud Karbasian, about the necessity "to find the best ways to implement agreements signed between the two sides, the signature of new ones, and encouraging public and private sectors to carry out joint projects" (cited in SANA 2018b). In addition, officials of both sides discussed the means of boosting their strategic cooperation in economic, commercial, investment, and services sectors, including the importance of a railway line connecting Syria, Iran, and Iraq in facilitating access to the Mediterranean Sea and Europe and the need to establish a joint free market among the three states (SANA 2018b). In October 2018, during a meeting in the framework of the Syrian-Iranian Businessmen Forum, several memoranda of understanding were signed between the two countries in different trade, investment, economic, and production domains, including one to establish a Joint Chamber of Commerce between the Federation of Syrian Chambers of Commerce and the Chamber of Commerce, Industry, Mines, and Agriculture of Iran (SANA 2018h). In

---

[9] According to *The Syria Report* (2018k), the agreement was believed to be funded by Iran's credit line to the benefit of the Syrian government. Meanwhile, the state-owned Agricultural Cooperative Bank would provide concessionary loans to individual farmers.

March 2019, there were increasing talks of the handing over of the container terminal of the Lattakia Port to Iran by Damascus.

Rumors and other information[10] (*The Syria Report* 2015e; Jedinia and Kajjo 2016) about Iranian individuals and institutions purchasing large tracts of land throughout Syrian territory were very hard to evaluate, and numbers were often exaggerated. The only exception to this was in the Sayyida Zeinab suburb of Damascus, which hosted a Shi'a shrine and witnessed Iranian investments and acquisitions (Yazigi 2019: 22).

Meanwhile, Iranian political, religious, and cultural influence has increased considerably in various parts of the country, especially in the coastal areas, Damascus, the Aleppo countryside, and Deir ez-Zor. Institutions linked to the IRI multiplied, providing social, medical, and educational activities, as well as religious academies and sites (Jaber 2015; al-Hal 2018; Sada al-Sham 2018). The establishment of these institutions served a number of purposes, including the Iranian government's desire to build a popular base and secure the loyalty of local populations. Iran also extended some of its companies and institutions in remote and underserved areas of the country, mainly in the countryside around Aleppo and Deir ez-Zor (Hatahet 2019: 6).

Since 2012, Syria's Shi'a community also developed institutionally with the Iranian, Hezbollah, and Iraqi Shi'a interventions in the Syrian uprising. This ranged from setting up scout movements, as was done in Homs and Damascus, to the community's own religious authority (namely, the Supreme Islamic Ja'fari Council in Syria, established in 2012 along the lines of the Lebanese Supreme Islamic Shi'a Council). The Supreme Islamic Ja'fari Council in Syria, headed by Sayyed Muhammad Ali al-Misky, developed a Khomeinist political position and was close to the pro-Iran militias fighting in Syria (Hage Ali 2017).

Iranian influence on Syrian society was also increasingly visible in the streets of Damascus before the establishment of Iranian-sponsored Shi'a fundamentalist militias and those loyal to them, especially in particular events such as Ashura (al-Souria Net 2016c; al-Hal 2018) or in high-profile celebrations of Iran's Islamic Revolution across Syria, including Aleppo, Damascus, and Lattakia, organized by Iranian government entities or Iranian-funded cultural and religious organizations. All of these events demonstrated the increasing political and cultural influence of Iran (Majidyar 2017b).

---

[10] For example, a journalist wrote on al-Modon's website that between 2015 and the end of 2018, more than 8,000 properties in Damascus and its surroundings were transferred from Syrians to "Iraqi and Iranian Shi'as," according to a private source in the Department of Real Estate Registration (Haddad 2019b).

More generally, through the Syrian uprising, Iran was able to expand its regional network of Shi'a militia-type organizations as follows (Smyth 2015: 1–5):

- Asaib Ahl al-Haqq, an Iraqi Shi'a proxy of Iran that funneled fighters to Syria
- Kataib Sayyid al-Shuhada, initially a shadowy Iran-backed organization based in Iraq, which announced its main goal of defending all Shi'a shrines worldwide, but limited its involvement in Syria and Iraq alone
- The Iranian proxy Harakat Hezbollah al-Nujaba, which announced the creation of Liwa Ammar ibn Yasir, an Iraqi Shi'a militia whose name echoed a shrine in Raqqa to Ammar ibn Yassir that was destroyed by Sunni jihadist forces
- Badr Organization, which was originally the military arm for the Islamic Supreme Council of Iraq's predecessor, the Supreme Council for the Islamic Revolution in Iraq, and served as a main IRGC conduit for man-ufacturing proxies in Iraq

The fighting permitted Tehran to diffuse the state's fundamentalist ide-ology more widely. Furthermore, the presence of Shi'a militants of many nationalities fighting in Syria allowed Iran to project its power in Shi'a com-munities worldwide (Smyth 2015: 1–5).

Throughout the conflict years, Syria continued to be presented as a stra-tegic asset for the IRI, as was reflected by the statement of Ali Akbar Velayati, a top adviser to Khamenei, saying that Syria was "the golden ring of resistance front." He added, "[I]f Assad and the Syrian people fail in their fight against Takfiri groups … their next target will be Iraq, followed by Iran" (Hafezi 2016). Tehran increasingly considered Syria a first line of defense against a joint effort by its regional and international enemies, not only to provoke regime change in Damascus and the end of its alliance with Iran, but also as a way to isolate and overthrow the IRI as part of a longer-term strategy.

Hezbollah

Hezbollah has long had a close relationship with the Syrian regime, an alliance that strengthened over time, especially following the death of Hafez al-Assad. Hafez al-Assad treated Hezbollah as a useful tool for strength-ening Syria's relations with the IRI, while also exploiting the group's attacks to pressure Israel during peace negotiations. The situation changed under Bashar al-Assad, especially following the withdrawal of Syrian armed forces from Lebanon in 2005 and the 2006 war between Israel and Hezbollah.

The Syrian regime increasingly viewed the relationship with Hezbollah not as a tactical and temporary alliance, as it had been under Hafez, but as a deep strategic alliance. Bashar deepened Syria's collaboration with the group, both politically and militarily (Blanford 2011: 337).

The eruption of the Syrian uprising in March 2011, as well as the subsequent military intervention by Hezbollah in support of the Assad regime, demonstrated that the relationship between the two actors had become strategic. In May 2011, during Hassan Nasrallah's first speech on Syria, he characterized the Assad regime as "the spine of the resistance" in Syria, its overthrow being a strategic objective favored by U.S. and Israeli interests (al-Muqâwama al-Islâmiyya 2011). In addition, Nasrallah claimed that Hezbollah's support for the Syrian regime was not only in the interests of the party and the Shi'a, but also for the sake of Lebanon and all its various religious communities, against the threats of *Takfiri* terrorist forces (al-Manar 2012). Since mid-2011, Hezbollah began training thousands of Lebanese and Syrian youths in combat camps (Itani 2014). Hezbollah's presence was confirmed with the first so-called martyrs in Syria as early as June 2012 (Ashkar H. 2014). In November 2013, Hassan Nasrallah finally publicly acknowledged Hezbollah's presence in Syria (al-Manar 2013).

Hezbollah's role in Syria took various forms, ranging from veteran fighters commandeering squads of Syrian soldiers, who essentially acted as noncommissioned officers, to the less experienced Syrian regular troops in street fighting (Blanford 2013). They took care of training some of the pro-regime militias, including NDF units (Nakhoul 2013) and some of the new recruits in the SAA (AFP and *Orient le Jour* 2014a). Hezbollah also participated in various military offensives alongside pro-regime forces throughout the country, including the offensive of Eastern Aleppo in late 2016 and in Dar'a Province in mid-2018.

Later on in the war, Hezbollah established several militias in Syria. Quwat al-Ridha was considered the strategic nucleus for Hezbollah in Syria, operating militarily under the leadership and supervision of the party. The new group was composed of native Syrian young fighters, mostly Shi'as from Homs Province, but also Alawis and Sunni, and the majority came from various countryside areas (Homs, Aleppo, Dar'a, and Damascus countryside) (al-Hadath News 2014). Hezbollah also participated in the establishment of smaller Shi'a militias such as Liwa al-Imam Zain al-Abidain, active in Deir ez-Zor (Al-Tamimi 2016b), and Jaysh al-Imam al-Mahdi al-Muqawama al-Watani al-Aqaidiya fi Suriya (Army of Imam al-Mahdi, the National Ideological Resistance in Syria) (Smyth 2015: 47). The Lebanese Islamic movement was responsible for organizing, training, and equipping between 10,000 and 20,000 militiamen, mostly Shi'as but also members of other religious denominations, including Alawis, Sunnis, and Druze (Alipour 2015; Alami 2017).

Estimates of Hezbollah fighters in Syria since 2013 have numbered between 7,000 and 9,000. They include elite fighters, experts, and reservists among their ranks, rotating in and out of the country on 30-day deployments (AFP and *Orient le Jour* 2014b; Alami 2016). The military importance of Hezbollah in Syria was also translated politically and socially, only increasing sectarian tensions and Sunni grievances over time. Some of the Syrian Shi'a militia, constituted with the help of Iranian and Hezbollah cadres, adopted the ideology linked with it: *wilayat al-faqih*[11] (Smyth 2016). Hezbollah further expanded its range of activities in Syria by establishing a branch of the Imam Mahdi Scouts in Syria, which had been operating since at least 2012 (al-Tamimi 2016a).

Assad's regime allies—deep understanding, but with some differences

Prior to the outbreak of the Syrian uprising in March 2011, Russian–Iranian relations had been deteriorating for a number of years, notably because President Dmitry Medvedev had supported UN sanctions against Iran in 2010 and signed a ban on the Russian delivery of the S-300 missile defense system to Tehran (Notte 2017: 25). However, Russia and Iran, the two main allies of the Assad regime, have seen their mutual interests and dependence increase throughout the years with the Syrian uprising and the major assistance that they provided to Damascus. Their collaboration has proven effective and strong, despite the existence of minor political differences. The most telling proof of this could be found in the process of preparation of Russian military aviation intervention at the end of September 2015, as explained by analyst Arun Lund (2016d):

> In July 2015, the Iranian Quds Force commander Qassem Suleimani reportedly visited Putin in Moscow to prepare for a joint intervention. A bilateral Russian-Syrian agreement legalizing the intervention was signed on August 26, 2015. Iran then opened its airspace to Russian planes en route to Syria and began airlifting reinforcements well in advance of the first Russian air strikes. In late September, the Iraqis announced the establishment of a joint Russian–Iranian–Iraqi–Syrian

[11] The theory of the *wilayat al-faqih* is that a guardianship of the jusrisprudent or jurisconsult should hold ultimate political power. It was initially led by Ayatollah Khomeini, and then Ayatollah Khamenei.

intelligence coordination center in Baghdad. Bombing began on September 30, and two weeks later, Iran launched an offensive near Aleppo under Russian air cover. The following month, Putin flew to Tehran for a meeting with Ayatollah Ali Khamenei, after which the two leaders praised each other's policies and stressed their "complete agreement" on the Syrian issue...

Iranian military cooperation with Russia in Syria considerably increased Tehran's capacity to plan and conduct complex conventional operations. Close cooperation between Russian and Iranian military personnel at the operational and tactical levels allowed military knowledge transfer between the two armies (Bucala and Casagrande 2017).

Political and economic relations between both countries also improved. Ali Shamkhani, secretary of Iran's Supreme National Security Council, declared in an interview in June 2017 that Russia and Iran had cultivated closer diplomatic, commercial, and military ties after the removal of most nuclear-related sanctions on Iran in January 2016.[12] Since then, Tehran has received advanced weapons from Russia, including the long-delayed S-300 missile defense system. Moscow and Tehran were also negotiating the supply of around USD 10 billion worth of arms and military hardware to Iran. The volume of trade between Russia and Iran increased by about 80 percent, reaching USD 2 billion in 2016, following the lifting of nuclear-related sanctions (Majidyar 2017c). Moscow officials also criticized Washington's unilateral withdrawal in May 2018 from the 2015 nuclear deal with Iran, which also included Britain, China, France, Russia, Germany, and the European Union as signatories. The agreement gave Iran relief from sanctions in exchange for restrictions on its nuclear program. The Trump administration not only restored its sanctions on Tehran, but in November, it imposed new sanctions on Iran's crucial oil, banking, and transportation sectors (Bezhan 2018).

The outcome of the war was undoubtedly more important to Tehran, causing it to be less flexible than Moscow on various issues related to peace and cease-fire negotiations or that would endanger its interests in Syria directly. This resulted in some divergences.

Having developed a close alliance with the Assad family and its security apparatus for over three decades, the leaders of the IRI considered the Syrian regime essential to its regional security structure and a key supply route to

---

[12] However, it should be recalled that Russia has started working with Tehran at the end of the 1990s to develop port and rail infrastructure in Iran. Moscow slowly built up its presence in the country, developing a quasi-monopoly in the area by the turn of the century (Esfandiary and Tabatabai 2018).

delivering weapons to Hezbollah. With the successive military victories of pro-regime forces from 2016, Russia was increasingly seeking to find a political solution to end the war in Syria, so long as its strategic interests were secured, while Iran still favored a total military victory and the consolidation of its proxies in the country for its broader regional agenda against both Israel and regional rivals such as Saudi Arabia (Majidyar 2017c).

Russia's relation with Israel proved to be another point of contention. Russia constantly avoided the risk of seriously alienating Israel, let alone associating itself with the anti-Israel rhetoric characteristic of the Iranian leadership. Russian–Israeli relations have evolved positively under Putin's presidency, with closer collaborations. Since the start of Russian air strikes in Syria, Russia and Israel coordinated their military activities along the Syrian–Israeli border to prevent accidents (Notte 2017: 28). Israeli authorities also publicly stated their opposition to any Iranian or Hezbollah troops close to their borders, calling on Russia to prevent such a scenario from happening.

In this context, Israel multiplied its attacks against Hezbollah and pro-Iranian targets in Syria, especially from the beginning of 2017. In September 2017, the former Israeli air force chief Amir Eshel declared that Israel had hit arms convoys of the Syrian military and its Hezbollah allies nearly 100 times since the beginning of 2012 (Lombardi 2014: 121; Dadouch and Heller 2017). Israel continued to expand its bombing campaign in Syria from the end of 2017 until 2019 against Iranian targets and groups linked to it.

In May 2018, the Israeli army took advantage of the U.S. decision to put an end to the nuclear deal with Tehran to pursue new attacks against Iranian targets in Syria. Iran responded by firing missiles from Syria toward Israeli military outposts in the occupied Syrian Golan Heights. Israel then launched an unprecedented round of air attacks against dozens of Iranian military and security installations in Syria. However, both Tehran and Tel Aviv called for calm and a deescalation of military tension between the two countries.

The increasing Iranian presence in Syria in recent years has been strongly contested by Israel, Saudi Arabia, and the United States. Even Russia, Iran's partner in assisting the Syrian regime to quell the Syrian popular uprising, tacitly accepted Israel's strikes. Israel was in fact pressing Moscow to get Iran to leave Syria, threatening to conduct more bombing of Iranian positions near its border or anywhere inside the country should it remain (Daragahi 2018). In July 2018, Israeli prime minister Benjamin Netanyahu declared that Israel did not object to Assad reexerting control over the country and stabilizing his regime's power, but warned that Israel would act to protect its borders against the Syrian military if necessary, as it had in the past. He added, "We haven't had a problem with the Assad regime, for 40 years not a single bullet was fired on the Golan Heights" (cited in Landau 2018). This position was nothing new, as Israel did not want to see any significant changes at its borders and was content with a weakened Syrian regime. Israel's primary objective in dealing with Russia included the removal of missiles aimed at its territory from Syria, the withdrawal of Iranian and Hezbollah forces, and the preservation of the 1974 disengagement agreements with Syria for the Golan Heights.

Similarly, the United States wanted to replace Iranian influence with Russian influence in Syria. U.S. secretary of state Mike Pompeo listed Iran's withdrawal from Syria in May 2018 as one of twelve preconditions for removing sanctions after the Trump administration withdrew from the nuclear deal (Daragahi 2018). Washington had the diplomatic cards to encourage and convince Russia to push Iran out of Syria, such as lifting U.S. sanctions affecting Russian energy companies and stopping its opposition to construction of the Nord Stream 2 pipeline that would convey Russian gas to Germany and beyond (Mamadov 2018).

However, there were limits to Russia's willingness and capacity to achieve the Israeli and U.S. demands. At the end of July 2018, Moscow's ambassador to Tel Aviv declared that Russia could not compel Iranian forces to quit Syria, while also stating that Moscow could equally do nothing to prevent Israeli military strikes against Iranian forces in Syria. This declaration came after Russia had offered to keep Iranian forces at least 100 kilometers (60 miles) from the Golan Heights cease-fire line. The offer was rejected by Israel as insufficient (Reuters Staff 2018b).

In addition, following the incident with the downing of a Russia Ilyushin-20 reconnaissance plane over the Mediterranean Sea, in which Israel was involved, Russia supplied S-300 systems to the Syrian army to reinforce its combat capacities. Prime Minister Netanyahu criticized as irresponsible Moscow's decision to provide advanced antiaircraft systems to Syria, but stated that Israel was committed to continued deconfliction with Moscow in its military operations in the region (Agencies and TOI Staff 2018). Israel, however, carried out new strikes in Syria in the end of December 2018 and beginning of January 2019 against alleged Iranian and Hezbollah targets outside Damascus. Another point of contention was Russia's improved political relationship with Iran's archenemy, Saudi Arabia, throughout the war in Syria (as discussed further later in this chapter).

The influence on the ground within the country was also distributed and implemented differently with consequences for the future. Moscow's forces took hold in economically strategic areas (through one military base in Hmeimem, near the port of Tartus, for the control of economic trade; and one in Palmyra, in the center of Syria, for the control of gas and oil fields, in addition to one big military base in Hama), and they worked on the reformation and reconstruction of the SAA's nucleus (through the establishment of the Fourth and Fifth Corps). Russia played a leading role in the SAA's restructuring that started in 2018, which led to a large wave of transfers, promotions, dismissals, and arrests affecting hundreds of officers in the regime's forces (Haddad 2019a). Moscow tried through these measures to implement a comprehensive plan to restructure the military institution and to strengthen the networks of officers loyal to it. These actions resulted in tension in the relations between a network of pro-Moscow regime officers on one side and a network of pro-Iran officers on the other, according to Think Tank Strategy Watch (2019).

Similarly, the operation to restructure the Syrian armed forces coincided with the Russian command adopting a plan aiming at weakening Iranian influence by dismantling the allied forces and militias loyal to Tehran. The Air Force Intelligence Directorate, for example, terminated the contracts of about 6,500 members of a militia loyal to it and dissolved the Ba'th Commandos and NDF militias in Barzeh and Qudisiyeh, as well as the Qalamoun Shield. In addition, it arrested NDF militia members in Deir ez-Zor (Strategy Watch 2019).

On the other hand, Tehran primarily relied on Shi'a fundamentalist militias (Lebanese, Iraqi, and Afghan) and Syrian paramilitary auxiliary forces (the NDF and the LDF). Tehran has also encouraged its Syrian local allies in some areas to penetrate the local economy, notably by purchasing real estate or land, and in transportation and the oil trade (Hatahet 2019: 6–7). At the same time, this has not prevented Iran from increasing its power through networks on the ground and supporting financially particular Ba'thist candidates, militia commanders, tribal leaders, and other groups close to Tehran during the municipal elections in 2018 (Khatib 2018). At the end of August 2018, Iran and Syria concluded a fresh military deal between the defense ministers of the two countries in Damascus, thus consolidating their defense ties and demonstrating once again their deep strategic links (al-Frieh 2018a).

The existence of these disagreements nevertheless did not translate or transform into rival or competing interests in Syria, even in the economic arena, where both sides were increasingly eager to benefit from the reconstruction process in Syria and the country's natural resources. Both states continued to stress their strong cooperation and mutual interests in Syria. More generally, Russia and Iran had common shared interests on many issues, as argued by the academics Leonid Issaev and Nikolay Kozhanov (2017):

> While Russia and Iran have a lot of issues to argue about, they also have a number of common interests in Syria, Iraq, and Afghanistan,

in Eurasian transit routes, the situation in Transcaucasia and Central Asia, as well as in oil and gas markets.

United States—no Libya scenario in Syria

Western states were particularly cautious in their criticisms of the regime's repression of protesters in the first few weeks, as they had pursued a policy of rapprochement with Damascus in the previous years. A U.S. congressional delegation by Senator Richard Shelby visited Syria as late as February 2011. On March 28, U.S. secretary of state Hillary Clinton described Bashar al-Assad as different from his late father and predecessor, Hafez, adding that "many of the members of Congress of both parties who have gone to Syria in recent months have said they believe he's a reformer" (Goodenough 2011). She declared that the United States "would not enter the conflict in Syria as it had in Libya," arguing rather that "each of these situations is unique" (Goodenough 2011).

Indeed, the United States had less of a strategic interest in regime change in Syria than it did in Libya. Unlike Libya, Syria was not a major oil exporter. Syria's significance came mostly with regard to its location bordering Turkey, Iraq, Lebanon, and Israel, and its relationship with Iran and role in the Israeli–Arab conflict. Syria was far from a top priority at this period for Washington. Obama's administration had broken away from President George W. Bush's policy of isolation of Damascus because it served other U.S. objectives in the region, including helping to stabilize Iraq before the U.S. army's withdrawal and making certain that Damascus did not allow the reactivation of the flow of jihadi fighters through its territory and networks. Furthermore, President Obama had been elected at least in part on the basis of his criticisms of his predecessor's military interventions, especially in Iraq in 2003. The U.S. army withdrew from Iraq in December 2011, after Baghdad and Washington signed an agreement in 2008 requiring Washington to withdraw its forces.[13] The Obama administration diminished U.S. activity in the region prior to the uprisings in 2011, pursuing counterterrorism policies through increased use of drone warfare and the killing of Osama bin Laden in 2011 (Phillips 2016: 23–27).

In the following months, as the regime continued the crackdown on protests and soldiers began to peel away from the army, U.S. intelligence officials identified officers from the Alawi sect who could potentially topple

---

[13] At the time the withdrawal was announced, there were fewer than 3,000 troops and one base, Contingency Operating Base Adder, south of Baghdad (Logan 2011). The rise of the IS in the following years would increase the numbers of U.S. soldiers in Iraq in response.

Bashar al-Assad. Washington's policy in 2011 was to get to the point of a transition in Syria by finding cracks in the regime and offering incentives for people to abandon Assad, but regime cohesiveness held and the crackdown intensified (Lee and Malas 2015). At the end of April 2011, Washington took its first concrete steps in response to the bloody crackdown on protests by imposing sanctions on personalities deemed responsible for human rights abuses, notably in Syria's intelligence agency and the IRGC, which was accused of assisting Damascus in the repression of protesters (Hosenball and Spetalnick 2011). In August 2011, President Obama publicly called for Assad to step down, without changing the core of U.S. policy regarding Syria as explained previously: The regime must be maintained with only superficial changes and integrating opposition actors linked to Western nations, Turkey, and Gulf monarchies, represented first by the SNC and then by the Coalition.

At the end of the summer of 2011, and following the Western-led military interventions to overthrow the Qaddafi regime, the specter of the Libyan model was mentioned in Syria and even encouraged by segments of the Syrian-exiled opposition in the SNC. For varying reasons, the Western powers were hesitant, so they limited their involvement. The United States and most Western states, with the exception of France, could be characterized as relatively passive toward the uprising in Syria with regard to challenging the Assad regime. Early on, from Washington to the NATO headquarters in Brussels, they made clear that they had no intention of intervening in Syria to overthrow Assad's regime.

In August 2012, U.S. secretary of defense Leon Panetta explained:

> The best way to preserve that kind of stability is to maintain as much of the military and police as you can, along with security forces, and hope that they will transition to a democratic form of government. That's the key ... (Reuters 2012d)

He added that it was important not to make the same mistakes that Washington made in Iraq, referring to the disbanding of security forces and the army.

This unwillingness to change the status quo radically vis-à vis the regime in Syria was notably reflected by the absence of any kind of large, organized, and decisive military assistance of the United States, Western states, or both to the Syrian armed opposition groups. Western governments provided only "nonlethal" support and humanitarian assistance while resisting pleas to arm opposition forces or establish safe zones or no-fly zones (Entous 2015). In addition, the United States opposed supplying various FSA forces with antiaircraft missiles (or Manpads) capable of taking down warplanes

(Reuters 2014), which would have curtailed to some extent the murderous and destructive air strikes, particularly of low altitudes. U.S. officials opposed the introduction of such weapons in the country, citing long-standing fears that they might fall into the hands of groups that would use these weapons against Western targets or commercial airlines. In July 2012, the United States halted the provision of at least 18 Manpads sourced from Libya (Malas 2012).

In the Obama administration, Secretary of State Hillary Clinton, along with David Petraeus, the then-CIA director and former U.S. commander in Afghanistan and Iraq, differed with this line and recommended training and equipping Syrian armed opposition groups. This position, however, was promoted and defended in order to not overthrow the Assad regime. Clinton was also very interested in preserving state institutions and their integrity, especially its security infrastructures, so as not to repeat a scenario akin to Iraq following the fall of Saddam Hussein. The objective of arming some segments of the armed opposition groups was to create a partner in Syria that Washington could work with and that had the capacity to persuade Assad and his backers that a military victory was impossible (Clinton 2014: 386–394).

The rise of ISIL and the establishment of its caliphate in June 2014 following the conquest of Mosul in Iraq pushed Washington to re-engage its forces more deeply in the region. In September 2014, President Obama announced the establishment of a broad international coalition, composed of nearly 60 states at its peak, to defeat the jihadist group; however, only a few participated effectively in the campaign in Syria (five states) and Iraq (eight states), as the United States conducted approximately 85 percent of its total combat missions in Syria and Iraq in 2015 (European Parliament 2015: 8). Washington developed a strategy of "IS first," with the objective of defeating the group, which former U.S. director of national intelligence James Clapper called the "preeminent terrorist threat" to the United States (Stein 2017: 5).

With this perspective, and alongside the creation of an U.S.-led international coalition to combat IS in the autumn of 2014, there was a plan by the Obama administration, approved by Congress in 2014, to provide the equivalent of USD 500 million to arm and equip 5,000–10,000 Syrian opposition armed forces. The objective was not aimed at overthrowing the Assad regime, but rather concentrated on fighting ISIS, as written in the text of the resolution:

> The Secretary of Defense is authorized, in coordination with the Secretary of State, to provide assistance, including training, equipment, supplies, and sustainment, to appropriately vetted elements of

the Syrian opposition and other appropriately vetted Syrian groups and individuals for the following purposes:
- Defending the Syrian people from attacks by ISIL and securing territory controlled by the Syrian opposition.
- Protecting the United States, its friends and allies, and the Syrian people from the threats posed by terrorists in Syria.
- Promoting the conditions for a negotiated settlement to end the conflict in Syria. (Belasco and Blanchard 2015)

However, this program was a total failure, with only 100–120 fighters trained by September 2015 (Ackerman 2015). In addition, numerous fighters withdrew from the U.S. Defense Department's train-and-equip program after refusing to sign a contract guaranteeing not to fight Assad regime forces (Hamidi 2015). At the end of September 2015, the program was terminated following the attacks of Jabhat al-Nusra on two small groups of trained fighters that were sent into northern Aleppo and that could not face its brutal power.

In October 2015, even Senator Lindsey Graham challenged Defense Secretary Ashton Carter and Joint Chiefs of Staff Chair General Joseph Dunford on the U.S. strategy in Syria. He asked about the possibility of overthrowing Bashar al-Assad, saying, "This is a half-assed strategy at best" (C-SPAN 2015).

More generally, as argued by Gilbert Achcar (2016: 20–21):

Rather than lack of confidence in the opposition's military skills, there are some grounds to believe that Washington did not seriously support any particular group of the Syrian opposition because it could not guarantee their loyalty to U.S. interests.

This is when in the framework of the strategy of "IS first," and following the complete failure to assist FSA forces in northern areas, the United States increasingly supported YPG forces through the coalition known as the SDF, as mentioned in Chapter 5. The United States and French and British allied forces advised and assisted local ground forces, while also facilitating the delivery of arms and ammunition to SDF forces on the ground (Stein 2017: 5). Washington considered the SDF the most effective fighting force in Syria against IS (The New Arab 2016a), although it was not ready to support Kurdish national rights in Syria and elsewhere.

The U.S. policy of "IS first" in the framework of the war on terror led to some degree of rapprochement with the Russians. The U.S. president clearly stated in his speech at the UN General Assembly on September 28, 2015, his willingness to work with Russia and Iran to find a solution in Syria, while emphasizing the implausibility of maintaining "a prewar status quo" (Halawi 2015). The beginning of the Russian air strike campaigns on September 30 in Syria to assist the Assad regime was not objected to by the United States (ISW Research Team 2015). On December 15, 2015, then–secretary of state John Kerry told reporters in the Russian capital after meeting President Vladimir Putin that "the United States and our partners are not seeking so-called regime change" (Taranto 2015). A similar tendency was observed among European states to concentrate on the war on terror and not demand the departure of Bashar al-Assad, at least in the short term.

The election of Trump as U.S. president and his arrival to power in January 2017 did not change the strategic positioning of Washington in Syria (the priority was still the war on terror and maintaining the structures of the regime), despite a more aggressive and firm policy toward the Assad regime to make it respect the boundaries set by the U.S. administration in the country. Iran's influence in some regions of Syria was also checked. Washington did not hesitate to bomb the Syrian regime's military bases or forces on several occasions, such as in April 2017, in response to chemical attacks in Khan Sheikhoun city in Idlib Governorate carried out by Syrian air forces, killing more than 70 civilians (Lynch 2017).[14] However, the way that the U.S. bombing occurred showed that they did not want to hit Damascus too hard. Moscow officials confirmed that they received advance warning from the United States about its strike on Syria, while still condemning it. According to some testimonies, regime soldiers were informed about the strike by Russian officials ahead of time, promptly evacuating personnel and moving equipment out of the area (The Daily Beast 2017). Within 24 hours of the strike, the regime's warplanes were taking off from the bombed Shayrat air base.

Similarly, the U.S. government, in alliance with the United Kingdom and France, launched air strikes in Syria in mid-April 2018, officially in response to the Assad regime's use of chemical weapons against the city of Douma a few days earlier that killed at least 70 civilians and wounded a few hundred more. The three Western powers reportedly targeted three sites in Damascus and Homs, which were accused of developing, fabricating, and stockpiling chemical weapons. These strikes caused no casualties, and

---

[14] The chemical attack also showed that the deal between the United States and Russia to get rid of the chemical weapons in the hands of the regime had been a failure. The SNHR (2016) documented 139 attacks using a toxic substance between September 2013 and August 2016. The Syrian regime focused its use of poison gases on opposition-held areas; 97 percent of its chemical attacks targeted opposition-held areas, while 3 percent of the attacks were carried out in IS-held areas, showing once again the priority of the regime's repression (SNHR 2016).

most of the installations were evacuated a few days before the attack, thanks to warnings from Russia. The United States, the United Kingdom, and France said that the strikes were not aimed at paralyzing the Syrian regime's defenses or provoking "regime change," but rather to dissuade Assad from using chemical weapons. Russian foreign minister Sergey Lavrov also declared that before the U.S. strikes against Syrian targets, Russia had told U.S. authorities which parts of Syria represented "red lines" for Moscow, and U.S. military action had not crossed these lines (Reuters 2018).

At the same time, following the election of Donald Trump as U.S. president, the U.S.-led coalition in its struggle against IS boosted support for the SDF, supplying armored vehicles for the first time as they prepared for a new phase in a campaign to capture Raqqa. The mission was carried out in the autumn of 2017 by SDF forces, dominated by the YPG contingent, with U.S. soldiers participating in the offensive as well. In July 2017, Turkey's state-run Anadolu Agency provided detailed information about ten U.S. bases in northern Syria, including troop counts and a map of the U.S. military presence (Bilgic and Harvey 2017).

In February 2018, about 300 men working for a Kremlin-linked Russian private military firm were either killed or injured in Deir ez-Zor during a confrontation between U.S. forces and their SDF allies on one side, and pro-regime forces comprised mainly of Russian mercenaries on the other (Tsvetkova 2018). After this event, a Pentagon spokesman declared that Washington "did not seek a conflict with the regime" (Barthe, Kaval Paris, and Zerrouky 2018). The U.S. air strikes, which killed hundreds of Russian mercenaries in Syria, marked the bloodiest confrontation between the two states in decades. However, the incident did not spark a political crisis between Moscow and Washington. Washington still wanted to maintain its influence in this area of Syria for various political purposes, including the complete elimination of IS and the countering of Iranian influence (Savage 2018; C-SPAN 2018).

Despite this firmer policy, from the beginning of 2018, there was an increasing debate within the Trump administration about whether to maintain U.S. troops in Syria and continue the collaboration with Kurdish-led SDF forces. President Trump declared in April that he wanted to get U.S. forces—about 2,000 soldiers on the ground, including special operations forces—out of Syria relatively soon, agreeing only to keep them a while longer to defeat IS but unwilling to back a long-term commitment (Hirschfeld Davis 2018). At the same time, Trump called for increased engagement in Syria from their partners on several occasions, including Saudi Arabia, the UAE, Qatar, and others to ensure that Iran did not take advantage of the eradication of IS (al-Monitor 2018).

In August 2018, the State Department announced it was pulling back the USD 230 million of funding that it had allocated to rebuild parts of Syria once held by IS. Instead, Washington secured USD 300 million in financial donations for regions of Syria previously held by IS, including USD 100 million by Saudi Arabia and USD 50 million by the UAE, alongside smaller amounts from coalition partners, to replace its own funding. This financial assistance came after Trump demanded that allies help carry the costs of the war (Wroughton 2018). However, this was far from U.S. expectations on the matter. Following the U.S. decision, the British government declared that it was also ending funding for some aid programs in opposition-held areas of Syria, including projects that funded local councils (Singh 2018).

In September 2018, the U.S. administration redefined its objectives to include the exit of all Iranian military and proxy forces from Syria, not limiting itself to the defeat of IS (Kube and Lee 2018); however, in mid-December 2018, Trump once again announced the withdrawal of U.S. troops from Syria, declaring that they had succeeded in their mission to defeat IS and therefore that they were no longer needed in the country. This decision drew widespread criticism among a number of U.S. officials and administrations, while prompting Defense Secretary Jim Mattis and Pentagon chief of staff Kevin Sweeney to resign in protest. The departure from Syria was seen as contradicting not only the antijihadist struggle, but also Washington's number one priority in the region: counteracting Iran's influence.

Before too long, though, Trump's original decision of a rapid, 30-day withdrawal seemed postponed once more. U.S. officials announced that there were no fixed timetable, while initially the departure was unconditioned, it became explicitly based on receiving assurances from Ankara not to attack the regions under the control of YPG forces—a demand that caused Turkish president Recep Tayyip Erdogan to snub National Security Adviser John Bolton during Bolton's visit to Ankara in the beginning of January 2019 (Dobbins 2019). Trump warned Turkey of economic devastation if it attacked SDF forces in Syria. By mid-to-late January 2019, no U.S. troops had withdrawn from Syria, and only some equipment had moved out, while SDF forces were continuing their military operations against IS with support from U.S.-led coalition air strikes and artillery (Holland, Stewart, and Wroughton 2019).

Despite the confusion over Trump's strategy in Syria, U.S. policy did not radically change toward the Assad regime throughout Obama's and Trump's early mandates, focusing on a political transition favoring stability and the maintenance of the regime's structures, as well as the war on terror. As mentioned earlier, the major difference was Trump's focus on opposition to Iran and seeing its influence diminished in Syria.

Saudi Arabia, Qatar, and the Gulf Cooperation Council (GCC)

Prior to the uprising, many Gulf monarchies enjoyed relatively good relations with Damascus, especially the two main protagonists, Qatar and Saudi Arabia, with high levels of investment in the country. Sheikh Hamad of Qatar championed the international rehabilitation of Assad against Damascus's ostracizing by the United States, Europe, and other Arab states. Damascus and Doha worked very closely together on a number of regional issues throughout the 2000s (Fielding-Smith and Khalaf 2013). Saudi Arabia's relations with Syria improved considerably prior to the uprising after a period of high tension, especially following the assassination of Rafic Hariri in 2005 in Lebanon. This was due to the strong political and economic links between Hariri and Saudi rulers, in which Damascus was accused of being the orchestrator of the operation.

This animosity reached its highest level with the boycott of the Arab League summit in Damascus in March 2008 by Saudi Arabia and many other states following Riyadh. Later in 2008, relations gradually began to improve. Bashar al-Assad and Abdullah bin Abdul al-Aziz exchanged a series of letters, political delegations, and even personal visits. Relations warmed considerably between 2009 and 2010, with Assad visiting Riyadh three times and the Saudi king visiting Damascus (Hassan 2013b). Muhammad al-Jasser, governor of the Saudi Arabian Monetary Agency, announced new loans to Syria in March 2010 worth USD 140 million, following a second visit to Damascus by the Saudi monarch. Relations between the two countries were stable on the eve of the uprising. The Syrian regime even supported the Saudi-led military intervention of the GCC Peninsula Shield Force to crush the uprising in Bahrain in March 2011, while Iran opposed it (Wieland 2012: 55).

In the early stages of the uprising, Gulf rulers tried to engage with the regime to facilitate a peaceful solution and prevent a repressive military response. They were not prepared to see Assad ousted from power. Saudi Arabia was especially worried about the regional trend of uprisings, and Qatar wanted to maintain its good relations with Damascus. Saudi King Abdullah sent his son, Prince Abdulaziz bin Abdullah, to Damascus three times, while Qatari Emir Hamad sent his son, Tamim, to try to convince Bashar al-Assad to end the repression of demonstrators and engage in some superficial reforms in a unity government (Phillips 2016: 68–69). At the same time, Riyadh continued to develop economic relations with Damascus. In April 2011, Saudi Arabia signed a contract to finance the construction of a power plant in Deir ez-Zor worth USD 375 million. As late as August 2011, Saudi Arabia and the UAE paid USB 4 billion to the Central Bank of Syria (Said H. 2016). For its part, Qatar's first reaction was very cautious, and al-Jazeera, the Qatari-owned television channel, was criticized for downplaying the first demonstrations.

This situation changed over time, as it became clearer to the Gulf monarchies that reaching a sort of understanding with the regime and steering Damascus away from Tehran to strengthen their regional influence were increasingly impossible. In the mid-to-late summer of 2011, Saudi Arabia and Qatar became the most important and vocal actors demanding the removal of Bashar al-Assad from power. It was indeed in large measure as a result of Saudi and Qatari pressure that regional and Muslim world organizations aligned themselves against the Assad regime, including the Arab League (which in March 2013 awarded Syria's seat to the Syrian Coalition), the Organization of Islamic Conference, and the Gulf Cooperation Council (GCC) (Heydemann 2013a: 10).

Undermining Iran's influence was the core issue for Saudi Arabia in relation to Syria. Since 2003, Riyadh has been worried about the growth of Tehran's influence in Iraq and in the region, perceiving it as a military and ideological threat to provide another Islamic model of rule. Saudi Arabia, which had generally in the past relied massively on its financial power to conduct its foreign policy objectives and neutralize rival actors rather than intervening directly, increasingly took the leading role in opposing Iran's growing influence in the region (particularly Lebanon, Iraq, and Yemen). The election of Barack Obama in the United States in 2009 did not appease the fears of Riyadh—on the contrary, the new president wanted to progressively disengage from the region and try to seek some form of détente with Tehran (Phillips 2016: 19–20, 33–37; Matthiesen 2017: 46).

In the background of the Saudi–Iranian cold war, Qatar had considerably deepened its influence in the region in the years prior to the MENA uprisings. The decision in the early 1990s to build up Qatar's energy infrastructure and exploit the country's massive reserves of natural gas allowed Doha to increase its foreign influence and power. Its wealth expanded massively, with its GDP surging from USD 25 billion in 2001 to USD 200 billion in 2013. Long-term liquefied natural gas (LNG) contracts linked foreign partners' energy security needs to Qatar's domestic stability, while large accumulations of capital were invested both in Qatar and abroad in the form of high-profile acquisitions and investments. LNG gave Qatar the choice of diversifying its international relationships by making a range of countries stakeholders in Qatari stability. This massive wealth and diversification of international and regional relations enabled Qatari leaders to become important regional actors by playing a very active role in mediating regional crises and conflicts, including in Yemen (2008–10), Lebanon (2008), and Darfur (2008–10). In addition, Qatar's television channel al-Jazeera brought the emirate a good deal of popularity in the Arab world for its anti-Israel and anti-U.S. coverage. This was the case despite Qatar having welcomed the opening of the largest U.S. military base in the region, the al-Udeid Air Base, as well as hosting the U.S. Central Command after 2003 and becoming the first GCC state to grant Israel de facto recognition following a visit by Israeli prime minister Shimon Peres in 1996.

The beginning of the MENA uprisings saw a new opportunity for Doha to advance its regional power and influence, first through direct participation in military intervention in Libya, and later through assistance to Islamic fundamentalist groups. This assistance was perhaps most notable through the political and economic support for branches of the MB throughout the region, most notably Egypt and Tunisia (Ulrichsen 2014; Matthiesen 2017: 54). In Egypt, for example, Doha delivered a total of USD 5.5 billion to President Mohamed Morsi's government, constituting USD 4 billion in deposits at the Central Bank of Egypt, as well as various grants and shipments of LNG. In addition, Qatar announced in 2012 that it would undertake an investment program in Egypt worth USD 18 billion over the next five years, but this commitment was abandoned following the military coup in July 2013 that ousted the MB from power (Khan and Lebaron 2013).

Given the conditions on the ground, Riyadh and Doha saw an opportunity in Syria to establish a Sunni-friendly regime as a means for increasing their standing in the region. In Iraq, this meant pressuring the government led by al-Da'wa, a Shi'a Islamic fundamentalist party allied with Tehran, and at the same time strengthening Iraqi Sunni parties. In Lebanon, the fall of the Assad regime would help to bolster Saudi allies, the March 14 coalition led by Saad Hariri, to the detriment of Hezbollah and other Syrian-allied parties. As argued by Hassan Hassan (2013b):

> For the Gulf States, the Syria conflict is thus a critical battle for control of a key pivot state in the region. Drawing Damascus away from the Iranian camp is seen as a way of cementing broader regional influence in the Levant, and reestablishing the more favorable regional balance of power that they lost following the U.S. occupation of Iraq in 2003.

As the militarization of the uprising deepened, Saudi Arabia and Qatar became the primary financial and military backers of the Syrian armed opposition, shipping military materials via Turkey to the various armed groups in early 2012, although they differed over which armed groups and which elements of the political opposition to support. As we have seen,

Saudi Arabia and Qatar funded various armed opposition groups, from the FSA to Islamic fundamentalist movements.

Indeed, Saudi Arabia and Qatar did not see eye to eye in the Syrian conflict, and significant divergences of opinion remained. In Syria, Qatar collaborated more closely with Turkey than Saudi Arabia, while Doha saw an opportunity to promote the interests of its long-standing regional client in the MB and other Islamic fundamentalist movements in Syria. Saudi Arabia, on the other hand, sponsored opposition members that would serve its interests, while it sought to prevent the rise of two main forces in Syria: the MB and jihadist forces.

Although it did not radically oppose the Syrian MB as its regional counterpart, the Saudi kingdom still considered the Brotherhood movement a threat, notably influencing the Saudi Islamic fundamentalist opposition al-Sahwa. Saudi Arabia supported the MB from the mid-1950s until 1991. That year, relations were broken off following the MB's declaration of support for Saddam Hussein's regime against the Western-led intervention backed by the Saudi kingdom. In 1992, the emirate of Qatar, which had maintained a long-standing relationship with the MB for decades by hosting one of its most influential members, Sheikh Yusuf al-Qardawi replaced Saudi Arabia as the MB's main supporter (Achcar 2013: 149).

Similarly, it was the deployment of the U.S. army on Saudi soil during the 1991 military intervention against Iraq that led al-Qa'ida to oppose the Saudi kingdom, while it was funded by Riyadh in the 1980s in the war in Afghanistan against the Soviet Union. Leaders of al-Qaida and IS have both launched attacks in Saudi Arabia in the past and openly called for the overthrow of the Saudi kingdom (Porter 2017). In March 2014, Saudi Arabia named the MB a terrorist organization, alongside major jihadist groups fighting in Syria including Jabhat al-Nusra, the al-Qa'ida branch in Syria (Lacroix 2014a).

This is why, except in Bahrain—where both Saudi Arabia and Qatar intervened to assist in the crushing of popular protests—Riyadh and Doha have had different policies on the uprisings in the region. Saudi Arabia generally supported the maintenance of the old regimes throughout the region and opposed protest movements, with the exception of Libya, where it remained neutral, and Syria. Saudi Arabia's top Islamic scholar, Grand Mufti Sheikh Abdul-Aziz al-Sheikh, condemned the MENA uprisings in 2011 as a plot by the enemies of Islam to break up Arab Muslim nations and spread instability (Reuters 2012a). With the exception of Bahrain, as mentioned previously, Qatar welcomed the uprisings by boosting its support to the MB and other Islamic fundamentalist movements to expand its political and economic influence at the expense of Saudi Arabia and the UAE.

Relations between Doha and Riyadh continued to worsen through the years because of competing objectives in the uprisings, leading to a first crisis in 2014 and a second in June 2017. Saudi Arabia, the UAE, Bahrain, and Egypt cut diplomatic and transport ties with Qatar in June 2017, accusing the country of supporting terrorism, fomenting regional unrest by backing movements such as the MB and Hamas, and getting too close to Iran—all of which Doha denied. Saudi Arabia wanted above all to discipline Qatar's independent policies and subject it to Riyadh's regional agenda. This crisis rendered even weaker the position of the Syrian opposition, both armed and political, by deepening its divisions. Throughout the uprising, Saudi Arabia and Qatar became increasingly isolated and less able to expand or deepen their support to armed opposition forces in Syria. Saudi Arabia was stuck in a quagmire in Yemen, while Qatar rhetorically supported the armed opposition forces without acting (Finn and Maclean 2016).

Progressively, Saudi Arabia and Qatar also faced increasing obstacles in their campaigns to isolate the Assad regime politically and diplomatically in the MENA region. Egypt and Jordan had long indicated ambivalence about the future of Assad, while formally supporting measures against the regime in the Arab League and the Organization of Islamic Cooperation (Ibish 2016: 21). The Egyptian state showed signs of rapprochement with the Syrian regime. In October 2016, Egyptian officials at the United Nations rejected the resolution led by France at the UNSC, demanding an end to all bombing in Aleppo and instead favoring the Russian resolution, while Syria's national security chief, Ali Mamlouk, met a senior Egyptian intelligence official, Khaled Fawzi, in Cairo. In their meeting, the two sides agreed to coordinate politically on fighting the violent extremism that both countries were facing (Aboulenein 2016). In November 2016, the secretary-general of the Arab League, Ahmed Aboul Gheit, said in an interview on Egyptian television that Assad could stay in power if he continued to win future elections, while he advocated for a unity government between the government and the opposition (*Middle East Eye* 2016).

At the same time, a series of agreements was reached between Russia and the Gulf states to cooperate in areas of common strategic interest. Gulf monarchies increasingly sought a consensus with Moscow, including Syria. In December 2016, Russia brokered the first deal in 15 years between the Organization of Petroleum Exporting Countries (OPEC) and non-OPEC countries to cut oil production, and secured a USD 5 billion investment by Qatar in oil giant Rosneft PJSC (Blas and Champion 2016). In late May 2017, following a visit of Deputy Crown Prince Muhammad bin Salman to Russia to discuss the oil market and the situation in Syria with President Vladimir Putin, officials in Moscow said that "relations between Saudi Arabia and Russia are going through one of their best moments ever" (Issaev and

Kozhanov 2017). In September 2017, Saudi Arabia assured Russia that it supported the gradual processes of negotiating local cease-fires and establishing "de-escalation zones" in Syria (Akram 2017).

More generally, relations between Saudi Arabia and Russia continued to improve as they agreed on output cuts under an OPEC deal aimed at bolstering prices (Carey and Meyer 2017). In October, it was Saudi King Salman bin Abdul Aziz's turn to visit Russia, during which billions of dollars on investment deals in energy, trade, and defense were reached, including the possible purchase of Russia's advanced S-400 Triumf missile defense system (Borshchevskaya 2017). In the same month, Moscow and Doha signed a joint intergovernmental agreement on military technical cooperation on the sidelines of Russian defense minister Sergei Shoigu's visit to Doha (*Middle East Monitor* 2017a). At the end of March 2018, Qatar Airways announced plans to buy a 25 percent stake in Russia's Vnukovo Airport, the third largest in the Moscow area (Reuters Staff 2018a).

Russia welcomed the role of Saudi Arabia in uniting the Syrian political opposition, guaranteeing the participation of Moscow representatives and Cairo groups for talks with the regime and pressuring them to seek a political solution with Damascus (see Chapter 4). Saudi Arabia and Qatar, therefore, became less able to seek the overthrow of Assad (and to some extent less interested in doing so). However, Riyadh maintained its primary focus on countering the influence of Iran in Syria, as reflected in an interview by Saudi Crown Prince Muhammad Bin Salman in March 2018 asserting that Bashar al-Assad was staying, but hoping that he would not become a "puppet" for Tehran (Hennigan 2018). The Saudi kingdom and the UAE were also interested, although to a lesser extent than Iran, in countering the influence of Turkey, perceived as a close ally of Qatar.

By summer 2018, a form of political détente and rapprochement was occurring between some Gulf monarchies and Damascus. The UAE,[15]

---

[15] It is important to note that despite UAE initially following Saudi Arabia's opposition to the Assad regime following the outbreak of uprising in Syria, the UAE opened its doors to a number of Assad's close relatives, including his mother, Anisa, and his sister Bushra and her children. Moreover, several internationally sanctioned pro-Assad businessmen continued to do business without any problem in the UAE, including his cousin, Rami Makhlouf. In 2014, many UAE-based individuals and companies actively aided Assad's war efforts. Some provided the Syrian regime with the fuel it needed to operate its war machine; others, like the Dubai-based Yona Star, acted as shipping agents for the Syrian air force, the Syrian Air Force Intelligence, the Army Supply Bureau, and the Scientific Studies and Research Center, which has been developing the regime's biological and chemical capabilities.

Many other Emirati businessmen known to be close to the UAE authorities have also maintained their relations with the Syrian government long after the eruption of the Syrian uprising. Some established new companies in Syria, opened branches for their UAE-based companies in which sought to normalize its relations with Damascus, took the lead in this process. Visits from junior Emirati representatives in Syria became more frequent, while UAE officials sent more than one maintenance team to inspect its Damascus embassy in a sign that some activity could resume. In May 2018, the UAE also announced the resumption of the air route between the Syrian province of Lattakia and the emirate of Sharjah (Qanso 2018). In June 2018, UAE foreign affairs minister Dr. Anwar Gargash stated, "I think it was a mistake to kick Syria out of the Arab league" (al-Wasmi and Macmillan 2018). A month later, Lebanese newspaper al-Akhbar revealed that the Deputy Head of the Supreme National Security Council in the UAE, Ali Muhammad bin Hammad al-Shamsi, visited Damascus and met with an officer in the Assad regime, believed to be the head of the general administration of the General Intelligence, General Deeb Zeitoun. The newspaper reported that Shamsi discussed security issues with the Syrian officer and potential means of restoring relations between the two countries. But there were concerns from Abu Dhabi not to anger Riyadh, so al-Shamsi suggested the possibility of resuming indirect relations between the two parties by tasking the UAE ambassador in Beirut, Hamad Saeed al-Shamsi, with managing affairs of the embassy in Damascus from his base in the Lebanese capital (Qanso 2018).

This process continued after the summer. In October 2018, on the sidelines of the UN General Assembly, there was a public exchange of hugs, followed by a brief verbal exchange between the Syrian foreign minister, Walid al-Muallem, and his Bahraini counterpart. Khalid bin Ahmed Al Khalifa, the Bahraini foreign minister, told Saudi-run al-Arabiya TV that it was not the first meeting with "my brother," the Syrian minister. But he said that the meeting had been unplanned, while other planned ones weren't caught on camera. He added, "The Bahraini government is … working even with the countries that we disagree with. We do not work with those who try to topple these countries." The minister also affirmed Bahrain's support to the extension of the government's sovereignty over all Syrian territories (Associated Press 2018).

A few days later, Bashar al-Assad praised Kuwait and his ruler's positions in an interview with the Kuwaiti newspaper *al-Shâhed*. In the interview, he described Amir Sheikh Sabah al-Ahmad's political stance toward Syria as "honorable," while stating that Damascus had reached an understanding with many Arab states, and that Western and Arab delegations have already started to come to Syria to arrange their return (*al-Shâhed* 2018).

---

the country, or both. The UAE also never really fully broke diplomatic relations with Damascus, and the Syrian embassy continued to operate in Abu Dhabi (Bakeer 2019).

In December 2018, the situation accelerated once more toward a relegit-imation and rehabilitation of the Assad regime among its Arab counterparts. First, Sudanese president Omar al-Bashir, a close ally of Saudi Arabia, Qatar and Turkey, visited Syria in mid-December, becoming the first Arab League leader to visit the country since the beginning of the uprising in March 2011, while on December 27, the UAE reopened its embassy in Syria after seven years. A day later, Bahrain followed suit. Both states justified their decision by the necessity to reactive an Arab presence and role in Syria, but also to counter the deepening influence of Turkey and Iran the country (Bakeer 2019). In the beginning of January 2019, Lebanon's *al-Joumhouria* newspaper, citing unnamed sources, reported that Major General Ali Mamlouk, Syria's national security chief, traveled to Saudi Arabia in late December to discuss the restoration of relations (The New Arab 2019).

Turkey, expanding its role in Syria

The relations between Turkey's AKP government and the Syrian regime after Bashar al-Assad's arrival had improved considerably, particularly since 2004. Both states organized common cabinet meetings and spoke of "family bonds" when they referred to bilateral relations. Erdogan used to spend va-cations with Assad's family (Wieland 2012: 57). The 2007 Free Trade Agreement and the 2009 Visa Exemption Agreement further reinforced Syrian–Turkish relations. Trade volume rose from USD 796 million in 2006 to USD 2.5 billion in 2010, greatly advantaging Turkey, as mentioned in Chapter 1. As late as February 2011, during the foundation stone for a joint "friendship dam" on the Orontes with Syrian officials, Erdogan declared that "we have always said that there should be no problems between brothers" (Davis and Ilgıt 2013).

Prior to 2011, under the leadership of the AKP, Turkey had increased significantly its political and economic influence in the region following the U.S.-British-led invasion of Iraq in 2003. Its export-driven economy expanded considerably with new markets opening in the Middle East (Phillips 2016: 35).

Following the beginning of the Syrian uprising in March 2011, Erdogan advised Assad to make some concessions to the protesters in the form of minor reforms to appease them rather than radically modifying the Syrian state's composition. However, relations started to worsen following a visit to Damascus of Turkey's foreign minister, Ahmed Davutoglu, on August 9, 2011, during which he delivered a message from Erdogan that called for an end to violence and the approval of a Turkish-sponsored peace plan. Assad and regime officials rejected Turkey's mediation and propositions. Eventually, the Syrian regime's refusal to engage with any Turkish recommendations, coupled with strong official encouragement from the United States, prompted then-prime minister Erdogan to publicly call on Bashar al-Assad to step down in early September 2011. A final attempt occurred in October with another visit of the Turkish foreign minister, but once again no political settlement sponsored by Turkey could be found (Wieland 2012: 57).

From the beginning of 2012, arms purchased by Saudi Arabia and Qatar were delivered to various opposition groups through the Turkish airport of Esenboğa in Ankara. The Turkish government remained aware of and part of the operation, monitoring shipments as they moved by land into Syria.

Very quickly, however, the main concern of Turkey became the rising influence of the PYD and its control of Syria's Kurdish-majority regions following the regime's withdrawal in the summer of 2012 of some areas close to the Turkish border. To counter the growing influence of PYD forces, the Turkish government turned a blind eye to foreign-fighter flows across the Syrian border from the end of 2011 through 2014. This provided Islamic fundamentalist and jihadist groups with recruits and freedom of movement and allowed cross-border networks to develop, which assisted these groups to sustain themselves economically (Chivers and Schmitt 2013; Itani and Stein 2016: 7–8). The Turkish government saw some benefit in their development, as they were fighting the PYD and the Syrian regime. Turkey also supported other key armed groups in northwestern Syria, including Faylaq al-Sham and al-Jabha al-Shamiyeh, which had connections to the MB and several Turkmen armed groups raised and armed by Ankara. Jaysh al-Islam, previously close to Saudi Arabia, also came under increasing Turkish influence following the group's forced departure to the northern regions of Syria from Eastern Ghoutha as the regime took control of these areas in April. As mentioned previously, in the summer of 2018, Turkey supported the establishment of the National Liberation Front, which gathered various opposition armed forces, especially Islamic fundamentalist forces, and acted as a proxy force for Ankara.

The Turkish government also initially resisted moves to join the U.S.-led international coalition against ISIL, arguing that the war should not be limited to the jihadist group, but rather also include a focus on overthrowing the Syrian regime. They refused the use of the Turkish Incirlik and Diyarbakir air bases by the United States to carry out bombing operations against IS targets in Syria until July 2015. However, Ankara changed its position after the killing of a Turkish soldier in an IS attack and a suicide bombing in the Turkish town of Suruc on July 20 against the cultural center of Amara. The center had been hosting a meeting of 300 young Kurdish leftists, members of the Federation of Socialist Youth Associations. The suicide bomber, a Turkish citizen and member of IS, resulted in the death of thirty-two people. In the wake of this tragedy, Turkey finally took the decision in mid-2015 to launch a bombing offensive against a number of IS sites in Syria and allow the use of its military bases to U.S. planes (Ackerman, Letsch, and Shaheen 2015). However, the Turkish air force continued to prioritize Kurdish targets over those of IS.

Ankara maintained an ambivalent attitude toward the other main jihadist group, Jabhat al-Nusra, providing support to the Jaysh al-Fateh coalition (led by Jabhat al-Nusra and Ahrar Sham, accompanied by Islamic and FSA groups, with various other small groups affiliated with the FSA) (Itani and Stein 2016: 8; Tokmajyan 2016: 5). Similarly, in October 2017, Turkish soldiers were provided an armed escort into Idlib by the jihadist coalition HTS,[16] allowing Turkish troops to monitor and contain YPG units in their stronghold of Afrin. In an interview with al-Jazeera channel, HTS political bureau chief Yousuf Al-Hajar said that his organization had a close relationship with Turkey, which he described as an ally (MEMRI 2018). More generally, HTS engaged pragmatically with Turkish intelligence but refused to fully submit to Ankara's diktat to dissolve the group and join the National Liberation Front's coalition, led by Ahrar al-Sham, Jaysh al-Islam, Nour a-Din al-Zinki, and armed groups close to the MB, supported by Ankara in Idlib in August 2018. Following this refusal, Turkey designated HTS a terrorist organization and continued to put pressure on it (Lund 2018b), by trying to create divisions within it, while maintaining contacts with the jihadist orgnaization. In the beginning of January, HTS leader, Abu Muhammad Jolani, even declared that he supported Turkey's goal to control the east of the Euphrates under PYD's rule, deemed as an enemy of the revolution by the jihadist organization (Rudaw 2019).

By 2016, and especially after the failed coup d'état of a fraction of the army in Turkey in July, Ankara did not consider the fall of Assad a priority, but rather defeating the Kurdish national movements, in both Turkey and Syria. During this period, the AKP government operated a new rapprochement with the Russian government after nearly a year of heightened tensions (Nashashibi 2016). Russian jets assisted Turkish military forces for the first time in December 2016 throughout their operations in northern Syria, bombing IS targets as part of their larger Euphrates Shield campaign (Coskun and Karadeniz 2016). The operation succeeded both in rooting out IS from the Turkish border and preventing the PYD-YPG from connecting its main territory in northeast Syria with the city of Afrin.

The successive military interventions of Turkish troops within Syria from summer 2016 in the framework of the Euphrates Shield operation, and then in Afrin in March 2018, considerably increased Ankara's influence

---

[16] HTS grew out of what used to be the Nusra Front, Syria's official al-Qa'ida franchise.

over the newly conquered regions. They assisted in the return of services such as medical facilities, hospitals, and schools in regions previously occupied by IS, while imposing their own rule by disregarding local governance structures in Jarablus following the eviction of IS in 2016 (Haid 2017b: 9) and replacing former PYD structures in Afrin. Turkey's postal service opened branches in Jarablus, al-Bab, and Cobanbey (in Arabic al-Rayi) (All4Syria 2017b), while setting up towers for Turkish communications companies and establishing Turkish-sponsored universities in a number of cities (Tastekin 2018). They trained hundreds of Syrians to establish a new armed security force made up of regular police and special forces. Along with this policy, families of the armed opposition fighters who died in the Turkish-led Operation Olive Branch military campaign and subsequent occupation of Afrin in March 2018 also received death gratuity payments from the Turkish government (Tastekin 2018).

Mulham Jazmati, a researcher at the Syrian Economic Forum, stated that Turkey's aims in this area were not only military, but also economic. As an example, he cited large investments in the city of Qabsein in the al-Bab region in December 2017, where the local council signed a Memorandum of Understanding with a Turkish construction company to establish a residential project in the area, including 225 apartments and about 30 shops in the Turkish mold. He argued that Ankara wanted "to impose their stewardship on the northern region as it has strategic value, most importantly preventing the formation of a united Kurdish state on its borders in the future" (cited in Enab Baladi 2018b).

Under Turkey's auspices, the construction in northern Syria of First Industrial City, a few miles northwest of the city of al-Bab, was also launched in February 2018 with the cooperation of al-Bab's local council and a large group of industrialists and traders from the town. First Industrial City was expected to boost the local economy and provide work opportunities for thousands of young people (al-Khateb 2018). In mid-March 2018, the Azaz Local Council signed an agreement with a Turkish company called ET Energy to establish a power generator with a capacity of 30 megawatts to provide electricity to the city and its surroundings, demonstrating Ankara's willingness to invest and remain in this region (Enab Baladi 2018c). In July 2018, the city council of al-Bab issued new identification cards (around 140,000 total) to the population of the town and its surrounding areas, which were translated into Turkish and shared with Turkish officials (*The Syria Report* 2018q).

Through these policies and building of infrastructures to build a popular base, Ankara also envisioned the possibility of sectors of Syrian refugees residing in Turkey to come back to these areas. In March 2018, 140,000 Syrian refugees from Turkey had returned to these areas (Uras 2018). It was still a small portion compared to the approximately 3.4 million Syrian refugees in Turkey. The Turkish border police had in fact increasingly prevented Syrian refugees from crossing into Turkey through physical force, even shooting to kill in a number of instances. In 2014, as part of extra security measures to prevent the mass arrival of refugees, Turkey began to build a wall on the border with Syria.

Turkish flags, placards, and testimonies of support of Erdogan multiplied in territories under Turkey's control, promoted particularly by Turkish military and officials operating in this area and its Syrian armed proxies. However, Turkey's growing influence did not come without opposition. There were accusations levied against Turkish forces and the Sultan Murad Brigade, a majority-Turkmen opposition group established by Turkey about favoring the Turkmen minority of the Jarablus District receiving better services and taking most of the jobs. Meanwhile, Turkish interference in local affairs was condemned on numerous occasions, as when protesters demonstrated against the raising of Turkish flags over a school in Jarablus (Enab Baladi 2016b; Haid 2017b: 18). Turkey also restricted or simply banned humanitarian work by both Syrian and international organizations in Jarablus and other areas under its control, allowing only Turkish organizations to carry out such activities (Haid 2017b: 15).

In October 2018, a report by the website Syria Direct showed the deep influence and domination of Turkey in all aspects of society in territories where it had armed forces, stating that

> residents, rebels, and local opposition officials suggest that Turkey's role in northern Syria has gradually expanded from the security sector to encompass most aspects of political and civilian life—courts, schools, and religious authorities, right down to the minutiae of service provision and civil registration. Even local councils—civilian administrative bodies that once answered directly to the Syrian opposition's Interim Government—now operate under the authority of Turkish "walis" or governors in neighboring Turkish provinces ... (Brignola, Hamou, and al-Maleh 2018)

As mentioned in the previous chapter, Turkey's ambitions and interests in Syria changed throughout the conflict, focusing increasingly on Kurdish PYD forces over time, including by directly occupying territories through multiple interventions and proxies in the northern border areas, and building a local force that would allow it to maintain a political influence in Syria to serve its interests. This was symbolized by the declarations of Erdogan following the announcement of the withdrawal of YPG forces from Manbij and the entry of the Syrian regime's army in December 2018: "Turkey will have nothing left to do in the Syrian town of Manbij once 'terrorist organizations' [YPG] leave the area" (Yeni Safak 2018). Similarly, at the same time, Turkish foreign minister Mevlut Cavusoglu stated at the Doha Forum in Qatar that Ankara was prepared to engage with Damascus if the Assad government held and won free and fair elections (al-Jazeera English 2018). The idea of overthrowing the Assad regime was long gone.

International and regional actors seeking stabilization under the Assad regime

The failure of the various peace talks and conferences organized under the auspices of the United Nations in Geneva since 2012 between regime and opposition representatives led to increasing parallel channels of negotiations between the countries involved in the Syrian uprising. In mid-December 2016, a new rapprochement occurred among Iran, Turkey, and Russia following the conquest of Eastern Aleppo by pro-regime forces. The foreign and defense ministers of these countries met in Moscow to discuss the future of Syria on December 20, while the United States was not invited to participate. A common declaration was issued following the meeting, in which a road map was suggested for a cease-fire and potentially an end to the war in Syria. The declaration broadly affirmed that Russia, Turkey, and Iran were ready to help broker a peace deal, with one crucial point: that the priority was to fight "terrorism" in Syria rather than regime change (Reuters 2016). For its part, the United States backed the Syria peace talks being prepared by Russia in the Kazakh capital of Astana and hoped that they would prove to be a positive step toward peace (Wroughton 2017).

Similarly, relations between Turkey and Iran also witnessed a new rapprochement in August 2017 following the meeting of the chief of Iranian armed forces, Mohammad Hossein Bagheri, with President Erdogan and Defense Minister Nurettin Canikli in Ankara to discuss ways of strengthening bilateral defense relations and coordinating joint counterterrorism efforts. It was agreed that this would be carried out by launching common military operations against PKK and its branches in Syria and Iran, as well as reconciling the two countries' policy differences in Syria and Iraq. Both sides also agreed that Iraqi Kurdistan's independence referendum, which resulted in a "yes" vote, with over 92 percent in favor of independence in September 2017, destabilized Iraq and adversely affected the broader region (Majidyar 2017d; Medawar 2017). Tehran and Ankara were most vehement in their rejection of independence for Iraqi Kurdistan, and they both multiplied actions against Erbil in collaboration with the central government of Baghdad.

In September 2017, following new talks in Astana, a joint agreement was reached between Russia, Iran, and Turkey to deploy observers on the edge of a deescalation zone in Syria's Idlib Province, which was largely under the control of the jihadist coalition HTS. In reality, only Turkish armed forces deployed in the area, having twelve military observations by mid-May 2018. Three other deescalation zones were included in the various Astana meetings: Eastern Ghouta, northern rural Homs, and southern Syria (Quneitra and parts of Dar'a Governorate) (Beals 2017; Majidyar 2017e). However, these agreements did not stop the regime's forces and its foreign allies from attacking or besieging these regions, while Eastern Ghouta and southern Syria fell under the regime's control in April and mid-July 2018, respectively, as mentioned previously. Idlib remained threatened by a military offensive of regime forces throughout 2018 and beginning of 2019, while suffering from continuous bombings.

However, Russia, Iran, and Turkey continued to collaborate to advance parallel conference discussions to the Geneva Negotiations under the auspices of the United Nations, notably with the Syrian National Dialogue Congress sponsored by Russia and held in January 2018 in Sochi. However, the conference was boycotted by large segments of the opposition, including the Coalition and Kurdish political parties (i.e., the PYD and the KNC). At a summit in Ankara hosted by Turkish president Erdogan in April 2018, Turkey, Russia, and Iran affirmed their commitment to achieving a "lasting cease-fire" that will "protect civilians" in Syria and find a political solution to the conflict (AFP 2018).

In summer 2018, as the regime was consolidating its power in the country, Russia stepped up efforts to encourage regional host countries, including Jordan, Lebanon, and Turkey, to facilitate the return of Syrian refugees.

As international and regional actors increasingly sought to stabilize Syria under Assad's rule, encourage the return of refugees, and begin the process of reconstruction, Damascus was consolidating its power in the country by capturing new territories. By early August 2018, the Syrian regime now controlled over 60 percent of Syrian territory and 75 percent of the population, with its allies' assistance.

Conclusion

The failure of the U.S. invasion of Iraq and the global financial crisis of 2007–08 both dealt severe economic blows to the prestige of the American neoliberal model, causing a relative overall weakening of U.S. power that not only left more space for other global imperialist forces like Russia to operate, but also benefited regional powers that increasingly acted with greater independence. As a result of the relative weakening of U.S. power after its failure in Iraq, regional states like Iran, Turkey, Saudi Arabia, and Qatar played a growing role in the region and in the popular uprisings after 2011 by supporting various actors' efforts to increase their own political influence or by intervening directly. Sectarianism was also a useful tool to mobilize particular constituencies to serve political objectives by these states.

The United States was less eager than in the past to intervene militarily in the region, notably through the sending of massive numbers of soldiers on the ground, as a result of its defeat and the catastrophic consequences in Iraq. Washington's objectives were generally to maintain regime structures with only minor and superficial changes. The Syrian case was no different.

It was in this framework that the various interventions in Syria occurred. The assistance of Russia, Iran, and Hezbollah to the regime has been indispensable to its survival at all levels: political, economic, and military. These actors massively invested their forces to protect their own interests (mostly geopolitical). At the same time, their deepened involvement over time made it such that they eventually felt they had an even greater stake in the regime's survival than had been the case at the beginning of the uprising. The assistance given by these actors also allowed the regime to benefit from an authoritarian knowledge transfer, and thus produced significant adaptations in the scale and organization of the Assad regime's coercive apparatus, ameliorating its capacity to counter a popular armed insurgency (Heydemann 2013b: 67).

On the other hand, Turkey and the Gulf monarchies, led by Saudi Arabia and Qatar, radically changed their relations with a regime previously considered friendly, becoming the most vocal opponents of Assad. Saudi Arabia, and Qatar to a lesser extent, also saw the uprising as a tool to weaken Iran regionally. Ankara, Doha, and Riyadh participated in the division and fragmentation of the FSA by selectively sponsoring one brigade over another to serve their own respective political interests, while inadvertently bolstering Islamic fundamentalist forces. They contributed to the Islamization of the armed opposition and the deepening of sectarianism and Kurdish–Arab tensions among the opposition.

With the increasing success of regime forces against various opposition armed forces, the so-called Friends of Syria progressively concentrated on issues directly related to their national interests rather than the ousting of Assad from power. Turkey mainly focused its efforts on undermining and defeating PYD Kurdish forces in Syria, while the Gulf monarchies progressively diminished their assistance to opposition armed forces following several defeats to pro-regime forces, and then ceased it completely. Saudi Arabia and UAE increasingly sought a resolution of the conflict that would limit the influence of Iran, Turkey, and jihadist actors such as IS in Syria.

They also started by the end of 2018 a process of normalization with the Damascus regime. This process of normalization with the UAE, and possibly with Saudi Arabia in the near future, could be a way for the regime to win some independence and leverage in relations with Iran, and to a lesser degree Russia as well.

Qatar, for its part, was still suffering from its political isolation by the great majority of the Gulf monarchies and increasingly unable to pursue any independent policy in Syria except to support its Turkish ally. Further, the Western states, led by the United States, concentrated progressively and increasingly on IS and the war on terror, which served Damascus's agenda, and encouraged a resolution to the conflict that would stabilize the country without challenging Assad's regime.

Despite the rivalries among various imperial and regional powers, they held the common position that the Syrian civil war should not spill over into neighboring areas and that jihadist forces should be contained. Over time, they came to the agreement that it was necessary to put an end to the uprising in Syria, whose cohesion and vision had strayed far from the initial objectives of the protest movement that erupted in March 2011.

7. War Economy, Reconstruction, and Challenges

Introduction

After more than eight years of a popular uprising transformed into a murderous war, with major regional and international actors intervening in the country, the situation in Syria is catastrophic at all levels, especially in terms of human loss. An estimated 2.3 million people, approximately 11.5 percent of the population, were killed, injured, or maimed as a result of the armed conflict by 2015 (SCPR 2015: 51). With the increase in mortality rate, life expectancy diminished significantly for all age groups, especially among youth, with a male's life expectancy at birth declining from 69.7 in 2010 to 48.4 in 2015 (SCPR 2016b: 9). By the end of 2015, 85.2 percent of Syrian people lived in poverty (SCPR 2016a: 37, 45–46), while 69 percent of the population were estimated to still be living in extreme poverty at the end of 2017 (Humanitarian Needs Overview 2017).

More than half of Syria's population was internally or externally displaced as a result of the war. Life conditions for the majority of Syrian refugees in neighboring countries were characterized by poverty, exploitation, and discriminatory policies. Of the 5.5 million Syrian refugees worldwide, the majority of whom were displaced to neighboring countries, only a tiny fraction has returned to Syria. Forceful displacements of populations were still occurring in 2017[1] and 2018[2] (AFP and *Le Monde* 2018; UN News 2018).

The Syrian economy suffered greatly from the war. The regime's resources, reserves, and fiscal revenues were reduced considerably through the years, and in response, the government engaged in new austerity measures and diminution of subventions on essential products, worsening the condition of life of the country's popular classes. The war, alongside the development of a black market and trafficking of all kinds, resulted in the consolidation of crony capitalists and a surge of new economic actors affiliated with the regime.

The Assad regime, as it was accumulating new military victories and capturing new territories with the assistance of its foreign allies, began to

---

[1] This amounted to more than 900,000 persons.
[2] More than 1 million people had been displaced in Syria within the first six months of 2018.

envision the issue of reconstruction as a major tool for the regime to consolidate its power and networks in the aftermath of the war.

Effects of the war on society

The Human Development Index measure of 0.472 in Syria fell from the "medium human development" cluster of nations into the "low human development" group, largely as a result of weakening performance in education, health, and income. The healthcare system was severely affected through damage and destruction to medical facilities and healthcare infrastructure, the flight of healthcare professionals, the death and injury of medical staff, and the collapse of the pharmaceutical industry (SCPR 2014: 6). By 2016, almost half of the country's 493 hospitals had been directly affected in the five years of fighting, while the number of persons per doctor in the country rose from 661 in 2010 to 1,442 in 2015 (ESCWA and University of St Andrews 2016: 31).

The portion of the population with access to education fell from 95 percent in 2010 to less than 75 percent in 2015 due to the loss of infrastructure and a shortage of teachers. More than 27 percent of schools reported staff shortages in 2015, as opposed to 0.3 percent in 2010 (ESCWA and University of St Andrews 2016: 30). It was estimated that 45.2 percent of school-age children did not attend school in the 2014–15 school year. The school nonattendance rate was the highest in Raqqa and Deir ez-Zor, where it reached 95 percent as a result of the IS decision to close schools in areas under its domination. In relatively safer governorates, the school age nonattendance rate was comparably low, almost zero percent in Tartus, 16 percent in Damascus, and 17 percent in Lattakia (SCPR 2016a: 48). Economic factors also played an important role, with the rise in prices and inflation leading to a decrease in job opportunities and more families resorting to child labor to provide basic needs. Begging and child marriages also increased for the same reason throughout the years (Syria Untold 2016a, 2016b).

While the poverty rate increased in all governorates, those that witnessed intensive conflict and had higher historical rates of poverty suffered the most. Residents in Raqqa were the poorest, with 91.6 percent of their inhabitants living below the overall poverty line, while those in Idlib, in Deir ez-Zor, and rural Damascus also suffered from high rates of overall poverty. The lowest rate was in Suwayda, at 77.2 percent, followed by Lattakia, at 79.8 percent, Damascus, at 82 percent, and Tartus, at 82.4 percent (SCPR 2016a: 45).

The worsening economic situation had social consequences, with both divorce rates and polygamy rising in Syria over the course of the war. According to official figures, polygamous relationships accounted for

30 percent of marriages registered in Damascus in 2015, up from just 5 percent in 2010 (AFP 2016b). Further, Lana Khattab and Henri Myrttinen (2017) argued:

> While gender-based violence was relatively widespread in Syria before the war, the reality of the violent conflict exacerbated it. Various forms of sexual and gender-based violence, exploitation, and abuse have increased, be it early marriage of girls, sexual slavery, homophobic and transphobic violence, or sexualised torture of men, women, girls and boys in situations of detention.

Syrian women within the country and in exile encountered substantial barriers as they attempted to establish new livelihoods. Females represented 57 percent of the total number of IDPs in Syria, exceeding 70 percent in some areas (SCPR 2016b: 69).

At the same time, the sudden shortage of men in Syrian society due to war or emigration, as well as the lack of employable men as a result of injury or imprisonment, have created a space for women to occupy particular niches in society and the workforce that were previously male-dominated or unavailable to women. For example, according to 2015 FAO estimates, 65 percent of the economically active population in agriculture in 2015 were women, an increase of 6 percent since 2009. In some areas, women could constitute up to 90 percent of the agricultural labor force (cited in Aniyamuzaala and Buecher 2016: 31). As a result, by 2016, female-headed households constituted 12–17 percent of the population in Syria and up to one-third of the Syrian population in refugee-hosting countries (Aniyamuzaala and Buecher 2016: 4). This process continued throughout the years. In April 2018, an official at the Ministry of Social Affairs and Labour declared that there were four times more women than men in the labor market. In the public sector, the ratio was estimated at 3:1 in a recent report issued by the unit (*The Syria Report* 2018t).

However, gender participation in the economy was far from equal, with women receiving substantially lower pay and facing discriminations and barriers in the workplace. Income in female-led households tended "to be below that of male-headed households," according to the research assessment "Women, Work, and War," published by CARE (Aniyamuzaala and Buecher 2016: 5) in 2016. At the same time, in September 2018 at the local municipal so-called elections in regime-held areas, the common denominators of the various "national unity" lists led by the Ba'th Party was the very low female representation in most governorates, with male candidates constituting 95 percent of representatives in Aleppo and Suweida (Mashi 2018).

A destroyed economy, austerity measures, and rising cost of living

Between 2010 and 2016, Syria's GDP fell from USD 60.2 billion to USD 12.4 billion (cited in *The Syria Report* 2018w). National currency reserves dwindled from USD 20 billion in late 2010 to USD 0.7 billion by the end of 2015 (World Bank 2016), due in large part to the pressure on the SYP and to finance import trade. During that same period, the Syrian pound lost some 90–100 percent of its value, falling from SYP 47 per USD 1 before the uprising to around SYP 500 at the end of 2018.

In 2014, the regime's public debt had reached 147 percent relative to Syria's GDP. This included 76 percent in domestic debt and 71 percent in foreign debt, while the total debt measured against GDP was estimated at 23 percent in 2010. By November 2016, Syria's public debt had increased eleven times over (*The Syria Report* 2016l). The government became increasingly dependent on Central Bank advance payments, in addition to foreign assistance, which increased during the war due to a very limited fiscal income base. Fiscal revenues dropped from 23 percent of GDP in 2010 to less than 3 percent of GDP in 2015. In 2015, at least a third of government expenses were funded by long-term borrowing from the Central Bank of Syria (*The Syria Report* 2016j; World Bank 2017: VII).

The government tried to compensate this deficit by increasing the prices on some goods and decreasing subsidies on others throughout the years. At the same time, they increased the salaries of public and private registered workers to appease them, often without success. Rising opposition was voiced among the population in regime-held areas. These measures, which involved the curtailing of subsidies on staple goods while increasing public-sector salaries, were part of the concept of "subsidy rationalization" ('*aqlanat ad-da'm*), which was typical of neoliberal schemes in the region to better target subsidies to reach those in "most need" (Arslanian 2016).

This situation had consequences on the cost of living in the country and increased hardship for many families. In 2010, for example, the average worker in Damascus received a minimum of SYP 11,000 a month— approximately USD 220—while in autumn 2016, his salary was around SYP 26,500, or USD 53 (Samaha 2016). Prices of fuel oil surged tenfold from 2011 to 2015, while the price of rice and sugar increased 2.3-fold in the same period (World Bank 2017: VIII). In September 2017, the average monthly cost of living (including rent) in Damascus was around SYP 311,000 (just over USD 600) per month, while at the end of 2018, the Central Bureau of Statistics stated that the average estimated household expenditure for Syrian families was around SYP 325,000 (around $650) per month. Meanwhile, the average monthly salary of a government employee hovered between

SYP 30,000 and 40,000, while the average salary of private-sector employees could reach as high as SYP 65,000 (Samaha 2017c; Enab Baladi 2018o). Even if both parents worked full time, their wages were not enough to get through the month. As a result, people had to fill the gap in various ways, including having several jobs, increasing their revenues by demanding bribes, withdrawing children from school so they can go to work, renting rooms to refugees, selling cars and valuables, and demanding financial assistance from relatives abroad (Lund 2016a).

Moreover, the closure of many workplaces since the beginning of the uprising in March 2011 led to massive job losses. The economy lost 2.1 million existing and potential jobs between 2010 and 2015. Unemployment in 2015 reached 55 percent. Youth unemployment increased from 69 percent in 2013 to 78 percent in 2015 (ESCWA and University of St Andrews 2016: 28). The high level of unemployment and high cost of living encouraged segments of youth to get involved in the army or pro-regime militias, especially when the average militiaman could expect to make four times the salary of a university teacher (All4Syria 2017a). At the same time, by late 2017, businessmen in various Syrian industries were complaining of a lack of personnel despite the country's exorbitantly high unemployment rate, primarily as a result of massive outflow of working-age skilled, and less skilled, individuals (dead, injured arrested, in exiles, etc....) and the lack of mobility of Syrians due to economic insecurity. A few months before, in April 2017, a report by the FAO and the World Food Programme cited a shortage in farming labor as a challenge faced by the Syrian agricultural sector (*The Syria Report* 2017q). This situation was reflected in the massive drop in the number of individuals registered with the Social Security Organization (SSO), which included workers from the public and private sectors and pensioners. Around 2.2 million people were registered with the SSO in 2019, while their number was estimated at 3.7 million in 2012, a decrease of 40 percent (*The Syria Report* 2019a).

Remittances, which were sent by Syrians to their families inside the country, became one of the most important sources of income in the uprising. According to World Bank data, the value of Syrian expat remittances in 2016 reached about USD 1.62 billion—an average rate of about USD 4 million daily. This amounted to around SYP 651 billion, which was above the annual total for salaries and wages, estimated at SYP 478 billion. Remittances sent to Syria were often the main source of cash for tens of thousands of families in need of assistance (Damas Post 2018a). This marked a profound shift compared to before the uprising, when remittances accounted for just 3 percent of GDP annually (World Bank 2011: 49).

Structure of the economy

The structure of the Syrian economy changed dramatically since the beginning of the uprising, with agriculture and government services together accounting for 50 percent of total GDP in 2013 and 46 percent in 2014 (SCPR 2014: 4). In 2014, around 55 percent of employment was in public-sector jobs, indicating that the majority of formally employed persons were working in the government (SCPR 2015: 34). These sectors remained significant throughout the uprising, with agriculture accounting for between 26 and 36 percent of GDP by late 2016 and serving as an important safety net for 7.6 million Syrians, including IDPs (Enab Baladi 2018e; *The Syria Report* 2018j). In reality, however, these sectors contracted by more than 40 percent over time (Butter 2015: 13). In 2016, the World Food Programme stated that the losses of the agricultural sector in Syria since 2011 amounted to USD 16 billion (Enab Baladi 2018e).

The most severely affected sector was mining (including oil production), which observed a diminution of 94 percent in real terms since 2010. Manufacturing, domestic trade, and construction also decreased by more than 70 percent on average (Butter 2015: 13). In dire straits, the Syrian government beginning in early 2013 planned the transfer of state factories to "safe areas," such as coastal towns and cities or the Suwayda region, to enable them to continue production, while encouraging private manufacturers to relocate to these areas as well (*The Syria Report* 2013a).

The manufacturing sector was falling apart, its remnants consisting either of small, fragmented workshops with little productive output or competitive edge, or of scattered industrial establishments with direct ties to foreign powers whose financial support and protection allowed them to continue to operate (SCPR: 2016a: 6). In a Bertelsmann Stiftung's Transformation Index (2016: 15) report, the Syrian Center for Policy Research (SCPR) stated that up to 90 percent of industrial enterprises in conflict areas such as Aleppo had closed down, while the remaining facilities operated at only 30 percent capacity (*The Syria Report* 2016c). In the city of Aleppo itself, known as the main manufacturing center of Syria, only 10 percent of the city's factories and plants still operated by March 2016, according to data from the Ministry of Industry. Some 70 percent of the manufacturing base (i.e., around 28,000 factories) were damaged to a more-or-less serious degree, while the rest were relocated to other parts of the country (mainly the coast) or simply stopped because of the economic or security conditions.

A very slight improvement was witnessed from 2016 in the manufacturing sector, as the regime's forces increased their control over the territory, but it was still very far from pre-2011 levels. For instance, the Sheikh Najjar industrial city in Aleppo employed 18,000 persons in more than 500 industrial establishments in October 2018 (Suleiman A. 2018), while prior to the uprising, it contained more than 2,700 licensed companies and employed around 31,500 registered workers (World Bank 2011: 124). At the end of 2018, the number of Syrian industrial establishments was estimated at around 70,000 by the Syrian Ministry of Industry, while before 2011, the number was close to 130,000 (Ghanem 2018).

In 2017, after years of steep decline, some sectors of the Syrian economy saw improvement, including luxury hotels (Cham Palaces and Hotels[3]), transport and logistics companies (Syrianair, al-Ahliah Transport,[4] Lattakia International Container Terminal,[5] and Damascus Cargo Village[6]). Al-Badia Cement, the only private-sector cement company still operating in Syria, saw its revenues almost double, from SYP 13.8 billion in 2016 to SYP 26.7 billion in 2017 (*The Syria Report* 2018f, 2018d). The manufacturing sector also witnessed some recoveries in 2016 and 2017, as regime forces expanded their control over larger swathes of territory, while the first half of 2018 saw a stagnation in numbers of new companies and a decline in the value of these investments (*The Syria Report* 2018p). The government adopted a series of measures in early 2018 to encourage investment and reconstruction in industrial sites to reduce the reliance on imports. At the end of May, a presidential decree exempted all manufacturers from a construction license fee that was previously needed to start building a factory or expand an existing one in an industrial city or zone (Enab Baladi 2018f). Additional measures in favor of the industrial sector were implemented throughout 2018 and beginning of 2019. In 2018, 847 industrial ventures of all sizes started production compared with 771 in 2017. An important number of these, however, were very small craft projects. The official capital value of the projects was SYP 30.3 billion (USD 60.6 million) and they were expected to create 3,766 new job opportunities, while in comparaison in 2017, the total capital value of the projects that began production was SYP 25.9 billion and the number of jobs generated was 3,728 (*The Syria Report* 2019c).

However, the industrial sector was facing many challenges alongside the massive destructions it suffered, such as the high level of smuggling (especially from Turkish products) and of imported products in the country, the lack of workers, Western sanctions, low national consumption, lack of access to foreign markets and funding, and other factors. For example, in Aleppo alone, hundreds of ring-spinning factories closed in March 2019 as

[3] Cham Palaces and Hotels managed the largest chain of high-end hotel properties in Syria
[4] Al-Ahliah Transport operated a fleet of intercity passenger buses.
[5] Lattakia International Container Terminal managed the container terminal of the Port of Lattakia.
[6] Damascus Cargo Village operated a storage and logistical center at the Damascus International Airport.

they faced shortages of raw materials, competition from imports, power outages, and corrupt practices, according to a report published in the *Tishreen* newspaper.

The conquest of Eastern Ghouta and Dar'a Province by pro-regime forces in April and July 2018, respectively, would also have a positive impact on the economy for the regime, although it took time. In Eastern Ghouta, this would restore in the near future the production of hundreds of factories, still not destroyed or too severely damaged by regime bombing, while bringing more security to Damascus. This region was a major supplier of food products to Damascus, in addition to the localization of many factories in sectors such as textiles, chemicals, and furniture. However, the destruction of facilities was significant. The industrial companies' direct loss, according to the Ministry of Industry and the General Establishment for Chemical Industries, was SYP 81 billion, while the cost of rehabilitating these facilities and reactivating them amounted to double that figure (Enab Baladi 2018j). The return of investors and inhabitants was also delayed or prevented by the division of power of these areas by various security services.

In Dar'a Province, the conquest of the Nasib border crossing with Jordan became a major issue of economic and strategic importance that would reopen key trade routes for Damascus.[7] Syrian exporters would once again have access to Gulf countries, an important market before 2011, while imports from Jordan and the Gulf also would be available at a lower cost. Transit revenues to and from Lebanon would increase as a result, primarily because Syria is the only land route for Lebanese exports to the Gulf and Iraq (Enab Baladi 2018k; *The Syria Report* 2018l). At the same time, a few weeks before the takeover of the Nasib border, the Homs-Hama motorway reopened, facilitating the transport and exchange of merchandise.

In 2018, the value of the 102 projects licensed by the SIA amounted to SYP 895 billion (around USD 1.79 billion), with the possibility of creating 7,959 jobs when the projects started. The agency reported that work is underway during 2018 to implement 34 projects, with an investment cost estimated at SYP 10 billion (around USD 20 million) (SANA 2019).

The Syrian economy was still far from a national economic recovery, however, and many obstacles remain on the path ahead.

Regional changes

The regions of Syria that were insulated from the extensive destruction and unrelenting violence occurring elsewhere in the country profited

---

[7] The value of exports through the Nasib border crossing with Jordan since its opening in October 2018 until January 2019 amounted to SYP 3.16 billion (Enab Baladi 2019b).

economically during the war. The Wadi al-Nasara economy, for example, boomed as a result of a large influx of Syrian Christians, mainly from the city of Homs. This demographic shift led to greater investment flowing into Marmarita, Hwash, Mishtaya, and even Kafra, a small village that benefited from its proximity to the main regional highway (Masouh 2013: 91).

Suwayda also benefited from a greater share of investment throughout the years of the uprising due to its relative safety and proximity to the Syrian capital of Damascus. In 2015, for example, Suwayda hosted the highest number of investment projects by the SIA (17), followed by Tartus (12), the Damascus countryside (8), Aleppo (4), Lattakia (3), Hama (2), and Damascus city (1). Together, Suwayda, Tartus, and Lattakia hosted 68 percent of all projects licensed by the SIA. In 2010, their combined share was only 11 percent (*The Syria Report* 2016m).

It was, however, Syria's northwest coastal region that benefited economically from its relative stable situation throughout the war, with the exception of some protests at the beginning of the uprising in Baniyas, Lattakia city, and several villages in the Lattakia countryside (north of Lattakia and in the Haffe areas), which by 2013 were all repressed by regime forces (Khaddour 2016b: 6). Tartus observed an inflow of people fleeing other regions of the country, many of whom brought their savings with them. Investment in the province was higher than in other areas of Syria, although it was believed to be well below its levels prior to the uprising (*The Syria Report* 2016a), while many private companies relocated there. However, the majority of the population of Tartus remained dependent on the regime for their economic survival, whether as public servants or as employees of the army or security apparatus. Many public employees often had a second job as well. From 2012 to 2013, Tartus also witnessed the proliferation of construction sites for luxury hotels, restaurants, and shopping malls (Khaddour 2013b: 29–32).

In 2015, the provinces of Lattakia and Tartus attracted most real estate transactions in Syria, according to official data. Statistics from the General Directorate of Cadastral Affairs, affiliated with the Ministry of Local Administration, indicated that in 2015, the number of real estate contracts involving the transfer of property in the provinces of Tartus and Lattakia stood at 46,000 and 40,000, respectively. In 2010, the year preceding the uprising, Damascus countryside (90,000) came first, followed by Aleppo Province (75,000), which comprised both the city and the countryside. Overall, 219,000 real estate contracts were signed in Syria in 2015, down by 54 percent from 2010, when they reached 477,000 (*The Syria Report* 2016g).

Data from the SIA showed that 32 percent of licensed private investments in 2015 were on the coast, while slightly less—27 percent—were in the traditional economic powerhouses of Damascus and Aleppo. In the province of Tartus, the number of new individual companies increased from

867 in 2014 to 1,752 in 2015. The total registered capital value of these projects was SYP 530 million (around USD 1.23 million), although their real investment value was likely much higher, as not all the value of investments was usually declared (*The Syria Report* 2016b). In contrast, in 2010, Damascus and Aleppo attracted 40 percent of projects, while a meager 4.5 percent went to Lattakia and Tartus (Yazigi 2016c: 4, 7).

The economic growth witnessed in Tartus encouraged some business elites of the area to call for more economic openings. Wahib Merei, president of the Tartus Chamber of Commerce and Industry and a businessman close to the Syrian regime, called on the government to declare the province of Tartus a free-trade zone. He added that that this measure would help Tartus play a major role in the reconstruction of the country and allow it to become an important regional economic center, similar to Dubai (*The Syria Report* 2015c). However, this measure was still not implemented at this time.

Benefits from the war economy

The war economy has been described by scholar David Keen as the "continuation of economics by other means," with distinctive features including "the destruction or circumvention of the formal economy and the growth of informal and black markets." This is especially the case in civil wars, as well as "pillage, predation, extortion, and deliberate violence against civilians [that] is used by combatants to acquire control over lucrative assets ... and exploit labour." In addition, war economies tend to be highly decentralized, with fighters "thriv[ing] on cross-border trading networks" (cited in al-Mahmoud 2015).

At the same time, the informal sector was a significant part of the Syrian economy prior to the uprising. The informal economy is not in and of itself a distinctive element of a war economy, but an important sector of economic activity in countries on the periphery more broadly.

Similarly, illegal smuggling of goods had existed for a long time in Syria. The Assad regime's cronies were the main beneficiaries of trade in the smuggling of goods in the 1980s, as many goods during this period were not allowed into Syria. The subsequent liberalization of trade beginning in the 1990s led to a decline in some sectors of smuggling business, a trend that accelerated after Bashar al-Assad came to power in 2000 and began a new round of neoliberal reforms. At the same time, the 2003 U.S. invasion and occupation of Iraq ended Syria's direct involvement in various smuggling activities, especially oil; however, other illegal trafficking and smuggling activities began during this period, and in most cases, the Syrian government was not able to control or dominate these new illicit trafficking activities. In the early 2000s, for example, drug trafficking surged in the country, driven by new products and new routes, while as transborder smuggling in Iraq recovered and intensified in the following years after the invasion, the Syrian government reverted to taxing trafficking networks rather than controlling or dominating them (Herbert 2014: 73–74).

With the progressive militarization of the Syrian uprising, the Syrian research center explained that armed groups and security services

> tried to directly recruit people to be part of their armed battalion, or indirectly through "organizing" illegal activities like smuggling, monopoly, theft, pillage, weapons trade, and people trafficking. These illegal activities attracted around 17 percent of the active population inside Syria in 2014 ... (SCPR 2016a: 37)

More generally, the share of the informal economy considerably increased throughout the uprising. This situation saw the development of "war commanders" and the emergence of a "new guard" of *nouveaux riche* businessmen who accumulated enormous wealth since the beginning of the uprising. To launder their money, war traders turned to a number of methods, most importantly buying and trading real estate, luxury cars, gold, and land, or trading in currency (including U.S. dollars). This led to the emergence of new centers of power, although the regime was still the main one, with the entanglement between the new guard of businessmen and the army and security (Hamidi 2016). By accumulating such profit and power, they came to exert a large degree of control over the lives of Syrians living in regime-controlled areas.

At the same time, warlords were increasingly integrating into the formal economy by establishing formal companies, which were registered as LLCs, or participating in investment projects. For example, Bassam al-Hasan, the Republican Guards officer who participated in the creation of the NDF, and his nephew, Saqr Rustom, who led the Homs branch of the NDF, established a company named Damas Real Estate Development and Investment LLC, in order to invest in real estate projects (*The Syria Report* 2018k). In Hama, after Russia's willingness to dissolve regime militias and force them to join in the Fifth Corps, various militia leaders began to transfer and invest the money that they had accumulated in various trafficking networks, kidnappings, and armed robbery into the formal economy, including real estate, land, and businesses, controlling the increasing economic activity of the city. Heads of militias and high-ranked personalities of security services turned more and more into significant businessmen, controlling more than 65 percent of shops and real estate in Hama and its countryside, according to one activist from the city (Shahdawi 2018).

Similarly, in regions suffering sieges in opposition-held areas in which local populations were lacking food, water, electricity, and fuel, members of the SAA and of militias, as well as military opposition factions, took advantage of the situation to accumulate profit. The pro-regime armed forces erected checkpoints at strategic entry points to the besieged area, providing them with ample opportunities for many illegal economic practices, such as allowing goods in exchange for bribes (Todman 2016: 4, 8). Some traders, businessmen who lived or worked in the besieged areas before the conflict and who often had local connections with regime security forces, also benefited from the situation. They tried to secure contracts from the highest levels of the regime to have an effective monopoly over the supply of a certain good in a besieged area. These traders also had to have a relationship with the opposition armed groups operating there, and fees or goods had to be paid in order for the traders to pass between the checkpoints. Once these goods were within the besieged area, the traders often hid or kept them and sold them strategically to maximize their profit (Todman 2016: 4).

Muhy al-Din al-Manfush (known as Abu Ayman), for example, became one of the most prominent merchant smugglers in Damascus Province. He was a trader from the city of Mesraba near Douma and continued to manage a dairy farm there. Abu Ayman provided food and fuel, relying on personal relations with regime officials to get his supplies through the Harasta checkpoint (northeast of Damascus city). He then delivered the products to customers in the city, charging prices up to 20 times higher than in Damascus. He used some of the funds to try to win over local residents by paying salaries for teachers and administrators in several areas of Ghouta, while the regime benefited by taking a cut of his profits and maintaining networks of influence in opposition-held areas.

Abu Ayman protected his facility with a private militia. Around 1,500 people worked in his factory, which also supplied Damascus with cheese and dairy products. He was able to develop his facilities to produce canned and baked goods sold in Ghouta and Damascus (Sadaki 2016). Meanwhile, his local area of Mesraba was not a target of the SAA's military attacks, seemingly part of an arrangement with the regime. A resident of eastern Ghouta estimated that before the tunnels came into regular operation, Abu Ayman made a daily profit of at least USD 10,000 (Todman 2016: 5–8).

Another example was Hussam Qaterji in Aleppo. A trader who was little known before the beginning of the uprising, he operated as a middleman for the trade of oil and cereals among the regime, the PYD, and IS (Yazigi 2016c: 4). Qaterji and traders working for him bought up wheat from Raqqa and Deir ez-Zor and gave 20 percent of the shares to IS (El-Dahan and Georgy 2017; Khaddour 2017d: 12). He was rewarded by the regime through his "election" as an MP, representing the Aleppo Governorate.

In the meantime, Qaterji was also trying to formalize his business ventures by establishing two LLCs together with his brother, officially in
agricultural trade and economic consultancies, which were fronts for their
business activities (*The Syria Report* 2016n; El-Dahan and Georgy 2017).
He increasingly also started to be involved in real estate, by notably establishing the Aleppo Private Joint Stock Holding Company, with capital of
SYP 1 billion (around USD 2 million) by the end of 2018 (al-Iqtisadi 2018c).
He was part of a new business class filling the gaps of the traditional or
former bourgeoisie of the city who had left during the war and used their
contacts with the regime to become prominent economic actors.

Reinforcement of crony capitalists and clientelism

Crony capitalist businesspeople and elites affiliated with the regime largely
maintained and expanded their operations in the country. Their sustained
support allowed them the opportunity to enrich themselves by gaining preferential access to industries and economic sectors that were abandoned
when competitors fled Syria (Kattan 2014). Sanctions did not change the
situation. After Western powers imposed sanctions on Syria's oil sector early
in the war, Aymen Jaber became an important importer of oil products in
the country.[8] Muhammad Hamsho is also believed to have expanded his
businesses and influence, relying on his links with Maher al-Assad, Bashar's
brother (Younes 2016).

In the beginning of 2015, the new licenses governing the operations of
Syria's two mobile phone companies, MTN and Syriatel (a company owned
by Rami Makhlouf),[9] were replaced by new 20-year licenses, in which a
one-time fee of SYP 25 billion was paid by each company, along with a
general reduction of the taxes imposed on these companies in the next three

[8] With fiscal revenues declining and foreign currency reserves largely spent, the government was
also being forced to lift gradually its long-held monopoly over the oil sector and call the private
sector for help. In December 2014, the Syrian government offered investors the possibility of
importing crude oil, refining it at one of the two refineries in Homs or Baniyas, and reselling it
in either the local or export market. The government would collect a fee for the processing,
which could be paid in kind, in the form of the oil derivatives produced. A few weeks before this
decision, it had already allowed private traders to import oil derivatives, only restricting their
sale to manufacturers (*The Syria Report* 2014c).

[9] Syria's mobile phone sector has been marred in controversy for a long time, starting from the
award of the initial contracts in 2000 to two companies associated with people close to Bashar
al-Assad. One of the licenses went to Syriatel, a company established by his maternal cousin,
Rami Makhlouf, while the second went to Areeba, a company owned by the Mikati family of
Lebanon, close to the Assad family. Areeba's mother company later merged with South Africa's
MTN with the Mikati family holding a share in the newly established group.

years, from 60 percent in 2014 to 20 percent by 2018. This decision would generate huge losses for the Syrian state in the coming years, while increasing the profits of the two companies, official records showed. On an annual basis, the government was giving up an average of SYP 81 billion, or the equivalent of USD 270 million at the market exchange rate of SYP 300 per USD 1. The net loss, therefore, was SYP 1.665 billion, only very partially compensated by the SYP 50 billion in fees.

This decision was particularly surprising, as the government was in need of revenue, while at the same time it guaranteed higher long-term profits for the individuals associated with the regime, such as Rami Makhlouf (*The Syria Report* 2015b). During the first nine months of 2018, Syriatel's profits increased to SYP 46.08 billion, compared to SYP 24.3 billion in the corresponding period of 2017—an increase of 89.34 percent. The increase in profits was mainly the result of the reduction of the Syrian government's tax on the revenues of the company from 31.5 percent in 2017 to 21.5 percent in 2018 (al-Iqtisadi 2018b).

The deepening of neoliberal reforms, especially from the perspective of benefiting from the reconstruction of the country, tightened the grip of crony capitalists on the Syrian economy. Indeed, a number of well-connected Syrian investors were reportedly awarded licenses by the government to collect and sell scrap metal from the cities and towns that had witnessed massive destruction, overwhelmingly from regime bombing (*The Syria Report* 2016e). Similarly, in July 2015, the government approved a law that allowed the establishment of private-sector holding companies by city councils and other local administrative units (LAUs) to manage public assets and services, which opened the way for regime cronies to generate business from public assets (SANA 2016c). In the fall of 2016, a holding company named Damascus Cham Private Joint Stock Company was established with capital of SYP 60 billion (around USD 120 million), which was to be completely owned by the Damascus Governorate (*The Syria Report* 2016j). This holding was in charge of managing the reconstruction of the Basatin al-Razi area in Damascus Governorate. In 2018, the Homs governorate also announced the establishment of a holding company and in 2019 it was the turn of the Aleppo and Damascus countryside governorates. None of these, except Damascus Cham Holding Company, had however yet started its operations in the spring of 2019.

In December 2015, the regime introduced two pieces of legislation that demonstrated yet again that the crony capitalist associates of the Assad family were already preparing themselves for the reconstruction period. First, Bashar al-Assad issued a decree enacting a new Urban Planning and Construction Law, whose main provisions included the greater ease provided for the expropriation and redevelopment of illegal housing areas. This helped to ease the destruction of urban areas that supported the uprising against the regime (*The Syria Report* 2015h).

Second, the Syrian Metals and Steel Council was established with the aim of lobbying for a sector that would benefit from any reconstruction drive. The council would play the role of both a lobbying group and a regulator for the sector. It was comprised of a board of 17 members, including four representing the state and the public sector: the ministries of economy and trade, the General Organization for Cement and Building Materials, and Hama Steel. The president of the council was known crony capitalist Muhammad Hamsho, who was already active in the metal industry at the time (Rî'âsa majlis al-wizarâ` 2015). His company, Syrian Metal Industries, had a production capacity of 630,000 tons a year and was located in the industrial city of Adra, near Damascus. The other members of the board included a collection of the best-connected Syrian investors, three of whom were under Western sanctions: Ayman Jaber and the two other Hamsho brothers, Imad and Samir.

The Hamsho Group ran a major plant in Lattakia, with an annual capacity of 500,000 tons of reinforced steel, while Jaber was a shareholder in Arabian Steel Company, based in Jableh, near Lattakia. The building industry was expected to boom during the postwar reconstruction drive, with the metal industry benefiting in particular from the opportunities. In addition to the demands generated by new projects, many metal-related companies would benefit from the removal of all scrap metal from destroyed areas. The regime seemed to be positioning its capitalist associates in such a way that they would be able to reap the benefits of these new conditions (*The Syria Report* 2015i). However, this council was canceled by the new government of Prime Minister Imad Khamis in August 2016 without explanation, but most probably due to its lack of activities (SANA 2016a). This did not prevent personalities close to the regime from continuing to dominate this sector of the economy.

Trade, especially imports, became a major source of lucrative business deals in the country because of very low levels of economic production, the absence of regime investments, and the need for specific goods like foods, pharmaceuticals, and oil derivatives (SCPR 2015: 29). A Syrian pro-regime publication called *Sahibat al-Jalala* claimed in mid-2016 that a handful of traders controlled as much as 60 percent of all Syria's import trade, indicating that it was their connections with top regime members that allowed them to control such a large share of the market. A few weeks earlier, the same publication had indicated that the top two importers collectively controlled 20 percent of all import trade, the next two controlled 10 percent and 5 percent, respectively, and the following two controlled 3 percent each (Salam 2016).

In January 2016, the Public Private Partnership (PPP) Law was passed six years after it was drafted, authorizing the private sector to manage and develop state assets in all sectors of the economy except oil. Economy and Foreign Trade Minister Humam al-Jazaeri declared that the law was "a legal framework for regulating relations between the public and private sectors and [met] the growing economic and social needs in Syria, particularly in the field of reconstruction," while also providing the private sector with the opportunity "to contribute to economic development as a main and active partner" (cited in Sabbagh 2016c). This law was cited as a reference for the new economic strategy of the National Partnership, launched one month later in February by the government, which replaced the social–market economic model developed prior to the uprising. In practice, no details were provided about the objectives or policies that would guide this new strategy. The new PPP Law would likely continue to tighten crony-capitalist control over public assets at the expense of state and public interests (Yazigi 2016a). This PPP law also has to be understood in the context of deepening neoliberal dynamics, where economic sectors that were previously managed solely by the state became open to the possibility of capital accumulation by private actors (Hanieh 2018: 202–217).

In this framework, Prime Minister Khamis announced in September 2018 during a meeting with representatives of companies and businessmen participating in the Damascus International Fair that the government would probably open 50 infrastructure projects in the country to private investors under public-private partnerships (al-Frieh 2018b). Similarly, Fares Shehabi, MP and head of the Aleppo Chamber of Industry, in a session in Parliament in October 2018 called to deepen the PPP process in the public industrial sector to expand investment opportunities of the private sector (Economy 2 Day 2018a).

The crony capitalists, who generally benefited from their connections with the regime, were able to secure high-margin government contracts, exclusive import deals, and, since 2011, smuggling and other deals associated with the war economy. Given these perks, they were clearly not ready to let go of their dominating economic power, which increased even more throughout the war and positioned them even more closely with the regime. More generally, the Assad regime's favoring of neoliberal policies, presented as necessary and technocratic decisions to overcome the problems of war and destruction, should instead be understood as a means to transform and strengthen the general conditions of capital accumulation, benefiting crony capitalists as well as larger economic networks linked to Damascus.

Reconstruction, or consolidating the power of the regime

The cost of reconstruction was estimated between close to USD 400 billion in mid-to-late 2018 (Mcdowall 2018), and although the war was not yet finished, national and foreign actors already were looking for investment opportunities. Conferences in the neighboring countries of Jordan and Lebanon have been organized on the issue of reconstruction in Syria since mid-2016 (Heydemann 2017).

In August 2017, after a six-year absence, the regime organized the Damascus International Trade Fair in a bid to bring back foreign investors and promote an image of normalcy in the country. Among the many nationalities represented at the fair were Russian, Iranian, Chinese, Iraqi, Indian, South African, and Lebanese companies. Very few Western, Turkish, and Gulf companies were present, despite the fact that they were the largest investors in Syria prior to 2011 (al-Frieh and Said 2017a). One month later, between September 19 and 23, the Rebuild Syria Exhibition 2017 was held, attended by 164 companies from twenty-three countries of the Arab world and elsewhere (SANA 2017d).

Conferences continued throughout 2018 to promote investment in the country. Postwar reconstruction was one of the main issues through which the regime and crony capitalists would consolidate their political and economic power, while providing foreign allies with a share of the market to reward them for their assistance.

The regime enacted a series of decrees and laws to frame and benefit from the reconstruction. Decree No. 66 (Cham Press 2012), for example, which entered into force in September 2012, allowed the government to "redesign unauthorized or illegal housing areas" and replace them with "modern" real estate projects with quality services (Ajib 2017).

Initially, this decree allowed the Damascus Governorate to expel the populations of two large areas in Damascus,[10] including Basatin al-Razi, in the district of Mazzeh, where the development of the high-end real estate project of Marota City (which in the Syriac language means "sovereignty") is under construction. The inhabitants of these areas were mostly working- and lower-middle-class residents who had migrated in recent decades from rural areas. This decree, according to Syrian authorities, aimed to improve the living conditions of the inhabitants by eliminating informally built properties and replacing them with comfortable and modern ones. However, the decree selected two areas that supported the opposition, while the areas inhabited by supporters of the regime, where life conditions were no better, were left intact.

Decree No. 66 was inspired by some aspects of a 2007 Damascus Master Plan that had not been implemented because of the beginning of the uprising

---

[10] Two areas in Damascus, in its southern suburbs are involved. The first, already started, included Mazzeh, a residential area near the presidential palace, and Kafr Soussa. The area of the second zone included Mazzeh, Kafr Sousseh, Qanawat, Basatin, Daraya, and Qadam (Cham Press 2012).

in 2011. This area was and still is considered an immensely lucrative real estate opportunity: undeveloped farmland and informal housing in some places within walking distance of the center of Damascus (Rollins 2017).

The reconstruction programs planned the construction of 12,000 housing units for about 60,000 people, targeting mainly high-income households in the neighborhoods of Basatin al-Razi. The prices per square meter ranged from SYP 300,000 to SYP 500,000 according to the executive director of Damascus Sham Holding Company, Nasouh Nabulsi, who added that he believed prices of real estate in Marota City would be the highest in Syria over the long term (Damas Post 2018c).[11] The establishment of Marota City would also probably lead to the raising of rent in adjacent areas for being close to luxury neighborhoods. The reconstruction process included schools and restaurants, places of worship, and even a multistory parking garage and shopping center. According to the Syrian authorities, 110,000 job opportunities and 27,000 permanent jobs were to be created by this project (Ajib 2017; Sabbagh 2017).

Under Decree No. 66, residents who were entitled to new housing, built in an unspecified location, would receive the equivalent of a year's rent, paid for by a special fund created by the Damascus Governorate, until the construction was completed. Those who were not eligible would receive the equivalent of two years' rent, paid no later than one month after the eviction notice. The decree did not specify under what conditions the inhabitants were considered eligible to buy a new home. Only a small portion of the inhabitants have reportedly received either compensation or shares, but even that support is not sufficient to get by in a city suffering from rising rents and cost of living (Rollins 2019). Many inhabitants of the areas have complained throughout the years about reconstruction, including on regime or pro-regime television, as well as the absence of any alternative housing and the fact that other areas are too expensive to live (Channel Sama 2015; Syria TV Channels 1 2015; ORTAS Videos 2017), to say nothing of refugees living outside the country, who received no benefits at all.

In October 2017, Qassioun, the online media platform run by a branch of the Communist Party that was supportive of the regime, announced that Jamal Youssef had acknowledged that no alternative housing had yet been provided for the inhabitants of the project that were expelled under Decree No. 66 (*The Syria Report* 2017n). Another option suggested by Youssef was the possibility of offering to buy a property in Marota City on preferential

---

[11] The economic researcher Younes al-Karim (cited in Abdel Jalil 2018b) estimated that the price per square meter could reach up to SYP 3 million. In the end of 2018, an article of a regime's economic newspaper was titled "Skyscrapers in Damascus overlooking the ruins of war ... And the apartment at 400,000 dollars!" (Economy 2 Day 2018b).

terms: Residents would have the right to buy their properties at cost and to benefit from flexible loan terms (*The Syria Report* 2018c). However, there was still a problem with the latter proposition. The former residents of Basatin al-Razi were mostly from a lower- or middle-class background and could not afford a property in the new real estate project of Marota City, nor could they easily access bank financing. The authorities of the governorate knew this reality perfectly well. In other words, the vast majority of former residents would probably not be compensated in any way (let alone sufficiently) and would not receive any other housing, despite the provisions of the law.

In July 2018, following the total recovery of the Damascus countryside by regime forces, the Damascus Governorate announced a reconstruction plan for Basilia City (*basila* means "paradise" in the Syriac language). The area of Basilia City was 9 million square meters, and it included around 4,000 units. Just as with the project of Marota City, evictions of local residents had started in some areas concerned with Basilia City's plan, while they faced similar problems regarding alternative housing (Enab Baladi 2018l).

The reconstruction plan in Homs focused on three of the city's most de-stroyed districts—Baba Amr, Sultanieh, and Jobar—and committed to rebuilding 465 buildings, able to house 75,000 people, at a cost of USD 4 billion, according to Homs governor Talal al-Barrazi (cited in Mroue 2018a). The new urbanism plan took its inspiration from the "Homs Dream" (MsSyriano 2010) project directed by the former governor of Homs, Muhammad Iyad Ghazal, who was dismissed by Bashar al-Assad at the beginning of the demonstrations in 2011 because he was the main target of protesters at that time in the city. This project was announced in 2007 by Ghazal, who planned the destruction of parts of downtown to rebuild more modern buildings and skyscrapers. This urban plan was presented at that time as an opportunity to embrace modernization and urban improvement, but it was rejected by important sectors of the local population. For example, the project did not guarantee residents the right to stay in the traditionally middle-class neighborhood. Instead, the municipality suggested alternative housing in another neighborhood or financial compensation, which raised fears that the master plan would result in a form of gentrification and prevent residents from returning home (Aldeen, Syria Untold, and Syrian Independent Media Group 2018). Some locals also accused the former re-construction plan of using urban planning to push Sunnis and Christians out of central areas, while Alawi areas remained untouched (Solomon 2017).

In October 2018, Homs's city council announced on its official Facebook page that they had finalized the zoning plans for three districts in the city (Jourat al-Sheikh, al-Qarabees, and al-Qasour), which were former opposition-held areas and remained empty, as almost none of the former inhabitants had returned. The council added that property owners who wanted to obtain demolition and building permits must apply to the city council for licenses (Hurriya Press 2018b).

Aleppo, various suburbs of Damascus, and other areas could see the imposition of similar projects. In Aleppo, more than 50 percent of the buildings and infrastructure had been partially or totally destroyed, according to a preliminary assessment of the municipality in January 2017, while large sections of eastern neighborhoods of Aleppo's population had been forcefully displaced to other areas or left the areas as a result of the war. Of the 15 priority areas put forward by the Syrian government for reconstruction, eight were not located in Eastern Aleppo. The priority areas were neighborhoods in the west and center of the city that did not suffer the same level of destruction as the 52 neighborhoods in the East, which had been taken over by the regime's armed forces and their allies in December 2016 (Beals 2017; *The Syria Report* 2017a). In the same way as Homs, the reconstruction and rehabilitation of buildings had prioritized districts that were historically favorable to the regime, not the most damaged areas formerly under the control of the armed opposition or attacked by it.

Likewise, in September 2018, Suhail Abdul-Latif, the general manager of the state-owned General Housing Establishment, stated that his company had been contracted by the Damascus Countryside Governorate to rehabilitate 175 buildings in the Damascus suburb of Adra al-'Umalia, considered a regime stronghold and inhabited largely by religious minorities, particularly Alawis, who were located close to the Adra Industrial City. However, in this case, homeowners were demanded to pay 40 percent of the reconstruction cost of their properties, while the state committed to paying 60 percent.[12] This showed the willingness of the regime to pressure inhabitants to contribute directly to reconstruction efforts because of the lack of national resources (Hamidi S. 2018; *The Syria Report* 2018r).

The Syrian website SANA reported in July 2017 that the government had allocated SYP 25 billion (USD 48.5 million) of contracts for reconstruction in Aleppo. This figure was only a fraction of the amount needed for the reconstruction of the city, estimated at more than USD 5 billion and possibly even tens of billions of dollars (SANA 2017b). Aleppo was depleted to a third of its prewar initial population of 3 million people, with nearly 2 million people displaced outside the city, according to UN estimates in late 2017. Also, 44 percent of the city's housing stock had been destroyed and 86 percent of commercial infrastructure damaged. The bulk

---

[12] In December 2018, the reconstruction committee allocated SYP 1.8 billion (USD 3.6 million) to restore partially damaged houses in Adra al-'Umalia and remove the destroyed and damaged buildings (Damas Post 2018f). Restoration works had not yet begun at this time.

of the destruction and damage was in East Aleppo, where most of the city's informal housing was situated (Beals 2018).

Following a visit by Prime Minister Khamis in early January 2018, the Syrian government announced that Aleppo's share in the 2018 budget would be SYP 40 billion (or about USD 80 million), dedicated to reconstruction projects and to the rehabilitation of infrastructures and services destroyed in the city (Iqtissad 2017; SANA 2018a). In November 2018, the government held several sessions in Aleppo over a period of several days and ultimately voted in favor of a global strategy of development for Aleppo Province to encourage the reconstruction of the city and the boosting of its economy. Meanwhile, the third Industrial Conference was organized in Aleppo, with the participation of ministers of the governments and calls for a series of measures for the boosting and development of the industrial sector in the city of Aleppo and at a national level (al-Jazaeri 2018).

Another city that had suffered massive destruction was Raqqa. More than 80 percent of the city was uninhabitable or altogether destroyed, and basic infrastructure was practically nonexistent. Saudi Arabia's Gulf affairs minister, Thamer al-Sabhan, visited Raqqa in September 2017—following its recapture by the SDF with support from the U.S.-led international coalition—to meet with the civil council to discuss the reconstruction of the city. However, no investments have yet materialized in any concrete plan.

In April 2018, the Assad regime issued a new legislative law, Decree No. 10, a nationwide expansion of Decree No. 66 that raised new fears of stripping citizens who had been forced out of Syria of their property. Decree No. 10 was enacted as an amendment to Decree No 66 of 2012 and stipulated that property owners would have to submit their title deeds to relevant authorities, all LAUs, within one year after the announcement of reconstruction plans in the locality.[13] If they were not able to do so, they could ask their relatives to do so by procuration or be represented by an attorney. If they failed to do so, they would not be compensated, and ownership would revert to the province, town, or city where the property was located.

Those who have proved their property title can, as explained by Human Rights Watch (2018a):

1) register the sector in their names and receive a share of the profits from redevelopment; or 2) sell their shares in a public auction; or

---

[13] Decree No. 10 was slightly amended by deputies in Parliament in November 2018 following some criticisms on the international political scene, but without changing its main dynamics. The time allocated to owners to claim in-kind rights that were not recorded in the real estate registry, for example, were extended from one month to one year (al-Souria Net 2018b).

3) create a company to invest in and develop the division ... All the shareholders in a sector must agree to one option.

Under Decree No. 10, inhabitants in these zones must move out. Local authorities normally should guarantee compensation equivalent of two years' rent to tenants who do not qualify for alternative housing. Tenants with a right to alternative housing should be moved into that housing within four years, and in the meantime also will have their annual rent covered. It was not clear from the law who would qualify for alternative housing or how such a determination would be made (Human Rights Watch 2018a), but as previously mentioned in the case of Marota City, the process of alternative housing and compensation was far from being successful and indeed was very partial.

However, the main purpose of the law remained the seizure of real estate and property of civilians who had been forced to leave the country, especially in former opposition-held areas. As a result, this decree would be able to make new land registrations and exclude from these registers a plethora of real estate owners. De facto, through the reconstruction of the administrative structure, the property of civilians forced to flee would be seized.

Decree No 10, therefore, extended Decree No. 66 to the whole of the country, in that it permitted all LAUs throughout Syria, such as cities and governorates, to configure real estate development zones within their administrative boundaries and, based on that zoning, to expropriate their populations and rebuild them (*The Syria Report* 2018i). The minister of local administration Hussein Makhlouf, in an April 9 interview with the pro-regime newspaper *al-Watan*, declared that the first three areas to be included for new real estate development zones were Baba Amro, a suburb of Homs, and Harasta in Eastern Ghouta, areas that were significant and symbolically meaningful opposition strongholds (Hamimu 2018).

In September, the Damascus Governorate Committee issued a report announcing the destruction and rebuilding under Decree No. 10 of Tadamon District in Damascus, which included a mix of supporters and opponents of the regime. The head of the committee, Faisal Sorour, declared that 3,500 homes were inhabitable and residents who could prove the ownership of those properties would be able to return. For the rest of the residents who saw their housing completely destroyed, they would not be permitted to return to homes considered uninhabitable, and the reconstruction would take an estimated four to five years. The residents of al-Tadamon District strongly condemned and rejected the report of the Damascus Governorate Committee, while calling to oppose the decision legally and appealing to the judiciary. Other areas of Damascus, such as Jobar, Barzeh, and Qaboun, were also scheduled to be studied for reconstruction in early 2019 under Decree No. 10 (al-Saleh 2018; al-Watan Online 2018). In November 2018, the Damascus governorate established a plan to prepare new organizational plans for all informal areas in Damascus, including areas considered as loyalist, such as Mezze 86. However, specific dates have not been set for the implementation of any study on reconstruction projects (Emmar Syria 2019d).

By allowing the destruction and expropriation of large areas, Decree No. 66 of 2012 and Decree No. 10 of 2018 were used as efficient instruments for rapid and large development projects that would benefit regime cronies and attract possible foreign funding, while at the same time operating as a punishment against populations known to oppose the regime. They most probably would be replaced with higher social classes and new war elites, who were generally less inclined to rise up against the regime. The focus in providing housing for wealthy strata of society in the reconstruction plans launched by the government and the private sector was even criticized in pro-regime newspapers published in the country. For example, a real estate expert, Ammar Yousef stated in an interview with the newspaper *al-Ayam* that "all the residential projects that are being launched today are targeted at the wealthy, and the average income or even higher income-earning citizens cannot live in these houses" (cited in Suleiman L. 2018). He added:

> The government, if it continues in this orientation, will be unable to solve the housing crisis for the next 100 years, especially with 3 million homes destroyed, and the need in Syria of a million and a half homes annually, and this need increases between 100 to 150 thousand homes every year ... (Suleiman L. 2018)

The development of residential projects that could be built in these areas would in fact be carried out by holding companies owned by governorates or municipalities, but the construction and management of projects would likely be contracted to private-sector companies owned by well-connected investors (*La Libre* 2016; *The Syria Report* 2018i).

The return of civilians to certain areas was also complicated by various measures pertaining to the regime's security institutions. The war also demolished many Syrian land registries, including at the deliberate initiative of pro-regime forces in some recaptured areas, making it complicated for residents to prove home ownership (Chulov 2017). In a report by Human Rights Watch (2018b), inhabitants were not allowed to come back to Daraya, even with property titles, while certain neighborhoods of Qaboun remained restricted and demolitions have been ongoing in some of them since the city fell under the regime's control in 2017. According to approximate prewar estimates by the Ministry of Local Government, only about 50 percent of land in Syria was officially registered. Another 40 percent had boundaries delimited but had not yet been registered. The multiple land registries were paper based and often not properly stored (Prettitore 2016).

In addition, a significant percentage of displaced people had lost their ownership documents or never obtained them in the first place, according to Laura Cunial, a legal and housing expert at the Norwegian Refugee Council (NRC). Nearly half of Syrian refugees surveyed by the NRC and the United Nations High Commissioner for Refugees (UNHCR) said that their home had been destroyed or damaged beyond repair by the war, while only 9 percent had their property title deeds with them and in good condition, according to the survey published in 2017. Wide sections of those refugees came from informal areas, which as mentioned before, represented around 40 percent of all housing units in Syria (Yazigi 2017: 6; Zweynert 2018). However, even those who had the necessary documents often found it difficult to access their properties. The process of entry into the areas controlled by the regime often required the obtaining of entry permits from various branches of security to cross-checkpoints. This process involved blackmail, bribes, and threats of detention. Residents were also required to pay electricity, telephone, and water bills for years of absence during the war, which equated to nearly 50 percent of the cost of these assets (Aldeen, Syria Untold, and Syrian Independent Media Group 2018).

This is to say nothing of opposition activists and supporters, who are unlikely to return to Syria at all out of fear of detention and torture by the regime due to their political activities. In this framework, Decree No. 63 empowered the Ministry of Finance to seize immovable assets and property from individuals who fell under Law No. 19 of 2012, the counterterrorism law. According to Human Rights Watch, the former law provided "a dangerously broad interpretation of what constitutes terrorism, and unfairly criminalized a large segment of the population without any due process rights or fair trial" (cited in Othman Agha 2018). In November 2018, the Syrian Ministry of Finance published the findings of a study documenting over 40,000 cases of property seizures as a result of "terrorist activities" by their owners in 2017 and 30,000 seizures in 2016 (al-Modon 2018c).

A whole system of laws allowed the regime to expropriate individuals of their properties. In Hama, for instance, a real estate development project was announced in October 2018 in the neighborhood of Wadi al-Jouz, which was completely destroyed by regime forces in 2013. Under the PPP Law of 2016, the project involved the construction of 2,400 apartments worth SYP 40 billion (USD 86 million). The government used the urban planning law of 1982 (Law No. 5 of 1982) to destroy and rebuild Wadi Al-Jouz (*The Syria Report* 2018w).

During the same period, the Aleppo City Council announced the beginning of development works in sectors of al-Haidarieh's informal area, located northeast of Aleppo. al-Haidarieh was under opposition control during most of the conflict and was largely destroyed by regime and Russian air forces. It was among the largest informal housing districts in Syria. This project of reconstruction in this case was conducted on the basis of Law No. 15 of 2008,[14] which was the framework for large real estate projects and which regulated the establishment of real estate development zones, as well as investment in them. The land targeted by the reconstruction was expropriated land, without any information or compensation process to former inhabitants, the overwhelming majority of whom had left the city and the country and had not yet returned (*The Syria Report* 2018x).

Both areas, Wadi al-Jouz in Hama and al-Haidarieh in Aleppo, were part of a list of 23 areas to attract private investors selected by the Real Estate Development and Investment Commission and which would benefit from the incentives provided by Law No. 15 of 2008 (*The Syria Report* 2018x).

In addition to these laws, Law No. 3 in 2018 was one of the main ways in which the regime conducted demolitions and subsequently prevented the return of civilians. Presented as a law "concerning the removal of the rubble of buildings damaged as a result of natural or abnormal causes," the government was given significant leeway in defining what constituted rubble or damage, meaning that neighborhoods could be closed off and housing subsequently destroyed. More generally, the regime also used arbitrary, punitive demolitions, and antiterrorism legislation to raze whole areas of neighborhoods that fell to the opposition after 2011. Aside from Decrees No. 66 and No. 10, the Syrian government has passed more than 45 laws since 2011 related to housing, land, and property (Ahmad, Hourani, and Smiley 2018).

New personalities emerging

Some businessmen linked to the regime also started to appear and rise to prominence. They were usually individuals who were outside both crony capitalist circles and the dependent business elite networks built in past decades, who had accumulated some level of wealth before the uprising. This was particularly observed with the reconstruction process.

The most important rising figure was Samer Foz, who throughout the war became one of the country's most powerful businessmen. Multiple Syrian and Dubai-based businessmen interviewed by the *Financial Times* stated that Foz had close ties to the Assad regime. Prior to the uprising in

---

[14] The law was passed before 2011, at a period of deepening economic liberalization and with the objective of attracting funds and investments from the Gulf and expatriates into its real estate sector.

2011, he owned the Aman Group,[15] a contractor for real estate developments and food commodities. According to their website, the group had "strategic relations with an extensive network of suppliers in over 30 countries" (Aman Group 2017).

Throughout the war and through his close contacts with high regime's officials, Foz became an important business personality. He benefited massively from government contracts and acted as a broker for grain deals with the state-owned company Hoboob (Saul 2013; Enab Baladi 2017e), while he also acted as an intermediary with the PYD and the IS to trade wheat. In addition, he was involved in the purchase of assets of businessmen who left Syria and were facing difficult or tensed relations with the regime, such as Imad Ghreiwati.[16] In March 2018, Prince Alwaleed bin Talal sold his stake, representing 55 percent, in the Four Seasons Damascus hotel to Foz.[17] According to the *Financial Times* (cited in Kerr and Solomon 2018), the transaction generated more than USD 115 million. The Four Seasons Damascus was popular with UN agencies, aid groups, and visiting diplomats. At the time, it was believed to be the best-performing Four Seasons hotel of seventeen MENA locations. Foz's business interests rapidly and massively expanded beyond importing and trading grains and building materials to include aviation, the cable industry, steel, sugar, car assembly and distribution, hotel management, real estate development, pharmaceuticals, and even banking by buying stakes in the Syria International Islamic Bank[18] and al-Baraka Bank[19] (Emmar Syria 2019a).

Alongside his business activities, Foz also founded "the Association of the FOZ Charity," which carried out charitable projects in Lattakia and its

---

[15] The company had two subsidiaries: Foz for Trading, the group's commercial foundation, was one of the region's largest importers of basic commodities. Al-Mohaimen for Transportation & Contracting, the group's operational arm, provided unlimited logistics support to Foz for Trading through a large ground fleet.

[16] In early 2017, Ghreiwati's company, Syria Modern Cables (SMC), which produced insulated wiring and high-voltage power cables, was occupied by an armed militia linked to Muhammad Hamsho. The armed men finally left the factory, but in exchange, Foz acquired SMC and all of Ghreiwati's other Syrian assets, including the KIA car dealership, at a very steep discount (*The Syria Report* 2018g).

[17] Other shareholders in the Syrian Saudi Touristic Investments Company, the company that owned the property, included the Ministry of Tourism, the Damascus Governorate, and Kuwaiti Syrian Holding Company, which was affiliated with the Kuwaiti Kharafi group (*The Syria Report* 2018e).

[18] His holding company's share in the bank reached 7.6 percent, equivalent to SYP 9 billion in January 2019 (around USD 18 million).

[19] He bought shares equivalent to 1.18 percent of the bank's capital, worth about SYP 841 million (around USD 1.68 million).

rural areas and was planning to expand their services to Damascus and the countryside (Swedeh 2017). He was accused of funding the Quwat Dir' al-Amn al-Askari ("The Military Security Shield Forces"), which was affiliated with al-Amn al-Askari ("The Military Security"), and to use it for personal affairs as well (al-Sharq al-Awsat 2017).

His company, Aman Group, also announced in August 2017 its contribution in partnership with Damascus Governorate and Damascus Cham Private Joint Stock Company in the reconstruction of Basatin al-Razi area, in the Mazzeh District of Damascus. Aman Damascus, the company established by the Aman Group for this project, announced capital of USD 18.9 million (Damascus Cham 2017; Enab Baladi 2017e). In November, Foz's Aman Group was granted by Damascus Cham Holding the right to develop real estate properties worth around USD 312 million in the Basatin al-Razi project (*The Syria Report* 2017p). Marota City announced that a residential area of over 60,000 square meters would be built, with around 220 luxury apartments and duplexes of between 200 and 450 square meters, including a variety of services and gardens (Marota City 2018b).

Other business figures also benefited from lucrative contracts with Damascus Cham Holding as part of the reconstruction of Basatin al-Razi. There was, for instance, Zubaidi and Qalei LLC, owned by Khaled al-Zubaidi and Nader Qalei, a powerful Sunni businessman based in Damascus with connections to the regime. In early 2018, the Kuwait-based businessman Mazen Tarazi, active in a variety of economic sectors,[20] established a joint venture with Damascus Cham Holding to build a 120,000-square-meter shopping center and six other properties (Damascus Cham 2018a). The estimated value of these investments was USD 250 million. Tarazi would hold 51 percent of the shares of the joint venture, while Damascus Cham would own the rest, meaning that effective control of the company would be in the hands of Tarazi. In addition, he would purchase five other parcels worth an estimated USD 70 million (Iqtissad 2018; Abd al-Jalil 2018a; *The Syria Report* 2018b).

---

[20] In early January 2018, the Syrian Civil Aviation Authority granted a license to an airline established by Mazen Tarazi. Tarazi would hold 85 percent of the shares of the company, with his two sons, Khaled and Ali, holding the rest. The company operating the airline had a capital of SYP 70 million. Tarazi demonstrated his support for the regime on a number of occasions. In 2014, he allegedly financed the transport of many Syrians based in Kuwait to Damascus to vote in the presidential election. In 2015, he was credited by the Syrian official media for "providing financial assistance to the families of the martyrs and wounded of the Syrian army" and for "renovating schools in the suburbs of Homs and Damascus."

A few days later, it was the turn of the Talas Group,[21] owned by businessman Anas Talas, to sign a partnership agreement with Damascus Cham Holding worth SYP 23 billion (approximately USD 52.7 million) for the construction of four parcels within Marota City that would be divided into residential and mixed residential and commercial sectors. The distribution of investments in this partnership was as follows: The Talas Group had 25 percent, or SYP 5.7 billion, and the rest, or 75 percent or SYP 17.3 billion, remained under the control of the governorate (Damascus Cham 2018b; Eqtisad 2018). The last two individuals shared certain characteristics, including having accumulated wealth in the Gulf and being relatively unknown before 2011 in Syria.

In January 2018, Damascus Cham Holding established a new joint venture with Exceed Development and Investment, owned by private investors Hayan Muhammad Nazem Qaddour and Maen Rizk Allah Haykal. The value of this joint venture was SYP 9.2 billion (equivalent to around USD 21 million at the time). The company Exceed, established just a few months earlier, would hold 51 percent of the shares, representing SYP 4.7 billion, while Damascus Cham would own 49 percent (SYP 4.5 billion) and contribute plots of land. According to Damascus Cham Holding's website (Damascus Cham 2018c), the company was to develop three plots of lands in Marota: two devoted to housing with a total built-up area of 11,000 square meters, with the third being a commercial center used for the sale of building materials of 2,956 square meters.

At the end of March 2018, the Rawafed Damascus Private joint venture, owned by Rami Makhlouf and his close associates and composed of Ramak for Development and Humanitarian Projects LLC and four other companies, obtained a contract worth SYP 25.9 billion (USD 48.3 million) to develop real estate in Marota City: three properties with a combined built-up area of 38,000 square meters, two 15-story buildings, mostly residential with two commercial floors, and one twelve-story commercial property (Damascus Cham 2018d; Damascus Cham 2018e; *The Syria Report* 2018h).

In April 2018, Damascus Cham Holding signed its seventh joint venture with Bunyan Damascus, a partnership with two companies, Apex Development and Projects LLC and Tamayoz LLC. The joint venture had a capital of SYP 15.2 billion, equivalent to USD 34.8 million, and would develop two mixed-use properties with a total built-up area of 30,000 square meters. DCH held 60 percent of the shares, and its partners held the balance (Damascus Cham 2018e).

---

[21] The company is mainly active in the production and distribution of food products from its base in the UAE. The company has developed its own food brand, Tolido.

A few months before, in February, Damascus Cham Holding announced that it was collaborating with al-Baraka Bank and other banks in Syria to create a real estate financing company, which would participate in the funding of the development of Marota City. Al-Baraka Bank was notably headed by Muhammad Halabi, the former co-chief executive officer (CEO) of Syria International Islamic Bank, which was hit by sanctions internationally in 2011 and 2012 for its role as a front for the regime-owned Commercial Bank of Syria in funding the proliferation of weapons of mass destruction and other weapons of war (Goldsmith 2018).

Another significant business personality who emerged during the war was Wassim Qattan. In the summer of 2017, Qattan was assigned the management contract of the Qassioun Shopping Mall, at an annual cost of SYP 1.2 billion. A few months later, in mid-March 2018, the Ministry of Tourism awarded a 45-year contract to a company called Murooj al-Cham Investment and Tourism Company to develop a prime real estate location known as al-Jalaa, in Damascus. The proposal included the building of a large, five-star hotel and a shopping mall. In August 2018, Qattan's company was once again granted a controversial deal: the management of the Massa Plaza mall, located in the upscale district of Malki in Damascus, which was previously managed by the Hakim Brothers company. Qattan made the most lucrative offer: SYP 1.29 billion, which is equivalent to some USD 2.97 million. He was thought to be acting as a front for a powerful regime figure, probably Maher al-Assad (Enab Baladi 2018d, 2018m; *Syria Daily News* 2018).

The fact that all these personalities were issued from the Sunni community did not prevent them from having very close links to and benefiting from the regime, demonstrating once again the multiple strategies and tools of the regime to constitute a diverse popular base through clientelism, tribalism, and sectarianism.

These new business elites were able to capitalize, economically and in terms of political influence, on opportunities from the departure of the dependent business elite networks. Fares Shehabi, head of the Aleppo Chamber of Industry and a wealthy businessman, and a known supporter of the regime, was notably elected president of the Federation of Syrian Chambers of Industry in June 2012 (Abboud 2013: 6) and became an MP in 2016. Samer al-Debs, an industrialist close to the regime, became an MP in 2012 and then president of the Damascus and Countryside Industrial Chamber in 2014 (Iqtisadi 2018a). For his part, Muhammad Hamsho entered the Board of Directors of Damascus Chamber of Commerce at the beginning of 2014 as an alternative to Bassam Ghraoui by ministerial decision, where he assumed the position of secretary and continued to be an MP. He also served as chairman of the Syrian-Chinese Businessmen Council

(Iqtissad 2015b) and was nominated to other official positions. Wassim Qattan, mentioned previously, was nominated in February 2018 as president of the Damascus Province Chamber of Commerce, after the minister of domestic trade and consumer protection, Abdallah Gharbi, dissolved the former board of directors (Sahibat al-Jalala 2018).

Elections at the Chambers of Commerce in Aleppo and Damascus at the end of 2014, for instance, saw a significant change in their memberships. In Aleppo, ten of the twelve elected board members were new investors, many of whom were unheard of prior to the uprising. In Damascus, seven of the twelve were in the same situation (Yazigi 2016b: 4). In the beginning of 2014, the Ministry of Industry already had nominated new individuals to sit on the board of various Chambers of Industry in Hama, Aleppo, Homs, and Damascus, in a move largely seen as a reprisal against investors supporting the opposition or deemed not sufficiently supportive of the regime. This was the same as the parliamentary elections result in 2016, with some 70 percent of new entrants in the chamber reflecting significant changes that affected the power base of the Syrian regime (Sabbagh 2016a).

The 2018 municipal elections also reflected the consolidation of the regime's power networks at the lowest level of society, with Ba'thists, personalities linked to militias, and regime affiliates winning the great majority of municipalities, and with the domination of the National Unity list, for whom 70 percent of the seats of the local administration were reserved, while only 30 percent were for independent candidates. This was especially important, as local councils would officially assume responsibility for reconstruction, although operating under the rules from the Ministry of Local Administration, whose minister was Hussein Makhlouf, the cousin of Rami Makhlouf.

At around the same time, a new lobby of Syrian businessmen, the Global Group of Syrian Businessmen in the World, was established in November 2018 in Bucharest, Romania. The gathered investors consisted mostly of Sunni entrepreneurs from Damascus and Aleppo who now lived outside the country but who had maintained connections with the Syrian regime. Khaldoun al-Muwaqa, who since 2012 has been heading the regime-linked Grouping of Syrian Investors in Egypt, chaired this new body, while Rateb al-Shallah, a symbol of the traditional Damascene business class, was designated honorary president. The new organization declared that it had representatives and/or offices in 23 countries, and it aimed at supporting the Syrian economy in the reconstruction's process, notably through serving as an intermediary for foreign investors, whether by providing advice or by participating directly in the Syrian economy (*Industry News* 2018a; *The Syria Report* 2018y).

It was not surprising, therefore, that in December 2018, the first economic conference on investment opportunities in Syria was organized in Bucharest. The event was spearheaded at the initiative of the Romanian Institute for Political and Economic Studies, in cooperation with the Syrian Embassy and with the participation of many companies and chambers of commerce and industry from Romania (Damas Post 2018e).

Nevertheless, numerous challenges remained for the regime as it attempted to reattain political and economic stability within Syria and secure funds for reconstruction across the country.

The issue of national funding and foreign investments

These large real estate projects were expected to attract foreign capital, crucial for Syrian reconstruction. The investments of public and private actors were insufficient to rebuild the country, while as mentioned previously, the state was seriously indebted. The doubling of the reconstruction tax (called the National Contribution for Reconstruction), which was introduced in 2013 and was initially supposed to apply for only three years on various taxes and fees,[22] did not fix the problem. This tax did not generate much revenue, bringing the equivalent of SYP 13 billion, a mere USD 31 million, into the 2017 budget (*The Syria Report* 2017r). Oil revenues, which accounted for a large portion of revenues until 2012,[23] were nonexistent, while tax revenues had declined considerably. Indirect tax revenues constituted 70 percent of the government's official financial revenues in mid-2018, which indicated the lack of national revenue (Enab Baladi 2018n). The national budget for 2017 was SYP 2.6 trillion (USD 5 billion) passing in 2018 to SYP 3.1 trillion (SANA 2017e) and increasing once again in 2019 to SYP 3.882 trillion (al-Frieh 2018c).

The combined value of the government's project of the Reconstruction Committee, which was established in 2012 and is affiliated with the Ministry of Local Administration and Environment, in the 2018 budget was only SYP 50 billion and SYP 34.8 billion (USD 75.2 million) in 2019. The money allocated was spent mostly on the rehabilitation of destroyed equipment and buildings, although some projects listed were not necessarily damaged during the war, such as the Bassel al-Assad Airport in Lattakia, the Jableh Hospital, and the Sharqiyeh phosphate mines currently being developed by a Russian company (*The Syria Report* 2018u). The 2019 budget allocated for

---

[22] Taxes on business profits, exit fees, car license plate fees, and real estate license fees were among the many on which the tax was imposed. But the income tax on wage earners was exempted.

[23] In 2018, the daily oil production reached in 24,000 barrels of crude oil, about 6 percent of the precrisis production of 385,000 barrels per day (Kassioun 2019).

reconstruction was not more than SYP 50 billion, equivalent to USD 115 million (Haddad 2018).

Moreover, there were problems of funding as public-private partnership (PPP) schemes relied on financing from banks, which was clearly unavailable, as the total assets of 14 private-sector commercial banks operating in the country reached SYP 1.7 trillion at the end of 2016, equivalent at the time to only around USD 3.5 billion, while in 2010, it was USD 13.8 billion. In terms of assets, some of the six state-owned banks were larger than their private-sector counterparts, particularly the Commercial Bank of Syria. However, these banks had large bad debt portfolios (*The Syria Report* 2017l).

Therefore, the reconstruction required foreign funding, which would benefit the countries that were the staunchest supporters of the Assad regime, particularly Iran and Russia. Syrian officials have repeatedly declared that companies from Iran and other allied countries would be rewarded. Following the recapture of Eastern Aleppo in December 2016, Aleppo governor Hossein Diyab also stressed that Iran was going to "play an important role in reconstruction efforts in Syria, especially Aleppo" (Schneider 2017). In March 2017, the Iranian Reconstruction Authority publicized the renovation of 55 schools that it planned to restore across Aleppo Province (Schneider 2017). Iran also had the largest presence at the International Trade Fair in Damascus, with more than 40 Iranian companies taking part in the event (Heydemann 2017). In September 2017, Iranian officials declared that they would rehabilitate and reconstruct electricity infrastructure in Damascus and Deir ez-Zor, and an Iranian company was awarded a contract to supply electricity to Aleppo. If finalized, these deals would be worth hundreds of millions of dollars (al-Jazeera English 2017).[24]

In September 2018, a Memorandum of Understanding on cooperation in the electricity sector was signed between Syria and Iran, which included the provision by Tehran of new power stations in Lattakia and Banias and the refurbishing of existing stations in Aleppo, Deir ez-Zor, and Homs (SANA 2018e). A month later, Iran struck a new deal with Damascus to build a 400 million euro (USD 460 million) power plant in Lattakia. In August 2018, the Syrian Ministry of Public Works and Housing agreed with Iranian private companies to build 30,000 residential units as part of

---

[24] Improving electricity supply was a key element of helping the Syrian regime restore economic growth in territory under its control. Bassam Darwish, head of the electricity ministry's planning unit in the Syrian government, estimated that direct damages in the power sector throughout the war correspond to approximately between USD 4 billion and USD 5 billion, and the damages to the electrical system in Aleppo amounted to one-quarter of this total. Meanwhile, indirect losses resulting from lack of electricity to various sectors, residential zones, and institutions amounted to nearly USD 60 billion (Reuters 2017e).

the General Organization for Housing projects in Damascus, Aleppo, and Homs (Hurriya Press 2018a). Then Iraj Rahbar, the deputy head of the Mass Construction Society of Iran, announced in February 2019 that his company was planning to build 200,000 housing units in Syria, mostly around Damascus, as a result of a memorandum of understanding that had been signed a few weeks earlier in a meeting of the Joint Syrian-Iranian Higher Committee. The agreement, he explained, would be implemented within three months and be funded through a new, USD 2 billion Iranian credit line (Economy 2 Day 2019).

Regarding Moscow, a Russian delegation in October 2015 visited Damascus and announced that Russian companies would lead Syria's postwar reconstruction. Deals worth at least 850 million euros emerged from these negotiations. A further Russian parliamentary visit to Syria in November 2016 resulted in Syrian foreign minister Walid Muallem reportedly offering Russian firms priority in rebuilding Syria (Haeur 2017). In mid-December 2017, a delegation of Russian CEOs headed by Russian deputy prime minister Dmitry Rogozin came again to Damascus for talks with Bashar al-Assad on investment and reconstruction in the country, referring to "major economic projects," including projects "on oil, gas, phosphate, electricity, and petrochemical industries," as well as on transport and trade (AFP and *Le Figaro* 2017). In February 2018, Syria and Russia signed an agreement on cooperation in the electrical power field in the "framework of developing the electrical system through reconstructing and rehabilitating Aleppo thermal plant and installing Deir ez-Zor power plant, in addition to expanding the capacity of Mharda and Tishreen plants" (SANA 2018c). In March 2019, several private Russian companies announced their willingness to communicate their construction techniques and skills to Syrian builders working on the reconstruction process in collaboration with the Syrian Ministry of Public Work and Housing (Emmar Syria 2019e).

However, there was serious doubt about the implementation of some of these projects, especially massive reconstruction schemes, and memorandums of understanding mentioned in this discussion forged between Tehran and Moscow and Damascus, just like many other investment projects and economic agreements announced during the past few years (*The Syria Report* 2019b). The Syrian government, for example, failed to secure the necessary funds for its contribution in deals with Iran and Russia in the electricity sector and the construction or rehabilitation of power plants; as a result, the two nations pulled out (Hatahet 2019: 14).

The Chinese government, in August 2017, hosted the First Trade Fair on Syrian Reconstruction Projects, during which a Chinese-Arab business group announced a USD 2 billion commitment from the government for the construction of industrial parks in Syria (Heydemann 2017). Qin Yong, the vice president of the China-Arab Exchange Association, estimated investments in Syria of similar value in December 2017 and explained that the business leaders that he had accompanied to Damascus, Homs, and Tartus—including representatives of the China National Heavy Duty Truck Company—planned to build roads, bridges, airports, and hospitals and restore electricity and communications (Abu-Nasr, Arkhipov, Meyer, and Shi 2017).

China, however, remained reluctant to invest in such an unstable country. For Beijing, investments in emerging countries were often conditioned on privileged access to natural resources, as in Africa. However, Syria was quite weak in raw materials, and those that did exist were largely promised to Moscow and Tehran. Projects also could be awarded to India (*The Indian Express* 2017) and Brazil (Adghirni 2017) as a reward for their pro-regime position on the international stage.

Among Arab countries, several countries expressed their willingness to take part in the reconstruction process of Syria. A total of 30 Egyptian companies participated in the Damascus International Fair in August 2017, while union delegation of Egyptian engineers visited Syria in early 2017 and met with Bashar al-Assad (Abd al-Haleim 2018; Ray al-Yawm 2017). Oman, for its part, signed in November 2017 a Memorandum of Understanding with Syria for cooperation in the energy sphere, making the Syrian–Omani company a "springboard toward establishing other investment projects between the two countries" (Madan 2017). The cooperation between the two countries sought to aid in the rehabilitation and reconstruction of damaged oil facilities (Madan 2017; al-Frieh and Said 2017b).

In Lebanon, many business groups and figures expected to participate in the reconstruction process, including former parties and individuals opposed to the Assad regime. Raya al-Hassan, a former finance minister from northern Lebanon who was directing the Tripoli Special Economic Zone project that was planned to be built adjacent to the port, declared in August 2017 that "Lebanon is in front of an opportunity that it needs to take very seriously" regarding the benefits of reconstruction in Syria (Associated Press 2017). The city's location close to the Syrian border also attracted increasing foreign investment. Tripoli port signed a 25-year lease with the Emirati port operator Gulftainer in 2013, to manage and invest in the terminal. The CEO of Lebanon's subsidiary of Gulftainer, Ibrahim Hermes, argued that "our aim was to invest here in anticipation of Syria's reconstruction" (Associated Press 2017). Similarly, Future Movement MP Dima Jamali declared in August 2018 that Tripoli must play an important role in the reconstruction of Syria and "we must separate the economic and developmental aspects from the political aspect" (*Orient le Jour* 2018).

In July 2018, after the regime's capture of Nasib border a few weeks earlier, Jordan invited members of the Damascus Chambers of Commerce and Industry and the Federation of Syrian Chambers of Industry to visit Amman. This was the first visit since 2011, and Jordanian officials simultaneously called for the reopening of the crossing, alluding to the readiness of thousands of trucks to transport commodities into Syria, according to Muhammad Khair Dawood, the head of the Trucks Owners' Union. The invitation followed the visit to Damascus in May of a delegation led by al-Ragheb, the president of the Jordan Chamber of Industry (Enab Baladi 2018k; *The Syria Report* 2018o). The head of the Jordanian Businessmen Association, Hamdi Tabbaa, also called on Egyptian businessmen to benefit from the reconstruction of Syria by establishing alliances between Egyptian and Jordanian contracting companies and participating in reconstruction projects (Damas Post 2018b).

However, it was the possible future investments of Gulf monarchies that were a major element in the foreign funding of reconstruction plans.[25] The UAE was the first Gulf monarchy to show its interests. In August 2018, UAE citizen Abdul Jalil al-Blooki visited the premises of Damascus Cham Holding. Among other positions, al-Blooki was the deputy chairman of Aafaq Islamic Finance, a Sharia-compliant financial services firm, and head of the Syrian company Emirates Private Development and Investment Company LLC, which was established in 2013 to invest in the real estate sector (Marota City 2018a). In the end of December 2018, a delegation from the UAE-based company Damac Properties visited Damascus, headed by its senior vice president for international development, Wael al-Lawati. Damac is a real estate developer and one of the largest companies in the UAE and Arab world, with assets of more than USD 7 billion and annual revenues of more than USD 2 billion. Lawati met at the Four Seasons Damascus with representatives from two Syrian companies, Telsa Group and al-Diyar al-Dimashqiah[26] (Emmar Syria 2018; *The Syria Report* 2018z). In mid-to-late January 2019, the visit of a Damascus Cham Holding

---

[25] Already in January 2018, the Kuwait Syrian Holding Company (KSHC), established in July 2002 to invest in the country, purchased a plot of land in the upscale Yaafour suburb of Damascus estimated at USD 12.2 million, out of which KSHC was investing 5.5 million. KSHC was part of the Kharafi group of companies, a multisector group whose owner was believed to be close to Maher al-Assad, according to several Syrian businessmen contacted by *The Syria Report* (2018u). The investment was carried out in a joint venture with Syrian investors, although the names behind the project were not revealed. The plot of land was adjacent to another in the area, and the plan was to build a large residential complex on the two plots, which had a combined area of 180,000 square meters (Kuwait Syrian Holding 2018; *The Syria Report* 2018e).

[26] Both companies were established relatively recently—Tesla in 2015 and Diar al-Diyar al-Dimashqiah in September 2018. Maher al-Imam is the general manager of Tesla, while Muhammad

delegation to the UAE, represented by its chief executive Nassouh Nabulsi, accompanied by Syrian businessmen and industrialists led by Muhammad Hamsho, was announced to encourage economic investment in Syria. The delegation met with a number of UAE Chambers of Commerce and Industry, as well as with UAE businessmen (Emmar Syria 2019b).

As mentioned in the previous chapter, these visits took place in the broader context of major changes occurring in the relations between the UAE and Syria. In January 2019, the Lebanese newspaper *al-Diyar* published an article indicating that more than 570 Arab, international, and Asian companies have applied to participate or otherwise shown interest in the reconstruction process in Syria (Economy 2 Day 2019a).

The level of reconstruction funded by foreign capital remained unclear and insufficient, however, particularly as Russia and Iran were having increasing difficulty maintaining their level of financial and material support for the Syrian regime. The participation of other foreign actors in Syria's reconstruction also was linked to the development of other regional and international political affairs and negotiations, notably regarding Iran. In particular, the issue of sanctions imposed by the United States[27] and European Union[28] on Syria constituted an obstacle that could scare off foreign companies. In November 2018, the United States increased its pressure on Syria, announcing that it will seek to impose sanctions against any party (including shipping companies, insurers, vessel owners, managers, and operators) involved in shipping oil to Syria (World Maritime News 2018). These sanctions participated in the following months in the increase shortages of energy products in Syria, especially regarding petrol (gasoline) resulting in growing frustrations among the Syrian population. In addition, U.S. pressure has put the brakes on further rapprochement between some Arab regimes (notably Saudi Arabia) and Syria. For instance, momentum to get Syria back into the Arab League has ebbed. The threat of U.S. sanctions was also alienating most international and Chinese multinational companies such as Huawei, which recently announced its withdrawal from Syria

---

Ghazi al-Jalali, a former minister of communication and a board member of Syriatel (and who is under EU sanctions), is a founder of Diar (Emmar Syria 2018; *The Syria Report* 2018aa).

[27] They notably banned exports, sales or supply of services, and any new investments in Syria by any U.S. individual. They also forbade any dealings by U.S. individuals in Syrian oil and hydrocarbon products and their import into the United States (McDowall 2018).

[28] European Union sanctions include asset freezes, travel bans, trade restrictions, financial sanctions, and an arms embargo. They forbid trade in items that could be used militarily or for repression, luxury goods, precious stones and metals, and equipment or technology for some oil and gas sectors, including exploration and production, refining, and gas liquefaction. The European sanctions also target Syria's electricity network, banning European Union companies from building power plants, supplying turbines, or financing such projects (McDowall 2018).

and Iran (Hatahet 2019: 9). The European Union and the United States[29] have repeatedly declared that support for Syria's reconstruction and the end of sanctions would depend on a credible political process that leads to a real political transition. In this context, the European Union imposed new sanctions in January 2019 on eleven prominent businessmen, including Samer Foz, and added five entities to the list of those subject to restrictive measures against the Syrian regime and its supporters because of their involvement in luxury real estate developments such as Marota City and/or acting as middlemen on behalf of the regime (Council of the European Union 2019).

The dilemma of reconstruction was also connected to the capacity of the regime to provide stability in the regions under its control and a business-friendly environment favorable to foreign investment. This was endangered by three main elements: militias, jihadists, and crony capitalists.

The issue of stabilization of the regime and centralization of power

The capacity of the regime to stabilize the situation in areas it controlled and put an end to (or least control) the various militias, whose grievances against it had increasingly become public and outspoken, remain an important challenge. We have seen in previous chapters that the militias have been involved in criminal activities such as robbery, looting, murder, infighting, and especially checkpoint extortion, resulting in higher prices and further humanitarian suffering, as well as generating apprehension about re-creating a favorable business environment.

Being subjected to pro-regime militias and NDF units on a regular basis, local populations often complained about their behavior. In regime-held areas, the behavior of these militias caused increasing frustration. They carried out *tashbihiyyah* (meaning "thuggish" in Arabic) abuses against harmless regime supporters, who were unable to confront them. For example, following the establishment of militias in the Zahra neighborhood in Homs at the beginning of the uprising in 2011, segments of the Alawi population in the area could be heard complaining that they were being coerced into helping fund the war effort of the Shabiha. They feared for their security or were scared that their children could be kidnapped for ransom if they did not pay the Shabiha what they called "protection money" (Reuters 2012d). Similarly, an elderly Alawi cleric in 2013 from the village of Masyaf in

---

[29] In addition to the sanctions imposed in 2011, the U.S. Congressional Foreign Affairs Committee unveiled in December 2017 the No Assistance for Assad Act, which would prevent the Trump administration from using nonhumanitarian U.S. aid funds for the reconstruction of Syria in areas held by the Assad regime or associated forces (U.S. Congress 2017).

central Syria stated that "the head of the NDF here is a dirty man. Two years ago he had nothing. Now he has land, cars, houses. That is all from stealing under the name of 'nationalism'" (cited in Reuters Staff 2013). This was a reflection of a more general pattern. Coastal residents from Lattakia and Tartus also expressed anger on several occasions about the silence of the local police and security forces, pointing especially at the rise in kidnapping, and looting, and other crimes by pro-regime militias and the disregard for residents' safety (Zaman al-Wasl 2016a, 2016b).

In September 2016, local populations in regime-controlled areas of western Aleppo city showed frustration against regime officials as a result of an increase in the looting of homes by loyalist Shabiha groups after residents evacuated the area. Pro-regime militias also looted hundreds of factories and workshops in Ramouseh industrial neighborhood in Aleppo. Fares Shehabi (2016), an MP and head of Aleppo's Chamber of Industrialists, complained about the incident on his Facebook page:

What happened in Ramouseh was very wrong, shameful ... either we live in the jungle with no laws, or we live in a nation that respects itself and its laws ... No one is above the law, do not waste your victory, nor disrespect the blood of your martyrs...

The pro-regime Imam of Aleppo's al-Abara Mosque mentioned the matter in a Friday prayer following these complaints and explained that trading stolen products was banned under Islamic law. NDF members often justified these actions as *ghana'im* (war spoils) that they had earned through their efforts to defend the homeland against the enemy (Syria Untold 2016d).

In May 2017, the Syrian government tried to cancel levies extorted by regime checkpoints following growing opposition from traders and transporters alike, reflecting the exasperation of the population in various areas under the control of the regime. Businessmen in Aleppo were increasingly critical of these levies, while lorry drivers outside the city of Suwayda closed the motorway linking to Damascus for two hours in protest of the "fees" imposed by the various checkpoints along the road. In mid-May 2017, Zeid Ali Saleh, the head of the Military and Security Committee in Aleppo, finally issued an order forbidding the levying of these fees by regime checkpoints on lorries transporting goods within and outside the city under the pretense of providing protection. A few days after, the Damascus Chamber of Industry demanded a similar ban in the capital (Enab Baladi 2017b).

In response to this growing unrest, the prime minister declared that he would ban these practices, but resistance from militias continued (al-Fayha Net 2017). This situation reflected the fact that as the war was ending in large swathes of the country, the justification for these checkpoints was becoming less and less valid.

In mid-June 2017 in Aleppo, following a number of crimes connected to pro-regime militias, which were reported even in the pro-regime media, a major crackdown was launched against these forces. The presidential palace sent Lieutenant General Muhammad Dib Zeitoun, head of state security and one of Assad's most powerful intelligence chiefs, to put an end to militia lawless behavior. State Security and Air Force Intelligence troops started rounding up popular committee members in the Adhamiya, Akramiya, and Seif al-Dawla neighborhoods, with small skirmishes in some cases. In addition, the local head of the Ba'th Party, Fadel al-Najjar, also issued a decree tightening regulations on the Ba'th Battalions. Meanwhile, the Aleppo security chief, Zaid al-Saleh, withdrew government IDs provided to militia fighters and forbade armed groups from operating in many areas as part of an effort to restructure and centralize local forces (Lund 2017d; al-Watan Online 2017).

There were significant challenges to curb the power of militias on a national scale. As mentioned in the previous chapter, the main challenge was that leaders of militias were generally linked to the powerful security service agencies and high military officials, preventing municipal and city officials from acting against them without the support of top-level decision-makers.

On July 6, 2017, a demonstration of hundreds of protestors, organized by industrialists and businessmen of the city, was organized in the Sheikh Najjar industrial zone, denouncing the practices of the regime's militia in Aleppo. Demonstrators accused the militias of killing civilians and deliberately disrupting the return of key services such as water and electricity by maintaining their control over services and prices. Protestors condemned the extortion of money against workers by militias at military checkpoints both inside and outside the city, notably by threatening them with forced entry to the military service if they did not pay. Meanwhile, a similar demonstration took place in the city of Nubl in the countryside of northern Aleppo, a stronghold of Shi'a pro-regime militias, demanding that the authorities stop armed robberies by pro-regime militias and the removal of military barriers (Shabaka âkhbar nubl w al-zahrâ` al-rasmîyya 2017; Enab Baladi 2017d; al-Modon 2017). In the second half of 2018, the industrial zone of Sheikh Najjar witnessed the departure and closing of other heavy- and medium-level industrial facilities. The taxes and fines that were imposed by the security administrations and militias at military checkpoints contributed to raising costs and raising the prices of the products, which were subject to competition from imported and smuggled products (al-Souria Net 2019).

Although the regime started a process to dissolve some militias or include them in the SAA, sometimes with the assistance of Russia, this was only the beginning of a long battle to discipline and put an end to the militias in the country, which numbered around 100,000 soldiers in 2017, including local militias such as NDF and those controlled by Iran. As argued by a Syrian official, who foresaw the problem in 2013:

After this crisis, there will be 1,000 more crises—the militia leaders. Two years ago they went from nobody to somebody with guns and power. How can we tell these shabiha to go back to being a nobody again? (Baker 2013)

In the summer of 2017, lawless and violent pro-regime militias were still spreading chaos and creating insecurity in various regime-held territories. By the end of August, fighters from the Nusur Homs paramilitary group refused to be inspected on their way into the city of Homs, instead opening fire on the police patrol and brutally beating a police officer (Zaman al-Wasl 2017g). In the military campaign to recapture the city of Deir ez-Zor and to cleanse IS from the area, territories falling under the control of the regime's forces were also subject to looting by regime forces, in a similar fashion as Aleppo, at the end of 2017 (Deir Ezzor 24 2017). In early 2018, a medical student at Aleppo University was severely beaten by a Ba'th Brigade militia fighter at the main gate of the university. The incident sparked angry reactions, relying on social network posts by the regime's supporters in the city about the abuses committed by militia members in Aleppo against civilians, launching the #togetheragainstshabiha hashtag on social media (al-Souria Net 2018a).

This situation continued in the city of Aleppo throughout 2018, increasing the popular anger of its inhabitants because of the daily criminality of members of loyalist militias. In various parts of the city, these criminal acts have escalated to the point of kidnapping and killing children (al-Modon 2018b). In the beginning of 2019, discontent continued to grow in the city of Aleppo and its southeastern countryside as a result of the lack of basic goods, including gas, bread, water, electricity, and other necessary services, while the militias and security forces monopolize fuel and oil at the gas stations (al-Souria Net 2019).

The pro-regime militias and the NDF, although respecting to some extent Assad's regime authority, introduced forms of fragmentation at the local level. Some of these groups also engaged in violent intermilitia rivalries over the control of territory and resources (Balanche 2018: XV).

The power of these militias was evident, as their leaders acted with near-total impunity in the country. They had powerful patrons in the country's ruling family and among its allies, and the profits from stolen property and bribes collected at checkpoints tended to trickle upward, which made it dangerous for local officials to interfere in their affairs. The regime also depended on these militias to manage its security challenges. Thus, instead of trying to confront the problem, Assad's regime responded with censorship, arresting journalists sympathetic to it who had raised issues with militias' behaviours (Lund 2017b).

The regime, however, had to discipline the Jaber brothers' militias in 2016 and 2017 for stepping out of bounds on several incidents, notably for clashing with other militias in the streets of Lattakia, including one commanded by Munzer al-Assad, the cousin of Bashar (Samaha 2017a; Ahmed al-Ali 2016). Following new violent incidents in February 2017 involving Ibrahim Jaber, the brother of Muhammad and Ayman and a high official of the regime, Bashar al-Assad ordered the withdrawal of hundreds of members of the regime's forces serving in the militias of the Jaber brothers (Enab Baladi 2017a) and the subsequent inclusion of his militias in the army's Fifth Corps. In June 2018, Syrian security services stormed the offices of Ayman Jaber in Lattakia, while a judicial order froze his assets and those of his family. Both of the Jaber militias, the Desert Hawks and Sea Commandos, were subsequently disbanded, while the property of Ayman Jaber was confiscated and he was put under house arrest for a period of time (Mustafa 2018). These disciplinary measures against actors who had gained too much autonomy demonstrated the steadfastness of Damascus in remaining the sole Syrian decision-maker among other actors of the ground.

In other cases, pro-regime media targeted businessmen, some with close ties to the regime, accused of corruption. Wissan Qattan, for example, an investor at the Qasion Mall and the al-Jalaa Gate Hotel in Damascus, had been the target of criticism from the beginning of 2018 by pro-regime news media and websites. The pro-regime *Tishreen* newspaper published an article accusing Qattan of encroaching on state property by expanding the Damascus mall and by obtaining public funds to achieve these ends (Hage Ali 2018). This was part of the regime's propaganda and rhetoric to combat corruption. There was, however, no genuine and persistent campaign against Qattan—in fact, he continued to consolidate his economic and political influence. In January 2019, Wassim Qattan's company was awarded by the joint committee established by the prime minister, which included representatives from the ministries of tourism and religious endowments, the development of the Yalbagha compound, which was located on a 7,000-square-meter plot near Marjeh Square in central Damascus, with an annual average investment fee of SYP 1.725 billion (around USD 3.45 million) for a period of 45 years. The project to be developed involved the construction of a four-star hotel with restaurants, in addition to commercial and housing space (Emmar Syria 2019c).

Other security challenges also existed for the regime, including the change in strategy of retreating jihadist groups, who largely shifted toward suicide bombings in civilian areas with the purpose of destabilizing regime-controlled towns and cities.

IS and al-Qa'ida losing ground ... but still a threat

Between 2016 and 2018, IS territories were under attack by various local, regional, and international forces. Internationally, however, IS operatives were still able to carry out more than 1,400 attacks in 2016 and kill more than 7,000 people, a roughly 20 percent increase over 2015, according to the university's Global Terrorism Database (Bhojani 2017).

However, 2017 was a turning point. First, IS was defeated in the city of Mosul in June following a nine-month offensive with air and ground support from a U.S.-led multinational coalition, and then Raqqa fell in mid-October after a four-month offensive of the SDF supported by U.S. air forces. After Raqqa, the Syrian army and its allies took full control of Deir ez-Zor city from IS in November. However, this loss of territory did not prevent IS from increasing its suicide attacks and car bombings in various regions of the country, in addition to murdering civilians in the areas in which its soldiers were withdrawing (Reuters 2017a). For example, in December 2017, IS claimed responsibility for a public bus bombing that killed eight people and injured eighteen more in the neighborhood of Akrama, in Homs, mostly inhabited by Alawi (Nassar, Nelson, and al-Zarier 2017).

Similarly, HTS, which lost territory to pro-regime forces and became increasingly concentrated in the Idlib area in early 2017, also returned to its tactic of suicide attacks in the objective of regaining momentum. In February 2017, HTS executed suicide attacks on two security installations in the city of Homs, killing 50 people and injuring 24, and in March, two suicide attack operations targeted Damascus. First, on March 11, a double bomb attack targeted Shi'a visiting a pilgrimage site in Damascus, murdering 74 people (Perry 2017). A few days after, on March 15, two more suicide bomb attacks killed at least 31 people and wounded dozens more in central Damascus (Reuters 2017g).

In an audio statement on April 23, al-Qa'ida leader Ayman al-Zawahiri called on Syrian Sunni jihadists to wage guerrilla war ranging from Assad's regime and his Iranian-backed allies to Western powers, and to prepare for "a long battle with the Crusaders and their allies, the Shi'a and Alawis" (Reuters 2017b). In a new message in February 2018, Zawahiri called on jihadists in Syria "to unite and agree and gather and merge and cooperate and stack together as one rank," and urged the various factions to "bury the reasons of disagreement" (Hoffman 2018). HTS (led by Jabhat al-Nusra), although officially having cut ties with al-Qa'ida, has maintained links with military organizations connected to the jihadist networks in northern Syria, providing them with territories and resources. In the Idlib region, several jihadist factions remained officially linked to al-Qa'ida, including Hurras al-Din, composed of several thousand Syrian and foreign fighters, including veterans from Iraq and Afghanistan; and the Turkestan Islamic Party. They fought alongside HTS when the latter took control of the Idlib region against the NLF groups backed by Turkey (Moutot 2019).

The gradual loss of territory under the control of these organizations did not spell their end or their capacity to strike regime-dominated areas through terrorist attacks. In July 2018, for example, IS soldiers killed at least 250 civilians in a devastating and meticulously planned attack on Druze-majority Suwayda. The IS strategy was turning toward insurgency.

In August 2018, it was estimated by both the Pentagon and the United Nations that the IS still had more than 30,000 fighters in Iraq and Syria (Britzky 2018). In an annual report on the U.S. antiterrorism fight world-wide, the State Department stated that IS, al-Qa'ida, and their affiliates, despite being weakened, "have proven to be resilient, determined, and adaptable, and they have adjusted to heightened counterterrorism pressure in Iraq, Syria, Afghanistan, Libya, Somalia, Yemen, and elsewhere" (cited in Landay 2018). In mid-January 2019, a bomb attack claimed by IS killed 16 persons in the city of Manbij, including four Americans (two soldiers and two civilians working for the U.S. military) and five SDF fighters. The attack in Manbij was the deadliest on U.S. forces in Syria since they deployed on the ground there in 2015 (Mcdowall and Stewart 2019). In March 2019, the IS fighters were defeated at their last held enclave on the Euphrates at the village of Baghouz by the SDF, but the jihadist group remained a threat, with fighters operating in remote territory elsewhere and capable of mounting insurgent attacks.

Crony capitalists as rapacious capitalists

The militias were certainly one of the biggest challenges for the regime in restoring stability, but they were not the only ones to put an obstacle on the issue of reconstructing the country's economy. The crony capitalists, empowered throughout the war, were also impeding the possibility of enabling the return of sections of the bourgeoisie to reinvest in the country, and therefore of creating a business environment favorable for reconstruction by their willingness to dominate the economy and investment opportunities. The regime's military victories and increasing control over large portions of

Syrian territory encouraged Damascus to try to bring back investors and businessmen who had left the country because of the war. Damascus's motivations were based on attracting investment and increasing business activity, while manufacturers reduced the need for imports, as foreign currency was very scarce.

Crony capitalists did not hesitate to criticize some government measures that tried to bring Syrian businessmen back into the country. In February 2017, for example, Minister of Finance Maamoun Hamdan visited Egypt to meet with the "Syrian Businessmen Group—Egypt," (Tajammu' Rijal al-A'mal As-Suri Bi-Masr) (SANA 2015), many of whom were manufacturers. He offered them many incentives, such as a reduction in customs duties on production inputs, an exemption of all duties on machinery as well as on sales tax, in addition to a rescheduling of any debt owed to state banks. Hamdan also announced that the government was providing funds to establish an 8-megawatt power-generating set for the Sheikh Najjar Industrial City in Aleppo, as well as completing work on the Aleppo Airport. The investors responded with a list of requests, including a grace period of two years for their debts and an extension of the age of the used machinery allowed back in the country from seven to ten years. They also raised several issues with regard to customs duties and other business regulations. A week later, a delegation of Syrian investors based in Egypt visited Damascus to meet with various government officials (SANA 2017a; *The Syria Report* 2017f).

A week after the minister's visit to Cairo, the newspaper *al-Watan*, owned by Rami Makhlouf, published a commentary piece on February 26 titled "The Egyptian Industrialists," strongly condemning the investors for their alleged arrogance, the fact that they conditioned their return to Syria on incentives provided by the government, and the fact that they returned "only after the liberation of Aleppo." The article also mentioned that they should pay back all their dues, including debt arrears and taxes (Hashem 2017).

The Syrian investors who left Syria during the war came from very diverse backgrounds and operated in a variety of business sectors, but they had one thing in common: no privilege relations with the regime. Those located in Egypt, for example, were mostly industrialists in the textile sector; many came from Aleppo, meaning that they had an urban Sunni background; and the origin of their wealth bore little relation to their ties with state institutions, but rather was based on capital investment (*The Syria Report* 2017f).

At this time, there was no sign of a massive return of Syrian industrialists, while the Egyptian regime announced in March 2017 its intention to establish an integrated industrial zone and other facilities for Syrian industrialists in Egypt as a counterinitiative against attempts by the Syrian regime to reattract Syrian industrialists based in Egypt (Syrian Economic Forum 2017). Many elements certainly prevented the return of Syrian businessmen on a mass scale in summer 2017, but the behavior of crony capitalists did not help in any willingness to come back to Syria.

In the beginning of 2018, Egyptian ruler Abdul Fattah al-Sisi inaugurated a large textile factory in Sadat City, an industrial zone north of Cairo, owned by one of Syria's most prominent industrialists, Muhammad Kamel Sabbagh Sharabati, who was listed as one of the 100 most important businessmen in 2009 in Syria and was a member of the Aleppo Chamber of Industry prior to 2011 (Kabawat 2018 Eqtissad 2018).[30] He left Syria in 2012 following his refusal to fund the repression and war efforts of the regime and was accused of supporting the revolution (Zaman al-Wasl 2017i). Some of his factories in Aleppo were eventually burned down. In 2018, Sharabati owned and ran four large plants in Sadat City on a total area of 180,000 square meters under the name of Fourtex or al-Roubaia Textile Company for Spinning, Weaving, and Dyeing. Fourtex complex of textile factories in Cairo was one of the leading exporters to Africa and its value was estimated at $200 million (Sharabati-denim 2018; Abd al-Hamid 2018).[31] Sharabati notably declared in an interview on Egyptian television that improving business conditions and regulations in Egypt had encouraged him to increase his investments in the country (ON Live 2017).

In these conditions, the call by Foreign Minister Muallem in August 2017 for an "active economic diplomacy for preparing the right groundwork for the reconstruction phase in service of national interests" and "the importance of prioritizing expatriate contributions in the reconstruction process through enhancing communication and constructive interaction with the Syrian communities abroad" (SANA 2017c) proved rather difficult to achieve, except if collaborations with crony capitalists and other regime officials were made directly.

At the beginning of the summer of 2018, new measures were taken to try to bring back Syrian businessmen living abroad, particularly from Egypt, and to encourage investments in the country and the means to resume production of their facilities. At the end of June, a delegation of Syrian businessmen residing in Egypt visited the Syrian prime minister Imad Khamis in Damascus and the Aleppo governor in Aleppo. The meeting with Prime Minister Khamis resulted in several decisions in support of investment and industry, "including the establishment of a permanent expo for the Syrian goods at Damascus Fairground City, enhancing external

---

[30] He was also one of the founders of Arab Bank Syria, as well as one of the most important investors in Arabia Insurance and Cham Holding.

[31] His company produced up to 50 million running meters of denim and flat fabric per year, while they employed some 2,600 people. His products were sold under the Sharabati Denim brand across Africa, the Middle East, and Europe (Sharabati Denim 2018).

expos in order to expand the export markets, facilitating the importation of raw materials necessary to support the industry and provide facilitations for the industrialists whose facilities have been damaged to enable them to resume production, in addition to activating the economic office at the Syrian embassy in Egypt" (cited in SANA 2018d).

The Syrian businessmen's delegation had also made other more crucial demands to Khamis, who expressed his readiness to study these demands and establish committees to implement them. The most important of these were the creation of boards of directors of the affected industrial zones in Aleppo, the granting of loans for additional reconstruction facilities, and the rescheduling of loans (providing more time to repay them) for businessmen who defaulted on repaying their loans to Syrian banks. As a reminder, in Egypt, about 30 percent of Syrian businessmen had invested USD 800 million in a number of projects, particularly in textiles, restaurants, and cafés (Enab Baladi 2018i).

Most of these demands had been made the year before, as mentioned earlier in this book. However, signs of resistance among personalities of the regime could still be seen toward businessmen who had left the country or not supported the regime enough in the past. For example, the governor of the Central Bank, Duriad Dergham, declared in July 2018 that he would provide loans only to those who stood by the Syrian regime (Enab Baladi 2018j). In February 2019, the head of the Syrian Businessmen's Union in Egypt, a separate business association from the one mentionned above, Khaldoun al-Muwaqa, declared in the *Tishreen* newspaper that despite the willingness of many industrialists to come back to Syria, the conditions were not realized, and solutions to address their demands and problems were still to be implemented (*Industry News* 2019). For example, Ammar Sabbagh, an important Aleppo industrialist who resided in Egypt where his textile manufacture were now based, established a new textile factory in Armenia in March 2019. Asked in an interview wh did he not return to Syria, he replied that he had tried to restart his factory in Aleppo, but that he had closed shortly afterward because the production costs were too high if the factory could not work full time (24h), and they could not compete with the prices of smuggled products that were cheaper (Emmar Syria 2019).

Conclusion

The humanitarian, socioeconomic, and political status quo in Syria is catastrophic at all levels. The vast majority of the Syrian population inside the country suffer from unemployment, rising inflation, and worsening living conditions. The structure of the economy was modified considerably, with low-conflict regions benefiting from the transfer of companies and industries and witnessing significant growth in public and private investments in these areas.

At the same time, the regime was able to take control of the USD 30 billion international humanitarian aid delivered by UN agencies such as the World Health Organization (WHO). The international humanitarian organizations operating from Damascus also had to rely on local implementing partners and to choose their sponsors from a list of "national NGOs" by the Syrian Minister of Foreign Affairs, such as Syria Trust (founded and chaired by Syrian first lady Asma al-Assad), or charities such as al-Bustan, owned by Rami Makhlouf. The vast majority of these billions of U.S. dollars in diverted funds are from the same Western states that imposed the sanctions in the first place (Sparrow 2018).

By the start of 2019, the reconstruction process was very limited and the scale of destructions remained massive. The regime, however, was already using reconstruction plans as a means of strengthening its patrimonial and despotic character and its networks, while also serving as an instrument to punish or discipline former rebellious populations.

However, the endurance of the Assad regime with the assistance of its foreign allies did not signal the end of all problems for Damascus. On the contrary, the regime had to deal with a series of contradictions and challenges: on the one hand, satisfying the interests of crony capitalists and heads of militias, and on the other, accumulating capital through economic and political stability, while granting shares to its foreign allies in the reconstruction business and other economic sectors such as natural ressources. These objectives were rarely overlapping, and some contradictions and rivalries were already appearing. Mounting criticisms were levied increasingly by civilians in regime-held areas against the criminal practices of the pro-regime militias and socioeconomic difficulties, while areas conquered by the regime's forces in 2018, such as al-Ghoutha and Dar'a, witnessed some actions of dissent against the regime's symbol[32] and even sometimes targeting regime's security services affiliates, showing the volatility of the situation and the lack of the regime's hegemony. This does not even take into account the great potential of destabilization caused by jihadist forces turning increasingly to terrorist actions and particularly targeting urban populated areas with the loss of territory.

The resilience of the regime in its war against any kind of dissent came at a very high price—above all, in terms of human lives and destruction, but also politically.

---

[32] In March 2019, a demonstration occurred in the city of Dar'a refusing the rebuilding of Hafez al-Assad's statue, while calling for the overthrow of the Assad regime (Tube Rased 2019).

Conclusion

In this book, I have tried to delineate and analyze the origins, characteristics, and evolution of the Syrian uprising in relation to economic and political developments in Syrian society and in the regional and international arena. The Syrian revolutionary process, and uprisings in the MENA more generally, can be examined with the same theoretical and conceptual tools used to understand other popular mobilizations or revolutions in different regions of the world. I have sought to analyze the Syrian uprising in its totality from local socioeconomic and political developments to regional and international developments. Departing from there, the book has analyzed the resilience of the Assad regime.

The establishment of a despotic and patrimonial regime

The nature of the state built by Hafez al-Assad and the socioeconomic and political developments during his rule had profound impacts on Syrian society. The Ba'thist regime initially gained autonomy from the dominant elite and bourgeois classes by breaking their monopoly over the means of production and mobilizing sections of the workers and peasants through the party's institutions. After 1970, Assad achieved autonomy from each of the factions in his power base by balancing them against each other: He first used the army to liberate himself from the party's ideological restrictions. He then established and developed a *jamaa* (literally meaning "the group" or "the alliance" in Arabic), a core of largely Alawi personal followers, usually from his family, who were nominated to critical security and military commands, which provided him with even greater autonomy from the larger Ba'thist military. He widened the basis of the regime by including the urban middle class and bourgeois Sunni, especially from Damascus, coopting large sections of them into the top ranks of the party and many independent technocrats in the various levels of government. Progressive and gradual economic liberalization allowed him to promote a new, state-dependent bourgeoisie and build an alliance with a segment of the Damascene private bourgeoisie. Assad, therefore, was able to achieve autonomy within the state structure and autonomy from society by balancing statist and private-sector interests (Hinnebush 2001: 67). At the same time, the party structure still served as an instrument of mobilization, clientelism, and control among popular classes, especially in rural areas.

It was also the first period in postindependence Syrian history to witness such waves of violent repression against dissenting parties, ranging from universities to various civil society organizations like trade unions and independent professional associations, and opposition political parties. All who opposed the regime or refused to submit to its domination suffered harsh repression. This led some to characterize Syria as a "kingdom of silence" (Wikstrom 2011).

The patrimonial state built by Hafez al-Assad was then transferred to his son, Bashar. The corporatist nature of the state was undermined considerably compared to the Hafez period, as the new ruler relied massively on a smaller group of loyal personalities from his family, high officials in security services, and crony capitalists. The power and role of corporatist organizations were significantly weakened, reducing the social basis of the regime considerably. Bashar's accelerated neoliberal policies and consolidation of power against the old guard completely shifted the social base of the regime, composed initially of peasants, government employees, and some sections of the bourgeoisie, especially the "new class," to a social coalition with crony capitalists at its center, along with sections of the regime supporting factions of the bourgeoisie and urban higher-middle classes. These policies led to increasing poverty and social inequalities, along with increasing sectarian and ethnic animosities in some regions, as a result of the growing scarcity of resources on one side and regime patronage policies and absence of democracy on the other.

Meanwhile, the oppressive nature of the regime remained a constant feature, preventing any organized independent political organizations to exist on a wide scale, or even on a smaller scale. The only actors able to play an increasing role in society during this period were religious associations and institutions, notably assuming the role of the state in social services, which were constantly diminishing. In this framework, but moreover to serve the regime's foreign objectives such as preventing stability in Iraq following the U.S. and British invasions in 2003, Islamic associations and fundamentalist organizations, including jihadist actors, had significant space in which to organize and act relatively freely in Syria for several years.

The impoverishment of large sections of the population, in an atmosphere of corruption, absence of democratic rights, and growing socioeconomic inequalities, laid the groundwork for a popular insurrection that was only waiting for a spark. This would come from the regional uprising in Egypt and Tunisia, and then a local one following the events in Dar'a.

The origins and development of the uprising

Uprisings in Tunisia, Egypt, and elsewhere inspired large segments of the Syrian population to take to the streets with similar demands for freedom and dignity (in other words, democracy, social justice, and equality). This was demonstrated by the hegemony of an inclusive and democratic rhetoric among large sections of the protest movement in 2011 and 2012. Along with this element, the alternative institutions established by the protesters such as the coordination committees and local councils, by providing services to the local population, attempted to achieve a situation close to dual power in which the domination of the state vanished. The protest movement through these two elements provided a political alternative that could appeal to large sections of the population, especially in its first six months and before the mass militarization of the uprising. This situation was increasingly challenged as a result of the evolution and dynamics of the uprising. The inclusive and democratic message of the protest movement was progressively undermined throughout the uprising, although it remained in some sectors.

The analysis of class and state formation in Syria described in Chapter 1 outlined the origins and evolution of the uprising in Syria. The bulk of protesters originally came from the suburbs of Damascus, Aleppo, and Homs, midsized towns and rural areas, which were the regions where accelerated neoliberal policies had the greatest effect, while repression and corruption only increased their dissatisfaction toward the regime. At the same time, repressive and sectarian regime policies prevented large sections of the popular classes from religious minorities to join the revolt in great numbers, and demonstrations were limited. The sectarian strife and civil war in the neighboring countries of Iraq and Lebanon also led some from religious minorities to fear a similar fate. Activists from religious and ethnic minority backgrounds did play a role in the uprising. This reality refuted the claims that the protest movement was uniquely sectarian or opposed Sunni to minorities. Furthermore, a large majority of peaceful protesters in Sunni-populated areas did not mobilize on a sectarian basis, nor did they have sectarian objectives.

The repression of the protest movement and the lack of any overtures by the regime led to a radicalization of the language of the protesters, who ultimately demanded the fall of the regime. With no other avenue to make their voices heard (elections, parliaments, free press, etc....), they chose to revolt. As argued by Trotsky (2008: 740):

[P]eople do not make revolution eagerly any more than they do war ...
a revolution takes place only when there is no other way out.

These conditions also lay at the roots of the progressive militarization of the movement.

Repression, mobilization, and adaptation

After the outbreak of the uprising, the state prioritized violence and hindered any possibility of opening up to include sections of the opposition or meet demands of the protest movement. In tandem with repression, it mobilized its popular base and portrayed the protesters as extremist terrorists or armed gangs seeking to destabilize the country.

Peaceful, nonsectarian, and democratic activists were the main targets of the regime. The repression in the main square of Homs in April 2011 is one such example. At the same time, the regime freed significant numbers of Islamic fundamentalist and jihadist personalities with previous military experience from Iraq and other countries, and let them proliferate to realize its own characterization of an uprising led by religious extremists.

The regime also adapted its strategies and tools of repression according to regional variations in sectarian and ethnic composition. The aim of the regime's high officials was nevertheless consistent: to suppress the protests, divide people according to primordial identities, and instill fear and distrust among them to break the inclusive spirit of the movement. The massacres by pro-regime militias and Shabihas, many from Alawi backgrounds, targeted impoverished Sunni villages and popular neighborhoods in mixed regions, particularly Homs and Hama provinces and the coast, with Alawi and Sunni populations living side by side. They were executed for the purpose of stoking sectarian tensions. The regime also targeted women, with terrible human and social consequences.

The resilience of the regime also was rooted in the mobilization of its popular base through sectarian, tribal, regional, and clientelist connections, as well as in the massive foreign support from Russia, Iran, and Hezbollah. The sectarian aspect of the state's mobilization of the Alawi minority in its armed apparatus (SAA, militias, and security services) was particularly significant. The so-called homogeneity of the Alawi population nonetheless must be challenged, as significant political, socioeconomic, and regional dynamics differences existed within it.

Large numbers of Alawis relied on their employment in state-run economic and military institutions for their subsistence. At the same time, they feared for their lives, as the uprising was increasingly portrayed by the regime as an Islamic and sectarian armed uprising and an anti-Alawi movement, rather than as a popular revolution for democracy and social justice. This perception was reinforced by the reality of the rise of movements with anti-Shi'a and anti-Alawi positions. For many Alawis, the regime appeared to be the only option that would ensure their group survival, while opposing Bashar also risked devastating economic costs, as many worked in state institutions or were employed by the army, the secret services, or pro-regime militias. Thus, fears of revenge against Alawi, along with economic dependence, were the main reasons for standing with the regime, and loyalty was not necessarily associated with support for its policies. Finally, the lack of an alternative in the form of a credible opposition in exile, as well as the rise of Islamic fundamentalist and jihadist movements, discouraged support for the uprising.

The fear of violence was not limited to the Alawi minorities; it also extended to other religious minorities, especially the Christian population, which dreaded the collapse of the state and a similar fate as Iraqi Christians, who fled Iraq in droves after the U.S. and British invasion of 2003. The expansions of these movements and the multiplication of actions targeting Christians and other religious minorities also pushed many to abstain from joining the uprising even if they did not necessarily support the regime. This was particularly the case with Suwayda Province, mostly inhabited by Druze, which maintained a form of autonomy from the regime, notably through a movement to refuse the conscription of its youth, while otherwise not challenging or in limited ways the state.

The regime's popular base was not limited to religious minorities; it included Sunni supporters throughout the country, cultivated through patronage and informal networks rooted in clientelist, tribal, and regional connections. Sunnis were represented at all levels in state structures and institutions. The regime also played on deep social and rural/urban divides, particularly in Aleppo and to some extent in Damascus. Large sections of urban government employees, the middle class, and bourgeoisie in the two main cities of Damascus and Aleppo were passive or did not involve themselves in the protest movement, although some might have sympathized in the early days. There was also a general perception among many, including Sunnis, that an Islamic state or society was being imposed in opposition-held areas.

The main supporters of the regime were crony capitalists, security services, and high representatives of religious institutions linked to the state. The crony capitalists and security services helped to mobilize pro-regime demonstrations and funded various militias after the militarization of the uprising. This support for the regime came with expanding economic opportunities in the country through the war economy or the formal economy. New businessmen and networks played increasingly important roles in the economic and political landscape, in exchange for their loyalty and services to the regime, while other sectors of the bourgeoisie left the country.

The financial assistance given by the regime's allies, Iran and Russia, allowed it to maintain state institutions and provisions. The state remained the leading employee and provider of resources and services throughout the war. The catastrophic humanitarian and socioeconomic situation in Syria, therefore, reinforced the role of the state.

Weakening of the uprising and failure of the opposition

The regime's repression weakened the protest movement and isolated the activists, rendering contact and collaboration much more difficult and making it nearly impossible for the movement to constitute a centralized leadership. Moreover, the regime's war led to the gradual transformation of the uprising into an armed conflict. The initial successes of some FSA units, both militarily and in terms of some successful collaboration with the civilian protest movement, had raised hopes for some parts of the opposition. The combination of armed resistance and peaceful or civil actions (strikes and demonstrations) was put forward as the strategy to fight the regime. Hassan al-Ashtar, an FSA leader in Rastan, told a journalist in January 2012 when asked how to overthrow the regime that the answer lay in the three pillars of resistance—the continuation of peaceful demonstrations, the FSA, and civil disobedience (cited in Achcar 2013: 266).

The military asymmetry in favor of the regime, with the massive assistance of its foreign allies, rendered an FSA military victory nearly impossible. The FSA's networks lacked any comparable organized and stable support, and its units were never able to form an effectively centralized organization. This led to its progressive marginalization and weakening throughout the war. Islamic fundamentalist and jihadist movements increasingly dominated the opposition military situation. Foreign countries that claimed to support the uprising (i.e., Turkey, Saudi Arabia, and Qatar) also weakened and divided the FSA units by providing them support on an unstable basis and under strict conditions, while increasingly turning their support predominantly to Islamic fundamentalist movements. They were more interested in building their own proxies on the ground and advancing their own interests and political influence than in the protest movement per se.

The FSA never represented an independent social force that could bring people together around a distinct, inclusive political message. The diversity of FSA units in terms of geography and policies, although sharing similar local dynamics in the beginning, was never overcome. No leadership or centralized decision-making were developed, which allowed foreign countries and Islamic fundamentalist groups to instrumentalize the units or simply put an end to them.

Similarly, the opposition in exile, first represented by the SNC and then by the Coalition, failed to constitute a credible alternative. In both cases, the MB, other religious fundamentalists, and sectarian groups and personalities dominated these institutions while trying to portray an inclusive image in the media by appointing secular and liberal personalities in visible positions to appease fears among Western backers. Moreover, liberal and secular personalities (such as George Sabra and Michel Kilo) and political organizations in the various opposition bodies in exile defended and justified the presence of reactionary Islamic movements on the Syrian political and military scene within the country. They remained silent on the human rights violations committed by some Salafist groups and included some like Jaysh al-Islam in the opposition. The political head of the latter group, Muhammad Alloush, was appointed as the chief negotiator in the Geneva 3 conference and remained an important figure in the HNC.

Both sides had an interest in this collaboration, with the perspective of gaining power or at least playing a role in the negotiation processes. First, the liberal and secular individuals and groups in the Coalition saw cooperation with reactionary Islamic groups as a military necessity, even if the latter were antidemocratic and ruled in an authoritarian way in the areas they controlled, including attacking and kidnapping democratic activists. For their part, Islamic fundamentalist groups, including the MB and Salafist movements like Jaysh al-Islam, collaborated with the opposition in exile to demonstrate their moderation and reassure regional and Western states. One side was the main beneficiary of this collaboration, however: the Islamic fundamentalist movements. The relationship was unequal, though, as these movements had an organized political and military presence within the country and received massive funding and support from some states (Saudi Arabia, Qatar, and Turkey) and private networks from the Gulf monarchies, while democratic and secular groups, which were already weak on the ground, were severely repressed by the regime's forces and unable to organize later for various reasons.

The players within the SNC and the Coalition believed that the end justified the means, but the end is determined by the means used. These circumstances resulted in the absence of an organized democratic or progressive pole on a national level within or outside the country during these years, while letting reactionary Islamic groups occupy the political and military space. This led to a situation that the rhetorical commitments of the opposition bodies in exile to an inclusive democracy were not credible enough to persuade large sections of the population to abandon the Assad regime and join the uprising. Further, they were not able to develop any solid and inclusive alternative institutions to the state.

As argued by Syria researcher Tareq Aziza (2018):

This shameful atmosphere (within the opposition of the Syrian Coalition characterized by corruption and submission to foreign states

286 / SYRIA AFTER THE UPRISINGS

and interests) that has prevailed for years among opposition institutions (if indeed they are institutions) has facilitated the West and the supporters of the regime, of course, made it easier for them to repeat the lie of "the absence of alternative" or even "fear of the alternative" "Assad is bad but there is no mature alternative!", etc.

Riyad Turk, longtime leader of the dissident Syrian Communist Party–Political Bureau, which later was renamed the People's Party, and also a founding member of the SNC, acknowledged in September 2018 after his arrival in France that one of the initial problems with the SNC at its establishment was that the MB and groups linked to it dominated it (Atassi 2018).

The growth of reactionary Islamic fundamentalist and jihadist forces further reduced the capacities of the protest movement to provide an inclusive and democratic message, including to those who were not involved directly in the events but who sympathized with the initial goals of the uprising. The rise of those Islamic movements was the result of various causes, including the regime's initial facilitation of their expansion, the repression of the protest movement leading to radicalization among some elements, better organization and discipline, and finally support from foreign countries.

These various forces constituted the second wing of the counterrevolution after the Assad regime. They did not have the same destructive capacities as Assad's state apparatus, but their outlook on society and the future of Syria stood in complete opposition to the initial objectives of the uprising and its inclusive message for democracy, social justice, and equality. Their policies were equally repulsive to the most conscious sections of the protest movement and threatened groups like religious minorities, women, and many Sunnis who feared their ascension to power because they did not share their view of society and religion. Their ideology, political program, and practices proved to be violent not only against the regime's forces, but also against democratic and progressive groups, both civilians and armed groups, and ethnic and religious minorities.

The Kurdish issue in Syria

The rise of the Kurdish national question also raised important questions for the protest movement and challenged its inclusiveness. Despite an initial unity in demands and actions between Arab and Kurdish LCCs and groups, the Arab Syrian opposition, whether within the country or outside, was unable to accommodate the concerns of the Kurds in Syria. They instead showed an attitude of refusal and chauvinism similar to that of the regime, while the Coalition, allied with the Turkish government, supported its repressive policies against Kurds in Turkey and Syria. The Kurdish national question was completely denied by the main actors of the Arab Syrian opposition, both in the Coalition and in military groups such as Jaysh al-Islam that participated in negotiations.

For its part, the PYD, with the benevolent attitude of Damascus, used the opportunity of the uprising to become the dominant Kurdish political actor in Syria, while trying to advance its own interests. It concentrated on building its own institutions and an effective military force, with many advances and achievements in certain aspects, including secularization of laws, women's rights, and the inclusion of women and religious and ethnic minorities. They had authoritarian and repressive policies, however, particularly against rival Kurdish organizations and activists. The PYD was certainly the most organized nonstate actor in Syria, with its own institutions and international relationships, including to state actors such as the United States and Russia. These states, however, did not support Kurdish national demands in Syria, or elsewhere, but rather used the PYD to serve their own interests, especially in their war against IS. The Kurdish group, despite being a proxy for the interests of both Washington and Moscow at various times, maintained its autonomy and managed to advance its own interests as well through these collaborations.

The Kurdish national question reemerged on the Syrian political scene through the eruption of the 2011 protest movement. However, this gain is being threatened by multiple actors who do not wish to see the rise and creation of a Kurdish autonomous region in Syria. As Damascus consolidated its power and the elimination of large sectors of opposition armed forces was well advanced, pressure on the PYD increased by the end of 2016. The regime reiterated on several occasions its refusal of any autonomous Kurdish region and increasingly came into conflict with PYD forces in the north from mid-2016, while Turkey wanted to put an end to the PYD's presence at its borders. Washington and Moscow saw their relationship with Ankara and the stability of Syria as more important than Kurdish rights, which they never supported. Faced with this situation, the PYD was increasingly trying to find a form of consensus with Damascus to preserve its structures and institutions in areas that it controlled in the northeast, but with no concrete results to date.

The climate of continuous war and the increasing militarization of the uprising on one side and the upsurge of sectarian and ethnic tensions in the country on the other allowed less and less space for the protest movement to organize and provide an inclusive and democratic message. The initial objectives of the uprising were challenged more and more from all sides.

Regional and international political dynamics

The regional and international environment was most probably the most important factor in the resilience of the regime. The assistance provided by the Damascus allies Russia, Iran, and Hezbollah, in addition to foreign Shi'a fundamentalist militias sponsored by Tehran, allowed the survival of the regime on political, economic, and military levels. They viewed the protest movement in Syria and the possible fall of the Assad regime as a threat to their own interests, especially geopolitical interests. They intervened alongside the regime's forces early on and played a crucial role in the fighting. At the same time, they provided the regime with significant expertise in dealing with internal dissent, whether expressed in civilian protest or armed resistance.

These allies substantially increased their broader influence in the country, both in society and in state institutions, as their interventions deepened. The survival and stabilization of the regime, therefore, became even more important over time in order to preserve not only their geopolitical interests, but their growing economic ones as well. Tehran and Moscow particularly sought to benefit from the reconstruction process and Syrian natural ressources.

The majority of Western states, led by the United States, did not get deeply involved in the organization of the opposition. They initially rejected any plans to assist armed opposition forces, while opening up space to Saudi Arabia, Qatar, and Turkey to provide limited and specific weaponry to various armed groups. The unwillingness of the United States to envision a plan to overthrow the regime or intervene decisively against it weakened and divided FSA units and led to the rise of reactionary Islamic movements, while encouraging the regime's allies to deepen its military assistance without risking direct confrontation with Washington. The United States and Western states became increasingly focused on IS and the war on terror, following its announcement of its caliphate in 2014. This situation served the Syrian regime's agenda.

Syria was not seen as a strategic interest for the United States, notably because it lacked substantial oil reserves. The significance of Syria was related to its geographic location bordering Turkey, Iraq, Lebanon, and Israel, as well as its relationship with Iran and its role in the Israeli-Arab conflict.

U.S. officials were also reluctant to intervene massively in the region as they had done in the past in the framework of a "regime change" strategy, which they abandoned at the eve of the uprising. This was a direct consequence of the experience in Iraq and the numerous failures that followed. Rather, the objectives were to limit change in the region, mainly by seeking agreements and understanding between existing regimes (or sections of it) and the opposition groups linked to Western states, Turkey, and Gulf monarchies. In the Syrian uprising, these attempts, whether by Western states or Gulf monarchies and Turkey, were met with failure.

Gulf monarchies, led by Saudi Arabia and Qatar on one side and Turkey on the other, then adopted a more hostile position toward the Assad regime. Saudi Arabia, Qatar, and private networks from the Gulf monarchies funded and backed military and political groups, particularly Islamic fundamentalist and some jihadist movements, as a means of promoting forces on the ground that served their interests.

Riyadh's main objective in the Syrian conflict was to weaken Iran, seen as its main enemy in the region. Overthrowing the Assad regime, the main ally of Tehran in the region, was in Riyadh's interest to strengthen a Sunni axis led by Saudi Arabia against Iran. On its side, Qatar saw the uprising as an opportunity to increase its own regional influence, notably through the MB and other Islamic fundamentalist actors. The Gulf monarchies feared the establishment of a form of liberal democracy in Syria, which would threaten their own interests if democratic ideas and activities expanded in the MENA region. From this perspective, they preferred a sectarian war and encouraged a sectarian narrative through their media and funding.

Similarly, Turkey initially supported the overthrow of Assad's regime after failing to convince Damascus in the first months of the conflict to accept the integration of opposition forces close to Ankara in a unity government and superficial reforms. This objective was progressively abandoned, however, and the Turkish priority increasingly became the defeat of the Kurdish PYD and the cleansing of its forces at the borders. FSA groups and Islamic fundamentalist groups under Turkish influence were used as proxies in Ankara's war against the Kurds. The policies of Gulf monarchies and Turkey promoted jihadist forces while dividing the FSA units through diverse sponsoring. This situation amplified the sectarian effects of Iranian and Hezbollah interventions. This contributed to the Islamization of the armed opposition and the deepening of sectarian and Kurdish-Arab tensions.

The various international imperialist and regional dominant powers, despite their disagreements, did not want the Syrian crisis to extend beyond the country's borders. They especially wanted to limit the growth of the jihadist forces acting in Iraq and Syria. They increasingly shared a common interest in putting an end to the uprising and achieving a solution in which the structure of the regime was not radically changed. They wanted a stable political environment, which would allow them to build and develop their political and economic capital, regardless of the demands of the protest movement.

This focus was reflected in July 2017 on the international scene when neither U.S. president Donald Trump nor the new French president Emmanuel Macron called for the ouster of Bashar al-Assad; their priority continued to be the fight against IS and other similar jihadist forces. These countries were previously the most opposed (at least rhetorically) to Assad remaining in power. In August 2017, former U.S. ambassador to Syria Robert Ford declared, "There is no conceivable military alignment that's going to be able to remove him ... Everyone, including the U.S., has recognized that Assad is staying" (cited in Issa 2017). As the Assad regime consolidated its power in the country, along with the near-elimination of IS (territorially, if not as an organization), the increasing priority of the United States, alongside other Western states, Gulf monarchies, and Israel, became to roll back Iran's influence in Syria.

There was, however, a near-consensus between all the international powers around a number of points: to liquidate the protest movement, to stabilize the regime in Damascus with Bashar al-Assad at its head for a short to medium length of time, to oppose Kurdish autonomy, and to defeat jihadist groups militarily, such as IS and Jabhat al-Nusra. There was a general global trend aimed at liquidating the Syrian uprising in the name of the so-called war on terror, and what was considered as a return of an authoritarian stability. The main point of contention was Iran's influence in Syria.

The regime survives, but problems remain

The Assad regime emerged from the war as an even more brutal, narrowly sectarian, patrimonial, and militarized version of its former self. The uprising-turned-war forced Damascus to reconfigure its popular base, narrow its dependency on global authoritarian networks, adjust its modes of economic governance, and reorganize its military and security apparatuses (Heydemann 2013b: 60). Its repression continued as well, targeting former opposition fighters and civilians who participated in the so-called reconciliation agreements. Jamil Hassan, the fierce head of the Air Force Intelligence, said in the summer of 2018 that more than 3 million Syrians were wanted by the state and their judicial cases were ready, adding, "a Syria with 10 million trustworthy people obedient to the leadership is better than a Syria with 30 million vandals" (cited in *The Syrian Reporter* 2018).

The issue of reconstruction was an important challenge for the regime. Since 2017, Damascus has been hatching plans, but thus far, only one major real estate project was going ahead: the Marota City development in the Mazzeh District of Damascus, where all investments on the infrastructure of the project came from the state and private investors, mostly linked to the regime. The lack of national funding, whether private or public, the uncertainty of the scale of foreign funding despite growing interests of the UAE, and other potential Gulf monarchies to seek investments in Syria and international sanctions preventing the participation of significant economic actors were serious problems for a country with nearly USD 400 billion in projected costs for reconstruction. This was alongside the destruction of health and education services, large-scale internal and external displacement of Syrians, enormous losses of human capital, and a low level of international reserves.

The process of rehabilitation of Damascus on the Arab political scene led by the UAE and increasing interests by regional and international actors in the reconstruction did not solve all the abovementioned challenges and difficulties. The situation was also connected to regional and international political evolutions and negotiations, which could influence the reconstruction process.

Along with this situation, reconstruction efforts could differ from region to region according to the varying levels of influence and presence by foreign states in certain areas outside the sovereignty of the Syrian state. One example was the Euphrates Shield areas under Turkish domination, where Turkish authorities invested significantly in governing institutions and economic infrastructure. Differences in reconstruction plans between and within regions could affect local sectarian and ethnic dynamics in a postwar Syria.

At the same time, the issue of refugees and the possibility of their return was an important factor in reconstruction. Many neighboring countries, such as Lebanon and Turkey, did not recognize most Syrians living there as refugees. In these countries, there is growing domestic political pressure to return Syrians forcefully to Syria, with no security guarantees. So far, Syrian authorities have taken in only small flows of returnees. For many refugees, the Syrian regime still presented a threat to their safety, or at least it presented administrative obstacles to their returning to their original homes. Many refugees come from areas that have been completely destroyed.

A massive return of refugees would be a major challenge for the regime, politically, economically, and in terms of infrastructure, particularly if many were to return within a short period. In addition, remittances sent by Syrians to their families inside the country (as mentioned in the previous chapter) became one of the most important sources of national income, thus helping to boost internal consumption.

The economist Osama Qadi argued that "recovery might take 20 years, assuming Syria post conflict starts in 2018 at 4.5 percent growth" (FEMISE 2017). At present, this estimate seemed optimistic to say the least, not only because the war still was not over and the growing and deepening sanctions against the Syrian state. Furthermore, reconstruction plans are not limited to rebuilding infrastructure. The regime's socioeconomic and political policies were likely to exacerbate social, economic, and regional inequalities throughout the country, deepening problems of development that already had existed before 2011. Historical examples, such as those in Lebanon and Iraq, have shown that even adequate levels of national or international funding might not guarantee an effective reconstruction process.

More generally, the deepening of neoliberal policies, notably the new economic strategy of national partnership and the PPP law, presented as necessary and technocratic measures by successive Syrian governments, should be considered as a means to transform the general conditions of capital accumulation and empower economic networks linked to the regime. As argued by Adam Hanieh (2018: 201), capitalist states often seize crisis as moments of opportunity "to restructure and push forward change in ways that were previously foreclosed and significantly extend the reach of the market in a range of economic sectors that have hitherto been largely state dominated." Prior to the war, PPPs already had been considered as a key instrument to accelerate the mobilization of private capital, especially in the energy sector.[1] In this framework, the reconstruction plan of the Syrian government, which has remained largely underdeveloped thus far, probably would fortify and strengthen the patrimonial and despotic character of the regime and its networks, while being employed as a means to punish or discipline former rebellious populations and continue to impoverish the most disadvantaged parts of Syrian society.

Syrian officials also faced increasing frustrations from populations considered pro-regime, or at least that had not joined the protest movement. In coastal areas, Damascus notably allowed the proliferation of private charity organizations, but primarily those linked to figures allied to the regime, providing social services in place of the state. This was a way to maintain a clientelist and dependent relationship with local communities that supplied important personnel for the regime's army and militias. Criticisms from within the regime's popular base against state institutions and leaders for their corruption or inefficiency and socioeconomic problems also increased in this period. Frustration and suspicion of the government and its authority were very significant in the Suwayda Province, which preserved a form of autonomy vis-à-vis Damascus without a complete break

---

[1] Investments in electricity infrastructure, for example, were needed to attract private investments and reduce the cost of business operations. A report developed by the World Bank in cooperation with the Syrian Ministry of Electricity in 2010 estimated that about USD 11 billion of investments in new generating capacity (7,000 megawatts) and expansion of the transmission and distribution networks would be required through 2020 (World Bank 2011: 22–24).

from state institutions. The threats of jihadist groups such as HTS and IS still existed within the country, as well as their capacity to create instability through the use of suicide bombers.

The resilience of the regime did not mean the end of its contradictions or forms of dissent, especially in areas held by opposition forces. The absence of a structured and independent, democratic and inclusive Syrian political opposition, which appealed to the popular classes and social actors such as independent trade unions, made it difficult for various sectors of the population to unite and challenge the regime on a national scale.

A long-term revolutionary process

The material conditions in which the uprising emerged help to explain its origins and development. This is a different approach than that of those who argue that it is essentially a sectarian conflict or a conspiracy led by foreign actors, or who ignore the socioeconomic and political systems in place. This book has sought to explain the trajectory of the Syrian uprising, while also analyzing the resilience of the regime.

Syria, as well as the wider MENA region, was witnessing a revolutionary process. The mobilization of large sections of the population in opposition to the Assad regime challenged its authority, and various new sovereignties emerged with the purpose of establishing dual and multiple powers.

However, the protest movement was confronted by multiple forms of counterrevolutions opposing its initial objectives. The first and most brutal counterrevolutionary actor was the Assad regime, which aimed to crush the movement militarily. The establishment and rise of Islamic fundamentalist and jihadist military organizations constituted the second counterrevolutionary force, opposing the initial demands of the rebellion, attacking democratic elements of the protest movement, and seeking to impose a new authoritarian and exclusive political system. Finally, regional powers and imperialist international states acted in a counterrevolutionary manner. These included the allies of the regime, by providing the necessary military assistance and fighting alongside regime forces to crush the protest movement, and the so-called Friends of Syria (Saudi Arabia, Qatar, and Turkey), by advancing their own political interests by notably supporting the most reactionary elements of the uprising and the Islamic fundamentalist movements and trying to transform the uprising into a sectarian war to prevent the advent of a democratic Syria. The beginning of the process of rehabilitation and normalization of the Syrian regime by the end of 2018 and the acceptance of Assad remaining in power by former states that had demanded his overthrow also illustrated this situation.

The multiple forms of this counterrevolution thereby prevented any radical change of the class and political structure in Syria and were important factors in the resilience of the regime.

It is beyond the scope of this book to predict the future of Syria, but the incompleteness of the uprising signifies that the regime will still face challenges despite the repression of opposition within the country. Indeed, the resilience of the regime has come at a very high cost, in addition to the growing dependence on foreign states and actors. The sectarian and Alawi identities of some regime institutions have been strengthened, particularly the army and security services and to a lesser extent the state administration. The multiplication of militias has created problems due to their thuggish and criminal behavior. The catastrophic humanitarian and socioeconomic situation in Syria also begs the question of how the regime will deal with a large majority of the country's population suffering from unemployment, increasing inflation, and worsening living conditions. Even the regions considered as loyalist have seen increasing criticism of officials.

Revolutionary processes are long-term events, characterized by higher- and lower-level mobilizations according to the context. They can even be characterized by some periods of defeat. In Syria, the conditions that led to the uprisings are still present, and the regime is very far from resolving them and indeed actually has deepened them. Damascus and other regional capitals believe that they can maintain their despotic rules and orders at all cost by the continuous use of massive violence against their populations. This is doomed to fail, and new explosions of popular anger are to be expected, as demonstrated by new and massive popular protests in Soudan and Algeria, starting at the end of 2018 and beginning of 2019, challenging their own authoritarian regimes.

However, these conditions do not necessarily directly translate into political opportunities, particularly after more than eight years of a destructive and murderous war and the general fatigue of the population, most of whom simply desire a return to stability, even an authoritarian one under Assad's rule. No viable organized opposition has been apparent, with the failures of the opposition in exile and armed groups leaving many people who had sympathized with the uprising feeling frustrated and bitter.

Nevertheless, one factor that could play a role in shaping future events is the unprecedented documentation of the uprising, including video recordings, testimonials, and other evidence. In the 1970s, Syria saw strong popular and democratic resistance, with significant strikes and demonstrations throughout the country, but this history was not well known by the new generation of protesters in 2011. The revolutionary uprising of 2011, however, with its vast documentary archive, will remain in the popular memory and be a crucial resource for those who resist in the future.

Bibliography

Books

Abu Rumman, Mohammed (2013). *Islamists, Religion, and the Revolution*, Beirut, Friedrich-Ebert-Stiftung, FES Jordan and Iraq/FES Syria.

Achcar, Gilbert (2013). *Le peuple veut, une exploration radicale du soulèvement arabe*, Paris, Actes Sud.

Achcar, Gilbert (2016). *Morbid Symptoms: Relapse in the Arab Uprising*, Stanford, CA, Stanford University Press.

Allsopp, Harriet (2015). *The Kurds of Syria*, London, I.B. Tauris.

Ayboga, Ercan, Flach, Anja, and Knapp, Michael (2016). *Revolution in Rojava: Democratic Autonomy and Women's Liberation in Syrian Kurdistan*, translated by Biehl, Janet, London, Pluto Press.

Baczko Adam, Dorronsoro, Gilles, and Quesnay, Arthur (2016). *Syrie, Anatomie d'une guerre civile*, Paris, CNRS edition.

Batatu H. (1998). *Syria's Peasantry, the Descendants of Its Lesser Rural Notables, and the Politics*, Princeton, NJ, Princeton University Press.

Belhadj, Souhail (2013). *La Syrie de Bashar al-Asad, anatomie d'un régime autoritaire*, Paris, Editions Belin.

Blanford, Nicholas (2011). *Warriors of God: Inside Hezbollah's Thirty-Year Struggle Against Israel*, New York, Random House.

Bozarslan, Hamit (2009). *Conflit kurde, Le brasier oublié du Moyen-Orient*, Paris, Autrement, Mondes et Nations.

Clinton, Hillary Rodham (2014). *Hard Choices*, New York, Simon & Schuster.

Darwish, Sabr (2015). "Al-fasl al-thânî: 'indamâ hamal al-slâ ... Zamlakâ namûzajân," in *Sûriyyâ: tajraba al-mudun al-muharara*, Beirut, Riad El-Rayyes, Books.

Dik (-al), Majd (2016). *A l'est de Damas, au bout du monde, témoignage d'un révolutionnaire syrie*, Paris, Don Quichotte editions.

Donati, Caroline (2009). *L'exception syrienne, entre modernization et résistance*, Paris, La Découverte.

George, Ala (2003). *Syria, Neither Bread, Neither Freedom*, London, Zed Books.

Grojean, Olivier (2017). *La révolution kurde, le PKK et la fabrique d'une utopie*, Paris, La Découverte.

Haddad, Bassam (2012a). *Business Networks in Syria: The Political Economy of Authoritarian Resilience*, Stanford, CA, Stanford University Press.

Hanieh, Adam (2018). *Money, Markets, and Monarchies: The Gulf Cooperation Council and the Political Economy of the Contemporary Middle East*, Cambridge, UK, Cambridge University Press.

Hassan, Hassan, and Weiss, Micheal (2015). *ISIS: Inside the Army of Terror*, New York, Reagan Arts.

Hinnebusch, Raymond (1990). *Authoritarian Power and State Formation in Ba'thist Syria: Army, Party, and Peasant*, Boulder, CO, Westview Press.

Hinnebusch, R. (2001). *Syria Revolution from Above*, London and New York, Routledge.

International Business Publication (2010). *Islamic Financial Institutions (Banks and Financial Companies) Handbook*, Washington, DC.

Kannout, Lama (2016). *In the Core or on the Margin: Syrian Women's Political Participation*, UK and Sweden, Syrian Feminist Lobby and Euromed Feminist Initiative EFI-IFE.

Khatib Line (2011). *Islamic Revivalism in Syria: The Rise and Fall of Ba'thist Secularism*, London and New York, Routledge Studies in Political Islam.

Lefèvre, Raphael (2013). *The Ashes of Hama: The Muslim Brotherhood in Syria*, London, Hurst.

Lister, Charlie (2015). *The Syrian Jihad*, New York, Hurst.

Littell, Johnathan (2015), *Syrian Notebooks: Inside the Homs Uprising*, London, New York, Verso.

Matar Linda (2015). *The Political Economy of Investment in Syria*, London, UK, Palgrave Macmillan.

McDowall, David (1998). *The Kurds of Syria*, London, Kurdish Human Rights Project.

Middle East Watch (1991). *Syria Unmasked: The Suppression of Human Rights by the Asad Regime*, New Haven, CT, Yale University Press.

Pargeter, Alison (2010). *The Muslim Brotherhood: The Burden of Tradition*, London, Saqi Books.

Perthes, Volker (1995). *The Political Economy of Syria Under Asad*, New York, London, I.B. Tauris.

Perthes, Volker (2004). *Syria Under Bashar Al-Assad: Modernisation and the Limits of Change*, London, Oxford University Press, Routledge.

Phillips, Christopher (2016). *The Battle for Syria: International Rivalry in the New Middle East*, New Haven, CT, and London, Yale University Press.

Pierret, Thomas (2011). *Baas et Islam en Syrie*, Paris, PUF.

Rasheed (-al), Madawi (2010). *A History of Saudi Arabia*, 2d ed., Cambridge, UK, Cambridge University Press.

Richards Alan, and Waterbury, John (1990). *Political Economy of the Middle East: State, Class, and Economic Development*, London, Westview Press.

Schmidinger, Thomas (2018). *Rojava: Revolution, War, and the Future of Syria's Kurds*, London, Pluto Press.

Seale, Patrick (1988). *Asad: The Struggle for the Middle East*, London, I.B. Tauris.

Seurat, Michel (2012). *L'etat de barbarie Syrie, 1979–1982*, Paris, Presses Universitaires de France, Proche-Orient.

Tejel, Jordi (2009). *Syria's Kurds: History, Politics, and Society*, New York, Routledge.

Trotsky, Leon (2008). *History of the Russian Revolution*, Chicago, Haymarket.

Van Dam, Nikolaos (2011). *The Struggle for Power in Syria: Politics and Society Under Asad and the Ba'th Party*, London, I.B Tauris.

Wieland, Carsten (2012). *Syria—A Decade of Lost Chances: Repression and Revolution from. Damascus Spring to Arab Spring*, Seattle, Cune Press.

Zisser, Eyal (2007). *Commanding Syria: Bashar al-Asad and the First Years in Power*, London, I.B. Tauris.

Chapters of Books

Ababsa, Myriam (2015). "The End of a World Drought and Agrarian Transformation in Northeast Syria (2007–2010)," in Hinnebusch R. (ed.), *Syria: From Authoritarian Upgrading to Revolution?* (Syracuse, NY, Syracuse University Press, 2015), pp. 199–223.

Abbas, Hassan (2013). "Chapter 2: Reinforcing Values of Citizenship," in Kawakibi S. (ed.), *Syrian Voices from Pre-Revolution Syria: Civil Society Against All Odds*, HIVOS and Knowledge Programme Civil Society in West Asia (pdf). Available at: https://hivos.org/sites/default/files/publications/special20bulletin202-salam20kawakibi20_6-5-13_1.pdf (accessed March 3, 2014), pp. 17–22.

Abboud, Samer (2015). "Locating the 'Social' in the Social Market Economy," in Hinnebusch R. (ed.), *Syria: From Authoritarian Upgrading to Revolution?* (Syracuse, NY, Syracuse University Press), pp. 45–65.

Ahmad, Balsam (2012). "Neighborhoods and Health Inequalities in Formal and Informal Neighborhoods of Aleppo," in Ahmad B. and Sudermann Y. (eds.), *Syria's Contrasting Neighborhoods: Gentrification and Informal Settlements Juxtaposed*, St. Andrews Papers on Contemporary Syria (Fife, Scotland: Lienners Publishers), pp. 29–60.

Aous (al-), Yahya (2013). "Chapter 3: Feminist Websites Experience and Civil Society," in Kawakibi S. (ed.), *Syrian Voices from Pre-Revolution Syria: Civil Society Against All Odds*, HIVOS and Knowledge Programme Civil Society in West Asia (pdf). Available at: https://hivos.org/sites/default/files/publications/special20bulletin202-salam20kawakibi20_6-5-13_1.pdf (accessed March 3, 2014), pp. 23–28.

Balanche, Fabrice (2015). "Go to Damascus, My Son: Alawi Demographics Shifts Under Ba'th Party Rule," in Kerr M. and Larkin C. (eds.), *The Alawis of Syria: War, Faith and Politics in the Levant* (New York, Oxford University Press). pp. 79–106.

Darwish (al-), Daryous (2016). "Local Governance Under the Democratic Autonomous Administration of Rojava," in Collombier V., Favier A., and Narbone L. (eds.), *Inside Wars: Local Dynamics of Conflicts in Syria and Libya*, European University Institute Italy (pdf). Available at: http://cadmus.eui.eu/bitstream/handle/1814/41644/Inside%20wars_2016.pdf (accessed October 30, 2016), pp. 16–21.

Diaz, Naomi Ramirez (2018). "Unblurring Ambiguities," in Hinnebush R. and Imady O. (eds.), *The Syrian Uprising: Domestic Origins and Early Trajectory* (London and New York, Routledge), pp. 207–222.

Donati, Caroline (2013). "The Economics of Authoritarian Upgrading in Syria," Heydemann S. and Leenders R. (eds.), *Middle East Authoritarianisms: Governance, Contestation, and Regime Resilience in Syria and Iran* (Stanford, CA, Stanford Studies in Middle Eastern and Islamic Societies and Cultures), pp. 35–60.

Ezzi, Mazzen (2013). "A Static Revolution: The Druze Community (Sweida 2013)," in Stolleis F. (ed.), *Playing the Sectarian Card Identities and Affiliations of Local Communities in Syria*, Friedrich Ebert Stiftung (pdf). Available at: http://library.fes.de/pdf-files/bueros/beirut/12320.pdf (accessed September 11, 2015), pp. 39–70.

Favier, Agnès (2016). "Local Governance Dynamics in Opposition-Controlled Areas in Syria," in Collombier V., Favier A., and Narbone L. (eds.), *Inside Wars: Local Dynamics of Conflicts in Syria and Libya*, European University Institute Italy (pdf). Available at: http://cadmus.eui.eu/bitstream/handle/1814/41644/Inside%20wars _2016.pdf (accessed October 30, 2016), pp. 6–15.

Ghadbian, Najib (2015). "Contesting Authoritarianism: Opposition Activism Under Bashar al-Asad, 2000–2010," in Hinnebusch R. and Zintl T. (eds.), *Syria from Reform to Revolt. Volume 1: Political Economy and International Relations* (Syracuse, NY, Syracuse University Press), pp. 91–112.

Goldsmith, Leon T. (2015). "Alawi Diversity and Solidarity: From the Coast to the Interior," in Kerr M. and Larkin G. (eds.), *The Alawis of Syria* (London, Hurst and Company), pp. 141–158

Haddad, Bassam (2013). "Business Associations and the New Nexus of Power in Syria," in Aarts P. and Cavatorta F. (eds.), *Civil Society in Syria and Iran: Activism in Authoritarian Contexts* (Boulder, CO, Lynne Rienne Publishers), pp. 69–92.

Halhalli, Bekir (2018). "Kurdish Political Parties in Syria: Past Struggles and Future Expectations," in Tugdar, Emel Elif and Serhun, Al (eds.), *Comparative Kurdish Politics in the Middle East: Actors, Ideas, and Interests* (London, Palgrave Macmillan), pp. 27–56.

Hallaq (-al), Abdallah Amin (2013a). "Ismailis: A Minority–Majority in Syria (Salamiya 2014)," in Stolleis F. (ed.), *Playing the Sectarian Card: Identities and Affiliations of Local Communities in Syria*, Friedrich Ebert Stiftung (pdf). Available at: http://library.fes.de/pdf-files/bueros/beirut/12320.pdf (accessed September 11, 2015), pp. 102–113.

Hinnebush R. (1996). "State and Islamism in Syria," in Ehteshami A. and Sidahmed A. S. (eds.), *Islamic Fundamentalism* (Boulder, CO, Westview Press), pp. 199–214.

Hinnebush, R. (2015). "President and Party in Post-Bathist Syria, from the Struggle for Reform to Regime Destruction," in Hinnebusch R. and Zintl T. (eds.), *Syria from Reform to Revolt. Volume 1: Political Economy and International Relations* (Syracuse, NY, Syracuse University Press), pp. 21–44.

Hinnebush, Raymond, and Zinti Tina (2015). "Syrian Uprising and Al-Assad's First Decade in Power," in Hinnebusch R. and Zintl T. (eds.), *Syria from Reform to Revolt. Volume 1: Political Economy and International Relations* (Syracuse, NY, Syracuse University Press), pp. 285–312.

Kawakibi, Salam (2013). "The Paradox of Government-Organized Civil Activism in Syria in Civil Society in Syria and Iran," in Aarts P. and Cavatorta F. (eds.), *Civil Society in Syria and Iran: Activism in Authoritarian Contexts* (Boulder, CO: Lynne Rienner), pp. 169–186.

Kawakibi, Salam, and Sawah, Wael (2013). "Chapter 1: The Emergence and Evolution of Syria's Civil Society," in Kawakibi S. (ed.), *Syrian Voices from Pre-Revolution Syria: Civil Society Against All Odds*, HIVOS and Knowledge Programme Civil Society in West Asia (pdf). Available at: https://hivos.org/sites/default/files/publications /special2obulletin2o2-salam2okawakibi2o_6-5-13_1.pdf (accessed March 2, 2014).

Khaddam, Munzer (2013). "Al-âssâss al-îqtisâdî lil-âzma al-sûrîyya," in Bishara A. (ed.), *Khalfiyyât al-thawra al-sûrîyya, dirâsât sûriyya* (Doha, Qatar, Arab Center for Research and Policy Studies), pp. 71–94.

Khaddour, Kheder (2013a). "The Alawite Dilemma (Homs 2013)," in Stolleis F. (ed.), *Playing the Sectarian Card: Identities and Affiliations of Local Communities in Syria*, Friedrich Ebert Stiftung (pdf). Available at: http://library.fes.de/pdf-files/bueros /beirut/12320.pdf (accessed September 11, 2015), pp. 11–26.

Khaddour, K. (2013b). "A 'Government City' amid Raging Conflict (Tartous 2013)," in Stolleis F. (ed.), *Playing the Sectarian Card: Identities and Affiliations of Local Communities in Syria*, Friedrich Ebert Stiftung (pdf). Available at: http://library .fes.de/pdf-files/bueros/beirut/12320.pdf (accessed September 11, 2015), pp. 27–38.

Khatib, L. (2012). "Islamic Revival and the Promotion of Moderate Islam," in Hinnebush R. (ed.), *State and Islam in Baathist Syria: Confrontation or Co-optation?* St. Andrews Papers on Contemporary Syria (Fife, Scotland, Linners Publishers), pp. 29–58.

Landis, Joshua, and Pace, J. (2009). "The Syrian Opposition: The Struggle for Unity and Its Relevance, 2003–2008," in Lawson F. (ed.), *Demystifying Syria* (London, Middle East Institute at SOAS), pp. 180–206.

Lefèvre, Raphael (2017). "Syria," in Hamid, Shadi and McCants, William (eds.), *Rethinhking Political Islam* (New York, Oxford University Press). pp. 73–87.

Longuenesse, Elisabeth (1980). "L'industrialisation et sa signification sociale," in Raymond A. (ed.), *La Syrie Aujourd'hui* (online). Available at: http://books.open edition.org/iremam/747 (accessed January 18, 2013), pp. 327–358.

Marzouq, Nabil (2013). "Al-tanmiyya al-mafqûda fî sûrîyya," in Bishara A. (ed.), *Khalfiyyât al-thawra al-sûrîyya, dirâsât sûriyya* (Doha, Qatar, Arab Center for Research and Policy Studies), pp. 35–70.

Masouh, Samer (2013). "Tension in the Christian Valley (Wadi al-Nasara 2013)," in Stolleis F. (ed.), *Playing the Sectarian Card: Identities and Affiliations of Local Communities in Syria*, Friedrich Ebert Stiftung (pdf). Available at: http://library .fes.de/pdf-files/bueros/beirut/12320.pdf (accessed September 11, 2015), pp. 90–101.

Matthiesen, Toby (2017). "Renting the Casbah, Gulf States' Foreign Policy Towards North Africa Since the Arab Uprisings," in Ulrichsen K. C. (ed.), *The Changing Security Dynamics of the Persian Gulf* (London, Hurst/Georgetown University of Qatar), pp. 43–60.

Metral, François (1980). "Le monde rural syrien à l'ère des réformes (1958–1978)," in Raymond A. (ed.), *La Syrie Aujourd'hui* (online). Available at: http://books .openedition.org/iremam/744 (accessed January 18, 2013), pp. 297–324.

Om (-al), Tamara (2018). "The Political Voice of Syria's Civil Society," in Hinnebush R. and Imady O. (eds.), *The Syrian Uprising: Domestic Origins and Early Trajectory* (London and New York, Routledge), pp. 159–172.

Pinto, Paulo Gabriel Hilu (2010). "Les Kurdes en Syrie," in Dupret B., Ghazzal Z., Courbage Y., and al-Dbiyat M. (eds.), *La Syrie au présent* (Paris, Sindbad/Actes Sud and Ifpo), pp. 259–268.

Pinto, Paulo G. H. (2015). "God and Nation: The Politics of Islam Under Bashar al-Asad," in Hinnebusch R. and Zintl T. (eds.), *Syria from Reform to Revolt. Volume 1: Political Economy and International Relations* (Syracuse, NY, Syracuse University Press). pp. 154–175.

Pinto, Paulo G. H. (2017). "The Shattered Nation: The Sectarianization of the Syrian Conflict," in Hashemi N. and Postel D. (eds.), *Sectarianization, Mapping the New Politics of the Middle East* (London, Hurst and Company), pp. 123–142.

Qureshi, Jawad (2012). "Damascene 'Ulama and the 2011 Uprising," in Khatib L., Lefevre R., and Qureshi J. (eds.), *State and Islam in Bathist Syria, Confrontation or Cooptation?* St. Andrews Papers (Fife, Scotland, Lynne Rienner Publishers).

Roussel, Cyril (2006). "Les grandes familles druzes entre local et national," in Chiffoleau S. (ed.), *La Syrie au quotidien* (Culture et pratiques du changement, REMMM), pp. 115–116.

Ruiz de Elivra, Laura (2012). "State Charities Relation in Syria: Between Reinforcement, Control, and Coercion," in *Civil Society and the State in Syria the Outsourcing of Social Responsibility*, St. Andrews Papers on Contemporary Syria.

Ruiz de Elivra, L. (2013). "Chapter 4: Syrian Charities at the Turn of the Twenty-First Century: Their History, Situation, Frames, and Challenges," in Kawakibi S. (ed.), *Syrian Voices from Pre-Revolution Syria: Civil Society Against All Odds*, HIVOS and Knowledge Programme Civil Society in West Asia (pdf). Available at: https://hivos.org/sites/default/files/publications/special2obulletin2o2-salam2okawakibi2o_6-5-13_1.pdf (accessed March 4, 2014), pp. 29–33.

Said, Salam (2018). "The Syrian Military-Mercantile Complex," in Hinnebush R. and Imady O. (eds.), *The Syrian Uprising, Domestic Origins and Early Trajectory* (London and New York, Routledge), pp. 56–76.

Satik, Niruz (2013). "Al-hâla al-tâ'ifîyya fî al-întifâda al-sûrîyya al-massârât al-înmât," in Bishara A. (ed.), *Khalfîyyât al-thawra al-sûrîyya, dirâsât sûrîyya* (Doha, Qatar, Arab Center for Research and Policy Studies), pp. 373–426.

Seifan, Samir (2013). "Sîyâsât tawzî' al-dakhl wa dawrhâ fî al-înfijâr al-îjtimâ'î fî Sûrîyya," in Bishara A. (ed.), *Khalfîyyât al-thawra al-sûrîyya, dirâsât sûrîyya* (Doha, Qatar, Arab Center for Research and Policy Studies), pp. 95–146.

Valter, Stéphane (2018). "The Dynamics of Power in Syria," in Hinnebush R. and Imady O. (eds.), *The Syrian Uprising: Domestic Origins and Early Trajectory* (London and New York, Routledge), pp. 44–55.

Wieland, Carsten (2015). "Alawis in the Syrian Opposition," in Kerr M. and Larkin G. (eds.), *The Alawis of Syria* (London, Hurst and Company), pp. 225–244.

Wimmen, Heiko (2017). "The Sectarianization of the Syrian War," in Wehrey F. (ed.), *Beyond Sunni and Shia: The Roots of Sectarianism in a Changing Middle East* (London, Hurst), pp. 61–86.

Yazigi, J. (2016b). "Syria's Implosion: Political and Economic Impacts," in Collombier V., Favier A., and Narbone L. (eds.), *Inside Wars, Local Dynamics of Conflicts in Syria and Libya*," European University Institute Italy (pdf). Available at: http://cadmus.eui.eu/bitstream/handle/1814/41644/Inside%2owars_2016.pdf (accessed October 30, 2016), pp. 1–6.

Academic Articles

Ababsa, Myriam (2006). "Contre réformes agraire et conflits fonciers en Jazira Syrienne (2000–2005)," *Revue des mondes musulmans et de la Méditerranée* (online), Issue 115–116. Available at: http://remmm.revues.org/3033 (accessed November 15, 2016).

Abdulhamid, Ammar (2005). "Syria: Another Regime Fall Looming," *ISIM Review*, No. 16. Available at: https://openaccess.leidenuniv.nl/bitstream/handle/1887/17025/ISIM_16_Syria_Another_Regimefall_Looming.pdf?sequence=1 (accessed September 20, 2011).

Balanche, Fabrice (2011). "Géographie de la révolte syrienne," *Outre Terre* (online). Available at: http://www.cairn.info/revue-outre-terre1-2011-3-page-437.htm (accessed January 18, 2012).

Batatu, Hanna (1981). "Some Observations on the Social Roots of Syria's Ruling Military Group and the Causes for Its Dominance," *Middle East Journal*, XXXV, 3, pp. 331–344.

Batatu, H. (1982). "Syria's Muslim Brethren," *MERIP* (online). Available at: http://www.merip.org/mer/mer110/syrias-muslim-brethren (accessed February 20, 2013).

Bou Nassif, Hicham (2015). "'Second-Class': The Grievances of Sunni Officers in the Syrian Armed Forces," *Journal of Strategic Studies*, Vol. 38, Issue 5, pp. 626–649.

Chatty, Dawn (2010). "The Bedouin in Contemporary Syria: The Persistence of Tribal Authority and Control," *Middle East Journal*, Vol. 64, No. 1, pp. 30–49.

Drysdale, Alasdayr (1981). "The Syrian Political Elite, 1966–1976: A Spatial and Social Analysis," *Middle Eastern Studies*, Vol. 17, No. 1, pp. 3–30.

Gauthier, Julie (2005). "Les événements de Qamichli: Irruption de la question kurde en Syrie?" *Etudes kurdes*, No. 7, Paris, Institut kurde de Paris/L'Harmattan, pp. 97–114.

Goulden, Robert (2011). "Housing, Inequality, and Economic Change in Syria," *British Journal of Middle Eastern Studies*, Vol. 38, Issue 2, pp. 187–202.

Heydemann, Steven (2013b). "Syria and the Future of Authoritarianism," *Journal of Democracy*, Vol. 24, No. 4, pp. 59–73.

Heydemann, Steven, and Leenders, Reinoud (2011). "Authoritarian Learning and Authoritarian Resilance: Regime Responses to the 'Arab Awakening'," *Globalizations*, Vol. 8, No. 5, pp. 647–653.

Hinnebusch, R. (1997). "Syria: The Politics of Economic Liberalisation," *Third World Quarterly*, Vol. 18, No. 2, pp. 249–265.

Hinnebush, R. (2012). "Syria: From Authoritarian Upgrading to Revolution," *International Affairs*, Vol. 88, Issue 1, pp. 95–113.

Houcarde, Bernard (2008). "The Rise to Power of Iran's 'Guardians of the Revolution'," *Middle East Policy Council*, Vol. XVI, No. 3. Available at: http://www.mepc.org/journal/rise-power-irans-guardians-revolution (accessed March 20, 2018).

Imady, Omar (2016). "Organisationally Secular: Damascene Islamist Movements and the Syrian Uprising," *Syria Studies*, Vol. 8, No. 1, pp. 66–91.

Khalaf, Rana (2015). "Governance Without Government in Syria: Civil Society and State Building During Conflict," *Syria Studies*, Vol. 7, No. 3 (pdf). Available at: https://ojs.st-andrews.ac.uk/index.php/syria/article/view/1176/911 (accessed December 11, 2015).

Lombardi, Roland (2014). "Les evolutions du conflit syrien: La vision israélienne," Confluences Méditerranée, No. 89, *La Tragédie Syrienne*, pp. 119–132.

Moubayed, Sami (2006). "The Islamic Revival in Syria," *Mideast Monitor*, Vol. 1, No. 3 (online). Available at: http://www.nabilfayad.com/-335/قضايا/the-islamic-revival-in-syria.html (accessed January 3, 2010).

Perthes, Volker (1992a). "Syria's Parliamentary Elections: Remodeling Asad's Political Base." *MERIP,* No. 174 (January–February).

Perthes, Vo. (1992b). "The Syrian Private Industrial and Commercial Sectors and the State," *International Journal of Middle East Studies,* Vol. 24, No. 2, pp. 207–230.

Pierret, Thomas, and Selvik, Kjetil (2009). "Limits of 'Authoritarian Upgrading' in Syria: Private Welfare, Islamic Charities, and the Rise of the Zayd Movement," *International Journal of Middle East Studies,* Vol. 41, No. 4, pp. 595–614.

Roy, Olivier (1996). "Groupes de solidarité au Moyen Orient et en Asie central," *Les Cahier du CERI,* No. 16, pp. 1–25.

Stacher, Joshua (2011). "Reinterpreting Authoritarian Power: Syria's Hereditary Succession," *Middle East Journal,* Vol. 65, No. 2, pp. 197–212.

Talhamy, Yvette (2009). "The Syrian Muslim Brotherhood and the Syrian-Iranian Relationship," *Middle East Journal,* Issue 63, pp. 561–580.

Valenta, Jiri, and Valenta, Leni Friedman (2016). "Why Putin Wants Syria," *Middle East Quarterly,* Spring 2016 (online). Available at: http://www.meforum.org/5876 /why-putin-wants-syria#_ftnref11 (accessed December 15, 2016).

Van Bruinessen, Martin (2016). "Kurdish Identities and Kurdish Nationalisms in the Early Twenty-first Century," *Academia* (pdf). Available at: https://www.academia .edu/31059416/Kurdish_identities_and_Kurdish_nationalisms_in_the_early_twenty -first_century?auto=download (accessed August 20, 2017).

Zambelis, Chris (2017). "Institutionalized 'Warlordism': Syria's National Defense Force," *Terrorism Monitor* (online), Vol. 15, No. 6. Available at: https://jamestown .org/program/institutionalized-warlordism-syrias-national-defense-force/ (accessed January 20, 2018).

PhD Thesis

Rafizadeh, M. (2014). "The Syrian Civil War: Four Concentric Circles of Tensions," *University of South Florida,* Ph.D thesis. Available at: http://scholarcommons.usf .edu/cgi/viewcontent.cgi?article=7008&context=etd (accessed June 30, 2017).

Articles

Abbas, Hassan (2011). "The Dynamics of the Uprising in Syria," *Jadaliyya* (online). Available at: http://www.jadaliyya.com/pages/index/2906/the-dynamics-of-the -uprising-in-syria (accessed November 11, 2011).

Abboud, Samer (2013). "Syria's Business Elite Between Political Alignment and Hedging Their Bets," *Stiftung Wissenschaft und Politik (SWP) Comment.* Available at: http://www.swp-berlin.org/fileadmin/contents/products/comments/2013C22 _abo.pdf (accessed January 30, 2014).

Abboud, Samer (2016). "Syria's War Economy," *Carnegie Middle East Center* (online). Available at: http://carnegie-mec.org/diwan/54131 (accessed November 20, 2016).

Abboud, Samer (2017). "The Economics of War and Peace in Syria," *The Century Foundation* (online). Available at: https://tcf.org/content/report/economics-war -peace-syria/ (accessed February 15, 2017).

Abd al-Haleim, Ahmad (2018). "Egypt Eyes Extensive Role in Syria Reconstruction Efforts," *al-Monitor* (online). Available at: https://www.al-monitor.com/pulse/originals /2018/01/egypt-companies-reconstruction-syria-war.html (accessed January 5, 2018).

Abd al-Hamid, Ashraf (2018). "Haraba min jahîm al-âssad. wa îftitah âkbar masna' lil-nasîj fî misr," *al-Arabiya* (online). Available at: https://www.alarabiya.net/ar /arab-and-world/egypt/2018 /01 /21 /مصر- في- للنسيج- مصنع- أكبر- وافتتح- الأسد- جحيم- من- هرب .html (accessed January 25, 2018).

Abdallah, Tamam, Abd Hayy (al-), Tarek, and Khoury, Ernest (2012). "Stuck in the Middle: The Struggle for Syria's Kurds," *Al-Akhbar English* (online). Available at: https://www.shiachat.com/forum/topic/235000214-kurds-and-the-syrian-revolution/ (accessed July 30, 2012).

Abd al-Jalil, Mrad (2018a). "Âsmâ` jadîda li-rijâl â'mâl fî sûrîyyâ. man warâ`hum?" *Enab Baladi* (online), January 7. Available at: https://www.enabbaladi.net/archives /196755 (accessed January 10, 2018).

Abd Jalil, Mrad (2018b). "Hilm al-'âsimat âm hilm rijâl al-â'mâl," *Enab Baladi* (online), April 1. Available at: https://www.enabbaladi.net/archives/217667 (accessed May 20, 2018).

Abdel-Gadir, Ali, Abu-Ismail, Khalid, and El-Laithy, Heba (2011). "Poverty and Inequality in Syria (1997–2007)," United Nations Development Programme (UNDP) (pdf). Available at: http://www.undp.org/content/dam/rbas/doc/poverty/BG_15 _Poverty%20and%20Inequality%20in%20Syria_FeB.pdf (accessed December 20, 2011).

Abdulhalim, Fatma, Mohammed, Jan, and Van Wilgenburg, Wladimir (2016). "Rojava University Seeks to Eliminate Constraints on Education in Syria's Kurdish Region," *ARA News* (online). Available at: http://aranews.net/2016/08/rojava -university-seeks-eliminate-constraints-education-syrias-kurdish-region/ (accessed October 29, 2016).

Abdulssattar Ibrahim, Mohammad, Hamou, Ammar, and al-Maleh, Alice (2018). "Free Syrian Police in Northwestern Syria to 'Dissolve' amid HTS Takeover," *Syria Direct* (online). Available at: https://syriadirect.org/news/free-syrian-police-in-north western-syria-to-'dissolve'-amid-hts-takeover/ (accessed January 20, 2019).

Abdulssattar Ibrahim, Mohammad, Nassar, Alaa, and Schuster, Justin (2017). "Power Struggle Between Regime, Kurdish Self-Administration Plays out in Region's Largest Public Hospital," *Syria Direct* (online). Available at: http://syriadirect.org /news/power-struggle-between-regime-kurdish-self-administration-plays-out-in -region's-largest-public-hospital/ (accessed May 12, 2017).

Abdulssattar Ibrahim, Mohammad, and Schuster, Justin (2017). "Thousands of Arabs Excluded from Elections in Syria's Kurdish-Majority North," *Syria Direct* (online). Available at: http://test.syriadirect.org/news/%C2%A0-thousands-of-arabs-exclu ded-from-elections-in-syria's-kurdish-majority-north/ (accessed September 5, 2017).

Abdulssattar Ibrahim, Mohammad, and al-Maleh, Alice (2018). "US-Backed Opposition Authorities in Northern Syria Push for 'De-centralization' Agreement with Damascus: SDF," *Syria Direct* (online). Available at: http://syriadirect.org /news/us-backed-opposition-authorities-in-northern-syria-push-for-'de-centrali zation'-agreement-with-damascus-sdf/ (accessed August 20, 2018).

Abi Najm, Assi (2011). "Al-Tansîkîyât: Mawlûd min taht al-ârd," *al-Âkhbâr* (online). Available at: www.al-akhbar.com/node/22408 (accessed September 30, 2011).

Aboudi, Sami (2013). "Assad's Overthrow 'Red Line' for Iran: Supreme Leader's Aide," *Reuters* (online). Available at: http://www.reuters.com/article/us-syria-crisis-iran -idUSBRE90J08320130120 (accessed February 20, 2013).

Aboulenein, Ahmed (2016). "Syrian Security Chief Makes Public Cairo Visit— SANA," *Reuters* (online). Available at: http://uk.reuters.com/article/uk-mideast -crisis-syria-egypt-idUKKBN12H2AM (accessed November 10, 2016).

Aboultaif, Eduardo Wassim (2015). "Syria's Druze Are Caught in a Maelstrom," *The Daily Star* (online). Available at: http://www.dailystar.com.lb/Opinion/Commen tary/2015/Jun-01/299980-syrias-druze-are-caught-in-a-maelstrom.ashx (accessed September 20, 2016).

Abou Zeid, Rania (2012). "TIME Exclusive: Meet the Islamist Militants Fighting Alongside Syria's Rebels," *Time* (online). Available at: world.time.com/2012/07/26 /time-exclusive-meet-the-islamist-militants-fighting-alongside-syrias-rebels/ (ac cessed October 10, 2012).

Abu-Nasr, Donna, Arkhipov, Ilya, Meyer, Henry, and Shi, Ting (2017). "China Eyes Role Rebuilding Syria While Putin Spars with West," *Bloomberg* (online). Available at: https://www.bloomberg.com/news/articles/2017-12-21/china-arrives-in-syria -as-putin-fights-west-over-postwar-cash (accessed December 28, 2017).

Achcar, Gilbert (2018). "Will the Middle East Powder Keg Ignite?," *Socialist Worker .org* (online). Available at: https://socialistworker.org/2018/03/08/will-the-middle -east-powder-keg-ignite (accessed March 20, 2018).

Ackerman, Spencer (2015). "US Has Trained only 'Four or Five' Syrian Fighters Against ISIS, Top General Testifies," *The Guardian* (online). Available at: http:// www.theguardian.com/us-news/2015/sep/16/us-military-syrian-isis-fighters (September 20, 2015).

Ackerman, Spencer, Letsch, Constanze, and Shaheen, Kareem (2015). "Turkey Carries out First Ever Strikes Against Isis in Syria," *The Guardian* (online). Available at: https://www.theguardian.com/world/2015/jul/24/turkish-jets-carry-out-strikes -against-isis-in-syria-reports (accessed March 29, 2017).

Adghirni, Samy (2017). "Brazil Looks for Role in Syria's Reconstruction After the War," *Bloomberg* (online). Available at: https://www.bloomberg.com/news/articles /2017-10-19/brazil-looks-for-role-in-syria-s-reconstruction-after-the-war (accessed October 24, 2017).

ADN Kronos International (2016). "Mîshîl Kîlû: lâ tûjad ârd kurdistânîya fî sûrîya wa lan nasmah bi-îsrâ`îl thânîya" (online). Available at: http://www1.adnkronos.com /AKI/Arabic/Politics/?id=3.2.1612063814 (accessed February 20, 2017).

AFP (2011). "Syria's Muslim Brotherhood Open to Turkish 'Intervention'," *Ahram Online* (online). Available at: http://english.ahram.org.eg/NewsAFCON/2017/26813 .aspx (accessed December 10, 2011).

AFP (2016a). "Fewer Russian Strikes Targeting IS: Analyst," *al-Monitor* (online), October 9. Available at: http://www.al-monitor.com/pulse/afp/2016/10/syria-conflict -russia-military.html#ixzz4Ms9L8Hha (accessed October 10, 2016).

AFP (2016b). "Polygamy and Divorce on the Rise in War-Torn Syria," *The Economic Times* (online). Available at: http://economictimes.indiatimes.com/articleshow

/54285775.cms?utm_source=contentofinterest&utm_medium=text&utm_camp
aign=cppst (accessed September 30, 2016).

AFP (2017). "Chechens Serving as Russian Military Police in Aleppo: Kadyrov," *Yahoo News* (online), January 24. Available at: https://www.yahoo.com/news/chechens-serving-russian-military-police-aleppo-kadyrov-102122643.html (accessed January 25, 2017).

AFP (2018). "Russia Says over 63,000 Troops Have Fought in Syria," *Yahoo* (online). Available at: https://www.yahoo.com/news/russia-says-over-63-000-troops-fought-syria-141424820.html (accessed August 26, 2018).

AFP, and *Le Figaro* (2017). "Syrie: De grands projets économiques» évoqués" (online). Available at: http://www.lefigaro.fr/flash-eco/2017/12/18/97002-20171218 FILWWW00190-syrie-de-grands-projets-economiques-evoques.php (accessed December 20, 2017).

AFP, and *Le Monde* (2018). "Plus de 920 000 déplacés en Syrie en 2018, un record depuis le début du conflit" (online). Available at: https://mobile.lemonde.fr/syrie /article/2018/06/11/plus-de-920-000-deplaces-en-syrie-en-2018-un-record-depuis -le-debut-du-conflit_5312982_1618247.html?xtref=http://m.facebook.com (accessed July 20, 2018).

AFP, and *Orient le Jour* (2014a). "Marchands de légumes, commerçants ou étudiants, les hommes du Hezb fiers de combattre en Syrie" (online). April 12. Available at: http://www.lorientlejour.com/article/862890/-marchands-de-legumes-commer cants-ou-etudiants-les-hommes-du-hezb-fiers-de-combattre-en-syrie.html (accessed in April 12, 2014).

AFP, and *Orient le Jour* (2014b). "En Syrie, le Hezbollah a acquis et professe une précieuse expérience antiguérilla" (online). April 16. Available at: http://www .lorientlejour.com/article/863267/en-syrie-le-hezbollah-a-acquis-et-professe-une -precieuse-experience-antiguerilla.html (accessed April 16, 2014).

AFP, and *Orient le Jour* (2014c). "À Tartous, les partisans d'Assad s'offusquent de luxueux projets" (online), October 17. Available at: http://www.lorientlejour.com /article/891578/a-tartous-les-partisans-dassad-soffusquent-de-luxueux-projets .html (accessed October 20, 2014).

Agencies and Times of Israel (TOI) Staff (2018). "Netanyahu Says Russian Supply of S-300 Missiles to Syria 'Irresponsible'" (online). Available at: https://www.time sofisrael.com/netanyahu-says-russian-sale-of-s-300s-to-syria-irresponsible/ (accessed December 20, 2018).

Ahmad, Kadar, and Edelman, Avery (2017). "Kurdish Self-Administration Enforces Draft, Turning Kobane into 'Ghost Town'," *Syrian Voice* (online). Available at: http://syrianvoice.org/kurdish-self-administration-enforces-draft-turning-kobane -into-ghost-town/?lang=en (accessed December 20, 2017).

Ahmad, Reem, Hourani, Nourani, and Smiley, Sage (2018). "'A New Syria': Law 10 Reconstruction Projects to Commence in Damascus, Backed by Arsenal of Demo- lition, Expropriation Legislation," *Syria Direct* (online). Available at: https:// syriadirect.org/news/'a-new-syria'-law-10-reconstruction-projects-to-commence-in -damascus-backed-by-arsenal-of-demolition-expropriation-legislation/ (accessed November 25, 2018).

Ahmed a l -Ali , Asaad (2016). "Khilâf Ayman Jaber wa Munzher al-Âssad: harb shawâri' fî al-Lâzhiqîyya," *al-Modon* (online). Available at: http://www.almodon

‏خلاف-أيمن-جابر-ومنذر-الأسد-حرب-شوارع-في‎/com/arabworld/2016/7/12 - (accessed March 20, 2017).

Ahmed, Younes (2016). "Syria's Businessmen Invest in Post-war Reconstruction," *The Arab Weekly* (online). Available at: http://www.thearabweekly.com/News-&-Analysis /5343/Syria's-businessmen-invest-in-post-war-reconstruction (accessed June 6, 2016).

Ajib, Nadi (2017). "Mashrû' tanzîm 66 khalf al-râzî. tajruba râ`ida 'ala tarîq îâda ali'mâr—fîdîû," Syrian Arab News Agency (SANA) (online). Available at: https:// www.sana.sy/?p=683277 (accessed January 17, 2018).

Akhbar (-al) (2016). "Sâhibat al-jalâla" tubsir al-nûr fî sûrîyâ" (online). Available at: /http://www.al-akhbar.com node/262572 (accessed February 20, 2017).

Akhbar (-al) (2018). "Al-Marsûm al-tashrî'î raqm 16" (online). Available at: https:// al-akhbar.com/ArticleFiles/201810405931461636742115714611848.pdf (accessed October 20, 2018).

Akram, Fares (2017). "Russian FM Says Saudi Arabia Backs Syria Truce Deals," *AP News* (online). Available at: https://apnews.com/0ee23fc4e9a04566a1c4cabf2711f ab4 (accessed September 12, 2017).

Alam, Kamal (2016). "Why Assad's Army Has Not Defected," *National Interest* (online). Available at: http://nationalinterest.org/feature/why-assads-army-has-not -defected-15190 (accessed December 20, 2017).

Alami, Mona (2016). "Meet One of Hezbollah's Teen Fighters," *al-Monitor* (online). Available at: http://www.al-monitor.com/pulse/originals/2016/01/lebanon-hezbollah -teenagers-jihad-syria.html (accessed January 30, 2016).

Alami, M. (2017). "Hezbollah Embedded in Syria," *Atlantic Council* (online). Available at: http://www.atlanticcouncil.org/blogs/syriasource/hezbollah-is-embedded-in -syria (accessed March 30, 2017).

Aldeen, Sarah Najm, Syria Untold, and Syrian Independent Media Group (2018). "In Homs, Assad Accused of Using Military for Urban Planning Scheme," *Syria Deeply* (online). Available at: https://www.newsdeeply.com/syria/articles/2018/01 /02/in-homs-assad-accused-of-using-military-for-urban-planning-scheme (accessed January 5, 2018).

Ali, Idrees, Landay, Jonathan, and Wroughton, Lesley (2018). "Exclusive: U.S. Commanders Recommend Letting Kurdish Fighters in Syria Keep Weapons," *Reuters* (online). Available at: https://uk.reuters.com/article/uk-mideast-crisis-syria -usa-exclusive/exclusive-u-s-commanders-recommend-letting-kurdish-fighters-in -syria-keep-weapons-idUKKCN1OR1OH (accessed December 29, 2018).

Alipour, Farahmand (2015). "Syrian Shiites Take up Arms in Support of Assad's Army," *al-Monitor* (online). Available at: http://www.al-monitor.com/pulse /originals/2015/08/syrian-shiite-militia.html#ixzz3lQxXNYZE (accessed September 8, 2015).

All4Syria (2013). "Mubâdara nushatâ` kurd sûrîîn min âjl tal âbîyad" (online). Available at: http://www.all4syria.info/Archive/91463 (accessed December 10, 2013).

All4Syria (2016). "Top Syriac Priest Stripped of Cross for 'Abusing Reputation of the Church'," *The Syrian Observer* (online). Available at: http://syrianobserver.com/EN /News/31831/Top_Syriac_Priest_Stripped_Cross_Abusing_Reputation_the _Church (accessed October 30, 2016).

All4Syria (2017a). "Fî (sûrîyyâ al-âsad). îstâz fî al-jâmi'a yahsal 'ala râtib yuqal 'an rab' mâ yahsul 'alayhu muqâtl fî mîlîshîyyâ mûwâlîyya" (online), April 22. Available at: http://www.all4syria.info/Archive/404489 (accessed April 27, 2017).

All4Syria (2017b). "Mû`assa al-barîd al-turkîyya taftatah âwal furû'ihâ fî surîyyâ" (online), October 10. Available at: http://www.all4syria.info/Archive/448411 (accessed October 12, 2017).

Alous, Yahya (2015). "Sunnis Against Sunnis," *The Syrian Observer* (online). Available at: http://syrianobserver.com/EN/Features/28975/Sunnis_Against_Sunnis (accessed April 15, 2015).

Aman Group (2017). "Overview" (online). Available at: http://www.amangroupco .com/en/pages/6/Overview/1 (accessed August 20, 2017).

Amir, Narmin, and Fakhr ed Din, Yusuf (2012). "Interview with Abdalaziz al-Khair," Leading Figure of the National Coordination Body for Democratic Change, Syria, Anti-imperialist camp (online). Available at: http://www.antiimperialista.org/en /al_khair (accessed September 10, 2012).

ANF News (2018). "Statement from Afrin Canton Democratic Autonomous Administration" (online). Available at: https://anfenglish.com/rojava/statement-from -afrin-canton-democratic-autonomous-administration-24464 (accessed March 19, 2018).

ANHA Hawar News Agency (2016). "TEV-DEM Distributes Food to Migrants in Sheikh Maqsoud" (online). Available at: http://en.hawarnews.com/tev-dem-distri butes-food-to-migrants-in-sheikh-maqsoud/ (accessed December 18, 2016).

Aniyamuzaala, James Rwampigi, and Buecher, Beatrix (2016). "Women, Work, and War: Syran Women and the Struggle to Survive Five Years of Conflict," *CARE* (pdf). Available at: https://www.care.org/sites/default/files/documents/Syria_women _and_work_report_logos_07032016_web.pdf (accessed March 20, 2018).

A-Noufal, Waleed Khaled, and Clark, Justin (2018). "'We Don't Even Know if He's Alive': Despite Promises of Reconciliation, Rebels and Former Opposition Figures Disappear," *Syria Direct* (online). Available at: https://syriadirect.org/news/'we -don't-even-know-if-he's-alive'-despite-promises-of-reconciliation-rebels-and -former-opposition-figures-disappear/ (accessed November 20, 2018).

Arabiya (-al) (2013). "Muftî al-sa'ûdîya yushîd bi-mawqif al-qardâwî dud îrân wa hizb âllah" (online). Available at: https://www.alarabiya.net/ar/saudi-today/2013/06/06 /مفتي-السعودية-يشيد-بموقف-القرضاوي-ضد-إيران-وحزب-الله.html (accessed December 20, 2013).

Arafat, Hisham (2017a). "Kurdish Self-administration Ratifies Administrative Division of Northern Syria," *Kurdistan 24* (online), July 29. Available at: http://www .kurdistan24.net/en/news/81756dd2-033d-40a0-9954-ca05bb10c32d (accessed August 20, 2017).

Arafat, Hisham (2017b). "Syrian Kurdish PYD Elects New Co-chairs in Rojava," *Kurdistan 24* (online), September 30. Available at: http://www.kurdistan24.net/en /video/4861d542-8761-4ea6-a90a-38d6eb8233ed (accessed October 20, 2017).

Arfeh, Hasan (2016). "Governing the Most Dangerous City in Syria," *Syria News Deeply* (online). Available at: https://www.newsdeeply.com/syria/articles/2016/08 /04/governing-the-most-dangerous-city-in-syria, (accessed October 20, 2016).

Arfeh, Hasan (2018). "Sawa'id Al-Khair Interferes with Humanitarian Work in Idlib," *Atlantic Council* (online). Available at: http://www.atlanticcouncil.org/blogs

/syriasource/sawa-id-al-khair-interferes-with-humanitarian-work-in-idlib (accessed March 12, 2018).

Arhim, Zeina (2013). "Al-Raqqa al-muharara: shumû' madîyya` fî al-furât wa salâmât li-Dayr al-Zor bil-hijja al-hûrânîyya," *al-Quds* (online). Available at: http://www .alquds.co.uk/?p=44818 (accessed January 30, 2014).

Arif, Hassan (2015). "Al-mab'ûja ... shuhadâ` madanîyûn âm shabîha," *Rozana FM* (online). Available at: http://rozana.fm/ar/node/11405 (accessed December 20, 2015).

Arslanian, Ferdinand (2016). "Liberalization and Conflict in the Syrian Economy," *Syria Untold* (online). Available at: http://www.syriauntold.com/en/2016/12/liberali zation-conflict-syrian-economy/#_ftn44 (accessed December 22, 2016).

Asharq Al-Awsat (2012). "Nus watîqat al-'ahd al-watanî lil-mu'âradat al-sûrîyat" (online). Available at: http://archive.aawsat.com/details.asp?section=4&issueno =12273&article=684969#.W5KIfyOEjGJ. (accessed July 20, 2012)

Ashkar, Hisham (2013). "The Battle for Qusayr and the Fate of Saint Elias Church," *Al-Akhbar English* (online). Available at: http://english.al-akhbar.com/node/19828 (accessed December 10, 2013).

Associated Press (2017). "Lebanon Prepares for Syria's Post-war Construction Windfall," *VOA News* (online). Available at: https://www.voanews.com/a/lebanon-prepares -for-syria-post-war-construction-windfall-/3993378.html (accessed August 20, 2017).

Associated Press (2018). "Syria's Assad Reaches 'Understanding' with Arab States," *VOA News* (online). Available at: https://www.voanews.com/a/syria-s-assad-reaches-under standing-with-arab-states/4598574.html (accessed October 20, 2018).

Atassi, Basma (2013). "Qaeda Chief Annuls Syrian-Iraqi Jihad Merger" (online). Available at: http://www.aljazeera.com/news/middleeast/2013/06/2013699425657 882.html (accessed July 20, 2013).

Atassi, Mohamed Ali (2018). "Fî âwal hadith lahu ba'd khurûjihi mutasililân min sûrîyâ ... rîyâd al-turk: al-khalalu al-yawm lam ya'ud baqâ` "mujrim al-harb" bashâr al-âssad," *Al-Quds* (online). Available at: https://www.alquds.co.uk/%EF%BB%BF سور-من-متسللا-خروجه-بعد-له-حديث-أول-في/?fbclid=IwAR1Tdlfk4feWZQtue-t-IXRSnTrL kV2h_E2OFDKL3XVr2F3uvWiF-gq-kbQ (accessed October 20, 2018).

Atlas, Terry (2013). "U.S. Military Intelligence Warned No Quick Fall for Assad," *Bloomberg* (online). Available at: https://www.bloomberg.com/news/articles/2013-07 -21/u-s-military-intelligence-warned-no-quick-fall-for-assad (accessed December 20, 2013).

Awsat (-al), Asharq (2017). "'Haîtân â'mâl' jdad yatanâfisûn 'ala "î'âda al-îmâr" fî sûrîyâ" (online). Available at: https://aawsat.com/home/article/999986/«حيتان في-«الإعمار-إعادة»-على-يتنافسون-جدد-«أعمال-- (accessed February 20, 2017).

Awsat (-al), Asharq (2018). "Kurds Blame Russia for Allowing Turkish Ground Assault on Afrin," *The Syrian Observer* (online), January 22. Available at: http:// syrianobserver.com/EN/News/33746/Kurds_Blame_Russia_For_Allowing _Turkish_Ground_Assault_Afrin/ (accessed January 25, 2018).

Ayboga, Ercan (2107). "A Trip to Liberated Minbic in Northern Syria: From Hell to Paradise," *Open Democracy* (online). Available at: https://www.opendemocracy.net

/north-africa-west-asia/ercan-ayboga/trip-to-liberated-minbic-in-northern-syria
-from-hell-to-paradise (accessed July 20, 2017).

Aziza, Tareq (2018). "Târeq ʿazîza: al'îtilâf tahâluf sîyâssî hash mutaʾadad al-wilâ`ât
wa al-âjandât," *Democratic Studies Republic Center* (online). Available at: http://drsc
-sy.org/هش-سياسيٌّ-تحالف-الائتلاف-عزيزة-طارق/ (accessed April 20, 2018).

Azzouz, Ammar, and Katz, Irit (2018). "Fleeing Home at Home: Internal Displacement in Homs, Syria," *LSE Middle East Center Blog* (online). Available at: http://
blogs.lse.ac.uk/mec/2018/02/21/fleeing-home-at-home-internal-displacement-in
-homs-syria/ (accessed March 20, 2018).

Baczko Adam, Dorronsoro Gilles, and Quesnay, Arthur (2013). "Building a Syrian
State in a Time of Civil War," *Carnegie* (online). Available at: http://carnegieen
dowment.org/2013/04/16/building-syrian-state-in-time-of-civil-war-pub-51517
(accessed April 20, 2014).

Baker, Aryn (2013). "Syria's Assad May Be Losing Control over His Deadly Militias,"
Time (online). Available at: http://world.time.com/2013/09/11/syrias-assad-may-be
-losing-control-over-his-deadly-militias/ (accessed July 20, 2014).

Bakeer, Ali (2019). "Why Did the UAE and Bahrain Re-open Their Embassies
in Syria?" *al-Jazeera Emglish* (online). Available at: https://www.aljazeera.com
/indepth/opinion/uae-bahrain-open-embassies-syria-190107165601089.html (accessed
January 10, 2019).

Baladi News (2017). "Al-âssad yahujuzu ʿala âmûâl rajul al-â'mâl al-sûrî 'imâd
ghraywâtî wa 'âi`ltihi" (online). Available at: https://www.baladi-news.com/ar
/news/details/24017/الأسد-يحجز-على-أموال-رجل-الأعمال-السوري-عماد-غريواتي-وعائلته (accessed
December 20, 2017).

Balanche, F. (2016). "Status of the Syrian Rebellion: Numbers, Ideologies, and
Prospects," *The Washington Institute* (online). Available at: http://www.washington
institute.org/policy-analysis/view/status-of-the-syrian-rebellion-numbers-ideologies
-and-prospects (accessed November 30, 2016).

Balanche, Fabrice (2018). "Sectarianism in Syria's Civil War," *Washington Institute*
(pdf). Available at: https://www.washingtoninstitute.org/uploads/Documents/pubs
/SyriaAtlasCOMPLETE-3.pdf (accessed March 30, 2018).

Barazi (-al), Zahra (2013). "The Stateless Syrians," *Tillburg University* (pdf). Available
at: https://www.refworld.org/pdfid/52a983124.pdf (accessed January 20, 2014).

Barnard, Anne, Hubbard, Ben, and Kershner, Isabel (2018). "Iran, Deeply Embedded
in Syria, Expands 'Axis of Resistance'," *The New York Times* (online). Available at:
https://www.nytimes.com/2018/02/19/world/middleeast/iran-syria-israel.html
(accessed July 10, 2018).

Barnard, Anne, Saad Hwaida, and Schmitt, Eric (2015). "An Eroding Syrian Army
Points to Strain," *The New York Times* (online). Available at: http://www.nytimes
.com/2015/04/29/world/middleeast/an-eroding-syrian-army-points-to-strain
.html?_r=0 (accessed September 20, 2015).

Barrington, Lisa, and Said, Rodi (2016). "Kurdish, Syrian Government Forces Declare
Truce in Qamishli Area: Statement," *Reuters* (online). Available at: http://www
.reuters.com/article/us-mideast-crisis-syria-qamashli-idUSKCN0XK05I (accessed
August 30, 2016).

Barthe, Benjamin, Kaval, Allan, Paris, Gilles, and Zerrouky, Majid (2018). "Les forces américaines en Syrie repoussent une offensive des troupes pro-Assad," *Le Monde* (online). Available at: http://www.lemonde.fr/proche-orient/article/2018/02/09/les -forces-americaines-en-syrie-repoussent-une-offensive-des-troupes-pro-assad _5254089_3218.html#iov4VTM87TSxfQAb.99 (accessed February 9, 2018).

Bassam, Laila (2015). "Assad Allies, Including Iranians, Prepare Ground Attack in Syria: Sources," *Reuters* (online). Available at: http://www.reuters.com/article/2015 /10/01/us-mideast-crisis-syria-iranians-idUSKCN0RV4DN20151001?mod=related &channelName=worldNews&utm_source=Facebook (accessed November 12, 2015).

Bassam, Laila; Al-Khalidi, Suleiman, and Perry, Tom (2015). "Syria's Assad: Army Focusing on Holding Most Important Areas," *Reuters* (online). Available at: http:// www.reuters.com/article/us-mideast-crisis-syria-idUSKCN0Q007H20150726 (accessed August 2, 2015).

Bassiki, Mohammad, and Haj Hamdo, Ahmed (2016). "Amid War and Conscription–A City Without Men," *Syria News Deeply* (online). Available at: https://www.news deeply.com/syria/articles/2016/05/16/amid-war-and-conscription-a-city-without -men; (accessed June 1, 2016).

BBC News (2011a). "Middle East Unrest: Syria Arrests Damascus Protesters" (online). March 16. Available at: http://www.bbc.com/news/world-middle-east-12757394 (accessed May 30, 2011).

BBC News (2011b). "Mid-East Unrest: Syrian Protests in Damascus and Aleppo" (online). March 15. Available at: http://www.bbc.com/news/world-middle-east -12749674 (accessed May 30, 2011).

Beals, Emmanuel (2013). "Syria's Rebel Press Is Fighting Back Against Jihadists," *Vice* (online). Available at: http://www.vice.com/read/syria-radio-journalists-fight-back (accessed January 20, 2014).

Beals, E. (2017). "UN Allowing Assad Government to Take Lead in Rebuilding Aleppo," *Fox News* (online), November 16. Available at: http://www.foxnews.com /world/2017/11/16/un-allowing-assad-government-to-take-lead-in-rebuilding -aleppo.html (accessed January 10, 2018).

Beals, E. (2018). "Assad's Reconstruction Agenda Isn't Waiting for Peace. Neither Should Ours," *The Century Foundation* (online). Available at: https://tcf.org /content/report/assads-reconstruction-agenda-isnt-waiting-peace-neither/ (accessed June 10, 2018).

Becker, Petra (2013). "Syrian Muslim Brotherhood Still a Crucial Actor," *Stiftung Wissenschaft und Politik* (pdf). Available at: https://www.swp-berlin.org/fileadmin /contents/products/comments/2013C34_bkp.pdf (accessed February 24, 2014).

Belasco, Amy, and Blanchard, Christopher M. (2015). "Train and Equip Program for Syria: Authorities, Funding, and Issues for Congress," *Congressional Research Service* (pdf). Available at: https://www.fas.org/sgp/crs/natsec/R43727.pdf (accessed June 30, 2015).

Bertelsmann Stiftung's Transformation Index (2016). "Syria Country Report," available at https://www.bti-project.org/fileadmin/files/BTI/Downloads/Reports/2016 /pdf/BTI_2016_Syria.pdf (accessed September 20, 2018).

Berti, Benedetta (2016). "Syria's Weaponized Humanitarian Space," *Carnegie* (online). Available at: http://carnegieendowment.org/sada/64023 (accessed July 28, 2016).

Bezhan, Fred (2018). "What's So Tough About the 'Toughest Ever' U.S. Sanctions on Iran?" *Radio Free Europe Radio Liberty* (online). Available at: https://www.rferl.org /a/iran-toughest-ever-u-s-sanctions-explainer/29585958.html (accessed December 20, 2018).

Bhojani, Fatima (2017). "Despite Losing Terrain, Islamic State's Attacks Rose in 2016: Study," *Reuters* (online). Available at: https://www.reuters.com/article/us-islamic -state-attacks/despite-losing-terrain-islamic-states-attacks-rose-in-2016-study -idUSKCN1B115Q (accessed August 22, 2017).

Bilgic, Taylan, and Harvey, Benjamin (2017). "Turkish Report Exposes Locations of U.S. Troops in Syria," *Bloomberg* (online). Available at: https://www.bloomberg.com /news/articles/2017-07-19/turkish-leak-of-u-s-positions-in-syria-seen-endan gering-troops (accessed August 10, 2017).

Birnbaum, Michael (2016). "The Secret Pact Between Russia and Syria That Gives Moscow Carte Blanche," *Washington Post* (online). Available at: https://www .washingtonpost.com/news/worldviews/wp/2016/01/15/the-secret-pact-between -russia-and-syria-that-gives-moscow-carte-blanche/?utm_term=.f407e8118d5d (accessed December 20, 2016).

Blanchard, Ben (2016). "China Says Seeks Closer Military Ties with Syria," *Reuters* (online). Available at: http://www.reuters.com/article/us-mideast-crisis-syria-china -idUSKCN10R10R (accessed August 20, 2016).

Blanford, Nicholas (2013). "The Battle for Qusayr: How the Syrian Regime and Hizb Allah Tipped the Balance," *Combating Terrorism Center* (online), August 27. Available at: https://www.ctc.usma.edu/posts/the-battle-for-qusayr-how-the-syrian -regime-and-hizb-allah-tipped-the-balance (accessed in October 30, 2014).

Blas, Javier, and Champion, March (2016). "Putin's Oil and Gas Deals Magnify Military Power in Middle East," *Bloomberg* (online). Available at: https://www .bloomberg.com/news/articles/2016-12-20/putin-s-oil-and-gas-deals-magnify -military-power-in-middle-east (accessed December 21, 2016).

Bodner, Matthew (2015). "Why Russia Is Expanding Its Naval Base in Syria," *The Moscow Times* (online). Available at: https://themoscowtimes.com/articles/why -russia-is-expanding-its-naval-base-in-syria-49697 (accessed November 20, 2016).

Bonsey, Noah (2017). "What's at Stake in the Syrian Peace Talks in Astana?" *International Crisis Group* (online). Available at: https://www.crisisgroup.org/middle -east-north-africa/eastern-mediterranean/syria/what-stake-syrian-peace-talks -astana (accessed December 20, 2017).

Borshchevskaya, Anna (2013). "Russia's Many Interests in Syria," *The Washington Institute* (online). Available at: http://www.washingtoninstitute.org/policy-analysis /view/russias-many-interests-in-syria (accessed February 20, 2014).

Borshchevskaya, Anna (2017). "Will Russian-Saudi Relations Continue to Improve?" *Foreign* Affairs (online). Available at: https://www.foreignaffairs.com/articles/saudi -arabia/2017-10-10/will-russian-saudi-relations-continue-improve (accessed February 25, 2018).

Brignola, Jodi, Hamou, Ammar, and al-Maleh, Alice (2018). "'The Head is Turkish, the Body Syrian': Expanding Turkish Influence in Rebel-Held North Leaves Syrians Ambivalent About the Future," *Syria Direct* (online). Available at: https:// syriadirect.org/news/'the-head-is-turkish-the-body-syrian-expanding-turkish

-influence-in-rebel-held-north-leaves-syrians-ambivalent-about-the-future/ (accessed October 25, 2018).

Britzky, Halley (2018). "Reports: 30,000 ISIS Fighters Remain in Iraq and Syria," *Axios* (online). Available at: https://www.axios.com/isis-more-active-in-iraq-and -syria-than-1534426054-8876473a-bfe6-4b50-90b2-21c4b04dac44.html (accessed August 25, 2018).

Brown, Daniel (2017). "Russia Is Using Syria as a Testing Ground for Some of Its Most Advanced Weapons," *Business Insider* (online). Available at: http://www .businessinsider.com/russia-is-using-syria-testing-ground-some-advanced-weapons -2017-5?IR=T (accessed September 30, 2017).

Bucala, Paul (2017). "Iran's New Way of War in Syria," *The Critical Threats Project of the American Enterprise Institute and the Institute for the Study of War* (pdf). Available at: http://www.understandingwar.org/sites/default/files/Iran%20New%20Way%20 of%20War%20in%20Syria_FEB%202017.pdf (accessed May 20, 2017).

Bucala, Paul, and Casagrande, Genevieve (2017). "How Iran Is Learning from Russia in Syria," *The Institute for the Study of War* (online). Available at: http://www .understandingwar.org/backgrounder/how-iran-learning-russia-syria (accessed February 9, 2017).

Butter, David (2015). "Syria's Economy Picking up the Pieces," *Chatham House* (pdf). Available at: https://www.chathamhouse.org/sites/files/chathamhouse/field/field _document/20150623SyriaEconomyButter.pdf (accessed December 30, 2015).

Cagaptay Soner (2012). "Syria and Turkey: The PKK Dimension," *Washington Institute* (online). Available at: http://www.washingtoninstitute.org/policy-analysis/view /syria-and-turkey-the-pkk-dimension (accessed December 10, 2012).

Caillet Romain (2013). "The Islamic State: Leaving al-Qaeda Behind," *Carnegie Middle East Center* (online). Available at: http://carnegieendowment.org/syriain crisis/?fa=54017 (accessed April 13, 2014).

Caliskan, Mehmet Emin, and Toksabay, Ece 2018). "Erdogan Says Turkey May Extend Afrin Campaign Along Whole Syrian Border," *Reuters* (online). Available at: https://www.reuters.com/article/us-mideast-crisis-syria-afrin-turkey/erdogan -says-turkey-may-extend-afrin-campaign-along-whole-syrian-border-idUSKBN 1GV14U (accessed March 20, 2018).

Carey, Glen, and Meyer, Henry (2017). "Even the Saudis Are Turning to Russia as Assad's Foes Lose Heart," *Bloomberg* (online). Available at: https://www.bloomberg .com/news/articles/2017-09-08/even-the-saudis-are-turning-to-russia-as-assad-s -foes-lose-heart (accessed September 15, 2017).

Carlstrom, Gregg (2017). "What's the Problem With Al Jazeera?" *The Atlantic* (online). Available at: https://www.theatlantic.com/international/archive/2017/06/al-jazeera -qatar-saudi-arabia-muslim-brotherhood/531471/ (accessed June 26, 2017).

Carnegie (2011). "Saleh Muslim" (online). Available: http://carnegie-mec.org/publicat ions/?fa=48726 (accessed January 29, 2012).

Carnegie (2012a). "The Kurdish Democratic Union Party" (online). March 1. Available at: http://carnegie-mec.org/publications/?fa=48526 (accessed March 20, 2012).

Carnegie (2012b). "The Kurdish National Council in Syria" (online). February 15. Available at: http://carnegieendowment.org/syriaincrisis/?fa=48502 (accessed March 30, 2012).

Carnegie (2012c). "Local Coordination Committees of Syria" (online), December 20. Available at: http://carnegie-mec.org/diwan/50426?lang=en (accessed January 11, 2013).

Carnegie (2012d). "National Coordination Body for Democratic Change" (online), January 15. Available at: http://carnegie-mec.org/diwan/48369?lang=en (accessed February 13, 2012).

Carnegie (2012e). "Syrian Revolution General Commission" (online), December 20. Available at: http://carnegie-mec.org/diwan/50425?lang=en (accessed January 12, 2013).

Carnegie (2013a). "Charter of the Syrian Islamic Front" (online), February 4. Available at: http://carnegie-mec.org/diwan/50831?lang=en (accessed February 5, 2013).

Carnegie (2013b). "The Syrian National Council" (online), September 25. Available at: http://carnegie-mec.org/publications/?fa=48334 (accessed December 23, 2013).

Casey-Baker, Mary and Kutsch, Tom (2011), "Two suicide bombings rock Damascus as Arab League league monitors arrive", *Foreign Policy*, (online). Available at: https://foreignpolicy.com/2011/12/23/two-suicide-bombings-rock-damascus-as-arab-league-league-monitors-arrive/ (accessed January 11, 2012).

Cham Press (2012). "Marsûm 66..." (online). Available at: http://www.champress.net/index.php?q=ar/Article/view/7769 (accessed August 26, 2017).

Channel Sama (2015). "Liqâ` khâs ma' muhâfiz dimashq al-duktûr bashr al-sibân–al-marsûm 66," *YouTube Video*. Available at: https://www.youtube.com/watch?v=HKSgsV4kNRw (accessed August 30, 2016).

Chivers, C.J., and Schmitt, Eric (2013). "Arms Airlift to Syria Rebels Expands, with Aid from C.I.A.," *The New York Times* (online). Available at: http://www.nytimes.com/2013/03/25/world/middleeast/arms-airlift-to-syrian-rebels-expands-with-cia-aid.html (accessed March 28, 2013).

Choufi, Firas (2012). "Syria: Houran's Brush with Civil War," *Al-Akhbar English* (online). Available at: english.al-akhbar.com/node/7908 (accessed December 15, 2012).

Choufi, Firas (2014). "Syria's Valley of the Christians Under Fire," *Al-Akhbar English* (online), Available at: http://nena-news.it/syrias-valley-christians-fire/ (accessed December 10, 2014).

Chouikrat, Thilleli (2016). "Governing over Rubble: Aleppo's Exiled Opposition Council Leader Speaks," *al-Araby* (online). Available at: https://www.alaraby.co.uk/english/indepth/2016/12/9/mayor-of-rubble-aleppos-exiled-opposition-council-leader-speaks (accessed December 20, 2016).

Chulov, Martin (2017). "Iran Repopulates Syria with Shia Muslims to Help Tighten Regime's Control," *The Guardian* (online). Available at: https://www.theguardian.com/world/2017/jan/13/irans-syria-project-pushing-population-shifts-to-increase-influence (accessed January 18, 2017).

Clark, Justin, and Hamou, Ammar (2018). "One Week Since Deadly Attack, Latest Evacuations of Islamic State Fighters Leave Suwayda Residents 'Paralyzed by Fear'," *Syria Direct* (online). Available at: https://syriadirect.org/news/one-week-since-deadly-attack-latest-evacuations-of-islamic-state-fighters-leave-suwayda-residents-'paralyzed-by-fear'/ (accessed August 10, 2018).

Clark, Justin, and Hourani, Noura (2019). "HTS Continues Offensive Against Areas of Rebel-Held Northwest, 'Cutting off' and Seizing Nearly a Dozen Towns from

Factional Rivals," *Syria Direct* (online). Available at: https://syriadirect.org/news
/hts-continues-offensive-against-areas-of-rebel-held-northwest-'cutting-off'-and
-seizing-nearly-a-dozen-towns-from-factional-rivals/ (accessed January 10, 2019).

CNN (2012). "Obama Warns Syria not to Cross 'Red Line'" (online). Available at:
http://edition.cnn.com/2012/08/20/world/meast/syria-unrest/index.html (accessed
August 30, 2012).

Cojean, Annick (2014). "Le viol, arme de destruction massive en Syrie" *Le Monde*
(online). Available at: http://www.lemonde.fr/proche-orient/article/2014/03/04
/syrie-le-viol-arme-de-destruction-massive_4377603_3218.html (accessed January
20, 2017).

Coskun, Orhan, and Karadeniz, Tulay (2016). "Russian Jets Target Islamic State
Around Syria's al-Bab: Turkish Military," *Reuters* (online). Available at: http://www
.reuters.com/article/us-mideast-crisis-syria-turkey-idUSKBN14J0FS (accessed
December 31, 2016).

Council of the European Union (2019). "Council Implementing Decision (CFSP)
2013/255/CFSP Concerning Restrictive Measures Against Syria," *Official Journal
of the European Union* (online). Available at: https://eur-lex.europa.eu/legal-content
/en/TXT/PDF/?uri=CELEX:32019D0087&from=EN (accessed February 10,
2019).

Dadouch, Sarah, and Heller, Jeffrey (2017). "Israel Hits Syrian Site Said to Be Linked
to Chemical Weapons," *Reuters* (online). Available at: http://www.reuters.com
/article/us-mideast-crisis-syria-israel/israel-hits-syrian-site-said-to-be-linked-to
-chemical-weapons-idUSKCN1BI0MH (accessed September 8, 2017).

Dadouch, Sarah, and Perry, Tom (2017). "U.S.-Backed Syrian Fighters Say Will not
Let Govt. Forces Cross Euphrates," *Reuters* (online). Available at: https://uk.reuters
.com/article/uk-mideast-crisis-syria/u-s-backed-syrian-fighters-say-will-not-let
-govt-forces-cross-euphrates-idUKKCN1BQ27C (accessed September 18, 2017).

Dadouch, Sarah (2018). "Up to 15,000 Syrian Rebels Ready to Back Turkish Operation
in Northeast," *Reuters* (online). Available at: https://uk.reuters.com/article/uk-mideast
-crisis-syria/up-to-15000-syrian-rebels-ready-to-back-turkish-operation-in-north
east-idUKKBN1OC1IR (accessed December 13, 2018).

Dahan (El-), Maha, and Georgy, Micheal (2017). "How a Businessman Struck a Deal
with Islamic State to Help Assad Feed Syrians," *Reuters* (online). Available at:
http://www.reuters.com/article/us-mideast-crisis-syria-wheat-islamic-st/how-a
-businessman-struck-a-deal-with-islamic-state-to-help-assad-feed-syrians
-idUSKBN1CG0EL (accessed October 11, 2017).

The Daily Beast (2017). "U.S. Told Russia About Syria Raid in Advance" (online).
Available at: http://www.thedailybeast.com/cheats/2017/04/07/moscow-given-heads
-up-on-u-s-raid-of-syria.html?via=desktop&source=copyurl (accessed April 12,
2017).

Damascus Bureau (2016). "Idleb Students Chafe Under Restrictions," *The Syrian
Observer* (online). Available at: http://syrianobserver.com/EN/Features/31994
/Idleb_Students_Chafe_Under_Restrictions/ (accessed November 24, 2016).

Damascus Cham (2017). "Tawqî al-'aqd al-îdâfî bayn kul min sharika dimashq al-
shâm al-qâbida wa sharika âmân al-qâbida wa shata âmân dimashq al-musâhama

al-mighfala al-khâsa bi-qîma istathmârîya bi-hudûd mìa wa khamsûn milîyâr lîra sûrîya" (online). Available at: http://damacham.sy/الشا-دمشق-شركة-بين-الاضافي-العقد-توقيع/ (accessed January 10, 2018).

Damascus Cham (2018a). "Dimashq al-Shâm al-qâbida tabnî sharâka îstrâtîjîya ma' al-mustathmir 'mâzen al-tarazî'" (online), January 2. Available at: http://damacham .sy/ا-شراكة-تبني-القابضة-الشام-دمشق (accessed January 18, 2018).

Damascus Cham (2018b). "Dimashq al-shâm al-qâbida tuwaqi' 'aqd sharâka ma' sharika talas lil-tijâra wa al-sinâ'a bi-qîma 23 milîyâr lira sûrîya" (online), January 13. Available at: http://damacham .sy/مع-شراكة-عقد-توقع-القابضة-الشام-دمشق - (accessed January 15, 2018).

Damascus Cham (2018c). "Ijtimâ' al-hay'a al-tâ`sîssîya li-sharika al-mutawirûn al-musâhama al-maghfala al-khâsa" (online), February 1. Available at: http://dama cham.sy/المطور-لشركة-التأسيسية-الهيئة-اجتماع/ (accessed February 15, 2018).

Damascus Cham (2018d). "Ȋn'iqâd al-hay'at al-tâ`sîssîyat li-sharikat rawâfid dimashq al-istîthmârât" (online), August 4. Available at: http://damacham.sy/تأسيس-عقد-توقيع المساه-دمشق-روافد-شركة-/ (accessed April 15, 2018).

Damascus Cham (2018e). "sharikat bunîyân dimashq al-musâhamat al-maghfalat al-khâsa," April 4 (online). Available at: http://damacham.sy/شركة-لتأسيس-شراكة-عقد-توقيع دمشق-بنيان-/ (accessed April 4, 2018).

Damascus Cham (2018f). "Tawqî' 'aqd tâ`sîs sharikat rawâfid dimashq al-musâhama al-mughafala al-khâsa" (online), March 25. Available at: http://damacham.sy المساه-دمشق-روافد-شركة-تأسيس-عقد-توقيع/ (accessed April 1, 2018).

Damas Post (2018a). "Value of Annual Remittances to Syria at $1.5 Billion," *Syrian Observer* (online), March 1. Available at: http://syrianobserver.com/EN/News/33909 /Value_Annual_Remittances_Syria_1_Billion/ (accessed March 20, 2018).

Damas Post (2018b). "Da'wât li-înshâ tahâluf bayn sharikât masrîyat wa ûrdunîyat lil-îstithmâr bi-î'mâr sûrîyat" (online), September 5. Available at: http://damaspost .com/article/21009-سورية_بإعمار_للإستثمار_وأردنية_مصرية_شركات_بين_تحالف_لإنشاء_دعوات (accessed September 20, 2018).

Damas Post (2018c). "Al-Nâbulsî: Chaqaq 'mârûtâ sîtî' satakûn al-â'la sa'râ fî sûrîyâ" (online), October 9. Available at: http://damaspost.com/article/19972 شقق النابلسي الأعلى_ستكون_"سيتي_ماروتا"_ (accessed September 20, 2018).

Damas Post (2018d). "Al-Hukûmat tu'âqab al-mutaqâ'asîn 'an khidmat al-watân: Hatmân al-mutakhalafîn 'an al-khadmat al-'askarîyat min al-taqadum îla al-musâbaqât al-hukûmîyat" (online), October 30. Available at: http://damaspost.com /article/21746-من_العسكرية_الخدمة_عن_المتخلفين_حرمان_الوطن_خدمة_عن_المتقاعسين_تعاقب_الحكومة الحكومية_المسابقات_إلى_التقدم_ (accessed November 2, 2018).

Damas Post (2018e). "Al-yawm fî al-'âsimat al-rûmânîyat … ma'rad hawl furas al-îstithmâr fî sûrîyat" (online), December 11. Available at: http://damaspost.com /article/23244-سورية_في_الاستثمار_فرص_حول_معرض_الرومانية_العاصمة_في_اليوم؟fbclid=IwAR3qx vpjrCBKcuVLVe1otX7Pp8esy1Q8amxNSoJtw8BecI98RZafmzTetio (accessed December 12, 2018).

Damas Post (2018f). "1.8 milîâr lîrat li-tarmîm wa î'âdât tâ`hîl masâkin 'adrâ al-'umâlîyat" (online), December 23. Available at: http://damaspost.com/article /23745-18_العمالية_عدرا_مساكن_تأهيل_وإعادة_لترميم_ليرة_مليار؟fbclid=IwAR1qmHIlU9s

YYCfzKN4w_m1PPOkNVPXHQBi8dZ1eFkZ2uvcMovacOyDqggM (accessed December 27, 2018).

Daragahi, Borzou (2018). "Iran Wants to Stay in Syria Forever," *Foreign Policy* (online). Available at: http://foreignpolicy.com/2018/06/01/iran-wants-to-stay-in-syria-forever/ (accessed June 2, 2018).

Dark, Edward (2014a). "Pro-Regime Sunni Fighters in Aleppo Defy Sectarian Narrative," *al-Monitor* (online), March 14. Available at: http://www.al-monitor.com/pulse/fr/originals/2014/03/syria-aleppo-sunni-quds-baath-brigades.html #ixzz4PhygdiPM (accessed June 20, 2015).

Dark, E. (2014b). "Syrian Regime Ignores Supporters' Rising Anger," *al-Monitor* (online), October 7. Available at: http://www.al-monitor.com/pulse/originals/2014/10/homs-suicide-bombing-children-regime-syria-war-protests.html (accessed October 20, 2014).

Darwish, S. (2016a). "Cities in Revolution: Qamishli," *Syria Untold* (online), August 6. Available at: http://cities.syriauntold.com/#_ednref7 (accessed October 11, 2016).

Darwish, S. (2016b). "Cities in Revolution: Salamiyah," *Syria Untold* (online), August 9. Available at: http://cities.syriauntold.com/#_ftnref45 (accessed October 11, 2016).

Darwish, S. (2016c). "Al-sûrîyyûn al-muhâsirûn qirâ` fî âhwâl al-sûrîyin fî zhurûf al-harb," *Arab Reform Initiative* (pdf). September 2016. Available at: http://www.arab-reform.net/ar/node/976 (accessed October 2, 2016).

Darwish, S. (2016d). "Cities in Revolution: Baniyas," *Syria Untold* (online), October 4. Available at: http://cities.syriauntold.com/#_edn10 (accessed October 11, 2016).

Darwish, S. (2016e). "Cities in Revolution: Deir el-Zor," *Syria Untold* (online), September 10. Available at: http://cities.syriauntold.com/#_edn10 (accessed October 11, 2016).

Davis, Rochelle, and Ilgıt, Asli (2013). "The Many Roles of Turkey in the Syrian Crisis," *MERIP* (online). Available at: http://www.merip.org/mero/mero012813 (accessed February 20, 2014).

Davison, John (2016). "Seeing no future, deserters and draft-dodgers flee Syria," *Reuters* (online). Available at: http://www.reuters.com/article/us-mideast-crisis-syria-army-idUSKCN1001PY (accessed June 30, 2016).

Dawlaty (2015). "Syrian Nonviolent Movement: Perspective from the Ground," *Heinrich Boll Stiftung Middle East* (pdf). Available at: https://dawlaty.org/booklet /TheSyrianNonviolentMovement.pdf (accessed January 17, 2016).

Deir Ezzor 24 (2017). "Ba'd sarqa âhîyyâ` madîna dayr al-zûr wa ta'fîshihâ ... al-ta'fîsh yantaql îla qura rîf dayr al-zûr al-gharbî" (online). Available at: http://deirezzor24.net/archives/7426 (accessed September 25, 2017).

DeYoung, Karen, and Gearan, Anne (2013). "U.S. Announces Expanded Battlefield Aid to Syrian Rebels, but not Arms," *Washington Post* (online). Available at: https://www.washingtonpost.com/world/middle_east/us-announces-expanded -battlefield-aid-to-syrian-rebels/2013/02/28/f0a32414-819b-11e2-b99e-6baf4ebe 42df_story.html (accessed March 30, 2013).

DeYoung, Karen, and Sly, Liz (2012). "Syrian Rebels Get Influx of Arms with Gulf Neighbors' Money, U.S. Coordination," *Washington Post* (online). Available at: https://www.washingtonpost.com/world/national-security/syrian-rebels-get

-influx-of-arms-with-gulf-neighbors-money-us coordination/2012/05/15/gIQAds2
TSU_story.html (accessed November 10, 2012).

Dibo, Mohammad (2014). "Al-îshâ'at fî sûrîyâ: Bayn îstrâtîjîyat al-nizâm wa taktîk
al-mu'âradat," *Heinrich Boll Stiftung* (online). Available at: https://lb.boell.org/ar
/2014/11/25/lsh-fy-swry-byn-strtyjy-lnzm-wtktyk-lmrd (accessed May 10, 2015).

Dobbert, Steffen, and Neumann, Willi (2017). "Putin's Mercenaries," *Zeit Online*
(online). Available at: http://www.zeit.de/politik/ausland/2017-02/russia-vladimir
-putin-military-mercenary-soldiers-syria (accessed February 7, 2017).

Dobbins, James (2019). "Commentary: U.S. Should Review Its Approach to Syria's
Assad" (online). Available at: https://www.reuters.com/article/us-dobbins-syria
-commentary/commentary-u-s-should-review-its-strategy-on-syrias-assad-idUSK
CN1P220M (accessed January 9, 2019).

Drwish, Sardar Milla (2017a). "What Federalism Would Mean for Northern Syria,"
al-Monitor (online), March 27. Available at: http://www.al-monitor.com/pulse
/originals/2017/03/syria-kurdish-democratic-council-arab-leader-federal.html (accessed June 20, 2017).

Drwish, Sardar Milla (2017b). "Syrian Kurds Press on with Elections Despite
Divisions," *al-Monitor* (online), December 12. Available at: http://www.al-monitor
.com/pulse/originals/2017/12/syria-north-kurdish-federal-elections-rule.html#ix
zz5W4SVvab6 (accessed September 20, 2018).

Dunya Times (2012). "FSA Leader Asaad: We Will not Allow Kurdish Separatism"
(online). Available at: http://en.dunyatimes.com/article/FSA-leader-Asaad-We-will
-not-allow-Kurdish-separatism.html (accessed March 20, 2013).

DW (2016). "Fasâ`il muqatila sûrîya tarfud fîderâlîya al-kurd" (online). Available at:
http://www.dw.com/ar/الكرد-فيدرالية-ترفض-سورية-مقاتلة-فصائل/a-19127856 (accessed
April 25, 2017).

DW (2017). "New Russia-Syria Accord Allows up to 11 Warships in Tartus Port Simultaneously" (online). Available at: http://www.dw.com/en/new-russia-syria-accord
-allows-up-to-11-warships-in-tartus-port-simultaneously/a-37212976 (accessed
January 25, 2017).

Eakin, Hugh (2013). "Syria: Which Way to Kurdistan?" *The New York Review of Books*
(online). Available at: http://www.nybooks.com/daily/2013/08/28/syria-which-way
-kurdistan/ (accessed September 20, 2014).

Economy 2 Day (2018a). "Al-Shehâbî: Wâq' wizârat al-sinâ'at tahsad 'alayhi ... al-
matlûb î'adât binâ` mâ tam tadmîrihi qîmathi 1.8 milîyâr dûlâr" (online), October 24.
Available at: https://www.economy2day.com/new/الشهابي:-واقع-وزارة-الصناعة-لا-تحسد
عليه.المطلوب-إعادة-بناء-ما-تم-تدميره-وقيمته-1.8-مليار-دولار#.W8-Ty4Rknzs.facebook (accessed
December 20, 2018).

Economy 2 Day (2018b). "Nâtihât sahâb fî dimashq tutl 'ala înqâd al-harb. wa al-shaqat
bi-400 âlf dûlâr!" (online), November 30. Available at: https://www.economy2day
.com/new/ناطحات-سحاب-في-دمشق-تطل-على-انقاض-الحرب.-و-الشقة-بـ-400-ألف-دولار?fbclid=IwA
R1lto5Yd6qiVzXVmRupbYIJuHafalwYHd8wK4Rs5k_XjdPi2_1_pxnliAU#.XA
GkD2yEjAs.facebook (accessed December 1, 2018).

Economy 2 Day (2019a). "Âkthar min 570 sharikat 'arabîyat wa âjnabîyat tataqadam
bi-talabât lil-mushârakat fî î'âdat îmâr sûrîyat" (online), January 8. Available at:

https://www.economy2day.com/new/-بطلبات-تتقدم-وأجنبية-عربية-شركة- 570-من-أكثر
سورية-إعمار-إعادة-في-للمشاركة-?fbclid=IwARopTNwKO6iuiFMbgdPsGfUkZp3Ip5OG
SNEB2EOA2nOZkNsroXn3UfMd2Yg#.XDUfBnglptU.facebook (accessed
January 10, 2019).

Economy 2 Day (2019b). "Mashrû' binâ` îrânî dakhm fî sûrîyat ... binâ`madînat wa 200
âlf wahdat sakanîyat" (online), February 25. Available at: https://www.economy
2day.com/new/سكنية-وحدة-ألف-200و-مدينة-بناء..سورية-في-ضخم-إيراني-بناء-مشروع-?fbclid=IwA
Rofv2a5jmXhyhKFQXJRTuxIIjhoCHWKLB6VPiq54-t8wiejAUkP9ppENVg#
.XHRfEFwyYEw.facebook (accessed March 8, 2019).

Edwards, Madeline, and Hamou, Ammar (2018). "In Syria's Relatively Quiet, Majority-
Kurdish Northeast, Rumblings of Assyrian Discontent," *Syria Direct* (online).
Available at: https://syriadirect.org/news/in-syria's-relatively-quiet-majority-kurdish
-northeast-rumblings-of-assyrian-discontent/ (accessed November 1, 2018).

Emancipations (2015). "Une fenêtre sur l'histoire des coordinations et des conseils
locaux" (online). Available at: http://www.emancipation.fr/spip.php?article1126
(accessed December 20, 2015).

Emmar Syria (2018). "Dâmâk al-'iqârîyat al-îmârâtîyat tabhath fî dimashq sabil tanfîz
masârî' tatwîr 'iqârî" (online), December 20. Available at: https://www.emmarsyria
.com/post/62?fbclid=IwARoupRLDDSL5GZSMBRDF1JEfE7k437vXy-v
-acGI6kElqZRwkotISJCZOL0 (accessed December 24, 2018).

Emmar Syria (2019a). "Bi-mutawasit îstithmâr sanawî 1.7 milîyâr lîrat mujama' yalbaghâ
rasmîyân bi-îstithmâr wasîm al-qatân" (online) January 10. Available at: https://www
.emmarsyria.com/post/يلبغا%20مجمع%20استثمار?fbclid=IwARoa9bkHtjykCJreR7loLS1
LIgL7dw5bo3ovDr07_FLX13JS-c5VWcE3nQU (accesed January 10, 2019).

Emmar Syria (2019b). "Mârûtâ sîtî tuhat rihâlihâ fî âbû dhabî al-ûsbû' al-muqbil"
(online), January 15. Available at: https://www.emmarsyria.com/post/128?fbclid
=IwAR13JpmO-QFqqNuD1nCkZZnyz5dlqFL9qRN42yLgP4SpPEJKHlLRSy8
ZpxA (accesed January 18, 2019).

Emmar Syria (2019c). "9 milîyârat lîrat îstithmârât sâmer fûz fî bank sûrîyat al-îslami,
ma' safqat al-yawm wa nasbat tamlakahu tartafa' li-7.6%" (online), January 17.
Available at: https://www.emmarsyria.com/post/9-7.6?fbclid=IwAR3JenjidfkQ
vktoihH11H8tAwWAlipk-LEyvOOUHDb5NKQuCgroO9XTKTg (accessed
January 19, 2019).

Emmar Syria (2019d). "Muhâfazat Dimashq tuhadad mawâ'îd sudûr al-mukhatatât
al-tanzîmîyyat lil-qâbûn wa jûbar wa barazat" (online), February 24. Available at:
https://www.emmarsyria.com/post/244?fbclid=IwARoEQbf31pBoYDGmyPZ
YfXDpWkpNb1s-r4IdfMLeL6VLvlM-zTf1hfSmMCo (accessed March 1,
2019).

Emmar Syria (2019e). "Sharikât rûsîyat tabdâ` tawtîn taqnîyât al-tashîîd al-sarî' fî
sûrîyat wa tabâshar âwal mashrû' sakanî fî al-dîmâs" (online), March 2. Available
at: https://www.emmarsyria.com/post/261?fbclid=IwARoV7k21aVK3YrKKxmbG
1hj8yLTiXU89JhMZg8ei1VkSTiCOalZnLFU3FNU (accessed March 8, 2019).

Emmar Syria (2019f). "Sinâ'î halabî shahîr yaftatah ma'malân dakhmân lil-nasîj fî
ârmînîyâ wa yûwadh sabab îghlâq ma'malahu bi-halab" (online), March 8. Available
at: https://www.emmarsyria.com/post/280?fbclid=IwARoDHGi86omos9r5zsK
_Go9WR5NRoohL_Xk1LgkkVUcemK3-6hNScjIYSgQ (accessed March 9, 2019).

Enab Baladi (2015). "Tafâhumât bayn al-âkrâd wa ghurf al-'amalîyyât taqlibu al-tâwila fî halab" (online). Available at: http://www.enabbaladi.org/archives/56977 (accessed December 21, 2015).

Enab Baladi (2016a). "Nusra Front Closes Radio Fresh in Kafranbel 'Until Further Notice'," *The Syrian Observer* (online), June 16. Available at: http://syrianobserver.com/EN/News/31199/Nusra_Front_Closes_Radio_Fresh_Kafranbel_Until_Further_Notice (accessed June 17, 2016).

Enab Baladi (2016b). "Turkey Trying to Impose 'Turkmen' Council on Jarablus Administration: Sources," *The Syrian Observer* (online), September 7. Available at: http://www.syrianobserver.com/EN/News/31605/Turkey_Trying_Impose_Turkmen_Council_Jarablus_Administration_Sources (accessed October 15, 2016).

Enab Baladi (2016c). "Samira Masalmeh Proposes Inquiry into Coalition Spending" (online), December 20. Available at: https://english.enabbaladi.net/archives/2016/12/samira-masalma-proposes-inquiry-coalition-spending/ (accessed December 25, 2016).

Enab Baladi (2017a). "Ânbâ` 'an î'tiqâl al-âssad li-Îbrâhîm jabber wa âmrahu bi-hal mîlîshîyyâ maghâwîr al-bahr" (online), February 21. Available at: https://www.enabbaladi.net/archives/132633 (accessed March 30, 2017).

Enab Baladi (2017b). "Al-lajna al-âmnîyya fî halab talghy 'al-tarfiq'. Wa al-shehâbî: Al-âsad tadkhol" (online), May 20. Available at: https://www.enabbaladi.net/archives/150756?so=related (accessed August 28, 2017).

Enab Baladi (2017c). "Sinâ'iû dimashk yutâlibûn bi-îlghâ` 'al-tarfiîq' wa îqâf al-tahrîb min turkîyyâ" (online), May 21. Available at: https://www.enabbaladi.net/archives/150953 (accessed June 30, 2017).

Enab Baladi (2017d). "Sâ`iqûn yuqati'ûn tarîq nabl wa al-zahrâ`—halab îtijâjân 'ala 'al-âtâwât'" (online), July 8. Available at: https://www.enabbaladi.net/archives/160118?so=related (accessed August 30, 2017).

Enab Baladi (2017e). "Fawz. rajul al-î'mâl 'al-ghâmd' yuda' îduhu 'ala sukar sûrîyâ" (online), August 14. Available at: https://www.enabbaladi.net/archives/167188 (accessed December 30, 2017).

Enab Baladi (2018a). "Battle for Idleb: Is the Armed Opposition Losing Its Popular Base?" *The Syrian Observer* (online), January 17. Available at: http://syrianobserver.com/EN/Features/33729/Battle_Idleb_Is_Armed_Opposition_Losing_Popular_Base/ (accessed January 20, 2018).

Enab Baladi (2018b). "Turkish Hands Redraw the Economic Map of Aleppo's Countryside," *The Syrian Observer* (online), January 19. Available at: http://syrianobserver.com/EN/Features/33741/Turkish_Hands_Redraw_Economic_Map_Aleppo_Countryside (accessed January 20, 2018).

Enab Baladi (2018c). "Sharikat turkîya tu`aman al-kahrbâ`li-madînat â'zâz" (online), March 11. Available at: https://www.enabbaladi.net/archives/212457 (accessed March 20, 2018).

Enab Baladi (2018d). "Wasîm qattân min al-fanûn al-jamîlat îla "hût îqtisâdî" fî sûrîyâ" (online), March 14. Available at: https://www.enabbaladi.net/archives/213384 (accessed March 20, 2018).

Enab Baladi (2018e). "16 milîâr dûlâr khasâ`ir al-qitâ' al-zirâ'I fî sûrîyâ munzu 2011" (online), March 16. Available at: https://www.enabbaladi.net/archives/213747 (accessed March 20, 2018).

Enab Baladi (2018f). "Marsûm ya'fî al-sinâ'iîn min russûm tajdîd rakhs al-binâ" (online), May 27. Available at: https://www.enabbaladi.net/archives/231136 (accessed May 30, 2018).

Enab Baladi (2018g). "Al-âssad yazîd rawâtib al-'askariîn bi-nisbat 30%" (online), June 4. Available at: https://www.enabbaladi.net/archives/233015 (accessed June 5, 2018).

Enab Baladi (2018h). "Tatwîr îtifâqîyat 'al-tijârat al-hurat' bayn al-nizâm al-sûrî wa îrân" (online), June 19. Available at: https://www.enabbaladi.net/archives/236214 (accessed July 5, 2018).

Enab Baladi (2018i). "Tashîlât hukumîyat li-î'âdat al-mustathmirîn al-mughtarabîn îla sûrîyâ" (online), June 28. Available at: https://www.enabbaladi.net/archives /238001 (accessed July 5, 2018).

Enab Baladi (2018j). "Assad's Government Aims at Accelerating the Economic Cycle in Ghouta" (online), July 20. Available at: https://english.enabbaladi.net/archives /2018/07/assads-government-aims-at-accelerating-the-economic-cycle-in-ghouta /#ixzz5Q8JBUzH5 (accessed August 1, 2018).

Enab Baladi (2018k). "Economic Normalization: A Weapon in the Syrian Regime's Hands" (online), July 28. Available at: https://english.enabbaladi.net/archives/2018 /07/economic-normalization-a-weapon-in-the-syrian-regimes-hands/#ixzz5Q8Q PctnV (accessed August 1, 2018).

Enab Baladi (2018l). "Muhâfazat dimashq ta'lan 'an mukhatat tanzîm 'bâsîlîyâ sîtî'" (online), July 30. Available at: https://www.enabbaladi.net/archives/243806?so =related (accessed August 2, 2018).

Enab Baladi (2018m). "Ba'd mûl qâsîûn. wasîm qatân yastathmir mûl al-mâlakî" (online), August 20. Available at: https://www.enabbaladi.net/archives/247645 (ac-cessed August 29, 2018).

Enab Baladi (2018n). "'Adû majlis al-sha'b: Thalathâ îîrâdât al-hukumat min al-darâ'ib ghayr al-mubâshirat" (online), August 28. Available at: https://www.enabbaladi .net/archives/248920 (accessed August 29, 2018).

Enab Baladi (2018o). "Mall's Investment Lights up Damascus' Economic Activity" (online), September 1. Available at: https://english.enabbaladi.net/archives/2018 /09/malls-investment-lights-up-damascus-economic-activity/ (accessed September 3, 2018).

Enab Baladi (2018p). "Source: The 'Tiger' Cancels the Contracts of 6500 of Its Troops Throughout Syria" (online), September 20. Available at: https://english.enabbaladi .net/archives/2018/09/source-the-tiger-cancels-the-contracts-of-6500-of-its-troops -throughout-syria/ (accessed September 30, 2018).

Enab Baladi (2018q). "Fî Halab ... masîrat tabâruk al-zikra al-40 li-tâ`sîs 'PKK'" (online), November 27. Available at: https://www.enabbaladi.net/archives/266031 (accessed November 30, 2018).

Enab Baladi (2019a). "Munzu îftitâhihi. Thalâthat milîyârât lîrat qîmat al-sâdîrât min ma'bar nasîb" (online), January 3. Available at: https://www-enabbaladi-net.cdn .ampproject.org/c/s/www.enabbaladi.net/archives/275572/amp?fbclid=IwAR3 OZLSpxjegvrcIk-ZfJ4vQFAlOiKKTHlDsuvbDEMysOAgkHO5w1uSEn5U (accessed January 10, 2019).

Enab Baladi (2019b). "Îʿadat tafʾîl maʿmal al-samâd al-fûsfâtî fî homs bitâqat 400 tun" (online), January 9. Available at: https://www-enabbaladi-net.cdn.ampproject.org /c/s/www.enabbaladi.net/archives/274218/amp?fbclid=IwAR2hNp_-IkfZ31 KziW6ECYMLwT7jFGDISGOMdtOXwn2YNhz7JMWPaBMekTo (accessed January 10, 2019).

Entous, Adam (2015). "Covert CIA Mission to Arm Syrian Rebels Goes Awry," *Wall Street Journal* (online). Available at: http://www.wsj.com/articles/covert-cia-mission -to-arm-syrian-rebels-goes-awry-1422329582 (accessed January 30, 2015).

Enzinna, Wes (2015). "A Dream of Secular Utopia in ISIS' Backyard," *The New York Times* (online). Available at: https://www.nytimes.com/2015/11/29/magazine/a -dream-of-utopia-in-hell.html?_r=1 (accessed May 20, 2016).

Eqtisad (2017). "Râmî makhlûf yazûj 500 ʾaskarî wa ʾansar mukhâbarât min âbnâʿ al- sâhel" (online). Available at: https://www.eqtsad.net/news/article/18553/ (accessed January 20, 2018).

Eqtisad (2018). "Muhamad Kâmal sabâgh sharbâtî" (online). Available at: https:// aliqtisadi.com/شخصيات/محمد-كامل-صباغ- (accessed January 25, 2018).

Erhaim, Zeina (2014). "Karîmatuh al-harama tantasir ʾala zaîna al-sihafîya bi-fâriq sharît hudûdî." (online). Available at: https://zaina-erhaim.com/علي-تنتصر-الحرمة-كريمته ب-الصحفية-زينة/ (accessed February 20, 2015).

ESCWA, and University of St. Andrews (2016). "Syria at War, Five Years On," *UNRWA* (pdf). Available at: https://www.unescwa.org/sites/www.unescwa.org/files /publications/files/syria-war-five-years.pdf (acccesed November 20, 2016).

Esfandiary, Dina, and Tabatabai, Ariane (2018). "Moscow and Beijing Have Tehran's Back," *Foreign Policy* (online). Available at: https://foreignpolicy.com/2018/07/25 /moscow-and-beijing-have-tehrans-back/ (accessed August 2, 2018).

Euro News (2017). "The Economic Costs of Syria's Civil War" (online). Available at: http://www.euronews.com/2017/03/17/the-economic-costs-of-syria-s-civil-war (accessed March 19, 2017).

European Parliament (2015). "The International Coalition to Counter ISIL/Daʿesh (the 'Islamic State')" (pdf). Available at: http://www.europarl.europa.eu/RegData/etudes /BRIE/2015/551330/EPRS_BRI(2015551330_EN.pdf (accessed December 10, 2015).

Evans, Dominic, and Al-Khalidi, Suleiman (2013). "From Teenage Graffiti to a Country in Ruins: Syria's Two Years of Rebellion," *Reuters* (online). Available at: http://www.reuters.com/article/us-syria-crisis-uprising-idUSBRE92G0642020130317 (accessed June 30, 2014).

Ezzi, M. (2015). "The Druze of Suwayda: The Members of Dissent," *al-Jumhuriya* (online). Available at: http://aljumhuriya.net/en/sweida/the-druze-of-suwayda-the -embers-of-dissent (accessed September 30, 2015).

Ezzi, M. (2017). "How the Syrian Regime Is Using the Mask of 'Reconciliation' to Destroy Opposition Institutions," *Chatam House* (online). Available at: https://syria .chathamhouse.org/research/how-the-syrian-regime-is-using-the-mask-of -reconciliation-to-destroy-opposition-institutions (accessed June 30, 2017).

Fadel, Leith (2016). "Who Are the Syrian Desert Hawks?" *al-Masdar News* (online). Available at: https://www.almasdarnews.com/article/syrian-desert-hawks/ (ac- cessed July 7, 2016).

Fayha net (al-) (2017). "Khamîs yutâlib bi-mana' al-tarfîq 'ala al-hawâjiz ... wa al-'anâsir: 'mânak qadhâ'" (online). Available at: http://alfayha.net/منع-يطالب-خميس- ‎وا-الحواجز-على-التزفيق-/ (accessed March 20, 2017).

FEMISE (2017). "Reconstruction Cost of Syria Is Estimated at $300 Billion Five Times the 2010 GDP," FEMISE conference interview with Osama Kadi, president of Syrian Economic Task Force (online). Available at: http://www.femise.org /en/articles-en/reconstruction-cost-of-syria-is-estimated-at-300-billion-five-times -the-2010-gdp-femise-conference-interview-with-osama-kadi-president-of-syrian -economic-task-force/ (accessed August 26, 2017).

FIDA (2009). "République Arabe Syrienne, Programme d'Options Stratégiques pour le Pays" (pdf). Available at: https://webapps.ifad.org/members/eb/98/docs/french /EB-2009-98-R-22.pdf (accessed January 15, 2010).

Fielding-Smith, Abigail, and Khalaf, Roula (2013). "How Qatar Seized Control of the Syrian Revolution," *Financial Times* (online). Available at: https://www.ft.com /content/f2d9bbc8-bdbc-11e2-890a-00144feab7de?mhq5j=e2 (accessed May 20, 2013).

Finn, Tom, and Maclean, William (2016). "Qatar Will Help Syrian Rebels Even If Trump Ends U.S. Role," *Reuters* (online). Available at: http://www.reuters.com /article/us-mideast-crisis-syria-qatar-idUSKBN13L0X7 (accessed January 20, 2017).

Francis, Ellen, and Sharafedin, Bozorgmehr (2017). "Iran's Revolutionary Guards Reaps Economic Rewards in Syria," *Reuters* (online). Available at: http://uk.reuters .com/article/uk-mideast-crisis-syria-iran/irans-revolutionary-guards-reaps-econo mic-rewards-in-syria-idUKKBN1531TS (accessed January 30, 2017).

Frieh (al-) M. (2018a). "President al-Assad Stresses Importance of Developing Long-Term Cooperation Plans That Enhance Syrian-Iranian Steadfastness," Syrian Arab News Agency (SANA) (online), August 26. Available at: https://sana.sy/en/?p =145465 (accessed September 22, 2018).

Frieh (al-) M. (2018b). "Khamis: Large Infrastructure Projects Offered for Partnership," Syrian Arab News Agency (SANA) (online), September 10. Available at: https:// www.sana.sy/en/?p=146712 (accessed September 22, 2018).

Frieh (al-) M. (2018c). "Cabinet Approves State Budget Bill for 2019 at SYP 3882 Billion," Syrian Arab News Agency (SANA) (online), October 21. Available at: https://www.sana.sy/en/?p=149355 (accessed October 22, 2018).

Frieh (al-) Manar, and Said, H. (2017a). "Work Meeting to Effectively Invest Positive Outcomes of Damascus International Fair," Syrian Arab News Agency (SANA) (online), September 6. Available at: https://sana.sy/en/?p=113297 (accessed December 20, 2017).

Frieh (al-) M., and Said, H. (2017b). "Oman Activates Participation in Oil Investment in Syria," Syrian Arab News Agency (SANA) (online), November 22. Available at: https://sana.sy/en/?p=119022 (accessed December 22, 2017).

Ghaith Abdul-Ahad (2012). "Al-Qaida Turns Tide for Rebels in Battle for Eastern Syria," *The Guardian* (online). Available at: https://www.theguardian.com/world /2012/jul/30/al-qaida-rebels-battle-syria (accessed December 29, 2012).

Gall, Mark Landler Carlotta, and Schmitt Eric (2018). "Mixed Messages from U.S. as Turkey Attacks Syrian Kurds" (online). Available at: https://www.nytimes.com

/2018/01/23/world/middleeast/us-nato-turkey-afrin-manbij.html (accessed January 25, 2018).

Gambill, Gary C. (2013). "Syrian Druze: Toward Defiant Neutrality," *Foreign Policy Research Institute* (online). Available at: http://www.meforum.org/3463/syrian-druze -neutrality#_ftnref15 (accessed March 16, 2016).

General Command of the YPG (2014). "Statement of YPG General Command on Kobani and Fight Against ISIS," *Personal Website of Mutlu Civiroglu* (online). Available at: https://civiroglu.net/2014/10/19/statement-of-ypg-general-command -on-kobani-and-fight-against-isis/ (accessed November 20, 2014).

Geranmayeh, Ellie, and Liikhttp, Kadri (2016). "The New Power Couple: Russia and Iran in the Middle East," *European Council on Foreign Relations* (pdf). Available at: //www.ecfr.eu/page/-/ECFR_186_-_THE_NEW_POWER_COUPLE_RUSSIA _AND_IRAN_IN_THE_MIDDLE_EAST_PDFpdf (accessed December 10, 2016).

Ghanem, Hana (2018). "Khamîs: Lan nasmah bi-rijal â'mâl wa lâ mûwazaf fâsid," *al-Watan Online* (online). Available at http://www.alwatanonline.com/?p=94407 (accessed December 28, 2018).

Ghazzawi, Razzan (2014). "Women in Syria," *Rotefabrik* (pdf). Available at: http://www .rotefabrik.ch/_images/admin/zeitung/1394041288_fz_299_web.pdf (accessed December 20, 2014).

Ghazzawi, Razzan, Mohammad Afra, and Ramadan, Oula (2015). "'Peacebuilding Defines Our Future Now': A Study of Women's Peace Activism in Syria," *Badael* (pdf). Available at: http://badael.org/wp-content/uploads/2015/10/Syria_october 22.pdf (accessed January 11, 2016).

Glioti, Andrea (2016). "Rojava: A Libertarian Myth Under Scrutiny," *Al-Jazeera English* (online). Available at: http://www.aljazeera.com/indepth/opinion/2016/08 /rojava-libertarian-myth-scrutiny-160804083743648.html (accessed August 10, 2016).

Global Security (2016). "Russian Naval Base at Tartus/Tartous" (online). Available at: http://www.globalsecurity.org/military/world/syria/tartous.htm (accessed December 10, 2016).

Goldsmith, Jeff (2018). "After Decree 66, Some Residents Fear Reconstruction Means Eviction," *Syria Deeply* (online). Available at: https://www.newsdeeply.com/syria /articles/2018/04/06/after-decree-66-some-residents-fear-reconstruction-means -eviction (accessed April 10, 2018).

Goodenough, Patrick (2011). "Syrian President Assad Regarded as a 'Reformer,' Clinton Says," *CNS News* (online). Available at: http://www.cnsnews.com/news /article/syrian-president-assad-regarded-reformer-clinton-says (accessed March 29, 2011).

The Guardian (2011). "Syria Unrest: Homs Protest in Pictures" (online). Available at: https://www.theguardian.com/world/gallery/2011/apr/19/syria-homs-protests -shots (accessed May 3, 2011).

The Guardian (2012). "Al-Qaida Leader Zawahiri Urges Muslim Support for Syrian Uprising" (online). Available at: https://www.theguardian.com/world/2012/feb/12 /alqaida-zawahiri-support-syrian-uprising (accessed November 20, 2012).

The Guardian (2013). "Syria: Dozens Killed in Clashes After Suicide Attack in Damascus" (online). Available at: https://www.theguardian.com/world/2013/oct/19/syria-soldiers-killed-damascus-suicide-bombing (accessed November 25, 2014).

Hadath (al-) News (2014). "Qûwât al-ridâ'. fasîl sha'bî nû'î yundum lil-qitâl îla jânib al-jaysh al-sûrî" (online). Available at: http://www.alhadathnews.net/archives/121957 (accessed May 20, 2015).

Haddad, Bassam (2012b). "The Syrian Regime's Business Backbone," *MERIP* (online). Available at: http://www.merip.org/mer/mer262/syrian-regimes-business-backbone (accessed November 30, 2012).

Haddad, Ra'id al-Salhani Aleksandar (2019a). "Rûsîyâ tu'îd haykalat qûwât al-nizâm: Hân waqt al-taqâ'ud!" *al-Modon* (online), January 12. Available at: https://www.almodon.com/arabworld/2019/1/12/التقاعد-وقت-حان-النظام-قوات-هيكلة-تعيد-روسيا (accessed January 20, 2019).

Haddad, Ra'id al-Salhani Aleksandar (2019b). "Dimashq: Min yabî' 'iqârât al-ghâ`îbîn al-îîrânîîn," *al-Modon* (online), January 19. Available at: https://www.almodon.com/arabworld/2018/12/19/للإيرانيين-الغائبين-عقارات-يبيع-من-دمشق (accessed January 20, 2019).

Haddad, Wajih (2018). "Mûwâzanat 2019 al-sûrîyat: î'âdat al-î'mâr bi-115 milîyûn dûlâr," *al-Modon* (online). Available at: https://www.almodon.com/arabworld/2018/9/11/دولار-مليون-115ب-الاعمار-إعادة-السورية-2019-موازنة?fbclid=IwARoePIgD-hBniDv teonY-9kdA5Y6g11Ce6dx5sXCqPFrhb33esnP2qMVHBI (accessed November 20, 2018).

Hafezi, Parisa (2016). "Iran's IRGC Says Many Iranians Have Volunteered to Fight in Syria," *Reuters* (online). Available at: https://www.reuters.com/article/us-mideast-crisis-syria-iran-idUSKCN0Y92HD?rpc=401 (accessed September 24, 2017).

Hage Ali, Mohanad (2017). "The Shi'a Revival," *Carnegie Middle East Center* (online). Available at: http://carnegie-mec.org/diwan/69819?lang=en (accessed May 10, 2017).

Hage Ali, Mohanad (2018). "Limâzhâ yulâhiq al-âsad rijâl â'mâlihi," *al-Modon* (online). Available at: https://www.almodon.com/opinion/2018/6/1/أعماله-رجال-الأسد-يلاحق-لماذا (accessed June 10, 2018).

Haid, H. (2017a). "Can the Syrian Regime Expel Kurdish Forces out of Aleppo?" *Atlantic Council* (online), February 3. Available at: http://www.atlanticcouncil.org/blogs/syriasource/can-the-syrian-regime-expel-kurdish-forces-out-of-aleppo (accessed February 13, 2017).

Haid, H. (2017b). "Post-ISIS Governance in Jarablus: A Turkish-Led Strategy," *Chatham House* (online), October 26. Available at: https://www.chathamhouse.org/sites/files/chathamhouse/publications/research/2017-09-26-post-isis-governance-jarablus-haid.pdf (accessed October 25, 2017).

Hal (-al) (2018). "Iran and Shia Islam Spread in Old Damascus," *The Syrian Observer* (online). Available at: http://syrianobserver.com/EN/Features/34638/Iran_Shia_Islam_Spread_Old_Damascus (accessed August 20, 2018).

Halabi, Zayn (2019). "Al-Swûyadâ`: Hal badâ ântashâr quwât al-nizâm," *al-Modon* (online). Available at: https://www.almodon.com/arabworld/2019/2/21/السويداء-هل-النظام-قوات-انتشار-بدأ?fbclid=IwAR3wxXdMmXHk4eXWRT24CcycuepSZNL5SL AbQDXS-vOJPXLb6HtqNfu1CEc (accessed March 2, 2019).

Halawi, Ibrahim (2015), "Assad: Mass murderer to rational dictator", Middle East Eye, (online). Available at: http://www.middleeasteye.net/columns/assad-mass -murderer-rational-dictator-187936298#sthash.DTHu4OtC.dpuf (accessed 30 December 2015).

Hallaq (-al), Abdallah Amin (2013b). "Fî al-îslâm al-sîyâsî wa al-îslâm al-harbî fî sûrîyâ," Democratic Republic Studies Center (online), December 13. Available at: http://drsc-sy.org/السياسي-الإسلام-في%D9%90-الحربي-الإسلام-وال/ (accessed February 20, 2014).

Halliday, Joseph (2012a). "Syria's Armed Opposition," Washington Institute (pdf). March. Available at: http://www.understandingwar.org/sites/default/files/Syrias _Armed_Opposition.pdf (accessed November 5, 2013).

Halliday, J. (2012b). "Syria's Maturing Insurgency," Washington Institute (pdf), June. Available at: http://www.understandingwar.org/sites/default/files/Syrias_Maturing Insurgency_21June2012.pdf (accessed December 20, 2013).

Halliday, J. (2013). "The Assad Regime, from Counterinsurgency to Civil War," Washington Institute (pdf). Available at: http://www.understandingwar.org/sites /default/files/TheAssadRegime-web.pdf (accessed December 20, 2013).

Hamidi, Ibrahim (2015). "Syrian Opposition Fighters Withdraw from US 'Train and Equip' Program," The Syrian Observer (online). Available at: http://www.syrianob server.com/EN/News/29382/Syrian_Opposition_Fighters_Withdraw_from_US _Train_Equip_Program (accessed November 15, 2016).

Hamidi, I. (2016). "'The Walls of Fear' Return, Armed, to Damascus," The Syrian Observer (online). Available at: https://syrianobserver.com/EN/features/24873/the _walls_fear_return_armed_damascus.html (accessed November 15, 2016).

Hamidi, I. (2017). "Syrian Regime's Delay in Sealing Economic Agreements Cause Row with Tehran," The Syrian Observer (online). Available at: http://syrianobserver .com/EN/Commentary/32450/Syrian_Regime_Delay_Sealing_Economic _Agreements_Cause_Row_with_Tehran (accessed November 15, 2016).

Hamidi, Saleh (2018). "'Abd al-latîf li-'al-watan': takâlîf tâ'hîl masâkin 'adrâ 60 bil-mi'at 'ala al-hukûmat wa 40 'ala al-mûwâtin yadfa'uhâ taqsîtân," al-Watan (online). Available at: http://alwatan.sy/archives/163628 (accessed September 10, 2018).

Hamimu, Mohammad Manar (2018). "Al-qânûn 10 fursat li-mu'âlajat al-'ashwâ`iîât wa însâf âshâb al-hqûq … wazîr al-îdârat al-mahalîyat li-'al-watan': dirâsat li-tanzîm madkhal dimashq al-shmâlî wa bâb 'amrû fî hums wa 'ashwâ`iîât fî halab," al-Watan (online). Available at: http://alwatan.sy/archives/146475 (accessed April 10, 2018).

Hanna, Asaad (2016). "Syria's Sharia Courts," al-Monitor (online), February 11. Available at: http://www.al-monitor.com/pulse/originals/2016/02/syria-extremist -factions-sharia-courts-aleppo-idlib.html#ixzz4PVjdrSb1 (accessed March 30, 2016).

Haqq (al-), Tirwada Abd (2016). "The Islamist Factions' Judicial System in Idlib," Atlantic Council (online). Available at: http://www.atlanticcouncil.org/blogs /syriasource/the-islamist-factions-judicial-system-in-idlib (accessed October 30, 2016).

Hashem A. (2017). "Al-sinâ'iûn al-masrîyyûn," Al-Watan (online). (Available at: http://alwatan.sy/archives/93130 (accessed May 25, 2017).

Hassan, Hassan (2013a). "Saudis Overtaking Qatar in Sponsoring Syrian Rebels," *The National* (online), May 15. Available at: https://www.thenational.ae/saudis-over taking-qatar-in-sponsoring-syrian-rebels-1.471446 (accessed June 2, 2013).

Hassan, Hassan (2013b). "Syria: The View from the Gulf States," *Eurpean Council on Foreign Relations* (online), June 13. Available at: http://www.ecfr.eu/article/com mentary_syria_the_view_from_the_gulf_states135 (accessed January 2, 2016).

Hassan, H. (2013c). "The Army of Islam Is Winning in Syria," *Foreign Policy* (online), October 13. Available at: http://foreignpolicy.com/2013/10/01/the-army-of-islam -is-winning-in-syria/ (accessed January 2, 2017).

Hassan, H. (2016). "The Tale of Two Victories Against Syria's Worst Killers," *The National* (online), August 14. Available at: http://www.thenational.ae/opinion /comment/the-tale-of-two-victories-against-syrias-worst-killers (accessed September 20, 2016).

Hatahet, Sinan (2019). "Russia and Iran: Economic Influence in Syria," *Chatham House* (pdf). Available at: https://www.chathamhouse.org/sites/default/files/public ations/research/2019-03-08RussiaAndIranEconomicInfluenceInSyria.pdf?fbclid =IwAR2VzV4QdFeVBknWM7OODmMH1B8kt7u_foxgdYzceEyNoqtTZ5izYx nDMEI (accessed March 9, 2019).

Hauer, Neil (2017). "To the Victors, the Ruins: The Challenges of Russia's Recon struction in Syria," *Open Democracy* (online). Available at: https://www.opende mocracy.net/en/odr/to-victors-ruins-challenges-of-russia-s-reconstruction-in -syria/ (accessed December 31 2017).

Hayat (-al) (2017). "SDF Launches 'Raqqa Civil Council' as Battle to Free ISIS Capital Nears," *The Syrian Obesver* (online). Available at: http://www.syrianobserver .com/EN/News/32637/SDF_Launches_Raqqa_Civil_Council_as_Battle_Free _ISIS_Capital_Nears (accessed April 20, 2017).

Hayden, Sally (2018). "Portraits of War-Torn Syrian Cities," *New Internationalist* (online). Available at: https://newint.org/features/2018/04/01/portraits-three -syrian-cities (accessed December 29, 2018).

Hayek, Vincent, and Roche, Cody (2016). "Assad Regime Militias and Shi'ite Jihadis in the Syrian Civil War," *Bellingcat* (online). Available at: https://www.bellingcat .com/news/mena/2016/11/30/assad-regime-militias-and-shiite-jihadis-in-the -syrian-civil-war/ (accessed December 2, 2016).

Hemenway, Dan (2018). "Chinese Strategic Engagement with Assad's Syria," *Atlantic Council* (online). Avaialble at: https://www.atlanticcouncil.org/blogs/syriasource /chinese-strategic-engagement-with-assad-s-syria (accessed December 29, 2018).

Hennigan, W. J. (2018). "Saudi Crown Prince Says U.S. Troops Should Stay in Syria," *Time* (online). Available at: http://time.com/5222746/saudi-crown-prince-donald -trump-syria/ (accessed July 20, 2018).

Herbert, Matt (2014). "Partisans, Profiteers, and Criminals: Syria's Illicit Economy," *The Fletcher Forum of World Affairs*, Vol. 38, no. 1, pp. 69–86.

Heydemann, Steven (2013a). "Syria's Uprising: Sectarianism, Regionalisation, and State Order in the Levant," *FRIDE and HIVOS* (pdf) May 2013. Available at: http://fride.org/descarga/WP_119_Syria_Uprising.pdf (accessed January 10, 2014).

Heydemann S. (2017). "Syria Reconstruction and the Illusion of Leverage," *Atlantic Council* (online). Available at: http://www.atlanticcouncil.org/blogs/syriasource /syria-reconstruction-and-the-illusion-of-leverage (accessed May 23, 2017).

High Negotiation Committee (2016). "Executive Framework for a Political Solution Based on the Geneva Communiqué," *Riad Hijab English* (pdf). Available at: http:// english.riadhijab.com/userfiles/HNC%20Executive%20Summary%20-%20 English.pdf (accessed December 20, 2016).

Hindy, Lily (2017). "A Rising China Eyes the Middle East," *The Century Foundation* (online). Available at: https://tcf.org/content/report/rising-china-eyes-middle-east/ (accessed April 20, 2017).

Hirschfeld Davis, Julie (2018). "Trump Drops Push for Immediate Withdrawal of Troops from Syria," *The New York Times* (online). Available at: https://www .nytimes.com/2018/04/04/world/middleeast/trump-syria-troops.html (accessed December 20, 2018).

Hoffman, Adam (2018). "As Zawahiri Calls for Uniting the Ranks of Jihadists, A New al-Qa'ida Front Emerges in Syria," (online). Available at: https://dayan.org /content/zawahiri-calls-uniting-ranks-jihadists-new-al-qaida-front-emerges-syria (accessed April 20, 2018).

Hokayem Emile (2016). "'Assad or We Burn the Country': Misreading Sectarianism and the Regime in Syria," *War on the Rocks* (online). Available at: http://waronth erocks.com/2016/08/assad-or-we-burn-the-country-misreading-sectarianism-and -the-regime-in-syria/; (accessed September 30, 2016).

Holland, Steve; Stewart, Phil, and Wroughton, Lesley (2019). "How Trump Slowed Rush for Syria Exits After Huddle in Iraq," *Reuters* (online). Available at: https:// www.reuters.com/article/us-mideast-crisis-syria-trump-insight/how-trump -slowed-rush-for-syria-exits-after-huddle-in-iraq-idUSKCN1P92P9 (accessed January 20, 2019).

Homsi (al-), Fadel (2017). "Tal Rifaat: A Hill with Many Flags," *al-Jumhuriya* (online). Available at: https://www.aljumhuriya.net/en/content/tal-rifaat-hill-many-flags (accessed December 20, 2017).

Hosenball, Mark, and Spetalnick, Matt (2011). "U.S. Slaps New Sanctions on Syria over Crackdown," *Reuters* (online). Available at: https://www.reuters.com/article /us-syria-usa-sanctions/u-s-slaps-new-sanctions-on-syria-over-crackdown-idUS TRE73S4PP20110429?feedType=RSS&feedName=politicsNews&utm_source =twitterfeed&utm_medium=twitter&utm_campaign=Feed%3A+Reuters%2FPol iticsNews+%28Reuters+Politics+News%29 (accessed January 20, 2012).

Hossino, Omar (2013). "Syria's Secular Revolution Lives On," *Foreign Policy* (online). Available at: http://foreignpolicy.com/2013/02/04/syrias-secular-revolution-lives -on/ (accessed July 6, 2013).

Hossino, Omar, and Kanbar, Kinda (2013). "Syria's Women: Sidelined in Opposition Politics?" *Syria Deeply* (online). Available at: https://www.newsdeeply.com /syria/articles/2013/04/11/syrias-women-sidelined-in-opposition-politics (accessed September 20, 2014).

Hossino, Omar, and Tanir, Ilhan (2012). "The Decisive Minoriry: The Role of Syria's Kurds in the Anti-Assad Revolution," *The Henry Jackson Society* (pdf). Available at:

http://www.scpss.org/libs/spaw/uploads/files/Reports/03-2012_Henry_Jackson
_Soc_Rpt_re_Role_of_Syr_Kurds.pdf (accessed January 22, 2013).

Hourani, Nada (2017). "'People Can't Stand It Any Longer:' Regime Supporters in Latakia Fed up with 1 Hour of Electricity," *Syria Direct* (online). Available at: http://syriadirect.org/news/'people-can't-stand-it-any-longer'-regime-supporters -in-latakia-fed-up-with-1-hour-of-electricity/ (accessed January 25, 2017).

Human Rights Watch (2010). "A Wasted Decade Human Rights in Syria During Bashar al-Asad's First Ten Years in Power" (online). Availabe at: https://www.hrw .org/report/2010/07/16/wasted-decade/human-rights-syria-during-bashar-al -asads-first-ten-years-power (accessed February 20, 2011).

Human Rights Watch (2012). "Isolate Syria's Arms Suppliers" (online). Available at: https://www.hrw.org/news/2012/06/03/isolate-syrias-arms-suppliers (accessed November 12, 2013).

Human Rights Watch (2013). "Executions, Indiscriminate Shootings, and Hostage Taking by Opposition Forces in Latakia Countryside" (online). Available at: https://www.hrw.org/report/2013/10/10/you-can-still-see-their-blood/executions -indiscriminate-shootings-and-hostage (accessed November 12, 2013).

Human Rights Watch (2014a). "Razed to the Ground: Syria's Unlawful Neighborhood Demolitions in 2012–2013" (online), January 30. Available at: https://www.hrw.org /report/2014/01/30/razed-ground/syrias-unlawful-neighborhood-demolitions-2012 -2013 (accessed July 20, 2014).

Human Rights Watch (2014b). "Under Kurdish Rule Abuses in PYD-Run Enclaves of Syria" (pdf), June 14. Available at: https://www.hrw.org/sites/default/files /reports/syria0614_kurds_ForUpload.pdf (accessed July 20, 2014).

Human Rights Watch (2015). "'He Didn't Have to Die': Indiscriminate Attacks by Opposition Groups in Syria" (online). Available at: https://www.hrw.org/report /2015/03/22/he-didnt-have-die/indiscriminate-attacks-opposition-groups-syria (accesse December 20, 2015).

Human Rights Watch (2018a). "Q&A: Syria's New Property Law" (online), May 29. Available at: https://www.hrw.org/news/2018/05/29/qa-syrias-new-property-law (accesse September 20, 2018).

Human Rights Watch (2018b). "Syria: Residents Blocked from Returning" (online), October 16. Available at: https://www.hrw.org/news/2018/10/16/syria-residents -blocked-returning (accesse October 20, 2018).

Humanitarian Needs Overview (2017). "Syrian Arab Republic," *Relief Web* (pdf). Available at: https://reliefweb.int/sites/reliefweb.int/files/resources/2018_syr_hno _english.pdf (accessed July 20, 2018).

Hurriya Press (2018a). "Iran Commits to Residential Projects in Syria," *The Syrian Observer* (online), August 16. Available at: http://syrianobserver.com/EN/News /34640/Iran_Commits_Residential_Projects_Syria (accessed August 20, 2018).

Hurriya Press (2018b). "Assad Government Begins to Implement Zoning Plans in Homs," *The Syrian Observer* (online), September 21. Available at: http://syrianob server.com/EN/Features/34813/Assad_Government_Begins_Implement_Zoning _Plans_Homs (accessed October 20, 2018).

Ibish, Hussein (2016). "What's at Stake for the Gulf Arab States in Syria?" *The Arab Gulf States Institute in Washington* (pdf). Available at: http://www.agsiw.org/wp

-content/uploads/2016/06/Ibish_GCCSyria_Web.pdf (accessed September 30, 2016).

Iddon, Paul (2017). "The Power Plays Behind Russia's Deconfliction in Afrin" *Rudaw* (online). Available at: http://www.rudaw.net/english/analysis/10092017 (accessed September 12, 2017).

The Indian Express (2017). "India Welcome to Play a Role in Reconstruction of Syria, says Bashar al-Assad" (online). Available at: http://indianexpress.com/article/world /india-welcome-to-play-a-role-in-reconstruction-of-syria-says-bashar-al-assad -4689007/ (accessed July 20, 2017).

Industry News (2018a). "Al-i'lân 'an tâ`sîs munazamat tajamu' rijâl al-â'mâl al-sûrîin fî al-'âlam li-da'm al-îqtisâd al-watanî wa 'amalîyat al-i'mâr" (online), October 31. Available at: http://industrynews.sy/?p=14504 (accessed Decmber 20, 2018).

Industry News (2018b). "Tashmîl 97 mashrû'ân îstithmârîyâ jadîdân râsmâlihâ 874 milîyâr lîrat. hay`at al-îstithmâr: milîâr lira qîmat al-mashârî' al-munafizhat" (online), December 20. Available at: http://industrynews.sy/?p=14504 (accessed Decmber 20, 2018).

Industry News (2019). "Da'â mû`tamar 'qalmak âkhdar' âkhar … Al-Mûwaka': 'Aûdat al-sinâ'îin al-sûrîin min al-khârij yatatalab hulûlâ li-mu'adalâthum fî al-watan" (online). Available at: http://industrynews.sy/?p=14504 (accessed March 1, 2019).

International Crisis Group (ICG) (2011). "Popular Protest in North Africa and the Middle East (VII): The Syrian Regime Slow-Motion Suicide" (pdf). Available at: https://fr.scribd.com/document/59955127/International-Crisis-Group-Report-The -Syrian-Regimes-Slow-Motion-Suicide (accessed December 15, 2012).

International Crisis Group (ICG) (2012a). "Syria's Mutating Conflict" (pdf). August. Available at: https://www.crisisgroup.org/middle-east-north-africa/eastern-medit erranean/syria/syria-s-mutating-conflict (Accessed December 21, 2012).

International Crisis Group (ICG) (2012b). "Tentative Jihad: Syria's Fundamentalist Opposition" (pdf) October. Available at: https://d2071andvipowj.cloudfront.net /131-tentative-jihad-syria-s-fundamentalist-opposition.pdf (accessed December 20, 2012).

International Crisis Group (ICG) (2013). "Syria's Kurds: A Struggle Within a Struggle" (pdf). Available at: https://d2071andvipowj.cloudfront.net/syrias-kurds -a-struggle-within-a-struggle.pdf (accessed February 20, 2014).

International Crisis Group (ICG) (2014a). "Flight of Icarus? The PYD's Precarious Rise in Syria" (pdf), May 8. Available at: http://www.crisisgroup.org/~/media /Files/Middle%20East%20North%20Africa/Iraq%20Syria%20Lebanon/Syria /151-flight-of-icarus-the-pyd-s-precarious-rise-in-syria.pdf (accessed December 20, 2014).

International Crisis Group (ICG) (2014b). "Lebanon's Hizbollah Turns Eastward to Syria" (pdf). May 27. Available at: http://www.crisisgroup.org/~/media/Files /Middle%20East%20North%20Africa/Iraq%20Syria%20Lebanon/Lebanon/153 -lebanon-s-hizbollah-turns-eastward-to-syria.pdf (accessed May 30, 2014).

International Crisis Group (ICG) (2014c). "Rigged Cars and Barrel Bombs: Aleppo and the State of Syrian War" (pdf), September 9. Available at: https://d2071and-vipowj.cloudfront.net/rigged-cars-and-barrel-bombs-aleppo-and-the-state-of-the -syrian-war.pdf (accessed December 21, 2014).

International Crisis Group (ICG) (2017). "The PKK's Fateful Choice in Northern Syria" (online). Available at: https://www.crisisgroup.org/middle-east-north-africa /eastern-mediterranean/syria/176-pkk-s-fateful-choice-northern-syria (accessed May 20, 2017).

International Fund for Agricultural Development (IFAD) (2011). "Syrian Arab Republic 2011, Gouvernment Council" (pdf). Available at: https://www.ifad.org /documents/10180/7c26bd8a-48b6-4beb-a78b-6f4760883bdc (accessed February 20, 2012).

International Labour Organization (ILO) (2010). "Gender, Employment and the Informal Economy in Syria" (pdf). Available at: http://www.ilo.org/wcmsp5/groups /public/---dgreports/---gender/documents/publication/wcms_144219.pdf (accessed January 20, 2012).

Iqtissad (2015a). "Interview: Mohamad Mansour–How Syria's Media Tycoons, Control the Market" (online), December 11. Available at: http://syrianobserver .com/EN/Interviews/30269/Interview_Mohamad_Mansour_How_Syria_Media _Tycoons_Control_Market (accessed December 30, 2015).

Iqtissad (2015b). "Muhamad Hamshû mawzifân fî al-qitâ' al-'âm" (online), December 20. Available at: https://www.eqtsad.net/news/article/12455 (accessed December 28, 2015).

Iqtissad (2016). "Shiite Influence Increases in Damascus' Dummar District," *The Syrian Observer* (online). Available at: http://syrianobserver.com/EN/Features/31820 /Regime_Demographic_Change_Reaches_Lattakia_City_Slowly_Quietly (accessed May 10, 2017).

Iqtissad (2017). "Khamîs wa 16 wazîrân fî halab. wa 80 milîyûn dûlâr 'ala mada 'âm" (online). Available at: https://www.eqtsad.net/news/article/18831/ (accessed January 13, 2017).

Iqtissad (2018). "Mâzen al-tarazî, âw al-nisâb al-sûrî. îsm jadîd yaghzû 'âlam al-nizâm al-mâlî" (online), January 1. Available at: https://www.eqtsad.net/news/article/18780 / (accessed January 10, 2018).

Iqtisadi (-al) (2014a). "Sûrîyâ: Al-hajz 'ala âmûâl rajul al-â'mâl muwafaq al-qadâh" (online), July 8. Available at: https://aliqtisadi.com/392185-حجز-احتياطي-على-أموال-رجل-أعمال-- (accessed February 20, 2016).

Iqtisadi (-al) (2014b). "Al-hukûma al-sûrîya tusâdir malkîyat firâs tlâs fî ma'mal lâfârj" (online), August 21. Available at: https://aliqtisadi.com/441326-نقل-مكلية-فراس-طلاس-بلافارج-- (accessed August 30, 2015).

Iqtisadi (-al) (2018a). "Sâmer muhamad al-dibs" (online). Available at: https:// aliqtisadi.com/شخصيات/سامر-الدبس (accessed October 25, 2018).

Iqtisadi (-al) (2018b). "Ârbâh sîrîyatel tatajâwaz 46 milîyâr l.s fî 9 âshur" (online), November 13. Available at: https://aliqtisadi.com/1259018-أرباح-سيريتل-في-تسعة-أشهر/ (accessed November 15, 2018).

Iqtisadi (-al) (2018c). "Âbrazhum ma'tûq wa kaîyatî wa qâterjî ... rijâl â'mâl sûrîîn yû'asisûn sharikât qâbidat bi-râsmâl 3.5 miliâr lîrat" (online), December 26. Available at: https://www.emmarsyria.com/post/-.-3.5-?fbclid=IwAR1bK6Z9VEE LvDv9cAoc1S6onkHFimZLb2z_lGuILFUR4DXBAadLCmafSso (accessed December 28, 2018).

IRIN (2012). "As Kurds Enter the Fray, Risk of Conflict Grows" (online). Available at: http://www.irinnews.org/analysis/2012/08/02/kurds-enter-fray-risk-conflict -grows (accessed January 20, 2013).

IRIN (2013). "Syrian Refugees Suffer as Aid Agencies in Iraq Grapple with Sudden Influx" (online), August 21. Available at: http://www.irinnews.org/news/2013 /08/21/syrian-refugees-suffer-aid-agencies-iraq-grapple-sudden-influx (accessed August 30, 2013).

Isaac, Mardean (2015). "The Assyrians of Syria: History and Prospects," *Syria Comment* (online). Available at: http://www.joshualandis.com/blog/the-assyrians-of-syria -history-and-prospets-by-mardean-isaac/ (accessed April 29, 2016).

Issa, Auntun (2016). "Syria's New Media Landscape, Independent Media Born out of War," *The Middle East Institute*, MEI Policy Paper 2016–9 (pdf). Available at: http://www.mei.edu/sites/default/files/publications/PP9_Issa_Syrianmedia_web _0.pdf (accessed December 14, 2016).

Issa, Phillip (2017). "Syria Opposition Told to Come to Terms with Assad's Survival," *ABC News* (online). Available at: http://abcnews.go.com/International/wireStory /syria-opposition-told-terms-assads-survival-49396345 (accessed August 31, 2017).

Issaev, Leonid, and Kozhanov, Nikolay (2017). "The Russian-Saudi Rapprochement and Iran," *Al-Jazeera English* (online). Available at: http://www.aljazeera.com /indepth/opinion/2017/08/russian-saudi-rapprochement-iran-170817154056810 .html (accessed August 31, 2017).

ISW Research Team (2015). "Russia's First Reported Air Strikes in Syria Assist Regime with Targeting Broader Opposition," *Institute for the Study of War* (online). Available at: http://iswresearch.blogspot.it/2015/09/russias-first-reported-air-strikes -in.html (accessed October 2, 2015).

Itani, Faysal, and Stein, Aaron (2016). "Turkey's Syria Predicament," *Atlantic Council* (pdf). Available at: http://www.atlanticcouncil.org/images/publications/Turkey_s _Syria_Predicament.pdf (accessed October 20, 2016).

Itani, Fida (2014). "Haythu iufashil Nasr Allâh," *Now Media* (online). Available at: https://now.mmedia.me/lb/ar/analysisar/559886 (accessed August 12, 2014).

Jaber, Nawar (2015). "Influence iranienne en Syrie: la dimension confessionnelle," *Orient XXI* (online). Available at: http://orientxxi.info/magazine/influence-irani enne-en-syrie-la-dimension-confessionnelle,1081 (accessed January 18, 2016).

Jamal, Moutasem, Nelson, Maria, and Yosfi, Yaman (2015). "New PYD Curricula in Northern Syria Reveal Ideological, Linguistic Fault Lines," *Syria Direct* (online). Available at: http://syriadirect.org/news/new-pyd-curriculum-in-northern-syria -reveals-ideological-linguistic-fault-lines/ (accessed December 29, 2015).

Jamestown Foundation (2015). "The Struggle for Syria's al-Hasakah Governorate: Kurds, the Islamic State, and the IRGC, 3," *Terrorism Monitor* Vol. 13, Issue 7. Available at: http://www.refworld.org/docid/552b9f934.html (accessed November 11, 2016).

Jaulmes, Adrien (2012). "Une insurrection syrienne plus conservatrice qu'extrémiste," *Le Figaro* (online). Available at: http://www.lefigaro.fr/international/2012/07/30 /01003-20120730ARTFIG00409-syrie-une-insurrection-musulmane-conser vatrice.php (accessed August 30, 2012).

Jaysh al-Thûwar (2015). "Î'lân qûwât sûrîyâ al-dîmukrâtîyya fî halab wa îdlib" (online). Available at: http://jeshalthowar.com/?p=673 (accessed December 20, 2015).

Jazaeri (-al), Ruaa (2018). "3rd Industrial Conference Calls for Developing National Industry," Syrian Arab News Agency (SANA) (online). Available at: https://sana.sy/en/?p=150501 (accessed November 8, 2018).

Jazeera (al-) (2011). "Syrians Hold Strikes amid Battles in South" (online). Available at: http://www.aljazeera.com/news/middleeast/2011/12/201112119332270503.html (accessed June 11, 2012).

Jazeera (-al) English (2012). "Q&A: Nir Rosen on Syria's Armed Opposition" (online). Available at: http://www.aljazeera.com/indepth/features/2012/02/201221315020166516.html (accessed December 22, 2012).

Jazeera (al-) English (2017). "Iran Signs Deal to Repair Syria's Power Grid" (online). Available at: http://www.aljazeera.com/news/2017/09/iran-signs-deal-repair-syria-power-grid-170912162708749.html (accessed September 27, 2017).

Jazeera (al-) English (2018). "Turkish FM: EU Countries Turning Blind Eye to Khashoggi Murder" (online). Available at: https://www.aljazeera.com/news/2018/12/turkish-fm-eu-countries-turning-blind-eye-khashoggi-murder-181216103712249.html (accessed December 27, 2018).

Jedinia, Mehdi, and Kajjo, Sirwan (2016). "Iranians Buying up Land in War-Torn Syria," VOA News (online). Available at: https://learningenglish.voanews.com/a/iranians-buying-up-land-war-torn-syria/3252852.html (accessed November 29, 2016).

Jesr Press (2019). "Hamîdî dahâm al-hâdî al-jarbâ ya'ûd îla hudn al-âsad" (online). Available at: https://www.jesrpress.com/2019/02/19/4199/?fbclid=IwARorkLcQsvzHn4zUBnl7HK5of-SYJ8tqb183jH9qAqJjGgVwRlyPrusZ8GI (accessed March 3, 2019).

Jones, Rory (2017). "Israel Gives Secret Aid to Syrian Rebels," Wall Street Journal (online). Available at: https://www.wsj.com/articles/israel-gives-secret-aid-to-syrian-rebels-1497813430 (accessed June 20, 2017).

Kabalan, Marwan (2018). "Russia's New Game in Syria," Al-Jazeera English (online). Available at: https://www.aljazeera.com/indepth/opinion/istanbul-summit-failed-181029102112796.html (accessed December 29, 2018).

Kabawat, Hind Aboud (2018). "Al-muhandis muhamad kâmal sabâgh sharbâtî (âbû kâmal). min tanzif al-âlât îla âdkham masna' lil-ghazl," Souriyati (online). Available at: http://www.souriyati.com/2018/01/22/93716.html (accessed January 25, 2018).

Kajjo, Sirwan, and Sinclair, Christian (2011). "The Evolution of Kurdish Politics in Syria," MERIP (online). Available at: http://www.merip.org/mero/mero083111#_3_ (accessed September 30, 2011).

Karouny, Mariam (2012). "New Defense Minister a Symbol of Brutal War," Reuters (online). Available at: http://www.dailystar.com.lb/News/Middle-East/2012/Aug-03/183253-new-defense-minister-a-symbol-of-brutal-war.ashx (accessed August 20, 2013).

Karouny, Mariam (2013). "Saudi Edges Qatar to Control Syrian Rebel Support," Reuters (online). Available at: https://www.reuters.com/article/us-syria-crisis-saudi-insight/saudi-edges-qatar-to-control-syrian-rebel-support-idUSBRE94U0ZV20130531 (accessed September 10, 2013).

Kassioun (2019). "Ârqâm al-naft wa al-ghâz 2018" (online). Available at: https://kassiounpaper.com/economy/item/34308-2018?fbclid=IwAR2faqcagqGk8v181mMn neNgrEVEVhx6repJHZ_6tVVbxnuR2-LJMWwA4EQ (accessed January 10, 2019).

Kattan, Rashad (2014). "Syria's Business Community Decides," *Risk Advisory* (online). Available at: https://news.riskadvisory.net/2014/12/syrias-business-community -decides/; (accessed January 11, 2015).

Kattan, R. (2016). "Decisive Military Defections in Syria: A Case of Wishful Thinking," *War on the Rocks* (online). Available at: https://warontherocks.com/2016 /09/decisive-military-defections-in-syria-a-case-of-wishful-thinking/ (accessed December 20, 2017).

Kayali, Marwan (2018). "Sharikat rûssîyat tusaytir 'ala mujama' al-âsmadat al-wahîd fî suriyâ", *al-Modon* (online). Available at: https://www.almodon.com/print/607 ac4ab-1f1e-41e5-95e1-487ce7b405af/410ff364-8cf6-4a6a-8306-04b16ce67c38 (accessed January 2, 2019).

Kerr, Simeon, and Solomon, Erika (2018). "Prince Alwaleed Sells Hotel Stake to Assad-Linked Businessman," *Financial Times* (online). Available at: https://www.ft .com/content/47589da4-26b8-11e8-b27e-cc62a39d57a0 (accessed March 19, 2018).

Khaddour K. (2015a). "The Assad Regime's Hold on the Syrian State," *Carnegie Endowment* (pdf), July. Available at: http://carnegieendowment.org/files/syrian _state1.pdf; (accessed January 20, 2016).

Khaddour K. (2015b). "Assad's Officer Ghetto: Why the Syrian Army Remains Loyal," *Carnegie Endowment* (online), November 4. Available at: http://carnegieendowment .org/2015/11/03/assad-s-officer-ghetto-why-syrian-army-remains-loyal-pub-61449 (accessed January 20, 2016).

Khaddour K. (2016a). "Strength in Weakness: The Syrian Army's Accidental Resilience," *Carnegie Endowment* (online), March 14. Available at: http://carnegieendowment .org/2016/03/14/strength-in-weakness-syrian-army-s-accidental-resilience-pub -62968 (accessed April 20, 2016).

Khaddour K. (2016b). "The Coast in Conflict: Migration, Sectarianism, and Decentralization in Syria's Latakia and Tartus Governorates," *Friedrich Ebert Stiftung* (pdf), July. Available at: http://library.fes.de/pdf-files/iez/12682-20160725 .pdf (accessed September 20, 2016).

Khaddour K. (2017a). "Despite Its Weakness, the Syrian Army Remains Central to the Regime's Survival—Syrian Expert," *The Syrian Observer* (online), February 13. Available at: http://syrianobserver.com/EN/Interviews/32329/Despite_Weakness _the_Syrian_Army_Remains_Central_the_Regime_Survival_Syrian_Expert (accessed February 13, 2017).

Khaddour K. (2017b). "Eastern Expectations: The Changing Dynamics in Syria's Tribal Regions," *Carnegie Middle East Center* (online), February 28. Available at: http://carnegie-mec.org/2017/02/28/eastern-expectations-changing-dynamics-in -syria-s-tribal-regions-pub-68008 (accessed May 20, 2017).

Khaddour K. (2017c). "I, the Supreme," *Carnegie Middle East Center* (online), March 22. Available at: http://carnegie-mec.org/diwan/68348 (accessed May 20, 2017).

Khaddour K. (2017d). "Consumed by War: The End of Aleppo and Northern Syria's Political Order," *Friedrich Ebert Stiftung* (pdf), October. Available at: http://library .fes.de/pdf-files/iez/13783.pdf (accessed November 20, 2017).

Khaddour K. (2018). "Syria's Troublesome Militias," *Carnegie Middle East Center* (online). Available at: https://carnegie-mec.org/diwan/77635 (accessed November 20, 2018).

Khalaf, Rana (2015). "Governance Without Government in Syria: Civil Society and State Building During Conflict," *Syria Studies*, Vol. 7, No. 3 (pdf). Available at: https://ojs.st-andrews.ac.uk/index.php/syria/article/view/1176/911 (accessed December 11, 2015).

Khalaf, R. (2016). "Governing Rojava Layers of Legitimacy in Syria," *Chatham House* (pdf). Available at: https://www.chathamhouse.org/sites/files/chathamhouse/publi cations/research/2016-12-08-governing-rojava-khalaf.pdf (accessed December 22, 2016).

Khalaf, Rana, Ramadan, Oula, and Stolleis, Friederike (2014). "Activism in Difficult Times, Civil Society Groups in Syria 2011–2014," *Badael Project and Friedrich-Ebert-Stiftung* (online). Available at: http://badael.org/wp-content/uploads/2015 /01/Activism-in-Difficult-Times.-Civil-Society-Groups-in-Syria-2011-2014.pdf (accessed September 11, 2015).

Khalidi (al-), Suleiman (2017a). "Exclusive: U.S. Expands Presence in Syrian Desert, Rebels Say," *Reuters* (online), June 16. Avalaible at: http://www.reuters.com/article /us-mideast-crisis-syria-usa-exclusive-idUSKBN1951YX (accessed January 20, 2017).

Khalidi (al-), S. (2017b). "Syrian Rebels Say U.S. Allies Push for Retreat from Southeast Syria," *Reuters* (online), September 10. Avalaible at: http://www.reuters .com/article/us-mideast-crisis-syria-south/syrian-rebels-say-u-s-allies-push-for -retreat-from-southeast-syria-idUSKCN1BL0YP (accessed September 20, 2017).

Khalidi (al-), Suleiman, and Spetalnick, Matt (2017). "U.S. Warplane Downs Syrian Army Jet in Raqqa Province," *Reuters* (online). Avalaible at: http://www.reuters .com/article/us-mideast-crisis-syria-usa-idUSKBN1990XI (accessed June 20, 2017).

Khalidi (al-), Suleiman, Perry, Tom, and Walcott, John (2017). "Exclusive: CIA-Backed Aid for Syrian Rebels Frozen After Islamist Attack—Sources," *Reuters* (online). Available at: http://www.reuters.com/article/us-mideast-crisis-syria-rebels -idUSKBN1601BD (accessed February 21, 2017).

Khan, Mohsin, and Lebaron, Richard (2015). "What Will the Gulf's $12 Billion Buy in Egypt?" *Atlantic Council* (online). Available at: http://www.atlanticcouncil .org/blogs/menasource/what-will-the-gulfs-12-billion-buy-in-egypt (accessed December 20, 2013).

Kharon Brief (2018). "Top Assad Crony Positions Himself for Syrian Reconstruction" (online). Available at: https://brief.kharon.com/updates/top-assad-crony-positions -himself-for-syrian-reconstruction/ (accessed November 30, 2018).

Khateb (al-), Khaled (2018). "Turkey Props up Industrial Zone in Syria's al-Bab," *al-Monitor* (online). Available at: http://www.al-monitor.com/pulse/originals/2018 /02/syria-al-bab-euphrates-shield-industrial-area-turkey.html#ixzz58rwg8oSn (accessed March 2, 2018).

Khatib, Majd (2018). "Mâzâ turîd îrân min întakhâbât al-îdârat al-mahalîyat?," *al-Modon* (online). Available at: https://www.almodon.com/arabworld/2018/9/16/ماذا-تريد-إيران-من-انتخابات-الادارة-المحلية?fbclid=IwAR0oRA8Y-Cj99MTQl5cfmoMDjyNo KhllUdmgumKoLgSh61SIZkoeBU8CTGo (accessed October 20, 2018).

Khatib, Majd (2019). "Sûrîyâ: 75 àmnîyat khasat.. muta'didat al-wilâ`ât", *al-Modon* (online). Available at: https://www.almodon.com/arabworld/2019/3/11/سوريا-75 شركة-أمنية-خاصة-متعددة-الولاءات-?fbclid=IwAR2QL5jZ8fdLCvvuTrhHLqNDsB _D6IhzegqOl8CG1XUha-QoAC813YME2cM (accessed March 15, 2019).

Khattab, Lana, and Myrttinen, Henri (2017). "Why gender matters in Syria's re-building efforts," *LSE Gender Institute* (online). Available at: http://blogs.lse.ac.uk /gender/2017/08/29/why-gender-matters-in-syrias-rebuilding-efforts/ (accessed September 10, 2017).

Khodarenok, Mikhail (2016). "Here's Why Assad's Army Can't Win the War in Syria," *CI team* (online). Available at: https://citeam.org/here-s-why-assad-s-army -can-t-win-the-war-in-syria/ (accessed in September 13, 2016).

Khoshnawi, Hemin (2013). "Salih Muslim's Ankara Visit Marks Major Policy Change," Rudaw (online). Available at: http://www.rudaw.net/english/middleeast /syria/29072013 (accessed March 30, 2014).

Khoury, Doreen (2013). "Losing the Syrian Grassroots Local Governance Structures Urgently Need Support," *Stiftung Wissenschaft und Politik (SWP)* (pdf). Available at: http://www.swp-berlin.org/fileadmin/contents/products/comments/2013C09 _kou.pdf (accessed February 20, 2014).

Kilcullen, David, and Rosenblatt, Natt (2012). "The Rise of Syria's Urban Poor: Why the War for Syria's Future Will Be Fought over the Country's New Urban Villages," *PRISM* (pdf). Available at: http://cco.ndu.edu/Portals/96/Documents/prism /prism_4-syria/The_Rise_Of_Syrias_Urban_Poor.pdf (accessed November 20, 2013).

Kozak, Christopher (2017). "Iran's Assad Regime," *Institute for the Study of the War* (online). Available at: http://iswresearch.blogspot.ch/2017/03/irans-assad-regime .html (accessed May 20, 2017).

Kube, Courtney, and Lee, Carol E. (2018). "Trump Administration Has New Plan to Drive Iran out of Syria," NBC News (online). Available at: https://www.nbcnews .com/news/investigations/trump-administration-has-new-plan-drive-iran-out -syria-n919596 (accessed January 30, 2019).

Kurd Watch (2012a). "Abdussalam 'Uthman, Politician and Activist" (online). Available at: http://www.kurdwatch.org/syria_article.php?aid=2719&z=en&cure =240 (accessed February 20, 2013).

Kurd Watch (2012b). "Minutes of the Meeting" (online). Available at: http://www .kurdwatch.org/pdf/KurdWatch_D027_en_ar.pdf (accessed December 20, 2012).

Kurd Watch (2013a). "We Are Free and Independent, and We Are Pursuing Our Own Strategy" (online), June 4. Available at: http://kurdwatch.org/syria_%2oarticle.php ?aid=2846&z=en (accessed February 20, 2014).

Kurd Watch (2013b). "What Does the Syrian-Kurdish Opposition Want? Politics Between Erbil, Sulaymaniyah, Damascus, and Qandil" (pdf), September. Available at: http://www.kurdwatch.org/pdf/KurdWatch_A009_en_Parteien2.pdf (accessed May 30, 2014).

Kurd Watch (2018). "Home" (online), June 4. Available at: http://www.kurdwatch.org /?cid=1&z=en (accessed January 25, 2018).

Kurdish National Council (KNC) (2016a). "About the KNC" (online). Available at: http://knc-geneva.org/?page_id=49&lang=en (accessed February 2016).

Kurdish National Council (KNC) (2016b). "Release: The HNC's 'Executive Framework' Will Neither Bring Peace Nor Equality" (online), September 20. Available at: http://knc-geneva.org/?p=710&lang=en (accessed September 21, 2016).

Kurdish National Council (KNC) (2017). "Press Release: Kurdish National Council Suspends Participation in Current Round of Negotiations" (online), March 31. Available at: http://knc-geneva.org/?p=1310&lang=en (accessed April 3, 2017).

Kurdish Project (2017). "KDP: Kurdistan Democratic Party" (online). Available at: https://thekurdishproject.org/history-and-culture/kurdish-democracy/kdp-kurdistan-democratic-party/ (accessed August 30, 2017).

Kurdish Question (2016). "Final Declaration of the Rojava-Northern Syria Democratic Federal System Constituent Assembly" (online). Available at: http://kurdishques tion.com/oldarticle.php?aid=final-declaration-of-the-rojava-northern-syria-demo cratic-federal-system-constituent-assembly (accessed July 10, 2017).

Kureev, Artem (2016). "The Invisible Russian Military Presence in Syria," *Russia Direct* (online). Available at: http://www.russia-direct.org/opinion/invisible-russian -military-presence-syria (accessed September 10, 2016).

Kuwait Syrian Holding (2018). "Home" (online). Available at: http://www.ksh.com .kw/Home (accessed January 30, 2018).

Lacroix, Stéphane (2014a). "Saudi Arabia's Muslim Brotherhood Predicament" (online), March 20. Available at: https://www.washingtonpost.com/news/monkey -cage/wp/2014/03/20/saudi-arabias-muslim-brotherhood-predicament/?utm _term=.f6474b7aaabd (accessed February 20, 2016).

Lacroix, Stéphane (2014b). "Saudi Islamists and the Arab Spring," *Kuwait Programme on Development, Governance and Globalisation in the Gulf States and London School of Economics and Political Science* (pdf), May. Avaibale at: http://eprints.lse.ac.uk /56725/1/Lacroix_Saudi-Islamists-and-theArab-Spring_2014.pdf (accessed February 20, 2016).

Landau, Noa (2018). "Netanyahu: Israel Has No Problem with Assad, but Cease-fire Agreements Must Be Upheld," *Haaretz* (online). Available at: https://www.haaretz .com/israel-news/netanyahu-israel-has-no-problem-with-assad-agreements-must -be-upheld-1.6268158 (accessed July 20, 2018).

Landay, Jonathan (2018). "Islamist militants adapted after losses: U.S. State Dept.," *Reuters* (online). Available at: https://www.reuters.com/article/us-usa-security-extrem ists/islamist-militants-adapted-after-losses-u-s-state-dept-idUSKCN1LZ28E (accessed September 20, 2018).

Lang, Tobias (2014). "Druze Sheikhs Protest in Sweida," *Carnegie* (online). Available at: http://carnegie-mec.org/diwan/55356?lang=en (accessed September 20, 2017).

Lawson, Fred H. (1982). "Social Bases for the Hama Revolt," *MERIP* (online). Available at: http://www.merip.org/mer/mer110/social-bases-hama-revolt (accessed July 20, 2013).

Lee, Carol E., and Malas, Nour (2015). "U.S. Pursued Secret Contacts with Assad Regime for Years," *Wall Street Journal* (online). Available at: http://www.wsj.com /articles/u-s-pursued-secret-contacts-with-assad-regime-for-years-1450917657 (accessed December 30, 2015).

Lefèvre, Rafael (2016). "No More 'Hama Rules'," *Carnegie* (online). Available at: http://carnegie-mec.org/diwan/64609?lang=en (accessed September 21, 2016).

Legrand, Felix (2016). "The Strategy of Jabhat Al-Nusra/Jabhat Fath Al-Sham in Regarding the Truces in Syria," *Networks of Research of International Affairs* (online). Available at: http://www.noria-research.com/strategy-regarding-truces-in-syria/ (accessed October 3, 2016).

Leverrier, Ignace (2011). "Rami Makhlouf, 'de l'affairisme à l'illusionnisme'," *Blog le Monde* (online). Available at: http://syrie.blog.lemonde.fr/2011/06/28/rami-makh louf-de-laffairisme-a-lillusionnisme/ (accessed August 28, 2011).

La Libre (2016). "Défigurée par la guerre, Alep se prépare à une reconstruction titan-esque" (online). Available at: http://www.lalibre.be/actu/international/defiguree -par-la-guerre-alep-se-prepare-a-une-reconstruction-titanesque-58637ad2cd70138bd 425834a (accessed December 30, 2016).

Lister, Charlie (2016a). "Profiling Jabhat al-Nusra," *Brookings Institution* (pdf), July. Available at: https://www.brookings.edu/wp-content/uploads/2016/07/iwr_20160728 _profiling_nusra.pdf (accessed September 9, 2016).

Lister, Charlie (2016b). "The Free Syrian Army: A decentralized insurgent brand," *Brookings Institution* (pdf), November 26. Available at: https://www.brookings .edu/wp-content/uploads/2016/11/iwr_20161123_free_syrian_army1.pdf (accessed November 30, 2016).

Lister, Charles, and McCants, Will (2014). "The Syrian Civil War: Political and Military State of Play," *War on the Rocks* (online). Available at: http://warontherocks .com/2014/02/the-syrian-civil-war-political-and-military-state-of-play/ (accessed Decmber 10, 2014).

Local Coordination Committee (LCC) (2011b). "Dignity Strike. We Make Our Revolution by Our Own Hands" (online), December 8. Available at: http://www .lccsyria.org/3796 (accessed January 11, 2012).

Local Coordination Committee (LCC) (2011c). "Dignity Strike 11-12-2011" (online), December 11. Available at: http://www.lccsyria.org/3796 (accessed January 11, 2012).

Local Coordination Committee (LCC) (2012a). "A Year to the Revolution of Freedom and Dignity" (online), March 6. Available at: http://www.lccsyria.org/7189 (ac-cessed August 30, 2012).

Local Coordination Committee (LCC) (2012c). "Revolution of Dignity and Morals "Campaign Continues," *Syria Freedom Forever* (online), August 30. Available at: https://syriafreedomforever.wordpress.com/2012/08/30/372/ (accessed August 30, 2012).

Local Coordination Committee (LCC) (2013b). "Al-jumu'a 28 huzayrân: Al-îstibdâd wâhid, siwâ` bi-îsm al-dîn âw bi-îsm al-'almânîyya," *al-Manshûr* (online), July 28. Available at: http://al-manshour.org/node/4169 (accessed July 30, 2013).

Local Council of Douma (2016). "Min nahnu" (online). Available at: http://doumalc .com/?page_id=882 (accessed June 24, 2016).

Logan, Joseph (2011). "Last U.S. Troops Leave Iraq, Ending War," *Reuters* (online). Available at: https://www.reuters.com/article/us-iraq-withdrawal/last-u-s-troops -leave-iraq-ending-war-idUSTRE7BH03320111218 (accessed June 20, 2016).

Lowe, Robert (2006). "The Syrian Kurds: A People Discovered," *Chatam House* (pdf). Available at: https://www.chathamhouse.org/sites/files/chathamhouse/public /Research/Middle%20East/bpsyriankurds.pdf (accessed June 20, 2011).

Lund, Arun (2012). "Syrian Jihadism," *Sweedish Institute of International Affairs* (pdf). Available at: http://www.ui.se/upl/files/77409.pdf (accessed December 20, 2012).

Lund, A. (2013a). "Say Hello to the Islamic Front," *Carnegie Endowment* (online). November, 22. Available at: http://carnegieendowment.org/syriaincrisis/?fa=53679 (accessed December 31, 2013).

Lund, A. (2013b). "Showdown at Bab al-Hawa," *Carnegie Endowement* (online). December 12. Available at: http://carnegieendowment.org/syriaincrisis/?fa=53896 (accessed December 20, 2013).

Lund, A. (2014a). "The Politics of the Islamic Front, Part 1: Structure and Support," *Carnegie* (online), January 14. Available at: http://carnegieendowment.org/syriain crisis/?fa=54183 (accessed January 15, 2014).

Lund, A. (2014b). "The Politics of the Islamic Front, Part 2: An Umbrella Organisation," *Carnegie* (online), January 15. Available at: http://carnegieendowment.org/syriain crisis/?fa=54204 (accessed January 16, 2014).

Lund, A. (2014c). "Syria's Ahrar al-Sham Leadership Wiped Out in Bombing," *Carnegie* (online), September 9. Available at: http://carnegieendowment.org/syriain crisis/?fa=56581 (accessed September 10, 2014).

Lund, A. (2014d). "Al-Qaeda's Bid for Power in Northwest Syria," *Carnegie* (online), November 3. Available at: http://carnegie-mec.org/diwan/57107?lang=en (accessed November 22, 2014).

Lund, A. (2015a). "What's Behind the Kurdish-Arab Clashes in East Syria?" *Carnegie* (online), January 23. Available at: http://carnegie-mec.org/diwan/58814 (accessed June 11, 2015).

Lund, A. (2015b). "Who Are the Pro-Assad Militias?" *Carnegie* (online), March 2. Available at: http://carnegie-mec.org/diwan/59215 (accessed March 20, 2015).

Lund, A. (2015c). "Opposition Intrigue Revives an Old FSA Leadership," *Carnegie* (online), July 20. Available at: http://carnegie-mec.org/diwan/60774?lang=en (accessed July 20, 2015).

Lund, A. (2015d). "Syria's Kurds at the Center of America's Anti-Jihadi Strategy," *Carnegie* (online), December 2. Available at: http://carnegieendowment.org/syriain crisis/?fa=62158 (accessed December 22, 2015).

Lund, A. (2015e). "Syria's Opposition Conferences: Results and Expectations," *Carnegie* (online), December 11. Available at: http://carnegie-mec.org/diwan/62263 ?lang=en (accessed December 13, 2015).

Lund, A. (2016a). "Assad's Other War: Winning on the Ground, Defeated by the Pound?," *Carnegie* (online), April 5. Available at: http://carnegie-mec.org/diwan /63231?lang=en (accessed April 29, 2016).

Lund, A. (2016b). "Assad's Broken Base: The Case of Idlib," *The Century Foundation* (online), July 14. Available at: https://tcf.org/content/report/assads-broken-base -case-idlib/ (accessed August 11, 2016).

Lund, A. (2016c). "A Voice from the Shadows," *Carnegie* (online), November 25. Available at: http://carnegie-mec.org/diwan/66240?lang=en (accessed December 11, 2016).

Lund, A. (2016d). "Into the Tunnels," *The Century Foundation* (online), December 21. Available at: https://tcf.org/content/report/into-the-tunnels/ (accessed February 20, 2016).

Lund, A. (2017a). "The Syrian Rebel Who Tried to Build an Islamist Paradise," *Politico* (online), March 31. Available at: http://www.politico.com/magazine/story/2017/03/the-syrian-rebel-who-built-an-islamic-paradise-214969 (accessed April 20, 2017).

Lund, A. (2017b). "Eastern Aleppo Under al-Assad," *IRIN News* (online), April 12. Available at: http://www.irinnews.org/analysis/2017/04/12/eastern-aleppo-under -al-assad (accessed April 20, 2017).

Lund, A. (2017c). "Syria: East Ghouta Turns on Itself, Again," *The Century Foundation* (online), May 1. Available at: https://tcf.org/content/commentary/syria-east-ghouta -turns/ (accessed May 10, 2017).

Lund, A. (2017d). "Aleppo Militias Become Major Test for Assad," *IRIN* (online), June 22. Available at: https://www.irinnews.org/analysis/2017/06/22/aleppo-militias -become-major-test-assad (accessed June 23, 2017).

Lund, A. (2017e). "Winter Is Coming: Who Will Rebuild Raqqa?," *IRIN News* (online), October 23. Available at: https://www.irinnews.org/analysis/2017/10 /23/winter-coming-who-will-rebuild-raqqa?utm_source=FacebookAds& utm_medium=Social&utm_campaign=RebuildingRaqqa (accessed October 23, 2017).

Lund, A. (2018a). "Assad's Divide and Conquer Strategy Is Working," *Foreign Affairs* (online), March 28. Available at: http://foreignpolicy.com/2018/03/28/assads-divide -and-conquer-strategy-is-working/ (accessed April 23, 2018).

Lund, A. (2018b). "Syrian War: Understanding Idlib's Rebel Factions," *IRIN News* (online), September 3. Available at: https://www.irinnews.org/analysis/2018/09 /03/syrian-war-understanding-idlib-s-rebel-factions (accessed September 10, 2018).

Lundi Matin (2018). "Les révolutionnaires n'ont pas d'autre choix que de s'armer" (online). Available at: https://lundi.am/Les-revolutionnaires-n-ont-pas-eu-d-autre -choix-que-de-s-armer (accessed March 1, 2018).

Lynch, Sarah N. (2017). "U.S. Officials Say Russian Inaction Enabled Syria Chemical Attack," *Reuters* (online). Available at: http://www.dailymail.co.uk/wires/reuters /article-4395576/U-S-officials-say-Russian-inaction-enabled-Syria-chemical-attack .html#ixzz4ehvYS1cT (accessed April 13, 2017).

Macfarquhar, Neil, and Saad Hwaida (2012). "As Syrian War Drags on, Jihadists Take Bigger Role," *The New York Times* (online). Available at: http://www.nytimes.com /2012/07/30/world/middleeast/as-syrian-war-drags-on-jihad-gains-foothold.html ?_r=0 (accessed August 30, 2012).

Mackey, Robert, and Samaan, Maher (2015). "Caged Hostages from Syrian President's Sect Paraded Through Rebel-Held Suburb," *The New York Times* (online). Available at: http://www.nytimes.com/2015/11/02/world/middleeast/syrian-rebels -say-caged-hostages-will-die-with-them-if-shelling-continues.html?_r=0 (accessed November 20, 2015).

Macmillan, Arthur, and Wasmi (al-), Nasser (2018). "Dr Anwar Gargash: Solving the Qatar Crisis Must Involve Tackling the 'Trust Deficit'," *The National* (online). Available at: https://www.thenational.ae/world/mena/dr-anwar-gargash-solving -the-qatar-crisis-must-involve-tackling-the-trust-deficit-1.737701 (accessed July 20, 2018).

Madan, Aman (2017). "Opinion: Oman Set to Play Big Role in Post-War Syria," *al-Bawaba* (online). Available at: https://www.albawaba.com/news/oman-original -syria-iran-russia--1063100 (accessed January 20, 2018).

Madar al-Youm (2017). "Coalition Loses Fayez Sara for Being Stiff-Necked on Reform," *The Syrian Observer* (online), January 19. Available at: http://syrianobserver .com/EN/News/32227/Coalition_Loses_Fayez_Sara_For_Being_Stiff_Necked _Reform/ (accessed January 23, 2017).

Mahmoud (-al), Hamoud (2015). "The War Economy in the Syrian Conflict: The Government's Hands-off Tactics," *Carnegie* (online). Available at: http://carnegi eendowment.org/2015/12/15/war-economy-in-syrian-conflict-government-s-hands -off-tactics-pub-62202 (accessed January 11, 2016).

Majidyar, Ahmad (2017a). "Iran Recruits and Trains Large Numbers of Afghan and Pakistani Shiites," *Middle East Institute* (online), January 18. Available at: http://www.mei.edu/content/article/iran-s-recruitment-afghan-pakistani-shiites -further-destabilizes-south-asia (accessed January 25, 2017).

Majidyar, A. (2017b). "Celebrations of Iranian Revolution Across Syria Shows Iran's Soft Power Hegemony," *Middle East Institute* (online), February 13. Available at: http://www.mei.edu/content/io/celebrations-iranian-revolution-across-syria -shows-iran-s-soft-power-hegemony (accessed February 25, 2017).

Majidyar, A. (2017c). "Rouhani Visits Moscow to Bolster Iran-Russia Ties amid Fears of U.S.-Russia Partnership," *Middle East Institute* (online), March 23. Available at: https://www.mei.edu/content/article/io/rouhani-goes-moscow-bolster-iran-russia -ties-amid-fears-us-russia-partnership (accessed March 25, 2017).

Majidyar, A. (2017d). "Iran and Turkey Discuss Ways to Cooperate in Syria and Iraq," *Middle East Institute* (online), August 16. Available at: https://www.mei.edu /content/article/io/iran-and-turkey-discuss-ways-cooperate-syria-and-iraq (accessed August 25, 2017).

Majidyar, A. (2017e). "Tehran, Ankara, and Moscow Reach Agreement over Syria's Idlib," *Middle East Institute* (online), September 15. Available at: http://www.mei .edu/content/io/tehran-ankara-and-moscow-reach-agreement-over-syria-s-idlib (accessed September 20, 2017).

Malas, Nour (2012). "Syrian Rebels Get Missiles," *Washington Street Journal* (online). Available at: https://www.wsj.com/articles/SB10000872396390443684104578062 84292967307 (accessed April 20, 2014).

Maleh (-al), Alice, and Nassar, Alaa (2018). "Raqqa's Arab Tribes Navigate 'Uneasy Calm' Under SDF Rule," *Syria Direct* (online). Available at: https:// syriadirect.org/news/raqqa's-arab-tribes-navigate-'uneasy-calm'-under-sdf-rule / (accessed November 17, 2018).

Malik, Cyrus (2016). "Washington's Sunni Myth and the Civil Wars in Syria and Iraq," *War on the Rocks* (online). Available at: http://warontherocks.com/2016/08/washingtons -sunni-myth-and-the-civil-wars-in-syria-and-iraq/ (accessed September 15, 2016).

Mamadov, Rauf (2018). "On the Agenda for US-Russia Talks: Energy," *The Hill* (online). Available at: http://thehill.com/opinion/energy-environment/394528-on -the-agenda-for-us-russia-talks-energy (accessed August 1, 2018).

Manar (Al-) (2012). "Al-Sayyîd Nasr Allâh: mutamasikun bil-silâh. wa sanathâ`ru li-mughniyya thârân mucharifân" (online). February 16. Available at: http://www.almanar.com.lb/adetails.php?eid=185439 (accessed January 13, 2013).

Manar (Al-) (2013). "Nuss khitâb al-Sayyîd Nasr Allâh fî zikra 'Ashurâ` fî mal'ab al-râiyya fî al-Dâhiyya al-janubiyya" (online), November 25. Available at: http://www.almanar.com.lb/adetails.php?eid=356806 (accessed November 3, 2014).

Marchand, Laure (2011). "L'opposition syrienne rejette l'amnistie d'Assad," *Le Figaro* (online). Available at: http://www.lefigaro.fr/international/2011/06/01/01003-2011 0601ARTFIG00668-l-opposition-syrienne-rejette-l-amnistie-d-assad.php (accessed September 20, 2012).

Mardasov, Anton (2018). "Kremlin Pressed to Legalize Private Military Companies," *al-Monitor* (online). Available at: https://www.al-monitor.com/pulse/originals/2018 /07/russia-pmc-syria-putin.html (accessed September 20, 2018).

Marks, Simon (2018). "Greece Throws Lifeline to Assad by Buying Phosphates," *Politico* (online). Available at: https://www.politico.eu/article/syria-europe-greece -throws-lifeline-bashar-al-assad-by-buying-phosphates/ (accessed August 10, 2018).

Marota City (2018a). *Facebook* (online), August 7. Available at: https://www.facebook .com/Marota.city/posts/272057506858282 (accessed August 10, 2018).

Marota City (2018b). *Facebook* (online), September 17. Available at: https://www .facebook.com/Marota.city/posts/298255254238507?__xts__[0]=68.ARDKCnsV F3MN570cou4Qc4Z51mFHiGKwzqPJcR91d5YcZSAXdaBbiomc7EnLJ6gU3 EJewV9gbl-BhFaew6MPteG8uXRHpAotINJo7lXnrF3hUoaXXKpuTCNEJxJw ywHdD61NrsEihzKvSJvbhzsj9chUKXURJe95FaMU39pKRQlA7383Wk4Y&_ _tn__=-R (accessed October 10, 2018).

Marzouq, Nabil (2011). "The Economic Origins of Syria's Uprising," *al-Akhbar English* (online). Available at: http://english.al-akhbar.com/node/372 (accessed September 30, 2011).

Mashi, Marah (2012). "People's Committees in Syria: Patrolling Local Borders," *al-Akhbar English* (online). Available at: http://english.al-akhbar.com/node/11740 (accessed December 29, 2012).

Mashi, M. (2013a). "Mazbaha wâdî al-nasâra ... înjâzât "jund al-shâm" al-jadîda," *al-Akhbar* (online), August 19. Available at: http://www.al-akhbar.com/node/189101 (accessed November 29, 2013).

Mashi, M. (2013b). "Syria: Life Slowly Returns to Devastated Qusayr," *al-Akhbar English* (online), September 11. Available at: http://english.al-akhbar.com /content/syria-life-slowly-return-devastated-qusayr (accessed December 22, 2013).

Mashi, M. (2018). "Ta'îînât" al-îdârat al-mahalîyat: îhtikâr sîyâsî wa burûdat sha'bîyat," *al-Akhbar* (online). Available at: https://al-akhbar.com/Syria/257898 (accessed September 22, 2018).

Masry (-al), Abdulrahman (2017). "Analysis: The Fifth Corps and the State of the Syrian Army," *Syria Deeply* (online), January 11. Available at: https://www.news deeply.com/syria/articles/2017/01/11/analysis-the-fifth-corps-and-the-state-of-the -syrian-army (accessed January 18, 2017).

Mateo, Nelson, and Wilcox, Orion (2017), "The day after: What happens when IS is defeated?", *Syria Direct* (online). Available at: https://syriadirect.org/news/the-day -after-what-happens-when-is-is-defeated/ (accessed January 20, 2018).

McCants, William (2013). "Gulf Charities and Syrian Sectarianism," *Foreign Policy* (online). Available at: http://foreignpolicy.com/2013/09/30/gulf-charities-and-syrian -sectarianism/ (accessed February 20, 2015).

McDowall, Angus (2016). "Hundreds of Rebels Leave Syrian Town of Mouadamiya: witnesses," *Reuters* (online). Available at: http://www.reuters.com/article/us-mideast -crisis-syria-mouadamiya-idUSKCN12J244 (accessed October 20, 2016).

McDowall, Angus (2018). "Long Reach of U.S. Sanctions Hits Syria Reconstruction," *Reuters* (online). Available at: https://www.reuters.com/article/us-mideast-crisis-syria -sanctions/long-reach-of-u-s-sanctions-hits-syria-reconstruction-idUSKCN1LI06Z (accessed September 20, 2018).

McDowall, Angus, and Stewart, Phil (2019). "Blast Claimed by Islamic State Kills U.S. Troops in Syria," *Reuters* (online). Available at: https://www.reuters.com /article/us-mideast-crisis-syria-blast/blast-claimed-by-islamic-state-kills-u-s -troops-in-syria-idUSKCN1PA1GQ (accessed January 20, 2019).

Medawar, Sami (2017). "Coopération irano-turque contre le PKK: quels enjeux?" *Orient Le Jour* (online), August 26. Available at: https://www.lorientlejour.com /article/1068505/cooperation-irano-turque-contre-le-pkk-quels-enjeux-.html (ac- cessed August 26, 2017).

MEMRI (2011). "Syrian Oppositionist Mamoun Al-Homsi: If the Alawites Do Not Renounce Bashar Al-Assad, We Will Turn Syria into Their Graveyard" (online). Available at: https://www.memri.org/reports/syrian-oppositionist-mamoun-al -homsi-if-alawites-do-not-renounce-bashar-al-assad-we-will (accessed June 20, 2013).

MEMRI (2018). "Following HTS Decision to Grant Turkey a Military Presence in Idlib, Al-Qaeda Supporters Accuse It of Abandoning Its Principles, Seeking to Ingratiate Itself with the Enemies of Islam" (online). Available at: https://www .memri.org/reports/following-hts-decision-grant-turkey-military-presence-idlib -al-qaeda-supporters-accuse-it#_edn1 (accessed July 20, 2018).

Metransparent.net (2012). "Muqtal shaykh 'aql al-drûz âhmad al-hajarî: Hadith âm îghtîyyâl" (online). Available at: http://www.metransparent.net/spip.php?article17 992&lang=ar&id_forum=28677 (accessed March 20, 2015).

Middle East Eye (2016). "Arab League Chief Says Syria's Assad Can Run for President Again" (online). Available at: http://www.middleeasteye.net/news/arab-league -chief-says-assad-can-run-president-again-blasts-turkey-iran-1793764787 (ac- cessed December 2, 2016).

Middle East Monitor (2017a). "Russia, Qatar Sign Military Cooperation Agreement" (online), October 26. Available at: https://www.middleeastmonitor.com/20171026 -russia-qatar-sign-military-cooperation-agreement/ (accessed October 27, 2017).

Middle East Monitor (2017b). "Resigned Syrian Opposition Figure: We Were Asked to Accept Assad or Leave" (online), November 22. Available at: https://www.middle eastmonitor.com/20171122-resigned-syrian-opposition-figure-we-were-asked-to -accept-assad-or-leave/ (accessed December 10, 2017).

Modon (-al) (2017). "Halab: Tazhâhurât tutâlib bi-khurûj milîshîyyât al-nizhâm" (online), July 7. Available at: http://www.almodon.com/arabworld/2017/7/7/حلب-مظاهرات-تطالب-بخروج-مليشيات-النظام-وإزالة -- (accessed July 8, 2017).

Modon (al-) (2018a). "Sayf al-hajz 'ala riqâb al-muwâlîn: Hamîshû yadafi' 8.6 milîyâr lîrat" (online), October 21. Available at: https://www.almodon.com/arabworld /2018/10/20/سيف-الحجز-على-رقاب-الموالين-حميشو-يدفع-8-8-6-مليار-لیرة (accessed October 30, 2018).

Modon (al-) (2018b). "Police in Aleppo Are Unable to Stop the Kidnapping and Killing of Children," *The Syrian Observer* (online), October 31. Available at: http:// syrianobserver.com/EN/Features/34989/Police_Aleppo_Are_Unable_Stop _Kidnapping_Killing_Children/ (accessed November 1, 2018).

Modon (al-) (2018c). "Al-îrhâb al-iqtisâdî lil-nizâm: 70 âlf hajz îhtîyâtî" (online), November 8. Available at: https://www.almodon.com/arabworld/2018/11/8/الإرهاب-الاقتصادي-للنظام-70-ألف-حجز-احتياطي (accessed November 15, 2018).

Monitor (-al) (2014). "Christians in Homs Province Fear Jihadist Advance" (online). Available at: https://www.al-monitor.com/pulse/originals/2014/09/wado-al-nasara -syria-christians-fear-is-advance.html (accessed September 15, 2014).

Monitor (-al) (2018). "After Missile Strikes, Trump Resumes Exit Strategy for Syria" (online), April 15. Available at: http://www.al-monitor.com/pulse/originals/2018 /04/trump-syria-chemical-weapons-us-withdrawal.html#ixzz5DZkSkBCq (accessed May 20, 2018).

Moscow Times (2016). "Russian Election Commission Inadvertently Reveals Russian Troop Numbers in Syria" (online). Available at: https://Themoscowtimes.Com /News/Duma-Voting-Figures-Reveal-Over-4000-Russian-Troops-In-Syria-55439 (accessed December 6, 2016).

Moutot, Michel (2019). "HTS et el-Qaëda: les liaisons dangereuses" (online). *Orient le Jour and AFP*. Available at: https://www.lorientlejour.com/article/1152635/hts-et -el-qaeda-les-liaisons-dangereuses.html (accessed January 20, 2019).

Mouzahem, Haythem (2013). "Syrian Opposition Condemns Jihadists Targeting Alawites," *Al-Monitor* (online). Available at: https://www.al-monitor.com/pulse /originals/2013/08/syria-opposition-alawite-massacres-sectarianism.html (accessed December 20, 2013).

Mroue, Bassem (2018a). "Syria Starts Rebuilding Even as More Destruction Wreaked," *ABC News* (online), February 23. Available at: https://www.voanews .com/a/syria-starts-rebuilding-even-as-more-destruction-wreaked/4270776.html (accessed March 1, 2018).

Mroue, Bassem (2018b). "Clues but No Answers in One of Syria War's Biggest Mysteries," *Associated Press* (online), August 13. Available at: https://apnews.com/a b3868ab92f84b009e4b6d9bc8bdfbb3 (accessed September 1, 2018).

Munif, Yasser (2017). "Participatory Democracy and Micropolitics in Manbij, An Unthinkable Revolution," *The Century Foundation* (online). Available at: https://tcf .org/content/report/participatory-democracy-micropolitics-manbij/ (accessed March 27, 2017).

Muqâwama (Al-) al-Islâmiyya (2011). "Maharjân hâshed li-Hizb Allâh fî al-Nabî Shît fî 'aîd al-muqâwama wa al-tahrîr 2011" (online). May 25. Available at: http://www

.moqawama.org/essaydetails.php?eid=20819&cid=141#.VHrhTN7A1ss (accessed May 23, 2012).

Muslim World League (2013). "The MWL's Statement on the Escalation of Violence in Syria, and Participation of Hezbollah and Its Allies in the Killing of Its People" (online). Available at: http://en.themwl.org/content/mwl's-statement-escalation -violence-syria-and-participation-hezbollah-and-its-allies-killing (accessed February 20, 2014).

Mustafa, Hazem (2018). "Disbanding Iranian Militias on the Syrian Coast," *Syria Untold* (online). Available at: http://syriauntold.com/2018/10/ndf/ (accessed October 24, 2018).

Mustapha, Hassan (2015). "An Analysis of Jaish al-Thuwar (The Army of Revolutionaries)—a component of the Syrian Democratic Forces" (online). Available at: https://hasanmustafas.wordpress.com/2015/11/16/an-analysis-of-jaish-al-thuwar -the-army-of-revolutionaries-a-component-of-the-syrian-democratic-forces/ (accessed November 20, 2015).

Naharnet (2013). "Turkey Warns Syrian Kurd Leader Against Autonomy Plans" (online), July 27. Available at: http://www.naharnet.com/stories/92119-turkey -warns-syrian-kurd-leader-against-autonomy-plans/print (accessed February 24, 2014).

Nakhoul, Samia (2013). "Special Report: Hezbollah Gambles All in Syria," *Reuters* (online). Available at: http://www.reuters.com/article/2013/09/26/us-syria-hezb llah-special-report-idUSBRE98P0AI20130926 (accessed November 5, 2014).

Nashashibi, Sharif (2016). "Economics Trump Politics in Syria's Proxy War," *Syria Deeply* (online). Available at: https://www.newsdeeply.com/syria/community /2016/07/19/economics-trump-politics-in-syrias-proxy-war (accessed August 3, 2016).

Nassar, Alaa, Nelson, Maria, and al-Zarier, Bahira (2017). "Bus Bombing Rocks Alawite District in Homs City," *Syria Direct* (online). Available at: http://syriadirect .org/news/bus-bombing-rocks-alawite-district-in-homs-city/ (accessed January 10, 2018).

Nassar Alaa, and Wilcox Orion (2016). "US-Backed SDF Reportedly Opens Fire on Protestors, 1 Killed," *Syria Direct* (online). Available at: http://syriadirect.org/news /us-backed-sdf-reportedly-opens-fire-on-protestors-1-killed/ (accessed April 29, 2016).

Nasser, Rabie, and Mehchy Zaki (2012). "Role of Economic Factors in Political Movement: The Syrian Case," *The Economic Research Forum*, working paper 698 (pdf). Available at: http://erf.org.eg/wp-content/uploads/2014/08/698.pdf (accessed November 20, 2017).

Nebehay, Stephanie (2018). "U.N. Says It Has Credible Reports That China Holds Million Uighurs in Secret Camps," *Reuters* (online). Available at: https://www .reuters.com/article/us-china-rights-un/u-n-says-it-has-credible-reports-that-china -holds-million-uighurs-in-secret-camps-idUSKBN1KV1SU (accessed December 20, 2018).

The New Arab (2016a). "US Scrambles Jets to Protect Advisers in Syria: Pentagon," *Al-Araby* (online), August 20. Available at: https://www.alaraby.co.uk/english /news/2016/8/20/us-scrambles-jets-to-protect-advisers-in-syria-pentagon?utm _campaign=magnet&utm_source=article_page&utm_medium=related_articles (accessed August 20, 2016).

The New Arab (2016b). "Syrian Foreign Minister: 'Fighting IS not Our Prime Concern'," *Al-Araby* (online), September 1. Available at: https://www.alaraby.co.uk /english/news/2016/9/1/syrian-foreign-minister-fighting-is-not-our-prime-concern (accessed September 2, 2016).

The New Arab (2016c). "Tartous to Become Russia's Permanent Syria Naval Base," *al-Araby* (online), October 7. Available at: https://www.alaraby.co.uk/english/news /2016/10/7/russia-permanent-syria-military-presence-eyes-on-cuba-vietnam (accessed November 10, 2016).

The New Arab (2018a). "Iran to Recover War Losses by Exploiting Syria Natural Resources, Says Top Military Adviser" (online), February 19. Available at: https://www.alaraby.co.uk/english/news/2018/2/19/iran-to-recover-war-losses-by -exploiting-syrias-resources (accessed February 25, 2018).

The New Arab (2018b). "Russia Says It Has 'Tested' More Than 200 New Weapons in Syria" (online), February 22. Available at: https://www.alaraby.co.uk/english/News /2018/2/22/Russia-says-it-tested-over-200-weapons-in-Syria (accessed March 1, 2018).

The New Arab (2019). "Assad's Notorious Chief Security Adviser 'Visited Riyadh' to Discuss Syria-Saudi Rapprochement" (online). Available at: https://www.alaraby .co.uk/english/news/2019/1/9/assad-adviser-visited-riyadh-to-discuss-syria-saudi -rapprochement (accessed February 1, 2019).

The New York Times (2011). "In Syria, Crackdown After Protests" (online). Available at http://www.nytimes.com/2011/03/19/world/middleeast/19syria.html?_r=0. (accessed June 26, 2011).

Notte, Hanna (2017). "Russia's Role in the Syrian War–Domestic Drivers and Regional Implications," *Konrad Adenauer Stiftung* (pdf). Available at: http://www .kas.de/wf/doc/kas_47817-1522-2-30.pdf?170202155755 (accessed February 2, 2017).

Noufal, W. Khaled, and Wilcox O. (2016a). "Suwayda Protesters Remove Hafez al-Assad's Portrait, Call for Fall of Bashar," *Syria Direct* (online), April 17. Available at: http://syriadirect.org/news/suwayda-protesters-remove-hafez-al-assad's-portrait -call-for-fall-of-bashar (accessed April 20, 2016).

Noufal, W. Khaled, and Wilcox O. (2016b). "Sectarianism, Suicide Bombers, and Retaliation Along the Coast: 'The Monstrous Way This Hatred Can Manifest Itself," *Syria Direct* (online), May 23. Available at: http://syriadirect.org/news /sectarianism-suicide-bombers-and-retaliation-along-the-coast-'the-monstrous -way-this-hatred-can-manifest-itself'/ (accessed June 20, 2016).

Noureddine, Mohamed (2016). "PKK Foreign Relations Head Speaks Out," *al-Monitor* (online). Available at: http://www.al-monitor.com/pulse/politics/2016/07 /turkey-coup-pkk-kurds-rojava-us-intervention.html (accessed December 20, 2016).

Now (2016). "Syria Regime Establishing 'Tourism Security' Company" (online). Available at: https://now.mmedia.me/lb/en/NewsReports/567243-syria-regime-estab lishing-tourism-security-company (accessed August 30, 2016).

Oakford, Samuel (2017). "More than 1,800 Civilians Killed Overall in Defeat of ISIS at Raqqa, Say Monitors," *Airwars* (online). Available at: https://airwars.org/news /raqqa-capture/ (accessed October 22, 2017).

O'Bagy, Elizabeth (2012a). "Syria's Political Opposition," *Institute for the Study of War* (pdf) April. Available at: http://www.understandingwar.org/sites/default/files/Syrias _Political_Opposition.pdf (accessed November 11, 2012).

O'Bagy, E. (2012b). "Jihad in Syria," *Understanding War Institute* (pdf), September. Available at: http://www.understandingwar.org/sites/default/files/Jihad-In-Syria -17SEPT.pdf (accessed November 20, 2012).

O'Bagy, E. (2013). "The Free Syrian Army," *Institute for the Study of War* (pdf). Available at: http://www.understandingwar.org/sites/default/files/The-Free-Syrian -Army-24MAR.pdf (accessed February 14, 2014).

Omran for Strategic Studies (2016). "Dawr al-majâlis al-mahalîya fî marhala al-hâlîya wa al-întiqâlîya: qirâ`t tahlîlîya fî natâ`ij îstitalâ' râ`i" (pdf). Available at: https:// www.omrandirasat.org/الأبحاث-أوراق-بحثية-دور-المجالس-المحلية-في-المرحلة-الحالية-والانتقالية-قراءة/ تحليلية-في-نتائج-استطلاع-رأي.html (accessed March 29, 2017).

Orient le Jour (2011a). "La presse syrienne salue 'le retour bienvenu' du Caire" (online), February 13. Available at: http://www.lorientlejour.com/article/689082/La_presse _syrienne_salue_%22le_retour_bienvenu%22_du_Caire.html (accessed February 14, 2016).

Orient le Jour (2011b). "Plusieurs mesures adoptées pour désamorcer un éventuel soulèvement" (online), March 9. Available at: http://www.lorientlejour.com/article /692767/Plusieurs_mesures_adoptees_pour_desamorcer_un_eventuel_soulev ement.html (accessed March 10, 2011).

Orient le Jour (2011c). "La contestation s'étend dans le Sud syrien" (online). March 22. Available at: http://www.lorientlejour.com/article/695752/La_contestation_s%27et end_dans_le_Sud_syrien_.html (accessed March 23, 2011).

Orient le Jour (2011d). "Face à la révolte, Assad lâche du lest" (online). March 25. Available at: http://www.lorientlejour.com/article/696497/Face_a_la_revolte%2C __Assad_lache_du_lest_.html (accessed March 26, 2011).

Orient le Jour (2011e). "Assad fait un geste envers les Kurdes" (online). April 8. Available at: http://www.lorientlejour.com/article/698857/Assad_fait_un_geste_envers_les _Kurdes.html (accessed April 10, 2011).

Orient le Jour (2018). "Tripoli doit jouer un rôle important dans la reconstruction de la Syrie, selon la députée Jamali" (online). Available at: https://www.lorientlejour .com/article/1128549/tripoli-et-la-reconstruction-de-la-syrie-selon-la-deputee -jamali.html (accessed October 1, 2018).

Orient News (2015). "Bi-sayf 'fârsî': 'al-sanâdîd' âwal milîshîyyâ 'ashâ`irîyya li-dhabih al-sûrîyyîn" (online). Available at: http://orient-news.net/ar/news_show/85587/0/بسيف فارسي22%--الصناديد22%-%22أول-مليشيا-عشائرية-لذبح (accessed December 20, 2016).

Orient News (2016). *Shâhid … al-âwal mara fî sûrîyyâ al-'askar yakhsarûn al-întikhâbât bi-rahâba sadr wa al-dîmuqrâtîyya fafûz fî al-ghûta—hunâ sûrîyya, YouTube Video.* Available at: https://www.youtube.com/watch?v=YEIK1wpOUfM (accessed February 20, 2016).

Orton, Kyle (2016). "The 'Syrian Kurds' Helped Assad Take Aleppo City," *The Syrian Intifada* (online). Available at: https://kyleorton1991.wordpress.com/2016/11/30 /the-syrian-kurds-helped-assad-take-aleppo-city/ (accessed January 10, 2017).

Orton, K. (2017). "The Coalition's Partner in Syria: The Syrian Democratic Forces," *The Syrian Intifada* (online). Available at: https://kyleorton1991.wordpress.com

/2017/07/09/the-coalitions-partner-in-syria-the-syrian-democratic-forces/#more
-4002 (accessed July 9, 2017).

Osborn, Andrew, and Tattersall, Nick (2016). "Putin and Erdogan Push for Syria Talks Without U.S. or U.N.," *Reuters* (online). Available at: http://www.reuters .com/article/us-mideast-crisis-syria-putin-truce-idUSKBN1450NQ (accessed December 20, 2016).

Osman, Tamer (2017). "Manbij Residents Face off Against SDF over Conscription Policy," *al-Monitor* (online). Available at: http://www.al-monitor.com/pulse/origi nals/2017/11/syria-democratic-forces-forced-conscription-manbij.html#ixzz55J2w sMJ9 (accessed November 30, 2017).

Osseiran, Hashem (2018). "US Pull-out Exposes Oil and Gas Fields in Syria's East to Government Control," *The National* (online). Available at: https://www.thenational .ae/world/mena/us-pull-out-exposes-oil-and-gas-fields-in-syria-s-east-to -government-control-1.804568 (accessed December 30, 2018).

Othman Agha, Munqeth (2018). "Class and Exclusion in Syria," *Rosa Luxemburg Stiftung* (online). Available at: https://www.rosalux.de/en/publication/id/39119/class -and-exclusion-in-syria/ (accessed August 20, 2018).

Oudat (2018). "Russia's Syrian Army," *al-Ahram* (online). Available at: http://english .ahram.org.eg/NewsContent/2/8/308244/World/Region/Russia's-Syrian-army .aspx (accessed September 20, 2018).

Oweis, Khaled Yacoub (2013a). "Syrian Rebel Sheikh Calls for War on Assad's Alawite Heartland," *Reuters* (online), July 10. Available at: https://www.reuters .com/article/us-syria-crisis-coast/syrian-rebel-sheikh-calls-for-war-on-assads -alawite-heartland-idUSBRE9690PU20130710 (accessed September 20, 2013).

Oweis, Khaled Yacoub (2013b). "Insight: Saudi Arabia Boosts Salafist Rivals to al-Qaeda in Syria," *Reuters* (online), October 1. Available at: https://www.reuters .com/article/us-syria-crisis-jihadists-insight/insight-saudi-arabia-boosts-salafist -rivals-to-al-qaeda-in-syria-idUSBRE9900RO20131001 (accessed December 19, 2013).

Oweis, Khaled Yacoub (2014). "Struggling to Build an Alternative to Assad," *Stiftung Wissenschaft und Politik* (pdf). Available at: https://www.swp-berlin.org /fileadmin/contents/products/comments/2014C35_ows.pdf (accessed January 26, 2015).

Oweis, K. Y. (2016). "The Military Topography of Syria's South," *Stiftung Wissenschaft und Politik* (pdf), December. Available at: https://www.swp-berlin.org/fileadmin /contents/products/comments/2016C56_ows.pdf (accessed February 2, 2017).

People's Council of Western Kurdistan (PCWK) (2011). "The Declaration of the People's Council in Western Kurdistan," *Peace in Kurdistan* (online). Available at: https://peaceinkurdistancampaign.com/2012/01/04/the-declaration-of-the -peoples-council-in-western-kurdistan/ (accessed December 10, 2012).

Perrin, Jean Pierre (2008). "Damas remet l'opposition à l'ombre," *Libération* (online). Available at: http://www.liberation.fr/monde/0101165847-damas-remet-l-oppo sition-a-l-ombre (accessed June 30, 2011).

Perry, Tom (2016). "Federal Plan for Northern Syria Advances with U.S.-Backed Forces," *Reuters* (online). Available at: http://www.reuters.com/article/us-mideast -crisis-syria-federalism-idUSKCN0Z21FN (accessed June 26, 2016).

Perry, T. (2017). "Death Toll from Damascus Bombing Climbs to 74: Observatory," *Reuters* (online), March 12. Available at: http://www.reuters.com/article/us-mideast -crisis-syria-idUSKBN16J0AN (accessed March 16, 2017).

Perry, Tom, and Said, Rody (2016). "Syria Kurds Win Battle with Government, Turkey Mobilizes Against Them," *Reuters* (online). Available at: http://www.reuters .com/article/us-mideast-crisis-syria-kurds-idUSKCN10Y127 (accessed August 24, 2016).

Peterson, Scott (2011). "Syrian Opposition Forms Unity Council, Hoping to Continue Arab Spring," *Christian Science Monitor*. Available at: https://www.csmonitor.com /World/Middle-East/2011/1004/Syrian-opposition-forms-unity-council-hoping -to-continue-Arab-Spring (accessed July 19, 2012).

Pierret, T. (2013). "Implementing 'Sharia' in Syria's Liberated Provinces," *The Foundation for Law, Justice, and Society* (online). August 7. Available at: http://www .fljs.org/implementing-sharia-in-syria (accessed October 30, 2014).

Pierret, T. (2014). "The Syrian Baath Party and Sunni Islam: Conflicts and Connivance," *Brandeis University*, No.77 (pdf) February. Available at: https://www .brandeis.edu/crown/publications/meb/MEB77.pdf (accessed January 30, 2015).

Pizzi, Michael, and Shabaan, Nuha (2013). "Under Sectarian Surface, Sunni Backing Props up Assad Regime" (online). Available at: http://syriadirect.org/news/under -sectarian-surface-sunni-backing-props-up-assad-regime/ (accessed December 27, 2013).

Porat, Liad (2010). "The Syrian Muslim Brotherhood and the Asad Regime," *Brandeis University* (pdf). Available at: http://www.brandeis.edu/crown/publications/meb /MEB47.pdf (accessed February 10, 2011).

Porter, Tom (2017). "A Brief History of Terror in Saudi Arabia," *Newsweek* (online). Available at: http://www.newsweek.com/saudi-terror-isis-al-qaeda-628813 (accessed February 20, 2018).

Prettitore, Paul (2016). "Will Forcibly Displaced Syrians Get Their Land Back?" *Brookings* (online). Available at: https://www.brookings.edu/blog/future-develo pment/2016/07/21/will-forcibly-displaced-syrians-get-their-land-back/ (accessed December 20, 2017).

Putz, Ulrike (2012). "Christians Flee from Radical Rebels in Syria," *Der Spiegel* (online). Available at: http://www.spiegel.de/international/world/christians-flee -from-radical-rebels-in-syria-a-846180.html (accessed June 30, 2013).

Qanso, Wafiq (2018). "Al-îmârât turîd îsti`nâf al-'ilâqât ma' dimashq," *al-Akhbar* (online). Available at: https://www.al-akhbar.com/Syria/257980/الامارات-تريد-استئناف العلاقات-مع-دمشق- (accessed September 20, 2018).

Radio Rozana (2014). "Kîlû: lâ taqâranû "jabhat al-nusra" bi-"dâ'esh"," *An-Nahar* (online). Available at: https://www.annahar.com/article/97968-كيلو-لا-تقارنوا-جبهة النصرة-- (accessed March 20, 2015).

Rainey, Jonathan (2015). "Why Is Russia in Syria? The Historical Context of Russia's Intervention," *The School of Russian and Asian Studies* (online). Available at: https:// geohistory.today/russia-syria-history/ (accessed January 10, 2016).

Ray al-Yawm (2017). "Wafd masrî niqâbî fî dimashq" (online). Available at: http://www .raialyoum.com/?p=606807 (accessed December 23, 2017).

Reuters (2012a). "Saudi Top Cleric Blasts Arab, Egypt Protests—Paper" (online), February 5. Available at: http://www.reuters.com/article/egypt-saudi-idAFLDE 71403F20110205 (accessed February 20, 2012).

Reuters (2012b). "U.S. Defense Chief: Syria Military Must Remain Intact When Assad Goes" (online). July 31. Available at: http://www.reuters.com/article/us-syria -crisis-usa/u-s-defense-chief-syria-military-must-remain-intact-when-assad-goes -idUSBRE86T1KP20120730 (accessed August 3, 2013).

Reuters (2012c). "Minority Militias Stir Fears of Sectarian War in Damascus" (online), September 7. Available at: http://www.reuters.com/article/syria-crisis-militias /insight-minority-militias-stir-fears-of-sectarian-war-in-damascus-idUSL6E8K61 HT20120907 (accessed December 29, 2012).

Reuters (2012d). "Fearful Alawites Pay Sectarian Militias in Battered Homs" (online), September 25. Available at: http://www.reuters.com/article/syria-shabbiha-extortion -idUSL5E8KP4AZ20120925 (accessed July 12, 2013).

Reuters (2013). "Syrian Opposition Chooses Saudi-Backed Leader" (online). Available at: http://news.trust.org//item/20130706162516-fjpcv/ (accessed December 22, 2013).

Reuters (2014). "U.S. Opposes Supply of Shoulder-Fired Missiles to Syria Rebels" (online). Available at: http://www.reuters.com/article/us-syria-crisis-usa-missiles -idUSBREA1H0YI20140218 (accessed February 23, 2014).

Reuters (2016). "Russia, Iran, Turkey Say Ready to Broker Syria Deal" (online), December 20. Available at: http://www.reuters.com/video/2016/12/20/russia-iran -turkey-say-ready-to-broker-s?videoId=370761107&videoChannel=-13668 (accessed December 20, 2016).

Reuters (2017a). "Dozens Killed in Double Suicide Attack in Syrian Capital" (online), March 15. Available at: http://www.reuters.com/article/us-mideast-crisis-syria-blast -idUSKBN16M1J0 (accessed March 16, 2017).

Reuters (2017b). "Al Qaeda Chief Urges Jihadists to Use Guerrilla Tactics in Syria" (online), April 23. Available at: http://www.reuters.com/article/us-mideast-crisis -qaeda-syria-idUSKBN17P0WI (accessed April 23, 2017).

Reuters (2017c). "Turkey Warns on Syrian Kurdish Militia, Welcomes U.S. Weapons Pledge" (online), June 23. Available at: http://www.reuters.com/article/us-mideast -crisis-syria-turkey-idUSKBN19E0QJ (accessed June 23, 2017).

Reuters (2017d). "Damascus Says Syrian Kurdish Autonomy Negotiable: Report" (online), September 26. Available at: http://www.reuters.com/article/us-mideast -crisis-syria-kurds/damascus-says-syrian-kurdish-autonomy-negotiable-report -idUSKCN1C10TJ (accessed September 27, 2017).

Reuters (2017e). "Syria Producing More Energy After Army Recaptures Gas Fields— Ministry" (online), September 27. Available at: http://www.reuters.com/article/us -mideast-crisis-syria-electricity/syria-producing-more-energy-after-army-recaptures -gas-fields-ministry-idUSKCN1C12JY (accessed September 27, 2017).

Reuters (2017f). "YPG Fighters Credit Ocalan with Syria Victory" (online), October 23. Available at: https://www.reuters.com/article/us-mideast-crisis-syria -raqqa/ypg-fighters-credit-ocalan-with-syria-victory-idUSKBN1CS1J7 (accessed October 23, 2017).

Reuters (2017g). "Islamic State Killed More than 60, Dozens Missing in Syrian Town: Governor" (online), October 23. Available at: https://www.reuters.com/article/us -mideast-crisis-syria-town/islamic-state-killed-more-than-60-dozens-missing-in -syrian-town-governor-idUSKBN1CS0VD?il=0 (accessed October 23, 2017).

Reuters (2018). "Russia: U.S. Strikes Remove Moral Hurdles for S-300 Missiles for Assad—RIA" (online). Available at: https://www.reuters.com/article/us-mideast -crisis-syria-russia-lavrov/russia-u-s-strikes-remove-moral-hurdles-for-s-300 -missiles-for-assad-ria-idUSKBN1HR0LY (accessed September 20, 2018).

Reuters Staff (2012). "Syria Opposition Chiefs at Odds over Military Body" (online). Available at: https://www.reuters.com/article/us-syria-opposition/syria-opposition -chiefs-at-odds-over-military-body-idUSTRE8200SA20120301 (accessed April 20, 2012).

Reuters Staff (2013). "Insight: Battered by War, Syrian Army Creates Its Own Replacement" (online). Available at: https://www.reuters.com/article/us-syria-crisis -paramilitary-insight/insight-battered-by-war-syrian-army-creates-its-own-replace ment-idUSBRE93K02R20130421 (accessed April 20, 2014).

Reuters Staff (2018a). "Qatar Airways Plans to Buy Stake in Russian Airport as Emir Visits Moscow" (online), March 26. Available at: https://www.reuters.com/article /us-russia-qatar-airport/qatar-airways-plans-to-buy-stake-in-russian-airport-as -emir-visits-moscow-idUSKBN1H211O (accessed April 20, 2018).

Reuters Staff (2018b). "We Can't Force Iran out of Syria, Russia Tells Israelis" (online), July 30. Available at: https://www.reuters.com/article/us-mideast-crisis-syria-israel -russia/we-cant-force-iran-out-of-syria-russia-tells-israelis-idUSKBN1KK29O (accessed August 1, 2018).

Ri'âsa majlis al-wizarâ` (2015). "Al-qarâr raqm /3592/ li'âm 2015 al-mutadamin îhdâth a l- m a j l i s al-sûrî l il- ma' â di n wa al-salb" (online). Available at: http://www .pministry.gov.sy/contents/12510/القرار-رقم-/3592/-لعام-2015-المتضمن-إحداث-المجلس-السوري -للمعادن-- (accessed January 20, 2016).

Rollins, Tom (2016). "Unrest Grows Among Druze in Syria's Sweida," *Syria News Deeply* (online). Available at: https://www.newsdeeply.com/syria/articles/2016 /09/01/unrest-grows-among-druze-in-syrias-sweida (accessed September 20, 2016).

Rollins, T. (2017). "Decree 66: The Blueprint for al-Assad's Reconstruction of Syria?," *IRIN News* (online). Available at: https://www.irinnews.org/investigations/2017/04 /20/decree-66-blueprint-al-assad's-reconstruction-syria (accessed May 20, 2017).

Rollins, Tom (2019). "In Downtown Beirut, Signs of the Coming Cost of Syria's Reconstruction Plans," *Syria Direct* (online). Available at: https://syriadirect.org /news/in-downtown-beirut-signs-of-the-coming-cost-of-syria's-reconstruction -plans/ (accessed March 7, 2019).

Rose, Sunniva (2018). "Syria's New Religious Bill Angers Assad Loyalists," *The National* (online). Available at: https://www.thenational.ae/world/mena/syria-s-new -religious-bill-angers-assad-loyalists-1.777378 (accessed October 20, 2018).

Rosen, Nir (2012). "Islamism and the Syrian Uprising," *Foreign Policy* (online). Available at: http://foreignpolicy.com/2012/03/08/islamism-and-the-syrian-uprising/ (accessed March 20, 2013).

Rudaw (2015). "Moscow Pledges Help to Syrian Kurds, but Through Assad Government" (online). Available at: http://rudaw.net/NewsDetails.aspx?pageid=181385 (accessed December 23, 2015).

Rudaw (2016). "Kurds and Damascus Meet over Tensions, Future of Rojava" (online), December 29. Available at: http://rudaw.net/english/middleeast/syria/29122016 (accessed December 29, 2016).

Rudaw (2017a). "Turkish Official Says Afrin in Rojava Should Be Cleared of YPG" (online), July 29. Available at: http://www.rudaw.net/english/middleeast/turkey /29062017 (accessed July 29, 2017).

Rudaw (2017b). "Kurds Allied with US Are 'Traitors,' Says Assad" (online), December 18. Available at: http://www.rudaw.net/english/middleeast/syria/1812 20171 (accessed December 18, 2017).

Rudaw (2018a). "Mattis: Turkey Gave United States Advance Warning of Afrin Operation" (online), January 22. Available at: http://www.rudaw.net/english/middle east/syria/220120181 (accessed January 30, 2018).

Rudaw (2018b). "KNC Not Invited to Sochi for Calling on Kurdish Cause to Be Part of Agenda, Official" (online), January 28. Available at: http://www.rudaw.net /english/middleeast/syria/280120183 (accessed January 30, 2018).

Rudaw (2018c). "Syrian Rebels Allege Kurd-Assad Alliance to Justify Afrin Operation" (online), January 31. Available at: http://www.rudaw.net/english /middleeast/syria/300120183 (accessed February 1, 2018).

Rudaw (2019). "PKK Is 'Enemy' of Syria Revolution, Says Jihadist Leader" (online). Available at: http://www.rudaw.net/english/middleeast/syria/140120195 (accessed January 20, 2019).

Saadi (al-), Salam (2015a). "Iran's Stakes in Syria's Economy," *Carnegie* (online), June 2. Available at: http://carnegieendowment.org/sada/2015/06/02/iran-s-stakes-in-syria -s-economy/ (accessed December 10, 2015).

Saadi (al-), S. (2015b). "Russia's Long-Term Aims in Syria," *Carnegie* (online), October 6. Available at: http://carnegieendowment.org/sada/61521 (accessed November 19, 2015).

Sabbagh, Hazem (2016a). "Higher Judicial Committee for Elections Announces Results of People's Assembly Elections," Syrian Arab News Agency (SANA) (online), January 10. Available at: https://sana.sy/en/?p=74769 (accessed February 15, 2016).

Sabbagh, Hazem (2016b). "Civil Democratic Gathering of Syrian Kurds Marks Newroz and Mother's Day," Syrian Arab News Agency (SANA) (online), March 20. Available at: https://sana.sy/en/?p=32827 (accessed December 16, 2015).

Sabbagh, Hazem (2016c). "President al-Assad Issues Law on Public-Private Partnership," Syrian Arab News Agency (SANA) (online), April 16. Available at: https://sana.sy/en/?p=66150 (accessed April 20, 2016).

Sabbagh, Hazem (2017). "Stages of Implementation of al-Razi Regulation Project Area Discussed," Syrian Arab News Agency (SANA) (online). Available at: https://sana.sy/en/?p=121555 (accessed December 30, 2017).

Sabbagh, Hazem (2018). "Decree Exempting Martyrs and Injured People with Full Disability from Debts for Low-Income Loans," Syrian Arab News Agency

(SANA) (online), September 1. Available at: https://sana.sy/en/?p=125954 (accessed September 31, 2018).

Sabbagh, Rand (2013). "Attitudes of Christians in the Capital (Damascus 2013)," in Stolleis F. (ed.), *Playing the Sectarian Card Identities and Affiliations of Local Communities in Syria* (Friedrich Ebert Stiftung), pp. 71–89 (pdf). Available at: http://library.fes.de/pdf-files/bueros/beirut/12320.pdf (accessed September 12, 2015).

Sada al-Sham (2017). "Aleppans on the Syrian Coast: We Want to Return to Our City," *The Syrian Observer* (online). Available at: http://syrianobserver.com/EN/Features/32176/Aleppans_the_Syrian_Coast_We_Want_Return_Our_City/ (accessed January 10, 2017).

Sada al-Sham (2018). "'Unofficial' Cooperation Between Regime and Opposition at Commercial Crossings," *The Syrian Observer* (online). Available at: http://syrianobserver.com/EN/Features/33946/Unofficial_Cooperation_Between_Regime_Opposition_Commercial_Crossings (accessed March 20, 2018).

Sadaki, Yousssef (2016). "The Siege Economy of Eastern Ghouta," *Atlantic Council* (online). Available at: https://www.atlanticcouncil.org/blogs/syriasource/the-siege-economy-of-eastern-ghouta (accessed November 29, 2016).

Sahibat al-Jalala (2018). "Mustathmir mûl qâsîûn ra`isân li-ghurfat tijâra rîf dimashq" (online). Available at: https://majestynews.com/?p=41327#.WrF5FyOob_Q (accessed March 20, 2018).

Said, Hani (2016). "4 milîyârât dûlâr wa âshîyyâ` ûkhra: al-dawr al-sa'ûdî al-kbîr fî îjhâd al-thawra al-sûrîyya," *al-Ghad News* (online). Available at: http://www.elghad.co/arabic/news-212244#.WFOi9WbbcVh.twitter (accessed December 15, 2016).

Said, Rodi (2016). "Syria's Kurds Rebuked for Seeking Autonomous Region," *Reuters* (online). Available at: https://www.reuters.com/article/us-mideast-crisis-syria-federalism/syrias-kurds-rebuked-for-seeking-autonomous-region-idUSKCN0WJ1EP (accessed March 20, 2017).

Said, Yasser Nadim (2012). "Muqâraba thanâìyya (sunnî–'alawî) fî al-thawra al-sûrîyya: kayf wasalnâ îla al-majâzir al-hâlîyya," *al-Jumhuriya* (online). Available at: https://www.aljumhuriya.net/ar/131 (accessed March 20, 2012).

Salam, Tamam (2016). "Al-îhtikâr yûllad sirâ'ân 'ala nahesh al-lahem al-sûrî," *al-Araby* (online). Available at: https://www.alaraby.co.uk/supplementeconomy/2016/8/28/الاحتكار-يولد-صراعا-على-نهش-اللحم-ا (March 20, 2017).

Saleeby, Suzanne (2012). "Sowing the Seeds of Dissent: Economic Grievances and the Syrian Social Contract's Unraveling," *Jadaliyya* (online). Available at: http://www.jadaliyya.com/pages/index/4383/sowing-the-seeds-of-dissent_economic-grievances-an (accessed February 26, 2012).

Saleh (al-), Mahmoud (2018). "Surûr: 3500 manzil fî al-tadâmun sâlihat lil-sakan," *Al-Watan Online* (online). Available at: http://www.alwatanonline.com/?p=90933&fbclid=IwAR39tmKPDGIS2Kinj6DN6LJtZbigRgrFaFQwSHTGwpPw-WSrmtHyj_Cy9LI (accessed November 13, 2018).

Samaha, Nour (2016). "The Black Market Kings of Damascus," *Atlantic Council* (online). Available at: http://www.theatlantic.com/international/archive/2016/10/syria-war-economy-damascus-assad/502304/?utm_source=atltw (accessed October 15, 2016).

Samaha, N. (2017a). "Survival Is Syria's Strategy," *The Century Foundation* (online), February 8. Available at: https://tcf.org/content/report/survival-syrias-strategy/ (accessed May 20, 2017).

Samaha, N. (2017b). "How These Syrians Went from Opposition Fighters to Pro-regime Militiamen," *al-Monitor* (online), April 3. Available at: http://www.al-monitor.com/pulse/originals/2017/04/syria-south-opposition-defection-army-israel.html#ixzz5bUnsMzTU (accessed December 20, 2017).

Samaha, N. (2017c). "Long Read: Elites, War Profiteers Take Aim at Syria's Economic Future," *Syria Deeply* (online), September 18. Available at: https://www.newsdeeply.com/syria/articles/2017/09/18/long-read-elites-war-profiteers-take-aim-at-syrias-economic-future (accessed September 20, 2017).

Sarâj al-Dîn, Mû`min (2015). "Al-Nusra wa îkhwâtihâ, wa al-hurrîyya!!" *Sûrîyyatî* (online). Available at: http://www.souriyati.com/2015/09/21/22078.html (accessed November 30, 2015).

Sary, Ghadi (2016). "Kurdish Self-Governance in Syria: Survival and Ambition" *Chatam House, The Royal Institute of International Affairs* (pdf). Available at: https://www.chathamhouse.org/sites/files/chathamhouse/publications/research/2016-09-15-kurdish-self-governance-syria-sary_0.pdf (accessed October 10, 2016).

Saul, Jonathan (2013). "Exclusive—Assad Allies Profit from Syria's Lucrative Food Trade," *Reuters* (online). Available at: http://uk.reuters.com/article/uk-syria-food-idUKBRE9AD0U920131114 (accessed November 20, 2013).

Saul, J. (2014). "Exclusive: Russia Steps up Military Lifeline to Syria's Assad—Sources," *Reuters* (online). Available at: http://www.reuters.com/article/us-syria-russia-arms-idUSBREA0G0MN20140117 (accessed December 20, 2014).

Savage, Charlie (2018). "U.S. Says Troops Can Stay in Syria Without New Authorization," *The New York Times* (online). Available at: https://www.nytimes.com/2018/02/22/us/politics/isis-syria-american-troops.html (accessed February 25, 2018).

Sayigh, Yezid (2013). "The Syrian Opposition's Leadership Problem," *Carnegie* (online). Available at: http://carnegie-mec.org/2013/04/03/syrian-opposition-s-leadership-problem-pub-51373 (accessed June 20, 2013).

Sawah, Wael (2012). "Syrian Civil Society Scene Prior to Syrian Revolution" *HIVOS and Knowledge Programme Civil society in West Asia* (pdf). Available at: https://hivos.org/sites/default/files/publications/wp_21_wael_sawah_final.pdf (accessed December 21, 2012).

Schneider, Tobias (2016). "The Decay of the Syrian Regime Is Much Worse Than You Think," *War on the Rocks* (online). Available at: http://warontherocks.com/2016/08/the-decay-of-the-syrian-regime-is-much-worse-than-you-think/ (accessed September 3, 2016).

Schneider, T. (2017). "Aleppo's Warlords and Post-War Reconstruction," *Middle East Institute* (online). Available at: http://www.mei.edu/content/article/growing-warlordism-battle-scarred-aleppo (accessed June 17, 2017).

SDF General Command (2017). "SDF: We Will Not Stay Silent on Russian Attacks," *YPG Rojava* (online). Available at: http://www.ypgrojava.org/SDF%3A-We-will-not-stay-silent-on-Russian-attacks (accessed September 25, 2017).

Semenov (2017). "The Syrian Armed Forces Seven Years into the Conflict: From a Regular Army to Volunteer Corps," *Russian International Affairs Council* (online). Available at: http://russiancouncil.ru/en/analytics-and-comments/analytics/the -syrian-armed-forces-seven-years-into-the-conflict-from-a-regular-army-to -volunteer-corps-/ (accessed June 20, 2018).

Shadid, Anthony (2011). "Syrian Businessman Becomes Magnet for Anger and Dissent," *The New York Times* (online). Available at: http://www.nytimes.com/2011 /05/01/world/asia/01makhlouf.html?_r=0 (accessed May 3, 2012).

Shadid, Anthony (2012). "Bomb Kills Dozens in Damascus, Stoking Suspicions," *The New York Times* (online). Available at: http://www.nytimes.com/2012/01/07/world /middleeast/bomb-attack-in-syrian-capital-kills-25.html (accessed May 5, 2012).

Sh'abo, Rateb (2016). "On the Inevitability of Militarization in the Syrian Uprising," *Syria Untold* (online). Available at: http://syriauntold.com/2016/11/inevitability -militarization-syrian-uprising/ (accessed December 20, 2016).

Shâhed (-al) (2018). "Al-âssad: sûrîyat 'â`idat îla dawrhâ al-mihwarî al-'arabî" (online). Available at: http://www.alshahedkw.com/index.php?option=com_content& view=article&id=191290:2018-10-02-20-03-28&catid=1:02&Itemid=457 (accessed October 4, 2018).

Sharabati Denim (2018). "About Us" (online). Available at: http://sharabati-denim .com (accessed January 24, 2018).

Shekhani, Helbast (2018). "Russia Asks Kurds to Hand Afrin to Syrian Regime to Stop Turkish Attacks," *Kurdistan 24* (online). Available at: http://www.kurdistan24 .net/en/news/fbc1518b-a259-4b8d-9433-ebcoed802ca4 (accessed january 25, 2018).

Sheikh (-al), Omar (2013). "Musalahû al-dawla: al-jaysh al-radîf," *al-Akhbar* (online). Available at: http://www.al-akhbar.com/node/193595 (accessed February 22, 2014).

Sheikhi, Mahwash (2017). "Women's Activist: Rojava Laws a Dream Turned Reality," *Syria Untold* (online). Available at: http://www.syriauntold.com/en/2017/03/women - rojava-laws-dream-turned-reality/ (accessed June 22, 2017).

Sheikho, Kamal (2017). "Kurdish Women's Organizations: Awareness and Politics," *Syria Untold* (online). Available at: http://www.syriauntold.com/en/2017/04/kurdish -women's-organizations-spreading-awareness/ (accessed June 20, 2017).

Sheikho, Kamal (2018). "Over 19,000 Syrian Kurds Deprived of Citizenship, 46,000 Remain Stateless," *Asharq Awsat* (online). Available at: https://aawsat.com/english /home/article/1393276/over-19000-syrian-kurds-deprived-citizenship-46000 -remain-stateless (accessed December 20, 2018).

Sherlock, Ruth (2012a). "Syrian Activists Announce New Leadership," *The Telegraph* (online), June 19. Available at: http://www.telegraph.co.uk/news/worldnews /middleeast/syria/9342471/Syrian-activists-announce-new-leadership.html (accessed January 20, 2013).

Sherlock, Ruth (2012b). "Syria: 50 Dead in Damascus Car Bomb Attacks," *The Telegraph* (online), November 28. Available at: http://www.telegraph.co.uk/news /worldnews/middleeast/syria/9709945/Syria-50-dead-in-Damascus-car-bomb -attacks.html (accessed January 20, 2013).

Shiwesh, Ahmed (2016). "Rojava Administration Launches New Curriculum in Kurdish, Arabic, and Assyrian," *ARA News* (online). Available at: http://aranews .net/2016/10/rojava-administration-launches-new-education-system-kurdish -arabic-assyrian-2/ (accessed November 29, 2016).

Shocked, Shell (2016). "Friends or Foes?–A Closer Look on Relations Between the Kurdish YPG and the Syrian Regime," *offiziere.ch* (online). Available at: https:// offiziere.ch/?p=29051 (accessed September 10, 2016).

Singh, Kanishka (2018). "Britain to Stop Some Aid for Syrian Opposition in Rebel-Held Areas," *Reuters* (online). Available at: https://www.reuters.com/article/us -britain-syria-aid/britain-to-stop-some-aid-for-syrian-opposition-in-rebel-held -areas-idUSKCN1L40RW (accessed August 22, 2018).

Sinjab, Lina (2012). "Syria's Minorities Drawn into Conflict," *BBC News* (online). Available at: http://www.bbc.com/news/world-middle-east-19319448 (accessed February 12, 2013).

Slaytin, Bilal (2015). "Christian Evacuees Mourn Idlib," *al-Monitor* (online). Available at: http://www.al-monitor.com/pulse/culture/2015/04/syria-idlib-christians-jabhat -alnusra-.html#ixzz3zKwocTna (accessed June 10, 2016).

Sly, Liz (2013). "Islamic Law Comes to Rebel-Held Areas of Syria". *Washington Post* (online). Available at: https://www.washingtonpost.com/world/middle_east/islamic -law-comes-to-rebel-held-syria/2013/03/19/b310532e-90af-11e2-bdea-e32ad90d a239_story.html (accessed April 30, 2013).

Sly, Liz (2016). "Syrian Kurds Declare Their Own Region, Raising Tensions," *Washington Post* (online). Available at: https://www.washingtonpost.com/world /middle_east/syrian-kurds-declare-their-own-region-raising-tensions/2016/03/17 /db762950-ec4c-11e5-a9ce-681055c7a05f_story.html?utm_term=.e3710e9c41ca (accessed March 30, 2016).

SMART News Agency (2016). "Waqfa îhtijâjîyya fî 'Âmûdâ bi-rîf al-Hasaka lil-tandîd bi-tasrîhât 'al-Zu'bî wa "al-Ja'farî'," (online), March 28. Available at: https://smartnews-agency.com/ar/media/167515/وقفة-احتجاجية-في-عامودا-بريف-الحسكة -للتنديد-بتصريحات-الزعبي-و (accessed June 30, 2016).

SMART News Agency (2017). "Muzhâhara Dûmâ tutâlib bi-fik al-hisâr 'an ghûta dimashq al-sharqîyya" (online). Available at: https://smartnews-agency.com/ar /media/240307/ مظاهرة - في - دوما -تطالب - بفك - الحصار -عن -غوطة -دمشق -الشرقية (accessed September 20, 2017).

Smyth, Phillip (2015). "The Shiite Jihad in Syria and Its Regional Effects," *Washington Institute for Near East Policy* (online). Available at: http://www.washingtoninstitute .org/uploads/Documents/pubs/PolicyFocus138-v3.pdf (accessed September 30, 2015).

Smyth, P. (2016). "How Iran Is Building Its Syrian Hezbollah," *Washington Institute* (online). Available at: http://www.washingtoninstitute.org/policy-analysis/view /how-iran-is-building-its-syrian-hezbollah (accessed April 29, 2016).

Smyth, Phillip, and Zeilin, Aaron Y. (2014). "The Vocabulary of Sectarianism," *Syria Deeply* (online). Available at: https://www.newsdeeply.com/syria/community/2014 /01/31/the-vocabulary-of-sectarianism (accessed February 20, 2014).

Solomon, E. (2012a). "Feature—Rural Fighters Pour into Syria's Aleppo for Battle," *Reuters* (online), July 29. Available at: http://mobile.reuters.com/article/markets News/idUSL6E8IToTY20120729 (accessed August 20, 2012).

Solomon, E. (2012b). "Insight: Syria Rebels See Future Fight with Foreign Radicals," *Reuters* (online). August 8. Available at: http://www.reuters.com/article/us-syria -crisis-insight-idUSBRE8770BK20120808 (accessed August 20, 2012).

Solomon, Erika (2012c). "Rebel Rivalry and Suspicions Threaten Syria Revolt," *Reuters* (online), April 27. Available at: http://www.reuters.com/article/us-syria-rebels -idUSBRE83Q0S120120427 (accessed December 20, 2012).

Solomon, E. (2013). "Syria Rebels Reject Opposition Coalition, Call for Islamic Leadership," *Reuters* (online). Available at: http://www.reuters.com/article/us-syria -crisis-opposition-idUSBRE98O0LA20130925 (accessed December 29, 2013).

Solomon, E. (2017). "Syria: A Tale of Three Cities," *Financial Times* (online). Available at: https://www.ft.com/content/6710ab2a-7716-11e7-90c0-90a9d1bc9691 (accessed July 30, 2017).

Sottimano, Aurora (2016). "The Syrian Business Elite: Patronage Networks and War Economy," *Syria Untold* (online). Available at: http://www.syriauntold.com/en /2016/09/the-syrian-business-elite-patronage-networks-and-war-economy/#return -note-51304-5 (accessed October 30, 2016).

Souleiman, Dalil (2017). "Le double message de Damas sur l'autonomie du Rojava" (online). Available at https://www.lorientlejour.com/article/1074849/le-double -message-de-damas-sur-lautonomie-du-rojava.html (accessed September 27, 2017),

Souria (al-), Net (2016a). "Syrian Opposition Warns Against Kurdish Federalism," *The Syrian Observer* (online), March 17. Available at: http://syrianobserver.com/EN /News/30728/Syrian_Opposition_Warns_Against_Kurdish_Federalism/ (accessed March 30, 2016).

Souria (al-), Net (2016b). "Assad Regime Fears Its Popular Base, Bans Demonstrations in Loyalist Areas," *The Syrian Observer* (online), July 4. Available at: http:// syrianobserver.com/EN/News/31290/Assad_Regime_Fears_Popular_Base_Bans _Demonstrations_Loyalist_Areas (accessed July 30, 2016).

Souria (al-) Net (2016c). "Ashoura in Damascus: Publications in Farsi, Children Flogging Selves in Streets," *The Syrian Observer* (online), October 14. Available at: http://syrianobserver.com/EN/Features/31800/Ashoura_Damascus_Publications _Farsi_Children_Flogging_Selves_Streets/ (accessed November 10, 2016).

Souria (-al) Net (2016d). "'First- and Second-Grade Martyrs:' Loyalists Decry Regime's Discrimination in Dealing with Fighter Deaths," *The Syrian Observer* (online), October 24. Available at: http://syrianobserver.com/EN/Features/31847 /First_and_Second_Grade_Martyrs_Loyalists_Decry_Regime_Discrimination _Dealing_With_Fighter_Deaths%20; (accessed October 30, 2016).

Souria (-al) Net (2016e). "Best of 2016: Iran's Plan to Seize Damascus Continues with Support from Assad Regime," *The Syrian Observer* (online), December 30. Available at: http://syrianobserver.com/EN/News/30775/Iran_Plan_Seize_Damascus_Conti nues_With_Support_From_Assad_Regime/ (accessed January 20, 2017).

Souria (-al) Net (2018a). "Aleppo University Student Publicly Attacked by Pro-Assad Militiaman," *The Syrian Observer* (online), January 2. Available at: http://syrianob

server.com/EN/News/33663/Aleppo_University_Student_Publicly_Attacked
_Pro_Assad_Militiaman (accessed January 3, 2018).

Souria (-al) Net (2018b). "Parliament Amends Law No. 10," *The Syrian Observer*
(online), November 8. Available at: http://syrianobserver.com/EN/News/35031
/Parliament_Amends_Law_No/ (accessed November 30, 2018).

Souria (-al) Net (2019). "Aleppo Residents Rage at the Regime," *The Syrian Observer*
(online). Available at: https://syrianobserver.com/EN/features/47998/aleppo-residents
-rage-at-the-regime.html?fbclid=IwAR0FZlSNQGvwU1BT9P9hQrrF3IPn5Zcp
URiPUjjBQ4eai2qimKr7TJn2Vlw (accessed January 20, 2019).

Souriatna (2018). "HTS Religious Police Impose Fines for Smoking, Music, Mixing
Sexes in Idleb City," *The Syrian Observer* (online). Available at: http://syrianobserver
.com/EN/Features/33870/HTS_Religious_Police_Impose_Fines_Smoking
_Music_Mixing_Sexes_Idleb_City/ (accessed March 3, 2018).

Sparrow, Annie (2018). "How UN Humanitarian Aid Has Propped up Assad," *Foreign
Affairs* (online). Available at: https://www.foreignaffairs.com/articles/syria/2018
-09-20/how-un-humanitarian-aid-has-propped-assad (accessed September 29, 2018).

Spencer, Richard (2016). "Where Are the Syrians in Assad's Syrian Arab Army?" *The
Telegraph* (online). Available at: https://www.telegraph.co.uk/news/2016/04/09
/where-are-the-syrians-in-assads-syrian-arab-army/ (accessed February 20, 2017).

Sputnik News Araby (2016). "Al-liwâ` jamîl al-hassan: al-gharb yashbahu al-râ'î al-
lazhî yarbî zha`bân fî manzilihi" (online). Available at: https://arabic.sputniknews
.com/interview/201611031020677981-اللواء-جميل-الحسن-المخابرات- (accessed January 20,
2017).

Stack, Liam, and Zoepf, Katherine (2011). "Protesters in Syria Plan Large March
Near Capital," *The New York Times* (online). Available at: http://www.nytimes.com
/2011/04/08/world/middleeast/08syria.html (accessed November 12, 2011).

Stanford University (2016). "Jaysh al-Islam" (online). Available at: https://web
.stanford.edu/group/mappingmilitants/cgi-bin/groups/view/533#cite29 (accessed
November 10, 2016).

Statista (2018). "Syria: Gross Domestic Product (GDP) in Current Prices from 2000 to
2010 (in Billion U.S. Dollars)" (online). Available at: https://www.statista.com
/statistics/326864/gross-domestic-product-gdp-in-syria/ (accessed February 20, 2018).

Stein, Aaron (2017). "Reconciling U.S.-Turkish Interests in Northern Syria," *Council
on Foreign Relations* (pdf). Available at: https://www.cfr.org/sites/default/files/pdf
/2017/02/Discussion_Paper_Stein_Syria_Turkey_OR.pdf (accessed August 20,
2017).

Stewart, Phil (2017). "U.S. Tells Turkey It Supports Ankara's Fight Against PKK,"
Reuters (online). Available at: http://www.reuters.com/article/us-mideast-crisis
-turkey-mattis-idUSKBN1871F0 (accessed May 12, 2017).

Strategy Watch (2019). "Russia Curbs Maher al-Assad's Influence," *Syrian Observer*
(online). Available at: https://syrianobserver.com/EN/features/49024/russia-curbs
-maher-al-assads-influence.html (accessed March 9, 2019).

Stratfor (2015). "Iraq-Syria Battlespace: August 2015" (online). Available at:
https://www.stratfor.com/analysis/iraq-syria-battlespace-august-2015 (accessed
September 25, 2015).

Suleiman, Ali Mahmoud (2018). "Mudîr sinâ'at "al-shaykh najâr" li-'al-Watan'…," *al-Watan* (online). Available at: http://alwatan.sy/archives/170870 (accessed October 24, 2018).

Suleiman, Lujain (2018). "Mudun al-âhlâm" tataqadam fî hisâbât "hukûmat î'âdat al-î'mâr" 'ala mashârî' al-sukan al-sha'bî," *Al-Ayam* (online). Available at: http://alayam.sy/2018/12/23/|-مدن-الأحلام-تتقدم-في-حسابات-حكومة-|/ (accessed December 31, 2018).

Sultan (al-), Daham (2016). "Yâzijî: qad tûwajud âyâd khafîya tataqasad 'adm wûsûl al-dawâ` îla al-hasaka … makhlûf: sana'îd al-nazhr bi-bunûd al-'uqûd wa al-îstithmârât," *al-Watan* (online). Available at: http://alwatan.sy/archives/71395 (accessed September 30, 2016).

Suwayda 24 (2018). "Mashî'ûn shmâl al-sûwaîdâ' yataridûn al-muhâfiz wa qâ'id al-shurtat" (online). Available at: https://suwayda24.com/2018/07/26/مشيعون-شمال-السويداء-يطردون-المحافظ-و-/ (accessed August 20, 2018).

Syria Call (2018). "Palestinian Militia Recruits Young Guys of Eastern Ghouta in Exchange for Tempting Offers" (online). Available at: http://nedaa-sy.com/en/news/9290 (accessed October 25, 2018).

Syria Daily News (2018). "Al-qattân yafûz bi-îstithmâr funduq al-jalâ`" (online). Available at: http://syriadailynews.com/41217 (accessed March 20, 2018).

Syria Direct (2013). "EXCLUSIVE: FSA Says Muslim Brotherhood 'Must Act Like Any Opposition Group in Syria'" (online). Available at: http://syriadirect.org/news/exclusive-fsa-says-muslim-brotherhood-'must-act-like-any-opposition-group-in-syria'-1/ (accessed April 19, 2013).

Syria Direct (2014). "Kurds Detain Hundreds in Conscription Campaign" (online), October 15. Available at: http://syriadirect.org/news/kurds-detain-hundreds-in-conscription-campaign/ (accessed January 20, 2015).

Syrian4all (2013). "Mîshîl Kîlû: îltiqayt jabhat al-nusra wa âstaqbalet ka-al-âbtâl," *YouTube* (online). Available at: https://www.youtube.com/watch?v=_hdkkEFdROQ (accessed December 20, 2014).

Syrian Arab News Agency (SANA) (2015). "Syrians' Investments Abroad Would Not Prevent Industrialists from Return Home" (online). Available at: http://sana.sy/en/?p=61368 (accessed December 30, 2015).

Syrian Arab News Agency (SANA) (2016a). "Majlis al-wizarâ`yalghî ba'd al-majâlis al-'alîyâ wa al-khâsa wa yuqarar î'âda al-nazr bil-majâlis al-'alîyâ al-mushtaraka ma' ba'd dawl al-'âlam" (online), August 2. Available at: https://www.sana.sy/?p=412632 (accessed August 30, 2016).

Syrian Arab News Agency (SANA) (2016b). "New Governor of Hasaka Sworn in Before President al-Assad" (online), October 17. Available at: http://sana.sy/en/?p=90738 (accessed January 10, 2017).

Syrian Arab News Agency (SANA) (2016c). "Bi-râsmâl 60 milîyâr lîrat muhâfazat dimashq tatluq sharikat dimashq al-shâm al-qâbidat al-musâhamat al-mughfilat al-îdârat wa îstithmâr âmlâkihâ fî mintaqat mashru' tanzîm 66" (online), December 12. Available at: https://www.sana.sy/?p=481994 (accessed November 20, 2017).

Syrian Arab News Agency (SANA) (2017a). "Finance Minister Meets Delegation of Syrian Industrials Residing in Egypt" (online), February 19. Available at: http://sana.sy/en/?p=100509 (accessed February 21, 2017).

Syrian Arab News Agency (SANA) (2017b). "25 Billion Syrian Pounds Allocated for Construction Contracts in Aleppo," *The Syrian Observer* (online), July 11. Available at: http://syrianobserver.com/EN/News/32997 (accessed August 20, 2017).

Syrian Arab News Agency (SANA) (2017c). "Expats Should Be Urged to Contribute to Syrian Reconstruction: Muallem" (online), August 25. Available at: http://www.syrianobserver.com/EN/News/33179/Expats_Should_Urged_Contribute_Syrian_Reconstruction_Muallem (accessed August 25, 2017).

Syrian Arab News Agency (SANA) (2017d). "Rebuild Syria 2017 Expo Kicks Off at Fairgrounds" (online), September 26. Available at: https://sana.sy/en/?p=114208 (accessed September 30, 2017).

Syrian Arab News Agency (SANA) (2017e). "Cabinet Approves 3 Trillion Syrian Pounds for 2018 General Budget," *The Syrian Observer* (online), October 25, Available at: http://syrianobserver.com/EN/News/33428/Cabinet_Approves_Trillion_Syrian_Pounds_2_General_Budget (accessed January 15, 2018).

Syrian Arab News Agency (SANA) (2017f). "Foreign Ministry: Raqqa Still Occupied, Can Only Be Considered Liberated When Syrian Army Enters It" (online), October 30. Available at: https://sana.sy/en/?p=116827 (accessed November 30, 2017).

Syrian Arab News Agency (SANA) (2018a). "Al-bida` bi-tashghîl mahata tahwîl kahrabâ`bustân al-qasr. al-muhandis khamîs: rasada 60 milîyâr lîra li-îstakmâl tanfîz al-mashârî' al-khadmîya wa al-tanmawîya fî halab" (online), January 15. Available at: https://www.sana.sy/?p=687949 (accessed January 16, 2018).

Syrian Arab News Agency (SANA) (2018b). "Update—Syria, Iran to Enhance Economic, Trade Cooperation" (online), June 18. Available at: https://sana.sy/en/?p=140441 (accessed July 16, 2018).

Syrian Arab News Agency (SANA) (2018c). "Syrian-Russian Businessmen Council Adopts New Steps to Enhance Cooperation" (online), June 25. Available at: https://sana.sy/en/?p=140902 (accessed July 27, 2018).

Syrian Arab News Agency (SANA) (2018d). "Khamis, Syrian Businessmen in Egypt Discuss Means to Activate Investment in Syria" (online), June 27. Available at: https://sana.sy/en/?p=141073 (accessed July 27, 2018).

Syrian Arab News Agency (SANA) (2018e). "Syria, Iran Sign MoU on Electricity Cooperation" (online), September 12. Available at: https://www.sana.sy/en/?p=113707 (accessed September 27, 2018).

Syrian Arab News Agency (SANA) (2018f). "Khamis Inaugurates Number of Projects in Tartous and Lattakia Worth up to SYP 16 Billion" (online), October 3. Available at: https://www.sana.sy/en/?p=148119 (accessed October 30, 2018).

Syrian Arab News Agency (SANA) (2018g). "Khamis Inaugurates Road Projects in Lattakia Worth up to SYP 11 Billion" (online), October 4. Available at: https://www.sana.sy/en/?p=148184 (accessed October 30, 2018).

Syrian Arab News Agency (SANA) (2018h). "Syria, Iran Agree on Establishing Joint Chamber of Commerce" (online), October 21. Available at: https://sana.sy/en/?p=149294 (accessed October 30, 2018).

Syrian Arab News Agency (SANA) (2018i). "Presidential Decree on Raising Compensations and Allowances of Military Personnel" (online), December 23. Available at: https://sana.sy/en/?p=154173 (accessed December 30, 2018).

Syrian Arab News Agency (SANA) (2019). "102 Projects Included in Investment at a Value of SYP 895 Billion During 2018" (online). Available at: https://www.sana.sy /en/?p=155538 (accessed January 30, 2019).

Syrian Center for Policy Studies (2010). "Informal Labor," *Arab Watch* (pdf). Available at: http://www.annd.org/cd/arabwatch2016/pdf/english/18.pdf (accessed November 20, 2017).

Syrian Center for Political and Strategic Studies and Syrian Expert House (2013). "Syria Transition Roadmap" (pdf). Available at: http://syrianexperthouse.org /reports/Syria_Transition_Roadmap__Full_en.pdf (accessed January 20, 2014).

Syrian Centre for Policy Research (SCPR) (2014). "Syria. Squandering Humanity, Socioeconomic Monitoring Report on Syria," *UNRWA* (pdf). Available at: http://www.unrwa.org/sites/default/files/scpr_report_q3-q4_2013_270514final_3 .pdf (accessed June 20, 2014).

Syrian Centre for Policy Research (SCPR) (2015). "Alienation and Violence, Impact of Syria Crisis Report 2014," *UNRWA* (pdf). Available at: http://www.unrwa.org /sites/default/files/alienation_and_violence_impact_of_the_syria_crisis_in_2014 _eng.pdf (accessed January 30, 2016).

Syrian Centre for Policy Research (SCPR) (2016a). "Confronting Fragmentation! Syria, Impact of Syrian Crisis Report," *UNRWA* (pdf). Available at: http://scpr-syria .org/publications/policy-reports/confronting-fragmentation/ (accessed March 30, 2016).

Syrian Centre for Policy Research (SCPR) (2016b). "Forced Dispersion, Syrian Human Status: The Demographic Report 2016," *UNRWA* (pdf). Available at: http://scpr-syria.org/publications/forced-dispersion-syrian-human-status-the -demographic-report-2016/ (accessed December 3, 2016).

Syrian Coalition (2018). "Syrian Coalition Supports Syrian National Army's Efforts to Cleanse Syria of Terrorism" (online). Available at: http://en.etilaf.org/press/syrian -coalition-supports-syrian-national-army-s-efforts-to-cleanse-syria-of-terrorism .html (accessed January 25, 2018).

Syrian Economic Forum (2017). "The Egyptian Response!! Establishment of a Syrian Industrial Zone in Egypt" (online). Available at: http://www.syrianef.org/En/ (accessed April 18, 2017).

Syrian National Council (2011). "Syrian National Council Attends World Economic Forum Conference in Istanbul" (online). Available at: http://syriancouncil.org/en /press-releases/item/543-syrian-national-council-attends-world-economic-forum -conference-in-istanbul.html (accessed September 20, 2015).

Syria Needs Analysis Project (2013). "Impact of the Conflict on Syrian Economy and Livelihoods" (online). Available at: http://www.acaps.org/sites/acaps/ les/ prod-ucts/les/23_impact_of_the_conict_on_syrian_econo-my_and_livelihoods_july_2013 .pdf (accessed July 20, 2018).

Syrian Networks of Human Rights (SNHR) (2015). "The Society's Holocaust, Most Notable Sectarian and Ethnic Cleansing Massacre" (pdf). Available at: http://sn4hr .org/wp-content/pdf/english/The_Societys_Holocaust.pdf (accessed January 16, 2016).

Syrian Networks of Human Rights (SNHR) (2016). "139 Chemical Attacks in Syria After Security Council Resolution 2118" (pdf). Available at: http://sn4hr.org/wp

-content/pdf/english/139_attack_with_chemical_weapons_in_Syria_en.pdf (accessed January 16, 2017).

Syria News (2017). "Coalition's Bassam al-Malak Announces His Defection and Return to Damascus," *The Syrian Observer* (online). Available at: http://syriano bserver.com/EN/News/33142/Coalition_Bassam_Malak_Announces_His _Defection_Return_Damascus/ (accessed August 26, 2017).

Syrian Observatory for Human Rights (SOHR) (2015a). "More Than 1000 Protesters in the City of Lattakia Demand the Execution of Sulaiman al-Assad" (online), August 8. Available at: http://www.syriahr.com/en/?p=28298 (accessed September 20, 2015).

Syrian Observatory for Human Rights (SOHR) (2015b). "After the Agreement Held Between the Operation Room of Fateh Halab and YPG, a New Agreement Held Between the Operation Room of Mare' and al-Thuwar Army in the northern countryside of Aleppo" (online), December 20. Available at: http://www.syriahr .com/en/?p=40757 (accessed December 21, 2015).

Syrian Observatory of Human Rights (SOHR) (2016). "Madîna halab tushad khurûj kâmel al-qism al-shmâlî min âhîyâ` halab al-sharqîya 'an saytara al-fasâ`il" (online). Available at: http://www.syriahr.com/2016/11/28/مدينة-حلب-تشهد-خروج-كامل/ القسم-الـ- (accessed January 15, 2017).

The Syria Report (2012). "Syria Restricts Travels for All Males Aged Under 42–Report" (online). Available at: http://www.syria-report.com/news/economy/syria-restricts -travels-all-males-aged-under-42-report (accessed January 11, 2013).

The Syria Report (2013a). "Government to Relocate Plants in 'Safe Areas'" (online), April 9. Available at: http://www.syria-report.com/news/manufacturing/govern ment-relocate-plants-"safe-areas" (accessed May 30, 2013).

The Syria Report (2013b). "Businessman Becomes New Homs Governor" (online), July 22. Available at: http://www.syria-report.com/news/economy/businessman -becomes-new-homs-governor (accessed August 20, 2013).

The Syria Report (2014a). "Government Seizes Firas Tlas Shares in Lafarge Cement Syria–Report" (online), August 25. Available at: http://www.syria-report.com /news/economy/government-seizes-firas-tlas-shares-lafarge-cement-syria-report (accessed September 3, 2014).

The Syria Report (2014b). "Inauguration of New Leisure Facilities Draws Anger from Regime Supporters" (online), October 13. Available at: http://www.syria-report .com/news/economy/inauguration-new-leisure-facilities-draws-anger-regime -supporters (accessed October 14).

The Syria Report (2014c). "As Shortages Rise Government Offers Investors Right to Use Oil Refineries" (online), December 1. Available at: http://www.syria-report .com/news/oil-gas-mining/shortages-rise-government-offers-investors-right-use -oil-refineries (accessed December 12, 2014).

The Syria Report (2015a). "Government Highlights Economic Aid to Suweida Governorate as Tensions Rise" (online), February 2. Available at: http://www.syria -report.com/news/economy/government-highlights-economic-aid-suweida -governorate-tensions-rise (accessed February 20, 2015).

The Syria Report (2015b). "Syrian State to Give up Billions to the Benefit of MTN and Syriatel" (online), June 1. Available at: http://www.syria-report.com/news/telecoms -it/syrian-state-give-billions-benefit-mtn-and-syriatel (accessed June 6, 2015).

The Syria Report (2015c). "Syrian Businessman Wants Tartous Declared Free Trade Zone" (online), June 15. Available at: http://www.syria-report.com/news/economy /syrian-businessman-wants-tartous-declared-free-trade-zone (accessed June 16, 2015).

The Syria Report (2015d). "Idlib Falling Victim to Systematic Looting" (online), July 6. Available at: http://www.syria-report.com/news/economy/idlib-falling-victim-syste matic-looting (accessed July 30, 2015).

The Syria Report (2015e). "Factsheet: Syria-Iran Economic Relations Since 2013" (online), July 13. Available at: http://www.syria-report.com/news/economy/factsheet -syria-iran-economic-relations-2013 (accessed December 11, 2015).

The Syria Report (2015f). "New Rental Law Increases Fiscal Revenues and Loyalty of Regime Soldiers" (online), November 16. Available at: http://www.syria-report .com/news/real-estate-construction/new-rental-law-increases-fiscal-revenues-and -loyalty-regime-soldiers (accessed December 13, 2015).

The Syria Report (2015g). "Syrian Government Commits 30 Billion Pounds to Coastal Area and only 500 million to Aleppo" (online), November 16. Available at: http:// syria-report.com/news/economy/syrian-government-commits-30-billion-pounds -coastal-area-and-only-500-million-aleppo (accessed November 17, 2015).

The Syria Report (2015h). "New Urban Planning Law Issued" (online), December 14. Available at: http://www.syria-report.com/news/real-estate-construction/new-urban -planning-law-issued (accessed December 21, 2015).

The Syria Report (2015i). "Mohammad Hamsho Leads Newly-Established Syrian Metals Council" (online), December 22. Available at: http://www.syria-report .com/news/manufacturing/mohammad-hamsho-leads-newly-established-syrian -metals-council (accessed January 2, 2016).

The Syria Report (2015j). "Syrian President Expands Tartous University" (online), December 21. Available at: http://www.syria-report.com/news/education/syrian -president-expands-tartous-university (accessed December 22, 2015).

The Syria Report (2016a). "Data Confirm Attractiveness of Tartous to Syrian Investors" (online), February 16. Available at: http://www.syria-report.com/news/economy /data-confirm-attractiveness-tartous-syrian-investors (accessed February 20, 2016).

The Syria Report (2016b). "Syrian Private Investment Dives, Continues Move to Coast, Suweida" (online). March 1. Available at: http://www.syria-report.com/news /economy/syrian-private-investment-dives-continues-move-coast-suweida (accessed March 3, 2016).

The Syria Report (2016c). "Aleppo Lost 90 Percent of Its Manufacturing Capacity" (online), March 29. Available at: http://www.syria-report.com/news/manufac- turing/aleppo-lost-90-percent-its-manufacturing-capacity (accessed March 29, 2016).

The Syria Report (2016d). "Syrian Regime Pours Billions to Buy Loyalty of Coastal Region" (online), April 24. Available at: http://www.syria-report.com/news/econ omy/syrian-regime-pours-billions-buy-loyalty-coastal-region (accessed April 28, 2016).

The Syria Report (2016e). "Syrian Regime Seeking to Recycle Millions of Tons of Rubble" (online), June 14. Available at: http://www.syria-report.com/news/real -estate-construction/syrian-regime-seeking-recycle-millions-tons-rubble (accessed June 30, 2016).

The Syria Report (2016f). "Syria's Manufacturing Sector in Dire Straits" (online), July 19. Available at: http://www.syria-report.com/news/manufacturing/syrias-manufacturing-sector-dire-straits (accessed December 20, 2016).

The Syria Report (2016g). "Real Estate Investments Go to Tartous, Lattakia" (online), May 15. Available at: http://www.syria-report.com/news/real-estate-construction/real-estate-investments-go-tartous-lattakia (accessed June 27, 2016).

The Syria Report (2016h). "Syria, Iran Preferential Trade Agreement Enters into Force" (online), June 7. Available at: http://www.syria-report.com/news/economy/syria-iran-preferential-trade-agreement-enters-force (accessed July 20, 2016).

The Syria Report (2016i). "Regime Media Calls for Reducing Government Payments in Areas Outside Its Control" (online), September 20. Available at: http://www.syria-report.com/news/economy/regime-media-calls-reducing-government-payments-areas-outside-its-control (accessed September 30, 2016).

The Syria Report (2016j). "Report Highlights Government Dependency on Central Bank Funding and Limited Forex Disbursements" (online). September 20. Available at: http://www.syria-report.com/news/finance/report-highlights-government-dependency-central-bank-funding-and-limited-forex-disburse (accessed September 30, 2016).

The Syria Report (2016k). "Government Sends Ministers to Reaffirm Stake in Hassakeh" (online), September 27. Available at: http://www.syria-report.com/news/economy/government-sends-ministers-reaffirm-stake-hassakeh (accessed September 30, 2016).

The Syria Report (2016l). "Regime Cronies Business Ambitions Believed to Be Behind Destruction of Dozens of Shops in Jableh" (online), October 4. Available at: http://www.syria-report.com/news/real-estate-construction/regime-cronies-business-ambitions-believed-be-behind-destruction-dozen (accessed October 20, 2016).

The Syria Report (2016m). "PYD, Government Close Schools as They Seek to Impose Own Curriculum" (online), October 4. Available at: http://www.syria-report.com/news/education/pyd-government-close-schools-they-seek-impose-own-curriculum (accessed October 20, 2016).

The Syria Report (2016n). "Damascus Governorate Says Thousands Subscribe to Mazzeh Real Estate Development" (online). October 11. Available at: http://www.syria-report.com/news/real-estate-construction/damascus-governorate-says-thousands-subscribe-mazzeh-real-estate-devel (accessed October 25, 2016).

The Syria Report (2016o). "Founder of Large Syrian Conglomerate Dies" (online), October 25. Available at: http://www.syria-report.com/news/economy/founder-large-syrian-conglomerate-dies (accessed October 30, 2016).

The Syria Report (2016p). "Syria's Public Debt Multiplied by 11 Since 2011" (online), November 15. Available at: http://www.syria-report.com/news/finance/syrias-public-debt-multiplied-11-2011 (accessed November 16, 2016).

The Syria Report (2016q). "Iran Expected to Be Granted Syrian Mobile Phone License" (online), November 29. Available at: http://www.syria- report.com/news/telecoms-it/iran-expected-be-granted-syrian-mobile-phone-license (accessed November 30, 2016).

The Syria Report (2016r). "Prominent Intermediary Plays Key Role in Oil Deals Between Regime and ISIS" (online), Decmber 20. Available at: http://www.syria-report.com/news/oil-gas-mining/prominent-intermediary-plays-keyrole-oil-deals-between-regime-and-isis (accessed December 20, 2016).

The Syria Report (2017a). "Government Planning to Expand Use of Expropriation Law" (online), January 10. Available at: http://www.syria-report.com/news/real-estate-construction/government-planning-expand-use-expropriation-law (accessed January 12, 2017).

The Syria Report (2017b). "Government Decree Confirms as Civil Servants Dozens of Thousands of Sons of 'Martyrs', Youth" (online). January 17. Available at: http://www.syria-report.com/news/economy/government-decree-confirms-civil-servants-dozens-thousands-sons-"martyrs"-youth (accessed January 17, 2016).

The Syria Report (2017c). "Revolutionary Guards Get Hold of Syrian Mobile Phone Licence as Part of Broader Tehran Grab on Economic Assets," January 17. Available at: http://www.syria-report.com/news/economy/revolutionary-guards-get-hold-syrian-mobile-phone-licence-part-broader-tehran-grab-econ (accessed January 17, 2017).

The Syria Report (2017d). "In Boost to Coastal Area, Government Decides Sharp Rise in Tobacco Procurement Prices" (online). January 24. Available at: http://www.syria-report.com/news/food-agriculture/boost-coastal-area-government-decides-sharp-rise-tobacco-procurement-prices (accessed January 24, 2017).

The Syria Report (2017e). "Iran Grants USD 1 Billion to Damascus" (online). January 24. Available at: http://www.syria-report.com/news/economy/iran-grants-usd-1-billion-damascus (accessed January 24, 2017).

The Syria Report (2017f). "Regime Cronies Resist Government Attempts to Lure Back Investors into Syria" (online), February 27. Available at: http://syria-report.com/news/economy/regime-cronies-resist-government-attempts-lure-back-investors-syria (accessed February 22, 2017).

The Syria Report (2017g). "Syrian Government Promises Billions to the 'Capital of the Martyrs'" (online), April 18. Available at: http://www.syria-report.com/news/economy/syrian-government-promises-billions-"capital-martyrs" (accessed April 28, 2017).

The Syria Report (2017h). "Factsheet: Syria–Russia Economic Relations" (online), May 2. Available at: http://www.syria-report.com/news/economy/factsheet-syria-russia-economic-relations (accessed May 3, 2017).

The Syria Report (2017i). "Russian Company Wins Contract to Develop Syrian Phosphate Mine" (online), June 6. Available at: http://www.syria-report.com/news/oil-gas-mining/russian-company-wins-contract-develop-syrian-phosphate-mine (accessed June 7, 2017).

The Syria Report (2017j). "Russian Trading House Becomes Key Player in Syrian-Russian Economic Relationship" (online), June 13. Available at: http://www.syria-report.com/news/food-agriculture/russian-trading-house-becomes-key-player-syrian-russian-economic-relationship (accessed June 14, 2017).

The Syria Report (2017k). "Syria Cedes Oil and Gas Assets to 'Putin's Cook'–Report" (online), July 4. Available at: http://www.syria-report.com/news/oil-gas-mining/syria-cedes-oil-and-gas-assets-"putin's-cook"---report (accessed July 5, 2017).

The Syria Report (2017l). "Syrian Banks Unable to Finance Reconstruction," July 21 (online). Available at: http://www.syria-report.com/news/finance/syrian-banks -unable-finance-reconstruction (accessed July 21, 2017).

The Syria Report (2017m). "Syriatel Posts Sharp Increase in Revenues as Phone License to Iran Is Postponed" (online), September 12. Available at: http://www.syria -report.com/news/telecoms-it/syriatel-posts-sharp-increase-revenues-phone -license-iran-postponed (accessed September 16, 2017).

The Syria Report (2017n). "No Alternative Accommodation for Mazzeh District Residents—Government Outlet" (online), October 17. Available at: http://www .syria-report.com/news/real-estate-construction/no-alternative-accommodation -mazzeh-district-residents-government-outl (accessed October 19, 2017).

The Syria Report (2017o). "PM Visit to Coastal Area Highlights Discontent, Government Limitations" (online), October 24. Available at: http://www.syria -report.com/news/economy/pm-visit-coastal-area-highlights-discontent-government -limitations (accessed October 24, 2017).

The Syria Report (2017p). "Samer Foz Acquires Rights over Hundreds of Millions of Dollars in Basatin Al-Razi Project" (online), November 21. Available at: http:// www.syria-report.com/news/real-estate-construction/samer-foz-acquires-rights -over-hundreds-millions-dollars-basatin-al-ra (accessed November 22, 2017).

The Syria Report (2017q). "Syrian Businesses Complain of Labour Shortages Despite Massive Unemployment" (online), November 28. Available at: http://www.syria -report.com/news/economy/syrian-businesses-complain-labour-shortages -despite-massive-unemployment (accessed November 30, 2017).

The Syria Report (2017r). "Syrian Parliament Approves Doubling of Reconstruction Tax Rate" (online), December 12. Available at: http://www.syria-report.com/news /economy/syrian-parliament-approves-doubling-reconstruction-tax-rate (accessed December 24, 2017).

The Syria Report (2018a). "Government Prioritises Spending on Core Constituency" (online), January 9. Available at: http://www.syria-report.com/news/economy /government-prioritises-spending-core-constituency (accessed January 10, 2018).

The Syria Report (2018b). "Basatin Al-Razi Project Highlights Again Emergence of New Business Figure" (online), January 16. Available at: http://www.syria-report. com/news/real-estate-construction/basatin-al-razi-project-highlights-again -emergence-new-business-figure (accessed January 16, 2018).

The Syria Report (2018c). "Syrian Regime Drafting Law to Extend Decree 66 to All of Syria" (online), January 16. Available at: http://www.syria-report.com/news/real -estate-construction/syrian-regime-drafting-law-extend-decree-66-all-syria (ac-cessed January 16, 2018).

The Syria Report (2018d). "Transport, Tourism Data Confirm 2017 GDP Growth Trend" (online), January 16. Available at: http://www.syria-report.com/news/economy /transport-tourism-data-confirm-2017-gdp-growth-trend (accessed January 31, 2018).

The Syria Report (2018e). "Kuwait's Kharafi Group Announces Land Purchase Deal Outside Damascus" (online), January 30. Available at: http://www.syria-report .com/news/real-estate-construction/kuwait's-kharafi-group-announces-land -purchase-deal-outside-damascus (accessed January 31, 2018).

The Syria Report (2018f). "Company Filings Confirm Improved Business Activity in 2017" (online), March 6. Available at: http://www.syria-report.com/news/econo my/company-filings-confirm-improved-business-activity-2017 (accessed March 30, 2018).

The Syria Report (2018g). "Foz Acquires Four Seasons Hotel" (online), March 20. Available at: http://www.syria-report.com/news/tourism/foz-acquires-four-seasons -hotel (accessed March 30, 2018).

The Syria Report (2018h). "Makhlouf Invests in Marota City" (online), March 27. Available at: http://www.syria-report.com/news/real-estate-construction/makhlouf -invests-marota-city (accessed March 30 2018).

The Syria Report (2018i). "Syrian Regime Eases Expropriation of Informal Areas Across the Country" (online), April 9. Available at: http://www.syria-report.com /news/real-estate-construction/syrian-regime-eases-expropriation-informal-areas -across-country (accessed April 10, 2018).

The Syria Report (2018j). "Syria's GDP at Only a Fifth of Pre-Uprising Level" (online), May 15. Available at: http://www.syria-report.com/news/economy/syria's-gdp-only -fifth-pre-uprising-level (accessed May 20, 2018).

The Syria Report (2018k). "Warlords Increasingly Integrating into Syria's Formal Economy" (online), May 15. Available at: http://www.syria-report.com/news /economy/warlords-increasingly-integrating-syria's-formal-economy (accessed May 20 2018).

The Syria Report (2018l). "Iran Wins Contract to Supply Thousands of Tractors to Syrian Farmers" (online), May 28. Available at: http://www.syria-report.com/news /food-agriculture/iran-wins-contract-supply-thousands-tractors-syrian-farmers (accessed May 30, 2018).

The Syria Report (2018m). "Iran Gains Access to Syria's Large Phosphate Reserves" (online), June 19. Available at: http://www.syria-report.com/news/oil-gas-mining /iran-gains-access-syria's-large-phosphate-reserves (accessed June 25, 2018).

The Syria Report (2018n). "Russia to Take Control of Syria's Fertilizers Production Capacity–Report" (online), June 26. Available at: http://www.syria-report.com /news/manufacturing/russia-take-control-syria's-fertilizers-production-capacity ---report (accessed June 28, 2018).

The Syria Report (2018o). "Jordan Invites Syrian Business Chambers" (online), July 31. Available at: http://www.syria-report.com/news/economy/jordan-invites-syrian -business-chambers (accessed August 1, 2018).

The Syria Report (2018p). "Official Data Indicate a Decline in Already Low Manufacturing Investment" (online), August 28. Available at: http://www.syria -report.com/news/manufacturing/official-data-indicate-decline-already-low-manu facturing-investment (accessed September 10, 2018).

The Syria Report (2018q). "Turkish Hold on Syria's North Increases with ID Cards, Car Registration Plates, Electricity Supplies," August 28 (online). Available at: http://www.syria-report.com/news/economy/turkish-hold-syria's-north-increases -id-cards-car-registration-plates-electricity-suppl (accessed August 30, 2018).

The Syria Report (2018r). "Government Requires Loyalists to Part Finance the Rebuilding of Their Homes" (online), September 4. Available at: http://www.syria

-report.com/news/real-estate-construction/government-requires-loyalists-part-fin ance-rebuilding-their-homes (accessed September 10, 2018).

The Syria Report (2018s). "Russia, China Finance Syrian Imports of Heavy Machinery" (online), September 25. Available at: http://www.syria-report.com/news/real -estate-construction/russia-china-finance-syrian-imports-heavy-machinery (accessed September 28, 2018).

The Syria Report (2018t). "State-Owned Companies Report Manpower Shortages" (online), October 16. Available at: http://www.syria-report.com/news/econ omy/state-owned-companies-report-manpower-shortages (accessed October 28, 2018).

The Syria Report (2018u). "Reconstruction Committee Lists 2018 Projects" (online), October 23. Available at: http://www.syria-report.com/news/economy/reconstruc tion-committee-lists-2018-projects (accessed October 28, 2018).

The Syria Report (2018v). "Electric Generators as Part of Chinese Grants to Syria" (online), October 23. Available at: http://www.syria-report.com/news/power /electric-generators-part-chinese-grants-syria (accessed October 28, 2018).

The Syria Report (2018w). "Expropriation of Syrian Lands and Properties Likely to Continue Unabated" (online), October 23. Available at: http://www.syria-report .com/news/real-estate-construction/expropriation-syrian-lands-and-properties -likely-continue-unabated (accessed October 28, 2018).

The Syria Report (2018x). "Aleppo Announces Launch of Works on Informal Area" (online), October 30. Available at: http://www.syria-report.com/news/real-estate -construction/aleppo-announces-launch-works-informal-area (accessed October 31, 2018).

The Syria Report (2018y). "Syrian Investors Create New Lobby Group" (online), November 6. Available at: http://www.syria-report.com/news/economy/syrian-inv estors-create-new-lobby-group (accessed November 6, 2018).

The Syria Report (2018z). "UAE Companies Showing Growing Interest in Syria" (online), December 24. Available at: https://www.syria-report.com/news/economy /uae-companies-showing-growing-interest-syria (accessed December 28, 2018).

The Syria Report (2019a). "New Data Highlights Massive Drop in Syrian Workforce" (online), February 27. Available at: https://www.syria-report.com/news/economy /new-data-highlights-massive-drop-syrian-workforce (accessed March 2, 2019).

The Syria Report (2019b). "Iran Says It Plans to Build Large Housing Project Around Damascus" (online), March 6. Available at: https://www.syria-report.com/news /real-estate-construction/iran-says-it-plans-build-large-housing-project-around -damascus (accessdd 7 March 2019).

The Syria Report (2019c), "Manufacturing Data Paint Mixed Picture" (online). Available at: https://www.syria-report.com/news/manufacturing/manufacturing -data-paint-mixed-picture (accessed April 10, 2019).

The Syrian Observer (2013). "How Assad Junior Lost the Empire" (online). Available at: http://www.syrianobserver.com/EN/News/26367/How+Assad+Junior+Lost+the +Empire (accessed December 20, 2014).

The Syrian Reporter (2018). "Jamil al-Hassan: Any and All Opposition Will Be Eliminated," *The Syrian Observer* (online). Available at: http://syrianobserver.com

/EN/Features/34576/Jamil_Hassan_Any_All_Opposition_Will_Be_Eliminated/ (accessed August 10, 2018).

Syria Untold (2013a). "Union of Free Syrian Students" (online), May 6. Available at: http://www.syriauntold.com/en/work_group/union-of-free-syrian-students/ (accessed December 10, 2013).

Syria Untold (2013b). "Lessons from Raqqa: From Demanding Freedom to Creative State-Building" (online). May 28. Available at: http://www.syriauntold.com/en/2013 /05/lessons-from-raqqa-from-demanding-freedom-to-creative-state-building/ (accessed July 20, 2013).

Syria Untold (2013c). "The Strike of Dignity" (online), June 5. Available at: http://www .syriauntold.com/en/event/the-strike-of-dignity/ (accessed August 10, 2013).

Syria Untold (2013d). "Sisters Maisa and Samar Saleh Vs. Regime Forces and the Islamic State of Iraq and the Levant" (online), August 19. Available at: http://www .syriauntold.com/en/2013/08/sisters-maisa-and-samar-saleh-vs-regime-forces-and -the-islamic-state-of-iraq-and-the-levant/ (accessed September 23, 2013).

Syria Untold (2013e). "Darayya's Free Women" (online), December 19. Available at: http://www.syriauntold.com/en/work_group/darayyas-free-women// (accessed June 23, 2014).

Syria Untold (2013f). "The Free Women of Darayya's Crucial Role in the Syrian Uprising" (online), December 19. Available at: http://www.syriauntold.com/en /2013/12/the-free-women-of-darayyas-crucial-role-in-the-syrian-uprising/ (accessed June 23, 2014).

Syria Untold (2013g). "Our Right" (online). December 27. Available at: http://www .syriauntold.com/en/work_group/our-right/ (accessed January 3, 2014).

Syria Untold (2014a). "How Did Raqqa Fall to the Islamic State of Iraq and Syria?" (online), January 13. Available at: http://www.syriauntold.com/en/2014/01/how -did-raqqa-fall-to-the-islamic-state-of-iraq-and-syria/ (accessed January 14, 2014).

Syria Untold (2014b). "Kurdish-Arab Fraternity Coordination Committee" (online), February 21. Available at: http://www.syriauntold.com/en/work_group/kurdish -arab-fraternity-coordination-committee/ (accessed June 20, 2015).

Syria Untold (2014c). "Syrian Women and the Uprising: Fighting on Multiple Fronts" (online), February 26. Available at: http://www.syriauntold.com/en/2014/02/syrian -women-and-the-uprising-fighting-on-multiple-fronts/ (accessed March 11, 2014).

Syria Untold (2014d). "The Syrian Uprising, Through the Eyes of Three Syrian Women" (online), March 12. Available at: http://www.syriauntold.com/en/2014/03 /the-syrian-uprising-through-the-eyes-of-three-syrian-women/ (accessed March 30, 2014).

Syria Untold (2014e). "Syrian Women and the Politics of the Revolution" (online), March 17. Available at: http://www.syriauntold.com/en/2014/03/syrian-women -and-the-politics-of-the-revolution/ (accessed March 30, 2014).

Syria Untold (2014f). "The Women of Salamiyah Turn Houses into Protest Squares," May 10 (online). Available at: http://www.syriauntold.com/en/2014/05/the-women -of-salamiyah-turn-houses-into-protest-squares/ (accessed June 20, 2014).

Syria Untold (2015). "The Women of Mazaya in Response to the Attack: We Will Carry On" (online). Available at: http://www.syriauntold.com/en/2015/01/the

-women-of-mazaya-in-response-to-the-attack-we-will-carry-on/ (accessed June 11, 2015).

Syria Untold (2016a). "The Battle of School Curricula (1): Oppression and Mayhem" (online), February 21. Available at: http://www.syriauntold.com/en/2016/02/the -battle-of-school-curricula-1-oppression-and-mayhem/ (accessed February 21, 2016).

Syria Untold (2016b). "The Battle of School Curricula (2): Tampering with Syria's Future" (online), February 22. Available at: http://www.syriauntold.com/en/2016/02/the -battle-of-school-curricula-2-tampering-with-syrias-future/ (accessed February 23, 2016).

Syria Untold (2016c). "Women Now" (online), March 17. Available at: http://www .syriauntold.com/en/work_group/women-now/ (accessed November 11, 2016).

Syria Untold (2016d). "Tartusians and Aleppans, a Story of Mutual Benefits" (online), October 24. Available at: http://www.syriauntold.com/en/2016/10/tartusians-and -aleppans-a-story-of-mutual-benefits/ (accessed October 24, 2016).

Swedeh, Mike (2017). "Exclusive Interview: CEO of Foz Holding Samer Foz," *Arabisk London* (online). Available at: http://www.arabisklondon.com/exclusive-interview -ceo-of-foz-holding-samer-foz/ (accessed August 20, 2017).

Szakola, Albin (2016). "Druze Protesters Clash with Syria Regime Loyalists," *NOW* (online). Available at: https://now.mmedia.me/lb/en/NewsReports/566984-druze -protesters-clash-with-syria-regime-loyalists (accessed May 20, 2016).

Tahrir Institute for Middle East Policy (2017). "Summary" (online). Available at: https://timep.org/syrias-women/violence-against-women/ (accessed March 2, 2018).

Tamimi (-al), A. J. (2015a). "The New Druze Militia Factions of Suwayda Province," *Syria Comment* (online), August 8. Available at: http://www.joshualandis.com/blog /the-new-druze-militia-factions-of-suwayda-province/ (accessed September 30, 2015).

Tamimi (-al), A. J. (2015b). "Overview of Some Pro-Assad Militias," *Syria Comment* (online), September 1. Available at: http://www.aymennjawad.org/17800/overview -of-some-pro-assad-militias (accessed January 20, 2016).

Tamimi (-al), A. J. (2015c). "Rijal al-Karama After Sheikh Abu Fahad Waheed al-Bal'ous' Assassination," *Syria Comment* (online), October 26. Available at: http://www.joshualandis.com/blog/rijal-al-karama-after-sheikh-abu-fahad -waheed-al-balous-assassination/ (accessed November 30, 2015).

Tamimi (-al), A. J. (2016a). "Syrian Hezbollah Militias of Nubl and Zahara'," *Syria Comment* (online), August 15. Available at: http://www.joshualandis.com/blog /syrian-hezbollah-militias-nubl-zahara/ (accessed September 30, 2016).

Tamimi (-al), A. J. (2016b). "Liwa al-Imam Zain al-Abidain: Building a 'Resistance' in Eastern Syria," *Aymenn Jawad Al-Tamimi* (online), September 18. Available at: http://www.aymennjawad.org/19211/liwa-al-imam-zain-al-abidain-building (ac-cessed September 30, 2016).

Tamimi (-al), A. J. (2017a). "Administrative Decisions on Local Defence Forces Personnel: Translation and Analysis," *Aymenn Jawad Al-Tamimi* (online), May 3. Available at: http://www.aymennjawad.org/2017/05/administrative-decisions-on -local-defence-forces (accessed May 3, 2017).

Tamimi (-al), A. J. (2017b). "Rijal al-Karama Two Years After Bal'ous' Assassination: Interview," *Aymenn Jawad Al-Tamimi* (online), September 1. Available at: http://www.aymennjawad.org/2017/09/rijal-al-karama-two-years-after-balous (accessed September 3, 2017).

Taranto, James (2015). "Kerry Agonistes," *Wall Street Journal* (online). Available at: http://www.wsj.com/articles/kerry-agonistes-1450376950 (accessed December 20, 2015).

Tastekin, Fehim (2018). "Turkey Cultivating Ever-Deeper Roots in Syrian Territory," *al-Monitor* (online). Available at: https://www.al-monitor.com/pulse/originals/2018 /06/turkey-syria-turkish-university-in-al-bab.html (accessed August 20, 2018).

Todman, Will (2016). "Sieges in Syria: Profiteering from Misery," *Middle East Institute* (pdf). Available at: http://www.mei.edu/sites/default/files/publications/PF14_Tod man_sieges_web.pdf (accessed July 20, 2016).

Tokmajyan, Armenak (2016). "The War Economy in Northern Syria," *The Aleppo Project* (pdf). Available at: http://www.thealeppoproject.com/wp-content/uploads/2016/12 /War-Economy.pdf (accessed March 25, 2017).

Toumaj, Amir (2016). "Russian Influence Evident in Palestinian Militia in Syria," *FDD's Long War Journal* (online). Available at: http://www.longwarjournal.org /archives/2016/10/russian-influence-evident-in-palestinian-militia-in-syria.php (accessed November 10, 2016).

Tsvetkova, Maria (2018*)*. "Russian Toll in Syria Battle Was 300 Killed and Wounded: Sources," *Reuters* (online). Available at: https://www.reuters.com/article/us-mideast -crisis-syria-russia-casualtie/russian-toll-in-syria-battle-was-300-killed-and-wounded -sources-idUSKCN1FZ2DZ (accessed February 27, 2018).

Ufheil-Somers, Amanda (2013). "Iraqi Christians: A Primer," *MERIP* (online). Available at: http://www.merip.org/mer/mer267/iraqi-christians-primer (accessed January 20, 2016).

Ulloa, Silvia (2017). "Assyrians Under Kurdish Rule: The Situation in Northeastern Syria," *Assyrian Confederation of Europe* (pdf). Available at: http://www.aina.org /reports/ace201701.pdf (accessed July 20, 2017).

Ulrichsen, Kristian Coates (2014). "Qatar and the Arab Spring: Policy Drivers and Regional Implications," *Carnegie* (online). Available at: http://carnegieendowment .org/2014/09/24/qatar-and-arab-spring-policy-drivers-and-regional-implications -pub-56723 (accessed February 20, 2015).

Union of Free Syrian Students (2012). "Info" (online). Available at: http://ar.ufss.info/ %D8%A7%D9%86%D8%B6%D9%85%D8%A7%D9%85-%D8%A7%D8%A6%D 8%AA%D9%84%D8%A7%D9%81-%D8%B7%D9%84%D8%A8%D8%A9 -%D8%AC%D8%A7%D9%85%D8%B9%D8%A9-%D8%AF%D9% 85%D8%B4%D9%82-%D8%A5%D9%84%D9%89-%D8%A7%D8%AA%D8% AD%D8%A7/ (accessed January 27, 2012).

United Nations (2011). "Report of the Special Rapporteur on the Right to Food, Olivier De Schutter" (pdf). Available at: http://www.srfood.org/images/stories /pdf/officialreports/20110121_a-hrc-16-49-add2_country_mission_syria_en.pdf (accessed April 3, 2013).

United Nations High Commissioner for Refugees (UNHCR) (2018). "Syria Factsheet (January–November 2018)," *Reliefweb* (online). Available at: https://reliefweb.int

/report/syrian-arab-republic/unhcr-syria-factsheet-january-november-2018 (accessed January 4, 2019).

United Nations Relief and Works Agency for Palestine Refugees in the Near East (UNRWA) (2011). "Where We Work" (online). Available at: https://www.unrwa.org/where-we-work/syria (accessed July 20, 2015).

UN News (2018). "A Record One Million Syrians Displaced over Six Months, During Six Key Battles: UN Investigators" (online). Available at: https://news.un.org/en/story/2018/09/1019072 (accessed October 20, 2018).

Uras, Umut (2018). "Refugee Returns Expected After Afrin Operation: Turkey," *al-Jazeera English* (online). Available at: https://www.aljazeera.com/news/2018/02/refugee-returns-expected-afrin-operation-turkey-180222114439065.html (accessed April 4, 2018).

U.S. Congress (2017). No Assistance for Assad Act (pdf). Available at: https://www.congress.gov/115/bills/hr4681/BILLS-115hr4681ih.pdf (accessed March 26, 2018).

Van Wilgenburg, Wladimir (2014a). "Syrian Kurds Aim to Benefit from Islamist Infighting," *al-Monitor* (online), January 16. Available at: http://www.al-monitor.com/pulse/originals/2014/01/islamist-infighting-aids-syrian-kurds.html (accessed March 30, 2014).

Van Wilgenburg, W. (2014b). "Syrian Kurds, Rebels Find Common Enemy in ISIS," *al-Monitor* (online), March 27. Available at: http://www.al-monitor.com/pulse/originals/2014/03/syria-kurds-pyd-ypg-isis-rebels-kobani-afrin.html#ixzz4QNz7y4YC (accessed March 30, 2014).

Van Wilgenburg, W. (2014c). "Syrian Kurds Appoint Arab Governor in Hasakah, Bid for International Support," *Middle East Eye* (online), July 31. Available at: http://www.middleeasteye.net/news/syrian-kurds-appoint-arab-governor-hasakah-bid-international-support-1313083527 (accessed September 20, 2014).

Van Wilgenburg, W. (2017a). "Syrian Opposition Calls Kurdish Fighters 'Terrorists', Regime Rejects Federalism," *ARA News* (online), January 25. Available at: http://aranews.net/2017/01/syrian-opposition-calls-kurdish-ypg-fighters-terrorists-regime-rejects-federalism/ (accessed February 10, 2017).

Van Wilgenburg, W. (2017b). "If Bombed by Russia in Deir-Ezzor Again, the US Coalition and SDF Vow They Will Fight Back," *The Region* (online), September 17. Available at: http://theregion.org/article/11571-if-bombed-by-russia-in-deir-ezzor-again-the-us-coalition-and-sdf-vow-they-will-fight-back (accesed September 17, 2017).

Wall Street Journal (2011). "Interview with Syrian President Bashar al-Assad" (online). Available at: http://www.wsj.com/articles/SB10001424052748703833204576114712441122894 (accessed January 31, 2011).

Watan (al-) (2017). "Al-qarârât tatawâla al-âman fî halab" (online). Available at: http://www.alwatanonline.com/archives/34930 (accessed August 20, 2017).

Watan (al-) (2018). "Tâlabû bi-îlghâ'ihi wa tashkîl lajnat taqîîm jadîdat ta'mal bi-'nazâhat'" (online). Available at: http://alwatan.sy/archives/168168 (accessed October 26, 2018).

Waters, Gregory (2018). "The Tiger Forces, Pro-Assad Fighters Backed by Russia," *Middle East Institue* (pdf). Available at: https://www.mei.edu/files/publications/2%20UPLOAD%20VERSION_0.pdf (accessed October 30, 2018).

We Are All Syria (2017). "'I Do Not Want to Fight ... I Do Not Want to Die'," *The Syrian Observer* (online). Available at: http://syrianobserver.com/EN/Features/32717 /I_Do_Not_Want_Fight_I_Do_Not_Want_Die (accessed May 8, 2017).

Wehrey, Frederic (2013). "Syria's Sectarian Ripples Across the Gulf," *U. S. Institute of Peace, Peacebrief 161* (pdf). Available at: https://www.usip.org/sites/default/files /PB161.pdf (accessed February 20, 2015).

The White House (2013). "Statement by the President on Syria" (online). Available at: https://obamawhitehouse.archives.gov/the-press-office/2013/08/31/statement -president-syria (accessed December 20, 2013).

Wikstrom, Casja (2011). "Syria: 'A Kingdom of Silence," *al-Jazeera English* (online). Available at: http://www.aljazeera.com/indepth/features/2011/02/201129103121562 395.html (accessed June 20, 2011).

Williams, Jennifer (2016). "What Assad and Putin Are Doing in Syria 'Is Not Counterterrorism. It Is Barbarism'," *Vox* (online). Available at: http://www.vox.com /world/2016/9/22/13000276/assad-putin-bombing-syrian-hospitals-aleppo (accessed October 20, 2016).

Williams, Lauren (2011). "Syria Clamps Down on Dissent with Beatings and Arrests," *The Guardian* (online), February 24. Available at: https://www.theguardian.com /world/2011/feb/24/syria-crackdown-protest-arrests-beatings (accessed June 20, 2011).

Wimmen, Heiko (2016). "Syria's Path from Civic Uprising to Civil War," *Carnegie* (online). Available at: http://carnegieendowment.org/2016/11/22/syria-s-path-from -civic-uprising-to-civil-war-pub-66171?mkt_tok=eyJpIjoiTkdGbVpqqpqqqqqSTNOM kpoTkRRdyIsInQiOiJxSTFaeUdwSGpaQTNrTWZZMmJ5UGI5akp1M FA2eWFuRDRiRTVHWkVrVoVaZFwvYkFqOUxaOUFjRXFaW GYyMzhHMjQ3V21ObXRidVgxU2l5M3V1ZmRuQVU5ODhlQjlCQJl6dn NacoVETFM2cWM9Ino%3D (accessed November 29, 2016).

Wood, Paul (2013). "Syria's War in Miniature: Meeting the Christians Driven out of Qusayr," *The Spectator* (online). Available at: https://www.spectator.co.uk/2013/08 /syrias-war-in-miniature-meeting-the-christians-driven-out-of-qusayr/ (accessed November 20, 2013).

World Bank (2011). "Economic Challenges and Reform Options for Syria: A Growth Diagnostics Report (CEM, First Phase)" (pdf). Available at: http://siteresources .worldbank.org/INTDEBTDEPT/Resources/468980-1218567884549/5289593-122 4797529767/5506237-1270144995464/DFSG03SyriaFR.pdf (accessed November 20, 2018).

World Bank (2016). "Syria's Economic Outlook—Spring 2016" (online). Available at: http://www.worldbank.org/en/country/syria/publication/economic-outlook-spring -2016 (accessed June 20, 2017).

World Bank (2018). "Gross Enrolment Ratio, Tertiary, Both Sexes (%)" (online). Available at: https://data.worldbank.org/indicator/SE.TER.ENRR?locations=SY (accessed January 29, 2018).

World Bank Group (2017). "The Toll of War: The Economic and Social Consequences of the Conflict in Syria" (pdf). Available at: http://www.worldbank.org/en/country /syria/publication/the-toll-of-war-the-economic-and-social-consequences-of-the -conflict-in-syria (accessed January 20, 2018).

World Maritime News (2018). "US Treasury Warns Against Petroleum Shipments to Syrian Ports" (online). Available at: https://worldmaritimenews.com/archives /265186/us-treasury-warns-against-petroleum-shipments-to-syrian-ports/ (accessed January 20, 2019).

Wroughton, Lesley (2017). "Kerry Says U.S. Encouraging Astana Talks on Syria as Step to Peace," *Reuters* (online). Available at: http://www.reuters.com/article/us -mideast-crisis-syria-kerry-idUSKBN14P2FX (accessed January 10, 2017).

Wroughton, Lesley (2018). "U.S. Raises $300 Million from Allies for Syria Stabiliz ation," *Reuters* (online). Available at: https://www.reuters.com/article/us-syria-crisis -usa/u-s-raises-300-million-from-allies-for-syria-stabilization-idUSKBN1L21RV (accessed August 20, 2018).

Yahya, Huda (2017). "Idlib Local Councils Face Crisis of Trust Under Difficult Circumstances," *Syria Untold* (online). Available at: http://www.syriauntold.com /en/2017/09/idlib-local-councils-face-crisis-of-trust-under-difficult-circumstances / (accessed September 4, 2017).

Yalla Souriya (2016). "#Syria|Aleppo|PKK/YPG pulls out" (online). Available at: https://yallasouriya.wordpress.com/2016/12/29/syriaaleppopkkypg-pulls-out/ (accessed December 29, 2016).

Yazigi, Jihad (2013). "La guerre a transformé la communauté syrienne des affaires," *Souria Houria* (online). Available at: http://souriahouria.com/la-guerre-a-transforme -la-communaute-syrienne-des-affaires-par-jihad-yazigi/ (accessed November 25, 2015).

Yazigi, J. (2015). "Le projet autonomiste kurde est-il économiquement viable en Syrie?" (online), November 1. Available at: https://jihadyazigi.com/2015/11/01/le-projet -autonomiste-kurde-est-il-economiquement-viable-en-syrie/ (accessed November 12, 2015).

Yazigi, Jihad (2016a). "Tajdîd manzûma al-fasâd fî sûrîya," *al-Araby* (online). February 15. Available at: https://www.alaraby.co.uk/supplementeconomy/2016/2/14/تجديد-منظومة الفساد-ي- (accessed March 15, 2016).

Yazigi, J. (2016c). "No Going Back: Why Decentralisation Is the Future for Syria," *European Council on Foreign Relations* (pdf) September. Available at: http://www .ecfr.eu/page/-/ECFR185_-_NO_GOING_BACK_-_WHY_DECENT RALISATION_IS_THE_FUTURE_FOR_SYRIA.pdf (accessed October 11, 2016).

Yazigi, J. (2017). "Destruct to Reconstruct, How the Syrian Regime Capitalises on Property Destruction and Land Legislation," *Friedrich Ebert Stiftung* (pdf). Available at: http://library.fes.de/pdf-files/iez/13562.pdf (accessed July 30, 2017).

Yazigi, J. (2019). "Reconstruction or Plunder? How Russia and Iran Are Dividing Syrian Resources," *Adopt a Revolution* (pdf). Available at: https://www.adoptrevo- lution.org/wp-content/uploads/2019/01/Reconstruction_Web-EN_Final.pdf ?fbclid=IwAR1dqfvfzcSSqXfgs5xYsPDEGRSW70tzeaVTIMvj1jtF_O -FMdUMAZKa-OE (accessed January 20, 2019).

Yekiti Media (2014). "Al-majlis al-watanî al-kurdî yarfud fî îjtimâ'I al-yawm qarâr al- tajnîd al-îjbârî al-sâdr min hukûma kântûn al-jazîra" (online). Available at: http:// ara.yekiti-media.org/المجلس-الوطني-الكردي-يرفض-في-اجتماعه- (accessed September 20, 2014).

Yeni Safak (2018). "Erdoğan Says Turkey Has No Business in Syria's Manbij If YPG Terrorists Leave" (online). Available at: https://www.yenisafak.com/en/world /assad-forces-are-trying-to-run-a-psychological-operation-in-syrias-manbij-erdogan -3470351 (accessed December 30, 2018).

Yilmazkaya, Mahir (2016). "Education in Rojava After the Revolution," *ANF News* (online). Available at: https://anfenglish.com/culture/education-in-rojava-after-the -revolution-14891 (accessed December 20, 2016).

Young, Michael (2017). "Syriana," *Carnegie Middle East Center* (online). Available at: http://carnegie-mec.org/diwan/68366?lang=en (accessed April 20, 2017).

YPG (2018). "Our Forces Focus on the Fight Against ISIS" (online). Available at: https://www.ypgrojava.org/Our-forces-focus-on-the-fight-against-ISIS (accessed December 31, 2018).

Zainedine, Jalal (2018). "What Is Driving Rebel Defections to the Regime—and What Does It Mean for the Conflict and Its Participants?" *Chatham House* (online). Available at: https://syria.chathamhouse.org/research/what-is-driving -rebel-defections-to-the-regime-and-what-does-it-mean-for-the-conflict-and-its -participants (accessed August 20, 2018).

Zakwan, Hadid (2013). "'Âmûdâ -27-6-3013–îtlâq al-rasâs al-kathîf min qibl hizb PYD 'ala al-mutazhârîn," *YouTube* (online). Available at: https://www.youtube.com /watch?v=OmWDbTQokfA&feature=youtu.be (accessed June 27, 2013).

Zaman al-Wasl (2013a). "Al-sûrîyyûn yatamarnûn al-dîmuqrâtîyya fî al-manâtiq al-muharara ... îdâra zâtîyya bi-î'd mahalîyya taradd 'ala al-mukhawfîn min al-hurîyya" (online), February 20. Available at: https://www.zamanalwsl.net/read News.php?id=35864 (accessed July 20, 2013).

Zaman al-Wasl (2013b). "Presidential Decree to Legitimize Arming of Pro-Assad Militias Under 'Protection' Pretext" (online), August 6. Available at: https://en .zamanalwsl.net/readNews.php?id=1017 (accessed February 14, 2014).

Zaman al-Wasl (2016a). "Authorities Silent While Lattakia's Elderly a 'Soft Target' for Looters, Murderers," *The Syrian Observer* (online), August 22. Available at: http://syrianobserver.com/EN/News/31528/Authorities_Silent_While_Lattakia _Elderly_Soft_Target_for_Looters_Murderers (accessed August 30, 2016).

Zaman al-Wasl (2016b). "Loyalists Outraged by Shabeeha Looting in Regime-Held Aleppo," *The Syrian Observer* (online), September 7. Available at: http://www .syrianobserver.com/EN/News/31601/Loyalists_Outraged_Shabeeha_Looting _Regime_held_Aleppo (accessed September 12, 2016).

Zaman al-Wasl (2016c). "Major General al-Musa Appointed al-Hasakah Province New Governor" (online), October 17. Available at: https://en.zamanalwsl.net/news /article/19378 (accessed November 20, 2017).

Zaman al-Wasl (2017a). "Coalition Investigating Samira Masalmeh for Televised Comments," *The Syrian Observer* (online), January 5. Available at: http:// syrianobserver.com/EN/News/32168/Coalition_Investigating_Samira_Masalmeh _Televised_Comments (accessed January 17, 2017).

Zaman al-Wasl (2017b). "Fuel Crisis Stokes Resentment from Loyalists in Lattakia Province," *The Syrian Observer* (online), February 10. Available at:

http://syrianobserver.com/EN/Features/32325/Fuel_Crisis_Stokes_Resentment
_from_Loyalists_Lattakia_Province (accessed February 13, 2017).

Zaman al-Wasl (2017c). "Al-Baath Brigades, New Militia of University Student
Recruits," *The Syrian Observer* (online), February 21. Available at: http://www
.syrianobserver.com/EN/News/32368/Al_Baath_Brigades_New_Militia_University
_Student_Recruits (accessed February 21, 2017).

Zaman al-Wasl (2017d). "Assad Regime Forms New Militia from Hassakeh
Tribesmen," *The Syrian Observer* (online), April 11. Available at: http://syrianob-
server.com/EN/News/32593/Assad_Regime_Forms_New_Militia_from_Hassakeh
_Tribesmen (accessed April 12, 2017).

Zaman al-Wasl (2017e). "Militiamen of Shiite Villages Resettled in Qusayr Town:
Source," *The Syrian Observer* (online), April 27. Available at: http://www
.syrianobserver.com/EN/News/32674/Militiamen_Shiite_Villages_Resettled_Qusayr
_Town_Source (accessed April 30, 2017).

Zaman al-Wasl (2017f). "After Reconciliation Deal, Youths of Barzeh Join Pro-
Regime Militias," *The Syrian Observer* (online), July 17. Available at: http://
syrianobserver.com/EN/News/33019/After_Reconciliation_Deal_Youths_Barzeh
_Join_Pro_Regime_Militias (accessed June 20. 2017).

Zaman al-Wasl (2017g). "On-Duty Police Officer Hospitalized by Loyalist Militants
in Homs," *The Syrian Observer* (online), August 22. Available at: http://
syrianobserver.com/EN/News/33167/On_Duty_Police_Officer_Hospitalized
_Loyalist_Militants_Homs/ (accessed August 24, 2017).

Zaman al-Wasl (2017h). "Loyalists Denounce Assad for Abandoning Coastal War
Wounded," *The Syrian Observer* (online), August 24. Available at: http://syrianob
server.com/EN/Features/33184/Loyalists_Denounce_Assad_Abandoning_Coastal
_War_Wounded (accessed August 24, 2017).

Zaman al-Wasl (2017i). "Mohamad sabâgh sharabâtî. rajul al-à'mâl al-lazî lam tan-
fa'ahu shurâka râmî makhlûf" (online), October 22. Available at: https://www
.zamanalwsl.net/news/article/82244/ (accessed February 20, 2018).

Zaman al-Wasl (2018a). "Assad Ends Mission of Gen. Ali Diab, Man Who Armed
the PKK and YPG," *The Syrian Observer* (online), January 4. Available at:
http://www.syrianobserver.com/EN/Features/33677/Assad_Ends_Mission_Gen
_Ali_Diab_Man_Who_Armed_PKK_YPG (accessed January 5, 2018).

Zaman al-Wasl (2018b). "Pro-Assad Militias Complain Lack of Salaries and
Compensations" (online), February 24. Available at: https://en.zamanalwsl.net
/news/article/33137/ (accessed March 15, 2018).

Zaman, Amberin (2017). "Syrian Kurdish Commander: We're 'Ready to Engage' with
Damascus," *al-Monitor* (online). Available at: http://www.al-monitor.com/pulse
/originals/2017/09/turkey-kurdish-commander-says-us-should-stay-in-syria
.html#ixzz4tvJiDlBc (accessed September 27, 2017).

Zaza, Ahmad (2017). "To Work in Douma, Men Must Join Militants of Jaish Al-
Islam," Syria Deeply (online). Available at: https://www.newsdeeply.com/syria
/articles/2017/02/24/to-work-in-douma-men-must-join-militants-of-jaish-al-islam
?utm_campaign=a4913e06fc-EMAIL_CAMPAIGN_2017_02_24&utm_medium

=email&utm_source=Syria+Deeply&utm_term=0_d84f3fd103-a4913e06fc-1174
52141 (accessed February 28, 2017).

Zelin, Aaron Y. (2012). "Assad's Self-Fulfilling Prophecy," *Washington Institute* (online). Available at: http://www.washingtoninstitute.org/policy-analysis/view /assads-self-fulfilling-prophecy (accessed December 20, 2012).

Zurayk, Nisreen (2018). "Al-Marsûm 16" min zâwîyat îqtisâdîyat," *al-Akhbar* (online). Available at: https://www.al-akhbar.com/Syria/259130/المرسوم-16-من-زاوية-اقتصادي ?fbclid=IwAR1OskYaqWlrRtBly3JfE8yTUq7fWFZ97IrhNOUp1icJ7-NzQxrD _3juJWg (accessed October 20, 2018).

Zweynert, Astrid (2018). "Syria Faces 2 Million Lawsuits over Lost and Damaged Property: Experts," *Reuters* (online). Available at: https://www.reuters.com/article /us-syria-landrights-restitution/syria-faces-2-million-lawsuits-over-lost-and -damaged-property-experts-idUSKCN1GB300 (accessed March 20, 2018).

YouTube Videos

42maher (2011a). "Îzâla sûra Bachâr min mîdân Dar'â," YouTube (online), March 25. Available at: https://www.youtube.com/watch?v=H9_BOjkD2wY (accessed February 3, 2012).

42maher (2011b). "Tahdîm ramz al-zholm fî Dar'â–tamthâl habl al-Âssad," YouTube (online), March 25. Available at: https://www.youtube.com/watch?v=4f2XHZO _ohk (accessed June 10, 2011).

Abazeed, Iyad (2011). "Âzâr 2011 mudâkhala al-shaykh yûssef âbû rûmîyya tam hazhafihâ," YouTube (online). Available at: https://www.youtube.com/watch?v =UoaIyrpNVnU (accessed April 18, 2011).

Abd al-Hak, Mousa (2011). "Dârayâ–îtisâm nisâ`î imâm al-mahkama lil-mutâliba bil-mu'taqalîn," YouTube (online). Available at: https://www.youtube.com/watch?v =D7k-ocGoHMA (accessed January 22, 2012).

Abu Arab, Mustapha (2013). "Liqâ` ma' qâ'id harakat âhrâr al-shâm al-îslâmîya–hassân 'abûd 'ala qanâ al-jazîra," YouTube (online). Available at: https://www .youtube.com/watch?v=fL5dzLlmORI (accessed December 20, 2013).

C-SPAN (2015). "Senator Lindsey Graham on U.S. Strategy in Syria" (online). Available at: http://www.c-span.org/video/?c4557020/senator-lindsey-graham-us -strategy-syria (accessed November 2, 2015).

C-SPAN (2018). "Iran Strategy and Combating ISIS General Joseph Votel" (online). Available at: https://www.c-span.org/video/?441788-1/centcom-commander-general -votel-testifies-iran-strategy (accessed March 2, 2018).

Daraafree Syria (2011). "Thawra shabâb Sûrîyya–muhâfazha Dar'a wa al-qam'," YouTube (online). Available at: https://www.youtube.com/watch?v=IetDsvlm Ttk&feature=player_embedded (accessed February 11, 2012).

Fî sabîl âllah (2015). "Sheikh Adnan Arour Exposes Zahran Alloush," YouTube (online). Available at: https://www.youtube.com/watch?v=4RTc5y9pEhY (accessed February 20, 2016).

Freedom for Syria-Antakya (2011). "Înshiqâq al-muqadam Harmûsh," YouTube (online). Available at: https://www.youtube.com/watch?v=2XeIFv1B7no (accessed December 30, 2011).

Ghaith, Aal Fakhri (2013). "Dawla al-îslâm fî al-'irâq wa al-shâm dâ'esh: î'tisâm âmâm miqr al," YouTube (online). Available at: https://www.youtube.com/watch?v =Ox5jCIja9Mw (accessed July 23, 2013).

Î'tilâf (al-) al-watanî li-qûwa al-thawra wa al-mu'ârada al-sûrîya (2013). "Kalimat ra`îs al-îti`lâf al-shaîkh mu'âzh fî al-qumat al-'arabîya" (online). Available at: https:// www.youtube.com/watch?v=zNotoRrG2CI (accessed March 28, 2014).

Jazeera (-al) English (2016). "George Sabra: A Unity Government Is Unacceptable" (online). Available at: https://www.youtube.com/watch?v=h9fIH8Pq-Q4&feature =youtu.be (accessed December 20, 2016).

Kayani WebTV (2012). "Women of Zabdani," YouTube (online), December 29, 2013. Available at: https://www.youtube.com/watch?v=Otc6J9EQGiw (accessed December 29, 2013).

Loizeau, Manon (2017). "Syrie, Le cri étouffé" (online). Available at: http://primed.tv /syrie-cri-etouffe/ (accessed January 20, 2018).

MsSyriano (2010). "Helm Homs–al-mashârî' al-mustaqbalîya fî madîna homs al-sûrîya," *YouTube Video*. Available at: https://www.youtube.com/watch?v=Vxof2Ln _y30 (accessed February 20, 2016).

No Iran (2011). "Al-sha'b al-sûrî yutâlib lâ îrân wa lâ hizb âllah," YouTube (online). Available at: https://www.youtube.com/watch?v=2VW8Y2UgG3U (accessed November 22, 2012).

Nono Ali (2011). "Tashîî' al-shahîd al-batl mash'al al-tamû fî al-Qâmishlî âkbar mu-zhâhara," YouTube. Available at: https://www.youtube.com/watch?v=wKVf MPWyE78 (accessed November 10, 2011).

On Live (2017). "Liqâ` ma' m. muhamad kâmal al-sharbâtî ra'îs al-majmû'a al-ribâ'îya lil-nasjîyât: ON sabâh," *YouTube Video*. Available at: https://www.youtube.com /watch?v=KAv3NEqJok8 (accessed January 25, 2018).

Orient News (2016). "Mutazhâhirûn yaqtahamûn mabna muhâfazha al-sûwaydâ` lil-mutâliba bi-î'dâm mutahim bi-tasfîyya tâleb jâmi'î," *YouTube Video*, Available at: https://www.youtube.com/watch?v=eAsajMor3XY (accessed August 20, 2016).

ORTAS Videos (2017). "Al-mûwâtin wa al-mas'ûûl: mashrû' tanzîm al-maza 66 hal min jadîd. 02.12.2017," *YouTube Video*. Available at: https://www.youtube.com /watch?v=5r84-Dj59A8 (accessed January 3, 2018).

Sadam al-Majid (2011). "Lâ îrân wa lâ hizb âllah badna al-malek 'abd âllah," YouTube (online). Available at: https://www.youtube.com/watch?v=kkowPbipQlo (accessed January 12, 2012).

Shaam Network S.N.N. (2011a). "Sûrîyyâ muzhâhara Bânîyyâs," YouTube (online), March 18. Available at: https://www.youtube.com/watch?v=HWdtU IbPiH4&feature=player_embedded&oref=https%3A%2F%2F (accessed June 10, 2012).

Shaam Network S.N.N. (2011b). "Shâm–dar'â 17–hutâfât muzhâhara al-tashîî'," YouTube (online), March 29. Available at: https://www.youtube.com/watch?v =vQ5ktdYZbbQ (accessed April 20, 2011).

Shaam Network S.N.N. (2011c). "Shâm–Hamâ–Halfâîyyâ–masâ`îyyât rafad al-mû`tamar 27-6," YouTube (online), July 27. Available at: https://www.youtube.com /watch?feature=player_embedded&v=ari1HXh4PjU (accessed September 10, 2011).

Shahdawi, Yazan (2018). "Hamâ: Talâl al-Daqâq min za'îm milîshîyâ îlâ 'rajul al-â'mâl," al-Modon (online). Available at: https://www.almodon.com/arabworld /2018/8/19/أعمال-رجل-إلى-مليشيا-زعيم-من-الدقاق-طلال-حماة (accessed September 20, 2018).

Silent whisper2009 (2011). "Syrian Revolution 2011—Homs—Clock Tower—April 18 04-18". YouTube (online). Available at: https://www.youtube.com/watch?v=YVM l4VsGxqQ (accessed September 30, 2011).

SyriaFreePress (2011). "Vîdîû mutawal lil-thawra al-sûrîyya 18-3-2011 dar'â," YouTube (online). Available at: https://www.youtube.com/watch?v=nICh9dKhnr4 (accessed December 10, 2011).

Syria TV Channels 1 (2015). "Hiwâr khâs ma' d. bashr al-sibân muhâfiz dimashq hawl al-marsûm 66 li-'âm 2012," *YouTube Video*. Available at: https://www.youtube.com /watch?v=uhOENhG7CZc (accessed November 30, 2016).

Tansîqîyya al-Lâziqîyya (2011). "Al-Lâziqîyya âwal muzhâhara lil-hurrîyya wa nasra li-Dar'â 25-3-2011," YouTube (online). Available at: https://www.youtube.com /watch?v=F-uvURC4REAhttps://www.youtube.com/watch?v=U2zbQx2WPaQ (accessed April 19, 2011).

Tansîqîyya madîna Nawa (2011). "Îsqât awal tamthâl bi-Sûrîyya," YouTube (online). Available at: https://www.youtube.com/watch?v=-ugobzoJVvo (accessed June 26, 2011).

Tansîqîyya Salamîyya (2011). "Muzâharât madîna Salamîyya," YouTube (online). Available at: http://www.youtube.com/watch?v=oWYR8GZBitI (accessed September 10, 2011).

Tube Rased (2019). "Muzâharat fî darâ al-balad rafud î'adat nasb sanam hâfez al-âsad," YouTube (online). Available at: https://www.facebook.com/rased.tube /videos/vb.168528056848069/262045061385641/?type=2&theater (accessed March 9, 2019).

Ugarit NEWS Channel (2011). "Ûghârît î`lân tashkîl al-jaysh al-sûrî al-hur al-àqîd Rîyâd al-Âs`ad," YouTube (online). Available at: https://www.youtube.com/watch ?v=ItzI_AIFUWg (accessed November 30, 2011).

Blogs

Ashkar, Hisham (2014). "Funerals Hezbollah Fighters Syria 2012–2014," *Mostly Off* (blog). Available at: https://docs.google.com/a/soas.ac.uk/spreadsheet/ccc?key=oA m1WLKyxQY2ldEtQQzVBaE5KOU5tSoVIM1pJU2RYRnc&usp=drive_web #gid=0 (accessed October 30, 2014).

Darth Nader (2012). "Interview with Member of the 'National Unity Brigades' of the FSA" (online), September 17. Available at: https://darthnader.net/2012/10/17 /interview-with-member-of-the-national-unity-brigades-of-the-fsa/ (accessed December 20, 2012).

Syria Exposed (2005). "Myth No. 7: Alawie Is Still a Religious Sect," *Blog* (online). Available at: http://syriaexposed.blogspot.ch/2005/03/myth-no-7-alawie-is-still -religious.html (accessed February 20, 2016).

Syria Freedom Forever (2013a). "Statement by the Kurdish Youth Movement (TCK) About the Latest Events in the City of Amouda, and Videos and Pictures from the

Protests and Sit-ins" (online), June 23. Available at: https://syriafreedomforever
.wordpress.com/2013/06/23/statement-by-the-kurdish-youth-movement-tck-about
-the-latest-events-in-the-city-of-amouda-and-videos-and-pictures-from-the
-protests-and-sit-ins/ (accessed June 23, 2013).
Syria Freedom Forever (2013b). "Statement of the Civilian Movement in Syria
Regarding the Remarks of Mr. Zahran Alloush, Commander of the Army of Islam
on October 14, 2013," Available at: https://syriafreedomforever.wordpress.com/2013
/10/16/statement-of-the-civilian-movement-in-syria-regarding-the-remarks-of-mr
-zahran-alloush-commander-of-the-army-of-islam-on-october-14-2013/ (accessed
October 14, 2013).
Syria Freedom Forever (2013c). "Dynamics and Prospects for the Syrian Revolutionary
Process" (online), December 6. Available at: https://syriafreedomforever.wordpress
.com/2013/12/06/dynamics-and-prospects-for-the-syrian-revolutionary-process/
(accessed December 6, 2013).
Syria Freedom Forever (2016). "Friday of Dignity 18-03-2016–jumu'a al-karâma"
(online), March 18. Available at: https://syriafreedomforever.wordpress.com/2016
/03/18/10930/ (accessed March 18, 2016).

Facebook

Abboud, Ghassan (2015). *Facebook*. Available at: https://www.facebook.com/photo
.php?fbid=10155442871320591&set=p.10155442871320591&type=1&theater (accessed April 26, 2015).
Aziz, Omar (2011). "Al-âwrâq al-tâssîssîyya li-fikra al-majâlis al-mahalîyya bi-qalam
al-shahîd 'omar 'azîz," *Facebook* (online). Available at: https://www.facebook.com
/note.php?note_id=143690742461532 (accessed February 12, 2012).
Facebook (2018a). (online). Available at: https://www.facebook.com/tito.free.14
/videos/1595844353869530/ (accessed January 22, 2018).
Facebook (2018b). (online). Available at: https://www.facebook.com/amina.mesto
/posts/1533789510061243?pnref=story (accessed January 27, 2018).
Homs (2016). "Al-sha'ab yurîd îsqât al-muhâfizh," *Facebook* (online). Available at:
https://www.facebook.com/homs.City.khaled.ebn.alwaleed/videos/15387286
26419649/ (accessed February 22, 2016).
Local Coordination Committee (LCC) (2011a). "Founding Statement for the Union
of Free Syrian Students" (online), September 29. Available at: https://www
.facebook.com/notes/لجان-التنسيق-المحلية-في-سوريا/founding-statement-for-the-union-of
-free-syrian-students/291890390838104/ (accessed January 12, 2012).
Local Coordination Committee (LCC) (2012a). "A Year to the Revolution of Freedom
and Dignity," *Facebook* (online), March 6. Available at: https://www.facebook.com
/notes/لجان-التنسيق-المحلية-في-سوريا/a-year-to-the-revolution-of-freedom-and-dignity
/40237051979090 (accessed April 11, 2012).
Local Coordination Committee (LCC) (2012b). "New Battalions Sign the Code of
Conduct," *Facebook* (online), August 8. Available at: https://www.facebook.com
/notes/لجان-التنسيق-المحلية-في-سوريا/new-battalions-sign-the-code-of-conduct/50823
2342537240 (accessed August 30, 2012).

Local Coordination Committee (LCC) (2012c). "Revolution of Dignity and Morals Campaign Continues," *Syria Freedom Forever* (online), August 30. Available at: https://syriafreedomforever.wordpress.com/2012/08/30/372/ (accessed August 30, 2012).

Local Coordination Committee (LCC) (2013a). "Statement Issued by the Revolutionary Movement in Syria" (online), May 29. Available at: https://www.facebook.com /notes/سوريا-في-المحلية-التنسيق-لجان/statement-issued-by-the-revolutionary-movement-in -syria/664439210249885/ (accessed January 20, 2014).

Local Coordination Committee (LCC) (2013b). "A Statement Regarding the Acts of Violence Against the Kurdish Syrian Civilians," *Facebook* (online), July 1. Available at: https://www.facebook.com /notes/سوريا-في-المحلية-التنسيق-لجان/a-statement -regarding-the-acts-of-violence-against-the-kurdish-syrian-civilians/686341961 392943 (accessed July 20, 2013).

Local Coordination Committee (LCC) (2013c). "Messages from LCC to the World," *Facebook* (online), August 3. Available at: https://www.facebook.com/notes/70786 0739241065/ (accessed February 20, 2014).

Shabaka âkhbar nubl w al-zahrâ` al-rasmîyya (2017). "Âsbâb alwaqfa al-îhtijâjîyya wa matâlib al-muhtajîn," *Facebook* (online). Available at: https://www.facebook.com /Nubbol.Alzahraa.News/videos/1199800063458563/ (accessed July 30, 2017).

Shehabi, Fares (2016). *Facebook* (online). Available at: https://www.facebook.com /fares.shehabi/posts/10205546757183424?__mref=message (accessed September 21, 2016).

Syria Non-Violence Movement (2013). "Revolution's Civil Resistance Standing up to Armed Jihadists in the Eastern Ghouta, Damascus Countryside," *Facebook* (online). Available at: https://mbasic.facebook.com/SyrainNonviolence/photos/a.40417291 2958705.87158.262595243783140/606206429422018/?type=1 (accessed November 20, 2013).

Tansîqîya al-tâkhî al-kûrdîya (2011). "Home," *Facebook* (online). Available at: https://www.facebook.com/pg/SyriaBirati/about/?ref=page_internal (accessed December 10, 2012).

Women Now for Development (2012). "About" (online). Available at: https://www.face book.com/Women-Now-For-Development-253744368062815/ (accessed September 21 2014).

Interviews

Abdeh (-al), Maria (2018). Former member of peaceful protest movement, and current director of Women Now for Development, June 2018, Berlin.

Abd El-Krim, Aziz (2014). Former activist in 'Amuda, interview, May 2014, Lausanne, Switzerland.

Abdo, Youssef (2018). Former activist in Baniyas and former employee at the Afforestation Development Office project in the governorate of Tartous, interview, March 2018, Berlin.

Abu Zeed, Raed (2014). Former activist in Yarmuk Camp, Damascus, interview, October 2014, Paris.

Anonymous A (2014). Female activist in Dasmacus Province, 2014, email.

Anonymous B (2014). Female activist in Damascus Province in relief work, support for displaced persons and families of martyrs and detainees, 2014, email.

Anonymous C (2017). Former activist of Salamiyah, discussion July 2017, Paris.

Ghazzawi, Razan (2018). Former feminist activist in Syria, interview February 2018, London.

Hallaq (-al), Sabah (2018). Board member of the Syrian Women's League, 2018, Beirut.

Hassaf, Alan (2018). Former activist in Syria and member of the Union of Free Syrian Students, Geneva.

Ibrahim, Tareq (2013). Former activist in Yarmuk Camp, Damascus, interview May 2014, Lausanne, Switzerland.

Kalo, Aziz (2014). Former activist in Derik (Al-Malikiyah), discussion in June 2014, Geneva.

Othman, Fatmeh (2016). Former activist in Damascus and Qamishlo, discussion in July 2016, Lausanne, Switzerland.

Salameh, Salim (2014). Former activist in Yarmuk Camp, Head of the Palestinian League for Human Rights-Syria, Damascus, interview October 2014, Paris.

Youssef, Ciwan (2018). Former member of the Local Coordination Committees (LCC) and member of the Muwatana movement, interview July 2018, Geneva.

Youssef, Shiar (2016). Activist from Amuda in exile since 2014, interview May 2016, Paris.

Index